FEMINISM, QUEERNESS,
AFFECT, AND ROMANS

EARLY CHRISTIANITY AND ITS LITERATURE

Shelly Matthews, General Editor

Number 30

FEMINISM, QUEERNESS, AFFECT, AND ROMANS

Under God?

Jimmy Hoke

SBL PRESS

SBL PRESS

Atlanta

Copyright © 2021 by Jimmy Hoke

Library of Congress Control Number: 2021946563

This book is for the queer folks who were, are,
and evermore shall be there

Contents

Acknowledgments

For the best damn doctoral mentors who have been coaching me and this book from its beginning to this end: Althea Spencer Miller, Melanie Johnson-DeBaufre, and Stephen Moore.

For feminist and queer advice, mentorship, and book publication guidance: Shelly Matthews and Joseph Marchal.

For their labor and attention to perfect the manuscript, promote and advertise it, and transform it into a tangible book: my two anonymous reviewers and the staff of SBL Press: Bob Buller, Lindsay Lingo, Heather McMurray, and Nicole Tilford.

For conversation, collaboration, and good times at Drew University: Amy Chase, Arminta Fox, Christy Cobb, Elizabeth Freese, Eric Thomas, Jesse Mann (especially for Latin guidance), Karri Whipple, Linzi Guy, Lydia York, Matthew Ketchum, Midori Hartman, Minenhle Khumalo, Paige Rawson, Peter McLellan, and Sarah Emanuel.

For writing accountability and editing (and coffee breaks) at Luther College: David Faldet, Destiny Crider, and Melanie Batoff.

For creativity, diligence, and eagerness: all my students, especially my phenomenal research assistants Abby Trewin, Anna Luber, and Lucas Byl.

For everyone willing to take time (especially during a global pandemic) to read and comment on drafts: Arminta Fox, Christy Cobb, Christopher Zeichmann, Harry Hoke, Madison McClendon, Nan St. Clair, Paige Rawson, and Peter McLellan.

And, most especially, for their friendship and unwavering support and for continually shaping my feminism and queerness: Alyssa Henning, Ellis Arnold, Karen Esterl, Laura Wright, Madison McClendon, Mike Le Chevallier, Paige Rawson, Catherine ("Gran") Hoke, Lynn Williamson, and Chip, Harry, Kathy, and Michael Hoke.

Reading Guidance

I quote (and then translate—my own translations, unless noted otherwise) Greek and Latin passages frequently. Some readers—especially students and lay readers longing for accessible writing about Paul, sexuality, and gender—may find this off-putting, making the reading more dense and challenging than it is.[1] I ask (and thank you) for your patience: I want you to read my book, and I understand that including words, phrases, and large chunks in unfamiliar ancient languages creates a barrier.

Embrace that barrier; relish the unfamiliar. That is the reason I give all my readers the untranslated text: it is a visible reminder of the distance between us and these words.

There are a few Greek words that I refuse to translate. They are terms that have become too familiar, in my opinion. To provide readers with an orientation and guide they can turn back to, these terms are:

- ἐκκλησία (plural: ἐκκλησίαι): pronounced "eck-lay-see-uh" (plural, "eck-lay-see-ay"); means "assembly," broadly used, especially when people engaged in a democratic decision-making process; traditionally translated "church" within texts that describe assemblies of wo/men who gathered to follow Christ.
- ἔθνη (singular, ἔθνος): pronounced "eth-nay" (singular, "eth-nohs"); means "nations," used by Romans to refer to nations/peoples they conquered; often translated as "gentiles" in the New Testament, since it is the Greek equivalent of the Hebrew *goyim*, which frequently refers to the nations other than ancient Israel/Jews in the Hebrew Bible and other Jewish literature.

---

1. As I have come to understand from listening to disability activists, the issues addressed below are not barriers that keep academic writing from being accessible beyond the academy. Academic writing would be much more accessible if it were cheaper, open access, and available in formats such as large print or audiobook.

- πίστις: pronounced "pis-tis"; "trust" or "faith," typically translated in the New Testament and early Christian texts as "faith" or "belief" (πίστις has a verb form, πιστεύω, which I render "have/display/show πίστις").
- κύριος (plural, κύριοι): pronounced "koo-ree-os" (plural, "koo-ree-oy"); means "master" (especially in the context of slavery) and often translated as "lord" when Christian texts refer to Jesus (in Paul's letters) or when Jewish or Christian texts refer to God.
- δικαιοσύνη θεοῦ: pronounced "dee-kay-oh-soo-nay theh-oo"; means "God's justice" ("justice" = δικαιοσύνη), which, in Paul's letters and other Jewish and Christian texts, has been translated as God's "righteousness" or "justification"—words that efface its political roots and coat it with theological sentiment.

By using only the untranslated word, I transform these Greek words into terms themselves, which both you and I will imbue with meaning. But, even as we give them new limits, this allows them to exceed the limited containers in which English—often churchy—translation tends to place them.

Finally, beyond the Greek, some may find the theoretical orientation of this book dense and difficult. Though I won't provide full definitions here, I note them along with where in the book you can find where I define and detail them:

- Wo/men: pronounced "women"; term coined and theorized by Elisabeth Schüssler Fiorenza to call attention to and remind readers of the many differences among women (see further definition/discussion in chapter 1, starting on page 25).
- LGBTIA2Q+: acronym referring to lesbian, gay, bisexual, trans, intersex, asexual/ace/aromantic, two-spirit, and queer folks, with the plus (+) indicating the proliferation of other queer and trans identities not explicitly named in the acronym. There can be numerous variations on the acronym depending on the user (LGBT, LGBTQ, LGBTI/Q, etc.) as well as different meanings given to the letters (especially the A and Q). Any use of any acronym (and definition of each letter's meaning) is likely to become dated as discourse changes, and my usage reflects the acronym as LGBTIA2Q+ activists were using it in early 2021.
- Kyriarchy: pronounced "keer-ree-ARK-ee"; another term coined by Schüssler Fiorenza to point out how power is structured hier-

archically along many axes of privilege and oppression, including gender identity, race, sexual orientation, class, and ability (see further definition and discussion in chapter 1, starting on page 17).

+ Cruel optimism: concept theorized by Lauren Berlant to describe conditions when people attach to objects or promises that actively prevent their flourishing (see full definition and discussion in chapter 3, starting on page 139).

+ Homonationalism: term coined by Jasbir K. Puar to theorize the alliances between LGBTIA2Q+ folks and the project of nationalism, especially in (but not limited to) the post-9/11 United States' war on terror (see full definition and discussion in chapter 5, starting on page 237).

+ Fuck: okay, this is not a theoretical term, but it is an obscenity that may create barriers for some readers, even as it refreshes and empowers other readers who are weary of the sanitization (and romanticization) of academic/religious discourses on sex. In addition to being used in translations of Roman-era graffiti, I use the term several select times throughout the book as I think about the different (and sometimes obscene) sexual interactions that occurred in ancient Rome, including (but not limited to) those among ancient queer wo/men.

Again, I ask you to struggle with these terms and concepts and to enjoy that struggle. It took me years of reading theoretical texts before I finally felt like I had a foothold, and I still struggle when engaging new theories. I keep struggling because the payoff has always been worth it. I hope you will struggle with me, and I hope you will find it valuable—pleasurable, even.

Abbreviations

AB	Anchor Bible
ABRL	Anchor (Yale) Bible Reference Library
AcBib	Academia Biblia
Agr.	Philo, *De Agricultura*
AJP	*American Journal of Philology*
Ann.	Tacitus, *Annales*
ANTC	Abingdon New Testament Commentaries
Ant. rom.	Dionysius of Halicarnassus, *Antiquitates romanae*
AUSS	*Andrews University Seminary Studies*
BDSM	Bondage and discipline; domination and submission; sadism and masochism
BECNT	Baker Exegetical Commentary on the New Testament
Ben.	Seneca, *De Beneficiis*
Bibl. hist.	Diodorus Siculus, *Bibliotheca historica*
BibInt	*Biblical Interpretation*
BibInt	Biblical Interpretation Series
B.J.	Josephus, *Bellum judaicum*
BRPBI	Brill Research Perspectives in Biblical Interpretation
Carm.	Horace, *Carmina*
CBQ	*Catholic Biblical Quarterly*
CIL	*Corpus inscriptionum latinarum*
CJ	*Classical Journal*
CMP	Cultural Memory in the Present
Contempl.	Philo, *De vita contemplativa*
Contraversions	Contraversions: Jews and Other Differences
CP	Cultural Politics
CultRel	*Culture and Religion: An Interdisciplinary Journal*
CurBR	*Currents in Biblical Research*
Det.	Philo, *Quod deterius potiori insidari soleat*
dif.	*differences: A Journal of Feminist Cultural Studies*

Div	Divinations: Rereading Late Ancient Religion
ECL	Early Christianity and Its Literature
Fact.	Valerius Maximus, *Facta et dicta memorabilia*
Flacc.	Philo, *In Flaccum*
GLQ	*GLQ: A Journal of Lesbian and Gay Studies*
GTR	Gender, Theory, and Religion
Hermeneia	Hermeneia: A Critical and Historical Commentary on the Bible
HTR	*Harvard Theological Review*
HTS	Harvard Theological Studies
Ios.	Philo, *De Iosepho*
JCMAMW	Jews, Christians, and Muslims from the Ancient to the Modern World
JBL	*Journal of Biblical Literature*
JECH	*Journal of Early Christian History*
JECS	*Journal of Early Christian Studies*
JFSR	*Journal of Feminist Studies in Religion*
JHFCB	A John Hope Franklin Center Book
JHistSex	*Journal of the History of Sexuality*
JR	*Journal of Religion*
JSNT	*Journal for the Study of the New Testament*
JSP	*Journal for the Study of the Pseudepigrapha*
LCL	Loeb Classical Library
LD	*Lectio Difficilior*
Leg. 1, 2, 3	Philo, *Legum allegoriae* 1, 2, 3
Legat.	Philo, *Legatio ad Gaium*
Lib. aegr.	Plutarch, *De libidune et aegritudine*
LSJ	Liddell, H. G., R. Scott, H. S. Jones, *A Greek-English Lexicon.* 9th ed. with revised supplement. Oxford, 1996.
LXX	Septuagint
Metam.	Apuleius, *Metamorphoses*
MTSR	*Method and Theory in the Study of Religion*
NICNT	New International Commentary on the New Testament
NIGTC	New International Greek Testament Commentary
NovT	*Novum Testamentum*
NRSV	New Revised Standard Version
NTS	*New Testament Studies*

NW	Next Wave: New Directions in Women's Studies
OED	*Oxford English Dictionary*
P.Oxy.	*Papyrus* Oxyrhynchus
PCC	Paul in Critical Contexts
PM	Perverse Modernities
Post.	Philo, *De posteritate Caini*
Praec. ger. rei publ.	Plutarch, *Praecepta gerendae rei publicae*
Prov. 1, 2	Philo, *De providentia 1, 2*
PTMS	Princeton Theological Monograph Series
QT	Queering Theology Series
Res gest. divi Aug.	Res gestae divi Augusti
RTR	*Reformed Theological Review*
Saec.	Horace, *Carmen saeculare*
Sat.	Juvenal, *Satirae*
SBL	Society of Biblical Literature
SBLSP	Society of Biblical Literature Seminar Papers
SemeiaSt	Semeia Studies
SerQ	Series Q
SocT	*Social Text*
SP	Sacra Pagina
Spec.	*De specialibus legibus*
Syn	Synkrisis: Comparative Approaches to Early Christianity in Greco-Roman Culture
TSAJ	Texte und Studien zum antiken Judentum
TTC	Transdisciplinary Theological Colloquia
UCLF	*University of Chicago Legal Forum*
USQR	*Union Seminary Quarterly Review*
WBC	Word Biblical Commentary
WW	*Word and World*

Introduction: Under God?

One nation,
Under God.

—United States Pledge of Allegiance

We want villains. We look for them everywhere. People to pin our misfortune on, whose sins and flaws are responsible for all the suffering we see. We want a world where the real monstrosity lies in wicked individuals, instead of being a fundamental facet of human society, of the human heart.

Stories prime us to search for villains. Because villains can be punished. Villains can be stopped.

But villains are oversimplifications.

—Sam J. Miller, Blackfish City

This is a book about submission and subversion, injustice and justice, heroes and villains. It is also about Paul and the wo/men around Rome's ἐκκλησία; the Roman Empire and the nations it conquered and ruled; and the norms of straight cis men and resistant subcultures of queer wo/men.[1] Yet this oversimplifies my book's contents. In *Feminism, Queerness, Affect, and Romans*, I animate the impulses that move *in between* these simple divisions. This book is about *in-betweenness*.

In-betweenness is political because divisions are political. Heroes require villains: a villain's characteristics determine who and what is heroic. Villains, as the epigraph suggests, get imbued with all the injustices we wish to cast from the messy in-betweenness of the worlds we inhabit. Who is made a villain? How do heroic norms allow some villainous wo/men to

---

1. Feminist biblical scholar Elisabeth Schüssler Fiorenza coins *wo/men* to visibly represent the differences that exist among women. I explain this term and my usage of it more fully in chapter 1. It is pronounced aloud as "women" as though the slash were not present.

transform themselves into heroes? If we look in between the hero-villain divide, can we get beyond this norm and the injustices it paves over? *Feminism, Queerness, Affect, and Romans: Under God?* probes these questions and their intersections.

This book is political. The theo-political notion of "under God" is a problem that traps possibilities.[2] Paul's letter to the Romans traps and erases queer wo/men under God, just as Roman imperialism trapped and erased queer wo/men under a god-like Caesar. Indeed, Paul repudiates queerness *because* Rome did. Throughout this book, I argue that Paul's letter to the Romans submits to the norms that determined Rome's heroes and villains. Paul does this in hopes that he—and his audience of Christ-followers—can transform into Roman heroes. I call this *Romanormativity*.

These politics equally concern the present, as I emphasize with my book's subtitle. *Under God?* signals contemporary relevance by directing a query toward the US Pledge of Allegiance. Queer folks, especially queer folks of color, remain trapped and erased under present norms that heroicize the white straight cis men who rule over us. These men make queerness the villain, even as some of these villains regulate their queerness and submit to norms that promise to make them heroes. Just like Paul. I am concerned about Romans and the pasts it summons because they affect the present. The gridlock created by contemporary injustices is knotted to histories of intersecting oppressions in which Paul's letters participate. The twenty-first-century United States and first-century Rome declare: Under God, genuine change is an impossible fantasy. Justice and freedom are speculative fiction.

This book is oriented toward the past, the present, and the future. I refuse to uphold these temporal divisions. I gaze at the pasts in between the present and future, the futures in between the present and past. I am attempting to loosen theo-politics, particularly as expressed and influenced by Pauline interpretation, from this knotty gridlock. In *Under God?* I struggle to make the impossible plausible.

The scents of a plausibly utopian future drive this book. I do more than sniff out unjust divisions for critique. Critiquing these divisions resists their normalcy, but critique alone does not get out from under

---

2. Erin Runions has drawn wider attention to the biblical roots (beyond Paul's letters) of theo-politics and its affective and apocalyptic fantasies surrounding sex. See Erin Runions, *The Babylon Complex: Fantasies of War, Sex, and Sovereignty* (New York: Fordham University Press, 2014).

them. "Struggle includes the power to resist but it also seeks the power to change," writes feminist theorist, the*logian, and biblical scholar Elisabeth Schüssler Fiorenza.[3] *Feminism, Queerness, Affect, and Romans* struggles to move beyond villains and heroes, especially ones that take Pauline form. I bring to life the queer wo/men whose impulses oozed in between one another and Paul's words as they engaged his letter in Rome's ἐκκλησία.

A title orients a book. *Feminism, Queerness, Affect, and Romans* signals many orientations. Through *Feminism* and *Queerness*, I accentuate my political orientations. I am concerned about the inseparable oppressions of wo/men and LGBTIA2Q+ folks. This necessarily means this book concerns sexual orientation and gender identity, including how gender and sexuality are constructed. But feminist and queer orientations are always political: I care about *who* constructs sexuality and gender and *how* queer wo/men navigate norms. Feminism and queerness are central to this book because they demand justice. I insist that *queer wo/men were there*, a political refrain that demands a recognition that *does* something: I reconstruct queer wo/men in the past because they help us to imagine new futures in which queer wo/men are central.

Through *Affect*, I convey an orientation to *in-betweenness*. Some readers might be tempted to call this a theoretical orientation, since *affect* does signal that I am engaging with scholarship that is now characterized within affect theory. I cannot deny this theoretical orientation exists within these pages. But affect is more than just a theoretical orientation (just as feminism and queerness also gesture to theoretical fields). Affect orients us towards *feelings* and *sensations* that go beyond cognitive thinking. Affect is not disembodied from politics. Affect draws out these feelings and sensations and their in-betweenness and asks: Who produces or controls these feelings? What do these sensations *do*? By orienting *in between*, affect

---

3. Elisabeth Schüssler Fiorenza, *Transforming Vision: Explorations in Feminist The*logy* (Minneapolis: Fortress, 2011), 16. As she notes in this introduction to the volume, struggle is a long-present theme within her vast contributions to feminism, and it framed an older collection of her essays: Schüssler Fiorenza, *Discipleship of Equals: A Critical Feminist Ekklēsia-logy of Liberation* (New York: Crossroad, 1993). On pp. 2–3 of that volume, she observes how many liberal Protestants have questioned her ongoing work that struggles against the Catholic Church's restrictive positions toward women as well as how many feminists (often with understandable reasons) relinquish the struggle with religion or the Bible. Based in part on personal experience, a similar questioning (framed by a similar relinquishing) is often the reaction of queer folks to biblical scholars who continue to queerly probe biblical texts.

refuses to divide thinking from feeling: thinking is one among many sensations that move in between bodies. We already have seen this affective orientation at work in the book's first paragraphs: what (and who) moves in between justice and injustice, the villains and the heroes, Paul and first-century queer wo/men?

Finally, this book is about *Romans*. The title's final word signals its historical and textual dimensions. It orients my book toward an academic field, biblical studies, and this series, Early Christianity and Its Literature. Within biblical studies, *Romans* is shorthand for Paul's letter to the queer wo/men who assembled in the city of Rome in the late 50s CE.[4] This letter provides one starting point that allows us to see sensations that move in between this letter and the queer wo/men who came into contact with it.

Romans is an ambiguous term. Romans were *people*. Since they lived in the city of Rome, could we not also call the first-century queer wo/men

---

4. There is a rather wide range of dating for the epistle, which places its composition anywhere from 55 to 59 CE (or even as late as 64), and some older commentaries prefer a date in the earlier 50s, with the assumption that Paul writes this letter from Corinth. While I do not dispute this general dating, it should be noted that almost all of the commentaries appeal to Acts to establish some of the historical details of Paul's travels. See Joseph A. Fitzmyer, *Romans*, AB 33 (New York: Doubleday, 1993), 85–88; Thomas R. Schreiner, *Romans*, BECNT (Grand Rapids: Baker, 1998), 3–5; Robert Jewett, *Romans: A Commentary*, Hermeneia (Minneapolis: Fortress, 2007), 18 (Jewett prefers a date in late 56 or early 57); James D. G. Dunn, *Romans* WBC 38, 2 vols. (Dallas: Word, 1988), 1:xliii–xliv; Philip F. Esler, *Conflict and Identity in Romans* (Minneapolis: Fortress, 2003), 101; Douglas J. Moo, *The Epistle to the Romans*, NICNT (Grand Rapids: Eerdmans, 1996), 2–3 (Moo prefers to date to 57); Brendan Byrne, *Romans*, SP 6 (Collegeville, MN: Liturgical, 2007), 8–9 (Byrne gives early 58 the highest probability within this range); John B. Cobb Jr. and David J. Lull, *Romans* (Saint Louis: Chalice, 2005), 3; Arland J. Hultgren, *Paul's Letter to the Romans: A Commentary* (Grand Rapids: Eerdmans, 2011), 2–4. Scholars who give precise dates include: early in 56 CE, Frank J. Matera, *Romans*, Paideia (Grand Rapids: Baker Academic, 2010), 4–6; winter 56–57 CE, Ben Witherington III with Darlene Hyatt, *Paul's Letter to the Romans: A Socio-Rhetorical Commentary* (Grand Rapids: Eerdmans, 2004), 7; 57 CE, Leander E. Keck, *Romans*, ANTC (Nashville: Abingdon, 2005), 29–30; 56 or 57 CE, Elsa Tamez, "Romans: A Feminist Reading," in *Feminist Biblical Interpretation: A Compendium of Critical Commentary on the Books of the Bible and Related Literature*, ed. Luise Schottroff and Marie-Theres Wacker (Grand Rapids: Eerdmans, 2012), 698; winter 57–58 CE, Luke Timothy Johnson, *Reading Romans: A Literary and Theological Commentary* (New York: Crossroad, 1997), 4; Richard N. Longenecker, *The Epistle to the Romans: A Commentary on the Greek Text*, NIGTC (Grand Rapids: Eerdmans, 2016), 5–6.

who engaged Paul's letter Romans? Certainly, we can; yet, this designation is complicated. *Roman* can designate any inhabitant of the city, but it could also have a narrower meaning. One is Roman if one possessed Roman citizenship. It can also have a wider meaning, since Rome was both a city and an empire: A Roman could be anyone who dwelt within Rome's expansive territory. The meaning of *Roman* is as malleable as *American* is used today: inhabitant of the United States; US citizen; a person living anywhere in the Americas. Therefore, *Romans* also denotes this book's historical orientation. I am digging up the history of queer wo/men in first-century Rome, and I am situating Paul's letter as a primary source that offers a glimpse into this history.

The letter to the Romans did not affect queer wo/men only in first-century Rome: queer wo/men continue to be affected by it, sometimes unaware of subtle ways our lives bump against it. Romans 1:26–27 arguably contains the Bible's most infamous, overt, and encompassing condemnation of same-sex intercourse and its only explicit condemnation of queer *wo/men*. While I cannot ignore the impacts of these verses, the letter has more than one chapter; its effects on queer wo/men extends beyond two verses. Deeper dangers lurk beyond 1:26–27. How did Paul's theo-Christology (Rom 3–5) and ethics (Rom 12–15) affect first-century queer wo/men? And how do they continue to impact queer wo/men? A political orientation motivates my scrutiny of Romans. I desire change for how Romans affects queer wo/men and our politics.

Feminism, Queerness, Affect, and Romans. These are not four discrete orientations: they come together, even though they sometimes tug in different directions. These orientations are starting points: they shape the arguments that follow. My book shows some of the impulses that emerge *in between* these orientations. It is about what happens when feminism, queerness, affect, and Romans interact. What happens when we decenter Paul, as hero or villain? What ensues when queer wo/men become fully visible? Most importantly, it is about what *can* happen if these critiques and reconstructions move beyond the past. What justices are plausible when we try to get out from under God?

Reading Romans alongside Affect, Queerness, and Feminism

Feminism, Queerness, Affect, and Romans: Under God? reads Romans. As a work in biblical studies, it offers plausible meanings to passages in the letter. These meanings probe how queer wo/men who first encountered this letter could have engaged with it. It does historical work because it reconstructs the plausible responses and impulses of these wo/men. This work summons an assemblage where Paul is one among many queer wo/men. Paul's letter represents some of the many impulses—words, ideas, sensations, gestures, movements, scents, feelings, and so on—that moved in between queer wo/men in Rome's ἐκκλησία.

Submission provides a thematic lens for how I read Romans. Submission is often hidden due to the letter's hopeful anticipations of δικαιοσύνη θεοῦ ("God's justice"). Submission pulsates the pages of Romans, and submission's *affect* draws focus to particular texts where it is most explicit (such as Rom 13) or most cruel (such as Rom 3). When these pulses are intentionally wielded by systems of power, ignored, or left dormant, they enact or enable oppression. I direct my attention to two instances: submission's implicit appearance as faithful submission in Rom 3 and its explicit mention as ethical submission in Rom 13.[5] I draw out this submission by engaging *feminist and queer affective critique*. This is one way that the politics of feminism, queerness, affect, and Romans are drawn together throughout my book.

The second way engages in *subversion* alongside Rome's queer wo/men. I reconstruct queer wo/men in Rome through a praxis of ἐκκλησία-l assemblage, which draws attention to how bodies, forces, and sensations converge and collide alongside one another in complex and contradictory ways. Assemblages emphasize affect's in-betweenness: firm divisions break down; identities overlap. Assemblages help us see submission being subverted.

Subversion is different from inversion. Inversion implies a flipping or switching of positions: the powerless become powerful, the heroes transformed into villains. Imbalance inverts. This dismantles a specific oppression only to rebuild its same structures. Subversion seeks *interruption*. It destabilizes, sometimes subtly, sneakily. It can slowly bubble into a boiling point. In my use of the term, subversion struggles to dismantle oppression entirely, without rebuilding it. Subversion is hard work; it is an unending struggle.

The subversive ἐκκλησία-l assemblages I (re)build are part of my overall feminist and queer affective politics, inseparable from the work of

---

5. Though left untouched here, submission's pulse can also be found explicitly in Rom 8 and 10 and implicitly in many other unexamined spaces in the letter. See especially Rom 8:7, 20; 10:3.

critique. The queer wo/men of Rome—like queer wo/men today—have not fully embodied justice: there is always more critical work to do. Justices and injustices remain for us to unearth. The following six chapters engage in this critical work with the queer wo/men in between Romans.

The first chapter, "Romans and Romanormativity: Feminist and Queer Affective Critique," spells out the book's feminist and queer commitments. It begins with a discussion of foundational political-theoretical concepts, including intersectionality and difference; wo/men and kyriarchy; and heteronormativity and homonormativity. The chapter then places these feminist and queer concepts into dialogue with first-century Roman materials to demonstrate what I am calling Romosexuality and Romanormativity. Finally, I develop feminist and queer work around affect theory's emphasis on feelings, sensations, and in-betweenness, which shows how normativity, as an affective force, draws and compels bodies even when they may seem to resist dominant culture. This provokes new ways to read Romans. Feminist and queer affective critique, in dialogue with first-century socio-sexual-political norms, compels attention to how Roman constructions of sexuality and gender affect Paul's letter to the Romans beyond obvious passages. Affectively feminist and queer attention, I argue, reveals how an imperial-aligned ideal of submission "under God" undergirds Romans and drives an affectively aspirational Romanormativity.

In chapter 2, "Waking Up (from) Tired Texts: Feminism, Queerness, and ἐκκλησία-l Assemblages," I argue that feminist and queer deployments of assemblage move readings of Romans beyond "the heroic Paul" identified by Melanie Johnson-DeBaufre and Laura S. Nasrallah. The chapter engages feminist and queer affective critique to analyze Rom 1:26–27 and queer biblical scholarship's (literally) exhaustive focus on it. Looking to Rom 16 and material culture, I show how turning to the queer wo/men in and around Paul's audience aids in moving beyond the first chapter of Paul's letter. I argue that the site of the ancient ἐκκλησία offers a first-century space to expand feminist and queer affective renderings of assemblage. By thinking with assemblages alongside Schüssler Fiorenza's "ἐκκλησία of wo/men," I harness my own praxis of ἐκκλησία-l assemblage that the rest of the book uses to move beyond Pauline heroism. I feature this praxis by returning to Rom 1:26–27 as a test case at the chapter's conclusion. I bring to life the queer wo/men of Rome's ἐκκλησία by proliferating their plausible, diverging responses to these verses. Challenging presumptions of historical certainty, my speculatively plausible reconstruction imagines how queer wo/men interrupted and interacted with Paul and each other as their ideas and feelings clashed and mingled. My praxis of ἐκκλησία-l assemblage, in dialogue with feminist and queer affective critique, scrambles the sides in between queer wo/men and Paul and awakens this tired text.

The next two chapters turn to how first-century Christ-followers developed different theo-Christologies. Chapter 3, "Faithful Submission," considers the submissiveness of Paul's presentation of Jesus Christ and his πίστις in 3:21–31. I situate πίστις (traditionally translated as "faith") within the propaganda of Roman imperialism, which benefitted from promises of loyal πίστις to ensure the submissive behavior of its conquered ἔθνη. Rome's promises of πίστις enabled ancient fantasies of upward mobility into a Romanormative good life. These fantasies forge attachments akin to what Lauren Berlant calls "cruel optimism." I argue that faithful submission spreads from the letter's introduction in 1:5 into Rom 3–5 in ways that render Paul a purveyor of a cruel πίστις that is optimistically and impossibly attached to a fantasy of achieving the Romanormative good life under a Roman-without-Rome God.

Chapter 4, "Faithful Subversion," considers alternatives to Rome's cruel optimism based on different interpretations of Jesus, God, and πίστις (or lack thereof). Considering many affective impulses that were generated in between queer wo/men in Rome's ἐκκλησία, this chapter prolifer-ates several different interpretations of theo-Christology that could exist alongside those in Rom 1–5. Reconstructed alongside evidence from other first-century theologies (among Christ-followers, Jews, and other religious associations), these impulses aligned with and subverted Rome's kyriarchy as all of these bodies continue to tread in imperial waters. The chapter concludes by putting all of these impulses together and brings to life the theo-Christologies of Rome's queer wo/men as they interacted with Rom 3–5. These impulsive interactions simultaneously subvert and more strin-gently support cruel πίστις and faithful submission under God.

The final two chapters focus on how theo-Christology impacted Christ-followers' ethics: what they should *do*. Submission's pulse con-tinues through the epistle's closing chapters, as chapter 5, "Ethical Submission," shows. Jasbir Puar's "homonationalism"—a tactic that allows certain "queer" bodies to perform patriotic morality in order to become praiseworthy under a national/imperial gaze—resonates in a first-century Roman context. Many non-elite bodies, including but not limited to Paul, attempted to conform their ethics to those of Rome in order to benefit and rise in status. In this chapter, I exegete the ethical ideas in Rom 13 alongside imperial ethics and the kyriarchal structuring of morality. The regulations of sexual and ethical moderation in Rom 13:8–14 prove inseparable from 13:1–7's ethical mandate to submit to the ruling authorities of Rome. Romans 13 highlights how Pauline ethics participate in Roman-style homonationalism.

These homonational ethics were neither unique to Paul nor the only ethical ideas held by Christ-followers. If Paul's submissive notion of πίστις underlies his homonational ethics, then what different ethical responses might emerge from other theo-christological starting points? Chapter 6, "An Ethical ἐκκλησία," moves beyond the ethical questions of Rom 13 and considers other ethical impulses that plausibly emerged around Rome's ἐκκλησία. These plausible impulses engaged some of the pressing moral concerns that surrounded imperial politics, sexual praxis, and ethnic diversity. Emphasizing how Christ-followers were grappling with these concerns before receiving Paul's letter, this chapter situates Paul's ethical impulses as some among many ethical impulses that were sensed and embodied among queer wo/men in Rome's ἐκκλησία. Ultimately, it brings to life the complex and contradictory queerness that moved in between regulation and freedom and characterized this ἐκκλησία-l assemblage.

My book generates conversations in between theory and (biblical) text. This is a critical contribution. Feminist and queer affective critique and subversively feminist and queer assemblages are not methods applied to historical texts and contexts. Although this book *reads* Romans, the goal is not *a reading of* Romans. Its goal is to query what feminism, queerness, affect, and Romans can do when drawn together. Throughout this book, feminism, queerness, affect, and Romans twirl together in ways that affect each element. Feminism helps us read affect. Affect helps us feel Romans. Romans helps us engage queerness. These orientations draw many lines, move back and forth and in between many directions. The intersecting feminisms, queernesses, affects, and Romans that spill out of this constellation matter. Their politics impact queer wo/men in the present; their plausibilities intuit more just futures. From start to finish, *Feminism, Queerness, Affect, and Romans: Under God?* must, I insist, be political.

1

Romans and Romanormativity:
Feminist and Queer Affective Critique

Normal is overrated. Spoken like someone who didn't have to work so
hard at it. Who hadn't needed normal to survive.
—V. E. Schwab, *Vengeful*

What does normal feel like? Feminist and queer politics query what society
renders normal—maleness, cisness, straightness, whiteness—and critique
normativity. But queer wo/men, although deemed multiply abnormal, also
crave normalcy, like the character Eli Ever does in Schwab's novel. Feminist and queer affective critique probes the sensations that tug us toward
norms. This chapter places into conversation two broad areas of scholarship: (1) interdisciplinary and intersectional work within feminist, queer,
and affect theories and their contemporary politics; and (2) the experiences and regulations of gender and sexuality in the Roman Empire of
the first century CE, the historical setting of Paul's letter to the wo/men
of Rome's ἐκκλησία. Though first-century Rome and the globally connected twenty-first century have distinct differences, the critical lenses of
these contemporary politics resonate with ancient materials just as much
as ancient materials resonate in contemporary moments. The terms and
critiques developed by contemporary queer, feminist, and affect theories
provoke new questions that can be asked around ancient materials and the
wo/men who interacted with them.

First, "Intersectionality, Feminism, and Queer Theory" situates my
feminist, queer, and intersectional commitments. I introduce the terms
and theories from these movements that are critical for my approach to
Roman gender and sexuality and my development of affective critique
and assemblage. In "Queer Wo/men, Romosexuals, and Romanormativity," I transition into the first century and emphasize the lived sexual and

gender embodiments of Roman queer wo/men while also acknowledging the ways in which the politics of gender and sexuality were constructed and regulated by Roman imperial norms. The terms theorized at the intersections of feminism and queer theory bring new insights to the study of Roman sexual politics. Finally, in "The Forces and Feelings of Normativity: Affect Theories and Critiques," I emphasize how intersectionality, queerness, and feminism are foundational to affective critique, especially as manifested in the work of Jasbir K. Puar and Lauren Berlant. Drawing from Berlant and Puar, I cultivate an intersectionally feminist and queer affective critique.

Such a critique, I argue as the chapter concludes, is necessary for uprooting troubling dimensions of submission in first-century Rome and Paul's letters, both of which perpetuate a kyriarchal normativity through which oppressions based on gender and sexuality inseparably intersect with oppressions rooted in race/ethnicity and class. A queer and feminist *affective* critique attends to the forces and feelings of normativity that mingle in between the text of Romans. This in-betweenness challenges queer and feminist critiques to look beyond texts where wo/men and queer sexualities explicitly appear, such as Rom 1:18–32 or Rom 16. How do gender and sexuality—and their invariable intersections with race and class—affect the theologies and ethics of Romans?

Intersectionality, Feminism, and Queer Theory

The politics of feminism and queerness are my starting point for reading Romans. My situation in these fields relies on overlapping emphases in both theories that prioritize intersectionality. Attending to intersectionality means that we are also attuned to politics and scholarship that is rooted in critical race, postcolonial, disability, fat, and trans studies. So why choose to emphasize queerness and feminism? They are *my* starting points for intersectional interpretation: naming them admits where I start and that I might have seen things differently from another beginning.[1]

---

1. The admission of an interpreter's subjectivity has been (and is often still) denied among biblical scholars, but my situation of my personal, professional, political starting point is rooted in the work of biblical scholars working as feminist, queer, Black, Latinx, Asian/Asian-American, cultural, postcolonial, and disability critics of biblical texts and contexts. Elisabeth Schüssler Fiorenza signaled a "paradigm shift" to the subjectivity of biblical scholars—as opposed to their objectivity—in her 1987

The intersection of feminist and queer theories is my starting point because I am undeniably feminist and queer to my core. My identity as a scholar of the Bible is forever bound to these identities. Courses in feminist hermeneutics ignited my interest in research on Paul's letters, allowed me to find my scholarly voice and gave me confidence as a writer, and conscientized me to see how the political is personal, eventually leading to my claiming of a queer identity. While my queerness often means I am first associated with queer studies, I could not be queer without being feminist. Furthermore, *I will not be queer without remaining feminist.* The history of queer theory and feminism is rife with a supersessionism that presumes queerness supplants feminism, but my work and reading in queer theory pushes against this logic and allies with queer and feminist scholars who refuse this divide. Even if they sometimes involve tense interactions, I could bring queer theory into my scholarly identity only if it intersected with my feminist agenda. As a result, I will not allow my queerness to supplant my feminism. In what follows, I explain my engagement with feminist and queer studies and introduce concepts (intersectionality and difference; kyriarchy; heteronormativity and homonormativity; and wo/men) that are foundational to both affective critique and assemblage.

Intersectionality, originally coined by legal scholar Kimberlé Crenshaw in 1989, eschews a single-issue focus when analyzing discrimination.[2]

---

presidential address to the Society of Biblical Literature. She writes, "Once biblical scholarship begins to talk explicitly of social interests, whether of race, gender, culture, or class, and once it begins to recognize the need for a sophisticated and pluralistic reading of texts that questions the fixity of meaning, then a double ethics is called for." Elisabeth Schüssler Fiorenza, "The Ethics of Biblical Interpretation: Decentering Biblical Scholarship," *JBL* 107 (1988): 14. See also Fernando F. Segovia and Mary Ann Tolbert, eds., *Social Location and Biblical Interpretation in the United States*, vol. 1 of *Reading from This Place* (Minneapolis: Fortress, 1995); Segovia and Tolbert, eds., *Social Location and Biblical Interpretation in Global Perspective*, vol. 2 of *Reading from This Place* (Minneapolis: Fortress, 1995).

2. Kimberlé Crenshaw, "Demarginalizing the Intersection of Race and Sex: A Black Feminist Critique of Antidiscrimination Doctrine, Feminist Theory, and Antiracist Politics," *UCLF* 139 (1989): 139–67. Crenshaw's term participates in and draws from a long history of Black feminist work demanding attention to the interlocking oppressions and experiences of race, gender, class, and sexuality. Perhaps most notable is the 1977 statement of the Combahee River Collective, an organization of Black feminists committed to eliminating systemic oppressions of all people and emphasizing the particular nexus of oppressions that harmed working-class Black lesbians. At the outset of the statement, they proclaimed: "The most general statement of our politics at

Oppressions (specifically racism and sexism) intersect so that the resulting discrimination is greater than the sum of its parts.[3] This development of intersectionality resonates with how Audre Lorde writes about difference in ways that are important to emphases on the intersectionality of queerness.[4] Showing how sexuality intersects with race, gender, and class, Lorde acknowledges sexual orientation as one axis of difference among the many that she discusses. Both Lorde's discussion of difference and Crenshaw's analysis of intersectionality insist upon acknowledging and critiquing how multiple axes of oppression interact and affect people and society. Intersectionality and difference must be recognized in order to redefine power in a way that allows relations across these differences.[5]

Intersectionality, alongside the emphases of queer theory and feminism, can be seen in Lorde's analysis of how human difference gets cast as deviance. "We speak not of human difference but of human deviance." Lorde identifies a "mythical norm" deployed by those in power in American society. This norm is "white, thin, male, young, heterosexual, christian,

---

the present time would be that we are actively committed to struggling against racial, sexual, heterosexual, and class oppression, and see as our particular task the development of integrated analysis and practice based upon the fact that *the major systems of oppression are interlocking*. The synthesis of these oppressions creates the conditions of our lives." See "The Combahee River Collective Statement," Combahee River Collective, https://tinyurl.com/SBL4531a (emphasis added). Similar intersectional attention prior to Crenshaw's coining of the term includes bell hooks, *Ain't I a Woman? Black Women and Feminism* (Boston: South End, 1981); Cherríe Moraga and Gloria Anzaldúa, *This Bridge Called My Back: Writings by Radical Women of Color*, 4th ed. (Albany: SUNY Press, 2015); Audre Lorde, *Sister Outsider* (Berkeley: Crossing, 1984; repr. 2007); Patricia Hill Collins, *Black Feminist Thought: Knowledge, Consciousness, and the Politics of Empowerment*, 2nd ed. (New York: Routledge, 2000).

3. Crenshaw demonstrates how court rulings on Equal Opportunity Employment laws failed to address systemic hiring discrimination that disfavored Black women (because, courts ruled, companies were in compliance with laws preventing gender discrimination so long as they hired white women and were adhering to laws forbidding racial discrimination so long as they hired Black men). She writes, "The problems with exclusion cannot be solved simply by including Black women within an already established analytical structure. Because the intersectional experience is greater than the sum of racism and sexism, any analysis that does not take intersectionality into account cannot sufficiently address the particular manner in which Black women are subordinated" (Crenshaw, "Demarginalizing the Intersection," 140).

4. As emphasized in David L. Eng, with Jack Halberstam and Josè Esteban Muñoz, "Introduction: What's Queer about Queer Studies Now?," *Social Text* 23 (2005): 1.

5. Lorde, *Sister Outsider*, 123.

and financially secure."[6] By disenfranchising people based on any deviation from the norm (only those who deviate are considered different), those in power magnify difference along multiple axes, often meaning those who are oppressed focus exclusively on the way(s) in which only their particular group differs.[7] This "divide and conquer" mentality of difference connects with Crenshaw's emphasis on how a single-issue focus denies the intersectional experiences of those who deviate from the norm in multiple ways.[8] Intersectionality must be a starting point for any critique of injustice.

As feminists, we constantly critique and call out oppression and discrimination. Often, this means we appear as the "killjoy," as Sara Ahmed defines, the one or ones who become a problem by pointing out that a problem *already* existed.[9] Feminism calls out inequality because it is struggling toward an egalitarian world. The introduction framed this book in terms of struggle and drew from Schüssler Fiorenza's feminist situation of struggle. This situation participates in a long feminist history that locates feminism's politics, activism, and theories within contexts of struggle: "Feminism requires supporting women in a struggle to exist in this world," writes Ahmed.[10] Feminism centralizes women's struggles against gender-based oppressions at global, local, and national levels.[11] This struggle

---

6. Lorde, *Sister Outsider*, 116. Lorde's demands for attending to the intersections of all these oppressions—and her work on sexuality as part of that (additionally, see her essay "Uses of the Erotic: The Erotic as Power," in *Sister Outsider*, 53–59)—are an essence of the origins of a queerness that is intersectional. Her contributions should not and cannot be limited to queer theory; indeed, they should not even be said to primarily be concerned with queers or queerness, since she is equally—and often more—concerned with issues of racial oppression, along with oppressions based on gender and class.

7. "Those of us who stand outside that power often identify one way in which we are different, and we assume that to be the primary cause of all oppression, forgetting other distortions around differences, some of which we ourselves may be practising" (Lorde, *Sister Outsider*, 116).

8. "In our world, divide and conquer must become define and empower" (Lorde, *Sister Outsider*, 112).

9. Sara Ahmed, *Living a Feminist Life* (Durham, NC: Duke University Press, 2017), 36–39. Ahmed introduces the feminist killjoy in *The Promise of Happiness* (Durham, NC: Duke University Press, 2010), 50–87.

10. Ahmed, *Living a Feminist Life*, 14.

11. While the sources of such gender-based oppression are diverse and numerous, most feminist theorists acknowledge and critique a longstanding ideology of patriarchy,

involves becoming conscious—and helping others to become conscious—of how differences, especially gender differences, are experienced.

Far too often in patriarchal and even in feminist history, equality has been heralded as having arrived (reminiscent, perhaps, of Caesar's triumphal processions [παρουσίαι] that ushered in justice, equality, and πίστις to the nations he conquered). Yet these announcements have always been premature since, as killjoys show, equality today is still imagined in unequal terms. Even within feminism and its struggles, equality has been linked to the causes of white feminism, that is, a feminism that struggles only for the concerns of white, wealthier, straight, cis women.[12] This restricted vision of women and equality celebrates victories that enfranchised some women over others, ignores the differences and needs of women excluded from it, and often co-opts and celebrates all women's successes as a result of its work.[13]

---

which establishes and confirms male dominance across an array of sociopolitical institutions. Patriarchal ideology privileges maleness by presenting "men/male" as the natural/neutral category from which *difference* is defined. Repeated and reified over time, not only does this male perspective become the viewpoint of those who wield the most sociopolitical power, but it is also presumed to be universally applicable, thus neutral or objective. Feminist theory reveals these patriarchal perspectives that underlie such neutrality and shows how academic fields, scientific/medical research, and social institutions all presume that the generic human is, on further inspection, a man. Under such patriarchy, to prioritize or focus exclusively on women (or anything perceived as women's issues)—as well as any other deviation from the sociopolitically powerful man—is to be interested, biased, and subjective. See further Elisabeth Schüssler Fiorenza, *Rhetoric and Ethic: The Politics of Biblical Studies* (Minneapolis: Fortress, 1999), 1–14; Schüssler Fiorenza, *Wisdom Ways: Introducing Feminist Biblical Interpretation* (Louisville: Westminster John Knox, 2001), 102–17; Schüssler Fiorenza, *Transforming Vision: Explorations in Feminist The*logy* (Minneapolis: Fortress, 2001), 23–38; Amy Allen, *The Power of Feminist Theory: Domination, Resistance, Solidarity* (Boulder, CO: Westview, 1999); Joan Wallach Scott, *Gender and the Politics of History*, rev. ed. (New York: Columbia University Press, 1999); Patricia Hill Collins, *Black Feminist Thought: Knowledge, Consciousness, and the Politics of Empowerment*, 2nd ed. (New York: Routledge, 2000).

12. For example, in feminist struggles in the late nineteenth and early twentieth centuries ("first wave" feminism), feminist discourse focused its energy on the political movement for women's suffrage, trumping other concerns and excluding the voices and bodies deemed irrelevant or even detrimental to this cause, especially those who were not white. Despite insistences to the contrary, the dominant voices of this feminist movement presumed and portrayed (and thereby defined) women as racially white and more or less socioeconomically privileged.

13. See discussions in Moraga and Anzaldúa, *This Bridge Called My Back*, especially (but not limited to) sections 3 ("And When You Leave, Take Your Pictures with

Schüssler Fiorenza's theorization of kyriarchy displays the importance of a feminism that struggles with intersectionality and difference. Expanding the limitations of the term *patriarchy*, kyriarchy accounts for numerous axes upon which power is arranged in hierarchies that produce the most sociopolitical economic benefits for those at the top, that is, those who rule not only based on gender imbalances but also through imbalances created by class-based, racialized, and sexualized distinctions (among others). The term derives from the Greek roots of ἀρχή ("rule") and κύριος ("master" or "lord"), combining to denote "rule of the master/lord." Though in biblical texts κύριος is often a title affixed to God—and, more often in Paul's case, to Jesus—its more common usage in Greek is to refer to those men (and occasionally women) who are heads of households or major political leaders, or both. It is most often used (including numerous examples in New Testament literature) in relation to δοῦλαι, wo/men who have been enslaved by a κύριος as the master of the household.[14]

In using this root for her neologism, Schüssler Fiorenza renders explicit the fact that power is arranged along multiple axes. Kyriarchy's interlocking axes establish a small class of κύριοι (alongside some women as κυρίαι) at the top, with slowly decreasing gradations of lord-like authority moving in multiple directions downward on its complex hierarchy of power. Kyriarchy foregrounds the authority held and subtly manipulated by various lords and masters throughout history, from the citizen-male δῆμος ("people/citizens," i.e., the root of *demo*cracy) of ancient Greece and the imperial elite of Rome to kings, feudal lords, and today's 1 percent. The term emphasizes how their mastery has been sustained by ideologies of difference that enable sociopolitical division.[15]

Kyriarchy identifies and critiques the ways in which power controls and enforces oppressive hierarchies within these messy, intersecting networks of identity. It recalls Lorde's identification of a "mythical norm" that conveys a specific ideal "identity" most closely fitting any given society's

---

You: Racism in the Women's Movement," 55–97) and 4 ("Between the Lines: On Culture, Class, and Homophobia," 100–157); hooks, *Ain't I a Woman*, esp. 1–13, 119–58; Flavia Dzodan, "My Feminism Will Be Intersectional or It Will Be Bullshit!," *Tiger Beatdown*, 10 October 2011, https://tinyurl.com/SBLPress4531b1.

14. Schüssler Fiorenza, *Wisdom Ways*, 118–24; see also Schüssler Fiorenza, *Transforming Vision*, 8–11.

15. Schüssler Fiorenza, *Transforming Vision*, 8–11.

elite χύριοι. The ancient roots of kyriarchy remind us that mythical norms and deployments of deviance occur throughout history. Lorde cautions against "historical amnesia": "By ignoring the past, we are encouraged to repeat its mistakes."[16] We forget or ignore the historical and ongoing progression of kyriarchy at our peril.

Queer politics and theory also engage in critique, typically from the starting point of LGBTIA2Q+ oppressions. Traditionally, this has meant that queer theory has focused on sexuality and its regulation. However, sexual suppression intersects with oppressions based on class, race, and gender. Sex—meaning the actions of sexuality (not sex as gender)—"is a vector of oppression," writes Gayle Rubin.[17] Rubin emphasizes that sexual oppression has social, economic, and political motivations. Given the variety of sociopolitically oppressive uses of sex, which often rely on the "shock value" of particular sexual practices (e.g., BDSM), Rubin concludes, "Sexual acts are burdened with an excess of significance."[18] Because sexuality is excessively significant in society, it must be controlled by those in power and simultaneously becomes a site of resistance. Whether sexual acts are in the foreground or background, politics are fundamentally inseparable from sexuality and its effects.[19]

This excessive significance given to queer sexualities relies upon the shadow of heterosexual intercourse, which does not command the same attention—because it is considered *normal*. Resonating with Lorde's identification of a mythical norm, the emphasis in much queer theory has been on normativity and the ways norms oppress different (i.e., deviant) sexualities. This means subverting what lesbian feminist Adrienne Rich called "compulsory heterosexuality," the assumption (for her, especially problematic within feminist theory) that all women are heterosexual, which excludes and erases the experiences and histories of lesbian and queer wo/men.[20] Society operates under *heteronormativity*, the assumption that

---

16. Lorde, *Sister Outsider*, 117.

17. Gayle S. Rubin, *Deviations: A Gayle Rubin Reader* (Durham, NC: Duke University Press, 2011), 164. All citations of this volume refer to Rubin's 1984 essay, "Thinking Sex: Notes for a Radical Theory of the Politics of Sexuality."

18. Rubin, *Deviations*, 149.

19. "Like gender, sexuality is political. It is organized into systems of power, which reward and encourage some individuals and activities, while punishing and suppressing others" (Rubin, *Deviations*, 180).

20. Adrienne Rich, "Compulsory Heterosexuality and Lesbian Existence," *Signs* 5 (1980): 635.

all persons live like heterosexual couples.[21] Heteronormativity starts from the presumption that all people are straight and that anyone without a straight sexual orientation is crooked, that is, deviant vis-à-vis this norm. Although sexuality is the starting point for heteronormativity, queer theorists demonstrate how heteronormativity is structural and affects daily life, society, politics, culture, including perceptions of time (the workday, life rhythms) and the construction of space and architecture.[22]

Queer theory often interrogates, destabilizes, resists, and operates outside of dominant modes of social belonging, especially those structured by heteronormativity.[23] Queerness gets characterized by *subversion*, especially related to subverting norms and normativities. Increasingly, queer scholars demand an intersectional approach to normativities that considers how the "heterosexual" of Lorde's norm intersects with its "white,

---

21. "I am suggesting that heterosexuality, like motherhood, needs to be recognized and studied as a political institution—even, or especially, by those individuals who feel they are, in their personal experience, the precursors of a new social relation between the sexes" (Rich, "Compulsory Heterosexuality," 637). Michael Warner originally coined the term *heteronormativity*, to which Rich's *compulsory heterosexuality* could be called a precursor. Michael Warner, "Introduction," in *Fear of a Queer Planet*, ed. Warner, CP 6 (Minneapolis: University of Minnesota Press, 1993), vii–xxxi; orig. published in *SocT* 29 (1991): 3–17. My presentation of queer origins here is selective and does not purport to give a historical account so much as it attempts to highlight certain important—and most relevant—aspects among queerness's diverse beginnings. See Donald E. Hall and Annamarie Jagose, "Introduction," in *The Routledge Queer Studies Reader*, ed. Hall and Jagose with Andrea Bebell and Susan Potter (London: Routledge, 2013), xiv–xx, esp. xvi. See also the earlier introductory text, Jagose, *Queer Theory: An Introduction* (New York: New York University Press, 1996).

22. On queer approaches to time, see, for example, Jack Halberstam, *In a Queer Time and Place: Transgender Bodies, Subcultural Lives*, Sexual Cultures (New York: New York University Press, 2005); Elizabeth Freeman, *Time Binds: Queer Temporalities, Queer Histories*, PM (Durham, NC: Duke University Press, 2010); Halberstam's book on time also represents a queer approach to space and geography; on queer spatial orientations, see Samuel R. Delany, *Times Square Red, Times Square Blue*, Sexual Cultures (New York: New York University Press, 1999); Sara Ahmed, *Queer Phenomenology: Orientations, Objects, Others* (Durham, NC: Duke University Press, 2006).

23. Queer theory's origins (many of which precede the formal coining of the field of queer theory in 1990 by Teresa De Lauretis) are rooted in political activism and social change, even as they probe the often dense depths of academic theory. See Teresa De Lauretis, "Queer Theory: Lesbian and Gay Sexualities: An Introduction," *differences* 3 (1991): iii–xviii. The volume/essay was published in 1991, but the essay was originally delivered as a paper at a 1990 conference bearing its title.

young, financially secure, thin, christian, and male." How are politics and social formations structured by straightness also structured by whiteness and maleness? Indeed, how is heteronormativity itself foundationally tangled with racism, sexism, and classism—just as racism, sexism, and classism are all fundamentally based in heteronormativity?

The intersectional starting points of queer theory and its analysis of heteronormativity have not always been (and still frequently are not) emphatic. In 1997, Cathy J. Cohen criticized the narrow focus within queer politics and theories on the *hetero* of heteronormativity, which resulted in the casting of any and all straight people as the oppressors of LGBTIA2Q+ folks and, therefore, the villains of queer justice.[24] Cohen calls attention to the regulation and stigmatization of relationships and family structures especially found among poor, Black women (singled out in the 1965 Moynahan Report and presumed under Ronald Reagan's "welfare queens"). Although most of these women would be categorized as straight (and, therefore, outside of the work of the queer activism Cohen critiques), their sexualities are being cast as deviant from a heteronormativity that is clearly structured at the intersections of racialized and classed presumptions.[25]

Normativity is fluid. This fluidity maintains a mythical norm by shifting to include and exclude some bodies, in different times and spaces. When it comes to the intersectional regulation of sexuality, this means that (hetero)normativity not only excludes many straight folks but also can (temporarily) include certain queers. In the aftermath of US legal and political battles that have resulted in the permission of same-sex marriage nationwide, certain persons (particularly white gay affluent cis men) who were once clearly queer—that is, standing outside heteronormative social structures—now find that their sexual practices no longer exclude them from what were formerly heterosexual institutions.[26] Lisa Duggan

---

24. Cathy J. Cohen, "Punks, Bulldaggers, and Welfare Queens: The Radical Potential of Queer Politics?," *GLQ* 3 (1997): 437–65. Taking, as one example, the Queer Nation Manifesto (1990), she writes, "Screaming from this manifesto is an analysis which places not heteronormativity, but heterosexuality, as the central 'dividing line' between those who would be dominant and those who are oppressed" (Cohen, "Punks, Bulldaggers," 447).

25. Cohen, "Punks, Bulldaggers," 452–57. Cohen cites Lorde and emphasizes Crenshaw's theories of intersectionality (459).

26. Other victories include the repeal of the Defense of Marriage Act and of the US military's "Don't Ask Don't Tell" policy. This inclusion is, of course, contingent and

observes how a liberal LGBTIA2Q+ politics, especially centered upon the interests of folks who are affluent, white, cisgender, and male, distinguishes itself from a radical politics of queerness through a tactic and rhetoric of *inclusion* into already established, normative structures available only to straight folks (who are also primarily affluent and white). Duggan terms these politics *homonormativity*: conferring the normative benefits of heterosexuality onto "homos" who can become "the new normal" by being a *near* normal. With the exception of being a same-sex couple, their lives and families conform to the same monogamy and capitalist productivity as ideal, nuclear heterosexual couples.[27]

The focus on inclusion (in heteronormativity) represents the first dimension of homonormativity. The second dimension, usually entwined with the first, is its dependence on tactics of othering queer bodies who deviate from a normative, vanilla, and monogamous sexuality. Homonormativity *desexualizes* homosexuality in distinction to the embracing of different sexual relations emphasized within a norm-subverting or norm-refusing queerness.[28] Homonormative same-sex couples are just as vanilla and family oriented as heterosexual couples (at least as presumed under heteronormativity).

---

does not signal the complete downfall of heteronormativity, a point that Puar makes in her analysis of sexual exceptionalism (see ch. 5).

27. "New neoliberal sexual politics ... might be termed the new homonormativity—it is a politics that does not contest dominant heteronormative assumptions and institutions, but upholds and sustains them, while promising the possibility of a demobilized gay constituency and a privatized, depoliticized gay culture anchored in domesticity and consumption" (Lisa Duggan, *The Twilight of Equality: Neo-Liberalism, Cultural Politics and the Attack on Democracy* [Boston: Beacon, 2000], 50). See also Eng, with Halberstam and Muñoz, "Introduction," 11; Jasbir K. Puar, *Terrorist Assemblages: Homonationalism in Queer Times*, NW (Durham, NC: Duke University Press, 2007), 38–39; Halberstam, *In a Queer Time and Place*, 19. Duggan herself notes, *homonormativity* is meant to riff off of *heteronormativity*, as originally introduced by Warner; however, the term has taken on its own life in recent queer theory. Duggan does not intend the riff to be parallel to heteronormativity: "there is no structure for gay life, no matter how conservative or normalizing, that might compare with the institutions promoting and sustaining heterosexual coupling" (Duggan, *Twilight of Equality*, 94, n. 15).

28. David L. Eng details how this desexualization occurs in the 2003 Supreme Court decision *Lawrence and Garner v. Texas*, which ruled sodomy laws unconstitutional. See David L. Eng, *The Feeling of Kinship: Queer Liberalism and the Racialization of Intimacy* (Durham, NC: Duke University Press, 2010), 23–57.

During his popular (but ultimately unsuccessful) campaign in the 2020 Democratic presidential primaries, the nationally prominent, openly gay US politician Pete Buttigieg's deployment of his gay Christian identity exemplified homonormativity. As a gay Christian, Buttigieg's politics not only exemplified terms of queer critique (i.e., homonormativity and, as we will see in ch. 5, homonationalism); they also built upon the fantasies of imperial inclusion ("Romanormativity") that I am arguing are present in Paul's letters and other early Christian texts. A veteran married to his husband Chasten, Buttigieg cast himself as the beneficiary of homonormative LGBTIA2Q+ politics, whose emphasis on inclusion permitted him to marry and serve in the military. Buttigieg openly appealed to voters as the first gay presidential candidate and emphasized the importance of his election to rebalance the US Supreme Court in order to protect his marriage from the potential overturning of *Obergefell v. Hodges* (the 2015 decision to end marriage discrimination against same-sex couples).[29]

Buttigieg's emphasis on inclusion highlights the first dimension of homonormativity; his presentation of gay sexuality emphasizes the second. At a fundraiser for a prominent LGBTIA2Q+ organization, he recounted how he met his husband. In his narration, Buttigieg appealed to his youth (an ageism that distinguished him from older candidates) by saying they met through a dating app (common among millennials); however, he quickly cautioned "not the one you're thinking of," explicitly warding off any assumptions or associations with queer promiscuity, especially associated with gay-specific apps like Growlr, Grindr, or Scruff.[30] Later, the campaign canceled a fundraiser at a gay bar, centered around

---

29. "When I look at the Supreme Court, I can't help but remember that my marriage only exists by the grace of a single vote in that body," Buttigieg said in an interview. See Alexandra Whittaker, "Pete Buttigieg Wants to Restructure the Supreme Court to Be 'Less Political,'" *Cosmopolitan*, 24 October 2019, https://tinyurl.com/SBL4531b.

30. Chris Johnson, "Buttigieg Engages LGBT Crowd by Sharing Personal Struggle of Being Gay," *Washington Blade*, 7 April 2019, https://tinyurl.com/SBL4531c. The app he used was a general dating app—Hinge—developed primarily for straight folks to facilitate dates that lead to relationships that lead to marriage. He admits this in an interview with LGBTIA2Q+ magazine the *Advocate*, in which the interviewer also gives him a platform to emphasize his youth, since he would be the "first president to have met their spouse on a dating app" (Jeffrey Masters, "We Sat Down with Pete Buttigieg to Talk about Gay Stuff," *Advocate*, 23 April 2019, https://tinyurl.com/SBL4531d). Apps like Grindr, primarily centered around gay men looking for hookups, are not

an appearance by Chasten Buttigieg, reportedly because the bar refused to remove a "dancer pole" that Chasten deemed "inappropriate."[31] In this instance, we see Buttigieg attempting to appeal to his gay identity by campaigning in gay spaces but only if it conformed to an "appropriate" form of gayness not rooted in "inappropriate" overt displays of the *sex* of sexuality. Given how traditional Christian interpretations of sexual morality (at least partially rooted in Paul's letters) presume "good sex" occurs only in the private context of a monogamous marriage, Buttigieg's ongoing emphasis of his Christian faith and morals presumably played a role in these deployments of homonormative sexuality. These instances display how homonormativity dissociates certain same-sex couples from the elements of queerness that, under heteronormativity, make it impossible to include queerness within mythical normativity.

Buttigieg's rising-star status in national Democratic politics may soon fall into obscurity in the years after his unsuccessful primary bid. His example may feel less relevant if/when his name and campaign fade from our memories. History grants significance to the winners. But, when it comes to queer *national* politics, there are few—if any—other examples. The fact that concerns over relevance recommend excluding Buttigieg as an example signals just how Buttigieg's homonormative politics are *affective fantasies of inclusion*. At present, arguably the best example of a national, prominent gay politician—despite all his attempts to be as normal and moderate as possible—*still* isn't good enough to merit memory. Homonormative queer politicians can play into the fantasy of being normal, but their gayness will always fail them, forever an example to footnote and never destined to be the main bodies that the academy-nation desires or rewards.[32]

---

without problems, especially around racism, transphobia, sexism, fatphobia, and ableism, but these problems are not the associations about which Buttigieg was concerned.

31. Juwan J. Holmes, "Chasten Buttigieg Allegedly Abandons Fundraiser for Pete at 'Inappropriate' Gay Bar," *LGBTQ Nation*, 19 January 2020, https://tinyurl.com/SBL4531e.

32. As I complete this manuscript, Buttigieg's star has yet to fade, having recently been appointed US Secretary of Transportation in the cabinet of US President Joe Biden. This made him (as he and others remind the public) the first openly LGBTIA2Q+ cabinet member in US history. Buttigieg may someday be the first openly gay US president. If not him, someone else *will* be. Even as I hope and dream to make it otherwise, I suspect whoever becomes the United States' first openly LGBTIA2Q+ president (or, at least, a major party's nominee) is likely to draw upon Buttigieg's

Homonormativity signals how tactics that emphasize LGBTIA2Q+ inclusion merely redeploy heteronormativity in a way that permits certain privileged others to live according to its established norms. Homonormativity attends to some of the needs for intersectionality in queer critique. Homonormative inclusion is more likely to substantially benefit those already nearest to the mythical norm. It denies queer priorities that extend beyond marriage, including the recognition of other sexual relationships and bonds, discrimination and violence against trans folks, and systemic oppression that results in barriers to employment, housing discrimination, and unequal access to affordable health care.[33] All of these are political issues that become more urgent when the regulation of sexuality intersects with racism, sexism, and classism.

Difference and intersectionality insist on a new starting point for the work of queer and feminist politics: the oppression of women and LGBTIA2Q+ folks must account for the differences among these folks, acknowledge other forms of oppression, and critique feminist and queer approaches that replicate or continue any oppressive tactic. Kyriarchy and homonormativity are terms from feminism and queer theory that offer critique from an intersectional starting point.

Critique is only a starting point—just as the oppressions of wo/men and LGBTIA2Q+ folks represent only starting points for feminism and queer theory. If, as Lorde insists, "the master's tools will never dismantle the master's house," then intersectional politics must develop tools for such dismantling in order to keep building a society that reflects the "genuine change" Lorde envisions.[34] Such change neither imagines a return to an idyllic past nor rests its hope in easy visions of an anticipated future yet to come. Dismantling inequality and oppression is a necessary part of the struggle toward change: the killjoy is tearing down oppression's house and building something new, a new dwelling, with new tools.[35] This is an

---

tactics. Ultimately, his name may or may not stay relevant, but I insist on the significance that Buttigieg's *story* and its biblical resonances should have for our memories.

33. Especially vis-à-vis Buttigieg, the activist organization #QueersAgainstPete articulates the importance of these issues to intersectional queerness, opposing Buttigieg for his failure to address them. See especially "Open Letter," Queers Against Pete, https://tinyurl.com/SBL4531f.

34. Lorde, *Sister Outsider*, 112.

35. Ahmed, *Living a Feminist Life*, 14. She goes on to think of citation as a form of feminist building that, instead of bricks, uses straw—"lighter materials that, when put together, will create a shelter but a shelter that leaves you more vulnerable" (16).

equally (maybe even more) difficult struggle because the new equalities, the dwellings, and the tools that feminism and queerness seek to build have yet to be fully envisioned, defined, or invented.

If ignoring differences produces politics that "divide and conquer," naming, locating, and celebrating difference makes space for struggles to "define and empower."[36] Feminist and queer scholars have developed many tools that envision an intersectional embrace of difference. Given the ways in which the word *women* is impossible to fix with a stable definition, Schüssler Fiorenza inserts a slash into the term *wo/men* as a marking that does not change its pronunciation in oral contexts. The dividing slash in *wo/men* represents the differences among women, including differences in age, race, class, and sexual orientation, which grant them different access and relations to power. Some women oppress other women; indeed, some women oppress men (e.g., white women oppress wo/men of color as a result of racism; cis women oppress trans wo/men through transphobia and trans-exclusive radical feminism [TERF]; rich women oppress poor wo/men).[37] Visually representing these multiple, often complex divisions and power relations, *wo/men* captures some of gender's complexity and fractures any simplistic assertion of unity that could be presumed under the category of *women*.

The term works in a second political-theoretical direction. Emphasized by its homophonic pronunciation with *women*, *wo/men* sometimes— but not always—can include men—as a whole or some subset. Through such ambiguity, it performs a linguistic reversal that puts the burden on men—who have insisted on the inclusive ambiguity of terms like *men* and *guys*—to figure out whether they are (or should be) included when *wo/men* is used.[38]

My usage of *wo/men* fluctuates across this ambiguity: sometimes it (clearly) does not include men and other times it could or (obviously) does. When it comes to first-century ἐκκλησίαι, wo/men's presence and leadership has been erased and denied, which makes it crucial to emphasize their

---

36. Lorde, *Sister Outsider*, 112.

37. Schüssler Fiorenza, *Wisdom Ways*, 107–9. Schüssler Fiorenza, *Transforming Vision*, 6.

38. This consideration process, as Schüssler Fiorenza notes, is one in and to which wo/men have long been trained and accustomed. I go through this process myself when I use the term, especially in every instance below when I have made it clear that I have included myself among queer wo/men.

presence in these spaces as opposed to letting them be subsumed within *people*. When it comes to *queer wo/men*'s presence, the term combats a double erasure when used more inclusively: that of all wo/men (regardless of sexual orientation) and that of all queer folks (regardless of gender identity). However, some queer wo/men are more than doubly erased, and I often refer specifically to queer wo/men who are oppressed by *both* their gender identity *and* their sexual orientation.

Within one of queer theory's oft-celebrated origin texts, Eve Kosofky Sedgwick's axiom, "People are different," is especially relevant to queer's intersectional usages.[39] This admits that people experience queerness differently (and not always positively), especially as it intersects and interacts with other aspects of our identities. Sedgwick's axiom forges space for shifts toward thinking about queer destabilization. Such a subversion fosters the more fluid sense of identity that structures recent theorizations of queerness.

Struggling together with queer theory and feminism means starting with intersectionality and acknowledging that people are different and inhabit multiple identities and characteristics that affect perceptions, experiences, and sensations of belonging. As I struggle with oppressions held within Paul's letters that reflect injustices around first-century Roman imperialism, I draw from the critical lenses brought by the intersectional critique seen in queer theory's identification of normativities (especially homonormativity) and feminism's critique of interlocking oppressions as seen in kyriarchy.

This struggle is not only to unsettle Paul's letters: it also seeks genuine change. I assume that first-century queer wo/men struggled with kyriarchy as they too were working toward such change. By critiquing and decentering Paul, I draw from feminism and queer theory in order to carve out space for queer wo/men who were multiply marginalized by Roman kyriarchy and by Paul's letter. This takes seriously Crenshaw's intersectional conclusion: "It seems that placing those who are currently marginalized

---

39. Her actual axiom, word for word, is "People are different from each other"; but I prefer to use a more emphatic declaration: "People are different." See Eve Kosofsky Sedgwick, *Epistemology of the Closet* (Berkeley: University of California Press, 1990), 22, see further 22–27. This axiom is part of Sedgwick's set of axioms for antihomophobic inquiry, which confront epistemological methods that contain explicit and implicit reinforcements of a divisive heterosexual-homosexual binary (which, in turn, perpetuates homophobia).

in the center is the most effective way to resist efforts to compartmentalize experiences and undermine potential collective action."[40] By turning to Rome's ἐκκλησία, I harness the potential of feminist and queer visions of difference and change in order to reenvision this space. This turn centers the queer wo/men who are marginalized when focus centers exclusively and primarily on Paul as the hero or villain—even though the movement was originally an ἐκκλησία of different queer wo/men.

Queer Wo/men, Romosexuals, and Romanormativity

First-century Romans thought about, expressed, and regulated sex and gender in different ways from today. Despite these differences, it is crucial to draw attention to broader similarities. In both cases, sex and society are regulated by norms; different people have different experiences and expressions of sexualities within these societies and their norms. I distinguish three concepts—Romans' sexualities, Romosexuality, and Romanormativity—and connect scholarship on Roman sexuality and gender to feminist and queer theoretical concepts. Although I develop these three terms separately, it is crucial to note that their effects are inseparable: wo/men in the first-century Roman Empire were *affected* by the experiences of all three forces.

First, I emphasize Romans' sexualities: the evidence that queer wo/men existed and lived in Rome and that they embodied different experiences of sexuality and gender. Starting with queer wo/men reminds us that *they were there* despite arguments to the contrary. It is important to start with the queer wo/men who lived outside of expected first-century norms, because scholarship overwhelmingly focuses upon the various social, political, and legal norms that regulated sexuality, gender, and politics, which forms the bulk of what remains of Roman discourse. That said, we cannot ignore these norms, so I then turn to these regulations and describe them as Romosexuality, which can be compared to contemporary heteronormativity. However, if Romosexuality is akin to heteronormativity, then it follows that we might also be able to trace ancient manifestations of homonormativity, the attempt of *nearly* normal persons to conform to the terms of Romosexuality. I coin a new term: *Romanormativity*. This denotes the ways in which first-century persons could seek inclusion as Romans by

---

40. Crenshaw, "Demarginalizing the Intersection," 167.

conforming their social, sexual, and political practices with Romosexual norms, especially emphasizing sexual similarities in the hopes of making other differences less visible or significant.

Romans' Sexualities

Queer wo/men were there.

This statement bears emphasis because androcentric, heteronormative scholarship denies the existence of wo/men and queerness, only admitting their existence if their presence is explicitly mentioned.[41] Melanie

---

41. This point has long been affirmed by scholars working in and across feminist and queer biblical studies (and theologies). See especially Schüssler Fiorenza, *In Memory of Her: A Feminist Theological Reconstruction of Christian Origins*, 10th anniversary ed. (New York: Crossroad, 1994); Mary Rose D'Angelo, "Women Partners in the New Testament," *JFSR* 6 (1990): 65–86; Antionette Clark Wire, *The Corinthian Women Prophets: A Reconstruction through Paul's Rhetoric* (Minneapolis: Fortress, 1990); Robert Goss, *Jesus Acted Up: A Gay and Lesbian Manifesto* (San Francisco: HarperSanFrancisco, 1993); Nancy Wilson, *Our Tribe: Queer Folks, God, Jesus, and the Bible* (San Francisco: HarperSanFrancisco, 1995); Bernadette J. Brooten, *Love between Women: Early Christian Responses to Female Homoeroticism* (Chicago: University of Chicago Press, 1996); Cynthia Briggs Kittredge, *Community and Authority: The Rhetoric of Obedience in the Pauline Tradition*, HTS 45 (Harrisburg, PA: Trinity Press International, 1998); Robert E. Goss and Mona West, eds., *Take Back the Word: A Queer Reading of the Bible* (Cleveland: Pilgrim, 2000); Shelly Matthews, *First Converts: Rich Pagan Women and the Rhetoric of Mission in Early Judaism and Christianity*, Contraversions (Stanford: Stanford University Press, 2001); Matthews, "Thinking of Thecla: Issues in Feminist Historiography," *JFSR* 17 (2001): 39–55; Elizabeth A. Castelli, "The *Ekklēsia* of Women and/as Utopian Space," in *On the Cutting Edge: The Study of Women in Biblical Worlds*, ed. Jane Schaberg, Alice Bach, and Esther Fuchs (New York: Continuum: 2004), 36–52; Melanie Johnson-DeBaufre, *Jesus among Her Children: Q, Eschatology, and the Construction of Christian Origins*, HTS 55 (Cambridge: Harvard University Press, 2005); Deryn Guest et al., eds., *The Queer Bible Commentary* (London: SCM, 2006); Carolyn Osiek and Margaret Y. MacDonald, with Janet H. Tulluch, *A Woman's Place: House Churches in Earliest Christianity* (Minneapolis: Fortress, 2006); Joseph A. Marchal, *Hierarchy, Unity, and Imitation: A Feminist Rhetorical Analysis of Power Dynamics in Paul's Letter to the Philippians*, AcBib (Atlanta: Society of Biblical Literature, 2006); Mary Ann Beavis, "Christian Origins, Egalitarianism, and Utopia," *JFSR* 23 (2007): 27–49; Teresa J. Hornsby and Ken Stone, eds., *Bible Trouble: Queer Reading at the Boundaries of Biblical Scholarship*, SemeiaSt 67 (Atlanta: Society of Biblical Literature, 2011); Gillian Townsley, *The Straight Mind in Corinth: Queer Readings across 1 Corinthians 11:2–16*, SemeiaSt 88 (Atlanta: SBL Press, 2017); Kent L. Brintnall, Joseph A. Marchal, and Stephen D. Moore, eds., *Sexual Disorientations: Queer Temporalities,*

Johnson-DeBaufre reaffirms the basic feminist principle that *wo/men were there* because scholars often look at the textual and material evidence for women in 1 Thessalonians and ancient Thessalonikē, and, since they do not see women or "women's concerns" in these materials, they assert that women were not present in the ἐκκλησία of Thessalonikē.[42] The assumption that only particular issues or objects are women's erases women from the record, even though it is obvious that wo/men had to be present in the ancient world.

The same problem occurs with queer folks: queerness must be proved present. If texts or materials do not make evident deviant sexuality, then queerness is presumed absent. Furthermore, this evidence must describe *actual* bodies with orientations toward a chosen praxis or lifestyle. As with wo/men, these assumptions erase queerness from the historical narrative. By straightening the narrative, they make queernesses harder to see.

These erasures intersect: queer wo/men are more than doubly erased. Most queerness in the ancient world appears to be embodied by men, and ancient wo/men are (presumed) straight. Queer wo/men's presence is harder to find and prove. It is imperative, from the outset, to affirm unequivocally:

Queer wo/men were there.

Scholars working on homoeroticism among wo/men across Greco-Roman antiquity affirm the presence of these queer wo/men, most notably made visible by Bernadette J. Brooten's pioneering *Love between Women*.[43]

Affects, Theologies, TTC (New York: Fordham University Press, 2018); Christy Cobb, *Slavery, Gender, Truth, and Power: In Luke-Acts and Other Ancient Narratives* (Cham, Switzerland: Palgrave Macmillan, 2019); Joseph A. Marchal, ed., *Bodies on the Verge: Queering Pauline Epistles*, SemeiaSt 93 (Atlanta: SBL Press, 2019); Marchal, *Appalling Bodies: Queer Figures before and after Paul's Letters* (Oxford: Oxford University Press, 2019); Arminta M. Fox, *Paul Decentered: Reading 2 Corinthians with the Corinthian Women*, PCC (Lanham, MD: Lexington, 2020).

42. Melanie Johnson-DeBaufre, "'Gazing upon the Invisible': Archaeology, Historiography, and the Elusive Wo/men of 1 Thessalonians," in *From Roman to Early Christian Thessalonikē*, ed. Laura Nasrallah, Charalambos Bakirtzis, and Steven J. Friesen (Cambridge: Harvard University Press, 2010), 73–108.

43. Brooten analyzes primary sources that discuss sexual desire between women and analyzes both elite Roman imperial and early Christian discourse's constructions of it, including where it did and did not reflect reality. Other notable analyses of ancient lesbianism include Judith Hallett, "Female Homoeroticism and the Denial

Ancient discussions and portrayals of the τριβάς/*tribas* (Greek/Latin; pl. τριβάδες/*tribades*)—which, for the Greek term, the LSJ supplement glosses as "'masculine' lesbian"—receive much attention.[44] This figure emerges as evidence for the existence of ancient female homoeroticism. The so-called masculinity of the τριβάς comes from reading evidence of τριβάδες as women who penetrated others (primarily women but also men).[45] However, as Brooten first showed, even though they focused disdain on the *tribas* who penetrates, Roman authors applied the term more widely to any women erotically involved with one another. In a passage from Seneca the Elder's *Controversiae* (1.2.23), a man catches his wife in bed with another woman, and Seneca describes both women as *tribades*.[46] The evidence and descriptions of τριβάδες/*tribades* largely derives from male authors who clearly use the term in slanderous ways. As Brooten notes, the fact that the Latin term *tribas* is imported directly from the Greek τριβάς could indicate

---

of Roman Reality in Latin Literature," in *Roman Sexualities*, ed. Hallett and Marilyn Skinner (Princeton: Princeton University Press, 1997), 255–73 (original article published 1989); Nancy Sorkin Rabinowitz and Lisa Auanger, eds., *Among Women: From the Homosocial to the Homoerotic in the Ancient World* (Austin: University of Texas Press, 2002); Sandra Boehringer, *L'Homosexualité féminine dans l'Antiquité Grecque et Romaine* (Paris: Belles Lettres, 2007); Jen H. Oliver, "*Oscula iungit nec moderata satis nec sic a virgine danda*: Ovid's Callisto Episode, Female Homoeroticism, and the Study of Ancient Sexuality," *AJP* 136 (2015): 281–312; Kristina Milnor, *Graffiti and the Literary Landscape in Roman Pompeii* (Oxford: Oxford University Press, 2014), 191–232 (ch. 4, "Gender and Genre: The Case of *CIL* 4.5296").

44. LSJ, s.v. "τριβάς," supp., 295. The main volume defines the term as "a woman who practices unnatural vice with herself or with other women" (LSJ, s.v. "τριβάς, -άδος," 1816). Hallett's groundbreaking and influential article on the *tribas* in Rome analyzed how Romans constructed the term in ways that distanced the women it described from their elite reality. See Hallett, "Female Homoeroticism."

45. Hallett, "Female Homoeroticism," shows how the masculinization of the *tribas* was part of elite Roman writers' strategy to distance female homoeroticism from present-day Roman behaviors. As an example of this tendency, Martial writes: *pedicat pueros tribas Philaenis / et tentigine saevior mariti / undenas dolat in die puellas* ("The τριβάς Philaenis ass-fucks boys / and she is more savage than a husband's lust / she drills eleven girls in a day" [*Epigrams* 7.67.1–3]). This epigram is cited and analyzed by Deborah Kamen and Sarah Levin-Richardson, "Lusty Ladies in the Roman Literary Imaginary," in *Ancient Sex: New Essays*, ed. Ruby Blondell and Kirk Ormand (Columbus: Ohio State University Press, 2015), 243–44, as well as by Hallett, "Female Homoeroticism," 261–63; Brooten, *Love between Women*, 7, 46–48.

46. Hallett, "Female Homoeroticism," 258–59, 269; Brooten, *Love between Women*, 43–44, 75–76; Kamen and Levin-Richardson, "Lusty Ladies," 243.

how Roman writers cast the "unnaturalness" of female homoeroticism as a "foreign phenomenon" that threatened to infect Roman women.[47] These descriptions cannot be taken to accurately represent reality, even though they affirm the plausible existence of homoeroticism between women.[48]

The term itself indicates possibilities of erotic relations among wo/men that do not conform to the sexual imaginations of elite Roman men. τριβάς, remark both Brooten and Judith Hallett, derived from τρίβω, "to rub."[49] An alternative Latin term *fricatrix*, which seems to have been used synonymously with *tribas*, is an apparent derivative of *frico*, also "to rub."[50] Building off Hallett and Brooten, Maia Kotrosits suggests the *friction* of this rubbing offers erotic possibilities for wo/men beyond the presumptions of penetration made by male Roman authors (as well as many scholars who interpret them): "we might note that the term 'rub' depicts pleasure and relationships, not to mention the topography of the body, quite differently: as something like the interplay of two electrified fields."[51] This signals not only an alternative to penetration as the defining characteristic of sex but also a capacious imagining of sexuality and pleasure that could be mutually enjoyed and shared between bodies of many genders.[52] Even if we cannot confirm how the term was used or embodied by ancient queer wo/men, the

---

47. Brooten, *Love between Women*, 5. Hallett first draws attention to the trope of Hellenization in Roman literary depictions of the *tribas*, noting the term's Greek derivation (Hallett, "Female Homoeroticism," 259). Hallett concludes, "To them, female homoeroticism was an undifferentiated, unassimilated conglomeration of alien and unnatural Greek behaviors, which did not really take place in their own milieu, or—if it did occur—did so in a completely unrealistic way" (Hallett, "Female Homoeroticism," 269–70). Drawing especially from Hallett's insights, Diana Swancutt analyzes Roman representations of the *tribas* and argues that the Greekness of the *tribas* in Roman representations betrays anxieties around empire and threats to its control, both in terms of foreign and gendered others. See Diana Swancutt, "*Still* before Sexuality: 'Greek' Androgyny, the Roman Imperial Politics of Masculinity and the Roman Invention of the *Tribas*," in *Mapping Gender in Ancient Religious Discourses*, ed. Todd Penner and Caroline Vander Stichele, BibInt 84 (Leiden: Brill, 2007), 11–61, esp. 21–61.

48. Brooten, *Love between Women*, 7.

49. Hallett, "Female Homoeroticism," 259–60; Brooten, *Love between Women*, 5.

50. Brooten, *Love between Women*, 5.

51. Maia Kotrosits, "Penetration and Its Discontents: Greco-Roman Sexuality, the *Acts of Paul and Thecla*, and Theorizing Eros without the Wound," *JHistSex* 27 (2018): 356.

52. Kotrosits, "Penetration and Its Discontents," 356–57; Hallett, "Female Homoeroticism," 268; Joseph A. Marchal, "Bottoming Out: Rethinking the Reception of

possibilities that resonate around the term summon plausible experiences for queer wo/men whose erotic lives were "off the grid."[53]

Material culture confirms the presence of Roman queer wo/men. One clear example comes from Roman Egypt in the form of love spells, which Brooten compiles and discusses as evidence for reconstructing queer wo/men's history.[54] Queer wo/men commissioned these spells to bind other women to them: "Make Nike, daughter of Apollonous, fall in love with Pantous, whom Tmesios bore, for five months"; "Force Gorgonia, whom Nilogenia bore, to cast herself into the bath-house for the sake of Sophia, whom Isara bore, for her, so that she love her with passion, longing, unceasing love."[55] These spells reflect Rome's kyriarchal ideology of sexual domination (spelled out next as *Romosexuality*) and were almost certainly formulaic spells written by men who inserted names into them at the behest of their clients (regardless of genders of either the client or the object of their affection/obsession). However, as Brooten observes, these spells indicate not only the presence of female homoeroticism in Roman Egypt but also some level of acceptance and social support for women who loved other women, since they were able to commission these spells. Since the spells were formulaic, they show that women's homoerotic relationships existed, but they cannot tell us the true dynamics of these wo/men's relationships, which may not have mirrored the dominant androcentric cultural ideology.[56]

Closer to the city of Rome, graffiti from Pompeii attests to women's homoerotic attraction. In *CIL* 4.5296, found in the interior doorway of a house, the author wishes to entwine with and give kisses to her *pupula*

Receptivity," in *Bodies on the Verge: Queering Pauline Epistles*, ed. Marchal, SemeiaSt 93 (Atlanta: SBL Press, 2019), 228–29.

53. I draw this idea of "off the grid" existence from Kotrosits: "However, I am less interested in postulating a grand theory of eros or contact with the Other (a solidified, phallic concept itself) than with *carving out space for specific kinds of contact that appear 'off the grid'*" (Kotrosits, "Penetration and Its Discontents," 357, emphasis added). Kotrosits's use of "off the grid" also comes out of her discussion and critique of the "penetrative grid" model that provides the dominant framework for scholarly studies to Roman sexuality (as discussed in the following subsection).

54. Brooten, *Love between Women*, 73–113 (ch. 3, "'Inflame Her Liver with Love': Greek Erotic Spells from Egypt"). On the value of these spells for historical reconstruction, see especially 105–9.

55. Trans. Brooten, *Love between Women*, 92, 87.

56. Brooten, *Love between Women*, 73–77, 105–9.

("darling girl"). She describes herself as *perdita* ("lovesick" in feminine form).[57] Clearly, the graffito is an expression of the erotic desire of one woman for another, even proclaiming *crede mihi levis est natura virorum* ("trust me, trifling is men's nature").[58] Another example can be found in *CIL* 4.8321a: *Chloe Eutychiae s(alutem) non me curus Eutychia spe firma tua Ruf(um?) amas* ("Chloe greets Eutychia. You don't care about me Eutychia. With a firm hope you love your Ruf[us?]").[59] Like the love spells, this graffito plainly indicates desire by Chloe for Eutychia. Furthermore, it might be noted that, since the graffito is unfinished, *Ruf-* could be a man (Rufus) or a woman (Rufa).

Both graffiti—as well as the spells—point to two reasons for the difficulty of finding evidence of queer wo/men in Rome. The first is that the evidence is often less displayed or visible due to the restrictions and condemnations of female homoeroticism, especially in kyriarchal culture. There may be less of a material record because the record is lost or was never kept. Even in what remains, the evidence is often "straightened" out by androcentric and heteronormative scholarship: the homoeroticism of the two graffiti has been denied or the eroticism has been cast as heterosexual by arguing (against the grammatical evidence) that the authors were men.[60]

---

57. The full graffito reads: "O, would that it were permitted to grasp with my neck your little arms / As they entwine (it) and to give kisses to your delicate little lips / Come now, my little darling, entrust your pleasures to the winds / (En)trust me, the nature of men is insubstantial / Often I have been awake, [a] lovesick [woman] at midnight / You think on these things with me: many are they whom Fortune lifted high; / These, suddenly thrown down headlong, she now oppresses / Thus, just as Venus suddenly joined the bodies of lovers, daylight divides them and...." (*CIL* 4.5296; trans. Milnor, *Graffiti and the Literary Landscape*, 197–98).

58. See the discussion of this graffito and its history of (mis)translation to render its female author invisible in Milnor, *Graffiti and the Literary Landscape*, 191–232. See also Antonio Varaone, *Erotica Pompeiana: Love Inscriptions on the Walls of Pompeii* (Rome: L'Erma di Bretschneider, 2002; orig. published in Italian, 1994), 135. For more on this graffito as a queer material that can reorient archaeological approaches to Roman houses (and the ἐκκλησίαι that likely assembled in some of them), see James N. Hoke, "Orienting the *Domus*: Queer Materials and ἐκκλησίαι in Rome" (paper presented at the Annual Meeting of the Society of Biblical Literature, San Diego, CA, 25 November 2019).

59. Trans. Varaone, *Erotica Pompeiana*, 102.

60. "Our ignorance does not stem from a lack of sources, but rather from our ignoring and misinterpreting the available sources" (Brooten, *Love between Women*, 96). Similarly, Brooten shows how this has happened with the interpretation of love

The literary and material evidence affirms that wo/men sought after and engaged in sexual experiences with other wo/men—and men were aware of this fact, even if many of them disdained it. This evidence emphasizes the diversity of Romans' sexualities, especially among wo/men, and attests that queer wo/men were there, despite the ways in which Roman culture and contemporary scholarship worked to hide or erase them.

Beyond the evidence of women's homoeroticism, scholars have had to insist on affirming *queerness* in the ancient world, as an orientation itself and as a valid term to describe some Roman wo/men's relationships. Feminist classicists, especially Amy Richlin, have long established that subcultures existed within the Greco-Roman world, wherein wo/men were able to embrace and embody their desires with others in ways that deviated from the cultural norm.[61] Brooten, in particular, has established that, despite intense condemnation and erasure, some *women loved women* in ancient Rome. Those three italicized words contain much radicality, perhaps the *loved* even more that the *women*. When discussed (as in Rom 1:26), sexual intercourse between wo/men is not just castigated as (extremely) παρὰ φύσιν ("unnatural"); it is done so in a way that renders the acts *unthinkable* (from a male perspective).[62] Unlike the rich descriptions of various male sex acts (with any variety of partners), sex between wo/men is usually reduced to a single, brief mention, as if there is only one way women could have sex. The men condemning such practices have no sense of the myriad activities that can occur when they are not involved. In ancient Rome, the single instance of *women fucking women* was already quite radical.

But some women *loved* women.[63] Their desire differed from the penetrative prescription presumed by and for elite men, which was, to bluntly

---

spells between women, most notably in the case of Pantous (named in one of the spells quoted above), a rare and ambiguously gendered name. As a result of the ambiguity (the ending can be masculine or feminine), interpreters claimed Pantous must be male, essentially to "straighten" the woman's (Nike's) desire even though the relative pronoun used to introduce Pantous is ἥν (i.e., feminine), which, as Brooten argues, means Pantous should be identified as a woman (Brooten, *Love between Women*, 93–96).

61. Amy J. Richlin, "Not before Homosexuality: The Materiality of the *Cinaedus* and the Roman Law against Love between Men," *JHistSex* 3 (1993): 523–73.

62. Brooten, *Love between Women*, 240. See also Stephen D. Moore, *God's Beauty Parlor: And Other Queer Spaces in and around the Bible*, Contraversions (Stanford: Stanford University Press, 2001), 149, 171, 153.

63. My emphasis of the use—and distinction—between *fucking* and *loving* thinks with Halperin's unnecessarily scathing critique of Brooten's work. Early in this piece,

(over)simplify: any hole will do, as long as it is not yours. Such a "Priapic model," as Richlin names, defines sexuality exclusively through the lens of (male) domination and aggression.[64] Brooten's analyses of sexuality among women shows (many!) different sorts of yearnings, some similar to the desire to screw around and others more like the desire to have an erotic relationship with a particular wo/man (or even wo/men).[65] Some, she argues, are proximate to modern lesbianism. If contemporary lesbians love, fuck, or otherwise erotically engage with wo/men in myriad ways, then the similarity—in terms of the vast diversity—is quite striking.[66] Of course, these wo/men could not always avoid the restrictions and requirements of Romosexuality, even if they wanted to, but there is evidence that some wo/men and their desires deviated from these norms, even when those actions and desires were limited and pulled back by them.[67]

Halperin recounts a disagreement between two women in his classroom, who distinguished between *fucking* and *loving* with respect to ancient women (one student was interested in "women who loved other women" but not fucking; the other was interested in "women who fucked other women" but not loving). See Halperin, "David M. Halperin," in "Lesbian Historiography before the Name?," *GLQ* 4 (1998): 562. (I wholeheartedly disagree with his critique, and, it merits mention, Halperin's treatment of Brooten's work as "touristic," despite her vast scholarly credentials, is dismissive, condescending, and offensive. See Halperin, "David M. Halperin," esp. 560–62.) This distinction between fucking and loving draws an artificial boundary that often attributes violence, aggression, or nonmutuality to the former and presumes mutuality and (com)passion to the latter. However, professions of loving (and even uses of phrases like *making love*) are frequently voiced by abusive partners and other aggressive forms of sexuality in ways that mask love's violence. Likewise, although *fuck* can be used in contexts devoid of mutuality or relational bonds, it is also (perhaps even often) voiced in the throes of passion. It is important not to mistake the aggression the word carries for lack of mutual consent: many folks desire more aggressive or less intimate forms of sex. Although I do not want to draw too firm a distinction between fucking and loving, there is an importance in using *fuck* more expansively in ways that do not presume love to be the only context for mutual sexual pleasure (and do not limit *fuck* to its most aggressive and patriarchal usages, such as in graffiti).

64. Amy Richlin, *The Garden of Priapus: Sexuality and Aggression in Roman Humor*, rev. ed. (New York: Oxford University Press, 1992).

65. See Brooten, *Love between Women*, 29–186.

66. For any instance of difference between an "ancient lesbian" and a "modern lesbian," instances of similar difference could be found between two ancient (or two modern) lesbians.

67. In similar fashion, the queer archives being uncovered today from more recent pasts attest to the ways in which bodies have long resisted sexual norms (especially

These wo/men were not the only folks who embodied sexuality in ways that did not conform to imperial sexual norms. Textual and material remnants contain numerous references to men with unnatural preferences and desires, including men who prefer to bottom, men who desire too much sex, or men who have sex with women in less natural ways (e.g., cunnilingus). The first of these—men who preferred getting topped by other men—are represented with the term *cinaedus*. Although the term could be applied to any "lustful" men, it emphasizes a man's willing desire to bottom, even taking an active role when doing so—perhaps as participants in a "passive homosexual subculture," as Richlin argues.[68] As with *tribades*, the term is frequently used disparagingly. Elite male authors and writers of graffiti considered men being penetrated, even willingly and actively, as a signal of effeminacy and loss of power and control.

Although much of this evidence constitutes sexual slander (i.e., it may not be true), Richlin has demonstrated how its persistence, alongside the existence of these terms and ideas, makes a compelling case that

---

heteronormativity) despite regulation and attempts at erasure. These archives tell a different story from that which would be constructed from official, normative records and culture. As much as these archives show that deviant queers have long resisted normativity (sometimes in ways more resistant than more recent formulations), these archives always also bear signs of the ways that normative sexuality and its regulation affects their queernesses, defines their resistance, or subtly draws them back into the norm. See Ann Cvetkovitch, *An Archive of Feelings: Trauma, Sexuality, and Lesbian Public Cultures*, SerQ (Durham, NC: Duke University Press, 2003); Heather Love, *Feeling Backward: Loss and the Politics of Queer History* (Cambridge: Harvard University Press, 2009).

68. Richlin, "Not before Homosexuality." See also Deborah Kamen and Sarah Levin-Richardson, "Revisiting Roman Sexuality: Agency and the Conceptualization of Penetrated Males," in *Sex in Antiquity: Exploring Gender and Sexuality in the Ancient World*, ed. Mark Masterson, Sorkin Rabinowitz, and James Robson (London: Routledge, 2014), 453–55. Craig Williams contests this designation and argues that *cinaedi* primarily referred to gender identity as opposed to sexual orientation. See Craig Williams, *Roman Homosexuality*, 2nd ed. (Oxford: Oxford University Press, 2010), 177–245. While Williams makes important arguments about the effeminacy attributed to *cinaedi*, he draws too firm a distinction between ancient gender identities and sexual orientation that elides the ways in the preference to bottom is linked to the gendered portrayal of the *cinaedus* (both in slander and, potentially, by *cinaedi* themselves). His argument fixes a static notion of sexual orientation that cannot hold space for the fact that a man who prefers to bottom for other men might also, at times, top men or have sex with wo/men (just as queer wo/men such as a *tribas* might prefer sex with other wo/men but still be married and have sex with men).

these preferences and desires existed in real bodies. Homosexuality was embodied in different ways by wo/men and men in ancient Rome. Very rarely, if ever, could bodies have the luxury of being able to pursue same-sex intercourse exclusively; however, this restriction should not negate the probable queernesses of diverse Romans embodying sexualities that aligned with and deviated from and even resisted Rome's sexual norms.

Although Roman imperial culture produced and enforced sexual norms that affected all Romans' sexualities, Romans' sexualities cannot be contained within these norms. Romans' sexualities are vastly different from the Romosexuality we are now poised to consider. This distinction is important to remember because ancient norms are easier to see, even though Romans' sexualities were and are present: in the remains, between the lines, and off the grid. When we consider Romans' sexualities, we plainly see *queer wo/men were there.*

Romosexuality: Naturalizing Kyriarchal Politics

Starting with the diversity of Romans' sexuality reminds us that there were many different lived experiences of sexuality and gender in the first century. In practice, sexual agency, preferences, and participants were not restricted to a single gender, and queer wo/men were active shapers of their sexualities.[69] That said, Roman ideology (at least as expressed in the imaginations of mostly elite men at the top of an imperial kyriarchy) attempted to restrict how and when people *should* engage in sexual acts. Here, I outline this ideology, which I term *Romosexuality.*[70]

---

69. I am intentionally moving away from the use of *partner* to describe persons participating in sexual activity, as it presumes a level of mutuality/relationship and consent that is not inherently present. Though not perfect, using *participant* attempts to acknowledge that not all participants were *willing* participants in sexual encounters, and that many sexual encounters—ancient and contemporary—occur without the consent of all participants.

70. I am not the first scholar to use the term *Romosexuality*, which (according to Jennifer Inglehart on Twitter) was Craig Williams's original title for *Roman Homosexuality*. Classicists probing modern receptions of Roman sexuality have now begun to loosely use the term *Romosexuality* in their work. See Jennifer Inglehart, ed., *Ancient Rome and the Construction of Modern Homosexual Identities* (Oxford: Oxford University Press, 2015), especially her introductory essay "Introduction: Romosexuality: Rome, Homosexuality, and Reception," 1–35; Nikolai Endres, "From *Eros* to Romosexuality: Love and Sex in *Dorian Gray*," in *Oscar Wilde and Classical Antiquity*, ed.

By structuring sexuality, both heteronormativity and Romosexuality present particular sexual relationships as normal. These expressions
become most visible, effacing the many different sexualities present today
and in the Roman world. Even in the advent of same-sex marriage and
greater LGBTIA2Q+ visibility, heteronormativity structures contemporary society, sometimes restricting queer embodiments and making it
possible for queer existence to be forgotten, ignored, or denied. Similarly,
by disseminating this ideology in literary, legal, and visual forms and using
it to structure space and daily life, Romosexuality eclipses Romans' sexualities, driving them to the margins and making them harder to see. In
contemporary discourse around ancient sexuality, Romosexuality and
heteronormativity intersect to more than doubly hide, erase, or straighten
out ancient queernesses, especially that of queer wo/men.

One way that Romans categorized sexual acts was in terms of φύσις,
"nature." This can be seen in the *Oneirokritica* of Artemidorus, a second-
century author who analyzed sexual acts in dreams. Sex acts could be κατὰ
φύσιν ("according to nature" or "natural") or παρὰ φύσιν ("against nature"
or "unnatural").[71] While these terms present classification in binary terms,
authors make clear that some acts—generally under the *unnatural* head-
ing—are even less natural than others. It quickly becomes apparent that
what is natural is the sociopolitical hierarchy by which society has come to

---

Kathleen Riley, Alastair J. L. Blanshard, and Iarla Manny (Oxford: Oxford University
Press, 2017), 251–66. Stemming from a 2012 conference by this title, this work calls
attention to the ways in which *Roman* sexuality has often been ignored in its specific-
ity, and it has often been seen as derivative or degenerating from more ancient Greek
ideals, especially by modern receptions (Inglehart, "Introduction"). The volume Inglehart edited and introduces largely includes a selection of papers presented at this conference (16–18 April 2012 at Durham University). Although there is much potential
meaning for *Romosexuality*, this work largely employs the term for its playfulness.
As such, Romosexuality remains open for further definition. In what follows, I will
specify its meaning so as to make clear how I am theorizing and using the term in ways
that I hope will be beneficial and usable for others. However, to be clear, in specifying
my own definition of Romosexuality, I do *not* mean to limit its meaning.

71. Often alongside acts that are κατὰ/παρὰ νόμος ("according to/against law").
See discussions in Michel Foucault, *The Care of the Self*, vol. 3 of *The History of Sexuality* (New York: Vintage Books, 1986; repr. 1988), 17–25; John J. Winkler, *The Constraints of Desire: The Anthropology of Sex and Gender in Ancient Greece* (New York:
Routledge, 1990), 17–23; Brooten, *Love between Women*, 249–58, esp. 250–52, as well
as 175–86; Moore, *God's Beauty Parlor*, 140–43.

be naturally organized.[72] The natural that categorized and helped regulate Roman sexual experiences is essentially synonymous with uses of *normal* that regulate contemporary sexuality.

Artemidorus's dream analysis shows how sexuality was not a separate sphere from Roman society and politics. Dreams with "natural" sex acts foretell positive results, while dreams with "unnatural" ones could spell potential disaster.[73] In either case, the effects these dreams foretell do not correspond with the bedroom: they have implications for nonsexual life in Roman society, such as political success/failure, familial happiness, or economic downfall. These interpretations of dreams—sexual and not—rarely, if ever, foretell *sexual* results. Regardless of their actual sexual desires and practices, Romans do not appear to have looked to dream interpretation to reveal promises or pitfalls of their sex lives.[74] Sexuality affected society and politics; society and politics arranged sexuality.[75] One's sexual actions could affect one's placement on a socio-*sexual*-political hierarchy. This encouraged and enforced Romosexual behavior.

Artemidorus is not exceptional: his work has become the illustration *par excellence* for arrangements of Roman sexuality, because his treatment of sexual acts is the most comprehensive.[76] Rome's socio-*sexual*-political hierarchy can be confirmed by other, less systematic comments, including graffiti, fragments of papyri, and visual art.[77] Roman sexuality, in its elite

---

72. "This is to say that although it seems natural to us to discuss sex in terms of nature and 'unnature,' the 'naturalness' of these categories is itself a sort of cultural illusion. Like sexuality, 'nature' (as applied to sex) has a history" (Winkler, *Constraints of Desire*, 18). See also Brooten, *Love between Women*, 250–52; Moore, *God's Beauty Parlor*, 140.

73. Along these lines, see discussions of Artemidorus in Foucault, *Care of the Self*, 4–36; Winkler, *Constraints of Desire*, 17–44; Brooten, *Love between Women*, 175–186.

74. Brooten, *Love between Women*, 175; Winkler, *Constraints of Desire*, 27–28.

75. Brooten, *Love between Women*, 175–77; Winkler, *Constraints of Desire*, 24–25; Foucault, *Care of the Self*, 4–16. See also Moore, *God's Beauty Parlor*, 141–45.

76. Winkler terms Artemidorus a "ventriloquist" and concludes, "Thus, Artemidorus in his own way illustrates once more that 'nature' means culture" (Winkler, *Constraints of Desire*, 43, see further 41–44).

77. Brooten, *Love between Women*, 29–186; Natalie Boymel Kampen, ed., *Sexuality in Ancient Art* (Cambridge: Cambridge University Press, 1996); Williams, *Roman Homosexuality*, 177–245; John R. Clarke, *Looking at Lovemaking: Constructions of Sexuality in Roman Art 100 B.C.–A.D. 250* (Berkeley: University of California Press, 1998). Amy Richlin outlines the development of this history as it originates in feminist classics; see Amy Richlin, "Zeus and Metis: Foucault, Classics, and Feminism," *Helios*

presentations and regulation, confirmed the structure of its kyriarchal politics and society: elite men were on top and all others were under them in every sense.[78] These others—who were, in fact, almost the entirety of Rome—fell into various ranks below the most elite, and they often jockeyed for social standing and access to power, wanting to be seen by all others (especially those on top) as most proximate (and ideally identical) to the elite. One's natural sexual position or proclivities depended on one's position in society and politics (often also framed in natural terms). Less natural or unnatural sexuality, to differing degrees, disturbs or defies the sociopolitical order. Just as heteronormativity makes heterosexuality compulsory by penalizing and casting as abnormal anyone who deviates from its norm, Romosexuality deems deviations unnatural to enforce its own norms.

Kamen and Levin-Richardson map how studies of Roman sexuality (and Greco-Roman sexuality more broadly) have emphasized three major axes by which Romans talked about and attempted to regulate sex: penetration, agency, and self-control.[79] These axes did not function or affect Romans in clearly discrete ways. They worked in relation to one another. These axes intersect to produce Romosexuality's normative

---

18 (1991): 160–80; in particular, see 167–68, 172–75. See also, Marilyn B. Skinner, "Parasites and Strange Bedfellows: A Study in Catullus' Political Imagery," *Ranus* 8 (1979): 137–52; Richlin, *Garden of Priapus*; Judith P. Hallett, *Fathers and Daughters in Roman Society* (Princeton: Princeton University Press, 1984); and Eva C. Keuls, *The Reign of the Phallus: Sexual Politics in Ancient Athens* (New York: Harper and Row, 1985). See also Brooten, "Paul's Views on the Nature of Women and Female Homoeroticism," in *Immaculate and Powerful: The Female in Sacred Image and Social Reality*, ed. Clarissa W. Atkinson, Constance H. Buchanan, and Margaret R. Miles (Boston: Beacon, 1985), 61–87.

78. "The highly class-stratified nature of Roman society is an essential component in the construction of Roman sexuality—the two systems can hardly be understood independently" (Richlin, "Not before Homosexuality," 532). This is confirmed by Artemidorus's systematic treatment: "It needs to be understood, then, that for Artemidorus what determines the predictive meaning of a dream, and hence in a certain way the moral value of the act dreamed of, *is the condition of the partner, and not the form of the act itself*" (Foucault, *Care of the Self*, 18, emphasis added). Along similar lines, but looking specifically at those sexual acts classified as παρὰ φύσιν, Winkler observes: "The basic idea seems to be that unnatural acts do not involve any representation of human social hierarchy" (Winkler, *Constraints of Desire*, 38).

79. Kamen and Levin-Richardson, "Revisiting Roman Sexuality"; see also, Kamen and Levin-Richardson, "Lusty Ladies."

system that place elite Roman men at the top of the empire's socio-sexual-political kyriarchy.

In its most recorded formulations, Rome's sexual hierarchy is most often concerned with sexuality that affects elite men. It considers who penetrates whom and where?[80] The simple answer to this question is that elite men could penetrate just about whomever they wanted, wherever they wanted, and whenever they wanted. However, their penetrative unrestrictedness is countered by a general imperative that those on top should never bottom—that is, be penetrated. Employing Jonathan Walters's phrase, in order to enforce their sociopolitical dominance over all, Roman elite men must be "impenetrable penetrators."[81] Those who fall outside these proximities and are well below the elite tiers of society can be penetrated by the elite with indiscretion, with enslaved persons being the most vulnerable.[82] From the view of Rome's elite and their sexual protocol, since lower and lowest status bodies were naturally unnatural, they could penetrate and be penetrated however they liked among themselves so long as they did not penetrate into the uppermost echelons of Rome.

---

80. The "penetration model" of Roman sexuality, which follows the observations of the feminist scholars listed above in n. 77, especially Brooten, "Paul's Views on the Nature of Women and Female Homoeroticism." It is also developed and made the dominant model for discussing Roman sexuality through the work of Foucault, *Care of the Self*, 29–30; Winkler, *Constraints of Desire*, 11, 33–44; Williams, *Roman Homosexuality*, 177–245, esp. 177–83; Jonathan Walters, "Invading the Roman Body: Manliness and Impenetrability in Roman Thought," in *Roman Sexualities*, ed. Judith P. Hallett and Marilyn B. Skinner (Princeton: Princeton University Press, 1997), 29–43; Moore, *God's Beauty Parlor*, 144–46; Marilyn B. Skinner, *Sexuality in Greek and Roman Culture*, 2nd ed. (Malden, MA: Wiley Blackwell, 2014), 7.

Despite the frequent erasure or ignorance of their contributions, feminist classicists revealed and developed the penetrative model of Rome's sexual hierarchy before and at the same time as it was being articulated by other (male) classicists. On this erasure, see Brooten, "Response" in "Lesbian Historiography before the Name?," *GLQ* 4 (1998): 627, n. 1; Richlin, "Zeus and Metis."

81. Walters, "Invading the Roman Body," 30.

82. See especially Jennifer A. Glancy, *Slavery in Early Christianity* (Oxford: Oxford University Press, 2002), 16–29; Page duBois, *Slaves and Other Objects* (Chicago: University of Chicago Press, 2003), 82–100; Joseph A. Marchal, "The Usefulness of an Onesimus: The Sexual Use of Slaves and Paul's Letter to Philemon," *JBL* 130 (2011): 751–60; Brooten, *Love between Women*, 250–252; Michel Foucault, *The Use of Pleasure*, vol. 2 of *The History of Sexuality*, trans. Robert Hurley (New York: Vintage Books/Random House, 1985; repr. 1990), 215–16.

On its surface, the penetrative framework presents a sexist ideal: men should penetrate; women should be penetrated. Indeed, scholarship on Roman sexuality has often presumed that, while men could both penetrate and be penetrated, women could only be penetrated (at least in the elite Roman imaginary). This was not the case, as evidence discussed by Hallett, Brooten, Richlin, and Kamen and Levin-Richardson have all shown. Women are cast as penetrating participants in both graffiti and elite literary texts, specifically when named and discussed as *tribades*. As discussed above, *tribades* can describe sexual activities between women, which may not have involved penetration at all. But, when elite men mention women as *tribades*, they presume the penetrator/penetrated hierarchy and use the term to describe women penetrating women *and* men. Martial describes a *tribas*, Philaenis, as "ass-fucking boys" (*pedicat pueros*) in addition to "drilling" (*dolat*) girls (*Epigrams* 7.67.1–3).[83] Despite the natural prescription that (only) men should top, Roman men could and did imagine and admit that women penetrated too.

This does not mean Romosexuality *encouraged* women to be on top. The idea of women as penetrators threatened elite Roman men and their kyriarchal power. "Both literary sources and graffiti heap extra abuse upon those who don't hide their depraved sexual acts," write Kamen and Levin-Richardson.[84] The depravity, in this case, is tribadic penetration: women who penetrate—alongside those who enjoy or crave sex—are cast as monstrous. The penetrative norm of Romosexuality is not confirmed because it was impossible to exist outside it: it is established by *how* deviance from the norm was imagined and portrayed.

After all, the literary record almost exclusively focuses on the concerns of elite men. These texts are primarily anxious about the possibility of who could or might penetrate elite men and those most proximate to them (i.e., the men who may one day be among the elite and the women who may one day produce a new generation of elites).[85] Elite men who were penetrated signaled loss of control and, therefore, power; elite women who penetrated threatened the power and control of the men who pictured themselves on top of politics, society, and sexuality. These exceptions to the Romosexual

---

83. Kamen and Levin-Richardson, "Lusty Ladies," 243; see also discussion in Hallett, "Female Homoeroticism," 261–62.

84. Kamen and Levin-Richardson, "Lusty Ladies," 243.

85. Thus, the observations of Winkler and others above that sexuality merely reinforces the natural social order. See also Williams, *Roman Homosexuality*, 103–36.

norm existed, but Roman discourse, promulgated by the imperial elite and affecting the sexual mores of others (as seen in graffiti), casts the exceptional as unnatural—deviant, abnormal, and unfit to rule. Romosexuality structures sexuality and society through a penetrative norm that naturalizes men as the preferred penetrators.

Romosexuality's penetrative norm operates alongside an axis of *agency*: Is the sexual participant active or passive in the sexual encounter? Scholars have often conflated penetration with activity (i.e., the penetrator [a man] is the active participant who plays the active role) and being penetrated with passivity (i.e., a penetrated person [some men, all women] is the passive participant who plays the passive role).[86] Informed by contemporary sexist stereotypes about penetration, this conflation presumes there is nothing active about being consensually penetrated and nothing passive about penetrating, even if the penetrator just lies on their back and is ridden. Reflected onto first-century culture, this presumption almost always relegates women to passivity in yet another sphere of ancient life, especially when the same scholars ignore evidence that women were the penetrating as well as the penetrated person.

Contesting this conflation, Kamen and Levin-Richardson redefine active and passive roles based on ancient grammar, as in the active and passive voice of Latin (and Greek) verbs.[87] An active sexual participant is the active subject of the verb: Μόλα φουτοῦτρις ("Mola, who fucks" [*CIL* 4.2204]) or *Bononiensis Rufa Rufulum fellat* ("Rufa of Bononia sucks her Rufus" [Catullus 59]). A passive participant is acted upon: as the subject of a passive verb, as in *futata sum hic* ("I was fucked here" [*CIL* 4.2217]); or the object of an active verb, as in *L[ucius] Habonius sauciat / irrumat Caesum Fleic[e]m* ("Lucius Habonius wounds, face-fucks Caesus Felix" [*CIL* 4.1032a]), where Caesus Felix is the passive participant and Lucius Habonius the active.[88] Following this definition, neither activity nor passivity is defined purely by penetration. A person can actively engage in their own penetration by another, such as *cinaedi*—men who willingly

---

86. Kamen and Levin-Richardson, "Revisiting Roman Sexuality," 449.

87. Kamen and Levin-Richardson, "Revisiting Roman Sexuality," 450; Kamen and Levin-Richardson, "Lusty Ladies," 236–37.

88. Latin translations by Kamen and Levin-Richardson. I have drawn these examples from their catalogue of graffiti and texts from their analyses of Roman sexuality. The first three come from "Lusty Ladies," 231, 239, and 245 (respectively), and the last one from "Revisiting Roman Sexuality," 450.

bottomed.[89] Women could also be active sexual participants, including when they engaged in penetrative coitus with men, such as Mola above.[90] Agency and penetration were separate axes by which Romans described and regulated sexuality, which was imagined in ways that did not limit activity or passivity to any gender.

This does not mean that agency and penetration were unrelated: they were, via the regulative norms of Romosexuality. As with penetration, Roman discourse associated activity with men and passivity with women. This association was informed by an ancient conflation of penetrator = active/penetrated = passive, even though the arrangement of the agency axis was not limited by this. *Cinaedi*, as men who actively (and consensually) bottomed, were viewed more favorably than the *pedicatus/fututus*, men who were raped.[91] However, because both were penetrated, neither were considered "true" men who were fit to actively rule over others in the Roman elite imaginary. Invective against *cinaedi* is especially prominent (as noted above), which may belie the anxiety Roman men felt toward the proximity of men actively desiring to bottom, especially if an elite Roman man could be a *cinaedus*.

Similarly, Roman discourse idealized women as sexually passive, even though it could imagine women as active sexual participants, both when they penetrated and when they were penetrated. Romans praised the sexually passive Roman matron; meanwhile, they cast women who were active and penetrators as monstrous. When literary texts describe women as sexual actors, they clearly describe these women in negative terms (in contrast to the ideal Roman woman). When Catullus describes women like Rufa (see example above) as active when they perform oral sex, he does so in a section that condemns her for being an impious, thieving adulteress.[92]

Much of the evidence of women actively described as "fucking" or "fuckers" comes from graffiti, often found in Pompeii's purpose-built brothel.[93] This reflects women's agency in describing and reframing their

---

89. Kamen and Levin-Richardson, "Revisiting Roman Sexuality," 453–55.

90. Kamen and Levin-Richardson, "Lusty Ladies," 244–47.

91. Kamen and Levin-Richardson, "Revisiting Roman Sexuality," 450–52. A similar willing/unwilling distinction can be seen in oral penetration with *fellator* and *irrumatus* (respectively); see p. 455.

92. Kamen and Levin-Richardson, "Lusty Ladies," 239.

93. Levin-Richardson offers a comprehensive material analysis of the space, finds, and graffiti in Pompeii's brothel and uses this analysis to reconstruct the lives of the

own sexual experiences.[94] At times, it may also reflect Roman men's desires for women who were more active—even dominant—over them sexually. At the brothel, men could rule and be ruled simultaneously, for even if a prostitute played the active role, she was still playing a role dictated by her client. Since she was almost always an enslaved woman, in the Roman male imaginary, a prostitute was a sexual agent with no agency. Women could be active sexual participants in the brothel because their sexuality was regulated and condemned in other ways, both by enslavement and by invective that targeted prostitution and cast prostitutes as the antithesis of the Roman matron.[95] Through these idealizations and castigations, Romo-sexuality emerges as a normative ideal of sexual agency wherein normal Roman sex should involve an active man (as the penetrator) and a passive person (who was penetrated), either a woman or a man who was less powerful/elite.

Penetration and agency, as related but separate axes, do not capture the full picture of sexuality and its regulation in the Greco-Roman world. Sexuality, especially in terms of sexual desire, was also regulated in elite discourses by the terms of "self-control" (ἐγκράτεια) and "moderation" (σωφροσύνη).[96] A true Roman man of high social regard and worthy of high political position should not want to have too much sex, even if it is natural. His sexual appetite—or desire—should be controlled and orderly, regardless of his outlet for penetration. For the Roman elite, it is immoderation that often captures what is unnatural about sexuality. Desire for too much sex, desire to be penetrated, and desire to defy the social order all betray a lack of elite moderation.[97] If

---

female and male prostitutes within it and their relations and interactions with their male clients. See Sarah Levin-Richardson, *The Brothel of Pompeii: Sex, Class, and Gender at the Margins of Roman Society* (Cambridge: Cambridge University Press, 2019); on the term/distinction of the "purpose-built" brothel, see pp. 4–6.

94. See especially Levin-Richardson, *Brothel of Pompeii*, 111–28 (ch. 7, "Female Prostitutes").

95. Kamen and Levin-Richardson, "Lusty Ladies," 247–48. They note here an elite male desire for a μάτηρ "in the streets," πόρνη "in the sheets" when "the narrator of [Martial's] epigram XI.104 claims to want his wife to be Lucretia by day, a Lais (i.e., a prostitute) by night" (248).

96. See Foucault, *Use of Pleasure*, 63–77.

97. See further discussions throughout Foucault, *Use of Pleasure*, especially surrounding diet and economics.

one cannot moderate one's desire at a natural level, how can one be expected to govern others—family, society, empire?[98]

These regulations apply to bodies most proximate to Roman elite men, especially those who fall under their responsibility. A similar rule of moderation can be stated for the elite Roman women whom these men married: their desire should not be excessive and should be only for penetration by elite Roman men, ideally their husbands. However, according to the kyriarchal model, the status of these women is not the primary concern. Though their unnatural impulses may be taken as indication of non-elite birth and status, immoderation in elite women ultimately reflects the poor control *of a man*, most often her husband or father.

Penetration, agency, and self-control were all axes through which Roman discourse perpetuated norms about sexuality. Since the norms reinforced kyriarchal sexual politics, they had different implications and effects depending on one's gender, socioeconomic status, and ethnicity. Regardless of the sexual axis, elite Roman men always found themselves on top: the naturally self-controlled, active, impenetrable penetrator. Romosexuality encompasses *all* of these normative axes that render particular sexual embodiments natural while casting deviations as unnatural, that is, nonnormative.

The language of Rome's sexual axes derives from scholars who outline grids of Roman sexuality, which can visually demonstrate the sliding scale from top to bottom, especially when it comes to the intersecting axes of penetration and agency. Though useful, these sexual grids often cause a gridlock: scholars must prioritize particular axes at the expense of others. However, Romosexuality requires all three axes in order to confirm the normative sexuality of elite Roman men by casting all other sexual expressions as deviant—many as multiply deviant.

The gridlock proves how the Romosexual system works: multiple axes create multiple ways to regulate bodies. More axes multiply oppressions, confirming the status of those on top while making it difficult for anyone else to penetrate their way beyond the gridlock. This gridlock, often

---

98. Williams, *Roman Homosexuality*, 137–76; Dale Martin, *Sex and the Single Savior: Gender and Sexuality in Biblical Interpretation* (Louisville: Westminster John Knox, 2006), 65–76; Jennifer Wright Knust, *Abandoned to Lust: Sexual Slander and Ancient Christianity*, GTR (New York: Columbia University Press, 2006), 32–47; Colleen M. Conway, *Behold the Man: Jesus and Greco-Roman Masculinity* (Oxford: Oxford University Press, 2008), 21–29.

embodied in scholarship on Roman sexuality, shows how axes and grids can elide complex dynamics. This makes my turn to affective critique and assemblage critical to understanding Romosexuality and Paul's relation to it. Affect theory focuses on the forces and feelings that exist in between axial lines. These forces can motivate linear directions and sometimes compel systemic gridlock.

Like Romosexuality, we could outline multiple axes by which heteronormativity regulates contemporary sexual embodiments. Heteronormativity relies on regulating sexual embodiments beyond a norm of a (cisgender) man/woman couple, which include marital status, ability to procreate, and proper sexual practices (such as the missionary position). As Cathy Cohen argued, only particular straight people are accorded the economic and political power permitted through their heterosexual lifestyles. Romosexuality and heteronormativity are both constructions: though they theorize different axes of sexual power, they regulate bodies by enforcing a preferred norm, which is most accessible to those already near the top of the kyriarchal pyramid. Even among the elite men who define and benefit most from these sexual arrangements, their actual practices frequently deviate from the norm, often without consequences when he who made the exception also made the rules (e.g., Roman emperors, US Presidents).[99] Romosexuality represents the construction of imperial sexual norms that did not reflect most (if any) real Romans' sexualities. It is the system of norms—revolving around axes of self-control, agency, and penetration—that permitted the socio-sexual-political reality of empire and made elite Roman men Romosexuals.

Romanormativity

Romosexuality's norms create conditions that permit what I call *Romanormativity*. If Romosexuality is akin to heteronormativity, Romanormativity parallels homonormativity. Romanormativity denotes the tactics by which certain populations, who were deemed more marginal than elite Roman men, emphasized how they and their communities were

---

99. As Suetonius relates of Augustus's exploits with the wives of his political rivals (notably Antony's), see Suetonius, *Lives of Caesars* 2.69–71. See further discussion in Catharine Edwards, *The Politics of Immorality in Ancient Rome* (Cambridge: Cambridge University Press, 1993); Rebecca Langlands, *Sexual Morality in Ancient Rome* (Cambridge: Cambridge University Press, 2006), 348–51.

nearly Romosexual—that is, their sexual embodiments are as natural as the most virtuous Romans. Romanormativity attempts to take advantage of potentials for sociopolitical mobility under empire and strives toward inclusion at the top.[100]

The term *Romanormativity* riffs on *homonormativity*, but the *Roma* (and its blending into *Roman* with the *n* of *normativity*) also calls attention to how sexual norms are enforced by imperial interests. This reminds us how contemporary homonormativity cannot be separated from the interests of the US nation-state, which more and more resembles its own empire. The term *Roman*ormativity emphasizes the Romanness of the sexual embodiments taken on through Romanormative tactics. Romosexuality is the normative sexuality fostered by empire, so Romanormativity attempts to mirror not only this sexuality but also its Romanness. *Roma*normativity also reminds us how theologies can support imperial (and national) politics, as the goddess *Roma* was the divine embodiment of Rome itself. Roman imperialism was blessed by and with divine power, placing all other bodies under them and their gods.

Romanormativity frequently appears in the writings of Rome's ἔθνη, foreigners considered different from Rome's elite citizens. Elite men among these ἔθνη competed for Roman favor by aligning their sexual mores to Romosexuality. Philo of Alexandria's writings, for example, frequently show how Jewish Scriptures embody Roman virtues, especially in terms of sexual morality.[101] These Romanormative embodiments are apparent in Philo's biographies of biblical patriarchs, including Abraham, Moses, and Joseph. Maren Niehoff argues that Philo's patriarchs are portrayed in ideal alignment with the virtues of Roman Stoicism.[102] These virtuous alignments include sexualities that model Romosexuality, especially through Philo's portrayal of the women related to Jewish male heroes (i.e., their

---

100. James N. Hoke, "Be Even Better Subjects, Worthy of Rehabilitation," in *Bodies on the Verge: Queering Pauline Epistles*, ed. Joseph A. Marchal, SemeiaSt 93 (Atlanta: SBL Press, 2019), 90.

101. See Maren R. Niehoff, *Philo on Jewish Identity and Culture*, TSAJ (Tübingen: Mohr Siebeck, 2001) and Niehoff, *Philo of Alexandria: An Intellectual Biography*, ABRL (New Haven: Yale University Press, 2018). See also James N. Hoke, "*Homo Urbanus* or Urban Homos? Metronormative Tropes and Subcultural Queernesses around Philo and the Therapeuts," forthcoming.

102. Niehoff, *Philo of Alexandria*, 109–30 (ch. 6, "Character and History in the *Lives* of Biblical Forefathers").

wives, mothers, and daughters).[103] Looking at their wives' portrayals, Niehoff writes, "Biblical women have become Roman ladies who are beloved by
their husbands and trusted for their loyalty." Sarah, in particular, embodies
a steadfast wife whose enduring relationship with Abraham embodies the
ideal Roman matron—comparable to Augustus's wife Livia—who is both
loyal and not motivated by sexual desire.[104]

Joseph's biography exemplifies how the patriarchs embody Romosexual self-control. Philo displays Joseph's Romanormative persona in his
retelling of Gen 39:1–18, the episode with Potiphar's wife. Describing her
attempted seduction, Philo describes her as "unrestrainedly rabid around
her passion" (ἀκαθέκτως περὶ τὸ πάθος λυττῶσα) when she comes to him
with "dirty talk" (τοὺς περὶ μίξεως λόγους) (Ios. 40). Joseph models Roman
self-control: he refuses her "on account of propriety and moderation being
inherent [to him] by nature and practice" (διὰ τὴν ἐκ φύσεως καὶ μελέτης
ἐνυπάρξασαν κοσμιότητα καὶ σωφροσύνην) (Ios. 40). Not only is Joseph
self-controlled; he also does not allow himself to be made to seem passive
when facing the sexual agency of a woman who takes the active role in
initiating a sexual encounter.

In his restraint, Philo's Joseph emphasizes that it is because of the
Hebrews' (Ἑβραίων) singular customs and laws (ἐξαιρέτοις ἔθεσι καὶ
νομίμοις) (Ios. 42). He elaborates on the purity of Jewish marriages:

> πρὸ δὴ συνόδων νομίμων ὁμιλίαν ἑτέρας γυναικὸς οὐκ ἴσμεν, ἀλλ᾽ ἁγνοὶ
> γάμων ἁγναῖς παρθένοις προσερχόμεθα προτεθειμένοι τέλος οὐχ ἡδονὴν
> ἀλλὰ γνησίων παίδων σποράν.
> Before legal unions, we are not acquainted with intercourse with other
> women, but we, as chaste men, enter marriages with chaste virgins
> because we propose that its purpose is not pleasure but the bearing of
> legitimate children. (Ios. 44)

Joseph's emphasis on legal marriage and procreation stresses that Romosexual self-control is inherent to Jewish laws and customs in ways that
conform to imperial sexual regulations of adultery and childrearing. Philo
portrays Joseph as a hero who exemplifies Jewish values rooted in Scripture. This allows Philo, especially by stressing sexuality and self-control, to
present Jewish values as Romosexual.

---

103. Niehoff, Philo of Alexandria, 131–48 (ch. 7, "Biblical Ladies in Roman Garb").
104. Niehoff, Philo of Alexandria, 133–38.

Philo's emphasis on Joseph's natural restraint and rejection of adultery with Potiphar's wife demonstrates his political acumen. Just as Romosexuality linked sexual self-control and agency with natural ability to govern, Philo portrays Joseph as an astute politician, one who is as good as any of Rome's ruling political elite. He emphasizes the importance of his patience (τὸν καρτερικόν), as a form of self-control (ὁ εγκρατής): this is just as important as shepherding (ὁ ποιμενικός) and household management (ὁ οἰκονομικός), and all three of these political qualities were valued by Moses (*Ios.* 54).[105] Philo expounds: πρὸς μὲν οὖν ἅπαντα τὰ τοῦ βίου πράγματα λυσιτελὲς ἐγκράτεια καὶ σωτήριον, πρὸς δὲ τὰ πόλεως καὶ διαφερόντως ("Self-control is profitable and salvific for all life's affairs, especially for those of the polis" [*Ios.* 55]). He then warns of the dangers of its lack (ἀκρασία), which leads to civil dissents and wars (στάσεις ἐμφύλιοι καὶ πόλεμοι) and specifically points out: τῶν γὰρ πολέμων οἱ πλείους καὶ μέγιστοι δι' ἔρωτας καὶ μοιχείας καὶ γυναικῶν ἀπάτας συνέστησαν ("Most wars, especially the greatest, combine sexual passions, adulteries, and women's tricks" [*Ios.* 56]). Joseph's scriptural example of self-control—vis-à-vis Potiphar's wife's (Egyptian) lack of it—makes him an effective ruler. In Philo's accounting, self-control is not only endemic to Judaism, it is also what makes Jews like Joseph worthy of political inclusion among Rome's elite. Just as Buttigieg exemplified homonormativity by emphasizing his adherence to heteronormative monogamy and his politicized patriotism, Philo aligns sexual self-control in Joseph's story in ways that associate Judaism with Romosexuality and imperial political acumen, thus exemplifying Romanormativity.

Paul's letters similarly participate in Romanormativity. Indeed, the Romosexual ideas that Paul parrots in Rom 1:26–27 (as discussed in ch. 2) form the socio-sexual-political foundation for Paul's theology, which faithfully aligns to Roman kyriarchy (as discussed in ch. 3), and his ethics, which complete Paul's connection of Christ-followers as ideal embodiment of submitting to Romosexual morality (as shown in ch. 5). As with Philo and others, the root of Paul's Romanormativity is a hope for inclusion at the top.

Even when Romans' sexualities existed outside of the norm, their bodies and ideas were affected by Romosexuality. As we will see, feminist and queer studies in affect theory can reveal Romanormativity in ancient materials and foster understanding of their impacts on the wo/men who

---

105. Niehoff, *Philo of Alexandria*, 121–25, 145–47.

created and interacted with these materials. These varied affective resonances impact how we interpret Romans.

The Forces and Feelings of Normativity: Affect Theories and Critiques

Norms affect bodies and their interactions in ways that are neither obvious
nor simple. The study of affect theorizes these complexities: affect encap-
sulates potentials for change that are *felt* in the movements, sensations, and
forces that exist in/between bodies (which are not necessarily human or
organic).[106] "Affect arises in the midst of in-betweenness: in the capacities

---

106. Affect theories have formally been part of biblical studies since 2009 with
the publication of Erin Runions, "From Disgust to Humor: Rahab's Queer Affect," in
Bible Trouble: Queer Reading at the Boundaries of Biblical Scholarship," ed. Teresa J.
Hornsby and Ken Stone, SemeiaSt 67 (Atlanta: SBL Press, 2011), 45–74. This essay
was soon followed by Maia Kotrosits's 2010 article that explored the affective performances and construction of space in 1 Corinthians. See Maia Kotrosits, "The Rhetoric of Intimate Spaces: Affect and Performance in the Corinthian Correspondence,"
USQR 62 (2010): 134–51. However, Kotrosits points out a corrective genealogy of
affect. Since, at least in part, affect studies examine the circulation and production
of emotions and/as feelings, we must remember that critical analyses of emotions
and feelings predate the coining of affect. Kotrosits reminds readers that Virginia
Burrus's work on shame predates the formal entry of affect into biblical and early
Christian studies. See Maia Kotrosits, *How Things Feel: Affect Theory, Biblical Studies,
and the (Im)personal*, BRPBI (Leiden: Brill, 2016), 6. See also Virginia Burrus, *Saving
Shame: Martyrs, Saints, and Other Abject Subjects*, Div (Philadelphia: University of
Pennsylvania Press, 2008). Since these early forays, work on affect theory has begun
to expand in the field, beginning with a focused joint session of the Reading, Theory,
and the Bible and Bible and Cultural Studies program units at the Annual Meeting
of the Society of Biblical Literature, Chicago, 2012, which spawned the publication
of a special issue of *Biblical Interpretation* that includes essays by Jennifer L. Koosed,
Stephen D. Moore, Maia Kotrosits, Jennifer Knust, Amy C. Cottrill, and Alexis G.
Waller. See Jennifer L. Koosed and Stephen D. Moore, eds. *Affect Theory and the
Bible*, BibInt 22 (2014). Erin Runions's *The Babylon Complex* frequently discusses the
intersections and fantasies of affect, politics, and the Bible and draws from queer
and feminist scholars who work with affect. See Erin Runions, *The Babylon Complex:
Theopolitical Fantasies of War, Sex, and Sovereignty* (New York: Fordham University
Press, 2014). The first monograph to explicitly treat affect theory in both its title and
as the main emphasis in its pages is Maia Kotrosits, *Rethinking Early Christian Identity: Affect, Violence, and Belonging* (Minneapolis: Fortress, 2015). Further signal
works specifically within affect and biblical studies include Stephen D. Moore, *Gospel
Jesuses and Other Nonhumans: Biblical Criticism Post-Poststructuralism*, SemeiaSt 89
(Atlanta: SBL Press, 2017); Fiona Black and Jennifer L. Koosed, eds., *Reading with

to act and be acted upon."[107] Affect's *in-betweenness* makes it impossible to fully capture: how does one define or represent different unseen forces and feelings, especially ones that can be sensed and experienced differently?[108]

Though theories of affect will always fail to perfectly represent the "muddy, unmediated relatedness" that best expresses human existence and experience, considering the different dimensions of affect helps us account for how its in-betweenness exists around contemporary and

---

Feeling: Affect Theory and the Bible, SemeiaSt 95 (Atlanta: SBL Press, 2019); several essays on affect and biblical texts (as well as religion/theology more broadly) appear in both Karen Bray and Stephen D. Moore, eds., *Religion, Emotion, Sensation: Affect Theories and Theologies*, TTC (New York: Fordham University Press, 2019) and Brintnall, Marchal, and Moore, *Sexual Disorientations*. These two essay collections (both coming from papers first presented at Transdisciplinary Theological Colloquia held at Drew Theological School) further signal work on how scholars in theology and religious studies more broadly engage with affect theories, frequently in ways that overlap and interact with work in biblical studies. This work includes Donovan O. Schaefer, *Religious Affects: Animality, Evolution, and Power* (Durham, NC: Duke University Press, 2015); Jenna Supp-Montgomerie, "Affect and the Study of Religion," *Religion Compass* 9 (2015): 335–45; John Corrigan, ed., *Feeling Religion* (Durham, NC: Duke University Press, 2017); Karen Bray, *Grave Attending: A Political Theology for the Unredeemed* (New York: Fordham University Press, 2020). Corrigan's edited volume includes essays that look at emotion and affect in and across multiple religious traditions.

107. Gregory J. Seigworth and Melissa Gregg, "An Inventory of Shimmers," in *The Affect Theory Reader*, ed. Gregg and Seigworth (Durham, NC: Duke University Press, 2010), 1.

108. "What would it mean to give a logical consistency to the in-between? It would mean realigning with a logic of relation. For the in-between, as such, is not a middling being but rather a being *of* the middle—the being of a relation." See Brian Massumi, *Parables for the Virtual: Movement, Affect, Sensation* (Durham, NC: Duke University Press, 2002), 70. Massumi contrasts "foundationalist" approaches to the question of individual and society (presenting "which came first? The individual or society" as a chicken/egg problem) as privileging time with these approaches that privilege space and position in the form of "such notions as structure, the symbolic, semiotic system, or textuality" (68). He further contrasts affect's in-betweenness with that of recent theories (including obvious reference to both queer and postcolonial theories) that make use of the in-between in order to define and display their marginality, hybridity, or subversion, a move that ultimately leaves their spatial position in the middle as a determined position with respect to that which is normal, powerful, or central. Such theories represent the "middling beings" that Massumi claims for a theory that emphasizes "being *of* the middle." See further Massumi, *Parables*, 68–70.

ancient bodies.[109] Scholars who work on affect usually work along the lines of one of two vectors. One vector primarily thinks about affect in terms of being *forces* and considers its *intensity*; the other looks at how affect involves *feelings* and analyzes its relation to *emotion*.[110] Though these two scholarly vectors move along different directions and, at times, come into tension, both are necessary to understanding the intersectional politics of queer and feminist affective critique, especially since many feminist and queer studies of affect blur the lines.[111]

---

109. And it is out of such messy relations that affect emerges. Seigworth and Gregg, "Inventory of Shimmers," 4.

110. Seigworth and Gregg, "Inventory of Shimmers," 5–6. Puar gives different phrasing and framing to Seigworth and Gregg's vectors, calling them a split in affect's genealogy: one (the first vector) that emphasizes attachment and feeling (and thus "becomes interchangeable with emotion, feeling, expressive sentiment") and the other (the second vector) that looks at affect as what escapes various forms of perception. Thus, it becomes "a physiological and biological phenomenon, signaling why bodily matter matters." Puar, *Terrorist Assemblages*, 207–8.

111. Most work, especially monograph-length, in affect studies and religious/biblical studies maps out these trajectories in ways that call attention to (and typically query the fixity of) the split admitted more widely among scholars who work around affect (see previous note). As she develops her use of the word *sense*, which both attends to emotional sensations and feelings and attends to intuitive, preconscious forces, Kotrosits lays out and rejects the firm divisions in affect's genealogy (Kotrosits, *Rethinking Early Christian Identity*, 3–8). She further challenges the split, noting that the firm split relies particularly on Massumi's framing of the differences, in Kotrosits, *How Things Feel*, 7–12. Schaefer lays a "dual genealogy," labeling the two vectors as "Deleuzian" and "phenomenonological." In so doing, he provides a detailed summary of the signal works and different approaches in these two trajectories (Schaefer, *Religious Affects*, 23–34). Acknowledging Schaefer, both Bray and Bray and Moore admit this duality and then blur the binary and, to a degree, distance it from origins in particular theorists by pointing to how different affective approaches shift or focus their emphasis. They propose a "trinity" of "interconnected, yet distinct, lenses: a *psychobiological* lens, a *prepersonal* lens, and a *cultural* lens." See Karen Bray and Stephen D. Moore, "Introduction: Mappings and Crossings," in *Religion, Emotion, Sensation: Affect Theories and Theologies*, ed. Bray and Moore, TTC (New York: Fordham University Press, 2019), 5, see further 1–6. See also Bray, *Grave Attending*, 4–11, esp. 5–6 for her three lenses. Black and Koosed admit the split and also note how scholars (especially Kotrosits) have challenged its firmness. See Fiona Black and Jennifer L. Koosed, "Introduction: Some Ways to Read with Feeling," in *Reading with Feeling: Affect Theory and the Bible*, ed. Black and Koosed, SemeiaSt 95 (Atlanta: SBL Press, 2019), 1–5. My mapping here does not claim any innovative additions to these

One vector of affect considers how it moves in and between bodies as what motivates bodies and exists within them as potential capacities. In this theorization, affect describes a force that is "beyond conscious knowing" by which bodies are compelled or driven to forms of movement.[112] The forces represented as affect occur within a particular body—or between different bodies—*before* cognition produces change: "body—(movement/sensation)—change," as Brian Massumi describes it.[113] Affect connects the dual forces of movement and sensation that motivate bodies and produce some change in state (which can be quite minor in its individual scale).

Since these forces and their embodiments exist and move before or beyond cognition, affect is often experienced as excessive to the rational mind. Affect describes "intensity," or unassimilable excess. Thinking particularly in terms of language/imagery, which is important for applying these theories to texts like Paul's letter to the Romans, affect functions alongside an image's content (its qualities) and impacts its effect (including strength and duration).[114] Excessive, affect resists reduction to simplicity. Uncontainable, these intensities of movement and sensation comprise affect as it drives bodies to change.[115]

A theoretical focus on affect tries to better capture the complex intensities of moving bodies that are rarely, if ever, static. Returning to Paul's letter, we can use this idea of affect to acknowledge and examine the complex and intense movements that motivate Romans in ways that the author

---

previous maps; instead, I provide a map that guides readers through and to my own orientations to affect theories.

112. Like *queer*, *affect* is quite resistant to any stable definition. It exists in a somewhat sharp differentiation from cognitive knowing; however, they are not precisely opposites: the forces affect names exist "beyond, alongside, or generally *other than* conscious knowing." Seigworth and Gregg, "Inventory of Shimmers," 1.

113. As a force (albeit, one that is generally not forceful in a more violent sense), affect can be described as proprioceptive and autonomic, terms often used in neuroscience to describe brain functions that are involuntary and often imperceptible (at least in the moment). Massumi, *Parables*, 28–34. On distinguishing affect as a force that is not "violent," see also Seigworth and Gregg, "Inventory of Shimmers," 2; Massumi, *Parables*, 1. Massumi explains the parenthetical (movement/sensation) as the fact that these forces have been largely bracketed by cultural theory. See Massumi, *Parables*, 28–30.

114. Massumi, *Parables*, 24–28.

115. On a relational definition of change as an affective part of a "political economy of belonging," see Massumi, *Parables*, 77–80, as well as 68–88.

may have been unaware. Likewise, when considering the assembly who received this letter, Romans compelled unconscious affective forces that swirled *in between* the words being read and the bodies of the wo/men engaging with them.[116]

Affect exceeds the mind, but affect is often felt. It involves feeling and *feelings*. A second vector of affect theories focuses on the feelings that simultaneously are generated by and generate affect. This side of affect, as theorized by Sedgwick and Adam Frank, takes as a starting point the work of psychologist Silvan Tompkins, who described in detail how certain emotions operated as affects. "Tompkins considers shame, along with interest, surprise, joy, anger, fear, distress, disgust, and, in his later writing, contempt (he calls this 'dissmell'), to be the basic set of affects." In the case of sexuality, affect opens up and expands "different possibilities for sexual relevance (defined in this case by the distinct negative affects shame, anxiety, boredom, rage)." Focusing on affect as opposed to psychological drives (especially sexuality as a drive) multiplies possible motivations and effects for actions, thoughts, and feelings.[117]

Emotions may represent the most obvious and embodied forms of affect in terms of feelings. As Ahmed has shown, considering emotions affectively does not just mean studying what emotions are, it requires paying attention to what they *do*.[118] Emotions like disgust or happiness don't simply arise in individual bodies ex nihilo; they are produced through interactions and *histories* of interactions.[119] Emotions are affectively *sticky*, and they cling to inorganic objects and texts just as they stick

---

116. Along similar lines, Kotrosits argues for the affective forces and feelings that circulate in between (and attach to) biblical texts, early Christian history, and scholars studying them. She writes, "The affective resonances of texts are markers or symptoms of social and historical forces" (Kotrosits, *Rethinking Early Christian Identity*, 11–12, see further 7–13). Considering the study and theorization of religion more broadly, Schaefer calls attention to the emphasis on *logos* and a linguistic fallacy that overemphasizes language (and therefore text) in understanding and approaching religion, which misses "economies of affect." See Schaefer, *Religious Affects*, 9–10.

117. Eve Kosofsky Sedgwick and Adam Frank, "Shame in the Cybernetic Fold: Reading Silvan Tompkins," *Critical Inquiry* 21 (1995): 500, 504, see further 503–8.

118. Sara Ahmed, *The Cultural Politics of Emotion*, 2nd ed. (New York: Routledge, 2014), 1, 4.

119. See especially Ahmed, *Cultural Politics of Emotion*, 82–100 (ch. 4, "The Performativity of Disgust"), and Ahmed, *The Promise of Happiness* (Durham, NC: Duke University Press, 2010).

to human and organic/living bodies.[120] The circulation and production of emotions are political: certain emotions tend to affect and stick to certain populations. These affective effects follow histories of racism, sexism, heterosexism, and colonialism. As we will see in the next chapter, Rom 1:18–32 demonstrates the affective stickiness of emotions and how they can be held within and circulate in between bodies and texts, as the passage and its interpretations simultaneously contain and produce feelings of disgust and exhaustion.

Some affect theorists (Massumi notably among them) have been reticent of the theorization and study of emotion as affect, perhaps in part out of fear that this could cause a slippage and reduction: emotion is affect—affect is (only) emotion.[121] These fears often result in an attempt to separate emotion from affect. However, affectively speaking, such separation is impossible. Emotion is an affective sensation. Sara Ahmed captures it with a brilliant metaphor: "The activity of separating affect from emotion could be understood as rather like breaking an egg in order to separate the yolk from the white."[122] There are differences, some significant, in how these two trajectories of scholarship conceive of affect, but this does not mean they study different things when they speak of affect. The divergence of these two vectors shows how some scholars tend to focus on different

---

120. Ahmed, *Cultural Politics of Emotion*, 89–92, 97–100.

121. See further Sedgwick, *Touching Feeling: Affect, Pedagogy, Performativity*, SerQ (Durham, NC: Duke University Press, 2003). Unlike Sedgwick—who had already established deep roots in queer theory (and thus, her vector has perhaps been more easily applied in queer projects)—Massumi himself ignores the queer capacities of affect and its politics (indeed, judging from *Parables*, 69, he could be said to be mostly critical of [certain forms] of queer theory). However, Massumian affect exceeds its progenitor, as his theorization and development of Deleuze and Guattari have been essential to Puar and Berlant, among other queer theorists. Arguably, queer theory's development of Massumian/Deleuzian affect may better represent its force and political potentials (much like could be said for the feminist and queer developments of Deleuze and Guattari's assemblage; see ch. 2). Though Ahmed agrees with Massumi that emotions and sensations are not coterminous, she emphasizes the way in which the two often slide between one another (in a beside relationship, perhaps), particularly due to the "intensity of perception" implied by emotions. See Ahmed, *Cultural Politics of Emotion*, 25, 40 n. 4. Massumi draws an even sharper distinction between affect and emotion, emphasizing that the two are distinctly not synonyms: "But of the cleanest lessons of this first story is that emotion and affect—if affect is intensity—follow different logics and pertain to different orders" (27).

122. Ahmed, *Cultural Politics of Emotion*, 210.

manifestations of affect, but these vectors can converge. Studies of affect can scramble the whole egg.

This attempted separation of emotion from affect *genders* the so-called affective turn. Fears of reduction are not the only motivation for separating affect and emotion. The separation creates affect as a new theoretical innovation. After all, feminists (especially lesbian and queer wo/men of color) have long called attention to emotions, their importance to theory, and how they affect bodies.[123] An "affective turn" implies an origin story, one that is more recent in scholarly trends and one that can include straight white cisgender men among its pioneers.[124] As Ahmed insists, if emotion is essential to the study of affect, then there is *no* recent turn or discovery of affect as a whole: wo/men have been writing about affect for decades. Centuries, actually.[125]

The theorization of affect as emotions and feelings has also been pivotal for queer affective studies. It is not coincidental that Sedgwick—generally acknowledged as one of queer theory's foundational figures—focuses on shame as an affect. Shame is an affect that swirls around queerness when one considers the histories of queer folks hiding in the closet and experiencing rejection from families and close friends. Queer theorists have frequently analyzed and discussed experiences and portrayals of shame in society, politics, and literature.[126] Ahmed's work on emotions consid-

---

123. See, for example, Moraga and Anzaldúa, *This Bridge Called My Back*; Lorde, *Sister Outsider*, 124–33.

124. See Ann Cvetkovitch, *Depression: A Public Feeling* (Durham, NC: Duke University Press, 2012), 3–10, especially on her hesitation to refer to an "affective turn."

125. Ahmed, *Cultural Politics of Emotion*, 205–11. Kotrosits calls attention to the gendering of emotion and its relation to affective foci and genealogies (Kotrosits, *Rethinking Early Christian Identity*, 4). As noted above (see n. 106), Kotrosits has also reminded biblical scholars "turning" to affect that scholars, especially wo/men, in biblical studies and early Christianity have studied and called attention to the production and circulation of emotion in and around texts and histories (long) before more recent affect-theoretical attention—as well at the particular affective relationship among wo/men studying affect and biblical texts. See Kotrosits, *How Things Feel*, 6, 27–37. Similarly, Black and Koosed write, "Given this backstory, it is clear that affect-critical reading is not a sudden eruption ex nihilo; one wonders instead if it is less a new thing in biblical studies than an intensity of interests in poetics, cultural-critical approaches, receptions, and queer readings explored in a new critical vein" (Black and Koosed, "Introduction," 6–7).

126. In queer theory's "turn" to affect, Cvetkovich (thinking with the work of scholars, including Sedgwick, Ahmed, Heather Love, Jack Halberstam, José Esteban

ers the feelings of normativity: norms cause discomfort for queer bodies that refuse to inhabit them even as the politics of normativity continues to force queers to be "shaped by that which they fail to reproduce."[127] By considering how queer wo/men are often multiply affected by their failure to be "normal" in ways other than sexuality (e.g., race, gender, class, nationality), Ahmed's discussion of "queer feelings" stresses that studies of affect must attend to intersectionality. When Ahmed critiques the queer discomfort caused by norms, she also harnesses its potential. "Feeling queer" can mean "inhabiting norms differently" by embodying uncomfortable affects and making them generative.[128]

The distinction of two vectors imposes a binary on affect. But as a feminist genealogy of affect shows, it is a false distinction that tends to privilege the first vector as the truer form of affect. Many scholars who engage affect refuse to specify its meaning: "I tend to use *affect* in a generic sense, rather than in the more Deleuzian sense, as a category that encompasses affect, emotion, and feeling, and that includes impulses, desires, and feelings that get historically constructed in a range of ways," writes Ann Cvetkovich.[129] Like any binary, the distinctions are experienced in real ways, even if their inherent separation is produced as a fiction. It can be generative (as well as helpful for those new to affect theory) to break affect into diverging pieces in order to examine it closely and better understand its complexity—just

---

Muñoz, and David L. Eng) observes, "Especially important have been models for depathologization of negative feelings such as shame, failure, melancholy, and depression, and the resulting rethinking of categories such as utopia, hope, and happiness as entwined with and ever enhanced by forms of negative feeling" (Cvetkovich, *Depression*, 5). See also Sedgwick, *Touching Feeling*; Ahmed, *Cultural Politics*; Ahmed, *Promise of Happiness*; Love, *Feeling Backward*; Halberstam, *The Queer Art of Failure*, JHFCB (Durham, NC: Duke University Press, 2011); José Esteban Muñoz, *Cruising Utopia: The Then and There of Queer Futurity* (New York: New York University Press, 2009); Eng, *Feeling of Kinship*.

127. Ahmed, *Cultural Politics*, 152, see also 147–53. In her essay on disgust, queerness, and affect in the story of Rahab, Runions argues that queer approaches to biblical texts must attend to how feelings and bodily responses are generated from biblical texts and their histories of interpretation. As she does so, she calls attention to how feelings of disgust toward queerness cannot be cleaved from racism and the racialization of nonnormative sexualities. See Runions, "From Disgust to Humor," 45–74.

128. Ahmed, *Cultural Politics*, 155. Cvetkovich, *Depression*, does similar work with the feeling of depression and writes about how it can be put to politically generative use.

129. For example, Cvetkovitch, *Depression*, 4.

as it can be fruitful to let the pieces hook together and collide with one another to harness their productive tension and create new pieces.[130]

My engagement with affect travels along both vectors and refuses to separate affect's force and intensity from its feelings and emotional resonances. They all constitute affect and are necessary for approaching the affective dimensions of first-century texts and contexts. The affective critiques and analyses of Puar and Berlant, from which I draw most heavily when critically engaging Romans, consider both feelings and forces in ways that blur the vectors.[131] In what follows, I delve into Puar and Berlant, respectively, to show how both hone affect in order to engage in intersectional feminist and queer critique of contemporary politics and culture. To conclude, I show how Puar's and Berlant's critiques can complement one another in developing an affective critique that is both feminist and queer. This approach, I argue, raises new and relevant questions for critiquing and subverting submission in Paul's letter to the Romans.

Intimate Intersections of Affective Critique and Queer and Feminist Politics

Though it produces change, affect alone does not promise that this change will be *positive*. Intersectional feminist and queer critiques, such as Duggan's homonormativity, can be sharpened through affect theory's emphasis on complex feelings, sensations, and intensities that motivate capacities, belonging, relation, and connectivity. Jasbir K. Puar develops these feminist and queer analyses into an affective critique that is funda-

---

130. In her affective and rhythmic reading of the Samson narrative in Judges, A. Paige Rawson likewise blurs the boundaries between affect's vectored binary, poignantly summoning affect's rhythmic beats to hear the resonant harmonies the different (musical) lines reverberate. "In both the Tompkinsian and Deleuzoguattarian iterations of affect, *resonance*, like waves and wave frequencies in physics, is defined by the affect of one body upon another—*movement* in/of one body producing some sort of corresponding response (amplification) in another body." See A. Paige Rawson, "Reading (with) Rhythm for the Sake of the (I-n-)Islands: A Rastafarian Interpretation of Samson as Ambi(val)ent Affective Assemblage," in *Religion, Emotion, Sensation: Affect Theories and Theologies*, ed. Karen Bray and Stephen D. Moore, TTC (New York: Fordham University Press, 2019), 129.

131. Puar, for example, draws heavily from Massumi and Deleuze's affective work—especially to theorize assemblages—but she also engages Ahmed and the politics of feelings and emotions, especially how they structure the intersections of racialized, gendered, sexualized oppressions.

mentally intersectional. For Puar, affect provides an avenue to challenge a particular brand of identity politics that privileges a singular aspect of complex human identities (e.g., sexuality) while ignoring other aspects (e.g., race).[132]

Intersectionality can be considered in affective terms. Identities—and oppressions based on those identities—do not just intersect like an "X." The "lines" curve and twist and slide around based on any number of circumstances: identities depend on who, what, where, when, and how bodies are interacting and intersecting. It can be helpful to picture a traffic intersection: there are multiple things potentially affecting the intersection—cars (who is in them, what they are listening to), pedestrians, noises, animals, signals, and so on.[133] Puar relishes affect's complexifying of identity and, in so doing, intersectionally reimagines the "queer" of queer theory, unsettling it as an adjectival identity marker (which is equally implicit in its verbal usages). Puar prefers to speak of "queerness" rather than queer, transforming its force into an affective quality that cannot be possessed or fully embodied. Puar's *queerness* expresses its unsettledness: many (if not most) bodies are never perfectly captured by the term; one's relation to queerness shifts based on place and time; it is affected by racialized and gendered norms. Queerness creates capacities and relations while simultaneously enabling the querying and subverting of fixed patterns of uneven power and control.[134]

---

132. Such privileging produces, in Puar's language, a "cleaving of race and sexuality" that defines homonormative—and what she will further show to be "homonational"—politics, activism, and discourse (Puar, *Terrorist Assemblages*, 44). (For an elaboration of Puar's "homonationalism," see ch. 5, "Ethical Submission.") She discusses this cleaving at several other important junctures throughout the monograph (see especially 78, 131). Note that Puar wants to transform identity politics into a "politics of affect," but she acknowledges that identity politics are still necessary and that neither identity nor its politics can be entirely erased through such an affective transformation (see further 204–5).

133. See Crenshaw's analogy to a traffic intersection ("Demarginalizing the Intersection," 139). Puar reemphasizes this metaphor. See Jasbir K. Puar, "I Would Rather Be a Cyborg Than a Goddess: Becoming-Intersectional in Assemblage Theory" *philoSOPHIA: A Journal of Feminist Continental Philosophy* 2 (2012): 59–61.

134. "Queerness irreverently challenges a linear mode of conduction and transmission: there is no exact recipe for a queer endeavor, no a priori system that taxonomies the linkages, disruptions, and contradictions into a tidy vessel" (Puar, *Terrorist Assemblages*, xv). In her queer affective reading of Rahab, Runions draws from Puar to consider queerness as something other than liberatory alongside the Bible's role

Puar observes that queerness, while more malleable when defined affectively, can still be molded to support homonormativity: "queer as regulatory." Her theorization of queerness aims its critique at normative alignments in sources typically touted as allies of queer politics.[135] She situates and develops this critique in a US context where the inclusion of certain LGBTIA2Q+ subjects (those who mostly match the ideal categories of Lorde's mythical norm) enables a patriotic celebration of diverse inclusion while simultaneously excluding other bodies as perverse and deviant, typically along racial and religious lines (the Middle Eastern/Muslim terrorist, in particular). Via her affective theorization of queerness, Puar develops tactics and terminology for an intersectionally queer and feminist affective critique that aligns with these movements' political dimensions and provides new paths to engage its capacities for creative critique. Such an affective critique can help us uncover troubling Romanormative and imperial alignments in Paul's letter to the Romans, especially by considering how homonormativity intersects with US nationalism (what Puar terms "homonationalism"). Here I lay the groundwork for this reading of Romans by exploring Puar's critical development of an affective queerness.

The affective dimensions of a critically oriented queerness emerge most clearly in Puar's analysis of the 2003 US Supreme Court case *Lawrence and Garner v. Texas*.[136] Puar problematizes the notions of privacy

---

in producing national identity. See Runions, "From Disgust to Humor," esp. 49–56, 69–70.

135. Puar, *Terrorist Assemblages*, 11–23, 40, see further xiv–xvi, 37–78.

136. Puar, *Terrorist Assemblages*, 114–65 (ch. 3, "Intimate Control, Infinite Detention: Rereading the *Lawrence* Case"). This decision ruled that sodomy laws were unconstitutional and was widely heralded as a major victory for gay rights. Following Puar, I will hereafter refer to the case as *Lawrence-Garner*. That the victory is one of gay (as opposed to choosing to say LGBTIA2Q+) rights has particular valence because, as Puar points out, the acts specifically defined as sodomy involve phalluses, thus creating some conundrum as to whether lesbian sexual acts could be prosecuted under such laws to begin with. See Puar, *Terrorist Assemblages*, 122. Puar's point here echoes the 1811 British (well, Scottish) case of schoolteachers Marianne Woods and Jane Pirie, accused of having sexual intercourse but are ultimately acquitted, in part due to denying that such intercourse was possible (along with colonial/racial dimensions with regard to the social class of the teachers and the witness). See discussions of this case, with its relation to Rom 1:26–27, in Brooten, *Love between Women*, 189–90; Moore, *God's Beauty Parlor*, 148–69 (right column).

and intimacy deemed essential rights in the court's decision and discusses the unexamined race and class dimensions in the decision and most analyses of it (mirroring the erasure of Tyrone Garner, a Black man, from the case name).[137] According to the court, sodomy laws are unconstitutional (i.e., not American) because they violate individuals' rights to privacy, specifically within the context of *intimacy*; that is, they assume a conventional, stable, monogamous relationship between two persons (traditionally a man/woman, now extended to same-sex pairings).[138]

This definition of patriotic intimacy elides the "networks of contact and control" that regularize the bodies that can adhere to "its liberal fantasy form" and regulate and discipline deviant bodies for whom privacy and intimacy are impossible. In a comparison to the torture at Abu Ghraib (an extreme extension of the bodily violations enforced on racialized others in the name of national security against terrorism), sexual deviance and homophobia become the presumed norms of racial others, whose bodies are constantly scrutinized ("intimate control") in ways that emphasize a particular heteronormative domesticity in order to avoid further scrutiny, arrest, or imprisonment ("infinite detention").[139]

Affect exposes the homonormative intimacy presumed in the *Lawrence-Garner* decision and denied to countless others whose privacy is compromised by a constant threat of surveillance, scrutiny, and looming detention.[140] Its inhabitation of in-betweenness allows the consideration of affect to attend to the varying forces—usually fleeting and often barely detectable by sight, sensing, or feeling—that are at work or play in various

---

137. Puar notes that the erasure of names beyond the first plaintiff is typical in the titling of Supreme Court cases; however, the erasure and its impact cannot be ignored, especially when race is so rarely discussed in references to the case. See Puar, *Terrorist Assemblages*, 130–37, as well as 117–30.

138. Puar, *Terrorist Assemblages*, 117–30. Noting the ways in which this intimacy has racial assumptions embedded in this definition, she writes, "The ascendancy of whiteness does not require heterosexuality as much as it requires heteronormativity, or its mimicry in the form of homonormativity or what Franke calls the domestinormative" (128). Here Puar is working with Kathryn Franke's analysis of the case. See further Kathryn M. Franke, "The Domesticated Liberty of *Lawrence v. Texas*," *Columbia Law Review* 104 (2004): 1399–1426.

139. Puar, *Terrorist Assemblages*, 138–51. She observes how the ACLU focused on these issues of detention and deportation from the perspective that it splits and breaks up immigrant families. See Puar, *Terrorist Assemblages*, 143–48.

140. Puar, *Terrorist Assemblages*, 164.

structures of intimacy and surveillance.[141] The surveillance to which Puar refers serves the state but it is not solely (or even primarily) performed by the government and its official systems. Instead, surveillance of the self and others has become the task of patriotic citizens; it is a more intimate and affectively intense affair of policing bodies.[142] This intimate control of bodies illuminates the intimate ways Romosexuality affected bodies as a regulation that occurred through surveillance of bodies by individuals rather than through imperial force. Such surveillance and its affective Romanormativity is especially visible in the regulations and embodiments of sexualities among non-elite and conquered subjects such as Paul and (some of) his audiences.

As *Lawrence-Garner* released the surveillance of sexuality into the private sphere, sanctioning subjects to adhere to and police the boundaries of homonormative intimacy within their own homes, the decision demonstrates how affect moves between and within various bodies trained for such scrutiny, sexual or otherwise. Sensations of insecurity and security coincide. Their entanglement produces possibilities both for homonormative, patriotic alignment and for deviance from normalcy that must be surveilled and contained. The attention that Puar gives to homonormativity's connection to patriotic nationalism, a connection maintained by a fantasy of inclusion that is anything but simple or all-encompassing, would be impossible without the influence of affect's "muddy, unmediated relatedness" and its attention to the multiple belongings and nonbelongings of bodies in complex relations with themselves and others. These blurs and tensions—provocations, palpitations, sensations, or feelings—between exclusion and inclusion are based in complex, shifting, and *embodied* identities identified by affect theory.

Puar's critique is rooted in intersectionality so that it can account for unevenness in access to privacy and experiences of surveillance based

---

141. Puar observes, "Intimacy is a crucial part of an affective economy within surveillance systems that provoke, subsume, and muffle feelings and emotions, but also sensations, hallucinations, palpitations, yearnings of security and insecurity" (Puar, *Terrorist Assemblages*, 164).

142. One might ask whether paranoid reading strategies, as discussed by Sedgwick, is a form of affective textual surveillance, always assuming something is wrong, out of the ordinary, and in need of discipline in the form of theoretical critique. See further "Paranoid Reading and Reparative Reading, or, You're So Paranoid, You Probably Think This Essay Is about You," in Sedgwick, *Touching Feeling*, 123–51.

on race. "Without an intersectional analysis … the private is naturalized as a given refuge from state scrutiny." Puar's intersectional affective critique is also feminist: privacy, intimacy, and domesticity are also gendered concepts. *Lawrence-Garner*, after all, was a case involving two men, and, though it was lauded as inclusive to all LGBTIA2Q+ sexuality, sodomy has become a metonym for male homoeroticism.[143] When the decision determines certain sodomitic lives are now legitimate according to the nation, it also reifies how other lives are excluded and illegitimate, and it ignores wo/men's sexualities entirely: "What does the ruling say, if anything at all, to women? to lesbians?"[144] In raising these questions, Puar's affective analysis of *Lawrence-Garner* demonstrates the importance of intersectionality, wherein queer critique must also be informed by feminist and critical race studies. By situating *Lawrence-Garner* alongside Abu Ghraib and infinite detention, Puar develops an affective critique in which queerness can and must address kyriarchy's "interlocking nexus of power grids" that tend to fix identities in their multiple dimensions (including "race, gender, class, and nation").[145]

Puar's intersectional affective critique embodies the tension of what Seigworth and Gregg call "one of the most pressing questions faced by affect theory": "Is that a promise or a threat?"[146] Showing that the answer is both, Puar exposes the affective dimensions of US sexual politics, which more and more overtly take on the politics of empire.[147] Her critique reveals how queerness can align with power as easily and equally as it can

---

143. Puar, *Terrorist Assemblages*, 122, 125. See also Janet Halley, "Reasoning about Sodomy: Act and Identity in and after Bowers v. Hardwick," *Virginia Law Review* 79 (1993): 1721–80.

144. Puar, *Terrorist Assemblages*, 126.

145. Puar, *Terrorist Assemblages*, xiv. Alongside sexual exceptionalism (and its attendant homonationalism [see ch. 5, "Ethical Submission"]), Puar identifies and discusses "queerness as regulatory" and the "ascendancy of whiteness" as means of fixing and regulating identity in relation to power. See Puar, *Terrorist Assemblages*, 2, see further 3–32. See also Joseph A. Marchal, "The Exceptional Proves Who Rules: Imperial Sexual Exceptionalism in and around Paul's Letters," *JECH* 5 (2015): 87–115.

146. Seigworth and Gregg, "Inventory of Shimmers," 10.

147. Puar, *Terrorist Assemblages*, 1–3. Puar begins by quoting an article by Amy Kaplan that notes the use of "coming out" language by those owning the United States' emergence as an empire. See Amy Kaplan, "Violent Belongings and the Question of Empire Today: Presidential Address to the American Studies Association, October 17, 2003," *American Quarterly* 56 (2004): 1–18.

subvert it. Queerness poses affect's threat as it leaves these harmful effects in its sexually exceptional wake.[148]

Puar's critical analysis of intimacy, sexual regulation, and contemporary US politics offers a useful affective analogy for approaching Rome, Romans, and Romosexuality. Just as Puar's affective critique of intimacy reveals how "citizenship remains a critical yet undertheorized facet of sexual regulation in the United States," Roman imperial constructions of citizenship—vis-à-vis populations of conquered ἔθνη, *peregrini*, and enslaved folks—via regulative, Romosexual fantasies of social mobility and inclusion could be better theorized in scholarship on first-century texts and contexts, including Paul's letters.[149] The analogy is imperfect: there cannot be a one-to-one comparison between first-century Rome and the twenty-first-century United States. However, the resonances are striking.

For example, the valuation of "productive citizens" that Puar shows is a requisite determination for legitimate inclusion (i.e., homonormativity presents affluent gay families as having essential, high-paying jobs and help stimulate the economy[150]) can also been seen in who among conquered Romans get deemed worthy of Roman honors. This resonates with Puar's demonstration of how the policing of intimacy involves "regularizing queerness" to determine who gets "invited into life" and who becomes a queer population "through their perverse sexual-racial attributes and histories."[151] Through Romanormativity, certain queer populations could police and regularize their intimacy—in distinction to perverse sexual-racial others—in conformity with Roman norms in hope of gaining praise and benefits that might signal inclusion in Rome's elite. Puar's identification of affects of national belonging, therefore, can help to identify and critique ancient affects of imperial belonging that guided first-century Romosexual politics and cling to first-century materials.

---

148. However, by reformulating queerness as an affective assemblage and asking "what's queer about the terrorist," Puar's work also proves that analyses of affect offer promises as much as they threaten in our contemporary political context (promises that will be described more later). See also Puar, *Terrorist Assemblages*, xxiii–xxiv.

149. Puar, *Terrorist Assemblages*, 165.

150. Given the gendered and racialized wage gap, stereotypical affluent gay couples are white men.

151. Puar, *Terrorist Assemblages*, 165.

Cruel Affects and Queer (Anti)Normativity

We now turn to the affective lives of norms. Lauren Berlant shows that critiquing the existence of norms is not enough, even though this exposure is important work. It does not address the circumstances that motivate many people not only to follow norms but also to *actively crave them* because of the fantasies they help sustain. Ancient affects of imperial belonging motivated a Romanormativity that was sustained by fantasies of inclusion, especially via the idea of Roman citizenship. Although first-century Christ-followers, including Paul in his letter to Rome, envision God's justice as something that was different—sometimes radically different—from normal life under Roman rule, the new worlds they imagine often replicate the norms of their present context. Sometimes these visions crave the norms they replicate in ways that undermine the justice they seek. The affective lives of Romosexuality and Romanormativity render true justice impossible. Alongside Puar's affective critique of normative politics, Berlant's analysis of the subtle undertow of normativity's affective *ordinariness* allows us to see how.

The affective and intersectional dimensions of queerness confront an offshoot of queer theory's fluidity: its "fear of the ordinary."[152] Queer critique is often characterized by its subversive opposition to the norms and normativity it theorizes: normal is overrated. However, not all queer scholarship follows an antinormative imperative.[153] "Radical anti-normativity throws out a lot of babies with a lot of bathwater," writes Biddy Martin in her now-infamous critique of the then-just-burgeoning anti-normativity trend in queer theory. The title of her essay, "Extraordinary Homosexuals and the Fear of Being Ordinary," captures her critique of queerness's definitional subversion: it grants a preferred status to being something other than (and, implicitly, better than) ordinary, thereby privileging a fluid queer to a fixed feminism.[154] This privileging participates in

---

152. This "fear of the ordinary" is identified and examined in Biddy Martin, "Extraordinary Homosexuals and the Fear of Being Ordinary," in *Feminism Meets Queer Theory*, ed. Elizabeth Weed and Naomi Schor (Bloomington: Indiana University Press, 1997), 109–35.

153. Indeed, a special issue of *differences* queries queer theory's dependence on antinormativity and imagines queer possibilities that consider other relations to/with/around normativity. See Robyn Wiegman and Elizabeth Wilson, eds. *Queer Theory without Antinormativity*, special issue of *dif.* 26, no.1 (2015).

154. Martin, "Extraordinary Homosexuals," 110, 133.

a supersessionist logic wherein queer theory supplants and slowly replaces feminism and its relevance.[155] This has resulted in tensions between the two (allied) movements and difficulties for scholars who identify as both feminist and queer. At its publication, Martin's points sat uncomfortably with many queer scholars who emphasized queer's transgression and the importance of the "radical difference of queer ways of life" vis-à-vis heteronormativity.[156]

A queer and affective embrace of ordinary emphasizes how power slides in/between bodies—whether they conform, resist, or do a bit of both—as they live and move in more mundane ways. Martin's critique echoes in the emphasis on the everyday—"ordinary" life—that theories of affect add to queerness.[157] A focus on the everyday and ordinary is not a

---

155. On the realities and dangers of queer supersessionism, see Judith Butler, "Against Proper Objects," in *Feminism Meets Queer Theory*, ed. Elizabeth Weed and Naomi Schor (Bloomington: Indiana University Press, 1997), 1–30, esp. 4–9.

156. Heather Love, "Wedding Crashers," *GLQ* 13 (2006): 127. She goes on to observe that the tension between such radical antinormativity (exemplified in her quotations of Warner) and "Martin's call for a queer politics that makes space for attachment, kinship, and everyday life remains alive within queer studies" (128). While necessary, the sharpness of Martin's critique can be misread in ways that lend aid to homonormative impulses, but (as Love observes) this presumes a binary between normative ("gay neo-con") and antinormative ("queer radical") into which "few people can be fit completely" (128). Love's use of Martin emphasizes the essay's affective elements, namely, the space it makes for attachment and everyday life. Halberstam is critical of Martin's critique, noting that Martin does not contextualize the situations out of which theorists such as Rubin and Sedgwick wrote. See Jack Halberstam, *Female Masculinity* (Durham, NC: Duke University Press, 1998), 134–38. Muñoz calls Martin's critique a "more nuanced form" of "gay pragmatic thought." See Muñoz, *Cruising Utopia*, 21, see further 19–32. Ahmed's chapter "Queer Feelings" cites Martin more positively, noting that movement can be a privilege (Ahmed, *Cultural Politics*, 151–52). Halberstam may be more sympathetic (only implicitly in terms of its relation to Martin) to such an idea, or, at least, has observed more recently that movement—particularly to urban centers that may be safer for queer bodies (though such metronormativity is itself problematic)—implies a privilege of mobility that many queers (especially those without financial means or place-based roots) do not have. See Halberstam, *In a Queer Time and Place*.

157. Martin's analysis foreshadows affect's investigation of "regularly hidden-in-plain-sight politically engaged work—perhaps most often undertaken by feminists, queer theorists, disability activists, and subaltern peoples living under the thumb of a normativizing power—that attends to the hard and fast materialities, as well as the fleeting and flowing ephemera, of the *daily and the workaday, of everyday and every-night*

refusal to critique normativity. It does so alongside an acknowledgment of the complexities of the desire and the draw to *feel* normal.

Paul's audiences and letters, including Romans, were motivated by first-century apocalypticism and often exhibit a sense of urgency that responds to extraordinary sensations of time. Yet even in the rushed tempo of apocalyptic urgency, ordinary life persists. Even as some first-century wo/men and Paul anticipated the revelation of a new world, their daily lives continued and were affected by Roman kyriarchy. These ordinary affects structure urgent apocalyptic fantasies of a better life under God. Paul's theology is often considered *extraordinary* or, at least, responding to extraordinary events and conditions: what happens if we instead consider the *ordinariness* of Paul, his ideas, and his audiences?

Lauren Berlant shows how "normal" operates as an affective fantasy that impacts bodies and their everyday existence, often without their knowledge. At some point, we all crave feeling normal in some sense. As a fantasy, normalcy offers a vision of the good life, which assumes specific ideals and forms in Western capitalist culture. Even when the norms of such a good life attach ordinary subjects to harmful promises that prevent their flourishing (i.e., "cruel optimism"), there are *affective* costs to abandoning hope in something that feels better.[158] "We need to think about normativity as *aspirational* and as an evolving and incoherent cluster of hegemonic promises about the present and future experience of social belonging that can be entered into in a number of ways, in affective transactions that take place alongside the more instrumental ones."[159] These

---

life, and of 'experience' (understood in ways far more collective and 'external' rather than individual and interior)" (Seigworth and Gregg, "Inventory of Shimmers," 7, emphasis added). Bray's affect-driven political theology has also emphasized the important of attuning to the everyday: "This is a book about remaining with the everyday in ways that might change how such a day looks and feels" (Bray, *Grave Attending*, 25).

158. In an analysis of the film *Rosetta*, Berlant observes the title character's desire for and attachment to a job, which seems to be a requirement of normalcy for Rosetta. "Even in an extremely informal economy the goodness of the good life now *feels* possible to her and thus *feels* already like a confirming reality, calming her even before she lives it as an ongoing practice." See Lauren Berlant, *Cruel Optimism* (Durham, NC: Duke University Press, 2011), 163.

159. Berlant, *Cruel Optimism*, 163. In her essay on the affective and optimistic production of happiness in Jonah, Rhiannon Graybill draws from Berlant's language of a "cluster of promises" to describe Nineveh from Jonah's perspective. See Rhiannon Graybill, "Prophecy and the Problem of Happiness: The Case of Jonah," in *Read-*

(fantastical) attachments are experienced as *real* and provide structure to everyday life, structures that can be understood through analysis of the forces that sustain them and the sensations they provoke (i.e., affect). In Romans, Paul often betrays his own aspirational normativity through a Romanormative fantasy of inclusion on top yet under God.

Berlant's analysis permits an affective blurring of the boundary between normalcy and queerness. If affect marks a body's belonging (or nonbelonging), both in terms of a normative good life or to an antinormative queer one, then queer critique should attune to affect's pull upon ordinary and mundane lives and life. For *queer*, this implies that its traditional disruption and unsettling of established norms cannot avoid the broader affective draws that unconsciously attach bodies to some fantasy that promises a good life, defined at least in some part by structures of normativity. From Berlant, it is possible to expand upon Martin's insightful critique: perhaps radical antinormativity does not throw out "a lot of babies with a lot of bathwater" so much as it drowns babies by assuming they can and will swim in whatever water is retained.[160]

Normativity is easier to critique than it is to unsettle. As demonstrated in Berlant's discussion of being "Nearly Utopian, Nearly Normal," we are all, to some degree, waking up with a "normativity hangover" that we crave instinctively.[161] Berlant analyzes films that feature protagonists who repeat routines that they have established to give them an at least proximate sense of the good life, imagined differently by each character. Through their repetition of routines, the films leave ordinary viewers with the residue of the protagonists' craving of normativity. Like the characters, the audience *needs* the continuation of the routine, despite its dreariness, because it trains them to dread the interruption of this fragilely constructed normativity. Through the affective approximation of the characters' rut-inized sensations, the craving for such a "hangover" exemplifies normativity's pull as the subtlest (and, therefore, typically the strongest and most insidious)

---

ing with Feeling: Affect Theory and the Bible, ed. Fiona Black and Jennifer L. Koosed, SemeiaSt 95 (Atlanta: SBL Press, 2019), 102.

160. Martin, "Extraordinary Homosexuals," 133.

161. Especially as viewers (and Berlant's readers, to some extent), experience through the sense of "nearly" in the films *Rosetta* and *La Promesse*. "Both of these works thus end engendering in the audience a kind of normativity hangover, a residue of the optimism of their advocacy for achieving whatever it was for which the protagonists were scavenging" (Berlant, *Cruel Optimism*, 175–76).

of undertows that slowly pulls subjects into its hold as they "tread water" to float along at life's surface.[162] Insightful as queer theory's disruption of norms may be, the affective fantasies that undergird the normativity it critiques attach themselves to bodies who find such rhythms and attachments *comfortable* (despite their discomfort) if not actively alluring.

Admitting this, Berlant pursues answers to the question: why do subjects, especially those most marginal and missed, cling to bad "good lives" when abandoning them would obviously make space for change? In the two films, as Berlant reads them, both protagonists clearly desire objects that, for them, permit a fantasy of being normal according to the capitalist organization of life (e.g., the titular character Rosetta is attached to having a "real" job that permits her to participate in the formal, exchange economy as opposed to an informal, bartering one). Berlant identifies their attachments as examples of the "affects of aspirational normativity": "when the world exists between the routinized rut and the ominous cracks, [Rosetta] chooses the rut, the impasse." The sensation of risk of abandoning the objects and structures attaching them to aspirational—or a proximate— normativity prevents the characters from removing themselves from the cruelly optimistic impasse that they have entered through the fantastical lives they attempt to live. The rut appears to be a route, one on which that fantastical good life "*feels* possible," even though it ultimately prevents further flourishing.[163]

Uncovering its affective draw and delay, normativity, Berlant asserts, is not a "synonym for privilege," even as it largely benefits—materially and affectively—those privileged to be able to be most "normal."[164] Instead, normativity, through its promise of this good life, attaches subjects into its rhythmic rut, trains their bodies to tread water and survive (but not thrive), and convinces them to trust its strong sensation of the possibility of the good life.

Berlant's analysis of this question—why do subjects, especially those most marginal and missed, cling to bad "good lives" when abandoning them would obviously make space for change?—can aid us in asking and answering the question with respect to Paul and some of the wo/men in Rome's ἐκκλησία. Despite their apocalyptic anticipation of God's justice, Christ-followers in the first century were still stuck *anticipating*—wait-

---

162. Berlant, *Cruel Optimism*, 163–64, 169–73.
163. Berlant, *Cruel Optimism*, 163 with 164.
164. Berlant, *Cruel Optimism*, 167.

ing for—its arrival (παρουσία). As time continued to pass ordinarily, these wo/men existed at an impasse, in Berlantian terms—a delay (ἀνοχή) in Paul's words. Within this impasse, their lives remained structured by a *pax Romana* in which Rome's rulers made promises of a good life for conquered subjects who willingly submitted to their authority and embodied their morality. Examining the risks of subversion alongside the rut of submission, the rut seems to promise possibilities of a better life while awaiting another one under God. However, an affective exegesis of Romans can reveal how the submissive rut-inization of these promises motivates (and ultimately undermines) Paul's hopeful visions. A reading that is attuned to normativity's affect can situate Paul as one among many Christ-followers who were treading water under kyriarchy—all bodies struggling toward something different yet stuck in a Romanormative rut whose fantastic draws keep pulling undertow.

Feminist and Queer Affective Critique and Reading Romans

Can Puar's affective critique of normativity in US politics complement how Berlant scrutinizes the ordinary affective draws of norms? Assuming they do correspond, how can their analyses be woven together in feminist and queer affective critique? And can such an affective critique bring relevant insights for reading Paul's letter to the Romans? The affective resonances of intimacy across these texts offer connections.

The aspirational attachments to (an at least proximate) normativity that Berlant investigates reveal a creation of *intimacy* that epitomizes the fantasy of the good life.[165] This intimacy is not equated with sex/sexual-

---

165. The creation of such intimacy likely reveals its lack in the lives and experiences of the protagonists in the films Berlant discusses, even leading them to crave it and create it where it does not (and indeed, perhaps, cannot) exist. For example, in *La Promesse*, Igor—bound by a promise to a dying migrant man (whose death is attributable to Igor and his father's predatory business) to ensure the protection of the man's wife and child—hides the man's death to Assita (the wife) so that he can be better bound to her as her provider, enabling him to create and sustain a fantasy of himself as having a family (of sorts) not under the manipulative control of his father. See Berlant, *Cruel Optimism*, 164–66. Especially evident in Rosetta's awkward friendship with Riquet, a relation that helps her to acquire a job (the need that represents her primary attachment), the main characters in both films realize that their good lives can be maintained only through the intimacy they approximate with others (and which is lacking in their relations with their parents). See Berlant, *Cruel Optimism*, 171–75.

ity or marriage/family: at best, in her examples, sexuality forges or forces an intimacy that is imagined as having a friend or supportive partner, a relationship that provides the means for sustaining a subject's fantastical attachments.[166] It is a complex cluster of different and ever-shifting desires, each ultimately related to achieving stability—that is, a life that maintains a precise and perfect balance of economic, social, and political factors—and, thereby, success (in a capitalistic definition) that drives the construction of intimacy and its requirements. Intimacy nurtures normativity and its fantastical good life.

These affective connections of intimacy and normativity resonate with Puar's identification of intimate control in the realm of privacy and security in the context of US political interests. As "good life" fantasies instigate the need for particular intimacies that enable ideal (capitalist) behaviors, intimacy's normative portrayal fuses with a national network of control that regulates bodies and their rhythms in order to protect the "freedom" to live the good life. This requires bodily attachments to this fantasy in order to achieve and maintain a sensation of privacy and security on both personal and political levels. But, as Berlant shows, attachment to these fantastical provisions requires most subjects to operate their daily lives in an ongoing state of crisis ordinariness wherein their everyday experience of a private and secure good life is, in reality, not good at all.[167]

---

166. Though sex or sexual desire may play a (sometimes deeply submerged) role, the intimacy portrayed here is one more attuned to the affects of normativity—for normative intimacy is not only, or even primarily, defined or sustained by proper object choice (i.e., heterosexuality) or proper inhabitation of an ideal monogamy (i.e., homonormativity). For example, there is no obvious sexual desire between Rosetta and her friend Riquet, and certainly, it is not acted upon in the film, yet (as Berlant notes) she maintains this friendship because of his help in securing her job—and so she "awkwardly" dines with him, submitting to his "pleasure economy" by "imitating what it might be like sometime to have fun with a friend or in a couple." See Berlant, *Cruel Optimism*, 163, 177–78. This is in stark contrast to Rosetta's mother, who barters sex in exchange for her needs. Rosetta, as Berlant notes, refuses such an informal economy—in addition to refusing state welfare—and insists on providing for herself via what she deems a real job. See Berlant, *Cruel Optimism*, 171–74. However, her mantra that she repeats to herself as she falls asleep shows that her good life requires having found both a job and a friend: after affirming these facts, she says "I have a normal life" and "I won't fall through the cracks." See especially Berlant, *Cruel Optimism*, 161–62.

167. "Crisis," Berlant writes, "is not exceptional to history or consciousness but a process embedded in the ordinary that unfolds in stories about navigating what's

The sensation of treading water in such a state of cruel optimism can be compared to the sensation of drowning simulated while waterboarding, one of the torturous mechanisms used in infinite detention and the intimate control it helps enforce. To be clear, when someone like Rosetta treads water in order to sustain her fantasy, the subtle, ongoing torment of her specific situation is *not* equivalent to the intense pain experienced in the intentional torture inflicted upon suspected terrorists held in US detention centers. However, the eerie echoes of running water that simultaneously threaten yet sustain a not-quite-liveable life (and yet also not-yet-dead) in each instance emphasize the ways in which affective intimacy resonates between both instances of near-drowning.[168] This connection reveals that fantasies of security, intimacy, and inclusion, which mask their reliance upon networks of control, surveillance, and infinite detention, are integral dimensions of the (homo)normative good life that subtly pulls and disciplines subjects, particularly those most sociopolitically marginal, into the crisis ordinariness of Berlant's cruel optimism.

An affective critique informed by Puar and Berlant requires an intersectional approach that is both feminist and queer, drawing the movements of queerness and feminism together without erasing the tensions between them. Affect's focus on bodies and change shows that experiences and perceptions of sexuality, gender, and race (alongside other identity markers) shift and flow. Human identity affects and is affected by fantasies of the good life and the varying strategies of attaching to them; it regulates and is regulated in tandem with nebulous control networks that promise or threaten privacy and security through near-invisible processes of surveillance and detention. Drawn together, the critical force of Puar and Berlant's affective theorization in relation to queerness and feminism enable a critique of socio-sexual-political patterns while admitting that such patterns and problems affect diverse bodies (individually and as populations) differently, especially when seen on the more-focused scale of ordinary life.

Puar's affective understanding of queerness pushes past any notion of identity as fully fixed. However, in so doing, it cannot abandon or push

---

overwhelming" (*Cruel Optimism*, 10). Such an idea in Berlant's theorization specifically contrasts theories that promote trauma and the (singular) traumatic event as able to explain such sensations in populations. See further 9–10, 168–70.

168. On not-quite-liveable/not-quite-dead life, see Puar, *Terrorist Assemblages*, 138–43.

past identity politics.[169] As discussed above, a fixed identity poses problems for the critical and constructive attentions of queer theory's more fluid dimensions, especially for a meaning of queer that has come to privilege sexuality as its central focus or identity. Such privileging downplays intersections with race, gender, class, and the minute, mundane movements and sensations that affect bodies. Returning especially to sexuality, traditionally the turf where queer theory stakes its pride, affective critique further emphasizes that sexuality cannot be cleaved from the messiness of *bodies* that are constantly moving and sensing. This affective and intersectional understanding of queerness affirms the ongoing relevance of Rubin's observation that sexuality is still imbued with an "excess of significance" in society.[170] The excessive significance accorded to sexuality prevents its ordinariness.

Has a privileged focus on sexuality also caused queer theory to become burdened by such excess? Indeed, could *queer* be operating under an unspoken threat/promise that *if* sexuality is not (as) significant, then queer theory will become irrelevant or superfluous? Some queer scholars worry that the ever-expanding and everyday applications of queerness pose a threat to queer theory's ongoing relevance: "If everything is queer, then nothing is queer," some protest.[171] This threat might be of greatest

---

169. Identity politics become problematic when it is overemphasized in interpretation or politics, in particular formulations that attend to singular or fixed markers of identity, as observed in Puar's critique of networks of control (see especially *Terrorist Assemblages*, 159–62) and Berlant's attention to the ordinary complexities of the choices that individual and collective subjects make every day.

170. She observes that such excess is a problem because sexuality is not regarded as everyday: "Although people can be intolerant, silly, or pushy about what constitutes proper diet, differences in menu rarely provoke the kinds of rage, anxiety, and sheer terror that routinely accompany differences in erotic taste" (Rubin, *Deviations*, 149). Ken Stone draws inspiration from Rubin's comment as he probes queer readings at the intersection of the Bible, food, and sex. See Ken Stone, *Practicing Safer Texts: Food, Sex and the Bible in Queer Perspective* (London: T&T Clark, 2005).

171. See discussion of this in Janet Halley and Andrew Parker, "Introduction," in *After Sex? On Writing Since Queer Theory*, SerQ (Durham, NC: Duke University Press, 2011), 6–7. They refer specifically to the review essay of Sharon Marcus, who makes such a point and writes, "If everyone is queer, then no one is—and while this is exactly the point queer theorists want to make, reducing the term's pejorative sting by universalizing the meaning of queer also depletes its explanatory power." See Sharon Marcus, "Queer Theory for Everyone: A Review Essay," *Signs* 31 (2005): 196. I am understanding and sympathetic toward such a concern—and I am wary of

concern to (white) queer theorists for whom sexual orientation represents their primary lens or only deviation from mythical normativity.[172] Cathy Cohen's emphasis on the *transformative* politics of queerness, which offers "an acknowledgment that that through our existence and everyday survival we embody sustained and multisited resistance to systems (based on dominant constructions of race and gender) that seek to normalize our sexuality, exploit our labor, and constrain our visibility," reorients the issue.[173] If it is rooted in shared experiences of marginalization and attempts to critically undermine powerful systems that benefit from normativities, then intersectional and affective queerness makes a promise: *If queerness encompasses everything, then we've won.*

Yet neither of the above questions needs to be answered with a definitive yes or no. Affect exists in the ambiguous space between promise and threat, but, in this case, it can relieve that unspoken concern of queer irrelevance without the excesses of sexuality's significance. If, broadly speaking, sexuality still retains this excessive significance, then this excess invites affective analysis, which thrives in exposing the infinitesimal forces that eventually burst or bubble over. Excess manifests affect; and affect reveals sensations of extraordinariness to be an ordinariness overflowing. Embracing affect's in-betweenness, queerness does not abandon its important, historical contributions to the study of sexuality and the critique of regulatory norms, but, detaching such foci from a revered or privileged status, it emerges able to account for the ordinary but complex interplays of race, gender, sexuality, class, and other elements that affect identity, society, and politics.[174] An affective understanding of queer helps to ensure that the answer to that second question is no by creating space to theorize the ordinary alongside—but not equivalent to—the

---

the potential for privileged (largely white and male) heterosexuals to colonize queerness for their own gain—but I think such colonization (and its relations to kyriarchal power) is more antithetical to queerness than the term's expansion beyond and exceeding of its sexual container.

172. A point underscored in a tweet by Joshua Tranen in which he posited this concern over queer nothingness was motivated by a desire to remain an underdog within white queer theory. Tranen was responding to a post I made about Cathy Cohen on 16 October 2019.

173. Cohen, "Punks, Bulldaggers," 440.

174. While not supplanting or dismissing the insights of studying these issues in other fields such as feminism, critical race theory, postcolonial studies, disability studies, fat studies, and numerous other areas of inquiry.

normative. Understood affectively, queerness, alongside feminism, can continue to challenge and change society through movements that are both—even simultaneously—promising and threatening, extraordinary and ordinary.

This move toward queerness as an affective quality sheds the notion that queer must fix an identity governed by particular sexual practices. Likewise, feminism is relevant beyond instances and spaces when women and gender are explicitly acknowledged or posed as problems. Affect fosters the applicability of feminism, queerness, and their critiques to ancient contexts. Affective critique that draws from queerness is applicable to Romans beyond 1:18–32, when sexuality is explicitly mentioned. Similarly, affective critique that draws from feminism and queries gendered hierarchies can extend beyond places where women are explicitly mentioned (namely, Rom 16) or where gender is framed problematically, as also occurs in Rom 1:18–32. Paul's ideas and feelings about sexuality in the first chapter resonate around his theology and ethics in affective ways throughout the epistle; likewise, the wo/men named as leaders and participants in Rome's ἐκκλησία in the letter's closing chapter were present and responding to the entire letter, including ideas that are implicitly gendered throughout it. Most importantly, the letter's framing and its audiences' experiences of gender and sexuality *intersect* with one another and with issues and experiences of race/ethnicity and socioeconomic status. The next chapter uses this intersectional and affective approach to interpret Rom 1:18–32 and Rom 16 and harness a feminist and queer understanding of assemblages to reconstruct the queer wo/men of Rome's ἐκκλησία who were engaging with these impulses.

Applied to a first-century Roman context, affective feminism and queerness—especially in its Puarian and Berlantian conceptions—reveal first-century forms of networks of (intimate) imperial control and aspirational normativity. Romosexuality accorded natural sexuality (κατὰ or παρὰ φύσιν) with sociopolitical culture in ways that regulated ancient intimacy. Such an intimate definition, which operated along axes of race/ethnicity, gender, and class in addition to sexuality, could be used by the empire to control its subjects and ensure their ongoing submission. Rome's production of such control through various mediums of propaganda (whether intentional or less so) bears similarities to Puar's demonstration of how modern instances of intimate control do so through self-policing of sexual norms that enforce social, economic, and political security (i.e., forms of "regulatory queerness").

My development of the challenges of feminism, queerness, and affect brings new insights into the historical situation of the Roman Empire and, in so doing, challenges the theology, ethics, and politics of Paul's letter to that empire's central city. Since an imperially aligned ideal of submission, most notably to and under God, undergirds Paul's letter, these aspirational normativities and homonational impulses are deeply embedded in this submission. Even if Christ-followers are encouraged to submit "under God," this hierarchical and submissive logic cannot fully escape the networks of intimate imperial control in which these Romans have long been entangled. The impossibility of escape through placement under God opens the possibility that such submission leaves followers continuing to tread water as they hope for a divinely promised good life. Treading water hopefully, they continue to negotiate intimacy and community within a culture of controlled protocols that may still mimic those of the empire's elite. Such a reading of Romans through this feminist and queer affective critique prompts the question: *Is God's reign a promise, or could it also be a threat?*

2
Waking Up (from) Tired Texts:
Feminism, Queerness, and ἐκκλησία-l Assemblages

> History is written in sand, and a broom changes everything.
> —Maria Dahvana Headley, *The Mere Wife*

Like sand, queer wo/men cannot be swept away. We find nooks; we find crannies. Decades later, you will find us in your left shoe, in your bedsheets. No mere broom can sweep us away. This chapter takes a different sweep at history. It brings to life the queer wo/men who were there—standing, speaking, watching, moving, feeling, groaning, singing, screaming—in Rome's ἐκκλησία. Engaging in feminist and queer affective historiography, it moves beyond critique of Paul's letters and places Paul into Rome's ἐκκλησία of queer wo/men, as one among many. Drawing from feminist and queer affective renderings of assemblages, I argue that ἐκκλησία-l assemblages wake up interpretations of Romans. Bringing first-century queer wo/men to life involves *proliferating plausibilities* of queer wo/men's interactions with, beyond, against, and around Paul's singular letters.

The chapter begins and ends with Rom 1:18–32, that clobbering colossus that keeps capturing the attention of Romans's queer readers. "Waking Up Romans 1:18–32" demonstrates how a feminist and queer affective critique of this text brings out the Romanormative affects that surround it. I consider the affective dimensions of queer biblical scholarship's exhaustive treatments of this passage and suggest that Rom 1:18–32 might be a tired text from which queerness needs to awaken. "Going Beyond: The Queer Wo/men of Romans 16" stirs from this queer slumber by moving beyond 1:18–32 and toward the queer wo/men who, despite attempts to sweep them away, are present and named in Rom 16. While textual and material remnants affirm queer wo/men's presence and leadership, the full depth of their existence is harder to sense among these remnants. Assemblages offer a way to bring to life the first-century Roman queer wo/men and the ἐκκλησίαι in which they gathered. "Bringing Queer Wo/men to Life: Assemblages and the First Century," develops my conception of ἐκκλησία-l assemblage, which promises positive change even as it threatens to fold back into kyriarchy. The speculatively plausible reconstructions permitted by assemblages offer a way to imagine the ideas and participations of queer wo/men around Paul's letter. The chapter concludes with a return to Rom 1:18–32. Here, I reenvision how the queer wo/men in Rome's ἐκκλησία could have interrupted Paul's words and interjected their own thoughts, feelings, sighs, and expressions. These imagined interactions decenter Paul and *scramble the sides* in between the many different queer wo/men of Rome. This test case for my praxis of ἐκκλησία-l assemblage demonstrates the historicity of interactions whose specific content matters less than the process of enlivened, imaginative remembrance. Such a praxis awakens this tired text and prepares us to take ἐκκλησία-l assemblage beyond Rom 1.

Waking Up Romans 1:18–32

Romans 1:18–32 (especially 1:26–27) produces emotions. Homophobic readers feel increased disgust toward LGBTIA2Q+ bodies and practices. Heterosexist interpreters, crying "Love the sinner, hate the sin," feel sadness and hatred. Closeted LGBTIA2Q+ readers find shame and confusion. Knowing its histories of harm, proud(er) queers feel frustration and anger. These emotions, and others, swirl around 1:18–32 and its interpretations. Even Paul is emotional as he writes these words. They express his (and God's) disgust, sadness, shame, and frustration as his words degenerate into a spiraling cesspool of madness caused, at first, by refusal to live under God.

These emotions that surround 1:18–32 show how it produces and holds affect. Romans 1:18–32 affects the bodies of its hearers and author as their contact with it provokes these feelings.[1] Likewise, 1:18–32 (both its words and their interpretation) is affected by its contacts with its authors and hearers. Feelings radiate from the text; this text becomes associated

---

1. Ahmed develops the idea of a contact zone in relation to the affective stickiness and transfers of emotions in Sara Ahmed, *The Cultural Politics of Emotion*, 2nd ed. (New York: Routledge, 2014); see esp. chapter 4, "The Performativity of Disgust," 82–100.

with these feelings. We see how certain emotions *stick* to particular bodies and objects.[2] Romans 1:18–32 is a sticky text.

The emotions that stick to Rom 1:18–32 also get stuck onto queerness and queer bodies (or any body perceived as queer). Emotions—especially (but not limited to) disgust, hatred, and shame—have allowed Rom 1:18–32 to participate in the oppression of queer folks. LGBTIA2Q+ readers identify Rom 1:18–32 as a "clobber passage." The clobbering it legitimates is literal: Rom 1:18–32 is used by denominations and churches to deny to queer folk participation and positions of leadership; its words spat upon lesbian couples, by priests and county clerks alike, to deny marriage. The passage is a door slammed in the faces of gay men refused service in bakeries. It is a literal weapon when it is used to beat trans women, often to death. It leads LGBTIA2Q+ persons to question our self-worth, to attempt to cure ourselves, to harm ourselves, to hate ourselves. Romans 1:18–32 oppresses, silences, and harms queerness.

Disgust, oppression, and harm radiate from Rom 1:18–32 and get stuck to queer bodies. It is not without good reason that, when reading Romans, queer biblical scholarship gets stuck on 1:18–32. Given this harmful history, queer biblical scholars must debunk and limit its harm. In attempting to unstick Rom 1:18–32 from these harmful affective effects, queer biblical scholarship itself gets stuck in Rom 1:18–32. How can a queer and feminist affective critique of Romans address these sticky verses of its opening chapter—without getting stuck in them for the remaining pages?

"How can we get out of this morass?" Brooten laments at the outset of her three-chapter treatment of Rom 1:18–32. "The only way out of it is through it."[3] As an advisee struggles with any wise yet difficult advice, I cannot disagree, despite my own reluctance. Reader: I tried—*really* tried—to write a queer and feminist reading of Romans without a section on Rom 1:18–32, but my wise advisors told me I must because *you* expected it and needed it from a book with *queer* and *Romans* in its title. Now that I've gone through it, I see the wisdom: How can we understand Romanormativity's affective tugs upon Rom 3 and 13 without seeing the groundwork begun in chapter 1, where kyriarchy and Romosexuality seep through the verses? We can't get over Rom 1; we must go through it.

---

2. Ahmed, *Cultural Politics*, 12–14, 89–92.

3. Bernadette J. Brooten, *Love between Women: Early Christian Responses to Female Homoeroticism* (Chicago: University of Chicago Press, 1996), 192.

διὰ τοῦτο παρέδωκεν αὐτοὺς ὁ θεὸς εἰς πάθη ἀτιμίας, αἵ τε γὰρ θήλειαι αὐτῶν
μετήλλαξαν τὴν φυσικὴν χρῆσιν εἰς τὴν παρὰ φύσιν, ὁμοίως τε καὶ οἱ ἄρσενες
ἀφέντες τὴν φυσικὴν χρῆσιν τῆς θηλείας ἐξεκαύθησαν ἐν τῇ ὀρέξει αὐτῶν
εἰς ἀλλήλους, ἄρσενες ἐν ἄρσεσιν τὴν ἀσχημοσύνην κατεργαζόμενοι καὶ τὴν
ἀντιμισθίαν ἣν ἔδει τῆς πλάνης αὐτῶν ἐν ἑαυτοῖς ἀπολαμβάνοντες.
Because of this, God handed them over into passions of dishonor. For
their women traded their natural usage for that which is against nature;
and, likewise, the men, repenting the natural usage of women, were
burnt out in their yearning for each other, men who, with men, achieved
disfigurement and received their due retribution which was needed of
their error among themselves. (Rom 1:26–27)

Romans 1:26–27 are the two verses that address queerness and the point
from which queer (and anti-queer/heteronormative[4]) interpretations
expand. Romans 1:26–27 is far from clear: do the verses specifically address
homoeroticism and queerness, and, if so, are they limited to specific acts
and orientations, or do they encompass anything and everything? What
are the specific meanings of these terms and descriptions? Are they ethical condemnations? If so, what moral weight were they meant to impose
on their ancient audiences? A deeper look at these verses, in conversation
with other Roman texts and materials and within the context of 1:18–32,
can certainly yield some clarity. However, even with these considerations,
there are no clear answers. Paul offers only vague details. Affect's in-
betweenness might embrace both the ambiguities in any attempt at a clear
answer and the tensions of messy relatedness that occur when contradictory possibilities coexist within and among these attempts.

Is Rom 1:26–27 a comprehensive condemnation of homoeroticism?
This question, whose answer may be the least clear, hangs over these
verses and their effects on queer folks. This question breaks down into
two pieces. First, are these verses describing homoeroticism, and, if so,
what sorts of homoeroticism might it describe? Second, do these verses
condemn homoeroticism as part of a moral exhortation to follow "natural" sexual behavior—or, put differently, what are the purposes of 1:26–27
within the context of Romans? To consider the first question, we focus on
the text of 1:26–27; for the second, we turn to the wider passage, 1:18–32.

---

4. I do not take seriously any interpretation that renders anyone's humanity
invalid or up for debate. They do not deserve engagement or citation.

Romosexual Disgust and the Wo/men of 1:26–27

The question of what sorts of sex Paul and his earliest audiences would have associated with these words hinges on the definition of *nature*: what is being described when Paul uses the terms φυσικὴν ("natural") and παρὰ φύσιν ("against nature" or "unnatural") to describe the χρῆσις of these women and men?[5] First, what does χρῆσις—the noun described as natural/unnatural—mean? Translators (including those who produced the NRSV translation of Romans) often render it as "intercourse." Certainly, "[sexual] intercourse" is one of the many meanings ancient authors employ using χρῆσις, and—given that Paul uses the term to describe "passions of dishonor" (πάθη ἀτιμίας, 1:26) in which the men are "burnt out in their yearning for each other" (ἐξεκαύθησαν ἐν τῇ ὀρέξει αὐτῶν εἰς ἀλλήλους, 1:27)—the term certainly indicates that Paul is talking about fucking.[6]

Intercourse, however, is not the primary meaning of χρῆσις: when Romans described sexual intercourse, this term fit how many of them conceived it. As Brooten shows and as my translation above indicates, χρῆσις more generally—*and most often*—simply means "usage": how a person uses a tool or another object.[7] Paul defines sexual intercourse *as* usage:

---

5. Or, we might say, these men and *their* women (αἵ θήλειαι αὐτῶν). Only used when Paul describes the women, this genitive plural αὐτῶν (their) could be possessive, as in the prior sentence, or it could be partitive, indicating the women who are part of a particular group (i.e., ἔθνη/gentiles), which might alternatively be translated as "the women among them." If the latter, we might ask why Paul does not append an αὐτῶν in 1:27 to οἱ ἄρεσενες (the men) in 1:27.

6. As noted in the opening "Reading Guidance" and discussed in chapter 1, n. 63, I intentionally and expansively use this term to challenge ways it is often perceived and, especially, to prioritize its importance as a term of sexual expression for some queer folks.

7. Brooten, *Love between Women*, 245. Philo uses χρῆσις to talk about the use of particular animals as food (often within the context of Jewish customs and law [νόμος], e.g., *Legat.* 362; *Prov.* 2.64). He frequently employs it along with ἀπόλαυσις ("enjoyment," as in the act of enjoying something) to discuss virtue (ἀρετή [*Det.* 60]) as well as the "use and enjoyment of excessive pleasures" (πλεοναζούσης ἡδονῆς ἀπόλαυσίς τε καὶ χρῆσις [*Agr.* 108]). However, even if "pleasure" (here connected to Eve's temptation by the snake) connotes lack of sexual self-control, *using sex* as a form of "pleasure" is different from equating sex with the usage itself. For further discussion of the meaning of χρῆσις, see David E. Fredrickson, "Natural and Unnatural Use in Romans 1:24–27: Paul and the Philosophic Critique of Eros," in *Homosexuality, Science, and the "Plain Sense" of Scripture*, ed. David L. Balch (Grand Rapids: Eerdmans, 2000), 199–207. On

in other words, one person using another person. Paul's definition of sex matches a Romosexual conception of sex, as seen on the agency axis: sex involves the actor *using* another person (the willing or unwilling passive participant). Intercourse is a form of usage. This usage is gendered: in 1:27, "unnatural" men *repent from using women*—their "natural usage"— which their women have already abandoned, exchanging it for uses that are "against nature." In the Romosexual view that Paul adopts, intercourse naturally involves men using women for their purposes and perhaps pleasure, just like they might use a tool for a task or an animal for food.[8]

This "natural usage" is what Paul envisions as normal sexuality, and Paul's normal aligns with Romosexuality. Paul's emphasis is on those who have deviated from this norm. What are the unnatural uses that 1:26–27 wants its audiences to envision? Paul does not specify, especially in the case of the women. We are told only, in 1:26, that they "traded their natural usage for that which is against nature" (μετήλλαξαν τὴν φυσικὴν χρῆσιν εἰς τὴν παρὰ φύσιν). According to Romosexuality's naturalized norms, women could trade their "natural usage" and defy nature by being an active sexual participant (with a man or a woman), penetrating (a man or a woman), or being uncontrolled with sexual desire. Although it does not give details of the sorts of uses to which these women turn, it is noteworthy that they take an *active* role in the trade, that is, they are the subject of the verb μετήλλαξαν ("they traded"). To be sure, μετήλλαξαν is not a term with inherent sexual connotation. "Nevertheless," argues Brooten, "in the context of the widespread cultural view of women as sexually passive, for women to actively 'exchange natural intercourse for unnatural' stands out."[9]

While παρὰ φύσιν denotes more than just homoerotic activity, it is quite frequently invoked to describe homoeroticism, especially among

---

the connections between χρῆσις, sexuality, and ancient slavery, see Joseph A. Marchal, *Appalling Bodies: Queer Figures before and after Paul's Letters* (Oxford: Oxford University Press, 2019), 115–24; Marchal, "Bottoming Out: Rethinking the Reception of Receptivity," in *Bodies on the Verge: Queering Pauline Epistles*, ed. Marchal, SemeiaSt 93 (Atlanta: SBL Press, 2019), 211–12.

8. This is certainly an element of the text that affectively produces disgust, and not only for myself. When students read this text in my classes, I have them compare my translation to that in the NRSV. They always notice the change from "intercourse" to "usage," and their faces change to looks of repulsion as they realize this is what Paul thinks sex is. At this point, I lead us all in a collective groan.

9. Brooten, *Love between Women*, 246.

women. "The type of sexual relations engaged in by women most often called 'contrary to nature' (*para physin*) in the Roman world is sexual relations between women."[10] However, since the term was far from limited to homoeroticism, Paul *could* have in mind that the women were taking an active role when having sex with men (also, by extension, demonstrating uncontrolled desire), that these women were penetrating men, or that they were screwing around with the other women. Does Paul condemn them all? Or does he envision a specific act or subset of acts for which these women exchanged their natural usage?

If the vague 1:26 were all we had, it would be hard to tell. Paul cannot bear to describe women's unnatural sexuality—or, just as likely, he (like most men) cannot imagine what women might do outside of male dominance.[11] He is a little less skittish when it comes to the men. The men also abandon Romosexuality's naturalness: they repent (ἀφέντες)—as they might a sin—"the natural use of women" (τὴν φυσικὴν χρῆσιν τῆς θηλείας). As above, with just this detail, we could list a number of ways they might make their penance, including their being fucked by women (hail Mary, indeed). But Paul continues his description: "[the men] were burnt out in their yearning for each other, men who, with men, achieved disfigurement" (ἐξεκαύθησαν ἐν τῇ ὀρέξει αὐτῶν εἰς ἀλλήλους ἄρσενες ἐν ἄρσεσιν τὴν ἀσχημοσύνην κατεργαζόμενοι). Clearly, Paul envisions forms of male homoeroticism. Again, he specifies neither the exact sexual activities in which these men engaged nor what would make these acts unnatural.[12]

---

10. Brooten, *Love between Women*, 251.

11. A fact frequent across history: "Male lawyers, judges, poets, and theologians wonder again and again: 'What could women ever possibly do together without [an artificial instrument/phallus]?'" (Brooten, *Love between Women*, 190). Brooten discusses the use (and interpretation) of Rom 1 in the 1811 trial of teachers Marianne Woods and Jane Pirie in Edinburgh, Scotland, who had been accused of having a sexual relationship. While Rom 1:26 was cited as evidence of the immorality (and, therefore, illegality) of a woman having sex with another woman, the defendants were acquitted, in part, because—it was argued—such relations were impossible (and, therefore, 1:26 "referred to sodomy between a woman and a man") (Brooten, *Love between Women*, 189). See also Stephen D. Moore, *God's Beauty Parlor: And Other Queer Spaces in and around the Bible*, Contraversions (Stanford: Stanford University Press, 2001), 146–69, right column ("Things That Cannot Be Thought without Shame or Horror").

12. Edging? Fisting? Sucking? Rimming? Anal sex? Mutual masturbation? Piss play? All of the above?

Unlike in 1:26, Paul never calls the men's actions παρὰ φύσιν ("unnatural"). This accords with Romosexuality: the unnaturalness of male homoerotic activity depends on the participant, their roles, and their desires. For example, a man who topped another man was not unnatural; the man who bottomed would have been. What is (implicitly) less natural for Paul—and would have been according to elite Romans as well—is the repentance. Under Romosexuality, virtuous men were welcome to top other men (thus asserting their dominance over them) *but they were still expected to marry and make love to* their *women*. To be the rulers, true Roman men must marry good Roman women and make good Roman babies. Romans 1:27 discusses not the wholesale unnaturalness of male homoerotic activity but that of refusing (natural) sex with women. This flies in the face of wishful apologetic interpretations, for—at best—Paul condemns *orientations not acts*. (You can bang all the dudes you want, bro, but you'd better have a wife.)[13]

---

13. This is *not* to say that Paul and other first-century Romans conceived of sexual orientation in the ways we do today; however, there is a resonance between these ideas and contemporary theorizations of sexual orientations that merits acknowledgment (as with cross-temporal uses of queerness), thus admitting historical differences without drawing insistent divisions. I am arguing, in other words, that it is far more likely that Paul (like most Romans) would be less disdainful of mere homoerotic acts—or, at least, those of married men who occasionally, and as active impenetrable penetrators, top men of lower status. The idea of women or men pursuing exclusively homoerotic liaisons (whether as hookups or long-term marriage-like bonds) was unnatural and largely unthinkable—though such orientations and relationships are not entirely unattested, despite their being hidden. The "wishful apologist" argument essentially involves interpreting the passage in order to claim that, based on what he does condemn in his historical context, Paul does not have in mind—nor would he condemn—queer relationships today (or, at least, the subset of long-term, monogamous couples). Perhaps the quintessential example of a popular wishful apologist today (at least based on what my queer Christian students often cite as formative for them) is Matthew Vines, *God and the Gay Christian: The Biblical Case in Support of Same-Sex Relationships* (New York: Convergent Books, 2014), on Rom 1:18–32, see 95–115; for his firm distinction of difference with regard to sexual orientation, see 21–41. Although those most wishful are not writing in/for the academy, their arguments cite scholars whose arguments essentially align with theirs (i.e., although their interests/intentions may be neither wishful nor apologetic, their arguments are). These arguments tend to insist on the radical difference between ancient/modern when it comes to sexuality and sexual orientation. See, for example, Dale Martin, *Sex and the Single Savior: Gender and Sexuality in Biblical Interpretation* (Louisville: Westminster John Knox,

In 1:27, Paul does not specify the acts themselves as unnatural, but he does emphasize the men's yearning (ὄρεξις)—that is, their *desire*—for one another. This aligns with Romosexuality's axis of self-control. Too much desire led men and women to perform unnatural sexual activities: consumed with lust, men desired to fuck around, to bottom, or to top inappropriately (e.g., other men's wives, freeborn Romans), and women became active fuckers, adulteresses, or whores.[14] Philo (alongside other Greek and Roman authors, especially connected to Stoicism) associated ὄρεξις with negative discussions of ἐπιθυμία (desire) and the need to control pleasure (ἡδονή) (e.g., Philo, *Leg.* 3.115–116; *Post.* 27; Plutarch, *Lib. aegr.* 1).[15] In 1:27, the men's homoerotic activity displays their unnatural levels of desire: it proves they are aflame with a yearning they are unable to control. Paul never says the men's homoeroticism alone or itself is unnatural, although certainly it is a symptom of their unnatural yearnings. Ultimately, uncontrolled desire makes men burn up.

Romosexuality pervades Paul's definition of sexuality that is "unnatural" (παρὰ φύσιν) and how it relates to homoerotic acts and orientations. Since the two verses are linked, most notably with the adverb ὁμοίως ("likewise"), our considerations of the men of 1:27 clarifies some of the unanswered questions about the wo/men of 1:26 and vice versa. The unnaturalness of uncontrolled desire is already emphasized in the introduction to the unnatural wo/men in 1:26: God hands all of these folks over to "passions of dishonor" (πάθη ἀτιμίας). Passions and emotions are often discussed as needing to be controlled, alongside and in connection to terms of sexual

---

2006), esp. 51–64; Fredrickson, "Natural and Unnatural Use"; Thomas Hanks, "Romans," in *The Queer Bible Commentary*, ed. Deryn Guest, Robert E. Goss, Mona West, and Thomas Bohache (London: SCM, 2006). I will not go into detail here, but these arguments tend to assert difference by focusing on *one* element of the three-pronged axes of Romosexuality, typically self-control (i.e., condemning excess passion/desire, especially for Martin and Fredrickson) or penetration. They do not consider the interplay between penetration, agency, and desire/self-control in Romosexuality and Paul's replication of it.

14. See Diana Swancutt, "Sexy Stoics and the Rereading of Romans 1.18–2.16," in *A Feminist Companion to Paul*, ed. Amy-Jill Levine with Marianne Blickenstaff (London: T&T Clark, 2004), 53–59; Jennifer Wright Knust, *Abandoned to Lust: Sexual Slander and Ancient Christianity*, GTR (New York: Columbia University Press, 2006), 32–35.

15. Swancutt discusses the term and Rom 1:26–27 in the context of control of desires and passions within Stoic thought. Swancutt, "Sexy Stoics," 62–63.

desires and longings.[16] Wo/men who took an active role or penetrated during sex (regardless of the other participant's gender) displayed desire that they (and the men responsible for them) did not control. Uncontrolled passion results in wo/men abandoning their "natural use."

The ὁμοίως that associates 1:27 with 1:26 indicates that Paul strongly associates unnaturalness and homoeroticism for the women and the men. In 1:26 we noted that, on its own, Paul's description is too vague to say exactly what unnatural use the women take in exchange for the natural. Since 1:26 and 1:27 are linked as being "likewise," the women's unnatural exchange parallels that of the men, and, in 1:27, Paul specifies that the men want to have sex only with one another, that is, giving up using women. Although Paul is too skittish to directly name that women have sex with— and *love*—one another, he clarifies it through this linkage. If the men yearned for and achieved disfigurement with other men, then he and his audience almost certainly would have envisioned the wo/men's unnatural desires in "likewise" fashion.[17]

Have I taken us through this lengthy discussion of two verses just to conclude that the homophobes have been right all along: Paul condemns "homosexuality"?[18] Yes and no. Yes: Paul singles out homoeroticism here as emblematic of unnatural sexuality (as did many of his Roman contemporaries). But no: Paul does not limit unnatural sexuality to homoeroticism: his conception of unnatural sex parrots that of Romosexuality, which, as exemplified in Paul's term "natural use," is kyriarchal to its core. Paul's (and Rome's) opposition to homoeroticism is entwined, down to its root, with sexism. A succinct summary of 1:26–27 might be: in a way typical of first-century Roman authors, Paul strongly disapproves of unnatural sexuality—which encompasses the many sexual acts and desires that deviate from Romosexual norms—and singles out homoeroticism as

---

16. Swancutt, "Sexy Stoics," 62.

17. Here I concur with Brooten, *Love between Women*, 248–50. Her argument indicates that the ὁμοίως of 1:26 must describe female homoeroticism. Swancutt disagrees about this interpretation of ὁμοίως and cites passages where Paul uses the term in ways that do not imply this level of equation (1 Cor 7:3–4, 22) (Swancutt, "Sexy Stoics," 63–64).

18. I have not used the terms *homosexuality* or especially *homosexuals* because they are at this point dated among queer folks, but the terms do still tend to be found among conservative and homophobic interpreters. They are occasionally used by straight folks with better intentions (I hear them a lot in the classroom) in what might be called quaint anachronism in the present.

paradigmatic of what unnatural sexuality looks like among the wo/men and men he describes.

Why home in on homoeroticism? Homoeroticism was a frequent focus within Roman moral discourse and sexual slander. However, Paul makes more than just a cognitive argument. Romans 1:26–27 stems from and produces *feelings*. Paul describes unnatural sexuality in ways that affectively draw his audiences to *sense*, to *feel*, along with him, how certain sexual desires and activities are unnatural. Here is where an affective lens adds interpretive insight.

Disgust vibrates around the words strung together to form Rom 1:26–27.[19] Brooten alerts us to this affect, as she discusses why Paul waits until 1:26 to describe the passions and impurity that embody his argument about "impiety and injustice" (ἀσέβειαν καὶ ἀδικίαν) that begins at 1:18. "Paul's suspension of details for several verses may signal *disgust* concerning the degrading acts."[20] Paul is disgusted by the impulses of unnatural sexuality. His disgust did not develop in a vacuum. The unnatural associations that stick to homoeroticism make him skittish, since these associations tended to stick to nonelite, non-Roman bodies.

Romans 1:26–27 drips disgust. Paul funnels his Romosexually produced disgust into his words, which, in turn, affects his audience who are drawn into these sensations through Paul's disgusting descriptions.[21] Paul

---

19. Marchal, drawing from affective scholarship on disgust by Sara Ahmed, Eugenie Brinkema, and Sianne Ngai, also considers how Rom 1:18–32 produces and is produced by disgust. See Joseph A. Marchal, "The Disgusting Apostle and a Queer Affect between Epistles and Audiences," in *Reading with Feeling: Affect Theory and the Bible*, ed. Fiona Black and Jennifer L. Koosed, SemeiaSt (Atlanta: SBL Press, 2019), 113–40, esp. 123–31. The affective production of disgust in and around biblical texts is frequently a focus of biblical scholars working with affect theories; indeed, Erin Runions, in the first published essay in biblical studies to formally name affect, considers the disgust toward sexuality, especially sex work, that swirls around Rahab and Josh 2. See Erin Runions, "From Disgust to Humor: Rahab's Queer Affect," in *Bible Trouble: Queer Reading at the Boundaries of Biblical Scholarship*," ed. Teresa J. Hornsby and Ken Stone, SemeiaSt 67 (Atlanta: SBL Press, 2011), 45–74. Moore draws on Ahmed's work on the production of disgust (as well as hate) to analyze the violent portrayal of Jezebel and the woman Babylon in Revelation. See Stephen D. Moore, "Retching on Rome: Vomitous Loathing and Visceral Disgust in Affect Theory and the Apocalypse of John," *BibInt* 22 (2014): 502–26.

20. Brooten, *Love between Women*, 240, emphasis added.

21. This funneling does not require his rational intention, although it is possible that some of it is the result of his conscious intent.

gives just enough detail to draw out disgusting feelings. "Paul strategically employs a variety of terms that might *repel the reader* ('impurity,' 'degrading,' 'debased,' etc.) and names a number of actions that the reader might abhor," writes Brooten.[22] These terms, combined with Paul's vagueness, allow the audience (throughout history) to *feel* in the gaps with their own disgusting sensations of what unnatural sexuality could be.

Brooten labels Paul's sexual descriptions "strategic," which could imply Paul is in full cognitive control of his emotional productions. At the same time that he is a cognizant rhetorical author, Paul is also "merely a dummy on the knee of a ventriloquist culture that spoke through him," as Stephen D. Moore quips.[23] Paul is affected by Romosexuality's construction of nature, his own disgust a product of Rome's disgusting treatment of unnatural sexuality. He certainly creates his own strategic argument in these verses, but this does not mean Paul has any more control over his ideas and emotions than his audiences do.

However, the main argument here is *not* about homoeroticism. Paul is not setting out to address a question about sexuality, theology, and ethics. Romans 1:26–27 is a miniscule segment of a unit within Paul's argument in Romans (which is simultaneously strategic *and* ventriloquistic). Homoeroticism and the disgust it generates are just one plank that helps him make a larger point.

Spiraling out into Romanormativity: Romans 1:18–32

This argumentative unit begins at 1:18.

> God's anger is uncovered from heaven upon all impiety and injustice among people who, in their injustice, withhold the truth since God, as common knowledge, is apparent among them. After all, God made it clear to them. The invisible things about [God] that the mind can grasp are distinctly seen in [God's] deeds since the world's creation, which is [God's] eternal power and divinity. Thus, [these people] are inexcusable. Since even though they knew God, they did not esteem or thank God as a god; and they traded the esteem of the indestructible God for an image with the likeness of a person and ones of birds and mammals and reptiles. Therefore God handed them, with their hearts' desires, over to dirtiness so that they dishonored their bodies among them—that is,

---

22. Brooten, *Love between Women*, 258–59, emphasis added.
23. Moore, *God's Beauty Parlor*, 146.

these folks who traded God's truth for lies. They revered and served the creation instead of the one who created, the one who is praised forever, amen. (1:18–25)

Paul describes how and why God's anger (ὀργὴ θεοῦ) is provoked by impiety (ἀσέβεια) and injustice (ἀδικία) writ large. All impieties and injustices stem from a root problem: their refusal to esteem (ἐδόξασαν) or thank (ηὐχαρίστησαν) the one true God, despite the fact that they know God exists (γνόντες τὸν θεὸν) because God made Godself obvious (φανερόν), common knowledge (τὸ γνωστὸν) for them. Instead, they worship animals and idols—an act of exchanging God's truth for lies (οἵτινες μετήλλαξαν τὴν ἀλήθειαν τοῦ θεοῦ ἐν τῷ ψεύδει).

God, in turn, hands them over (παρέδωκεν) to dirtiness by dishonoring their bodies. Paul specifies that God hands them over "in their heart's desires" (ἐν ταῖς ἐπιθυμίαις τῶν καρδιῶν αὐτῶν). Put another way, God lets loose the desires these folks had been controlling and holding solely within their hearts, illustrating that their lack of honor for God stems from and leads to a loss of *self-control*.[24] Refusal to acknowledge, honor, and submit to God is their ultimate problem: further lack of self-control over their myriad desires, at this point unspecified, results in dirtiness and dishonor. Romans 1:26–27 follows this general description and illustrates one specific way these disgustingly dirty desires manifest among these people.[25] Romans 1:26–27 parallels the language Paul uses in the preceding verses, with God again handing these people over (παρέδωκεν) to passions, the women's trade (μετήλλαξαν) mirroring their earlier trading (μετήλλαξαν) of truth for lies. Refusal to esteem God leads to God letting them spin out of self-control, which, (un)naturally must include a lack of sexual virtue.

Although Paul refers generically to people/humanity in 1:18 (ἀνθρώπων), it is clear that he is describing the plight of *gentiles*, that is, those who do not follow or worship the only true God. Jews do acknowledge and worship God (and, when some do not, it is not on a large enough scale to concern Paul), and they have an established relationship to God

---

24. Fredrickson argues that loss of self-control, seen in the emphasis on *desire*, is Paul's primary concern (Fredrickson, "Natural and Unnatural Use," esp. 207–18). Fredrickson draws especially from Martin's argument in "Paul without Passion" (Martin, *Sex and the Single Savior*, 65–76).

25. After a rather random ἀμήν, perhaps a pause for everyone to take a breath before descending further into these disgusting desires.

through law.[26] Gentiles have, by and large, not done so, even though God has given them the ability. God is angry with them and poised to reveal it in judgment when God's justice comes (quite soon, Paul expects). Although Paul's audience in Rome primarily come from a gentile background, these followers are not included (any longer) in this description, because, through Christ's faith, they *have* submitted to being under God. Paul's description of the general plight of gentiles is comparable to ideas from other first-century Jewish texts, especially those coming from Jewish apocalyptic movements.[27] Like other first-century Jewish authors (including Philo), Paul thinks unnatural sexuality—and most often specified as homoeroticism—is a *gentile problem*.

However, (as with Philo) Paul simultaneously indicates that unnatural sexuality is an *ethnic problem*—that is, primarily among the ἔθνη, meaning, in his Romosexual context, the nations Rome controls or has conquered (including Judea).[28] Romans 1:18–32 echoes other decline narratives, including those written by Roman, Greek, and Jewish authors. Imperial rhetoric of a golden age, ushered in by Augustus and reinforced by his Julio-Claudian successors, heralded the restoration of Rome's most ancient virtues (*mos maiorum*), which had declined into the excesses of the chaotic Late Republican era.[29] This rhetoric cast other nations as morally inferior and frequently named sexual excesses as emblematic. Brooten observes, "Paul's depiction of sexual love between women as a result of idolatry resembles the Roman representation of such love as foreign."[30] These morally inferior nations included Germans and the snake-worshiping Egyptians (see Rom 1:24), but Romans also cast ire on the excesses of Greek culture—even as Rome lauded its philosophical virtues.[31] Romans

---

26. Stanley K. Stowers, *A Rereading of Romans: Justice, Jews, and Gentiles* (New Haven: Yale University Press, 1994), 91, see further 90–97.

27. Stowers, *Rereading of Romans*, 92–93, 185–87.

28. See Davina C. Lopez, *Apostle to the Conquered: Reimagining Paul's Mission*, PCC (Minneapolis: Fortress, 2008), 26–55, esp. 26–27, 55. In his affective consideration of disgust in this passage, Marchal also calls attention to "perverse racialization" of gentiles that enable Paul's generation of disgust (Marchal, "Disgusting Apostle," 125–26). See also Marchal, *Appalling Bodies*, 183–85.

29. Stowers, *Rereading of Romans*, 85–100, 122–25.

30. Brooten, *Love between Women*, 299.

31. On Roman prejudice against Egyptians, see Maren Niehoff, *Philo on Jewish Identity and Culture*, TSAJ (Tübingen: Mohr Siebeck, 2001), 48–60, see also 19–23. On their prejudice against Greeks, see Niehoff, *Philo of Alexandria: An Intellectual*

inherited and embodied the wisdom and virtue of Greek philosophy while the Greeks themselves lost their self-control, thus allowing Rome to conquer and replace them.

Drawing from these decline narratives, Rom 1:18–32 reinforces the naturalness of Romosexuality and replicates its presumptions of the superiority of Rome over other ἔθνη. Paul includes Christ-followers and Jews among those who naturally adhere to these norms. Unnatural sexuality is not inherent among those who follow God just as it is foreign to true Romans. This emphasizes how those who acknowledge and submit to God (i.e., Paul's audience and, by extension, Jews and all Christ-followers) are *not* among these ἔθνη prone to foreign sexual, immoral excess. Contra scholars who interpret Rom 1:18–32 as a veiled critique of the specific sexual infidelities and excesses of the Roman imperial family (Claudius, in particular), Rom 1:18–32 aligns with Roman imperialism and its sociosexual-political assumption that foreigners/ἔθνη are unnatural by nature.[32]

Biography, ABRL (New Haven: Yale University Press, 2018), 87, 137–58; Benjamin Isaac, *The Invention of Racism in Classical Antiquity* (Princeton: Princeton University Press, 2004), 381–405; on portrayals of Germans (exemplified in Tacitus), see Nancy Shumate, *Nation, Empire, Decline: Studies in Rhetorical Continuity from the Romans to the Modern Era*, Classical Interfaces (London: Duckworth, 2006), 81–127.

32. Stowers affirms the importance of this alignment: "Part of the power in Romans' discourse would have come not from the novelty of the message but from *the way in which it played on politically and culturally charged themes that readers met daily on images of coins, in public monuments, and in everyday discourse*" (Stowers, *Rereading of Romans*, 124, emphasis added). On this point, I am disagreeing with analyses in Neil Elliott, *The Arrogance of Nations: Reading Romans in the Shadow of Empire*, PCC (Minneapolis: Fortress, 2008), 77–83, and Theodore W. Jennings Jr., *Outlaw Justice: The Messianic Politics of Paul*, CMP (Stanford: Stanford University Press, 2013), 38, see further 30–40. Jennings's and Elliott's connection of this passage to the excesses of ancient empire and the ways in which the actions of the Roman 1 percent would have frustrated the majority of lower-status Christ-followers (among many other low-status Romans) make important points about the exceptional nature of Rome's emperors and the frustrations it likely engendered among some bodies, but (as becomes apparent in my own argument) I am interested in how many were willing to *ignore* these excesses so long as there were *possibilities* of upward mobility and socioeconomic success (which might, in turn, enable entrance into such an exceptional world). With Jennings especially, I find his interpretation problematic for its erasure of sexuality, especially when it comes to wo/men's (homo)eroticism (see pp. 38–39, where—when referring to imperial women—such behavior is broadened to include murder of husbands); indeed, Jennings erases the possibility of lesbian relationships in any form as the "sheerest fantasy" (39) without a mention of Brooten, let alone an engagement

Romans 1:18–32 does not critique Rome or its socio-sexual-political ideology; it replicates it.

When we consider how 1:26–27 tells a "decline narrative" about ἔθνη (as both "gentiles" and "nations") who do not submit to God in 1:18–25, we see that unnatural sexuality is symptomatic of a larger problem. The excess that Paul chooses to emphasize is emblematic of the chaos into which these impious ἔθνη have descended as a result of refusing God. Romans 1:28–32 completes their descent:

> Just as they did not approve of holding God with recognition, God handed them over to an unacceptable mentality—doing things that are not suitable. They have been filled with injustice, wickedness, vice; full of envy, rivalry, treachery, malignity; gossipers, slanderers, god-hating cocky people, overconfident braggarts, inventors of vices, disobedient to their parents, witless, uncommitted, unkind, merciless. They are folks who recognize God's judgment because the ones who are acting out such things are worthy of death. They are not just doing them, but they are even giving consent to those who act them out.

Structurally, as Rom 1:18–32 declines to its final declarations, it *spirals* out of control.[33] The spiral begins with the refusal to follow and submit to God, which slowly twirls into idolatry. It gains momentum as it swivels into unnatural sexual uses and homoeroticism, and, reaching a dizzying velocity, it spins out into a vice list of uncontrollably disgusting dimension.[34] The spiral whirls words with feelings. The words cannot be disconnected from either the sensations that produce them or those they produce. They swirl *in between* one another into an affective blend that motivates words, feelings, bodies, and actions. Like a tornado, this torrential text

---

with the tremendous amount of historical evidence contained in *Love between Women* that negates any claim that such a possibility is mere fantasy.

33. Brooten first identifies the spiral structure of Rom 1:18–32. "For this reason, attempts to discern a linear outline fail. Nor is the text circular. Instead it forms a spiral, beginning with the human rejection of the true God, climbing to God's response, and the winding back again to the human turn toward falsehood" (Brooten, *Love between Women*, 239).

34. The epic vice list is difficult to translate, signaling a loss of linguistic control as it spews a string of depraved nouns and adjectives in which it becomes less and less clear how to connect the terms. This bubbling-over disgust embodies the lack of control these vices exemplified. Ironically, Paul seems to lose his own control over his disgust at these vices.

spins around in its dizzying disgust. It grasps its audiences as well as anything in its path. Then, this tornadic text spits out the queer folks (within and beyond its audiences) and attempts to leave us dead in its dust, since, along with the many other vices in its spiral, 1:32 declares us ἄξιοι θανάτου ("worthy of death").

However, Rom 1:18–32 is not the death sentence its most dangerous interpreters have envisioned. "Worthy of death" does not mean *kill them* for Paul, although throughout history it has justified maiming murders of queer folks. Those who turn away from following God and spiral into this pit of depraved despair *deserve to die*, but 1:32 is not the end of Paul's letter. If God's anger were to be revealed right now, Paul says, these gentiles would be judged worthy of death for refusing to faithfully follow God. But, just prior to 1:18–32, Paul gives a summary of τὸ εὐαγγέλιον (the "good news" or "gospel"): "God's power is for salvation to everyone who shows faith, Jew first then Greek" (1:16). The Greeks, here a metonym for all other ἔθνη, are those who have yet to display faith and follow God, as 1:18–32 shows. As we will see, God *delays* the coming anger to make time for gentiles to straighten out this spiral and get up to speed.[35] They deserve death, but that death is not coming. Yay, good news.

Or not. For queerness still gets its death sentence. Queer folks may not be killed in Paul's vision, but they do become Romosexual—that is, natural, normal, straight. Queerness, according to Rom 1:18–32, will always be a symptom, the result of not following God—or not being *naturally faithful* to God. According to Paul, in the just world that God's revelation will bring, everyone will be faithful to God, which implies an end to unnatural sexuality. Problem solved: symptomatic queerness will be naturally cured, erased, *not there*.

This is not a satisfying conclusion to Rom 1:18–32, but it is where a feminist and queer affective lens leaves us. Enduring the whirling winds of its spiral structure, Paul's use of disgust and sexuality is an affective tactic (both intentional and beyond Paul's total control) that sows *feelings* and *sensations* in and in between its ideas. These tactics radiate from Paul's own feelings and normative cravings. As he parrots Romosexuality, his argument in 1:18–32 begins to employ the *Romanormativity* that runs through Romans. The Romanormative tactics of 1:18–32 use sexuality

---

35. Romans 1:16–17 and these ideas will be explained in detail in chapter 3 of this book.

to distinguish Paul and his audiences from Rome's other conquered subjects—that is, its ἔθνη. By reflecting Roman virtues onto himself and his
audience, he begins to cast them as natural vis-à-vis their disgust at these
unnatural wo/men and their behaviors.

A Tired Text?

Romans 1:18–32 is a tired and tiring text, politically and personally. In
Naomi Novik's novel *Uprooted*, Agnieszka picks a book from her lord's
library out of boredom, not realizing he is a wizard and all his books
are magical. The book is powerfully enchanted, and as she reads it she
understands page 1, page 2, but she gets to page 3 and realizes she's forgotten what the book was about. She starts again to review, and the same
thing happens.[36] This is how I feel reading scholarship on Rom 1:18–32,
especially when I have read much of it a number of times, by now in the
double digits. I *know* it. Yet when I sit down to write about it, *I don't know
what to say. I don't know what anyone says. I'm tired*. I am experiencing
my own exhaustion writing, rewriting, reviewing, revising this. Prior versions, which various editors and reviewers critiqued, skimmed the surface,
skipped over the tough questions, relied on summarizing others rather
than turning to the text and what I have to say about it. The text repels me,
not because it disgusts me, not even because it angers me, but because *it
exhausts me*. I'm tired before I even turn to it. I'm tired as I open the screen.
I don't say this to complain. But if we're going to talk about the affective
forces and tugs of ancient texts—and why they matter for interpretation—
then, at some point, I should admit my own emotional attachments toward
and away from these materials.[37]

---

36. Naomi Novik, *Uprooted* (New York: Del Rey Books, 2015), 27–28.

37. In her book's introduction, Karen Bray recounts vignettes of her and others'
everyday experiences (including, but not limited to, academic labor) that foreground
affective exhaustion in ways that resonate with my own recounting of exhaustion here.
See Karen Bray, *Grave Attending: A Political Theology for the Unredeemed* (New York:
Fordham University Press, 2020), 1–29, esp. 1–4, 13–14. Bray molds her attention to
texts, rituals, events, and theo-politics into an "affect hermeneutics" that also resonate
with my feminist and queer affective critique: "[Affect hermeneutics] would be an
approach to reading of text and world that would look for moments of emotional rup-
ture, dissonance, and overflow within spaces overtly and subtly marked as emotional"
(Bray, *Grave Attending*, 27).

If the stormy swirling in between Rom 1:18–32 and its audiences produces affect, then one dimension of this affect is *tiredness*. Because of its harmful effects, contemporary queer readers are affectively drawn to it: it compels us; we need to debunk it and discover ways to read it otherwise. We need to reorient its affective effects and show how Paul's comments on sexuality must be understood as temporally restricted products of a particular historical context, much as his comments on wo/men and slavery have been understood as having different meanings in the first century than in the twentieth and twenty-first.[38] Romans 1:18–32 captures Romans's queer readers in its spiraling sway: no matter how exhaustively queer interpretations may debunk and reframe its ideas, they can never exhaust the meanings, uses, and feelings that surround the text. And so, instead of exhausting 1:18–32 of its harmful effects, queer biblical scholarship has been exhausted *by* the text. Stuck within its affective grip, 1:18–32 tires queer readers and prevents us from looking beyond Paul's words here. Tiredness sticks to Rom 1:26–27. It is a *tired* text—discussed *ad nauseam* in queer biblical studies—even as it is a *tiring* text: exhausting readers before they can escape its sticky grip.

After all, the conclusion of 1:32 leaves us craving something else. Perhaps, as with the films Berlant discusses, we wake up groggy from the passage's twists and turns as we experience our own Romanormativity hangover. Perhaps this hangover compels our typical reactions: stopping and avoiding Romans entirely or, boldly, turning around and again facing its spiraling sway. The problem with getting stuck in 1:18–32 is that, at best, it seems to keep us in a creative loop that moves in a forwardly circular direction.

Yet there are fifteen more chapters in Romans. The feelings contained in 1:18–32 launch Paul into his theological ideas about faith, salvation, and ethics, all of which are affected by the Romanormativity we see in these early verses of the letter. Moore argues that Paul's "'theological system' (to the extent he can be said to have had *one*), traditionally thought to be encapsulated in his letter to the Romans, was not only *infected* by this sex-gender system but partly *produced* by it."[39] Moore's queer reading hints

---

38. That is, Marchal's "historical-contextual" approach to queer readings; see Joseph A. Marchal, "Queer Approaches: Improper Relations with Pauline Letters," in *Studying Paul's Letters: Contemporary Perspectives and Methods*, ed. Marchal (Minneapolis: Fortress, 2012), 214–16.

39. Moore, *God's Beauty Parlor*, 171.

at how taking a queer approach could move beyond Rom 1:18–32.[40] The rest of this book takes the hint and probes of other parts of Romans where Romanormativity can be found. Even if we get beyond the words of Rom 1:18–32, we can never entirely get over them and their affective effects.

Over the next two chapters in Novik's novel, Agnieszka discovers she is a witch as her lord requires her to learn his spells. The spells exhaust her; she hates it; she avoids learning. Over time, she starts to realize that with practice, magic is less exhausting; but it is not until she realizes learning magic might help save her family, friends, and village that she embraces the learning.[41] There can be value, even wisdom, in doing the tough, tiring work, at least when one can see the payoff. I would not go through the exegetical exhaustion of Rom 1:18–32 if I could not already envision getting beyond it, if I did not see the payoff that comes from critiquing the theology and ethics it influences in later chapters of Romans. If (as Brooten wisely intones) "the only way out of it is through it," then we must remember to get out—to wake up and keep moving. The only way out of it is through it *and beyond it*. It is toward an affectively feminist and queer beyond that I—*we*—now turn.

Going Beyond: The Queer Wo/men of Romans 16

We can go beyond Rom 1:18–32 by considering the queer wo/men around it. Brooten argues that Paul's views—and, by extension, those of Rome's elite—were not descriptive of all wo/men. After all, queer wo/men were there—*and this included in ἐκκλησίαι where Christ-followers gathered*.[42] Brooten concludes her analysis of Rom 1:18–32 with a reconstruction of how the first hearers of these words might have responded: a Jewish woman recognizes allusions to Leviticus; a man gets ideas for a sermon

---

40. Indeed, Moore's engagement with Brooten leads him to suggest that his essay might be a "prolegomenon" to a more subversive project that could centralize sex between women and "radically egalitarian behavior" and see what changes this might entail to Pauline (and, by extension, Christian) theology. See Moore, *God's Beauty Parlor*, 172.

41. Novik, *Uprooted*, 38–62, esp. 59–60.

42. Brooten, *Love between Women*, 300–302, 359–62. The diverse range of evidence Brooten's book compiles for female homoeroticism across early imperial Rome and into the early eras of its Christian empire affirms this as (highly) probable, even if this evidence is rarer, involves condemnations by authorities, and often gets erased from recorded view.

that takes Paul's idea about gentile idolatry and molds them to promote his own agenda; and a formerly enslaved man recognizes Stoic ideas he read aloud to his enslaver while his wife connects the words of 1:26 to some of the women she has served as customers at her food stall.[43] Brooten uses evidence of first-century queer wo/men to go beyond Paul's words and imaginatively proliferate several plausible responses, which include spoken words, thoughts, and feelings.

Going beyond Rom 1:18–32 does not merely indicate forward, linear movement into chapters 2–16. Following feminist hermeneutics, we must go beyond *Paul's words*, that is, his singular perspective, and bring into our gaze the wo/men around them. After all, Brooten writes, "After they read his letter, they probably talked about it."[44] Melanie Johnson-DeBaufre and Laura Nasrallah embrace this beyondness as they urge Pauline scholars to get "beyond the heroic Paul."[45] Typically, when interpreters analyze the political dimensions of Paul's letters, he must be either a hero: the champion of resistance to empire, who provides alternatives for Christ-followers confronting imperial oppressions ancient and contemporary; or a villain: the parrot of empire, repeating its kyriarchal values in Christo-theological form.[46] This binary approach offers two sides of the same Pauline coin: hero or villain, Paul's voice is centered exclusively.[47]

Drawing upon a rich tradition in feminist biblical scholarship inspired by Elisabeth Schüssler Fiorenza, Johnson-DeBaufre and Nasrallah decenter Paul.[48] They implore interpreters to leave behind his heroic status and get to

---

43. Brooten, *Love between Women*, 300. Of this reconstruction, she writes, "At a distance of over nineteen hundred years, we have to reconstruct academically what his first hearers knew experientially from their own culture: from Jewish literature, from the philosophy discussed in the marketplace and lecture halls, and from what people said on the streets and in the corner taverns" (300–301).

44. Brooten, *Love between Women*, 301.

45. Melanie Johnson-DeBaufre and Laura S. Nasrallah, "Beyond the Heroic Paul: Toward a Feminist and Decolonizing Approach to the Letters of Paul," in *The Colonized Apostle: Paul through Postcolonial Eyes*, ed. Christopher D. Stanley, PCC (Minneapolis: Fortress, 2011), 161–174.

46. Johnson-DeBaufre and Nasrallah, "Beyond the Heroic Paul," 162–68.

47. "Instead, two different portraits of Paul emerge: the rhetorical-textual Paul is either the organizer of the empire's subjugated nations or their imperial subjugator. Paul either undermines or wields dominant notions of masculinity" (Johnson-DeBaufre and Nasrallah, "Beyond the Heroic Paul," 166).

48. Although feminist biblical scholarship—especially that of Schüssler Fiorenza

and those influenced by her—has pioneered and insisted upon decentering methods within the guild of biblical studies, it is important to note that wo/men have long been decentering Paul from their readings of the Bible. This is especially the case with Black wo/men, which can be seen in stories of enslaved folks in the US South who walked out of white preachers' sermons when they insisted, according to Paul, enslaved folks should not resist or flee from their enslavers as well as when Howard Thurman's grandmother directed him not to read passages from Paul's letters (besides 1 Cor 13) because of their usage by enslavers to exhort submission and obedience. See Demetrius K. Williams, "African American Approaches: Rehumanizing the Reader against Racism and Reading through Experience," in *Studying Paul's Letters: Contemporary Perspectives and Methods*, ed. Joseph A. Marchal (Minneapolis: Fortress, 2012), 155–73, esp. 163–64; Brian K. Blount et al., eds., *True to Our Native Land: An African American New Testament Commentary* (Minneapolis: Fortress, 2007); Matthew V. Johnson, James A. Noel, and Demetrius K. Williams, eds., *Onesimus Our Brother: Reading Religion, Race, and Culture in Philemon*, PCC (Minneapolis: Fortress, 2012); Pamela R. Lightsey, *Our Lives Matter: A Womanist Queer Theology* (Eugene, OR: Pickwick, 2015), 36–50, esp. 39–40. Within feminist biblical studies, see especially Elisabeth Schüssler Fiorenza, *The Power of the Word: Scripture and the Rhetoric of Empire* (Minneapolis: Fortress, 2007), 69–109; Schüssler Fiorenza, "Paul and the Politics of Interpretation," in *Paul and Politics: Ekklēsia, Israel, Imperium, Interpretation; Essays in Honor of Krister Stendahl*, ed. Richard A. Horsley (Harrisburg, PA: Trinity Press International, 2000), 40–57. Although many scholars, including and following Schüssler Fiorenza, have included these urgings within Paul-and-politics volumes and panels (typically a solitary voice within them), their interventions have been largely ignored, especially outside feminist scholarship. In that same volume (*Paul and Politics: Ekklēsia, Israel, Imperium, Interpretation; Essays in Honor of Krister Stendahl*, ed. Richard A. Horsley [Harrisburg, PA: Trinity Press International, 2000]), see also the work of Cynthia Briggs Kittredge, "Corinthian Women Prophets and Paul's Argumentation in 1 Corinthians," 103–9, and Antionette Clark Wire, "Response: The Politics of the Assembly in Corinth," 124–29; and Wire, "Response: Paul and Those outside Power," 224–26. Other scholarship that has worked to decenter Paul includes Wire, *The Corinthian Women Prophets: A Reconstruction through Paul's Rhetoric* (Minneapolis: Fortress, 1990); Kittredge, *Community and Authority: The Rhetoric of Obedience in the Pauline Tradition*, HTS 45 (Cambridge: Harvard University Press, 1998); Joseph A. Marchal, *The Politics of Heaven: Women, Gender, and Empire in the Study of Paul*, PCC (Minneapolis: Fortress, 2008); Cavan W. Concannon, *"When You Were Gentiles": Specters of Ethnicity in Roman Corinth and Paul's Corinthian Correspondence*, Syn (New Haven: Yale University Press, 2014); Shelly A. Matthews, "A Feminist Analysis of the Veiling Passage (1 Corinthians 11:2–16): Who Really Cares That Paul Was Not a Gender Egalitarian After All?" *LD* 2 (2015), https://tinyurl.com/SBL4531g; Arminta M. Fox, "Decentering Paul, Contextualizing Crime: Reading in Light of the Imprisoned," *JFSR* 33 (2017): 37–54; Joseph A. Marchal, ed., *The People beside Paul: The Philippian Assembly and History from Below*, ECL 17 (Atlanta: SBL Press, 2015); Anna C.

the "networks of women and men who promote, resist, or ignore him while he is away."[49] Decentering allows us to go *beyond* Paul and his words (including those in Rom 1:18–32). When we speak of "going beyond," neither Johnson-DeBaufre and Nasrallah nor I want to *get over* Paul. Ahmed warns overing language often implies abandoning something's position, participation, and effects in politics and culture.[50] While getting beyond can have problematic meanings, *beyondness* also has creative and affective potential for intersectional politics, as José Esteban Muñoz's utopian queer beyond exemplifies.[51] Going "beyond the heroic Paul" refuses to place Paul on one side of a binary with an ἐκκλησία of wo/men on the other: the wo/men in these ἐκκλησίαι agreed and disagreed with one another as much as they did with Paul.[52] Johnson-DeBaufre and Nasrallah don't get over Paul; they place

---

Miller, *Corinthian Democracy: Democratic Discourse in 1 Corinthians*, PTMS (Eugene, OR: Pickwick, 2015); Katherine A. Shaner, *Enslaved Leadership in Early Christianity* (Oxford: Oxford University Press, 2018); Arminta M. Fox, *Paul Decentered: Reading 2 Corinthians with the Corinthian Women*, PCC (Lanham, MD: Lexington Books, 2020).

49. Johnson-DeBaufre and Nasrallah, "Beyond the Heroic Paul," 166.

50. Sara Ahmed, *On Being Included: Racism and Diversity in Institutional Life* (Durham: Duke University Press, 2014), 180.

51. "*Cruising Utopia* can ultimately be read as an invitation, a performative provocation. Manifesto-like and ardent, it is a call to think about our lives and times differently, to look beyond a narrow version of the here and now on which so many around us who are bent on the normative count. Utopia in this book has been about an insistence on something else, something better, something dawning. I offer this book as a resource for the political imagination. This text is meant to serve as something of a flight plan for a collective political becoming" (José Esteban Muñoz, *Cruising Utopia: The Then and There of Queer Futurity*, Sexual Cultures [New York: New York University Press, 2009], 189). My thinking here especially has resonance with his discussions of the queerness of utopia and proliferative and anticipatory queer futurity in his first chapter, "Queerness as Horizon: Utopian Hermeneutics in the Face of Gay Pragmatism" (Muñoz, *Cruising Utopia*, 19–32).

52. "Such a conceptualization of the *ekklēsia* of women as a democratic, public, feminist arena for practical deliberation and responsible choice does not repress but invites debates about different theoretical proposals and practical strategies." See Elisabeth Schüssler Fiorenza, *Discipleship of Equals: A Critical Feminist* Ekklēsia*logy of Liberation* (New York: Crossroad, 1993), 350. Miller draws out the disagreements among Paul and the wo/men of Corinth as participants in "*ekklēsia* discourse," which brought the democratic ideals of the ἐκκλησία, as they were being developed by first-century Greco-Roman philosophers to this less restricted gathering of Corinthian Christ-followers that included women and enslaved folks (Miller, *Corinthian Democracy*).

him as "*one voice among many*."[53] They *interrupt* him, like some of these wo/men probably did. Interrupting is not the same as silencing. The wo/men in Rome's ἐκκλησία did not just proliferate myriad ideas as they interrupted and responded to Paul's. They *had already been* conversing and debating these ideas *long before* Paul's letter arrived and was read in their assembly.[54] This suggests that the surviving (textual) remnants of Rome's ἐκκλησία were and are "contested spaces."[55] Paul's ideas were not novel to this group. Some could have held similar views and others were already shouting vigorously against them; maybe most others sat or stood and reacted through various sensations and postures from spaces in between.

What did the wo/men of Rome's ἐκκλησία look like? What roles did they play in the ἐκκλησία? How did they associate in smaller networks within this assembly? What sorts of feelings and sensations moved within and between them? *Who were these wo/men?*[56] The final chapter of Romans offers us a glimpse.

---

53. Johnson-DeBaufre and Nasrallah, "Beyond the Heroic Paul," 174, emphasis added. Their full sentence reads: "More importantly, if we place the assemblies at the center and hear Paul's letters as one voice among many, we can imaginatively reconstruct and reclaim a richer history of interpretation of Paul, a history populated with subjects struggling in different ways within the varied contexts of empire."

54. Describing how their approach could affect a reading of Romans, Johnson-DeBaufre and Nasrallah write, "The meaning of Romans might then be varied and its possibilities and limitations more fully unfolded. Such an approach takes Paul's letters as *partial inscriptions of the political visions and debates of the Christ-assemblies* rather than as a repository for Paul's thought alone" (Johnson-DeBaufre and Nasrallah, "Beyond the Heroic Paul," 166, emphasis added).

55. Johnson-DeBaufre and Nasrallah, "Beyond the Heroic Paul," 173. Similarly, with respect to the ἐκκλησία in Corinth, Miller's goal is to "place 1 Corinthians inside *a discursive space of contestation* over the nature of communal authority and leadership" (Miller, *Corinthian Democracy*, 9, emphasis added).

56. With regard to Romans, the task of reconstructing Rome's ἐκκλησία has traditionally been difficult. This is due both to Paul's lack of engagement with specific issues within the ἐκκλησία (since the letter is his first correspondence to an assembly he has not yet visited) and to the size and diversity of the city of Rome as the imperial capital. I am not the first to attempt to imagine the bodies that inhabited the Roman ἐκκλησία, as Peter Oakes has done so, appealing especially to the evidence of Pompeii. His reimaginative work helps provide one more avenue to pave the way for my proliferation. See Peter Oakes, *Reading Romans in Pompeii: Paul's Letter at Ground Level* (Minneapolis: Fortress, 2009), esp. 69–97.

Ἀσπάσασθε Πρίσκαν καὶ Ἀκύλαν τοὺς συνεργούς μου ἐν Χριστῷ Ἰησοῦ, οἵτινες ὑπὲρ τῆς ψυχῆς μου τὸν ἑαυτῶν τράχηλον ὑπέθηκαν, οἷς οὐκ ἐγὼ μόνος εὐχαριστῶ ἀλλὰ καὶ πᾶσαι αἱ ἐκκλησίαι τῶν ἐθνῶν, καὶ τὴν κατ' οἶκον αὐτῶν ἐκκλησίαν. ἀσπάσασθε Ἐπαίνετον τὸν ἀγαπητόν μου, ὅς ἐστιν ἀπαρχὴ τῆς Ἀσίας εἰς Χριστόν. ἀσπάσασθε Μαριάμ, ἥτις πολλὰ ἐκοπίασεν εἰς ὑμᾶς.

Say hello to Prisca and Aquila, my coworkers in Christ Jesus—who risked their own necks for my soul and whom not only I thank but also all the *ekklēsiai* among the *ethnē*—and the *ekklēsia* in their house. Say hello to my beloved Epaenetus, who is Asia's first offering to Christ. Greet Mary, who worked hard for you. (16:3–6)

These greetings tell us *who was there*. Of course, they cannot give us descriptions of everyone assembled there—let alone the objects they brought with them, the feelings of each individual, their gestures to one another, their words, the sensations they shared in between them. But they do give us a concrete starting point to see and name some of the many human differences each wo/man added to this ἐκκλησία.[57]

---

57. Scholars, in particular Schüssler Fiorenza and Peter Lampe, have analyzed these clues, especially the names mentioned in chapter 16, to assert probable details about the ἐκκλησία that aid reconstructing its discussions. See Elisabeth Schüssler Fiorenza, "Missionaries, Apostles, Coworkers: Romans 16 ad the Reconstruction of Women's Early Christian History," *WW* 6 (1986): 420–33; Peter Lampe, *From Paul to Valentinus: Christians at Rome in the First Two Centuries*, trans. Michael Steinhauser, ed. Marshall D. Johnson (Minneapolis: Fortress, 2003), chapter 16, "The Roman Christians of Romans 16," 153–83; Lampe's monograph was originally published in German: *Die Stadtrömischen Christen in den ersten beiden Jahrhunderten: Untersuchungen zur Sozialgeschichte* (Tübingen: Mohr Siebeck, 1987). Both Schüssler Fiorenza and Lampe reject the proposal that Rom 16 was not originally part of the epistle (and that it may not have originally been sent to Rome but to Ephesus). See Schüssler Fiorenza, "Missionaries, Apostles, Coworkers," 420; Lampe, *From Paul to Valentinus*, 153–64. Steven J. Friesen analyzed the persons named in Rom 16, among other "saints" named in Paul's letters, using a poverty scale, both to show the relative wealth/poverty of these saints and to show how even the wealthiest of these saints would not have been wealthy in the first century and would have been close to basic subsistence level (some just above, most/many below). See Steven J. Friesen, "Poverty in Pauline Studies: Beyond the So-Called New Consensus," *JSNT* 26 (2004): 323–61, see esp. 352–57 for discussion of those named in Rom 16. Drawing from much of the scholarship on Rom 16, Marchal reassembles these wo/men and their relations to one another and Paul's words by thinking at the intersections of their oppressions based on gender, sexual orientation, enslavement, and race/ethnicity. See Marchal, *Appalling*

Romans 16 emphatically affirms how *queer wo/men were there.* Its first words confirm wo/men's active leadership:

Συνίστημι δὲ ὑμῖν Φοίβην τὴν ἀδελφὴν ἡμῶν, οὖσαν καὶ διάκονον τῆς ἐκκλησίας τῆς ἐν Κεγχρεαῖς, ἵνα αὐτὴν προσδέξησθε ἐν κυρίῳ ἀξίως τῶν ἁγίων, καὶ παραστῆτε αὐτῇ ἐν ᾧ ἂν ὑμῶν χρῄζῃ πράγματι, καὶ γὰρ αὐτὴ προστάτις πολλῶν ἐγενήθη καὶ ἐμοῦ αὐτοῦ.

Let me introduce you to our sister Phoebe, who is also minister of Cenchreae's *ekklēsia*, so that, in *kyrios*, you can accept her in a manner worthy of holy folks, and assist her in whatever things she needs of you. She is, in fact, a leader of many, myself included. (16:1–2)

Romans 16 serves as a letter of introduction of Phoebe to the wo/men of Rome's ἐκκλησία, and it emphasizes that Phoebe is a significant leader among Christ-followers, a minister/preacher of another ἐκκλησία, and someone who is worthy of an esteemed welcome befitting "holy folks." Paul renders respect to her as a leader (προστάτις) with more authority than him, since he includes himself among the many whom she has led. Phoebe's leading role in this chapter is indicative of the emphasis on wo/men's presence and prominence among first-century Christ-followers found in Rom 16.[58]

Although the wo/men of Rome's ἐκκλησία might have needed an introduction to an unknown traveling minister, they would not have been skeptical of a woman who took active leadership in an ἐκκλησία or who traveled in a missionary-like capacity to other cities and their ἐκκλησίαι. About one-third of the twenty-six names in this chapter are clearly wo/men's, and, when counting those identified as taking active leadership and missionary roles, wo/men outnumber men.[59] If this many wo/men were worthy of such (positive) attention in Paul's letter, then it indicates a significant presence of wo/men beyond those named and a high level of participation, on equal levels to men, within one of the earliest ἐκκλησίαι. The wo/men of Rome's ἐκκλησία represent just the "tip of an iceberg"

Bodies, 185–98; and Marchal, "Bottoming Out," 230–32. Many scholars have worked on reconstructing and arguing for the prominent leadership roles of specific wo/men named in Rom 16, and their work will be cited below when I discuss specific passages and wo/men.

58. Schüssler Fiorenza, "Missionaries, Apostles, Coworkers," 423–27.

59. Schüssler Fiorenza, "Missionaries, Apostles, Coworkers," 427; Lampe, *From Paul to Valentinus,* 165–67.

of wo/men's engagement and activity in Rome and among first-century Christ-followers more widely.[60]

In 16:3–5 we meet Prisca and Mary. Prisca, along with her missionary partner Aquila, have worked alongside Paul, and he is in their debt since they have "risked their necks" (τὸν ἑαυτῶν τράχηλον ὑπέθηκαν) for him.[61] Since Paul almost always names the man first in a man-woman pairing, the fact that Prisca is named first in 16:3 indicates that her leadership role may be more significant to Paul or other Christ-followers.[62] Mary is quite active within Rome's ἐκκλησία, for she worked hard (κοπιάω) among them.[63] Unlike with Phoebe, Prisca, and Aquila, Paul may not have the same level of personal relationship with everyone he greets, since his greetings to folks like Mary indicate familiarity but not the same amount of indebtedness and friendship. From his and others' travels, he has encountered or heard about some of the leaders in Rome's ἐκκλησία, and, since he wants them to be open to his ideas (and warmly receive Phoebe), he greets these folks to establish an affective connection to them and their leaders.[64] Paul

---

60. Schüssler Fiorenza, "Missionaries, Apostles, Coworkers," 423, 427. In terms of the iceberg's unseen bulk, much is submerged in grammatically masculine language or has sunk away as historical sources lost to us forever.

61. Calling attention to the significance of risking their lives for Paul, Fox raises the plausibility that they may have risked their lives by visiting and ministering to Paul in prison, especially since, in Phil 2:25–30, Epaphroditus is described as having risked his life to visit the imprisoned Paul (Fox, "Decentering Paul, Contextualizing Crime," 47–51, esp. 50–51). In this article, Fox documents the risks and horrific conditions of Roman imprisonment (in conversation with the contemporary US prison-industrial complex) and the networks required to survive imprisonment. Prisca and Aquila are usually assumed to be husband and wife, as indicated in Acts 18:2 (where Πρίσκα becomes Πρίσκιλλα). Paul also mentions them together in 1 Cor 16:19, in which he relays greetings from them (and the ἐκκλησία in their house) to Corinth's ἐκκλησία. I will not assume their heterosexuality, since Romans does not mention their being married and Acts does not offer reliable portraits of Paul's travels and associations. (And, in its second-century context, attempting to align Christian and Roman virtues, it is plausible that the author would present such missionary couples as married to make them seem less subversive in terms of sexuality and gender.)

62. Schüssler Fiorenza, "Missionaries, Apostles, Coworkers," 428. See also Lampe, *From Paul to Valentinus*, 166–67.

63. Lampe observes that Paul uses only this verb, which indicates "active participation," to describe wo/men's engagement (Lampe, *From Paul to Valentinus*, 166).

64. Schüssler Fiorenza, "Missionaries, Apostles, Coworkers," 428; Yii-Jan Lin, "Junia: An Apostle before Paul," *JBL* 139 (2020): 202–3. See also Mary Rose D'Angelo, "Women Partners in the New Testament," *JFSR* 6 (1990): 73. When I explain this to

cannot ignore wo/men leaders if he wants his audience to welcome his ideas (and, he hopes, himself at a future date).[65]

Romans 16 confirms that *women were there*, but what about *queer wo/men* and differences in sexuality, status, and ethnicity this phrase affirms? Romans 16:12 names two wo/men as a couple: ἀσπάσασθε Τρύφαιναν καὶ Τρυφῶσαν τὰς κοπιώσας ἐν κυρίῳ ("Say hello to Tryphaena and Tryphosa, who work hard in *kyrios*"). Unlike the other greetings in Rom 16, where the wo/men Paul greets are either named individually or paired with a man, in this instance, Paul pairs two wo/men together. Tryphaena and Tryphosa are identified as a missionary couple, together working hard in Christ (their κύριος). Along with other New Testament examples of wo/men missionary couples, Mary Rose D'Angelo argues that Tryphosa and Tryphaena "emerge as evidence of partnerships of women in the early Christian mission."[66]

The naming of this partnership also draws attention to sexuality. D'Angelo observes, "These partnerships reveal a commitment between women that, in light of early Christian sexual mores, can be seen as a sexual choice." Their decision to work together is a choice, in the same way it would have been for other missionary couples like Prisca and Aquila (16:3) or Andronicus and Junia (16:7). If scholars attribute the bond of marriage to have motivated the choice of these heterosexual missionary couples, then it is just as plausible that a similar bond united Tryphaena and Tryphosa, in addition to other missionary couples of the same gender. In an imperial context where marriage was legally and socially encouraged,

---

students, I compare it to how, at a concert or a rally, speakers/singers might solicit connections with the audience by asking them to cheer as they name their hometowns.

65. Lin, showing that Junia (16:7) was an apostle despite arguments to the contrary, argues that, since Paul was less known to Rome's ἐκκλησία, Paul's greetings are meant to establish and confirm his status and credibility to the rest of the audience—certainly not those whom he greets (since the wo/men in Rome's ἐκκλησία would already know them and their prominence). She writes, "With regard to the first point, that Paul would not ingratiate himself with a prominent apostle, it seems rather that he is ingratiating himself by aligning prominent apostles with *him*" (Lin, "Junia," 201, see further 200–208). (Of course, we do not know what wo/men like Junia would have said about Paul when/if others in the ἐκκλησία checked his references.)

66. D'Angelo, "Women Partners in the New Testament," 68. The other pairs she discusses are Martha/Mary in Luke 10:38–42 and John 11–12 and Euodia and Syntyche in Phil 4:1–2.

missionary couples offered some women Christ-followers a marriage-like bond that made space for their sexual desires.[67]

The queerness of these missionary bonds does not have to involve sexual activity. "For such women," writes D'Angelo, "partnership in the mission would have consecrated female friendship as a means to supply the support, protection and intimacy lost in the disruption of familial bonds and the rejection of marriage."[68] Upholding the bonds and intimacies of wo/men's friendships does not require dismissing these wo/men as just friends in a way that associates friendship with nonsexual intimacy and romance with sexual activity. Such an association enforces artificial and problematic divisions between friendship and romance. Some of these wo/men may be homoromantic asexuals while others might be an ancient parallel to friends with benefits, either of which could offer forms of the "support, protection and intimacy" idealized within marriage bonds. If Schüssler Fiorenza calls the glimpse that Rom 16 gives us into wo/men's engagement and leadership in these ἐκκλησίαι the "tip of an iceberg," this small glimpse we get into queer wo/men's engagement and leadership presents us, according to D'Angelo, "the tip of a very deeply submerged iceberg."[69] Despite this deep submersion, Tryphaena and Tryphosa offer the glimpsing reminder that queer wo/men were there.[70]

The Greek origin of Tryphosa's and Tryphaena's names offer evidence of status differences among Rome's Christ-followers. D'Angelo places their coupling alongside a funerary relief (which Brooten first cited as evidence of artistic representations of female homoeroticism) depicting two women with Greek names (Eleusis and Helena) who are depicted shaking hands (a gesture typically associated with Roman marriage vows).[71] Since "bearers

---

67. D'Angelo, "Women Partners in the New Testament," 68, 73, 82–83.

68. D'Angelo, "Women Partners in the New Testament," 83.

69. Schüssler Fiorenza, "Missionaries, Apostles, Coworkers," 423; D'Angelo, "Women Partners in the New Testament," 85.

70. Marchal draws from D'Angelo's work on Tryphaena and Tryphosa to look at the wo/men of Rom 16 (especially those who likely bore the traumas of enslavement) and consider their "look from the bottom" in conversation with Paul's (Roma-normative) sexual ideologies (Marchal, "Bottoming Out," 230–32). Hanks also draws attention to how the wo/men of Rom 16 were "overwhelmingly sexual minorities," noting that very few were married couples (and even those couples might be "gender-benders") (Hanks, "Romans," 583–84, see also 604–5).

71. D'Angelo, "Women Partners in the New Testament," 68–71, 75; Brooten, *Love between Women*, 59–60. Christy Cobb beautifully brings the "queer materials" of Ele-

of Greek names in first century Rome were mostly descendants of slaves," it is "most probable" that these women "have a slavery background."[72] In the case of the relief, this background is certain, since its inscription indicates that Eleusis and Helena are Roman freedwomen. Considering Rom 16 through the lens of this relief, D'Angelo notes that Tryphaena and Tryphosa's familial association could have begun when they were enslaved within the same Roman *familia* and that they could have maintained a familial bond as *conlibertini* "as an aid to work and life."[73]

Tryphaena and Tryphosa are not the only names indicating some of the wo/men in Rome's ἐκκλησία were or had been enslaved. Analyzing the backgrounds of these names, Lampe notes most of them indicate lower socioeconomic status, and many of the names frequently occur in populations who were enslaved and formerly enslaved (having freedperson status according to Rome).[74] Lampe includes Junia (16:7), Ampliatus (16:8), Persis (16:12), Hermes (16:14), Julia (16:15), and Nereus (16:15) among those most likely to indicate enslavement at some point in the person's life.[75] He concludes that at least nine (and likely more) names have origins in Roman slavery.[76] Those whose names carry the possible associations with Roman slavery were also more likely to be poorer in socioeconomic terms, since many freedpersons were legally and economically dependent on their former enslavers' patronage.[77] Finally, Paul greets some who had never been enslaved, since a few of the names, including Prisca, Aquila, Urbanus (16:9), and Rufus (16:13), do not have any associations with slav-

---

usis and Helena to life through her own "homohistorical" imagination. See Christy Cobb, "A Voice after Death: Gender, Class, and Sexuality on Ancient Funerary Monuments" (paper presented at the Annual Meeting of the Society of Biblical Literature, San Diego, CA, 25 November 2019).

72. Lampe, *From Paul to Valentinus*, 171, 183.

73. D'Angelo, "Women Partners in the New Testament," 75.

74. Lampe, *From Paul to Valentinus*, 170–83.

75. Lampe, *From Paul to Valentinus*, 183. With Junia, Fox calls further attention to her imprisonment with Paul and Andronicus and reconstructs the particular ways that her gender—in addition to her low, possibly enslaved status—would have made prison a far more dangerous place for her (Fox, "Decentering Paul, Contextualizing Crimes," 44–47).

76. Lampe, *From Paul to Valentinus*, 182–83.

77. Although we must be wary of automatically associating all freedpersons with poverty, since some did accrue wealth and elevated social status. The status and citizenship of freedpersons will be considered more in the next chapter.

ery. Paul's greetings blend all of these names together, suggesting that he is not grouping them based on these status associations. Romans 16 shows how people with different statuses (according to Roman social distinctions) and with implicitly different degrees of poverty and wealth (though largely poor and relatively not wealthy) assembled in and were active in leading Rome's ἐκκλησία.[78]

Romans 16 also attests to ethnic differences. Most names do not bear traces of Roman heritage or citizenship, and many derive from Greek and other more eastern territories. Most of the assembly would have been noncitizen Roman ἔθνη.[79] Several names of Roman origin were created by Roman enslavers and given to the wo/men they enslaved, including Ampliatus, Nereus, and Persis, which means these wo/men could have come from any of the ἔθνη Rome conquered.[80] While a few names attest to Jewish background, it seems most of the wo/men were non-Jews.[81] It is reasonable to assume—as many commentators do—that Paul's letter to Rome was largely addressed to a non-Jewish audience of ἔθνη, in both the Jewish and Roman senses of the term.[82] However, as Stowers emphasizes,

---

78. Schüssler Fiorenza, "Missionaries, Apostles, Coworkers," 427–28; Friesen, "Poverty in Pauline Studies."

79. Lampe assesses the ethnic background of the names in Romans and concludes that at least half are clearly immigrants of eastern origin; however, though the rest could be native to Rome, that is, "autochthon," he is less conclusive on this second point (Lampe, *From Paul to Valentinus*, 167–70). Indeed, names that seem autochthonous may just be more native in the sense of belonging to persons whose families migrated several generations prior and eventually adopted more Roman names despite not being citizens or natives.

80. Lampe, *From Paul to Valentinus*, 174–75.

81. Lampe argues that three wo/men are Jews: Andronicus, Junia, and Herodion, based on Paul's designation of them as τοὺς συγγενεῖς μου ("my kinsfolk"). The remainder of those named are likely gentiles—presumably with the exception of Aquila (whom Acts 18:2 identifies as Jewish) and Prisca. He notes three names (Rufus, Julia, Mary/Maria) are attested in inscriptions of Jews in the city of Rome and two more (Andronicus, Tryphaena) when looking at evidence beyond the city, but these names are also typically Latin and are also attested among non-Jews (Lampe, *From Paul to Valentinus*, 74–75).

82. The question of the Jewish make-up of Rome's ἐκκλησία is hotly debated. The evidence within the letter makes clear that there were Jews present in the assembly to whom Paul wrote; however, based upon its content and Paul's self-appellation as "apostle to the gentiles," gentiles seem to be the letter's main audience. While Paul's letters to other communities make clear that questions about Judaism were contested,

this is Paul's *intended audience*.[83] Although his letter addresses the situation of non-Jewish Christ-followers in Rome, this does not mean he did not know that Jews were included within his *actual audience*, even if the theology and ethics in his letter do not directly pertain to them.[84] It also does not mean these Jewish wo/men—alongside their gentile companions—did not indicate their agreement or disagreement with Paul's views or express their own theological and ethical ideas and practices.

there is no reason to assume such contestation in Rome—at least as the *only* possibility, even if Paul's letter may appear to assume these conflicts based on his past experience. My own interpretation, then, follows the more radical version of the new perspective on Paul that carries forward the implications of Krister Stendahl, "The Apostle Paul and the Introspective Conscience of the West," *HTR* 56 (1963): 199–215. This radical perspective emphasizes that Paul—in terms of his intended audience (as well as, likely, the majorities of his actual audiences)—was writing to *gentiles* about following Christ, and he was not concerned with spreading this gospel to other Jews. Indeed, as scholars such as Stowers, John G. Gager, Lloyd Gaston, and Pamela Eisenbaum emphasize, Paul sees *two ways* to God's justice/salvation, one for Jews (through the laws, traditions, and faith of Israel) and one for gentiles (made possible through Christ and implied in following him). Paul does not say that Jews cannot follow Christ, but he does not believe Jews *need* to follow Christ in order to participate in God's justice/salvation. See Stowers, *Rereading of Romans*; Lloyd Gaston, *Paul and the Torah* (Vancouver: University of British Columbia Press, 1997); John G. Gager, *Reinventing Paul* (Oxford: Oxford University Press, 2000); Pamela Eisenbaum, *Paul Was Not a Christian: The Original Message of a Misunderstood Apostle* (San Francisco: HarperOne, 2009); Eisenbaum, "Jewish Perspectives: A *Jewish* Apostles to the Gentiles," in *Studying Paul's Letters: Contemporary Perspectives and Methods*, ed. Joseph A. Marchal (Minneapolis: Fortress, 2012), 135–53. On Paul's intended *gentile* audience in Romans, see, in addition to Stowers, A. Andrew Das, *Solving the Romans Debate* (Minneapolis: Fortress, 2007); Das, "The Gentile-Encoded Audience of Romans: The Church outside the Synagogue," in *Reading Paul's Letter to the Romans*, ed. Jerry L. Sumney (Atlanta: Society of Biblical Literature, 2012), 29–46; Ben Witherington III with Darlene Hyatt, *Paul's Letter to the Romans: A Socio-Rhetorical Commentary* (Grand Rapids: Eerdmans, 2004), 7–8. Mark D. Nanos agrees that gentiles are Paul intended audience, but he asserts they are meeting in the synagogue. See Mark D. Nanos, *The Mystery of Romans: The Jewish Context of Paul's Letter* (Minneapolis: Fortress, 1996); Nanos, "To the Churches within the Synagogues of Rome," in *Reading Paul's Letter to the Romans*, ed. Jerry L. Sumney (Atlanta: Society of Biblical Literature, 2012), 11–28.

83. Stowers details this in terms of Paul's "encoded audience" (*Rereading of Romans*, 21–33). Ultimately, as Stowers argues, "Romans tries to clarify for gentile followers of Christ their relations to law, Jews, and Judaism and the current place of both Jews and gentiles in God's plan through Jesus Christ" (*Rereading of Romans*, 36).

84. Stowers, *Rereading of Romans*, 29–30.

The greetings of Rom 16 offer textual insights that help us specify the different wo/men who would have heard Paul's letter and engaged, questioned, debated, and ignored its ideas together as an assembly. Material culture from first-century Rome affirms how queer wo/men were not unique to Rome's ἐκκλησία. This evidence helps us imagine additional sensations these wo/men experienced as some among many queer wo/men inhabiting the city of Rome.

First-century remains consistently make evident that women inhabited almost every space in Roman cities, in Italy and throughout Rome's imperial dominion.[85] Pompeiian graffiti affirm that wo/men were active

---

85. "*Wo/men were there*," Johnson-DeBaufre recounts her students exclaiming when they see just how apparent the fact is in the archaeological remnants she visits with them. See Melanie Johnson-DeBaufre, "'Gazing upon the Invisible': Archaeology, Historiography, and the Elusive Wo/men of 1 Thessalonians," in *From Roman to Early Christian Thessalonikē*, ed. Laura Nasrallah, Charalambos Bakirtzis, and Steven J. Friesen (Cambridge: Harvard University Press, 2010), 73. Wo/men's obvious visibility is more often downplayed and rendered invisible by biblical scholarship (Johnson-DeBaufre, "Gazing upon the Invisible," 83–92). When women are named or specified in texts, they are frequently assumed to be exceptions that prove the rule of women's absence among Christ-followers or exceptionally present among Christ-followers in ways that could not occur in wider, patriarchal Roman society. Similarly, when interpreters appeal to material evidence, women's archaeological presence is cast as an anomaly: when women *are* visible, it must be because these spaces were (exclusively) *for* women. Women are deemed absent and silent unless reliably proven otherwise (Johnson-DeBaufre, "Gazing upon the Invisible," 92–103). Archaeological invisibility influences the interpretation and translation of texts that affirm women's active presence, whether when claiming that only men gathered and participated in Thessalonikē's ἐκκλησία or when Junia, whom Paul names as being "distinguished among the ambassadors" (οἵτινές εἰσιν ἐπίσημοι ἐν τοῖς ἀποστόλοις) along with her partner Andronicus (16:7), was unquestionably taken to be Junias (a textual variant) until Brooten proved Junia to almost certainly be the original name. See Bernadette J. Brooten, "Junia … Outstanding among the Apostles," in *Women Priests: A Catholic Commentary on the Vatican Declaration*, ed. Leonard Swidler and Arlene Swidler (New York: Paulist, 1977), 141–44. This interpretive erasure, justified by androcentric assumptions, defies not only the textual evidence of Rom 16 but also the archaeological evidence from first-century Rome. Despite Brooten's definitive evidence and argument that Paul names Junia in Rom 16:7, androcentric bias remains central to discussion of Rom 16:7. Lin discusses how, after they (finally and begrudgingly) accepted Junia as a woman, male scholars challenged her leadership role, claiming that she (and Andronicus, by association) was not actually an apostle, arguing she is distinguished *by* the apostles rather than among them. Lin definitively debunks the grammatical/lexical acrobatics of these arguments and then argues (convincingly) that rhetorically,

in city life, assembling in houses, serving in *tabernae*, and keeping shops. Enslaved wo/men certainly would have been moving throughout these cities, and they would have met other enslaved wo/men as they did. Some of these wo/men left their marks on the spaces they inhabited and moved through. Rebecca Benefiel notes that Pompeii's "active graffiti culture" offers visible transcripts of first-century conversations, many of which involved wo/men.[86] Wo/men greeted one another and conversed within the House of the Four Styles: "its graffiti thus tells the story of women gathering together, of someone learning to draw a boat, and about the act of inscribing graffiti as a social activity in the central and most visible spaces of the home."[87] These remnants make obvious wo/men's visible and active presence in first-century spaces and emphasize the ways they interacted and conversed with other wo/men. These varied interactions raise new possibilities for reconstructing ways the wo/men of Rome's ἐκκλησία (who also assembled in and moved through houses) could have interacted with one another.

When archaeology approaches sex and sexuality, sexuality is only materially visible if it is depicted in painting, sculpture, or graffiti just as it is only textually apparent when it deviates. As Brooten and others uncover, textual depictions of sexual deviancy and depravity indicate the practices in question likely occurred often enough to require regulation and castigation. The material evidence of graffiti confirms the existence and frequency of these terms of practices beyond the bounds of the more elite authors whose writings and ideas survive.[88] However, presentations of material culture portray first-century sexual spaces and remnants as separate from the rest of society, treating the evidence of sexuality as an

---

Paul would name Junia's distinction among the apostles not to confirm *her* status but *his* (Lin, "Junia"). On Junia in Rom 16 and her role in Rome's ἐκκλησία, see also Eldon Jay Epp, *Junia: The First Woman Apostle* (Minneapolis: Fortress, 2005); Fox, "Decentering Paul, Contextualizing Crimes," 44–47.

86. Rebecca R. Benefiel, "Dialogues of Graffiti in the House of the Four Styles at Pompeii (*Casa Dei Quattro Stili*, 1.8.17, 11)," in *Ancient Graffiti in Context*, ed. Jennifer A. Baird and Claire Taylor (New York: Routledge, 2011), 38–39.

87. Benefiel, "Dialogues of Graffiti," 21.

88. See especially discussions of nonelite sexuality and the material evidence of its practice in John R. Clarke, *Looking at Lovemaking: Constructions of Sexuality in Roman Art 100 B.C–A.D. 250* (Berkeley: University of California Press, 1998) (including discussions of its relation to elite regulations and its socio-sexual-political hierarchy).

anomaly.[89] Many spaces are deemed sexualized because they contain erotic artwork (and occasionally graffiti), but any room, any street corner, any nook or cranny could have been used sexually.

Just as wo/men's presence does not simply occur when women are mentioned, depiction of sexuality does not itself indicate practice. Sexual-

---

89. Nowhere is this more apparent than in the material evidence from Pompeii, one of the best sources of material evidence for first-century Rome/Italy, given its more reliable preservation. Largely a result of religious prudery, most of the sexual images and artifacts from Pompeii have been removed from their original location and relegated to a single "Secret Cabinet/Museum" (the "Gabinetto Segreto" in Italian: an important phrase to know, as it is otherwise difficult to find, if one now desires to see this evidence). Not only does this mean an archaeologist/scholar (such as myself) cannot view the imagery *in situ* to consider for oneself how it might have affected the space, but it also fetishizes sexuality in Pompeii, making it exceptionally excessive in the minds of scholars and tourists alike—when more than likely, Pompeiians were no more sexually brazen than other Roman inhabitants (we just happen to actually have some of their sexual artifacts). To see the truth of this, one need spend only thirty minutes in the Secret Cabinet to hear the giggles and gaga of enthralled tourists marveling at this rare glimpse of Roman sexuality. Indeed, one frequently hears the cry of the tour guide perpetuating the uniqueness and separability of Pompeiian sexuality: "Pompeiians were much more brazen and overt about their sexual pursuits than the more refined residents of Herculaneum" (or something similar with the same effective yet unsubstantiated implication). Beyond the assumption of sexuality as relegated to secret spaces, constantly reinforced by archaeological displays and reconstructions, the definition of sexual evidence encompasses very contemporary (or perhaps dated modern) notions of what is sexual. While perhaps every appearance of a giant phallus needs to be separated from view (if one worries about petite impressionable minds seeing such anomalous human anatomy), there is no evidence such depictions had sexual meanings within Roman culture. Additionally, the racial and racist dimensions of excessive Roman sexuality are not discussed: images of pygmies engaged in all manners of brazen sexual practice in public—part of stock images within many elite Roman homes—are likewise displayed as evidence of Roman sexuality at large, in ways that are totally different from current social mores. In fact, these images support the notion of racism in antiquity, showing how non-Roman, especially African, bodies are commonly portrayed as sexually immoderate. These images function less as erotica and more as elite justification of conquest based on the stereotyping of barbarians as unable to rule themselves or conform to Roman mores. Much of this analysis is determined by my own time spent analyzing these depictions and attempting to think with them *in situ* during my own research in Pompeii in September 2015. See also Clarke, *Looking at Lovemaking*, where the Pompeiian evidence is frequently discussed. For using Pompeiian evidence to read Romans, see Oakes, *Reading Romans in Pompeii*.

ity and gender were experienced and embodied everywhere and anywhere. Given the evidence of its diverse existence, it is equally important to insist that it did. *Queer wo/men were there*, and this includes ancient iterations of bi, lesbian, gay, ace, intersex, trans, pan, and poly folks alongside some straight Romosexuals.[90] Wo/men loved, and they loved differently and for different reasons. Even when they may also have been forced to submit and conform to Romosexuality, wo/men practiced and preferred sexual acts differently, in ways that conformed to and deviated from the compulsory Roman sexual hierarchy.[91]

When we look beyond the tightly contained materials stereotypically deemed erotic, wo/men's sexuality emerges in many different forms. As D'Angelo shows, funerary reliefs could depict women like Eleusis and Helena gesturing a marital bond that indicates loving and intimate associations between these two women.[92] The relief is located with enough proximity to Rome to provide evidence that affirms queer wo/men's presence and ability to visibly exist (even if not "out," i.e., openly queer) and affirm their relationships.[93] Thus, D'Angelo can read Rom 16 alongside this relief in order to plausibly bring Tryphaena and Tryphosa to life.[94] Since the remains of Pompeii offer a similar proximity, evidence of Pompeiian queer wo/men—such as the graffiti discussed in chapter 1 under "Romans' Sexualities"—can further add plausibility to reconstructions of

---

90. As verified by examples in Brooten, *Love between Women*, 29–186. These queers, broadly speaking, likely thought and looked different in their differing contexts, but they bear continuous resemblances, *strikingly similar in their affect*, with contemporary and other historical queernesses. Though my own arguments and distinctions may differ in certain methods and articulations, they carry the same sociopolitical impulses and concerns that drive works such as Brooten's, as well as that of other LGBTIA2Q+ biblical interpreters, who find import in identifying the ways in which queer bodies have always been present and resistant within biblical texts and their interpretation. See, as major examples, Nancy Wilson, *Our Tribe: Queer Folks, God, Jesus, and the Bible* (San Francisco: HarperSanFrancisco, 1995); Robert E. Goss and Mona West, eds., *Take Back the Word: A Queer Reading of the Bible* (Cleveland: Pilgrim, 2000); Deryn Guest et al., eds., *The Queer Bible Commentary* (London: SCM, 2006).

91. Following Brooten's insistence in *Love between Women*, esp. 359–62.

92. D'Angelo, "Women Partners in the New Testament," 68–72.

93. Queer folks throughout history have been able to creatively embody visual existence while not being fully out, taking advantage of how heteronormativity only sees the norm it craves.

94. D'Angelo, "Women Partners in the New Testament," 75.

the queerness of Rome's ἐκκλησία. The lovesick woman who inscribed the poem longing for her *pupula* ("darling girl") on the entryway to her house could furnish it with a queerness designed to reorient the typical Romosexual orientation of the *domus*.[95] As the wo/men of the House of the Four Styles remind us how wo/men interacted in Roman spaces, this smaller *domus* helps us brings to life how queer wo/men interacted in such spaces in ways that offer us parallels to consider among the queer wo/men Christ-followers of Rome.

The trend of archaeological invisibility extends to enslaved wo/men. Like elite texts, Roman material objects were possessed in greater quantity by wealthy, elite men and their families, and Romans constructed spaces so that their architecture drew attention toward elite men and kept enslaved wo/men out of sight.[96] Archaeologists (and their funding sources) have frequently prioritized the material remains of elite households that are most opulent. They discuss spaces in ways that reconstruct the views based on what elite men wanted to be seen.[97] Katherine A. Shaner argues, "Just as most ancient texts about women reflect an androcentric perspective, so do literary and archaeological materials about enslaved persons reflect slaveholding perspectives."[98] Enslaved wo/men remain unseen in these materials, even though they almost certainly held them, cleaned them, and used them when working for their enslavers. As Sandra Joshel and Laura Hackworth Peterson show, enslaved wo/men developed tactics to take advantage of the corners, corridors, and spaces that were beyond sight lines of elite viewers. While archaeologists are trained to follow elite sight lines through the front doors and into the most opulent rooms, Joshel

---

95. I develop this argument in full detail in James N. Hoke, "Orienting the *Domus*: Queer Materials and ἐκκλησίαι in Rome" (paper presented at the Annual Meeting of the Society of Biblical Literature, San Diego, CA, 25 November 2019). We can only speculate on whether the author resided in this house, but calling it *her* house names the fact that she has taken ownership of, at least, this single interior space and reminds readers that women could and did take ownership over homes.

96. Joshel and Peterson discuss "master strategies" that control and silence enslaved persons, but they emphasize that "slave tactics" develop alongside and within these strategies, especially from outside of enslavers' sight lines. See Sandra R. Joshel and Lauren Hackworth Peterson, *The Material Lives of Roman Slaves* (Cambridge: Cambridge University Press, 2014), esp. 8–17.

97. "Indeed, modern authors often repeat ancient silences" (Joshel and Peterson, *Material Lives*, 33).

98. Shaner, *Enslaved Leadership*, xiv.

and Peterson point out that most of these buildings have backdoors, leading to alleyways, which enslaved wo/men would have traveled through to do their work.[99] In these spaces, outside of their enslavers' view, wo/men could interact, take a break, delay completing their work, and resist the strategies of control that were imposed upon them.[100]

The material lives and presence of enslaved wo/men remind us they were active in Roman society, despite the dehumanizing limitations and brutal conditions imposed upon them. Since wo/men who were or had been enslaved are named as leaders in Rom 16, it is clear that slavery did not prevent Christ-followers from leadership in Rome's ἐκκλησία. The enslaved participants in Rome's ἐκκλησία were some among many enslaved wo/men who actively shaped Rome's streets, houses, marketplaces, shops, and public buildings and who participated leading roles in Roman associations.

Just as enslaved wo/men were present and active in all areas and aspects of city life, religious cults and other associations in Rome depended on enslaved leadership and labor to function, and many enslaved wo/men participated (willingly and unwillingly) in religious activities.[101] Shaner illustrates how this provides context for enslaved participation and leadership in early Christianity, especially by considering first-century inscriptions from Ephesos. In particular, a decree of Paullus Fabius Persicus, Ephesos's proconsul from 44 to 45 CE, regulated changes for the leadership and financial practices of the city's Artemis cult, including specific limitations for the roles for enslaved persons. Emphasizing that

---

99. "In this regard, the back doors of houses are the material spaces of slave life, spaces where they could disrupt the owner's choreography within, by avoiding the cleaning of a room or the moving of furniture while the owner was otherwise preoccupied. They were what we might call the spaces of a backdoor culture of Roman houses" (Joshel and Peterson, *Material Lives*, 99, see further 87–117, ch. 3, "Slaves in the City Streets"). Shaner similarly discusses such "containment strategies for keeping enslaved persons both out of the way and on display" within Roman houses (*Enslaved Leadership*, 20).

100. In similar ways to Joshel and Peterson, Sarah Levin-Richardson considers tactics of enslaved women in Pompeii's purpose-built brothel. See Sarah Levin-Richardson, *The Brothel of Pompeii: Sex, Class, and Gender at the Margins of Roman Society* (Cambridge: Cambridge University Press, 2019), 111–28.

101. In Ephesos, inscriptions that publicly named benefactors included the names of enslaved wo/men and freedpersons, both as individual donors and as being enslaved members of a household of donors. See Shaner, *Enslaved Leadership*, 6–9.

enslaved persons must remain in subordinate roles within the temple in order to reflect the kyriarchal order of Rome, Persicus demanded that enslaved persons only inhabit roles and perform tasks designed for enslaved persons, leaving other more prestigious roles (e.g., priesthoods) for free persons.[102] Persicus's decree attempts to shift practice and make leadership roles more kyriarchally distinct than they were in the lived reality of first-century Ephesos.[103] Enslaved persons could *and did* hold leadership roles and priesthoods in the Roman world, and these leadership roles could enable some enslaved wo/men to gain a degree of power and additional wealth and prestige, including access to "privileged seating for enslaved priests" within Ephesos's theater.[104]

Shaner's analysis affirms the reality of enslaved wo/men's presence throughout Rome, including in religious associations, while acknowledging how lived realities always contain ambiguities and tensions.[105] While Roman kyriarchy consistently asserted and reasserted itself and structured the daily lives and practices of all Romans (enslaved or not), its control was never complete (thus requiring its reassertion).[106] Romans could and did deviate from prescribed norms while simultaneously maintaining their social distinctions. These ambiguous tensions could help explain the implicit distinctions Paul makes between enslaved and free participants in the ἐκκλησίαι he addresses, including the fact that, in Rom 16, Paul attributes the status of συνεργός ("coworker") only to the people whose names indicate they had never been enslaved (specifically, Aquila, Prisca, and Urbanus).[107]

By placing the enslaved wo/men of Rom 16 alongside material evidence, we see the status and socioeconomic differences, tensions, and ambigui-

---

102. Shaner, *Enslaved Leadership*, 23–24, 31–37.

103. "He would not need to make such arguments and implications, however, if the actual practices in Ephesos matched this rhetoric. Instead, actual practices left an ambiguity in the distinctions between slave/free status and roles in the cult" (Shaner, *Enslaved Leadership*, 36).

104. Shaner, *Enslaved Leadership*, 28–29.

105. "Reframing our historical inquiry to allow for the possibility that enslaved persons were priests, religious specialists, and cultic leaders gives a richer picture of ancient religious practices, one that accommodates existing evidence more fully" (Shaner, *Enslaved Leadership*, 40).

106. Shaner, *Enslaved Leadership*, 26–29.

107. Lampe notes this distinction and inquires, "Is their being a 'συνεργός' connected with their origin as free persons?" (*From Paul to Valentinus*, 183).

ties that the slash in *wo/men* emphasizes. This continues to bring to life the different ways in which *queer wo/men were there* in Rome and Rome's ἐκκλησία. These enlivened queer wo/men take us beyond Paul's words.

Bringing Queer Wo/men to Life: Assemblages and the First Century

Queer wo/men were there. We cannot stop coming back to this refrain: representation matters. But a song is more than its refrain; it is more than its words, rhythm, meter, notes. It is how all these elements interact; it is what the song *does*.[108] Feminist and queer theorizations of assemblages move beyond representation, but this does not mean they do not continue emphasizing representation's refrains. Bringing assemblages to the queer wo/men of first-century Rome allows us to affirm *how* queer wo/men were there; to proliferate plausible ways they interacted, things they said, things they did, their relations to objects and spaces, the movements that occurred in between them. Queer wo/men were there. Assemblages help us *bring them to life*.

In the following pages, I explain how my rendering of assemblages can continue bringing to life the queer wo/men Christ-followers who assembled in Rome's ἐκκλησία (in addition to many other ἐκκλησίαι). First, I develop ἐκκλησία-1 assemblages, a notion that foregrounds the interactions between bodies, forces, feelings, ideas, and sensations in, around, and as a result of these gatherings. Next, I discuss how kyriarchy operates as an assemblage, one that can overlap and converge with an ἐκκλησία-1 assemblage. I then show how ἐκκλησία-1 assemblages help us bring first-century queer wo/men to life by building up from the postholes we find when reading Romans.

ἐκκλησία-1 Assemblages

Assemblages are porous conglomerations (*assemblies*) of human and non-human bodies, sensations, and forces that are always in flux: individually,

---

108. On sensing rhythm and musical orality to hear the Samson narrative in conversation with both theories of affect and assemblage, see A. Paige Rawson, "Reading (with) Rhythm for the Sake of the (I-n-)Islands: A Rastafarian Interpretation of Samson as Ambi(val)ent Affective Assemblage," in *Religion, Emotion, Sensation: Affect Theories and Theologies*, ed. Karen Bray and Stephen D. Moore, TTC (New York: Fordham University Press, 2019), 126–44.

grouped, or collectively moving, bumping, stopping, shifting, oozing, flashing. These bodies—singular or plural, loosely defined, and certainly not exclusively human or even organic/living—inevitably group and regroup (and participate in multiple, simultaneous groupings) as they form numerous networks.[109] Assemblages, Puar writes, let us "move from What does this body mean? to What and who does this body affect? What does this body do?"[110] Assemblages impact experience and perception on individual and sociopolitical levels. They catch how identities are always mobile; they shift and are produced in and through our relations to other bodies and forces; they attune to some, repel others, and awkwardly sit alongside a few. They morph over time and in different spaces. Assemblages help capture the difficulties and gridlocks that occur when moving toward a fully intersectional vision.

Rome's ἐκκλησία was a "community of belonging" that can be thought of as an assemblage.[111] More than an assembly (ἐκκλησία) of human bodies, ἐκκλησία-l assemblage highlights the gatherings, minglings, and dispersions of Christ-followers' bodies; their voices, silences, ideas, and feelings; objects, creatures, plants, breezes; and the myriad forces and sensations that could move in between these always-changing groupings. My invocation of ἐκκλησία-l assemblage develops the ways feminist and queer assemblages prioritize affective belonging, multiplicity and proliferation, and the tensions and dynamics of change that can be both promising and threatening, utopian and dystopian. ἐκκλησία-l assemblage makes it possible not only

---

109. As they do, identity and power are produced as two effects of these networked interactions. See Jasbir K. Puar, *Terrorist Assemblages: Homonationalism in Queer Times*, NW (Durham, NC: Duke University Press, 2007), 215.

110. Puar, *Terrorist Assemblages*, 172.

111. My notion of this ἐκκλησία-l assemblage picks up on Marchal's denotation of the ἐκκλησία as an "eccentric assemblage" of bodies, especially as described in Joseph A. Marchal, "'Making History' Queerly: Touches across Time through a Biblical Behind," *BibInt* 19 (2011): 393–94; see also Marchal, "Bio-Necro-*Biblio*-Politics: Restaging Feminist Intersections and Queer Exceptions," *CultRel* 15 (2014): 170–71. Maia Kotrosits notes how "*assemblage* bears more than a minor resemblance to the meaning of the word *ekklēsia*" (*Rethinking Early Christian Identity: Affect, Violence, and Belonging* [Minneapolis: Fortress, 2015], 57, see further 56–58). I begin to develop this notion in James N. Hoke, "Unbinding Imperial Time: Chrononormativity and Paul's Letter to the Romans," in *Sexual Disorientations: Queer Temporalities, Affects, Theologies*, ed. Kent L. Brintnall, Joseph A. Marchal, and Stephen D. Moore, TTC (New York: Fordham University Press, 2018), 76–83.

to see these queer wo/men but also to hear, feel, sense, and smell them—to bring them to life with multiple, contradictory proliferations.

Feminist and queer theorizations of assemblages offer affective models that embrace such complex and contradictory plausibilities.[112] An event, issue, text, or moment can have two seemingly opposite narratives that emphasize different meanings or crossings with respect to gender or sexuality, or both.[113] Biddy Martin insists that queer and feminist politics must

------

112. Multiplicity and change—that is, the imagination of *infinite* possibilities, given bodies' unbound capacity for interaction—characterize assemblage. The conception of *assemblage*, as a term denoting "affective conglomerations," originates from the work of Gilles Deleuze and Felix Guattari, but the term has since expanded into a life of its own as feminist and queer theorists have developed and deployed it. In their original formulation, Deleuze and Guattari write, "An assemblage is precisely this increase in the dimensions of *a multiplicity that necessarily changes in nature* as it expands its connections. There are no points or positions.... There are only lines" (*A Thousand Plateaus: Capitalism and Schizophrenia*, trans. Brian Massumi [Minneapolis: University of Minnesota Press, 1987], 8, emphasis added). Also quoted in Puar, *Terrorist* Assemblages, 212. See further Deleuze and Guattari, *A Thousand Plateaus*, 8–9, 88–91. This idea of assemblages as "affective conglomerations" draws from Puar's development of assemblages (*Terrorist Assemblages*, 211). This development relies on Deleuze and Guattari's theories but employs it in ways that give them increased capacities for affective change within politics related to the meetings and differences of identities. The limited engagement in this project with Deleuze/Guattari (largely limited to footnotes) is due to the fact that these ideas of assemblage, while rooted in their original conception, have exceeded their idea in ways that are far more interesting and beneficial for queer and feminist thought but that ultimately have transformed the original theories in ways that make them differ enough to refer directly to these theorists (i.e., Puar in particular) and their conceptions of affect and assemblage. On the issue of orthodox Deleuzianism and its productive reframing in a more heterodox form, see the discussion in Alexander G. Weheliye, *Habeas Viscus: Racializing Assemblages, Biopolitics, and Black Feminist Theories of the Human* (Durham, NC: Duke University Press, 2014), 47–48. In addition to Puar's rearticulations of assemblages, Weheliye includes among these heterodoxies Rosi Braidotti, *Metamorphoses: Towards a Materialist Theory of Becoming* (Boston: Polity, 2002); Kara Keeling, *The Witch's Flight: The Cinematic, the Black Femme, and the Image of Common Sense*, PM (Durham: Duke University Press, 2007); Manuel DeLanda, *A New Philosophy of Society: Assemblage Theory and Social Complexity* (New York: Continuum, 2006). See also Elizabeth Grosz, *Becoming Undone: Darwinian Reflections on Life, Politics, and Art* (Durham, NC: Duke University Press, 2011); Manuel DeLanda, *Assemblage Theory* (Edinburgh: Edinburgh University Press, 2016).

113. Biddy Martin, "Sexualities without Genders and Other Queer Utopias," *Diacritics* 24 (1994): 112. As in her essay on extraordinary homosexuals ("Extraordinary

be able to "imagine both possibilities."[114] Feminism and queerness should imagine multiple possibilities (some of which may contradict) in ways that hold bodies in tension while also expanding and including more, and always different, bodies, forces, and sensations within their wider view.

Assemblages *proliferate* possibilities.[115] This proliferation makes room for the many contradictory tensions Martin identifies within feminism's and queerness's overlapping movements and allows their tensions to be both threat *and* promise. They allow us to suggest and elaborate multiple and divergent identities, ideologies, and interpretations and discover the myriad ways they interact with one another. Such proliferation encourages

---

Homosexuals and the Fear of Being Ordinary," in *Feminism Meets Queer Theory*, ed. Elizabeth Weed and Naomi Schor [Bloomington: Indiana University Press, 1997], 109–135), Martin intervenes in the trend to separate the analytical work and foci of queer theory and feminism, which often separates their objects of analysis (queer theory studies sex; feminism studies gender).

114. Martin, "Sexualities without Genders," 112. On this particular point, she discusses two possible interpretations of the murder of Venus Xtravaganza in *Paris Is Burning*, with specific reference to that found in Judith Butler, *Bodies That Matter: On the Discursive Limits of "Sex"* (Routledge: New York, 1993), 121–40 (ch. 4 "Gender is Burning: Questions of Appropriation and Subversion").

115. See Puar, *Terrorist Assemblages*, 205–11. My rendering of assemblage draws heaviest inspiration from Puar. It also takes inspiration from the work of Elizabeth Grosz. Grosz's corporeal feminism accounts for the complexity of bodies not only as gendered, racialized, sexualized, and classed entities but also as complex organisms in which all of these factors (and more) combine and interact in a dynamic ebb and flow. This compels her move to assemblages as a way to envision contradictory and volatile interactions in between bodies. See Elizabeth Grosz, *Volatile Bodies: Toward a Corporeal Feminism* (Bloomington: Indiana University Press, 1994), esp. vii–xiii, 13–24. Grosz also considers whether and how Deleuze and Guattari's oeuvre relates to feminism, given the problems that she and other feminists have critiqued in the ways their ideas have the potential to erase women. Acknowledging these serious concerns, she draws out pieces of their theories that feminism could work with and expand. This includes the feminist potential of thinking about multiplicity, difference, and desire through the lens of assemblages and their proliferations. See Elizabeth Grosz, "A Thousand Tiny Sexes: Feminism and Rhizomatics," in *Gilles Deleuze and the Theater of Philosophy*, ed. Constantin Boundas and Dorothea Olkowski (New York: Routledge, 1994), 187–210. In terms of race, Arun Saldhana uses assemblages to propose a similar proliferation of race as opposed to an attempt to eliminate race entirely or to quantify it into separable, discrete racial identities. See Arun Saldanha, "Reontologising Race: The Machinic Geography of Phenotype," *Environment and Planning D: Society and Space* 24 (2006): 9–24.

debate—through which more possibilities proliferate—and seeks everything that emerges from these interactions, common grounds as well as disagreements and contradictions. Assemblages lay out a wide but never complete variety of characteristics, feeling, experiences, and interactions—past, present, and possible—that bodies hold in/between them.[116] Forever coming together and separating, they can represent the complexities of feminism, queerness, and their interactions.

Puar emphasizes the multiple, contradictory possibilities held within any assemblage, possibilities that can be promising and threatening. This is evident when Puar considers queerness as an assemblage. Emphasizing queerness's promise, Puar writes, "Queer and gurdwara organizing may open up creative political junctures that are not bound through identity politics but gel instead, in a manner however transitory and contingent, through the politics of affect."[117] These "creative political junctures" make room for positive change and sensations of belonging, transitory though such feelings always are. Yet queerness simultaneously threatens when it is regulatory. There are no simple heroes or villains in an assemblage. Even promising moments of queerness bring unintended changes that cause harm, just as queerness's threatening regulations can occasionally make space for unintended change that positively benefits those it excludes.[118]

Assemblages admit that any identity is but a momentary capture of a body or bodies in flux. They encompass the infinite identities left behind and about to be produced by affect. They are difficult to conceptualize concretely because the descriptions they enable are messier and always

---

116. Puar, *Terrorist Assemblages*, 191–202.

117. Puar, *Terrorist Assemblages*, 202.

118. Assemblages on a more bodily and even microscopic level can also be considered in terms of promises and threats. Although she does not use the term *assemblage*, Denise Kimber Buell's consideration of ontological relationality that urges her "to lean into this *risky, messy interconnectedness* that I cannot avoid so long as I still breathe" certainly gestures toward the interconnections of assemblages and the fact that their scope is far beyond the human. See Denise Kimber Buell, "The Microbe and Pneuma that Therefore I Am," in *Divinanimality: Animal Theory, Creaturely Theology*, ed. Stephen D. Moore, TTC (New York: Fordham University Press, 2014), 87. Her essay reads early Christian texts (especially the Gospel of Thomas along with Gospel of Philip and writings of Irenaeus) alongside the animality of microbes and their promises and threats to the health of humans and the global environment highlights the organic—and inorganic—complexity of forces and bodies, individually or as infinitesimal groupings.

changing. Assemblages complement intersectionality and identity: they do *not* abandon or get over them.[119] Assemblages, Puar notes, point back to Crenshaw's original formulation of intersectionality, which used the image of a traffic intersection: there are many different bodies, gestures, systems, and forces at play in any given moment.[120] In their constant moves and shifts, assemblages capture a process of "becoming-intersectional."[121] Like affect, in a slight shimmer, assemblages move elsewhere; in a new moment or a different position, they sense and are sensed otherwise.[122]

This utopian side-scrambling emphasizes the *beyondness* that Johnson-DeBaufre and Nasrallah urge and that assemblages' affective excess enables. Feminist and queer assemblages *proliferate possibilities*: a thousand tiny microcosms of belonging based in the complex identities and their affective interactions.[123] ἐκκλησία-1 assemblages imaginatively multiply queer

---

119. Ahmed worries how concepts like assemblages can participate in "overing"—a "need to 'get beyond' categories of gender and race" (Ahmed, *On Being Included*, 180). She clarifies, "I am not saying that we need to dismiss these new theoretical vocabularies: we need resources to think differently as we encounter worlds. I am suggesting that the hope invested in new terms can mean *turning away* from social restrictions and blockages with the old terms that we need to move beyond" (181). See further 173–87. I agree with Ahmed's concern with overing, and so it is crucial to emphasize that assemblage help move *forward* and prompt change *in tandem with* identity categories and politics as well as intersectionality.

120. Jasbir K. Puar, "I Would Rather Be a Cyborg Than a Goddess: Becoming-Intersectional in Assemblage Theory," *philoSOPHIA: A Journal of Feminist Continental Philosophy* 2 (2012): 59–60; Kimberlé Crenshaw, "Demarginalizing the Intersection of Race and Sex: A Black Feminist Critique of Antidiscrimination Doctrine, Feminist Theory, and Antiracist Politics," *UCLF* 139 (1989), 149.

121. Puar, "I Would Rather Be a Cyborg."

122. On the idea of shimmers (taken from Roland Barthes) and affect, see Gregory J. Seigworth and Melissa Gregg, "An Inventory of Shimmers," in *The Affect Theory Reader*, ed. Gregg and Seigworth (Durham, NC: Duke University Press, 2010), 10–11.

123. Saldhana thinks about assemblages and emphasizes viscosity and proliferation for thinking about race and the numerous narratives and embodied experiences of race, even as it is socially constructed. "Race should not be eliminated, but *proliferated*, its many energies directed at multiplying racial differences so as to render them joyfully cacophonic." (Saldhana, "Reontologising Race," 21, see further 18–22, especially for Saldhana's discussion of viscosity). Grosz draws out the feminist potentials of assemblages to consider multiplicities of genders, sexualities, and desires. "A multiplicity is not a pluralized notion of identity (identity multiplied by *n* locations), but it is rather an ever-changing, nontotalizable collectivity, an *assemblage* defined, not by its abiding identity or principle of sameness over time, but through its capacity

wo/men's proliferations among first-century Christ-followers. These queer wo/men's *impulses* included words and ideas, but they also *go beyond them* to encompass the feelings, movements, and gestures that moved in between these folks.[124] Engaging the available evidence to proliferate speculative plausibilities, ἐκκλησία-1 assemblage gets beyond the iceberg's tip and allows us to better sense, feel, hear, see, and engage the queer wo/men of Rome's ἐκκλησία (among many other assemblies). ἐκκλησία-1 assemblage takes Paul's words and adds other words, ideas, movements, feelings, and gestures alongside, against, within, and beyond them—emphasizing that Paul is, indeed, "one among many."[125]

Framing the ἐκκλησία as assemblage draws attention to affects of belonging; they illuminate the feelings, the emotional bonds, and the forces that draw together shared elements of identity, an affective tug for some, a push away for others, and a force that is more or less comfortable depending on the body. Assemblages acknowledge that community is an imperfect ideal, one that is often regulatory and normativizing. Invocations of "the LGBTIA2Q+ community" frequently pave over the disparities between gay men and lesbians, cisgender queers and trans folks, Black queers and Asian queers, and—arguably most often—white queers and queers of color. Jack Halberstam cautions "that quests for community are always nostalgic attempts to return to some fantasized moment of union and unity," which "reveals the conservative stakes in community for all

---

to undergo permutations and transformations, that is, its dimensionality" (Grosz, "A Thousand Tiny Sexes," 192, emphasis added). Later she emphasizes proliferation and desire: "Desire does not take for itself a particular object whose attainment it requires; rather it aims at nothing above and beyond its own proliferation or self-expansion. *It assembles things out of singularities, and it breaks down things, assemblages, into the singularities*" (Grosz, "A Thousand Tiny Sexes," 196). The language of "thousand tiny" (specifically with sexes) comes from Deleuze and Guattari, *A Thousand Plateaus*, 213. Puar discusses the ideas of proliferating race and gender, drawing from Saldhana especially, as well as Grosz (Puar, *Terrorist Assemblages*, 209).

124. Thus, I add affect into the typical focus on discourse/verbal responses among first-century Christ-followers. This affective emphasis *beyond words* that assemblages bring to the ἐκκλησία of wo/men is critical for queer and feminist decentering and urges scholars to consider participation beyond words and (rational) argument, which can limit who/how we imagine accessed (and led) these spaces. Chapter 4 will further develop my affective usage of *impulses* to bring to life plausible responses of Rome's queer wo/men.

125. Johnson-DeBaufre and Nasrallah, "Beyond the Heroic Paul," 162.

kinds of political projects."[126] Belonging is contingent; it shifts based on who, what, where, when, and how things are assembled.

Idealized and conservative constructions of community are not limited to contemporary contexts. Similar constructions can be found in the New Testament and in historical scholarship that discusses an "early Christian community."[127] Although contemporary interpreters are guilty of uncritically perpetuating "romantic and communitarian conceptions of community," Stowers designates to Paul the primary responsibility for rhetorically crafting the ἐκκλησίαι to whom he wrote into unified, coherent communities.[128] Paul frequently presents unity (in Christ) as characteristic of an ἐκκλησία, and such unity should overcome and erase differences and divisions between Christ-followers (e.g., 1 Cor 1:10–17 as well as his rhetorical using of the baptismal formula in Gal 3:28 and 1 Cor 12:13).[129] Paul's fictionalization of a unified ἐκκλησία-1 community paves over dissent and attempts to dismiss debates and tensions as divisive.[130]

By complicating identities, assemblages rethink notions of community. For Puar, assemblages become crucial tools for emphasizing "the import of *communities of belonging*." Communities are never as stagnant as their idealization imagines them to be. In the aftermath of the 2001 attacks on New York's World Trade Center, a Pakistani Muslim queer man remarks, "My sexuality has taken a backseat to my ethnicity," especially in the context of more pronounced racism and Islamophobia within and beyond the queer "community." Communities of belonging describe sites (physical or otherwise) where bodies group based upon an affective sense of belonging, which can be sensed from shared characteristics, ideals or goals, or from something less tangible.[131] Feelings of belonging are unpredictable,

---

126. Jack Halberstam, *In a Queer Time and Place*, Sexual Cultures (New York: New York University Press, 2005), 154.

127. Stanley K. Stowers, "The Concept of 'Community' and the History of Early Christianity," *MTSR* 23 (2011): 238–56.

128. Stowers, "Concept of 'Community,'" 242.

129. Miller shows how Paul in 1 Corinthians genders democratic participation—especially through his construction of wisdom and speech in 1 Cor 1–4—in order to construct and cement his (singular) authority, especially over and against the wo/men of Corinth (Miller, *Corinthian Democracy*, 90–114, 130–53).

130. See Wire, *Corinthian Women Prophets*; Miller, *Corinthian Democracy*, esp. 155–86.

131. See Puar, *Terrorist Assemblages*, 173, 208, see further 207–9. On issues of race and national belonging related to this idea—and the ways in which this reveals

contextual, and complicated: it is impossible to know when any particular body—with its own complex assemblage of characteristics, experiences, and emotions—will sense connection with others.[132] Inclusion and exclusion, belonging and not belonging are transitory; they affect bodies and are also affected by bodies. As assemblages, communities of belongings fluctuate and are sometimes impermanent: new bodies become attached; bodies within them may lose their belonging-sensation and dissociate, or bodies within may regroup or splinter as senses shift.

I write not about an ἐκκλησία-l community but an ἐκκλησία-l *assemblage*. ἐκκλησία-l assemblage evokes a community of belonging, wherein belonging is always affectively contingent. This framing allows us to raise the question: what drew these queer wo/men together? This may be more—and something entirely other—than agreements and shared commitments. They may have thrived *because* they could quarrel and deviate together. Like an assemblage, these ancient ἐκκλησίαι refused the binary logics of acceptance or rejection and resistance or complicity in favor of a less positional and more complex—and therefore far more *realistic*—understanding of conversation and disagreement.[133] This emphasizes how Paul's letters are "sites of debate, contestation, and resistance," as Johnson-DeBaufre and Nasrallah and other feminist interpreters have long presented them.[134]

---

tensions with Massumi—see also José Esteban Muñoz, "Feeling Brown: Ethnicity and Affect in Ricardo Bracho's *The Sweetest Hangover (and Other STDs)*," *Theatre Journal* 52 (2000): 67–79.

132. Indeed, their devaluation—experienced in the discomfort or unease with discord and implied in desires for agreement—often works to perpetuate networks of power and control (Puar, *Terrorist Assemblages*, 208).

133. "Taking seriously the differences, the rifts, and the discontinuities between our own identities and those of our contemporaries (as well as the overlaps and the possibilities for solidarity) can facilitate our reconstruction of similar difference in antiquity" (Johnson-DeBaufre and Nasrallah, "Beyond the Heroic Paul," 165). See further examples of such work in Schüssler Fiorenza, *Power of the Word*, 82–109; Kittredge, *Community and Authority*; Wire, *Corinthian Women Prophets*.

134. Johnson-DeBaufre and Nasrallah, "Beyond the Heroic Paul," 162. The dynamic tensions and potential promises of ἐκκλησία-l assemblage emphasize the radically utopian potential of the "ἐκκλησία of wo/men." Schüssler Fiorenza names the ἐκκλησία of wo/men a "radical *democratic* space" that fosters and foregrounds solidarity among all wo/men. Schüssler Fiorenza reclaims democracy's definition and demands a return to its roots as truly and fully representing *all* voices, interests, perspectives, and bodies. "A feminist ethics of solidarity therefore presupposes as sine qua

ἐκκλησία-l assemblage reminds us that there could be many different groupings and alliances within this ἐκκλησία of queer wo/men. They did not have clear boundaries or a unified, singular result as their goal. These queer wo/men may have found some common ground and tensions that could not be reconciled. These heated gatherings—which involved not only discussion but also awkward or intentional silences, eating, moving, feeling, smelling, arousing, glaring—are integral for creating and sustaining communities (ancient and contemporary alike) and for continually moving toward potentially positive social change.

If the ἐκκλησία, as an assemblage of bodies sometimes in tandem and sometimes in tension, was more democratic and dynamic, then Paul's ideas *were* one among many. As his letters were read, wo/men commented, inserted, interjected. They cheered and groaned, ignored and embraced, gestured and interjected. Queer wo/men entered, left, felt alienated, sensed belonging, found energy, and got exhausted within an ἐκκλησία-l assemblage.

Kyriarchy as Assemblage

Does a heroic ἐκκλησία emerge as the assemblage-antidote to Paul and Roman imperialism? Bringing these queer wo/men to life proliferates

---

non the democratic agency and self-determination of women" (Schüssler Fiorenza, *Discipleship of Equals*, 351, see further 332–52, ch. 23, "The Ethics and Politics of Liberation: Theorizing the *Ekklēsia* of Women"). See also Schüssler Fiorenza, *In Memory of Her: A Feminist Theological Reconstruction of Christian Origins*, 10th anniversary ed. (New York: Crossroad: 1994), 343–51; Schüssler Fiorenza, *Wisdom Ways: Introducing Feminist Biblical Interpretation* (Louisville: Westminster John Knox, 2001), 127–30; Schüssler Fiorenza, *Transforming Vision: Explorations in Feminist The*logy* (Minneapolis: Fortress, 2011), 17–20. This radical democracy is a utopian vision: its ideal has never been fully and permanently realized, but its possibility is one that has been felt within history and always remains on the horizon. "A radical democratic conceptualization of the '*ekklēsia* of women' is at once a historically accomplished and an imagined future reality" (Schüssler Fiorenza, *Discipleship of Equals*, 369). See also Elizabeth A. Castelli, "The *Ekklēsia* of Women and/as Utopian Space," in *On the Cutting Edge: The Study of Women in Biblical Worlds*, ed. Jane Schaberg, Alice Bach, and Esther Fuchs (New York: Continuum: 2004), 36–52. This utopian vision is, therefore, one toward which feminist theories, politics, and the*logies must strive. By emphasizing change, ἐκκλησία-l assemblage helps continue to make space to concretely move toward justice with utopian hope while also admitting that the changes these assemblages motivated have never been completed and can threaten injustice and oppression even as they promise subversion and liberation.

historical plausibilities that make better history, but these plausibilities—and the queerer lives that motivate and are motivated by them—are not always *better*. ἐκκλησία-l assemblage can never alone promise the complete social change toward which utopian visions aspire. Assemblages are not inherently positive, and their hopeful changes are momentary. In the same moment they promise utopia, they can also threaten injustice. Romanormativity—like regulatory queerness—also motivates ἐκκλησία-l assemblage and the queer wo/men encompassed within it, drawing their movement back into kyriarchy.

Assemblages are not alternative models for power: they are neutral in that their capacities can be directed toward either stasis or change. When the contradictions and movements of assemblages are regulated by power, they produce opposing turfs with less-porous borders. They create divisions that quell the potential change that can emerge from engaging, rather than dispelling, tensions—the kind of change that encourages real community and diversity.[135] When underexamined, their complexity can enable the identitarian gridlock that supports regimes and societies of control.

These ways in which assemblages can work to tangle bodies into networks of control that sustain stasis and systems of uneven power enhance our understanding of kyriarchy.[136] Schüssler Fiorenza's term captures the idea of complex, intersecting networks of power that lock bodies into hierarchal grids of oppression: "However, this kyriarchal pyramid must not be seen as static, but as an *always changing net* of relations of domination."[137] Kyriarchy functions *as an assemblage*. As assemblage, kyriarchy divides

---

135. Here, I am assuming a distinction between *difference* and *division* essentially: difference being the more or less natural or organic ways bodies are dissimilar, and division being the creation of hard lines between differences that establish clear borders and prevent or make more difficult their crossings.

136. "Grids happen," writes Massumi. They are unavoidable in an assemblage's constant shifts: "Indeterminacy and determination, change and freeze-framing go together" (*Parables for the Virtual*, 8). Drawing from Massumi's insight, Puar stresses the necessary tension between the orderly grid of intersectionality and the chaotic fluidity of assemblages. Grids are included within *and formed by* assemblages. Grids lock, yet grids need the freer movement of assemblages to establish them—and to deconstruct them. Admitting their capacity for gridlock, assemblages probe the movements that underlie kyriarchal power networks and the ever-multiplying axes through which they function.

137. Schüssler Fiorenza, *Transforming Vision*, 9.

and conquers so as to maintain control in the hands of the powerful bodies it produces. Its maintenance of a hierarchy along multiple axes encourages bodies to stay locked on kyriarchy's *grid*, following one line and its individual intersections instead of seeing the divergences, curves, or connections that appear impossible, contradictory, or paradoxical on such a flexibly fixed plane of positions. The rule of the master advances its portrayal of characteristics like gender, race, class, and sexuality as separate categories that produce distinct identities, all of which can be aligned on its hierarchical grid that places the κύριοι, the elite, on the top lines.[138]

Kyriarchy, as assemblage, can shift just enough so that minor movements are sensed to be propelling change. Minor shifts are made to seem major, when, in actuality, such small shifts merely foster the flexibility that perpetuates kyriarchy's control—despite the reality that its network of power encompasses the bodies and forces that could dislodge it. Meanwhile, major shifts become less possible; they occur (or commence) but are made to seem minor or disruptive. The capacity for major movement is redirected into a minor shift, turning back toward stasis: gridlock.[139]

Assemblages and Reading Romans

Despite such dangers, assemblages contain capacities for changes that can unsettle and rearrange power in a less kyriarchal manner. Although any assemblage, always fleeting and constantly forming, reforming, and unforming, aligns with dominant power even as it curves away from it, thinking in terms of assemblages attempts to expose and dismantle some

---

138. Marchal develops and elaborates similar connections between the intersectionality of Schüssler Fiorenza's kyriarchy and the transdisciplinary benefits of thinking about kyriarchy and/as assemblage (Marchal, "Bio-Necro-*Biblio*-Politics," 172–74).

139. Such gridlock can be seen in Schüssler Fiorenza's discussion of the multiple axes (as in an intersectional grid) along which power functions, explained in an early formulation of kyriarchy. She writes, "In short, patriarchal power as the power of the master and lord operates not only along the axis of the gender system but also along those of race, class, culture, and religion. These axes of power structure the more general, overarching system of domination in a matrix- (or better patrix-) like fashion. When one shifts the analysis for investigating the axes of power along which this patrix of domination is structured, one can see not only how these systems of oppression constitute the kyriarchal social pyramid, but also *how they criss-cross the identity positions offered to individuals by the politics of domination*" (Schüssler Fiorenza, *Discipleship of Equals*, 365–66, emphasis added).

of the affective structures that create and support kyriarchal networks, instead of only untangling some of their effects.

When Puar calls queerness an assemblage, she moves beyond *queer* as an identity marker ("queer persons" or even "queer theory") or an action to be applied or done to objects or subjects (queering biblical texts or Paul, for instance).[140] "A queer praxis of assemblage" emerges in Puar's theorization that attempts to move beyond the grids and binaries that cannot contain contradictions (for fear of disorder or breakdown) and purport to relieve tensions (through isolation). Such a praxis "allows for a *scrambling of sides* that is illegible to state practices of surveillance, control, banishment, and extermination."[141] Queerness-assemblages attend to these small and sometimes barely perceptible changes and can slowly shift society and undermine kyriarchy even as each assemblage (re)aligns with dominant power, which is also always shifting into newer forms.[142]

Similarly, a praxis of ἐκκλησία-l assemblage encourages continual movement and ongoing proliferation, resisting demands for complete agreement, categorization, and unambiguousness.[143] ἐκκλησία-l assemblages *scramble the sides* that emerge in Pauline interpretation: between Paul and queer wo/men Christ-followers, between Paul and kyriarchy, between kyriarchy and its subversion. When ἐκκλησία-l assemblage

---

140. "Queerness as an assemblage moves away from excavation work, deprivileges a binary opposition between queer and not-queer subjects, and, instead of retaining queerness exclusively as dissenting, resistant, and alternative (all of which queerness importantly is and does), it underscores contingency and complicity with dominant formations" (Puar, *Terrorist Assemblages*, 205).

141. Puar, *Terrorist Assemblages*, 221, emphasis added.

142. On this movement to queerness and/as assemblage, Puar invokes an idea of "queer praxes of futurity," which points to affinities with work being done in queer temporalities, particularly the affective work of José Esteban Muñoz on utopias (Puar, *Terrorist Assemblages*, 204). Like Muñoz (and perhaps even more so than Muñoz), Puar is critical of Lee Edelman's insistence on queer negativity (and thus, presentism) as the best rejection of heteronormative "reproductive futurism" (Puar, *Terrorist Assemblages*, 211). See also Muñoz, *Cruising Utopia*, esp. 22, 90–95; Lee Edelman, *No Future: Queer Theory and the Death Drive*, SerQ (Durham, NC: Duke University Press, 2004).

143. My praxis of ἐκκλησία-l assemblage thinks alongside how Kotrosits discusses Puar's theorization of assemblage and queerness as assemblage and how it unfixes identity categories as she proposes an unexceptional queerness that unhinges the exceptionalisms of early Christian identity (Kotrosits, *Rethinking Early Christian Identity*, 54–61, esp. 54–55 for her discussion of Puar's work on assemblage/queerness).

proliferates plausibilities, these proliferations—and the tensions, contradictions, changes, and shifting alliances toward which they gesture—blur the lines between heroes and villains within Rome's ἐκκλησία. The queer wo/men in this ἐκκλησία-l assemblage, with Paul as one among many within it, are always and simultaneously heroic and villainous and everywhere in between.

Applying a feminist and queer affective-critical praxis of ἐκκλησία-l assemblage to Romans enables us to discern the affective threats of Paul's letters, which, as with Rom 1:18–32, frequently envision God's justice in kyriarchal and Romanormative terms. But this affectively driven exegetical analysis is not enough for an interpretive praxis of assemblage. Elizabeth Grosz writes, "It is thus no longer appropriate to ask what a text means, what it says, what is the structure of its interiority, how to interpret or decipher it. Instead, one must ask *what it does, how it connects with other things* (including its reader, its author, its literary and nonliterary context)."[144] ἐκκλησία-l assemblage cannot just leave Romans's threats behind when it proliferates other plausible ideas, movements, and interactions among Rome's queer wo/men. ἐκκλησία-l assemblage places these proliferations—including Paul's (which are oppressive and liberatory)—together and investigates what new sensations, ideas, and feelings emerge from their convergences, clashes, and tensions.

A praxis of ἐκκλησία-l assemblage engenders readings that are incomplete and imperfect, as unstable as the affect that motivates them. By holding contradictory (as well as complementary) capacities in tension, assemblages challenge interpreters and historians to contemplate *how these proliferations coexisted within bodies and spaces* and *how such coexistence might open new avenues for change.*[145] Such questions prove unanswerable in any firm or complete sense, but attempts to answer them—or, more realistically, just to *struggle* with their multiple possibilities—produce meanings and interpretations with the capacity to effect change.

Through this feminist and queer praxis of ἐκκλησία-l assemblage that I am invoking, I revisit and reconstruct some plausible versions of the debates, ideas, and feelings that we can say reliably *occurred*, even if we lack any reliable witnesses to attest to the content of these conversations. If conventional historiography might call my reconstructions imaginative

---

144. Grosz, "A Thousand Tiny Sexes," 199.
145. Puar, *Terrorist Assemblages*, 216–22.

musings (a label I deny only insofar as it typically carries derogatory implications), then this endeavor poses the question: to what degree does the
exact or accurate content *matter*?[146] If we know these conversations *must*
have occurred—but we have no firsthand witness—then we can, at least,
reconstruct numerous *probabilities*. We *can imagine*—as we draw from the
best available textual and material evidence. A concrete, stable historical
record is not truly *historical*.[147]

There is a hole in our history, a hole left by these voices, gestures, ideas,
and bodies of queer wo/men. It's a hole in which Paul's singular voice has
echoed, a hole that has, over centuries, been filled by the dirt of (heroically)
Pauline interpretation. "We are working up from postholes, working back
from the (im)material to the material."[148] Theater historian Odai Johnson
evokes this image of postholes—literally the holes left by the wood posts
of a colonial Williamsburg theater—long ago disintegrated, filled in, and
buried. From these indentations left in the dirt, an entire theater can be
recreated: a *speculatively plausible reconstruction*. When we decenter Paul,
we see the postholes. We can build up from them.

We began this (re)construction by bringing together material evidence of the ubiquitous presence of queer wo/men across the city of Rome
with the textual remnants of the queer wo/men whom Paul addresses
in Rom 16. These details give us a firmer sense of the myriad different
people who assembled, for different reasons and across different times, in
Rome's ἐκκλησία. This ἐκκλησία assembled wo/men with different gender
identities and sexual orientations, who came from many different ethnic
backgrounds, whose lives and social positions were affected differently by
Roman slavery, who had been dwelling in Rome for varying periods of
times, and who experienced differing degrees and periods of poverty or
wealth. This picture begins to build up from Pauline and Roman postholes.

---

146. Kotrosits raises similar questions in her affective approach to history
(Kotrosits, *Rethinking Early Christian Identity*, 25–27).

147. "Indeed, *we might read moments of methodological founding as pervasively
anti-historical acts*, beginnings which fabricate their legitimating histories through a
retroactive narrative, burying complicity and division in and through the funereal
figure of the 'ground.'" See Judith Butler, "Against Proper Objects," in *Feminism Meets
Queer Theory*, ed. Elizabeth Weed and Naomi Schor (Bloomington: Indiana University Press, 1997), 9.

148. Odai Johnson, *Absence and Memory in American Colonial Theatre* (New
York: Palgrave Macmillan, 2006), 18.

But as we gaze into these postholes to render visible the invisible, material the (im)material, it feels like there is so much more that could—*should*—materialize. Did these wo/men listen to Paul? How did they respond to his ideas? What else did they say to each other? Whose voices dominated? Whose held back, got paved over? What smaller groupings, bonds, or associations formed or existed between them? How did they feel?

With Rom 16 and some material evidence, we have reconstructed the frame, but there are so many more gaps we might fill in. We have the beams and poles, but we might rebuild some walls, furnish it with objects, and let queer wo/men *inhabit* the space: move around, say things, move things, break things, make friends, make enemies, find lovers, glare, huff, storm out, slip in. These postholes and materials suggest how much more we could find and how much we may never be able to find. They also give us the framework of a structure that can support some speculation. They can hold the weight of more imaginative proliferations like Brooten's *speculatively plausible* reconstruction of wo/men's responses to Rom 1:18–32. With the added support of ἐκκλησία-1 assemblage, they can bear the imaginative weight of something like this.

Romans 1:18–32: A Brief Test Case

διὰ τοῦτο παρέδωκεν αὐτοὺς ὁ θεὸς εἰς πάθη ἀτιμίας· αἵ τε γὰρ θήλειαι αὐτῶν μετήλλαξαν τὴν φυσικὴν χρῆσιν εἰς τὴν παρά..., *Because of this God handed them over to shameful passions, for their women traded their natural usage for that which is against* ... ἅλις ἤδη, *Enough already!* She sighs. Immediately another groan rises in agreement. From across the room, someone rolls her eyes, and another whispers to her neighbor οἷα φίλει γίνεσθαι, *As usual.* A slight tension fills the room. The words read are not new, nor is the spiraling madness into which they will later proceed. A few feel especially uneasy, remembering the frustration into which conversation around these issues has previously descended. They align with the usual Roman ideologies, though some mutter hopefully that they hear a critique of imperial sexual excess in the way this Παῦλος has framed them. That leads to other whispers (suddenly growing louder, perhaps). *Stop hearing critique of Rome in* everything, *what have they done to us?... Shhh, that kind of talk makes us too suspicious* ... more sighs and groans ... *Why can't you critique Rome in ways other than "shameful passions"?* By the time the lector, having had to repeat several words and phrases, reads ἀλλὰ καὶ συνευδοκοῦσιν τοῖς πράσσουσιν, *but they also sympathize with those who do such things* (1:32), it is apparent that these words have unearthed a few of the gathering's ongoing tensions that could only ever be held in a fragile stasis for so long.

Within this imagined scenario, several plausible positions—or, better put, impulses that include unvoiced reactions and gestures—resurface or are generated as a result of Paul's "voice" in this assembly. Some impulses largely agree with Paul: like this apostle, they have no reason to question the prevailing cultural assumptions about nature as it pertains to the prevailing sex/gender system. Some sense, with different levels of anxiety, that arranging sexuality in another (i.e., unnatural) way signals the potential decline of civilization. Those who agree most strongly may feel the pulsation of increasing madness (in both the term's senses, insanity and anger). Such madness may bubble out in these bodies especially when they are confronted with others who see—or even *do*—things differently, who disagree with the definition or presentation of what is natural in a variety of ways and degrees.

(Un)naturally, it follows that other wo/men feel differently. To some extent, they do have *reason to question* the prevailing assumptions about sex and its relation to society. There are wo/men who have reason to question based on personal experience, that is, those whose sexual practices or desires do not conform to the "natural" Romosexual hierarchy.[149] "Enough already" is the sigh of exasperation that represents this "other side."[150] Regardless of whether they have revealed their sexual proclivities (or they are otherwise known), some of these wo/men, to varying degrees, could raise suspicions about the naturalness of the sexual order; some may question why wo/men cannot love—or just fuck—other wo/men. Others may notice some of the problems of a hierarchically arranged sexual system. They may raise the question few Romans considered: can sex occur between two *equals*?[151] If so, how?

---

149. As scholars such as Brooten have shown, at least *some* in the Roman ἐκκλησία practiced "unnatural" sex, although such practice does not require rejection of the prevailing definition of *nature* or the socio-sexual-political hierarchy.

150. That is, the wo/men whose sexual practices or preferences did not align perfectly with the established order or those who understood such practices in ways that lead them to question and reject their condemnation.

151. Questions of equality within the ἐκκλησία and as an alternative relation to God—equal to rather than under—will be a recurring theme within my discussions of probabilities in an ἐκκλησία-l assemblage.

Such questions have more than sexual ramifications: they imply changes to society and politics as well. If the sexual side of the kyriarchal pyramid is altered to be more equal, this deconstruction prompts other sides held within the assemblage to be questioned and potentially shift. If sexual positions or objects adhere to the power differentials of the sociopolitical ladder (or redefine/eliminate power dynamics entirely), then are these other power dynamics and positions necessary? Should politics be different? Should there be an emperor, a voting body restricted to elite men, a scale of citizen/ free/foreign/slave? Should the empire be overturned—or better yet, could it be *shifted* to allow newer, dynamic movements and changes?

While it is possible that such revolutionary thoughts could be prompted by revolutionary sexual experiences or ideas, they do not automatically or necessarily follow a praxis for which assemblage theory accounts. As an assemblage, kyriarchy produces and maintains power and a dynamic stasis, making it effective because of its fluid ability to adapt to revolutionary shifts and to make them feel/seem smaller within their wide ebbs and flows. Someone whose sexual practices did not conform to the kyriarchal mold (an elite woman and an enslaved prostitute in love as equals, perhaps) might still prefer to maintain the political status quo (e.g., the elite woman enjoys her wealth). Normativity has an affective draw that motivates these assemblage dynamics: one can question the status quo just enough to feel normal within it—to keep treading water.

I do not want to deny the potential existence for revolutionaries within Rome's ἐκκλησία; however, it is more likely that this extreme was rare or an amalgamation of semirevolutionary bodies, actions, thoughts, and gestures produced through assemblage.[152] Within Rome's ἐκκλησία, this means that some wo/men, who were resistant to Roman imperial power and who wanted to overthrow or rethink it, may have heard imperial critique in Paul's contribution and been eager to point it out in support of questions they had already been raising in the assembly. Their rejection of Rome does not have to entail rejection of its sexual or social order any more than two women's rejection of Roman disdain for their unnatural coupling entails a rejection of the empire or their social statuses within it. The variety of possibilities are endless with so many points and lines held within ἐκκλησία-l assemblage. The plausible positions proliferate infinitely.

---

152. Extremes are, in other words, often produced by assemblages and are often held onto for their stability. Fictive binary sides help maintain the status quo.

While Paul's framing may have prompted some wo/men to articulate their ideas in different or new ways, much of 1:18–32 offered little new in terms of prevalent ideas about sex, gender, and society. It is just as likely that the assembly expressed their usual comments—or maybe some just sighed, smiled, groaned, or eye-rolled—before continuing to a different conversation with their Pauline participant.[153] Their affective, embodied reactions set up a framework for ἐκκλησία-1 assemblage and serves as a reminder that the ἐκκλησία's interactions were ongoing. Paul's letter entered into a history of the Roman assembly that existed before and continued to move and develop after his moment of entry.

Based on this beginning, it becomes more possible (quite probable, even) that Paul's contributions to the gathering's thoughts and feelings about sexuality added nothing particularly new. This is not to say that Paul's ideas did not matter or affect how these wo/men—and their reading of Paul's contribution as a participant among them—proceeded. Those who approved of what he says in Rom 1 might be more willing to embrace or consider the parts of his argument that follow, even if his ideas do not conform to their own theo-Christologies. Likewise, those who disagreed with this sexual ideology may have been on alert and looking for ways that these sexual and hierarchal ideas appear in his ethics and theology. Others had different reactions. Some could have completely forgotten these words by the time 2:2 was in their ears.

These early interruptions begin to give us a sense of how Paul's letter participates as *one voice among many* in an ongoing gathering of bodies that included queer wo/men. This interruption cannot be entirely for-

---

153. Fox also imagines Corinthian wo/men rolling their eyes as they interact with Paul's letters (Fox, *Paul Decentered*, 91). When it comes to gestures (such as eye-rolling), it must be noted that gestures and their meanings are cultural. When I imagine the gestures of queer wo/men in Rome's ἐκκλησία, I draw from the meanings common to twenty-first-century, US culture. These gestures, of course, express ideas and feelings in ways that differ from voicing them (and often cannot be voiced). Although I do not do so, it would be possible to imagine ancient gestural interactions, drawing from, for example, work done on ancient physiognomy, especially as it pertains to gender, such as Maud Gleason, *Making Men: Sophists and Self-Presentation in Ancient Rome* (Princeton: Princeton University Press, 1995). Instead, I see my gestural representations as an imaginative act of translation, much like trying to render the feelings and meanings of ancient languages into contemporary English. These translations allow Roman queer wo/men to come to life for queer folks living in twenty-first-century contexts.

gotten or ignored as the dialogue continues onto new topics like πίστις ("faith") and ethics. With its talk of honoring and thanking (from δοξάζω and εὐχαριστῶ, see 1:21) and of revealing God's anger (ἀποκαλύπτεται γὰρ ὀργὴ θεοῦ, 1:18), what, more broadly, does 1:18–32 say about God?[154] How does or will sexuality and the Romosexual hierarchy relate to following Jesus? Questions beyond those related to sexuality surface as well, both from 1:18–32 and the entire chapter: Who is God more broadly, and how do the members of this gathering relate to or belong to this God? How does this relate to the traditions and histories of Judaism? What is Jesus's relation to God, what example does he give the ἐκκλησία; and what does it mean to follow him? What does it mean that Jesus is κύριος ἡμῶν, our *master*? What is God's rule—and how does it affect the present rule of Rome? How does Jesus and showing πίστις to God affect our roles and behaviors in society? What ethical rules do we live by?

Rome's ἐκκλησία-l assemblage—and Paul's partial role within it—flows and shifts through theology, ethics, politics, nation, society, economics, race/ethnicity, gender, *and* sexuality. These various subjects ebb and flow, cross and collide, are crucial, ancillary, and irrelevant at different moments within and around it. Like the epistle itself, ἐκκλησία-l assemblages move on from sexuality but never leave it behind.

The various ideas and movements presented here are unattested (since we have no historical record) and represent my own imaginative reconstruction of some of this ἐκκλησία's interactions. These musings draw from historical records to confirm their plausibility. At the same time, they reflect my own contemporary experiences, biases, and concerns. What is *historical* about this reconstruction is *not* the individual content of any particular statement, body, idea, or context. It is the *conversation without specific content*—the mingling of different impulses and bodies through a feminist and queer praxis of ἐκκλησία-l assemblage—that is profoundly historical. It is urgent for history—both for accuracy in representing the past and for its role in determining the future—to reconstruct more than individual heroic ideas and positions and instead examine the far less tangible ways in which an assembly of ideas, bodies, objects, and forces affect and move toward change of historical proportions. Placing these historical musings in conversation, as I have just done and will continue to do

---

154. In the case of honoring/thanking God in 1:21, 1:18–32 reveals the results of *not* doing so, but this implies that followers in the assembly should honor and thank God.

through this praxis of ἐκκλησία-l assemblage, proffers a plausible representation of historical *interactions*, minglings that do not merely include the
words spoken. This never claims to be a perfect or final representation. In
resurrecting a dynamic ancient dialogue, I provoke contemporary interactions with other assemblages, which will disagree with my representations
or be sparked by them to add their own. The ἐκκλησία-l assemblage that
I present is just a beginning. It is definitionally incomplete with infinite
space for disagreement and development. We must keep sweeping and
proliferate plausible historical interactions, feelings, and sensations.

3
Faithful Submission

Faith is only a word, embroidered.
—Margaret Atwood, *The Handmaid's Tale*

Is God's reign a promise, or could it also be a threat? A praxis of ἐκκλησία-l assemblage emphasizes that it can be both. Far too often, readers of Romans encounter only its promises of justice under God. The concept of *faith*, especially as Paul develops it in Rom 1–5, is pivotal to these promises, particularly within Christian (and especially Lutheran) theo-Christology. Through faith, justice—under God's reign.

This chapter destroys that faith. Faith is, after all, only a word—embroidered on a cushion, as the narrator of *The Handmaid's Tale* laments. Reading Rom 1–5 through the lens of feminist and queer affective critique reveals unseen threats that motivate faith's promises.[1] By imbuing promising attachments, faith turns out to be more than a word: it is an affective force.

Faith resembles Lauren Berlant's rendering of *optimism*. Berlant defines optimism as an affective attachment to an object of desire, which is really "a cluster of promises we want someone or something to make to us and make

---

1. Though my critique specifically examines the contemporary Christian construction of faith through one of its primary exegetical foundations in Rom 3–5, this critique—especially as we see faith's connections to salvation—aligns with Karen Bray's broader diagnosis "of a soteriological and theological impulse in neoliberalism that demands we be productive, efficient, happy, and flexible in order to be of worth and therefore get saved out of the wretched experience of having been marked as worthless. The theological underpinnings of neoliberalism offer *a caged freedom in the guise of opportunity*" (Bray, *Grave Attending: A Political Theology for the Unredeemed* [New York: Fordham University Press, 2020], 4, emphasis added). This "caged freedom in the guise of opportunity" is essentially synonymous with Berlant's "cruel optimism" (which Bray draws from, especially in her book's second chapter) and can be seen in the faith constructed by Rome for its conquered inhabitants, as we will see below.

possible for us." Optimism is inherently neither promising nor threatening. We all need optimistic attachments to clusters of promises embedded in certain people, objects, texts, smells, ideas, routines, or institutions.[2]

What happens when we attach ourselves to promises that threaten our flourishing? This chapter concerns how faith's attachments sustain what Berlant calls *cruel optimism*. Cruel optimism occurs when the object one attaches oneself to, strives toward, and hopes for *inhibits* one's ability to attain its promises. Cruel optimism hopes for something that is "actually *an obstacle* to your flourishing."[3]

Cruel optimism sustains fantasies of *the good life*, a fantasy of goodness that, in the twenty-first century, tends to look productive (i.e., capitalist) and hetero- or homonormative: fulfilling job, stable and disposable income, home, spouse, nuclear family, and so forth.[4] Cruel optimism traps its victims in an *impasse* as they maintain unachievable fantasies. These impasses are a "temporary housing" that one cannot see (or refuses to admit) has become a permanent abode, an infinite holding pattern of treading water that prevents drowning yet never swims, never reaches stable ground.[5] Impasses and good life fantasies are characteristics that reveal cruel optimisms.

This chapter uncovers similar fantastic promises within the concept of πίστις (and *fides*, its Latin equivalent), the term that is most commonly translated "faith" in the New Testament and other Greco-Roman texts. πίστις and *fides* were critical to the maintenance of imperial rule, kyriarchy, and Romosexuality. Rome's πίστις/*fides* involved submission for those of lower status, especially in the case of conquered ἔθνη ("nations") that had been incorporated into the empire as participants in the *pax Romana*. Written and first heard in this context, Rom 1–5 uses πίστις to incorporate ἔθνη into God's plan for justice and salvation under divine rule. Paul's argument assumes the same submissive postures seen in imperial πίστις. πίστις in Romans, as in Rome, requires faithful submission.[6]

---

2. Lauren Berlant, *Cruel Optimism* (Durham, NC: Duke University Press, 2011), 23.

3. Berlant, *Cruel Optimism*, 1.

4. In other words, good life fantasies motivate the "aspirational normativity" discussed in chapter 1, particularly in Berlant's discussion of *Rosetta*. See especially, Berlant, *Cruel Optimism*, 163–64.

5. Berlant, *Cruel Optimism*, 4–5, 10.

6. And so, the heart of Christianity is also, in other words, part of the bedrock that sustained Roman kyriarchy.

This submissive aspect of faith points toward its potential for cruel optimism. By reading Berlant alongside Rom 1–5, this chapter moves from capitalist contexts to an imperial context, from hetero- and homonormative fantasies to ones that are Romosexual and Romanormative, from cruel optimism to cruel πίστις.

In this chapter, I discuss imperial portrayals of πίστις and its relation to ἔθνη alongside the appearance of these portrayals in Rom 1–5. First, I show how Berlant's conception of optimism applies to Roman conceptions of πίστις/fides, which frame it in affectively relational terms. I specify how, in hierarchal contexts, these optimistic πίστις-relations tended to involve submission and hopes of benefit for those of lower status who made faithfully submissive displays. Since cruel optimism sustains "good life" fantasies, I then turn our attention to the situation of ἔθνη conquered by and living in the city of Rome and exhibit how fantasies of a first-century, imperial good life developed around them. Finally, I draw out the cruelty—and the impasse—of πίστις's optimistic attachments: for ἔθνη the promises of inclusion in the imperial good life traps them in a bad life, one that actively inhibits their flourishing. Given the socio-sexual-political reality of Rome's ἔθνη, their faithful submission ultimately makes impossible their fantasies: cruel optimism. Throughout the chapter, I show how Rome's πίστις-relations with its conquered ἔθνη inform Paul's portrayal of πίστις in Rom 1–5. Paul's theo-Christology sustains relations of this same cruel πίστις for his audience of ἔθνη: they faithfully submit to God and hopefully await God's reign, which is, in essence, Roman without Rome.

Optimistic πίστις and Faithful Submission

In first-century Rome, πίστις and *fides* bound bodies as an *affective force*. Reading πίστις/*fides* through a feminist and queer affective lens, I demonstrate, first in Rome generally and then in Paul's letter specifically, how the affective forces of πίστις/*fides* epitomize Berlant's optimism. The optimistic attachments πίστις forged bound subjects in relations structured kyriarchically, such as enslaved persons to enslavers, loyal subjects to their emperor, or Jesus to God. πίστις in Rome and Romans required faithful submission.[7]

---

7. I use the term πίστις, generally untranslated, to refer generally to first-century conceptions of this term as "trust" or "faith," as opposed to translating the term, since it is difficult to render with one precise English equivalent (as will be discussed below).

The Optimism of Roman πίστις and fides

"And many other nations [*gentes*, ἔθνη] experienced the faith [*fidem*, πίστεως] of the Roman people during my rule, nations with whom there had never been an exchange of embassies or friendship" (Res gest. divi Aug. 32). These words, inscribed by Augustus in his monumental Res gestae, can be found near the end of the emperor's account of his territorial expansion of Rome.[8] His expansive conquest ensured an era of peace and prosperity for inhabitants across the empire, especially for Roman citizens (the *populus Romano*). Rome's first emperor asserts that through his territorial expansion, the peoples added to the empire were able to experience the πίστις that characterized Roman citizens. In being conquered (whether militarily or diplomatically) by Rome, the experience of "faith" for these ἔθνη, as Caesar conceives it, is one of submission. By submitting to his imperial authority, these non-Roman peoples take their place on the hierarchy of imperial politics and ultimately bolster Rome's prosperity, in which these ἔθνη—though distinct from Rome's citizenry— will implicitly share.

πίστις plays a fundamental role in establishing and maintaining relations, as Teresa Morgan has emphasized.[9] πίστις relies on reciprocity: relations based on πίστις presume that it will be displayed in both direc-

---

It should be noted that when I refer to πίστις as a concept in the first century CE, I am *not* excluding the Latin concept of *fides*, as both terms were roughly equivalent in usage in this period. On this issue, see Teresa J. Morgan, *Roman Faith and Christian Faith* (Oxford: Oxford University Press, 2015), 7–8, as well as 5–15. Because my discussion of Romans will look exclusively to the Greek term, I prefer to use the Greek when speaking about the general concept, as opposed to having to render it "πίστις/ *fides*" in order to denote their interchangeability. When I do refer specifically to *fides*, it is because I am referring to the use of the term in a specific text. I am not considering *fides* separately or differently from πίστις at any point.

8. In the preceding sections of the text (starting roughly at Res gest. divi Aug. 25), Augustus gives a summative account of the various ἔθνη whom he added to Rome's population, whether by military victory (as in Egypt) or by more peaceful arrangement (such as the establishment of client kingdoms as with Judea).

9. She observes, "But *pistis/fides* (along with justice, mercy, and a few others) is one of those qualities that can only be practised socially: it is inherently relational and characteristically expressed in action towards other human beings (or, occasionally, animals)" (Morgan, *Roman Faith*, 472). Throughout the book, she emphasizes the ways in which relationality is central to the concept of πίστις through her discussion of various examples, such that, by p. 444, she can declare this fact to be uncontroversial.

tions, even when only one party's πίστις is mentioned.[10] πίστις and the relations it maintains generally promise benefits to the parties in exchange for their mutual trust and loyalty. To establish trust/loyalty is to create a relationship upon which all parties can depend. In the case of a preexisting relationship, it is essential for the maintenance of that relationship, particularly if it is to remain beneficial for those involved.

πίστις is *relational*. Accounting for the experiential dimensions and practical benefits that function within its relations, πίστις operates beyond a simple cognitive function of "trust" or (especially) "belief."[11] It displays an *affective* means of creating and maintaining relations that helped structure kyriarchy.[12] πίστις's relational force attaches bodies through shifting sensations whose description and definition is uncapturable. Sometimes it involves trust, sometimes loyalty, sometimes belief; usually it is an oddly shifting combination of (at least) all three.

Binding bodies into relations and sustaining these relations through its sensations, πίστις's affective force can be specified further as the form of attachment that Berlant calls "optimism": "the force that moves you out of yourself and into the world in order to bring closer the satisfying *something* that you cannot generate on your own but sense in the wake of a person, a way of life, an object, project, concept, or scene."[13] It denotes a relationship that a person has based on the hope or expectation that this relation will

---

10. Morgan, *Roman Faith*, 53, see further 52–53.

11. This cognitive definition is probably most apparent in its theological translation as "faith" and its longstanding function as propositional "belief" in the New Testament and its interpretation. However, "the way in which the term 'belief' is used in modern English, to translate *pistis/fides* with a strongly cognitive and propositional accent, makes it easy to forget that cognitive processes and propositional belief are primarily expressed in Greek and Latin using the language of *thinking* (*putare, nomizein,* etc.)" (Morgan, *Roman Faith*, 75).

12. It is affective in affect's meaning as a proprioceptive force or sensation that occurs in between bodies and binds them into a complex relationality. Because Morgan comments that affective dimensions of πίστις are not present in Roman depictions—and, indeed, that such dimensions are largely emphasized by New Testament scholarship in exclusivity—I should note that Morgan's use of *affective* connects affect closely with emotion (i.e., they are virtually synonymous for her), and she argues that πίστις is not an emotion (Morgan, *Roman Faith*, 54). I agree with Morgan's assessment, but we diverge in how we use the term *affective*. As elaborated in chapter 1, emotions can be affective (i.e., manifest affect), but affect (and forces described as affective) cannot be limited to emotions.

13. Berlant, *Cruel Optimism*, 1–2.

help to bring about something beneficial, especially in terms of everyday, ordinary life. By maintaining these relations, optimism *attaches* its subjects to objects of relation, which can be concrete (a person or a physical object) or intangible (a concept like freedom or security). Optimism often seems positive (i.e., glass half full) because the relations and attachments it forges are connected to conceptions of the good life: one becomes attached via the promise that this attachment will yield satisfaction or improvement in some aspect of one's (daily) life.[14]

πίστις operated along a similar affective structure in order to attach a subject to their object, thereby forging a relationship with a person, sensation, group, or thing.[15] Though πίστις generally involves some degree of reciprocity between the subjects it binds, it is almost always spoken in terms of existing between a subject and an object. Thus, in Augustus's description, Rome, the subject, displays its πίστις/*fides* to the ἔθνη/*gentes*. Since Rome shows its trust in these nations after their surrender to its power, Rome becomes attached to them through their incorporation into its empire. Like Berlant's optimism, such attachments via πίστις are based upon the hope of benefit and satisfaction. By trusting these nations to remain peaceful and obedient in their faithful submission to Caesar and his empire, the Roman people expect the continuation of their prosperity and peace. In its reciprocal relation, the people of these now-submissive ἔθνη display πίστις to the Romans.

Since it generates a relationship between Rome and an ἔθνος, both the empire and these subjects must behave in ways that maintain the relationship. Rome realigns resources and protection to include more subjects. Likewise, the people of an ἔθνος adapt their lives to conform with Roman standards of living and its hierarchies in order to prove themselves submissive and worthy of inclusion under the *pax Romana*. Though their particular experiences of this πίστις-encounter differ, both parties partici-

---

14. Along these lines, Berlant notes, "Whatever the experience of optimism is in particular, then, the affective structure of an optimistic attachment involves a sustaining inclination to return to the scene of fantasy that enables you to expect that this time, nearness to this thing will help you or a world to become different in just the right way" (Berlant, *Cruel Optimism*, 2). Already, then (with words like "fantasy" deployed to make the hope less possible), one can see how Berlant will emphasize the ways in which optimism easily becomes "cruel," that is, that the fantasy is not just unattainable but also actively hindering one's ability to achieve its promises.

15. Indeed, "optimism is not a map of pathology but *a social relation involving attachments that organize the present*" (Berlant, *Cruel Optimism*, 14, emphasis added).

pate in an attachment that affects the structure and pace of their everyday lives. Peace and prosperity offer a cluster of promises and expectations that, as a result of these πίστις-relations, everyday lives will become or will remain good.[16]

The reciprocity and relationality of πίστις do not indicate egalitarian relationships, nor do all relations of πίστις involve some level of intimacy or knowledge between the parties.[17] In the case of the πίστις shown in the Res gestae, the *populus Romanae*, as native Romans, are implicitly of greater status than the ἔθνη, and neither the majority of this *populus* nor the emperor (to the extent he stands for them) has any sort of relational intimacy with these ἔθνη.[18] πίστις's affect draws and binds these subjects into an assemblage, one motivated by the imperial interests of Roman kyriarchy. One must conform to Roman virtues to merit faithful inclusion in Rome's good life: a form of Romanormativity.

The instances of its usages in enslaver/enslaved relations exemplify this. Valerius Maximus devotes a section of *Memorable Works and Deeds* to the *fides* of enslaved persons (*De fide servorum*, *Fact.* 6.8). "What is left to discuss is the *fides* of slaves towards masters, which is less expected and so more praiseworthy," he begins (*Fact.* 6.8 preface). Valerius narrates how an unnamed man, enslaved by Urbinius Panapio, saved Panapio's life by voluntarily taking Panapio's clothing and place in bed when soldiers were coming to kill Panapio. After the enslaved man is killed in his stead,

---

16. Perhaps especially for elite Romans who embody the good life, πίστις's optimistic attachment sustains the fantasy through the promise of *not* changing. Berlant observes, "One of optimism's ordinary pleasures is to induce conventionality, that place where appetites find a shape in the predictable comforts of the good-life genres that a person or world has seen fit to formulate" (Berlant, *Cruel Optimism*, 2).

17. The relationality of πίστις emphasizes its social function, which operates like a puzzle that fits together only when all persons take their proper place in society. "*Pistis/fides* exists in relationships between social equals and unequals, and it is a quality of both superior and subaltern partners in relationships. It can be characterized as holding all partners together in a shared enterprise (such as the thriving of a household), or as structuring their complementarity: fitting them together like the pieces of a social jigsaw" (Morgan, *Roman Faith*, 52).

18. On the Latin equivalent, *gentes*: "These and similar references to the *gentes* represent the empire as a composite of different peoples, united in their subjection to the *populus Romanus* or *genus Romana*." See Myles Lavan, *Slaves to Rome: Paradigms of Empire in Roman Culture* (Cambridge: Cambridge University Press, 2013), 34. Lavan overall assesses and tracks the metaphors used by the empire to convey its relations to its subjects.

Panapio erects a monument to his loyalty (*pietatis*). "How admirable the *fides* of Urbinius Panapio's slave," Valerius exclaims of this incident (*Fact.* 6.8.6). The *fides* and πίστις of enslaved persons may garner them praise and glory (in this case, only posthumously), but their faithful submission benefits the interests of their (often elite) enslavers.

Roman enslavers had to trust the persons they enslaved to act according to their best interests, even if an enslaved person was given the opportunity to betray them. This included instances—at least from the enslavers' perspectives—where enslaved persons prove their πίστις by saving their enslaver's lives (even though, the sources imply, this would mean the potential for escape and freedom). In reciprocity, enslavers are assumed and occasionally said to display πίστις toward slaves through positive treatment and the promise for future freedom.[19] In cases of uneven power, πίστις keeps its subjects attached in relations that, for the greater party (enslaver, patron, etc.), sustains their authority (while often improving their wealth and control) and, for the lesser party (enslaved person, client, etc.), permits their basic sustenance while promising eventual rewards for faithful behavior directed upward.[20]

Something similar can be said for πίστις within larger-scale political relationships, in particular between an emperor and his subjects, as seen in the Res gestae quotation. In the imperial regime of the first century CE, all inhabitants of every Roman territory were subjects under the authority of a

---

19. Morgan, *Roman Faith*, 51–55, esp. n. 70. "The promise of future manumission was an incentive for slaves to work hard and remain loyal to the interests of their masters." See Matthew J. Perry, *Gender, Manumission, and the Roman Freedwoman* (Cambridge: Cambridge University Press, 2014), 53.

20. A similar power dynamic can be found between an elite patron and clients of lower status (whether citizens or freedpersons), and hierarchal relations informed by πίστις also occur within families, such as between parents and children or husband and wives (Morgan, *Roman Faith*, 45–51, 60–65). The patron/client relationship cannot be fully separated from enslavement, since freedpersons were typical clients of Roman patrons (who could also be freedpersons) (Perry, *Gender*, 69–70). Faithful service that benefitted the client as former enslaver characterized the good freedperson. "This insistence on fidelity [*fides*] and obedience [*obsequium*] went hand-in-hand with a demand for industriousness and occupational skill. Such prescriptions ensured that patrons would benefit from their freedman's labor, thereby promoting slaveowners' economic interests together with their social ascendancy." See Rose MacLean, *Freed Slaves and Roman Imperial Culture: Social Integration and the Transformation of Values* (Cambridge: Cambridge University Press, 2018), 37.

single emperor.[21] Philo writes in *Legatio ad Gaium*: δοῦλοι δὲ αὐτοκράτορος οἱ ὑπήκοοι ("Subjects are slaves of the emperor" [*Legat.* 119]).[22] Philo's word for "subject" (ὑπήκοος) is a form of the Greek word expressing "obedience": subjects, then, are definitionally obedient and submissive toward their ruler.[23] His statement demonstrates the general perceptions of imperial authority that were being negotiated in elite discourse as they adjusted to new rule by emperor that became firmly established by the end of the Julio-Claudian years.[24] While the enslaved/enslaver relation between subject and emperor was commonly used to describe the empire's relation to inhabitants of its conquered territories (or "allies," i.e., the ἔθνη), elite, native Romans preferred to describe their own hierarchal relation with the emperor using the terms of father/child or patron/client relations.[25] Regardless of the metaphor, the relation chosen always involves a hierar-

---

21. Unlike in the era of Rome's Republic, where Roman society was hierarchically structured but ruled by an elite class, none of whom considered themselves subject to the others.

22. He goes on to emphasize that this is most true of Caligula, whom he portrays as a tyrant, and that it may not be true of his predecessors who ruled more moderately. However, despite this qualification, the statement itself stands as true for Philo, as the qualification merely indicates that those more moderate predecessors ruled in such a way that the subjects were not made to feel as though enslaved, even though they were, effectively, in such a position. Philo is not alone among elite Romans in his application of a enslaved/enslaver metaphor to describe particularly poor governance, as Matthew B. Roller discusses. Indeed, Caesar uses a similar metaphor in the Res gestae to describe the rule of Antony's faction (Res gest. divi Aug. 1). See Matthew B. Roller, *Constructing Autocracy: Aristocrats and Emperors in Julio-Claudian Rome* (Princeton: Princeton University Press, 2001), 214–15.

23. LSJ, s.v. "ὑπήκοος," 1871–72. See also Cynthia Briggs Kittredge, *Community and Authority: The Rhetoric of Obedience in the Pauline Tradition*, HTS 45 (Harrisburg, PA: Trinity Press International, 1998), 37–51.

24. See Roller, *Constructing Autocracy*, 213–87. Broadly, Roller's project in his monograph is to show the various ways Rome's early emperors fashioned themselves and presented themselves to the elites so they would accept their new relationship to an emperor/autocrat. See also Lavan, *Slaves to Rome*, 73–155, on the slave-master metaphor as used (strategically) by Rome's elite.

25. On father/child: Roller, *Constructing Autocracy*, 233–64; on patron/client: Lavan, *Slaves to Rome*, 176–210. On Philo's use of Rome's "public transcript" and its relation to Caligula's reign, see Neil Elliott, *The Arrogance of Nations: Reading Romans in the Shadow of Empire*, PCC (Minneapolis: Fortress, 2008), 36–37, 52. Note that Elliott does not explicitly mention the Claudian context of Philo's work.

chy in which πίστις plays a sustaining role.²⁶ Whether a father to a child or enslaver to enslaved wo/man, the emperor provides protection and stability to his subjects provided that they faithfully submit to and obey his authority.²⁷

This relation of πίστις that existed between an emperor and his subjects was crucial to the continued control and prosperity of the imperial state.²⁸ Valerius Maximus devotes another section of his work to public *fides* (*De fide publica*) in which he lauds the *fides Romana* (*Fact.* 6.6.2). Valerius emphasizes how Rome's *fides* has been extended to parties who seem to have broken the bond through enmity, granting them mercy and trust when they could have punished them (see especially, *Fact.* 6.6.2, 5). The *fides Romana* abounds to the point that Rome trusts—and expects that trust—from its allies, just like the nations (ἔθνη/*gentes*) whom Augustus entrusted with peace and prosperity. If subjects, enslaved persons, ἔθνη, and allies are all submissively faithful toward Rome, *fides Romana*, the faithfulness of empire, is a benevolent trust that affirms Rome's ruling power.

The optimistic attachments forged by *fides publica* are not without instability. Without public trust in the emperor and his government, tyranny and rebellion were likely to replace the peace and stability that allowed the state to thrive. Though hierarchical, the reciprocality of πίστις means that the good life is always precarious, even for those at the kyriarchal top for whom the good life may actually be good: there is optimism, with all its fragility, in desiring things to stay the same.²⁹ Though this pre-

---

26. See Morgan, *Roman Faith*, 85–95. Elite Romans adapted metaphors of slavery and freedom to describe their relationship to the emperor, especially as they adjusted to the limits that autocracy set on their access to power (compared to their greater ability/access to the most power/highest positions in the republic). This was especially the case to describe their position under so-called bad emperors (MacLean, *Freed Slaves*, 75).

27. Notably, talk of πίστις/*fides* for an emperor is more likely to emerge under more tyrannical or unstable conditions (Morgan, *Roman Faith*, 93). Here, πίστις has the hopeful effects of optimistic attachment: if its lack/failure caused the political disruption, its embodiment, even toward an autocrat, will restore stability.

28. Morgan, *Roman Faith*, 83–85. See also Elliott, *Arrogance of Nations*, 72–75. Elliott's discussion of such uses of *fides* and friendship as Rome's public transcript draws attention to the euphemistic nature of Augustan language, which elided the coercion involved in subjection.

29. What Berlant calls conventionality; see n. 16 above and Berlant, *Cruel Optimism*, 2.

carity certainly entails risk for the emperor and the imperial system, the assemblage that motivates kyriarchy makes it difficult to unravel the ideal of faithful submission.

Imperial propaganda emphasized the importance of πίστις in the relation between emperor and people, both Roman and ἔθνη. One way this was done was through coins celebrating the *fides publica*, the "public trust" or "trust of the people."[30] Since this phrase was placed on coins, an indication of wealth, and disseminated across the empire, it connects the public πίστις of subjects toward their emperor to ongoing economic prosperity ushered in by imperial rule. Analyzing these coins, Morgan asserts, "the cumulative effect … is to emphasize the interdependence of all the benefits of *fides*. Peace, ensured by armies, together with strong government, brings prosperity, trade, fair prices, and satisfaction to all the subjects of empire."[31] This cumulative effect emphasizes the goodness of the Roman/imperial *good life*. In order to realize these benefits, it is necessary for the people— the subjects—to trust, through *fides*/πίστις, the emperor. Official rhetoric of πίστις helped sustain the hierarchal relation between the emperor and his various subjects. Supported by its everyday maintenance of hierarchal relations, πίστις—as a form of Berlantian optimism that attaches subjects, hoping for the benefits of the Roman good life, to empire—involves faithful submission for all those under imperial authority.[32]

Jesus's Submission and πίστις in Romans 3:21–26

How do Berlantian optimism and the kyriarchal attachments forged through Roman πίστις/*fides* affect Paul's letter to Rome? Paul employs πίστις to discuss the relation between God and Jesus. Romans 1–5 explains how ἔθνη have been incorporated (alongside Jews) into God's plan for justice and salvation (1:16–17)—made manifest in Jesus's display of πίστις

---

30. The subjective genitive reading of the Latin phrase is most well attested (πίστις of the public; or public πίστις), but Morgan notes that the coins may actually play on the ambiguity since an objective reading (πίστις in the public, on the part of the emperor/state) is plausible. This second meaning could "allow the reader to remember the emperor's loyalty to the army [and the people more broadly]" (Morgan, *Roman Faith*, 83). Elliott also discusses the role of these coins and their dissemination of "public faith" in the empire's public transcript (Elliott, *Arrogance of Nations*, 38).

31. Morgan, *Roman Faith*, 84.

32. See Elliott, *Arrogance of Nations*, 31–32, where he claims the threat of punishment was more necessary for lower classes in order to guarantee/enforce their submission.

(3:21–26)—by means of their own πίστις that follows Jesus's example (3:27–5:11).[33] While understanding Paul's use of πίστις throughout Rom 1–5 is critical to understanding its argument, God's plan for justice (and the inclusion of both Jews and ἔθνη in it) is the central point of Paul's letter. God's justice (*not* the meaning and significance of πίστις) directs and necessitates its argumentative order and flow.[34] Since this chapter focuses

---

33. Arguing against numerous, strict divisions in Rom 1–5, Stowers writes, "Paul did not write in paragraphs, and paragraphs should not be assumed as the only way to arrange the sense of an ancient prose text." See Stanley K. Stowers, *A Rereading of Romans: Justice, Jews, and Gentiles* (New Haven: Yale University Press, 1994), 231. Stowers argues that Romans cannot be seen as a generalized "theological treatise" and particularly that 2:17–5:11 is a single, closely united, unit. Among Romans commentators, similar points are made by Leander E. Keck, *Romans*, ANTC (Nashville: Abingdon, 2005), 23–25; John B. Cobb Jr. and David J. Lull, *Romans*, Chalice Commentaries for Today (Saint Louis: Chalice, 2005), 22–23. On the rhetorical argument and a detailed overview, see Robert Jewett, *Romans: A Commentary*, Hermeneia (Minneapolis: Fortress, 2007), 23–46. He divides 1:18–4:25 as the "first proof," and 5:1–11 is then the start of the second; see similarly, Douglas J. Moo, *The Epistle to the Romans*, NICNT (Grand Rapids: Eerdmans, 1996); Joseph A. Fitzmyer, *Romans*, AB 33 (New York: Doubleday, 1993), 96–98; Brendan Byrne, *Romans*, SP 6 (Collegeville, MN: Liturgical, 2007), 26–28. James D. G. Dunn places a hard break between 1:18–3:20 and 3:21–5:21, saying 5:1–21 is part of this "crucial central section." See James D. G. Dunn, *Romans*, WBC 38, 2 vols (Dallas: Word, 1988), 1:161. Ben Witherington, arguing it is epideictic rhetoric, makes a soft divide between chapters 4 and 5. See Ben Witherington III with Darlene Hyatt, *Paul's Letter to the Romans: A Socio-Rhetorical Commentary* (Grand Rapids: Eerdmans, 2004), 16–22. A. Katherine Grieb keeps 1:18–3:31 as a unit, with 4:1–25 as a separate part of the story, followed by chapters 5–8 as another unit. See A. Katherine Grieb, *The Story of Romans: A Narrative Defense of God's Righteousness* (Louisville: Westminster John Knox, 2002), xxiii. A number of scholars put hard breaks into sections for 1:18–3:20, 3:21–4:25, and 5:1–8:9. See Thomas R. Schreiner, *Romans*, BECNT (Grand Rapids: Baker, 1998), 25–27; Arland J. Hultgren, *Paul's Letter to the Romans: A Commentary* (Grand Rapids: Eerdmans, 2011), 23–25; Frank J. Matera, *Romans*, Paideia (Grand Rapids: Baker Academic, 2010), 12–18.

34. "The argument of this book is that from its very first lines, Paul's letter burns with the incendiary proclamation of God's justice, and with a searing critique of the injustice (*adikia*) of those who smother and suppress the truth" (Elliott, *Arrogance of Nations*, 6). See also Theodore W. Jennings Jr., *Outlaw Justice: The Messianic Politics of Paul*, CMP (Stanford: Stanford University Press, 2013), 1–12, 27–29; Jennings, *Reading Derrida/Thinking Paul: On Justice*, CMP (Stanford: Stanford University Press, 2003), 1–8. Beyond Romans, πίστις and δικαιοσύνη are closely connected as virtues, critical to the maintenance of the Roman imperial state. "Together with *dikaiosynē*, it [*pistis*] is foundational to every society" (Morgan, *Roman Faith*, 502). Additionally,

first on Paul's πίστις and then how that πίστις affects Paul's argument, it requires analyzing Rom 1–5 nonlinearly. Romans 3:21–26 is where Paul's emphasis on πίστις reaches its climax: these verses reveal Jesus's πίστις as the crucial element needed for God's plan. By starting here, *in medias res*, the role of πίστις and its relations of faithful submission become clear enough to analyze the use of πίστις at the beginning and thesis (1:5, 16–17) and hortatory conclusion (4:23–5:11) of Paul's argument.

In Rom 3:21–26, Paul elaborates how Jesus Christ models a relation of πίστις toward God that makes God's justice (δικαιοσύνη) apparent and available for all who display such πίστις. He writes: δικαιοσύνη δὲ θεοῦ διὰ πίστεως Ἰησοῦ Χριστοῦ, εἰς πάντας τοὺς πιστεύοντας ("God's justice, through Jesus Christ's *pistis*, is for all who show *pistis*" [3:22]). This verse offers Jesus's πίστις as the means through which (διά) all others will be able to experience justice from God.[35] Paul's use of πίστις—along with its

---

"the text does not reveal what the sinner has to do in order to be saved (that is, have faith). Rather it tells how God has shown himself *to be righteous by justifying* the gentile people through Jesus' faithful death" (Stowers, *Rereading of Romans*, 223, see also 195–98). Furthermore, throughout Romans, *God* not Jesus is the central topic.

35. This interpretation and my translation of Rom 3:21–31 follows scholars who have made the convincing argument that there are firm grounds for taking πίστεως Ἰησοῦ Χριστοῦ as a subjective genitive ("faith of Jesus Christ") as opposed to an objective genitive ("faith in Jesus Christ," as another grammatical possibility). The debate over this genitive has a long history, and, although messy, the theological differences in interpretation between the two grammatical options are profound. In particular, Stowers's *Rereading of Romans* argues for this meaning, and thus he insists that the πίστις under discussion in Romans, and especially in these verses, belongs to and is the "action" of Jesus—toward God—and is *not* the action/belief of other humans toward Jesus. Thus, the πίστις under discussion in Rom 3:21–26 (as well as in many cases beyond these verses) is Jesus's and not that of his audience, ἔθνη, nor Jews, though it is related to their πίστις as it is discussed elsewhere in chapters 1–5. Stowers asserts that the fact that these instances employ a subjective genitive has been "proven decisive" (Stowers, *Rereading of Romans*, 194–95). Stowers cites Richard B. Hays as laying the definitive and even decisive argument for this translation. See Richard B. Hays, *The Faith of Jesus Christ*, 2nd ed. (Chico, CA: Scholars Press, 2002), which establishes this within Paul's rhetoric and theology in Galatians; see his discussion of Romans on pp. 156–61. Heliso affirms that both are grammatically possible, but the context of πίστις and its usage in Romans affirm a subjective genitive. See Desta Heliso, *Pistis and the Righteous One: A Study of Romans 1:17 against the Background of Scripture and Second Temple Jewish Literature* (Tübingen: Mohr Siebeck, 2007), 223–31, 234–42. See also Morna D. Hooker, "Πίστις Χριστοῦ," in *From Adam to Christ: Essays on Paul* (Cambridge: Cambridge University Press, 1990),

meaning for many of the ἔθνη in Paul's Roman audience—cannot be separated from the term's general first-century meaning in imperial Rome. All

---

165–84; Leander E. Keck, "'Jesus' in Romans," *JBL* 108 (1989): 443–60; Sam K. Williams, "The 'Righteousness of God' in Romans," *JBL* 99 (1980): 272–78; Williams, "Again *Pistis Christou*," *CBQ* 49 (1987): 431–47; J. J. O'Rourke, "*Pistis* in Romans," *CBQ* 36 (1973): 188–94; Donald W. B. Robinson, "'The Faith of Jesus Christ': A New Testament Debate," *RTR* 29 (1970): 71–81; Ian G. Wallis, *The Faith of Jesus Christ in Early Christian Traditions* (Cambridge: Cambridge University Press, 1995); Sigve Tonstad, "Pistis Kristou: Reading Paul in a New Paradigm," *AUSS* 40 (2002): 37–59; Richard N. Longenecker, "Πίστις in Romans 3:25: Neglected Evidence for the 'Faithfulness of Christ'?," *NTS* 39 (1993): 478–80. For the argument for the objective genitive, see James D. G. Dunn, "Once More, *Pistis Christou*," *Society of Biblical Literature 1991 Seminar Papers*, SBLSP 30 (Atlanta: Scholars Press, 1991): 730–44; Roy A. Harrisville III, "ΠΙΣΤΙΣ ΧΡΙΣΤΟΥ: Witness of the Fathers," *NovT* 36 (1994): 233–41; Harrisville, "Before ΠΙΣΤΙΣ ΧΡΙΣΤΟΥ: The Objective Genitive as Good Greek," *NovT* 48 (2006): 353–58; Brian J. Dodd, "Romans 1:17: A *Crux Interpretum* for the πίστις Χριστοῦ Debate?" *JBL* 114 (1995): 470–73. In terms of commentaries, the subjective genitive is used by Witherington, *Paul's Letter to the Romans*, 101–2; Richard N. Longenecker, *The Epistle to the Romans: A Commentary on the Greek Text*, NIGTC (Grand Rapids: Eerdmans, 2016), 408–13 (though he denies Stowers and Gaston's assertions of decisiveness); Luke Timothy Johnson, *Reading Romans: A Literary and Theological Commentary* (New York: Crossroad, 1997), 58–61 (with emphasis on "Jesus's faithful death"); Keck, *Romans*, 104–5; Cobb and Lull, *Romans*, 37–38; Grieb, *Story of Romans*, 37–38. The objective genitive is preferred by Jewett, *Romans*, 268, 275; Philip F. Esler, *Conflict and Identity in Romans* (Minneapolis: Fortress, 2003), 155–59; Moo, *Epistle to the Romans*, 225–26; Fitzmyer, *Romans*, 345–46; Byrne, *Romans*, 124–25, 130; Dunn, *Romans*, 1:166–67; Schreiner, *Romans*, 181–86; Hultgren, *Paul's Letter to the Romans*, 623–61 (devoting an entire appendix to overview the debate's intricacies). For other more summative discussions that represent the history of the debate as well as its continuation from both views, see Michael F. Bird and Preston M. Sprinkle, eds., *The Faith of Jesus Christ: Exegetical, Biblical, and Theological Studies* (Peabody, MA: Hendrickson, 2009). This listing of the various approaches, from a variety of perspectives, shows that this debate has a long history in contemporary scholarship; while I find the arguments—grammatical, exegetical, and theological—convincing, it should be noted that there are equal arguments for the objective genitive that have grounding, especially in terms of Greek grammar, but I find the theological implications and arguments of the objective genitive problematic and based largely on a history of Christian theology that has become too dependent on a "faith in Christ" that does not appear to be concretely existing in the first century. Finally, given that the grammatical/exegetical arguments are likely forever indecisive, theological argumentation seems to be the only compelling reason for either choice, but this—unfortunately—is often deemphasized or seen as a less legitimate argument by many scholars (from both sides of the debate).

πίστις in Romans centers around a relation with (and attachment to) God.[36] Pauline πίστις optimistically attaches Jesus and others to God and the cluster of God's promises.

In Romans, Jesus's πίστις involves Jesus's death and its role in God's plan for justice and salvation, which is most explicitly referenced in 3:21–26. Paul writes:

Νυνὶ δὲ χωρὶς νόμου δικαιοσύνη θεοῦ πεφανέρωται μαρτυρουμένη ὑπὸ τοῦ νόμου καὶ τῶν προφητῶν, δικαιοσύνη δὲ θεοῦ διὰ πίστεως Ἰησοῦ Χριστοῦ εἰς πάντας τοὺς πιστεύοντας. οὐ γάρ ἐστιν διαστολή, πάντες γὰρ ἥμαρτον καὶ ὑστεροῦνται τῆς δόξης τοῦ θεοῦ δικαιούμενοι δωρεὰν τῇ αὐτοῦ χάριτι διὰ τῆς ἀπολυτρώσεως τῆς ἐν Χριστῷ Ἰησοῦ· ὃν προέθετο ὁ θεὸς ἱλαστήριον διὰ πίστεως ἐν τῷ αὐτοῦ αἵματι εἰς ἔνδειξιν τῆς δικαιοσύνης αὐτοῦ διὰ τὴν πάρεσιν τῶν προγεγονότων ἁμαρτημάτων ἐν τῇ ἀνοχῇ τοῦ θεοῦ, πρὸς τὴν ἔνδειξιν τῆς δικαιοσύνης αὐτοῦ ἐν τῷ νῦν καιρῷ, εἰς τὸ εἶναι αὐτὸν δίκαιον καὶ δικαιοῦντα τὸν ἐκ πίστεως Ἰησοῦ.

Now, apart from law, God's justice is revealed, and it is attested by the law and the prophets. God's justice, through Jesus Christ's *pistis*, is for all who show *pistis*. For everyone erred and lacks God's glory, but they are freely made just by God's grace through the ransom-payment that was in Christ Jesus, whom God set out as a *hilasterion* through *pistis* in his blood for the display of God's justice on account of the dismissal of previous errors during God's delay toward the display of God's justice in the present moment; this results in God's being just, and God makes just the person by Jesus's *pistis*. (3:21–26)

As a unit, this miniclimax most clearly conveys that Jesus's πίστις involves faithful submission.[37]

---

36. "Romans is from start to finish theocentric," Hays states. As such, he continues, "In Romans 3, Paul's fundamental concern is to assert the integrity of God" (Hays, *Faith of Jesus Christ*, 156, 159, see further 156–61). Hays's analysis of Rom 3:21–26 affirms the subjective use of the genitive in πίστεως Ἰησοῦ Χριστοῦ, a phrase also found and used similarly in Galatians. See also Stowers, *Rereading of Romans*, 194–95, 225–26. Furthermore, "Paul did not believe in faith. He believed in God and emphasized faith—not because faith is powerful but because God is" (Keck, *Romans*, 133). Johnson also emphasizes God's primary role in Romans (Johnson, *Reading Romans*, 50–54, 60–61).

37. Stowers argues that the significance of Jesus's death here forms the "miniclimax" of Paul's argument in Rom 1:18–5:11, allowing the argument to transition from the depravity and salvation (bringing God's justice) of the ἔθνη to their incorporation (alongside Jews) into the lineage of Abraham (Stowers, *Rereading of Romans*,

According to Stowers, in 3:21–4:2, Paul reveals the significance of the fact that Jesus came into the world as the Χριστός, or the Davidic Messiah, who had the power to immediately bring about the final judgment of the world upon Jews and gentiles. This would have been catastrophic for most gentiles, who have no way to be in right relation with God and whom God has in fact handed over to depravity, in the form of various immoral behaviors (see Rom 1:18–2:16).[38] Unlike Jews, who can be made right with God through the provisions of the law and receive punishment for wrong-doings in the present, these gentiles will not be punished for wrongdoing until the final judgment, when they will have to account for all these compounded wrongs. Though Jesus had the power to immediately bring about God's final judgment and reign, he chose to *delay* (ἀνοχή) this power and instead be punished for treason (as a "messianic pretender") via crucifixion at the hands of the Roman state. In so doing, Jesus *trusted* that God (thus, Jesus's πίστις) would accept this delay as part of God's plan and promise to bring justice to all peoples (a promise elaborated in Paul's exegesis of Abraham's πίστις in Rom 4). The crux of the "good news" (εὐαγγέλιον), then, is that Jesus's trust in and obedience to God's promises has affected this delay, wherein all of the unrepentant and wicked gentiles are able to follow Jesus's trusting example and repent so that they can also be spared at the coming judgment (which will happen upon Jesus's return).[39]

202–6). Stowers emphasizes the continuity of these verses with Paul's preceding argument: "Whereas 1:18–3:21 argues that God by his nature must treat gentiles equally, 3:21–4:2 announces how God has in fact acted impartially toward gentiles and thus made known his righteousness" (Stowers, *Rereading of Romans*, 203). Similarly, Grieb calls this Paul's "first rhetorical climax" (Grieb, *Story of Romans*, 35). See also Moo, *Epistle to the Romans*, 91, 219; Schreiner, *Romans*, 178–79. Many indicate that these verses return to Paul's thesis (1:16–17, see further below) and returns to God's righteousness, having dealt with God's wrath. See Jewett, *Romans*, 268–70; Fitzmyer, *Romans*, 342, Byrne, *Romans*, 122–23; Witherington, *Paul's Letter to the Romans*, 99; Longenecker, *Epistle to the Romans*, 398, 391; Johnson, *Reading Romans*, 50–54. Some make the above points but also emphasize that, as they return to the thesis at a climactic point, these verses arrive abruptly, shift Paul's argument, and are ultimately quite extraordinary. See especially, Hultgren, *Paul's Letter to the Romans*, 151; Matera, *Romans*, 91.

38. As elaborated in chapter 2, the behaviors condemned of the ἔθνη in Rom 1:18–32 are all behaviors that elite Romans would have similarly eschewed and critiqued.

39. This paragraph provides a condensed summary of Stowers's hypothesis, "the Messiah who delayed," which he establishes exegetically and is (as my use and exegetical and theological continuation of it show) quite convincing (Stowers, *Rereading*

Within this context, πίστις—and Jesus's πίστις in particular—puts its subjects into a relationship with God. It affectively attaches them to God by means of a relationship that (as with that of ἔθνη to Rome) involves submission and obedience.[40]

While most of Paul's references to πίστις in Romans refer to the human side of the relation, Paul does occasionally refer to its reciprocity, namely, that God shows πίστις toward humans. He inquires in 3:3: τί γὰρ εἰ ἠπίστησάν τινες; μὴ ἡ ἀπιστία αὐτῶν τὴν πίστιν τοῦ θεοῦ καταργήσει; ("For what if some people break pistis? Doesn't their un-pistis nullify God's pistis?") Paul argues that God's πίστις toward humans remains constant, even if they do not adhere to their part of the relation by showing πίστις to God in turn.[41] Paul's understanding of πίστις aligns with first-century understandings of it as an offering or display of trust that establishes and maintains a relation. πίστις in Romans is also optimistic:

---

of Romans, 213–26). It is often ignored or dismissed in Romans scholarship, with its dismissals being brief and based largely on a refusal to reconsider Pauline/Christian theology in light of the hypothesis's major shift of core historical tenets. (Part of the problem may be rooted in the fact that Stowers offers a strong exegetical argument but himself refuses to consider or acknowledge its theological impact.) This "good news" is mentioned specifically in 1:16–17, a segment that will be discussed later in this chapter.

40. When speaking of humans (including Jesus), Stowers specifies, "Paul associates pistis with obedience to God, and 'trusting obedience' is sometimes a possible translation" (Stowers, Rereading of Romans, 199).

41. Thus, Romans establishes that God has proven God's πίστις to Jews throughout history (and will continue to do so for Jews, as promised, regardless of their actions), and, therefore, (and more importantly for a non-Jewish audience), "Rom 1–3 sets out to show that God's character as revealed in scripture and history leads to the conclusion that he will provide a just and merciful deliverance for the gentiles" (Stowers, Rereading of Romans, 197, see further 196–98). Along similar lines with relation to God's πίστις, "this question [in 3:3] cuts to the heart of monotheistic faith: Is God reliable and trustworthy, or not?" (Johnson, Reading Romans, 42). See also Witherington, Paul's Letter to the Romans, 93–94. Dunn's less radical "new perspective" notes in this verse a tension in Paul's thought between πίστις as a possession of God toward God's people (in Jewish ideas) and πίστις as a possession of humans toward Christ (in Christian ideas) (Dunn, Romans, 1:132). Most commentators devote less attention to God's πίστις and its importance or relevance in Romans, preferring to turn to consider who is unfaithful in relation to it. See Jewett, Romans, 244–245; Byrne, Romans, 109; Moo, Epistle to the Romans, 183–85; Cobb and Lull, Romans, 61–62; Longenecker, Epistle to the Romans, 343–44; Schreiner, Romans, 150–51; Hultgren, Paul's Letter to the Romans, 136–37.

through God's displays of πίστις, God becomes attached to humans—both Jews and ἔθνη.

Although God has demonstrated that God will continue to display πίστις despite the fact that some (τινες) do not respect the reciprocity of the relation and display ἀπιστία ("not-*pistis*," i.e., "faithlessness") instead of πίστις, these persons *should* show πίστις to God. The revelation of God's justice presumes the πίστις of all Jews and ἔθνη—the πᾶσαι αἱ πιστεύουσαι ("all who display πίστις") of 3:22 and 1:16. However, as Paul explains in 1:18–3:20, ἔθνη—in particular here, those who are not Jews—are incapable of such actions due to their ongoing condition, handed to them by God, of being unable to end (i.e., repent) their depraved behaviors.[42]

This is where Jesus as the Christ enters. The latter half of 3:21–26 describes the importance of God's public placement of Jesus.[43] Jesus's public death enacts a plan that requires (1) a means for these ἔθνη to be made just and thereby incorporated into God's establishment of salvation and justice (διὰ τὴν πάρεσιν τῶν προγεγονότων ἁμαρτημάτων, "on account of the dismissal of past errors") and (2) the time for this incorporation (ἐν τῇ ἀνοχῇ τοῦ θεοῦ, "during God's delay").[44] Jesus's death enables both

---

42. Paul insists that God's intent is salvation (σωτηρία) for all who show πίστις, regardless of ethnic status (1:16), but these non-Jewish ἔθνη also need a path, separate from Jewish law, to πίστις that assists them in understanding how to maintain such a relation with this God. Otherwise, it is their (human) nature to be unable to do so (Stowers, *Rereading of Romans*, esp. 104–9, 195–206).

43. This is a rather long sentence (spanning vv. 23–26), whose length is predominated by a relative clause that contains a string of prepositional phrases and few connecting verbal forms. Indeed, there are no verbs or words that function as verbs (infinitives, circumstantial participles, etc.) from προέθετο (at the very beginning of 3:25) until εἶναι (in the second half of 3:26), and in this space, there are seven independent prepositional units. In the sentence, Paul expands on *how* God's justice is being given to all ἔθνη, despite their errors (as explained in 1:18–3:20), as a result of a "payment of ransom" (ἀπολύτρωσις) in the actions of Jesus (τῆς ἐν Χριστῷ Ἰησοῦ).

44. See LSJ, s.v. "ἀνοχή," 148. Stowers prefers to use "held back punishment" for ἀνοχή, which seems overly wordy when "delay" brings out his hypothesis and still captures this holding back (i.e., delaying of punishment) (Stowers, *Rereading of Romans*, 223). On this idea of delay in Second Temple Judaism, see Stowers, *Rereading of Romans*, 104–7. Generally speaking, translators prefer to give this idea of respite or delay a much more decidedly theological or comforting meaning, using terms like *forebearance* and *patience*. See Jewett, *Romans*, 290–91; Fitzmyer, *Romans*, 351–53; Byrne, *Romans*, 133–34; Dunn, *Romans*, 1:173–74; Moo, *Epistle to the Romans*, 237–41; Keck, *Romans*, 111; Hultgren, *Paul's Letter to the Romans*, 159–60. Some com-

the time and the means for God to reveal justice to all people. By trusting God to delay the coming judgment, Jesus perfectly models the πίστις, also required of the ἔθνη, that allows him to maintain a right relation with God and bring about salvation and justice. Jesus's model provides a path (previously inaccessible to ἔθνη) to pardon past wrongdoings, for which these ἔθνη previously would have been held accountable at the now delayed judgment.[45] Jesus's πίστις submits to God's placement and trusts God to display justice.

Jesus's πίστις functions in accordance with Roman conceptions of πίστις and Berlant's optimism. In 3:21–26, Jesus's obedience/submission demonstrates that he has a relationship with God and that he trusts God to adhere to God's plan. For Jesus, according to Romans, the benefit of such an optimistic attachment is the hope that this delay allows for the opportunity for all people to be made just by God. As an experience, optimism attaches subjects to an object (just as πίστις attaches Jesus to God); meanwhile, "the *affective structure* of an optimistic attachment involves a sustaining inclination to return to the scene of fantasy that enables you to expect that *this* time, nearness to *this* thing will help you or a world to become different in just the right way."[46] Jesus's πίστις maintains an optimistic attachment to God, both in the specific experience of his death as implied in 3:21–26 and in the ways in which this πίστις sustains a relation that trusts the promise of *a world becoming different in just the* δίκαιος *way*.[47]

In 3:21–26, Jesus's optimism toward this plan emphatically involves submission to God, as the highest authority. Romans 3:25 explains that, through the πίστις-relation established between Jesus and God (διὰ

---

mentators mention (especially in its relation to the "forgiveness of sins") or prefer a translation of "clemency." See Longenecker, *Epistle to the Romans*, 433–35; Matera, *Romans*, 94. Jewett is alone in following a contention that 3:25–26 is a hymn fragment (Jewett, *Romans*, 270–71).

45. Jesus's death is of most importance in this model. "The best explanation lies in the narrative sketched above: Jesus's act of forgoing messianic powers and privileges meant, for Paul, that although Jesus was the messiah, his all-important act was his dying for the ungodly and his assumption of the status and role given to him when God approved his faithful act by vindicating him in the resurrection" (Stowers, *Rereading of Romans*, 215).

46. Berlant, *Cruel Optimism*, 2.

47. To explain this pun for those less familiar with Greek: though δίκαιος is better rendered "just," translators of biblical texts traditionally gloss the term as "right." (You may laugh now.)

πίστεως), God publicly placed Jesus as a ἱλαστήριον, an act or object that brings about reconciliation or appeasement.[48] Stowers notes that the closest parallel in extant literature comes from 4 Macc 17:22, where it is said that God saves Israel through the ἱλαστήριον of the Maccabean martyrs' deaths.[49] "The martyrs' example leads to national repentance and Antiochus's defeat, and thus to the propitiation of God's anger.… *The faithful resistance (not their deaths)* of the martyrs certainly wins God's favor, but at the same time the effects of their examples on other Jews and on Antiochus bring about the salvation of the nation from Antiochus."[50] In this instance, their "faithful resistance" submits to God (and not Antiochus) as their highest authority.[51]

In the context of Romans, Jesus's placement by God as a ἱλαστηριον provides an example of πίστις to God. A proper πίστις-relation with God will allow ἔθνη to appease God's wrath. Jesus's πίστις is characterized by his obedience to this plan that requires him to die still submissive to God.

---

48. The meaning of ἱλαστήριον is discussed heavily. It has traditionally (and more commonly) been taken to refer to a sacrificial offering according to the Jewish sacrificial system, with Jesus representing a sacrificial (sin) offering of atonement. Stowers makes a compelling case against this interpretation by showing how the idea of a *person* fulfilling the role of sacrificial offering in this way does not make sense with any evidence of Jewish thought or practice in the first century (Stowers, *Rereading of Romans*, 206–13). Drawing from the term's cognates and their uses in the Greco-Roman world, Stowers observes, "Even though *hilastērion* does not seem to have been a common word, there is nothing mysterious about its meaning in everyday speech. In fact, the use of its word group was part of everyday language. Its relation to the more common cognate forms would be clear even for a Greek speaker who had never heard the word before; either an adjective meaning propitiatory/conciliatory or, when used as a substantive, a conciliatory/propitiatory thing, place, or act. There is nothing sacrificial about the concept of propitiation or conciliation that the hilask-words denote, although the words had associations with the divine and cultic activity. People in everyday speech could use *hilaskomai* in reference to appeasing another person's anger or conciliating someone (e.g., Philo, *Spec. Leg.* 1.237; Plato, *Phd.* 1c; Plut., *Cat. Min.* 61)" (Stowers, *Rereading of Romans*, 210). Stressing a broader meaning with similarities to Stowers are Johnson, *Reading Romans*, 56–58; Witherington, *Paul's Letter to the Romans*, 108–9.

49. Stowers explains that the martyr's death is not sacrificial (an interpretation that assumes later Christian theological views) but serves as an example that permits Israel's salvation (Stowers, *Rereading of Romans*, 213).

50. Stowers, *Rereading of Romans*, 212–13, emphasis added.

51. However, as we will see in chapter 5, 4 Maccabees may be anti-Antiochus, but it is not anti-Rome.

He performs proper πίστις to God and allows God to show God's πίστις to him and, by extension, all people.

Related to this segment of Romans, the Christ hymn of Phil 2:6–11 indicates the connection between submission/obedience and Jesus's death and its central role in Paul's theology and Christology.[52] Philippians 2:8 proclaims of Christ Jesus: ἐταπείνωσεν ἑαυτὸν/γενόμενος ὑπήκοος μέχρι θανάτου/θανάτου δὲ σταυροῦ ("He humiliated himself/He became obedient to the point of death/of the cross's death").[53] Jesus is called ὑπήκοος, "obedient," a term that emphasizes his lower and submissive status.[54] Obedience is the act of "hearing under"—in other words, submission by

---

52. The Christ hymn is connected to Rom 3:21–26 by Stowers, who says it particularly emphasizes the theme of adaptability in Paul's Christology (Stowers, *Rereading of Romans*, 219–23). This emphasis on adaptability is what gives Paul's framing of Jesus its uniqueness. For summaries on histories of Phil 2:6–11 as a hymn and its terminology and structure, see Kittredge, *Community and Authority*, 75–77; John Reumann, *Philippians: A New Translation with Introduction and Commentary*, AB 33B (New Haven: Yale University Press, 2008), 333–39; Gregory P. Fewster, "The Philippians 'Christ Hymn': Trends in Critical Scholarship," *CurBR* 13 (2015): 191–98. Peter-Ben Smit prefers to call 2:6–11 an encomium, arguing, "Given that the term *hymnos* was, at least in the classical period, typically used in text addressed to gods that included prayer, *enkomion* seems to be the preferable form-critical classification, especially as the text does precisely what *enkomia* usually did: describing (and lauding) someone by recounting one's origins, deeds (*res gestae*) and end." See Peter-Ben Smit, *Paradigms of Being Christ: A Study of the Epistle to the Philippians* (London: Bloomsbury, 2013), 87. The comparison of the Christ hymn (as encomium) to ancient Res gestae is especially noteworthy here.

53. Within the context of its quotation in Philippians, Kittredge draws the important distinction between how Paul *uses* the hymn to enforce his rhetoric of obedience and how the hymn itself presents Jesus and his submission (Kittredge, *Community and Authority*, 72–86). The Christ hymn is often noted as presenting Jesus (especially in terms of his submission to death/crucifixion) as a model or example. See especially Peter Oakes, *Philippians: From People to Letter* (Cambridge: Cambridge University Press, 2001), 190; Carolyn Osiek, *Philippians, Philemon*, ANTC (Nashville: Abingdon, 2000), 55–69; Bonnie B. Thurston and Judith M. Ryan, *Philippians and Philemon*, SP 10 (Collegeville, MN: Liturgical, 2005), 90–91; Gerald F. Hawthorne, *Philippians*, WBC 43 (Waco, TX: Word, 1983), 79; L. Gregory Bloomquist, *The Function of Suffering in Philippians* (Sheffield: JSOT Press, 1993), 168.

54. See Kittredge, *Community and Authority*, 79–80. On the connection of Greco-Roman praise of such obedience to its praise of πίστις, see Reumann, *Philippians*, 371. See also Bloomquist, *Function of Suffering*, 166. Marchal notes that the hymn's emphasis is on this obedience (especially with respect to Jesus's death) and its need to be imitated by the epistle's audience. See Joseph A. Marchal, *Hierarchy, Unity,*

hearing and then adhering to another's command.[55] Such a hearing, then, implies placing oneself (or being placed) at lower level in order to hear and obey; whoever issues a command that requires such obedience has authority. Indeed, this is the same term Philo used above, translated as "subjects," when he describes them as "slaves of the emperor."[56]

As 2:7 states, Jesus takes the form of an enslaved person (μορφὴν δούλου λαβών), putting himself below all others in social terms: he becomes the ultimate submissive subject.[57] Jesus's obedience is a form of submission that results from his πίστις-relation with God. This submission has status implications when the terms describing his death are read in the context of Roman imperial hierarchy. Jesus's submissive status is further emphasized by the

---

and Imitation: A Feminist Rhetorical Analysis of Power Dynamics in Paul's Letter to the Philippians, AcBib 24 (Atlanta: Society of Biblical Literature, 2006), 134–35.

55. As with the Greek term for submission (ὑποτάσσω, "place under"), ὑπήκοος is an adjectival form from the same root as the verb ὑπακούω, "to obey," formed from the verb "to hear" (ἀκούω) and the same prepositional prefix for "under" (ὑπό). Kittredge considers both terms to be "within the language of obedience" and lays out the semantic uses of both terms in Greco-Roman literature (Kittredge, Community and Authority, 37–51, quotation from 51).

56. In other words, "subjects" are "obedient ones."

57. "Thus, to Roman imperial eyes, Jesus' form is that of an enslaved barbarian woman." See Katherine A. Shaner, "Seeing Rape and Robbery: ἁρπαγμός and the Philippians Christ Hymn (Phil. 2:5–11)," BibInt 25 (2017): 361, see further 360–61. Sheila Briggs draws attention to the problems of the hymn's kyriocentric use of slavery: "It Does not challenge the interests or beliefs of slavemasters." See Sheila Briggs, "Can an Enslaved God Liberate? Hermeneutical Reflections on Philippians 2:6–11," Semeia 47 (1989): 149, see further 142–46, in which she compares Jesus's "lowering" to that of highborn persons who become slaves in Greco-Roman novels: they are never really slaves, just as Jesus is not when read in light of 2:9–11. In other words, this hymn does not seem to fully reflect the reality of slavery as "social death." Kittredge discusses the hymn's use of slavery, acknowledging Briggs, and argues that the hymn's proclamation transforms the conventional (Roman imperial) understanding of slavery (Kittredge, Community and Authority, 79–81). The exaltation of 2:9–11 cannot be ignored, but I am especially interested in what the first half of the hymn can proclaim without too quickly skipping to the exaltation and resurrection of the latter verses (see more in the following chapter, "Faithful Subversion," where the Christ hymn returns). Relating the imagery of slavery to Paul's command to obey (ὑπακούσατε, 2:12, cf. ὑπήκοος 2:8), Marchal notes, "The communal obedience is compulsory, with 'fear and trembling,' as in a slave/master relationship." See Joseph A. Marchal, The Politics of Heaven: Women, Gender, and Empire in the Study of Paul, PCC (Minneapolis: Fortress, 2008), 52. See also Reumann, Philippians, 349; Stowers, Rereading of Romans, 220.

mention of his humiliation. To make oneself humble or lower (ἐταπείνωσεν) is a form of submission, being placed under (by choice or force) another's authority, an indication of lowness on Rome's hierarchy.[58] The hymn makes explicit that Jesus's obedient actions are those that makes him lower, even lowest, according to imperial terms.

Expanding on the degree of this humiliation, the emphasis on the form of Jesus's death confirms the shame and ultimate submission it entails: θανάτου δὲ σταυροῦ, "the cross's death." As a form of capital punishment, Roman crucifixion was particularly brutal and reserved for the worst and lowest of criminals.[59] Taking enslaved form, Jesus does not merely accept the harsh conditions of Roman slavery; he submits to being placed in the lowest of enslaved positions, that of an unfaithful slave convicted of heinous crimes (as defined by the imperial state) and publicly sentenced to death. Jesus's humiliation is submission: in God's hands, he is lowered and placed under to the point of being crucified in enslaved form.

---

58. This verb, ταπεινόω, means "to lower or decrease in height or size" and was often used to mean "to disparage, humble, or abase"—in other words, to be put in a position considered lower in social and political terms. "Humility was a slave virtue" (Thurston and Ryan, *Philippians and Philemon*, 83). See also Reumann, *Philippians*, 351–52; Kittredge, *Community and Authority*, 79–80.

59. See John Granger Cook, *Crucifixion in the Mediterranean World* (Tübingen: Mohr Siebeck, 2014), 359; Wenhua Shi, *Paul's Message of the Cross as Body Language* (Tübingen: Mohr Siebeck, 2008), 20–52. On its public nature, and how this embodied display was critical to maintaining peace/order, see Shi, *Paul's Message of the Cross*, 41–45; Martin Hengel, *Crucifixion: In the Ancient World and the Folly of the Message of the Cross* (Philadelphia: Fortress, 1977). On broader reactions to crucifixion in Jewish sources of the first centuries BCE/CE and early Christian texts, see David W. Chapman, *Ancient Jewish and Christian Perspectives of Crucifixion* (Tübingen: Mohr Siebeck, 2008). Chapman's overall argument emphasizes that both types of sources ultimately reflect similar views. These studies affirm the general assessment that crucifixion was the punishment typically used for the worst crimes, slaves, and poor foreigners/noncitizens, and it would seem logical to conclude (though no one makes the connection) that this would have perpetuated an idea that those of lowest status were most likely to commit the worst crimes (not entirely unlike such stereotypical correlations in modern society and the death penalty). Studies note its occasional usage on citizens (to qualify its application to lowest classes), but it is noteworthy that ancient sources spend much more time on these deaths *because* they must be justified—that is, if those of lowest status were more depraved and prone to commit the worst crimes, then how could someone of high, native Roman status ever deserve such a punishment (and the answer often seems to be because they had some slavish association/influence).

Returning to Rom 3, verses 25–26a emphasize God's role in setting him out to be crucified. προτίθημι (literally, "to set before") denotes action of setting or placement in a public or visible manner.[60] Although a rarer meaning, it could be used in contexts of death ("to hand over for burial"), including references to the practice of exposing children.[61] His death represents a public display for which the verb προτίθημι would be used. In 3:25, προέθετο describes God's placement of Jesus into a situation of death through a treasonous condemnation. Through his πίστις (διὰ πίστεως) toward God, Jesus acts submissively by allowing God to place him however God sees fit in order to accomplish God's plan for justice. By trusting God in this public placement, Jesus takes a passive role and displays πίστις in order to faithfully submit to God's authority. He is under God.

In Romans, God holds all power and authority, just like the emperor who mercifully displays the *fides Romana* and expects *fides publica* in return. Paul emphasizes the public nature of God's placement and authority—and, by extension, Jesus's submission—by twice describing Jesus's faithful submission as a "display" (ἔνδειξις).[62] The repetition of this display

---

60. LSJ, s.v. "προτίθημι," 1536. Its base meaning renders English translations such as "institute, propose"; "display, bring forward"; or (more temporally) "put first." The typical temporal meaning of the preposition πρό is largely absent in most uses of this compound, as in composition the preposition more often derives from the local meaning ("in front of"). See Herbert Weir Smyth, *Greek Grammar*, rev. Gordon M. Messing (Cambridge: Harvard University Press, 1920, 1984), 384 (§1694). See further Jewett, *Romans*, 283–84; Fitzmyer, *Romans*, 349; Byrne, *Romans*, 132; Matera, *Romans*, 98–99; Longenecker, *Epistle to the Romans*, 425–26; Hultgren, *Paul's Letter to the Romans*, 157–58 (with particular emphasis on cultic usage); Cobb and Lull, *Romans*, 67–70. A few commentaries note God's action and that this is God's plan. See Witherington, *Paul's Letter to the Romans*, 191–92 (however, qualifies it as "not grotesque"); Schreiner, *Romans*, 193–94 (stemming from the assumption that Jesus is of divine origin).

61. LSJ, s.v. "προτίθημι," 1536. See also Josephus, *B.J.*, 1.454 for a potentially similar usage with regard to a father and his adult children (however, there is a textual discrepancy and disagreement on whether προτίθημι is the verb used, and LCL prefers the variant).

62. God's placing action that entails Jesus's death and faithful submission is twice described as ἔνδειξις, a "pointing out" or "indication"—put more specifically into common usage, a "demonstration" or "display" (LSJ, s.v. "ἔνδειξις," 558). Commentators generally use "demonstration" or "manifestation." See Jewett, *Romans*, 291; Fitzmyer, *Romans*, 350–51; Schreiner, *Romans*, 194, 196; Byrne, *Romans*, 128; Longenecker, *Epistle to the Romans*, 433.

language emphasizes that Jesus's πίστις and his resulting placement (in God's hand) onto the cross ultimately benefits God: Jesus's faithful submission permits God to display God's justice and, by extension, God's power.[63] Displaying this submissive πίστις toward God proves that God is indeed πίστος and will bring justice to ἔθνη as well as to Jews.

Acknowledging this πίστις-relation and his attachment to God, Jesus reciprocates the relation according to its terms: he submits to God's authority, to God's power of placement. For Jesus, this πίστις-relation with God involves being passive to God's authority. He trusts that God will use him to display justice. In Rom 3:25, Paul alludes to the brutal humiliation of Jesus's death by indicating that Jesus's πίστις and his placement as a ἱλαστηριον requires his blood (ἐν τῷ αὐτοῦ αἵματι).[64] This short descriptive phrase indicates these details of Jesus's crucifixion by Rome: "By referring to Jesus's death through 'blood,' Paul underlines the violent nature of his death, the readers knowing that Jesus died by crucifixion."[65] He trusts that, since his crucifixion as condemnation for treason is caused by God's placement of him as a ἱλαστήριον, "with his blood" his death will lead into an ultimate demonstration of justice from God (εἰς ἔνδειξιν τῆς δικαιοσύνης αὐτοῦ). Rome typically reserved this brutal punishment for enslaved persons who committed acts of treason that disrupted or threatened imperial order—acts that indicated a grave lack of πίστις toward one's overlords, both one's master and the imperial state. Paradoxically, Jesus proves πιστός in his relation to God by appearing ἄπιστός in his condemnation to crucifixion.[66]

---

63. Indeed, in the first instance, God's public placement of Jesus is εἰς ἔνδειξιν τῆς δικαιοσύνης αὐτοῦ, "into a display of God's justice." After two other prepositional phrases, the term occurs again, in an almost similar phrasing: πρὸς τὴν ἔνδειξιν τῆς δικαιοσύνης αὐτοῦ, "toward the display of God's justice." Also noting the doubling and emphasis are Jewett, *Romans*, 291; Fitzmyer, *Romans*, 353.

64. Just as the Christ hymn highlights, Jesus's πίστις requires his submission to the point of death: he must be convicted of treason and sentenced to crucifixion at the hands of Rome's empire. Most commentators discuss the blood in relation to the language of atonement and sacrifice, only quickly mentioning the actual crucifixion/death. See Jewett, *Romans*, 187; Moo, *Epistle to the Romans*, 237; Fitzmyer, *Romans*, 348–49 (who translates ἐν as "through"); Schreiner, *Romans*, 194–95; Dunn, *Romans*, 1:170–72; Longenecker, *Epistle to the Romans*, 430–432; Matera, *Romans*, 98–99; Johnson, *Reading Romans*, 57–58.

65. Stowers, *Rereading of Romans*, 210.

66. However, this unfaithful appearance cannot necessarily be called an example for Christ-followers to mimic his treason in a subversive move against the empire.

Jesus's death trusts God's plan and God's authority to the point of ultimate submission to God and to the state. Jesus's πίστις is faithful submission. Jesus acknowledges God's ability to enact justice for all people, so long as he (and they) accept God's ultimate power and control, giving God all authority to set (προτίθημι) their lives in order to realize God's justice, power, and authority for and over all people. Through its faithful submission, Jesus's πίστις attaches him to God and the optimistic promises of God's plan for justice.

πίστις ἐθνῶν

Next, we prepare for the cruelty of πίστις by setting up a contradiction between the situation of Rome's conquered ἔθνη and the good life fantastically possessed by Roman citizens. Optimism, according to Berlant, attaches subjects to clusters of promises. In the case of cruel optimism, optimism's cluster of promises take the form of fantasies of the good life. In Berlant's contemporary context, these fantasies generally amount to capitalism's normative notions of success (financial, familial, political, and so on) and, more importantly, the *kinds* of lives people who have such success *seem* to lead: a well-paying job with regular hours, a well-behaved and properly-sized family, and participation in socially acceptable leisure activities.[67] The good life displays a life that has attained these goals—or is sufficiently upwardly mobile to attain them in the near future.

In what follows, I outline the promises of a Roman good life in the first century CE as fantasized for and by the conquered nations (ἔθνη) whom Rome affectively drew into optimistic πίστις-relations. The situation of Roman ἔθνη—including their status and portrayal under empire and its conquest of foreign nations—informs their submission to empire and the πίστις they are expected to display in reciprocity for the ongoing display of πίστις from the emperor and his people, as promised in the Res gestae.

Such an interpretation does not seem to represent Paul's use of Jesus's death. Jesus's submission to God is seemingly supposed to represent an *extreme* lowering and humiliation that, in so doing, emphasizes the extent of his πίστις toward God, that he is willing to be placed in this extreme situation if it will bring about salvation of all ἔθνη (compare, then, to the extremity of the examples of the Maccabean martyrs that results in Israel's salvation).

67. See Berlant's description/summary of *Rosetta* especially, as well as and in conversation with *La Promesse* (Berlant, *Cruel Optimism*, 161–71).

Roman good-life fantasies draw these conquered subjects toward Romo-sexual conformity: they are promised that the good life can be achieved by faithfully performing Romanormativity. Echoing the beneficial prom-ises of Rome's good life, Paul draws these ἔθνη (Paul's primary audience in the imperial capital) into performances of πίστις that follow the model of Jesus's faithful submission. This πίστις-relation fantasizes a good life for ἔθνη under a Roman-without-Rome God.

The Faithful Submission of Rome's ἔθνη

Though all were under the emperor as his subjects, inhabitants of Rome could be distinguished by various status designations along a hierarchy. In somewhat simplified form, senators and elite patricians were above freeborn plebs, who were in turn above freedpersons, who were above enslaved persons. Within and beyond this hierarchy, citizens were distin-guished from those not granted citizenship.[68] Among those excluded from citizenship status were most ἔθνη/gentes, who were differentiated from the δῆμος/populus ("people") of Rome, a mark of both citizenship and terri-torial belonging, as opposed to being a foreigner.[69] Though some elites among certain ἔθνη were granted the privileges of Roman citizens, they were still thought to be separate from those born in the original Roman state. In the context of the Roman empire, ἔθνη is a signifier for "others," that is, "the non-Roman peoples of the Roman Empire."[70]

To be any ἔθνη under Roman control was to be conquered, in the empire's view. Imperial imagery reinforced its hierarchy of conquest and domination over ἔθνη, as Davina Lopez has demonstrated. The imagery on the massive Sebasteion in Aphrodisias repeated this ideology on a massive scale. Images depicting Rome's conquest over many ἔθνη comprised the

---

68. Clarke provides a concise (and visualized) rendering of these distinctions. See John R. Clarke, *Art in the Lives of Ordinary Romans: Visual Representation and Non-Elite Viewers in Italy, 100 B.C.–A.D. 100* (Berkeley: University of California Press, 2006), 1–13, esp. 6.

69. See Lavan, *Slaves to Rome*, 32–37.

70. Davina C. Lopez, *Apostle to the Conquered: Reimagining Paul's Mission*, PCC (Minneapolis: Fortress, 2008), 26. As will be seen below, Lopez situates the language of ἔθνος/ἔθνη within its Roman imperial context. She argues, "As a result of such a broader, non-idealist analysis bolstered by attention to gender, sexuality, ethnicity, and militarism, the meaningful hierarchy for Pauline studies emerges as not Jews/Gentiles but Romans/nations" (Lopez, *Apostle to the Conquered*, 26).

lower row of panels on either main wall of the imperial worship complex.[71] The most well-known of these panels depicts the emperor Claudius (representing a masculinized Rome) towering over and suppressing a defeated Brittania (representing a feminized Britain). By repeating this imagery to encompass a multitude of the nations now comprising Rome, the empire reenforced its domination over these and other ἔθνη now submissive to its rule.[72] These stone representations cleave ἔθνη from native Romans.

Gender and sexuality intersect with race/ethnicity in order to perpetuate the necessity of imperial rule.[73] Rome's domination is presented as masculine and penetrative over the feminine and penetrated conquered nations. Romosexual protocols of properly gendered sexuality and properly sexualized gender informs the panels' positioning of the always male victor standing above and over (on top) of the conquered women. The depictions of the Roman victor often have a sexualized sense, with swords poised to penetrate the conquered women who assume more or less sexually receptive positions.[74] According to Romosexuality, these ἔθνη—by being conquered, penetrated, and passive—are not only unfit to rule themselves, but they are also unfit to be of the same status as the impenetrable

---

71. Lopez, *Apostle to the Conquered*, 26–28, 42–48, see also 16–17. The Sebasteion of Aphrodisias, alongside other Roman imperial images, is a visual representation of Rome's ideology of conquest, as Lopez argues. Shaner also analyzes the Aphrodisian imagery of imperialism (Claudius and Brittania, in particular) alongside other imperial representation of the inevitability and divine nature of Roman rule. Shaner writes, "an argument for the inevitability of divine imperial power emerges. Those who struggle against divinely ordained submission are no match for the beautiful, serene, imperial god-figure" (Shaner, "Seeing Rape and Robbery," 358, see further 350–58). On this massive visual representation of Roman imperial power and conquest, ἔθνη are under Romans and their gods, politically or otherwise.

72. As Lopez observes, these panels present Roman victory over the nations as decisive military victories that reinforce Rome's right to rule and imply the need for imperial rule and hierarchy as necessary for the provision of peace and prosperity for Rome and for each conquered ἔθνος (Lopez, *Apostle to the Conquered*, 50–55). Despite this portrayal, historical sources reveal that the conquest was ultimately only finalized through diplomacy, with several setbacks for Rome prior to this victory (in addition to uprisings that occurred afterward) (Lopez, *Apostle to the Conquered*, 44).

73. Lopez, *Apostle to the Conquered*, 50.

74. Lopez, Apostle to the Conquered, 44. Shaner emphasizes the assaultive sexual violence of these representations: "Thus in the visual rhetoric of these reliefs, the imperial god's divinity is confirmed in the act of seizure and victory; said another way, robbery and rape equals God" (Shaner, "Seeing Rape and Robbery," 358).

Roman elite. Regardless of their gender, those classified as ἔθνη are lesser on the hierarchy and should only be placed under (socially and sexually) the proper rule of Roman men.[75] This gendered and sexualized stability complements and affirms the stability of Rome's racial and class hierarchies, all of which entwined and enforced a peaceful imperial regime.

Although Augustus and his successors faithfully incorporated these ἔθνη into Rome and portrayed themselves offering to these peoples the benefits of Roman life, the empire considered them lesser, as persons needing to be placed under, or submitted.[76] Through the gendered and sexualized dimensions of this ideology, the emperor and those on top reminded these peoples of their conquered position that placed them under Rome's elite. As gender, sexuality, race/ethnicity, and social status intersect, they more than quadruple many wo/men's marginalization and oppression under the reign of Rome's πίστις. Who is farthest from the cluster of benefits πίστις promises?

At Rome (the city), the situation of these ἔθνη was more complicated. Whereas in provinces like Galatia one can easily assume that the majority of the population were not native, freeborn Romans, it is difficult to even estimate the number of foreigners (free or enslaved) present in the city of Rome and its immediate surroundings.[77] These foreigners living in Rome, whether they came for a limited time or permanently, were deemed *peregrini* by Romans.[78] Those labelled *peregrini* represented a variety of social positions, as they could have been free, freedpersons, or enslaved. Their reasons for residence (permanent or otherwise) could vary.[79]

---

75. "Roman peace is achieved through patriarchy: feminine submission stabilizes Roman masculinity" (Lopez, *Apostle to the Conquered*, 54).

76. In the early years of his reign, Nero bolstered public projects that "reinforced the inevitability and rightness of the imperial regime" (Elliott, *Arrogance of Nations*, 40, see also 40–42). See further Edward Champlin, *Nero* (Cambridge: Harvard University Press, 2003).

77. David Noy discusses the difficulties of estimation, primarily due to lack of firm censorial evidence and the fact that much evidence of foreign presence at Rome is dependent upon what was recorded and preserved in epigraphs (largely funerary). Further evidence, often about the more general population, can be gleaned from information about the amount of grain supplied to Roman residents, the extent of dwelling spaces (more telling for fourth century Rome), and other similar factors. See David Noy, *Foreigners at Rome: Citizens and Strangers* (London: Duckworth, 2000), 15–29.

78. Noy, *Foreigners at Rome*, 1–4.

79. That is, an enslaved person's reasons for coming to Rome would largely be determined (though perhaps not exclusively) by her of his enslaver at the time. Among

Despite this variety, it is clear that *peregrini*, as foreigners not coming from the immediate Italian provinces, refers to persons who originated from the foreign, often conquered, ἔθνη who have taken up residence in Rome. The difference between ἔθνη (and *gentes*) and the term *peregrini* is that *peregrini* specifies those ἔθνη who have become foreigners by leaving their homelands to reside in the imperial capital.[80] The term denotes their difference from the citizen class and emphasizes the fact that ἔθνη, as foreigners living in Rome (even those who have resided in the city for several generations) are of a different status of those granted Roman citizenship.

As with ἔθνη who resided in their home territories, some foreigners could become Roman citizens, but this was the exception and not the rule. Freeborn *peregrini* were likely to remain separated as noncitizen foreigners for generations, making the likelihood of a significant rise in status unlikely (though certainly some immigrants to Rome found material success and were able to finagle citizen status).[81] This legal and social distinction emphasizes to these ἔθνη who have immigrated to Rome (whether recently or long ago) that they are still lower on the imperial hierarchy, in large reason because their homelands have been conquered and brought under the empire's rule. Whether living in an occupied territory or as a *peregrinus* in Rome, one's origin as part of an ἔθνος, and not a natural Roman, lowered one's social and political status.

Enslaved persons—most of whom would have origins among Rome's conquered ἔθνη—who were freed were supposed to be granted citizenship as freedpersons. Freeborn ἔθνη/*peregrini* were treated with more suspicion and generally restricted from citizenship. Matthew

---

those of free status, reason could vary based on class and occupation: some may have come to Rome for financial opportunity (Noy, *Foreigners at Rome*, 85–139).

80. Though these contexts show the term was used elsewhere and can refer generally to foreigners, there is ample evidence of its use in the city of Rome to differentiate natural-born citizens from ethnic foreigners. See Noy, *Foreigners at Rome*, 1–4, 31–52; Lavan, *Slaves to Rome*, 32–37; Esler, *Conflict and Identity*, 84–86.

81. Noy, *Foreigners at Rome*, 23–26, 75–78. Indeed, if a law under Claudius is descriptive of on-the-ground conditions, some *peregrini* may have tried to present themselves as citizens despite not having been legally granted the right. This emphasizes the reality that the distinction between a citizen and a *peregrinus* in Rome could be minimal and nonexistent, especially for foreigners who were more able to blend in as Romans (for reasons of means, easier ability, or having lived in Rome for generations). However, even if some *peregrini* were able to become citizens by passing, others were not (Noy, *Foreigners at Rome*, 24–26).

Perry, discussing the distinctiveness of Rome's granting of citizen status to freedpersons, emphasizes how this distinguishes freedpersons from free foreigners: "The practice was all the more remarkable given that Romans attached substantial meaning to citizenship, routinely hesitating to bestow full citizen rights upon freeborn foreigners." Though remarkable, freedpersons were likely seen as less threatening subjects—that is, worthy of incorporation into citizenry. Roman law passed in the Augustan era, including the *lex Fufia Caninia* (2 BCE) and the *lex Aelia Sentia* (4 CE), defined the freedperson-patron relationship and restricted the number of enslaved persons who could be freed.[82] These laws participated in a discourse about manumission as a citizen-building process that required enslaved persons to prove themselves *worthy* of citizenship if they were to be freed, meaning they should be loyal and faithful to their enslaver and, by extension, Rome.[83] In theory, the promise of manumission and citizenship motivated fidelity among enslaved persons.[84] By attempting to restrict citizenship to only those who *proved* most faithfully submissive, Rome ensured its newest citizens would sustain the *fides publica*. Citizenship and manumission help motivate Roma-normativity.[85] Furthermore, through the process of enslavement and manumission, enslaved wo/men had their ethnic heritage erased from public view: their enslavers gave them names when they were enslaved, and, if freed, their citizenship gave them *Roman* names, associated with the *familia* of their patron/enslaver.[86] Freeborn ἔθνη/*peregrini*, though certainly benefitting from never having been enslaved, could not be controlled and molded toward faithful citizenship in the same way. As a result, it was less possible for them to disassociate from their lesser status as foreigners (vis-à-vis citizens).

This lesser status, particularly justified through the portrayal of ἔθνη as conquered, submissive subjects, was emphasized in the Roman capital

---

82. Perry, *Gender*, 4, 64–65.

83. Perry, *Gender*, 59–67. See also MacLean, *Freed Slaves*, 3, 37–41.

84. In practice would be another story, since many enslaved persons resisted and rebelled, and some may have more subtly resisted the system to use manumission and citizenship promises for their own agendas. Elite texts tell us only their idealized versions of freedom and citizenship.

85. Indeed, as Perry shows, marriage—especially for freedwomen—signified their successful, productive citizenship. See especially Perry, *Gender*, 88–93.

86. MacLean, *Freed Slaves*, 3; Perry, *Gender*, 99–106.

at least as much as it was in cities like Aphrodisias.[87] Lopez observes that it is conceivable that the Sebasteion depictions in Aphrodisias were similar to those seen in the "images of nations" (*simulacra gentium*) mentioned as having been on the portico in Pompey's theater in Rome (though they are lost), and similarly gendered depictions of Roman dominance and ethnic/ barbarian submission can be seen on the cuirass of Augustus's Prima Porta statue, which was found close to Rome.[88]

Literary examples describe triumphal processions that occurred in Rome to commemorate Roman victories over various ἔθνη. In these processions, the emperor would parade through the streets, along with the army. They were accompanied by some of those captured in the vanquished territories, an embodied representation of the ἔθνη as conquered and submissive to Rome's imperial might.[89] According to Josephus's account of the procession that followed Rome's destruction of Jerusalem, Vespasian led his soldiers through the city as they displayed the treasure, the captives, and—most impressively according to Josephus—floats that depicted battle scenes so spectators could experience the drama of Rome's victory (*B.J.* 7.131–152). These captive representatives were not only paraded as captives of Rome's great army but also dressed in a fashion that would have been stereotypical of their ἔθνος. These processions highlighted the foreignness, difference, and lower status of these submissive ἔθνη as compared to the native Roman citizenry.[90]

---

87. Or in central Turkey, where the only extant monuments of the Res gestae has been found (though evidence suggests similar monuments were erected throughout the empire, including in Rome). In addition to the Sebasteion images, Lopez discusses the Res gestae and its role, as both literary and visual representation, in perpetuating imperial propaganda that presented the ἔθνη as conquered by Rome (in gendered terms). See Lopez, *Apostle to the Conquered*, 88–100.

88. Lopez, *Apostle to the Conquered*, 1, 38–42.

89. Lopez, *Apostle to the Conquered*, 113–17. In addition to her general account and analysis, she observes how, in an instance of a procession under Caligula (described by Suetonius), captured Gauls were fashioned into Germans through dress, height, and the changing of hair length and color (p. 116). For the full account of such a procession, Lopez relies on and cites Josephus, *B.J.* 7.131–153. See also Emma Dench, *Romulus' Asylum* (Oxford: Oxford University Press, 2005), 37–41; Mary Beard, "The Triumph of Flavius Josephus," in *Flavian Rome: Culture, Image, Text*, ed. Anthony Boyle and William J. Dominik (Leiden: Brill, 2002), 543–58.

90. The processions constitute a performance that enforces the hierarchy of Romans over nations, citizens over foreigners. Lopez observes, "It allows the specta-

If the Roman citizens who participated in such a spectacle experienced these processional performances as the conquerors, then what of the *peregrini*—the transplanted ἔθνη—who also would have viewed these processions? This embodied ritual would have communicated to these ἔθνη similar messages to those in the panels of nations and other instances that Lopez identifies: Rome has conquered the ἔθνη and forced them into submission to Rome. Their conquered, feminized, penetrated status—as emphasized in the procession—confirms their lower social status and justifies their failure to attain citizen status.[91]

Peregrini who came from ἔθνη that had been conquered in the more distant past may have incorporated themselves into Roman life and a more citizen-like mindset, even if they had not attained such a status. These *peregrini* might have joined with their fellow Romans in celebrating the victory. By also participating in Rome's conquest, these foreigners could see themselves as better incorporated and more Roman (i.e., less conquered and penetrated) compared with more recently defeated ἔθνη.[92] While these *peregrini* are still below citizen status, they can imagine and present themselves as politically and socially above new groups of conquered others. Their optimistic πίστις attaches them to a fantasy of a good life that requires seeing themselves rising over others on the kyriarchal pyramid. Unfortunately, the public performance reaffirms the ongoing sociopolitical difference between *peregrini* and the *populus Romano*. Under the eyes of the empire, all foreigners are still distinct from and lower than the citizen class.

Although these ἔθνη are still conquered and of lower status, their ability to show and be shown πίστις as willingly submissive subjects draws them into potential relationships with their imperial conquerors. Reciprocal trust offers ἔθνη the possibilities for satisfying benefits of Roman rule (such as those experienced by many of Rome's [elite] citizens) in exchange for their willing submission to this rule. When Augustus declares on his Res gestae that, via his military conquests, he has allowed many ἔθνη to experience the πίστις of Rome's people (i.e., the citizen-body of those naturally born Romans), he is describing the relationship of the

---

tors at the city of Rome to participate safely—on a highly constructed, managed, and censored level—in Roman world conquest" (Lopez, *Apostle to the Conquered*, 114).

91. Lopez, *Apostle to the Conquered*, 114–17.

92. Indeed, one expects, some fraction of their ἔθνος would have been conscripted as part of Rome's military.

imperial state to these newly conquered peoples. At the mercy of these Roman people, headed and represented by the emperor, the future peace and prosperity of these foreign subjects depended upon how well they were incorporated into the Roman state as conquered ἔθνη. Magnanimously, Augustus suggests that he (and through him, all Rome) is willing to display πίστις—trust and loyalty—to these ἔθνη, even if once considered enemies of the Roman people.

Augustus does not speak directly of the πίστις that these conquered persons must show toward Rome.[93] However, the reciprocity is implicit. In the case of the Res gestae, reciprocal πίστις from the ἔθνη is implied in the terms of their submission: these ἔθνη display their πίστις by remaining loyal and trustworthy—and therefore, obedient—subjects of the empire. Consequently, to behave in less submissive ways—breaking the πίστις-relation—meant risking military suppression, for those residing in ethnic territories, or expulsion from Rome, in the case of peregrini.[94] Whether

---

93. This is not surprising: Morgan observes that most sources avoid discussing the πίστις of both parties within the same text, especially in cases where there is a status difference that might be mitigated if the reciprocal nature of πίστις is stated directly (Morgan, Roman Faith, 53).

94. Noy notes the threat of expulsion of foreigners—usually of a particular ethnic group—was common (Noy, Foreigners at Rome, 37–47). Such a point contextualizes the Edict of Claudius, through which Claudius reportedly ordered the expulsion of all Jews from the city of Rome around 49–50 CE. Noy's point emphasizes how Jews in Rome were in the same situation as any other ἔθνη/peregrini there. This expands the possibilities for how Jews in Rome—and/as ἔθνη in the ἐκκλησία—may have responded to such an expulsion and its ongoing threat within as a normal part of their lives (surely a "crisis ordinary" for those affected more by such expulsions). Claudius's edict is only directly attested in two first/second century accounts: Suetonius, Lives of the Caesars, 5.25.4: Iudaeos impulsore Chresto assidue tumultuantis Roma expulit ("Since the Jews constantly made disturbances at the instigation of Chrestus, he expelled them from Rome") as well as in Acts 18:2. I find the evidence too scant to attribute this expulsion to disagreements/dissent between Christ-followers and Jews. Following Mark D. Nanos, I do not use the edict as part of a historical basis for reading Romans, since the evidence is not nearly firm enough to establish historical certainties upon which to base interpretation. See Mark D. Nanos, The Mystery of Romans: The Jewish Context of Paul's Letter (Minneapolis: Fortress, 1996), 372–87; see also, Witherington, Paul's Letter to the Romans, 11–13; Elliott, Arrogance of Nations, 97–98. See other discussions in Jewett, Romans, 59–61, 764–766; Fitzmyer, Romans, 77–79; Dunn, Romans, 1:xlviii–lii; Esler, Conflict and Identity, 98–102; Moo, Epistle to the Romans, 4–5; Byrne, Romans, 11–13; Neil Elliott, The Rhetoric of Romans: Argumentative Constraint and Strategy and Paul's Dialogue with Judaism (Sheffield: JSOT Press,

residing in their homeland or a *peregrinus* in Rome, the lives of these ἔθνη were structured by πίστις, as it both was shown to them by Rome and required them to order their lives in ways that displayed their trust in their imperial rulers.

The promises implied for these ἔθνη by submissively displaying such πίστις to Rome consist of more than the guarantee of security in terms of military protection and belonging. Relations of πίστις promise additional benefits, particularly related to the rhetoric of Roman prosperity, to those who possess their ability to demonstrate this Roman value. Since πίστις is simultaneously characterized as a Roman value and a submissive one, proving possession of the ability to display it (individually or collectively) contributes to an appearance of being more Roman. This creates the potential for upward mobility, via increased individual status, preferential treatment for a particular ἔθνη as a group, or even the bestowal of Roman citizenship. This mobility—"a fantasy of endless upwardness"—gazes up toward a promise of the Roman good life that is always above.[95] It promises that one could always keep working to get to the top.[96]

With regard to displays of πίστις as a path toward citizenship, one example can be seen in the *Tabula Banasitana* from second-century North Africa: the inscription displays the official communications granting Roman citizenship to Julian the Zegrensian (*Iulianus Zegrensis*) by the emperor Marcus Aurelius.[97] The *fides* of Julian and his family is lauded as

---

1990), 47–52; Keck, *Romans,* 29–30; Matera, *Romans,* 9–10; Hultgren, *Paul's Letter to the Romans,* 9–11; Schreiner, *Romans,* 12–14; Stowers, *Rereading of Romans,* 23; Grieb, *Story of Romans,* 6–7; Johnson, *Reading Romans,* 4; Elsa Tamez, "Romans: A Feminist Reading," in *Feminist Biblical Interpretation: A Compendium of Critical Commentary on the Books of the Bible and Related Literature,* ed. Luise Schottroff and Marie-Theres Wacker (Grand Rapids: Eerdmans, 2012), 698.

95. Berlant, *Cruel Optimism,* 179.

96. This constant focus upward prevents alternative futures that might be better—or, at least, less cruel. "Given these conditions, if one is an informal or unofficial worker, there is little room for imagining revolution or indeed any future beyond the scavenging present, though it happens" (Berlant, *Cruel Optimism,* 179). Earlier she alludes to how hopes for capital/inheritance (as a form of upward mobility) divorces individuals from the communities that permitted some forms of resilience and creativity: "it sutures them both to life lived without risk, in proximity to plenitude without enjoyment" (Berlant, *Cruel Optimism,* 41).

97. Morgan, *Roman Faith,* 62–63. Morgan discusses this evidence alongside other evidence of πίστις in patron-client relations (see pp. 60–65). This example differs from others in which the ethnic status of the client (alongside the patron) is Roman or

a primary reason for his deserving citizen status: "since you assert that he is one of the leading men of his people and is very loyal [*fidissimum*] in his readiness to be of help to our affairs...."[98] Demonstrated πίστις/*fides* toward Rome alongside "leading" status within one's ἔθνη proves that a person both is loyally aligned with as well as accepting of one's position under Roman rule. Therefore, one is able to serve as a leader, modeling the benefits of being exceedingly loyal, for fellow members of their ἔθνος. Such extension of the rights and benefits of citizenship to certain *exceptionally faithful* ἔθνη (*fidissimum*) highlights the promises of political and social benefits that can result from πίστις with the *populus Romano*.

πίστις often signals a hope that this trust will engender and maintain a beneficial relation.[99] Reminiscent of the risks, routines, and ruts of optimism Berlant discusses, Morgan calls the πίστις required to forge such relationships a "hopeful risk" for both parties, who stand to gain significant benefits from a πίστις relationship but have an equal chance of losing what benefits they have if the other party turns out to be untrustworthy (ἄπιστος).[100] For Augustus and his successors who offered experiences of Rome's πίστις to many ἔθνη, the emperor and his people take a risk by displaying such πίστις to various ἔθνη, who could take the benefits of Rome's

---

unspecified. It is *also* (and importantly for my argument) an instance of the πίστις relations that are established and maintained between ἔθνη and the Roman people and, specifically, their emperor.

98. Translation James H. Oliver, "Text of the Tabula Banasitana, A.D. 177," *AJP* 93 (1972): 339; for Latin text, see p. 336.

99. "*Pistis/fides* is also often connected, explicitly or implicitly but clearly, with hope" (Morgan, *Roman Faith*, 453). On p. 64, Morgan observes that πίστις can be seen as a means to forge new relationships, which offer new social networks and benefits to parties involved in the relation.

100. Morgan, *Roman Faith*, 64. She observes such hope in an example from Plutarch, *Praec. ger. rei publ.* ("Precepts of Statecraft," πολιτικά παραγγέλματα), in which Plutarch advises a young colleague as he considers and prepares to commence a political career. The specific example of client/patron πίστις that Morgan uses is where Plutarch recommends a patron advocate for a "weak client" (ἀσθενοῦς) as having been ἀρχὴν πολιτείας ἔνδοξον ("the start of a highly reputable citizenship [i.e., here, meaning a political career]" [*Praec. ger. rei publ.* 805b]). The context of this example as political advice (with several discussions of issues of trust in politicians by their subjects) indicates that her observations about patron-client πίστις apply similarly to πίστις in the political climate of Rome's empire. As the prior discussion of the evidence in the *Tabula Banasitana* showed, these patron-client relations can be seen to apply similarly to the relation of an emperor-patron to his client-ἔθνη (kingdoms).

protection and prosperity to eventually mount rebellion against Rome or ally with its enemies. However, having already proven its power and might over these ἔθνη, Rome has the upper hand as the patron displaying πίστις because, like an individual elite patron, the empire has more resources at its disposal for protection and security.

Such hope is more of a necessity in the cases of lower status parties who grant πίστις toward those in higher positions. Although their hopeful risk is more necessary, it is also more precarious, another cruel paradox of optimistic πίστις. For conquered ἔθνη, their faithful submission to Rome, which hopes for both protection and better status, entails a more serious risk, one with a less secure safety net. The Roman people, guided by their emperor, could decide to force these ἔθνη into further submission. Though there is hope in the (implicit or explicit) promises of political and social incorporation of ἔθνη into the Roman state via status benefits (including citizenship), the πίστις required for their fulfillment is riskier since Rome could refuse this incorporation, if it is secure in the knowledge that many of these ἔθνη could not effectively rebel. Though πίστις may be more risky—and the good life it promises more precarious—for Rome's ἔθνη, the risk is harder to refuse when the rut feels otherwise inescapable. ἔθνη must retain their hope in these promises by displaying πίστις to Rome or else they risk greater decline under its military might.

By displaying πίστις, the hope for ἔθνη is that they will be better integrated into the Roman state, given good governance and attention from the emperor when requested, and even potentially granted citizenship and a permanent belonging as full members of the state. The reciprocal πίστις expected of Rome's ἔθνη involves their ongoing faithful submission to the goals of empire, permits the political and socioeconomic stability of the *pax Romana*, and promises the possibility of benefits for their ongoing obedience. Via submission to Rome, πίστις permits ἔθνη to hope for the cluster of social, economic, and political benefits promised to true, loyal Romans: optimistic inclusion in the Roman good life.

πίστις and Paul's ἔθνη in Romans 1:1–17

How do these faithfully submissive promises of a Roman good life for ἔθνη play out in Romans's optimistic presentation of πίστις? In Rom 1:5, ὑπακοὴν πίστεως ("*pistis*'s obedience") makes explicit the submissive connotations of πίστις: [Ἰησοῦ Χριστοῦ τοῦ κυρίου ἡμῶν] δι' οὗ ἐλάβομεν χάριν καὶ ἀποστολὴν εἰς ὑπακοὴν πίστεως ἐν πᾶσιν τοῖς ἔθνεσιν ὑπὲρ τοῦ ὀνόματος αὐτοῦ ("[Jesus Christ our Lord], through whom we received grace and sending off into *pistis*'s obedience in all of the *ethnē* on behalf of his name").[101] πίστις describes the obedience into which these Christ-followers should enter: submission directed to God.[102] By displaying πίστις, a person simultaneously demonstrates obedience.[103] From the outset of Romans, obedience entails submission, and it requires πίστις.

This faithful obedience introduced in 1:5 directly involves ἔθνη: ἐν πᾶσιν τοῖς ἔθνεσιν ("in all the *ethnē*"). Even if Paul employs ἔθνη as a technical term for "gentiles," since his audience consisted largely of non-Jews *and* members of conquered Roman territories, it is almost impossible that they would not have heard in the term its imperial meaning of "conquered nations."[104] Living in Rome alongside a greater number of native Roman

---

101. The bracketed subject of the clause (Jesus) comes from 1:4. Don B. Garlington calls it the "pivotal point" of this introduction because it connects him to this ὑπακοὴν πίστεως, which further represents "his own articulation of the design and purpose of his missionary labors." See Don B. Garlington, *Faith, Obedience, and Perseverance: Aspects of Paul's Letter to the Romans* (Tübingen: Mohr Siebeck, 1994), 12–13. ὑπακοή is the noun form of ὑπηκοός, the term for obedience and subjection discussed in relation to Jesus's submission in Phil 2:8 and the slavish nature of all subjects with respect to Rome's emperor in Philo, *Legatio ad Gaium*. As in these contexts, obedience in Romans represents a specific form of submission, a "hearing under," wherein the obedient subject submits to commands that they have heard, implicitly or explicitly, from another, almost certainly of higher status.

102. Relating this term to 3:21–26, "the righteousness of God is enacted through [Jesus's] own faithfulness, his faithful obedience unto death on the cross" (Grieb, *Story of Romans*, 37). With no note of submission, some say this is obedience to God, specifically God's grace, however. See Byrne, *Romans*, 40; Witherington, *Paul's Letter to the Romans*, 34–35. Some commentators stress this obedience as toward Christ. See Moo, *Epistle to the Romans*, 53; Hultgren, *Paul's Letter to the Romans*, 50. Jewett claims this is a "special sort of obedience produced by the gospel" and situates it as a *favorable* notion in the context of Roman honor (Jewett, *Romans*, 110).

103. "Indeed, the semantic range of *pistis* overlaps with that of *hypakoē*, 'obedience,' so that Paul can use the terms almost interchangeably in Romans" (Elliott, *Arrogance of Nations*, 45, see further 45–46). Garlington argues that πίστις describes ὑπακοὴν (as an "adjectival genitive") that can be translated "faith's obedience" with connections to ideas of submission (Garlington, *Faith, Obedience, and Perseverance*, 30–31, see further 10–31). See also Longenecker, *Epistle to the Romans*, 79; Matera, *Romans*, 30–31; Johnson, *Reading Romans*, 23; Schreiner, *Romans*, 34–36.

104. Lopez, *Apostle to the Conquered*, 166–68. Her conclusion comes from her reading of Galatians in the preceding chapter, "Re-Imagining Paul as Apostle to the Conquered," 119–63. Certainly, such a differentiation appears in the LXX and in

citizens, including those among the highest echelons of the empire's elite, both Jews and non-Roman gentiles would have been considered foreigners (*peregrini*) and very aware of their different ethnic status under the gaze of their imperial rulers. According to 1:5, ὑπακοὴν πίστεως, faithful obedience to God, is to be practiced among all these ἔθνη. This obedience resembles how these ἔθνη have submitted to Roman rule and experienced the πίστις of its people.[105] Whether through violence or the threat of violence (elided from mention in the Res gestae), the πίστις that πλεῖστα ἄλλα ἔθνη ("many other nations") experience requires taking a faithfully obedient posture toward the Roman people as a gesture that maintains the reciprocity implied in first-century πίστις-relations.[106] In Rom 1:5, these same conquered ἔθνη have been brought into a similar πίστις-relation—now directed toward God instead of Caesar—through the actions of a different and new master/κύριος, Jesus Christ, whose faithful submission resulted in his raised status.[107] Paul's introductory invocation of ὑπακοὴν πίστεως makes clear that, through (διά) the actions of Jesus Christ, all these conquered persons not only receive benefits from God (i.e., χάρις and ἀποστολή) but also are brought into an affective πίστις-relation with God, a relation that necessitates their obedience.

Romans 1:16–17 continues the emphasis on πίστις and shows how it is critical to understanding the establishment of God's justice:

Οὐ γὰρ ἐπαισχύνομαι τὸ εὐαγγέλιον, δύναμις γὰρ θεοῦ ἐστιν εἰς σωτηρίαν παντὶ τῷ πιστεύοντι, Ἰουδαίῳ τε πρῶτον καὶ Ἕλληνι· δικαιοσύνη γὰρ θεοῦ ἐν αὐτῷ ἀποκαλύπτεται ἐκ πίστεως εἰς πίστιν, καθὼς γέγραπται· ὁ δὲ δίκαιος ἐκ πίστεως ζήσεται.

Jewish literature roughly contemporaneous with Paul; indeed, when Paul refers to ἔθνη, this distinction is implied in the reference, but the term can contain multiple meanings, both within its usage by Paul (as author) and as it was heard by a diverse audience in Rome's ἐκκλησία. See also Elliott, *Arrogance of Nations*, 45.

105. "It evokes a scriptural vision in which the establishment of *God's dominion over the earth* included the subduing of hostile and oppressive nations" (Elliott, *Arrogance of Nations*, 46, emphasis added). For Elliott, this dominion must be in "inevitable conflict" with the Augustan imperial vision; see pp. 46–47.

106. See Elliott's discussion of the Res gestae as part of the imperial ideology that informs (or constrains) Romans (Elliott, *Arrogance of Nations*, 38–39, 50–57).

107. Indeed, Paul goes on to praise those assembled in the Roman ἐκκλησία because they have already become known for their displays of πίστις toward God. See Rom 1:8.

> For I am not ashamed of the gospel because God's power is for salvation to everyone who shows *pistis*, Jew first, then Greek. For God's justice is revealed in it from *pistis* into *pistis*, just as it is written, "The just one will live from *pistis*."

God's power of salvation can be compared to similar language used by and of Caesar and Rome's empire, who are said to have been the saviors (σώτηρ) of many peoples from barbarism, bringing them stability and "better" living conditions.[108] In Rome's kyriarchal view, whoever has the most power is most able to bring about the salvation of others (over whom, therefore, that person has authority). Salvation is an effect of having power/ability (δύναμις), so it is beneficial to be aligned with such power (whether that power is God's or the empire's).[109] According to 1:16, persons should want to be included in the salvation into which God's power leads.

In Romans, God is on top. By extending them salvation, God displays πίστις toward these now saved people. Salvation—along with the better life it presumes—requires inclusion and participation in a πίστις-relation with God. It is the possession of παντὶ τῷ πιστεύοντι, "everyone who shows πίστις."[110] As in the Res gestae, the hierarchical power dynamics between savior and peoples are implicit in God's power for salvation and the πίστις-relation this offers: the powerful party offers πίστις and protection in exchange for loyalty. Typically, those who are most loyal reap the most benefits of salvation from the one in power. Since God occupies the savior-position at the top, all others must be submissive and obedient in order to display πίστις toward God, as a demonstration of trust in and loyalty to God's power.

Romans 1:17 gives this πίστις-relation more detail and anticipates the climax of 3:21–26. This verse connects πίστις to the revelation of God's

---

108. "In the Roman cultural context, it is important to recall that priestly, military, and administrative forms of power were celebrated as effective means of salvation" (Jewett, *Romans*, 138). See also Cobb and Lull, *Romans*, 33; Longenecker, *Epistle to the Romans*, 164–65. Likewise, Elliott emphasizes how εὐαγγέλιον is an imperial term reclaimed by Paul: "For Paul, as for Roman political and diplomatic rhetoric, the *euangelion* is the *announcement* of a sovereign's impending triumph and, necessarily, the establishment of the sovereign's claim on obedience" (Elliott, *Arrogance of Nations*, 74–75); see also p. 29 on how the language of *pax Romana* as "peace" appears in Paul.

109. See Jewett, *Romans*, 138–39. Byrne notes power's distinction as capacity in contrast to weakness (Byrne, *Romans*, 56–57).

110. Cf. 3:22. See Jewett, *Romans*, 139–40.

justice (δικαιοσύνη θεοῦ). In similar fashion to how Caesar's promises of justice (*iustitia*) and establishment of a *pax Romana* allayed concerns over his new imperial regime, in Romans, God promises a regime change that also centers on establishing true justice.[111] As with imperial πίστις extended to numerous ἔθνη, God promises to justly extend benefits of it (as with citizenship status with Caesar) to all peoples who faithfully submit to God's rule—to those who display πίστις as part of a reciprocal relation with *and under* God. Romans 1 establishes the import of πίστις and connects it to the benefits that come from faithfully submissive displays (as in 3:21–26). As under Caesar, in Paul's presentation, πίστις affectively promises the good life to ἔθνη—under God.

πίστις appears three times in 1:17, preceded either by the preposition ἐκ ("from, out of, by") or εἰς ("into, to, toward"). The meaning of ἐκ πίστεως in the quotation of Hab 2:4 is integral to understanding its usage in 1:17 and Paul's letter: ὁ δὲ δίκαιος ἐκ πίστεως ζήσεται ("The just one will live from πίστις").[112] Referring to Jesus, Paul's citation of this passage foreshadows the point he elaborates in 3:21–26: as the Christ, the just one, Jesus displays πίστις toward God by submitting to God's authority and plan to suffer death, trusting that he will live and this will enact a delay of his messianic judgment (which God schedules).[113] In addition to living by his

---

111. See Elliott, *Arrogance of Nations*, 70–85; Jennings, *Outlaw Justice*, 60–70. On the broader role of δικαιοσύνη in Romans, generally as some form of "righteousness" or "justification," see Stowers, *Rereading of Romans*, 195–98; Dunn, *Romans*, 1:40–43; Grieb, *Story of Romans*, 20–25; Jewett, *Romans*, 141–44; Fitzmyer, *Romans*, 105–7, 257–63; Byrne, *Romans*, 57–60; Witherington, *Paul's Letter to the Romans*, 52–54; Schreiner, *Romans*, 63–71; Hultgren, *Paul's Letter to the Romans*, 605–15 (making very explicit it should *not* be translated as "justice," in contrast to scholars like Stowers or Elliott); Longenecker, *Epistle to the Romans*, 168–76, 403–8.

112. "Hab 2:4 is a key to the meaning of *pistis* in Romans" (Stowers, *Rereading of Romans*, 199, see further 199–202). See also Jewett, *Romans*, 145–47. Dunn argues this quotation begins to prove Paul's thesis in continuity with Jewish tradition (Dunn, *Romans*, 1:48–49). Within more traditional interpretations, Paul's use of Hab 2:4 confirms faith as a requirement for God's δικαιοσύνη. See Moo, *Epistle to the Romans*, 76–79; Matera, *Romans*, 35–36; Longenecker, *Epistle to the Romans*, 186; Fitzmyer, *Romans*, 264–65; Hultgren, *Paul's Letter to the Romans*, 79.

113. Following Stowers, who compares the variations (in the Greek LXX and Hebrew MT) of the passage, the substantive ὁ δίκαιος is not a generic referent to any just person but refers to *a specific human being*, namely, Jesus as the Christ, "the just one" (Stowers, *Rereading of Romans*, 199–202). Heliso's monograph on this particular figure in Romans affirms this interpretation that ὁ δίκαιος refers specifically to Christ,

πίστις toward God, Jesus the just also lives ἐκ πίστεως, from *God's* πίστις: Jesus trusts that God will remain trustworthy (πιστός) toward him as well.

This usage of ἐκ πίστεως applies to its meaning at the beginning of 1:17, where God's justice is revealed ἐκ πίστεως εἰς πίστιν. ἐκ πίστεως refers to the πίστις Ἰησοῦ Χριστοῦ (Jesus Christ's πίστις, cf. 3:22): God's justice is revealed from Jesus's πίστις, seen in his trust in God's plan and his submission and obedience to God to the point of death (cf. 3:21–26; Phil 2:5–11).[114] The πίστις of ἐκ πίστεως refers to a πίστις different from that referred to by εἰς πίστιν.[115] From Jesus's πίστις, God's justice is revealed *into* πίστις (εἰς πίστιν), which now refers not to Jesus's relation of trust with God but to that of his followers: their πίστις in God is the *result* of Jesus's model of faithful submission—from his πίστις into that of others.[116]

As in Hab 2:4, ἐκ πίστεως can also allude to God's fidelity that is displayed in Christ's submission to God: Christ submits fully to God's plan, *and* God upholds fidelity to this plan and raises him from death. Jesus exemplifies ideal submission in his πίστις toward God, embodying a per-

---

although his final conclusion admits the other meaning is plausible but less convincing (Heliso, *Pistis and the Righteous One*, 254, 163–64, see further 122–64). See similar interpretations in Johnson, *Reading Romans*, 28–29; Cobb and Lull, *Romans*, 35–36. Making general comparisons between the different ancient (and modern) versions of Hab 2:4 is frequent in commentaries; however, ὁ δίκαιος refers to generic humans in these interpretations. See Jewett, *Romans*, 145–46; Byrne, *Romans*, 60–61; Keck, *Romans*, 53–54; Moo, *Epistle to the Romans*, 76–77; Fitzmyer, *Romans*, 264–65; Dunn, *Romans*, 1:44–46; Hultgren, *Paul's Letter to the Romans*, 77–79; Longenecker, *Epistle to the Romans*, 182–86.

114. Stowers, *Rereading of Romans*, 202.

115. As Stowers emphasizes, the doubling of πίστις here signals *two different metaphors* (to use his language) "of physical movement: out of something and into something" (Stowers, *Rereading of Romans*, 202). Schreiner says the doubling emphasizes the centrality of "faith" (in Christ) for Paul (Schreiner, *Romans*, 71–72). Hultgren agrees both refer to a believer's πίστις, but the movement signals "the progression of the righteousness of God to accomplish what God seeks to do" (Hultgren, *Paul's Letter to the Romans*, 77). Jewett connects this movement to Paul's effort for missionary expansion (Jewett, *Romans*, 143–44).

116. Stowers, *Rereading of Romans*, 202. Heliso agrees that ἐκ πίστεως is christological (equivalent to the πίστις Ἰησοῦ Χριστοῦ) and contends that 1:17 is "introducing and providing a framework for the idea of *God's act of salvation through Christ's faithfulness-to-death* (πίστις Χριστοῦ), the knowledge of which triggers the human act of faith response" (Heliso, *Pistis and the Righteous One*, 254, see further 165–242). See further Johnson, *Reading Romans*, 28.

fect πίστις-relation between an emperor and his loyal subject. The πίστις of Jesus allows others to follow this model and enter into a πίστις-relation with God. It allows every person to display πίστις (πᾶς ὁ πιστεύων).

The language in Rom 1 establishes the affective relation between ἔθνη (who form Paul's primary audience) and πίστις, which affectively binds them in relation to God and promises of justice. In addition to the ὑπακοὴ πίστεως that is encouraged among all the ἔθνη in 1:5, 1:16–17 specifies that God's power toward salvation—belonging to all who display πίστις (as discussed above)—belongs Ἰουδαίῳ τε πρῶτον καὶ Ἕλληνι, "first to Jew and then to Greek."[117] Paul's "Jews and Greeks" can be taken as representative of "all the ἔθνη," just as they were certainly included among the πλεῖστα ἄλλα ἔθνη to whom Caesar extended his Roman πίστις. While Jesus's πίστις is an example that specifically directs non-Jewish ἔθνη into relation with God, Paul makes clear that all people—Jews and these other ἔθνη—are included under God's justice and expected to display πίστις toward God.

πίστις and Paul's ἔθνη in Romans 3:27–5:11

If 1:16–17 forms the thesis of Romans, providing a preview of Paul's main points, then it is evident that πίστις and the relations it maintains are important to the letter's central theme of δικαιοσύνη θεοῦ. In 3:27, Paul returns to the impact this has upon ἔθνη and their actions moving forward.[118] Romans 3:27–4:22 explains how ἔθνη are able to participate in God's promises alongside Jews, who, having an established πίστις-relation with God, already participate in these promises.[119] Jesus's πίστις that leads

---

117. "The phrase is routinely found on the lips of Romans (and Judeans under Roman rule) as they describe *the world's peoples as Rome's subjects*" (Elliott, *Arrogance of Nations*, 51).

118. Generally speaking, 1:18–3:20 covers the various details of the need for justice and the judgment under "God's wrath"—especially needed for non-Jews, as Stowers argues, since they are not covered by the justice under the torah. In other words, only non-Jews require something that will make them just when God's reign is established (and hence the need for delay).

119. On this point, Stowers make two important arguments. First, the phrase διὰ πίστεως refers to Jesus's πίστις even when Jesus is not named with the subjective genitive. Second, the relation established by this prepositional phrase specifically relates to ἔθνη/non-Jews. Jews have another means of πίστις-relation (i.e., ἐκ πίστεως) to God that does not require Jesus's death as an example for their inclusion in God's promises for justice. Paul does not address how Jews relate to Jesus and his πίστις, because such

to his death as God's ἱλαστήριον provides the means necessary for these ἔθνη, who were previously incapable of such action, to enter into πίστις-relation with God, thus receiving full share in its benefits.[120]

The impact of Jesus's πίστις for this audience and their actions culminates at 4:23–5:11, what Stowers calls the "hortatory conclusion" to this particular segment of Paul's argument.[121] Connecting ἔθνη to the effects on Abraham's πίστις, Paul writes:

> Οὐκ ἐγράφη δὲ δι' αὐτὸν μόνον ὅτι ἐλογίσθη αὐτῷ, ἀλλὰ καὶ δι' ἡμᾶς οἷς μέλλει λογίζεσθαι, τοῖς πιστεύουσιν ἐπὶ τὸν ἐγείραντα Ἰησοῦν τὸν κύριον ἡμῶν ἐκ νεκρῶν, ὃς παρεδόθη διὰ τὰ παραπτώματα ἡμῶν καὶ ἠγέρθη διὰ τὴν δικαίωσιν ἡμῶν.
>
> Not only on account of him is it written that it [Abraham's πίστις] was considered [justice] for him, but also on account of us, for whom it is going to be considered [justice], for those who display *pistis* to the one who raised Jesus, our Lord, from the dead, [Jesus] who was handed over on account of our blunders and raised on account of our claim for justice. (4:23–25)

Now included in the justice accorded to Abraham and his descendants, these ἔθνη should respond to God's πίστις by displaying their πίστις to God, following Jesus's example of submission, with the promise of receiving the benefits of justice (as opposed to God's wrath).[122]

Jesus's placement—here, having been passively "handed over" and then "raised" by God—again confirms God's authority and πίστις toward all people, including these Roman ἔθνη, to whom God reveals God's jus-

---

a relation is unnecessary in his understanding of bringing everyone into relation with God as part of God's plan for establishing justice (Stowers, *Rereading of Romans*, 241).

120. The phrase ἐκ πίστεως, then, refers to the "generative activity" that displaying submissive πίστις toward God can have for God's πίστις-relation with entire populations, which includes the display in Jesus's death as well as Abraham's πίστις, which generates a relation between the Jews and God. Romans 4 makes clear that the πίστις that Jesus's example provides permits ἔθνη to be adopted into Abraham's lineage and participate in the benefits of a πίστις-relation with God. See Stowers, *Rereading of Romans*, 237–50.

121. Stowers, *Rereading of Romans*, 247–50.

122. It is crucial to observe that the πίστις of those addressed in 4:24 is displayed toward God, as always the primary actor (who handed over and raised Jesus since Jesus submitted to and trusted God's plan). Again, πίστις is not directed to Jesus but always to God.

tice.[123] By recalling Jesus's placement and death here, Paul makes clear that the πίστις these ἔθνη should display is one that submits to God in a fashion similar to Jesus. They trust God to place them so that God's justice might be best revealed to all people according to God's faithful plan. Like Jesus, these ἔθνη should submit fully under God's power of placement and should acknowledge and obey God's authority, a demonstration of perfect and pleasing πίστις in relation to God's power.

The submissive πίστις that attaches these ἔθνη to God becomes optimistic based upon the promise of benefits from God's reciprocal displays of πίστις. Through this cluster of beneficial promises, πίστις forges a good-life fantasy. As 1:16–17 already established, God's power to bring salvation (σωτηρία) and offer the revelation of justice (δικαιοσύνη θεοῦ), generated by the faithful examples (ἐκ πίστεως) of Jesus (3:21–26) and Abraham (4:1–22), is for those in a πίστις-relation with God. These benefits are the inheritances of those who are (now) able to display reciprocal πίστις to God (εἰς πίστιν) through their faithful submission. God's establishment of justice originates from and confirms the fact that God is πιστός and also possesses the most power. It reinforces the relation between God and God's subjects.[124]

Justice and salvation represent some of the benefits of a πίστις-relation with God.[125] Submission to God's authority best permits all

---

123. Commentators who likewise emphasize God's action in these verses include Witherington, *Paul's Letter to the Romans*, 129; Schreiner, *Romans*, 243; Matera, *Romans*, 118. Longenecker isolates 4:25 in his commentary, making it a "concluding early Christian confessional statement" and emphasizing the passive nature of the verbs (i.e., God's action toward Christ, as above) but only because of human sin. Longenecker, *Epistle to the Romans*, 535–37. However, it is as common to ignore God's role in favor of trying to find or emphasize potential parallels to the gospel tradition (often arguing Paul is making reference to it). See Jewett, *Romans*, 341–43; Byrne, *Romans*, 161–62; Dunn, *Romans* 1:223–25; Fitzmyer, *Romans*, 389–90 (who also relates these verses to "justification by faith").

124. Indeed, drawing from E.P. Sanders's identification of δικαιοσύνη as a "transfer term," Stowers observes, "It concerns how one gets into a relation with God" (Stowers, *Rereading of Romans*, 243). While my analysis of πίστις shows how this term does significant work in establishing relations and attachments between God and subject, it is clear from the import of δικαιοσύνη in Romans and its relation to Paul's use of πίστις that God's δικαιοσύνη complements πίστις and frames these relations. See further E. P. Sanders, *Paul and Palestinian Judaism: A Comparison of Patterns of Religion* (Philadelphia: Fortress, 1977), 470–72.

125. Using the language of benefit, Stowers observes, "Abraham and Jesus Christ

persons to reap these benefits. According to 4:25, God raises Jesus from his ignoble death to these great heights διὰ τὴν δικαίωσιν ἡμῶν, "on account of our claim [or need] for justice." This justice, needed and hoped for by these ἔθνη, offers a raising, an elevation, for those who receive it. If Jesus's faithful submission to God is what permits his elevation in status, then, in following this example, the πίστις of Christ-followers trusts in and hopes that God's justice will allow a similar rising in their status and situation.[126]

Romans 5 expands the benefits of this relation, showing that the justice that God reveals as a result of Jesus's πίστις leads to increasing prosperity, including the promise of peace, for Christ's submissive followers.

> δικαιωθέντες οὖν ἐκ πίστεως εἰρήνην ἔχομεν πρὸς τὸν θεὸν διὰ τοῦ κυρίου ἡμῶν Ἰησοῦ Χριστοῦ, δι' οὗ καὶ τὴν προσαγωγὴν ἐσχήκαμεν [τῇ πίστει] εἰς τὴν χάριν ταύτην ἐν ᾗ ἑστήκαμεν, καὶ καυχώμεθα ἐπ' ἐλπίδι τῆς δόξης τοῦ θεοῦ.
>
> Thus, being made just from *pistis*, we have peace with God through our *kyrios*, Jesus Christ, indeed through whom we have obtained access by *pistis* to this grace in which we are standing and boast about the hope of God's glory. (5:1–2)[127]

With God's authority and power affirmed through faithful submission, God's establishment of justice leads to the possession of peace for those

---

are essential for Paul precisely as individuals who have made possible divine benefits inherited by whole peoples" (Stowers, *Rereading of Romans*, 243). Thus, the examples of Jesus and Abraham discussed above are paradigm-shifting examples of proper πίστις and of the benefits one receives from faithful submission: these benefits are the fulfillment of God's promises toward both those individuals and, by extension, the peoples on whose behalf they serve as exemplary.

126. "Paul certainly preached that gentiles should believe in the one true God and what he had done through Jesus Christ, but he did not proclaim that their salvation hinged on their own act of believing" (Stowers, *Rereading of Romans*, 248). As opposed to returning this to the language of atonement (already discussed as irrelevant to Romans above). See Jewett, *Romans*, 343.

127. Many commentators (however, neither Stowers nor myself, among others) see Rom 5 as beginning an entirely new section of Paul's argument. See Jewett, *Romans*, 344–49; Moo, *Epistle to the Romans*, 290–95; Fitzmyer, *Romans*, 393–94; Longenecker, *Epistle to the Romans*, 551–52; Hultgren, *Paul's Letter to the Romans*, 202; Byrne, *Romans*, 162–64. Keck keeps 5:1–11 in the same section of Paul's argument but says it represents a major turn (Keck, *Romans*, 133).

who participate in πίστις with God.[128] This peace is πρὸς τὸν θεὸν, toward or with God: these ἔθνη are now promised peace, provided they faithfully (and peacefully) submit to God's power to establish God's justice across the earth, to all peoples, all ἔθνη. According to Paul's theological presentation, peace, alongside justice, is a benefit of this participation in God's promises. πίστις optimistically attaches faithfully submissive ἔθνη to the cluster of benefits God promises: the good life under God.

For these ἔθνη, the good life under God is strikingly similar to the Roman good life under Caesar. If Rome brought justice and salvation to (certain) suffering ἔθνη, they claimed to do so through the stability of peace—the *pax Romana*—which brought prosperity throughout Rome's territories. Paul's language relies upon terms that had imperial connotations in the first-century Roman world. Just as πίστις was used by the empire to establish and maintain relations of uneven power between its rulers, people, and conquered ἔθνη, terms like δικαιοσύνη (and its various δικ- cognates)—along with εἰρήνη ("peace"), δόξα ("glory"), σωτηρία ("salvation"), κύριος ("master" or "lord"), and εὐαγγέλιον ("gospel")—were used in imperial rhetoric that would have been familiar to Paul and his audience of Roman ἔθνη.[129] Rome's peaceful prosperity was proclaimed (εὐαγγελίζομαι)

---

128. "The language of obtaining peace on the basis of justice/righteous action was familiar and regularly used of the pacification efforts of the Roman emperor, who, it was claimed, was being just as he established the *Pax Romana*" (Witherington, *Paul's Letter to the Romans*, 133–34). My translation and argument assume that ἔχομεν in 5:1 is indicative, describing something Paul's audience possesses thanks to God, following the decision of the Nestle-Aland text (though there is significant discrepancy with several major ancient sources attesting ἔχωμεν). Thus, I disagree with Stowers here that this verb is a hortatory subjunctive, although I do agree that this segment of Paul's argument has hortatory force (which does not hinge on the function of this verb). Ultimately, Stowers and I agree that "Romans does not consist of a theological argument (1:18–11:34) followed by ethical exhortations (12:1–15:13). Chapters 1–11 have a strongly argumentative character but the letter is hortatory throughout" (Stowers, *Rereading of Romans*, 249, see further 248–49). The indicative meaning is affirmed by Moo, *Epistle to the Romans*, 295–96; Byrne, *Romans*, 169–70, n. 17; Witherington, *Paul's Letter to the Romans*, 133; Fitzmyer, *Romans*, 395; Schreiner, *Romans*, 258; Dunn, *Romans*, 1:245–47; Johnson, *Reading Romans*, 79; Cobb and Lull, *Romans*, 80. Preferring the subjunctive are Hultgren, *Paul's Letter to the Romans*, 676–80; Jewett, *Romans*, 344, 346.

129. "By using such loaded terms as *euangelion, pistis, dikaiosynē, and eirēnē* as central concepts in Romans, he evokes their associations to Roman political thought." See Dieter Georgi, "God Turned Upside Down," in *Paul and Empire: Religion and*

in imperial rhetoric, linked to actual and potential glory, and possessed by those of and elevated to elite status (κύριοι). It is these promises that the *pax Romana* and Caesar's πίστις have not realized for most ἔθνη, who largely remained around the bottom of the Roman sociopolitical hierarchy.

Roman language pervades Paul's theology. The use of these concepts reveals alignments with the ideology of Rome's empire, even when Roman rulers are replaced. The benefits that God promises are not especially different from those Rome has promised to its subjects. Even if Paul does not imagine an empire with Caesar and other native Romans at the top, God's promised rule establishes justice and brings peace in Roman terms. Paul's theology is *Roman without Rome.*[130]

Paul's use of imperial language in Romans has deeper alignments with imperial ideologies when the situation of his audience of Roman ἔθνη is considered alongside this Roman-without-Rome theology. Paul's explication of πίστις and its extension to ἔθνη via Jesus's example echoes the approach of Caesar's conquest that incorporated many ἔθνη into a πίστις-relation with Rome. In Romans, the imperial relations that these ἔθνη have are no longer directed toward Rome and its emperor; instead, God emerges as the ultimate authority, the new emperor who ushers in peace and justice for all people. Jesus is set in his final (raised) placement as God's κύριος, a lord or master. God's justice and peace—and the submissive πίστις required to receive their benefits—is ultimately oriented to best benefit those at the top, namely, God, whose glory (δόξα) should be their greatest concern.[131]

Now incorporated into a πίστις-relation with God and God's divine power and authority, these ἔθνη are told, following Jesus's submissive example, to display πίστις, a πίστις that resembles the πίστις that ἔθνη were

---

Power in Roman Imperial Society, ed. Richard A. Horsley (Harrisburg, PA: Trinity Press International, 1997), 148.

130. However, "without Rome" does not need to be, as Elliott (citing Taubes's political philosophy) reveals, "a declaration of war." In my view, Paul's (political) theology is less anti-Rome and more pro-God, which are not always or necessarily in (binary) opposition—that is, Paul's theology really hopes for a (Roman) Empire ruled (by God) in his (and his audience's) favor. See Elliott, *Arrogance of Nations*, 61–62. See further Jacob Taubes, *The Political Theology of Paul*, trans. Dana Hollander, ed. Aleida Assmann and Jan Assmann (Stanford: Stanford University Press, 2004).

131. In addition to 5:2, ἡ δόξα τοῦ θεοῦ is mentioned several times in the argument of Rom 1–5: at 1:23, 3:7, 3:23, and 4:20. From these usages, δόξα is both God's possession as the ultimate authority and, by extension, something that faithful followers of God should acknowledge (see especially 4:20).

implicitly expected to show Caesar in exchange for his own. These ἔθνη still trust a power with imperial-like authority—in this case, God—to provide them with the benefits they need to survive and ideally thrive. In Romans, Paul's theology replicates imperial ideology only with new beings, God and then Jesus, at the top of the hierarchy.

Sitting atop this imperial-like hierarchy, God possesses the power of placement over all these submissive ἔθνη. In this regard, ἐλπίς ("hope") emerges as critical to understanding the significance of πίστις toward and with God. This hope provides final confirmation that their πίστις is an optimistic attachment, one that binds subjects to good-life fantasies. According to 5:2, the "hope of God's glory" is something the Roman ἔθνη can boast about, as Paul exhorts them to do (καὶ καυχώμεθα ἐπ᾽ ἐλπίδι τῆς δόξης τοῦ θεοῦ).[132] Exhorting his audience to boast of this hope—and, as Jesus did, to boast of their afflictions that ultimately produce hope (5:3–8)—Paul presumes a good life will arise from proper πίστις with God, as his argument assumes throughout Rom 1–5. Since God's glory confirms God's power and reputation for justice and peace, the hope for these ἔθνη is that this true justice and peace will actually accomplish for them the promise of the good life and its benefits—such as upward social mobility and better placement—in a coming Roman-without-Rome society ruled by God.[133]

Cruel πίστις

Recalling Morgan's discussion of the "hopeful risk" involved in πίστις alongside its connections with Berlant's notion of optimism, the optimistic

---

132. Stowers, *Rereading of Romans*, 249–50. Jewett provides context between honor and boasting in the Greco-Roman world (Jewett, *Romans*, 351–52). Others note this as a reversal of Paul's ideas of boasting in other contexts. See Dunn, *Romans*, 1:249; Fitzmyer, *Romans*, 396–97 (where he, quite problematically, contrasts Christian boasting in Paul to the "Jewish boasting" previously criticized).

133. This upward social mobility presumes (as it seems Paul's rhetoric often does) that the fundamental structure of society does not change: that is, if kyriarchy in an imperial political structure remains the same in God's reign, it makes sense to expect that God will leave unchanged the foundational socioeconomic patterns as well, even though this God may put God's faithful followers in positions of power and, therefore, better socioeconomic positions, *at the expense* of those currently in power who will move to the political and the socioeconomic bottom. Paul's hope in socioeconomic mobility is rarely made clear, but it is more apparent than any vision of true socioeconomic reform.

attachment represented by πίστις could become what Berlant calls "cruel optimism." This is especially the case when we consider Romanormative fantasies of the good life and the hope and difficulties this presented to conquered ἔθνη and *peregrini*. The good life, Berlant observes, "is for so many a bad life that wears out the subjects who nonetheless, and, at the same time, find their conditions of possibility within it."[134] What constitutes a good life is often a fantasy whose conditions are unattainable, or, even if they are achieved, the result is not as satisfying as the fantasy implies. Cruel optimism flourishes when subjects trust in its promises that such a good life is desirable, regardless of whether it is actually attainable.

Cruel optimism, as Berlant defines it, is "a relation of attachment to compromised conditions of possibility whose realization is discovered either to be *im*possible, sheer fantasy, or *too* possible, and toxic."[135] The optimistic attachment promises satisfaction and benefits but, in reality, this attachment actively prevents and works against the subject's ability to attain such satisfaction.[136] Whatever the object or fantasy, cruel optimism attaches a subject to it and makes its loss feel more unbearable than the cruelty that attaching to it sustains.

It is possible to claim that *all* optimism is cruel since its promises are always potentially fleeting and their inability to be fulfilled cruelly inhibits not only the final promised satisfaction but also alternative modes of flourishing during the duration of attachment. What makes optimism (more) cruel is when subjects are attached to promises that both can *never* be fulfilled and the ongoing conditions of the optimistic attachment are what *actively prevent* their fulfillment.[137] Such attachments leave subjects stuck in states of unfulfilled promises, always expecting that this time things will improve.

Cruel optimism holds its subjects at an impasse. *Impasse* denotes a holding pattern wherein, though one's optimism prevents further flourishing, the rhythms of life it sustains become routine: treading water.[138]

---

134. Berlant, *Cruel Optimism*, 27.

135. Berlant, *Cruel Optimism*, 24.

136. That is, flourish. It bears repeating Berlant: "A relation of cruel optimism exists when something you desire is actually an obstacle to your flourishing" (Berlant, *Cruel Optimism*, 1).

137. Berlant, *Cruel Optimism*, 24–25.

138. "An impasse is a holding station that doesn't hold securely but opens out into anxiety, that dogpaddling around a space whose contours remain obscure. An impasse

The impasse allows subjects to retain something "normal," even if that something also hinders satisfaction or prolongs a sense of misery.[139] The risk or fear of *letting go* of such an attachment—losing that normative pattern—holds subjects in optimism, regardless of how aware they may be of its cruelty.[140] These subjects tread water waiting for a buoy of assistance that is never going to come.

Impasse marks affect's stickiness: bodies are stuck in routines that have become ruts that exhaust them but never quite end them. Treading at this impasse involves molding life to sustain cruel optimism while permitting some normative experience of comfort (even while such comfort proves profoundly uncomfortable). The need to cling to an impasse's affective normativities—a craving reminiscent of the normativity hangover discussed in chapter 1—stem from the perception that these norms structure their lives as if they are already living a/the good life.[141]

Cruel optimism creates and perpetuates a state that Berlant calls "crisis ordinariness," wherein crisis can be experienced beyond and even apart from a momentary or contained event. A sensation of crisis ordinariness affects life in ways that elongate the variety of experiences contained in a crisis in such a way that they *feel* normal.[142] What appears to an observer as a crisis, Berlant notes, is often for the subject "a fact of life, and has been a defining fact of life for a given population that lives that crisis in ordinary time."[143] Even though the constant strain of the crisis sensation tires and threatens destruction, its ordinariness permits subjects to attain a sense of

---

is decompositional—in the unbound temporality of the stretch of time, it marks a delay" (Berlant, *Cruel Optimism*, 199). See further, pp. 199–200, where they name three broad types of impasse: (1) that caused by forced, often dramatic, loss; (2) that which occurs when one is "adrift in the normative;" (3) one that is improvisational and finds pleasure in lost sureties.

139. See my discussion above in ch.1 on the affective impulse to feel normal and Berlant's "normativity hangover."

140. Berlant, *Cruel Optimism*, 30.

141. Berlant discusses the impasses in the context of two films, *Time Out* and *Human Resources*, where characters actively *fake* the good life (performing a lie to their friends/family) despite having already failed to attain it or having lost it. This ultimately leads to an implosion for the main character. See "After the Good Life, An Impasse" (ch. 6) in Berlant, *Cruel Optimism*, 191–222.

142. See Berlant, *Cruel Optimism*, 170–80, also 8–10, 81–82.

143. Berlant, *Cruel Optimism*, 101. Earlier, Berlant notes that cruel optimism is sometimes more easily noticed by an observer (Berlant, *Cruel Optimism*, 24).

normalcy that is affectively hard to lose. Cruel optimism holds bodies at an impasse where apocalypse now has become *apocalypse normal.*

Cruel optimism, its unattainable good-life fantasies, and the normative impasses they affectively sustain take first-century form through discussions of πίστις/*fides* and how they affect ἔθνη/*peregrini.* This ultimately cements the destruction of Pauline πίστις. The πίστις that binds ἔθνη under Caesar/God is, in fact, the faithful submission that actively inhibits their upward ascent: cruel πίστις.

Cruel πίστις for Roman ἔθνη

When is πίστις's risk actually a faithfully submissive rut?[144] Cruel πίστις operates in contexts where its relational benefits prove to be a fantasy. For persons lower on the Roman sociopolitical hierarchy—and those from conquered ἔθνη in particular—the promises contained by displaying πίστις offer opportunities for upward mobility, forming a Roman version of the capitalist fantasy of the good life. In theory, as Augustus's Res gestae suggests, Rome offers its newly secured ἔθνη full incorporation into the social and political apparatuses of the state, including the benefits of citizenship and the hopeful possibility of rising up the social ladder to attain elite status—so long as they upheld πίστις and submitted to Roman rule.

In practice, however, this rise was difficult—if not impossible—for most foreigners to achieve. While the (already) elite among the ἔθνη, residing within their home territory, might be granted citizenship status, such status was primarily a confirmation of one's high social status in addition to one's political allegiance to Rome (i.e., the elite leaders within an ἔθνη will ensure that those below them remain submissively aligned with Rome). In the first century, it is rare to find ἔθνη made Roman citizens *en masse.*[145]

For *peregrini*—those foreign ἔθνη living in Rome—the conditions for citizenship and, by extension, further upward mobility were equally limited. Manumission from slavery was the most common method for attaining Roman citizenship (and "most common" in this scenario can be

---

144. Recalling the affective rut of aspirational normativity in *Rosetta* discussed above in chapter 1, which is (now more clearly) the rut of cruel optimism.

145. It is not until 212 CE under Caracalla that Roman citizenship is extended widely to all the ethnic territories. See Noy, *Foreigners at Rome,* 77–78.

taken to mean neither "widespread" nor "easy").[146] Even in this case, a manumitted wo/man, though now a Roman citizen, retains a lesser freedperson status, which limited aspects of social and political involvement and rise.[147] While one's children would be freeborn citizens (if born after manumission), the stigma of the former enslavement would carry and limit increases in sociopolitical status.

---

146. Noy, *Foreigners at Rome*, 23–26, 286–87. Although the promise of citizenship was tightly (and distinctively) woven into Roman manumission, it was not necessarily a guarantee in the first century. The *lex Iunia* (circa 17 BCE) created a formal category for freedpersons who had been informally manumitted: Junian Latins, essentially granting them a similar status to Roman *peregrini*/freeborn migrants. The law did offer a route to full citizenship for these freedpersons, primarily through the *anniculi probatio*, a process by which a Junian Latin provided a magistrate with evidence of (a) having born a child who had reached the age of one as the result of (b) a marriage that was legitimated through the presence of seven witnesses and was expressly for the purpose of having children. A little later (but before the fire of Rome under Nero), another route to citizenship became possible for Junian Latins: performing specific forms of civil service. These services options all benefit the economic life of the imperial capital (Perry, *Gender*, 65–66). See also MacLean, *Freed Slaves*, 50–51. Service in the Roman army was another route to citizenship, as Clarke notes. However, it was granted only at the completion of successful military service— often a twenty-five-year period and may have required the demonstration of valor on the field (as a form of loyalty to Rome against other ἔθνη). See Clarke, *Art in the Lives of Ordinary Romans*, 37–41.

147. This is not to say that every freedperson was limited, but the stigmas affected their perception and participation in society. Just as some women have more access to power than some men (as Schüssler Fiorenza's wo/men reminds), some freedpersons had more wealth and sociopolitical capital than some freeborn citizens. Throughout their monographs, both Perry and MacLean show the diversity among freedwo/men and emphasize the ways in which some were able to attain great success and wealth. "Economic opportunities, many of which were afforded by continued involvement with patrons, galvanized a privileged subset of the urban freed population, including wealthy artisans and those who served in elite households—above all, in the *familia Caesaris*" (MacLean, *Freed Slaves*, 170). While the reminder that not all freedpersons lacked power or were economically disenfranchised is crucial, I cannot help but query the *privileged subset*: What is the size of this subset? *Who is still being missed?* Many freedpersons could not leave permanent markers of their presences (or they did but have been lost or ignored), and their experiences of manumission and citizenship may have been more precarious and crueler than the ones we see in the sources MacLean and Perry bring into view—for example, some informally manumitted Junian Latins who never achieved citizenship.

Despite the πίστις these ἔθνη may have in being able to realize the good life, its promises prove to be a fantasy, difficult if not impossible for the vast majority of non-Roman foreigners to achieve. Sustained by their πίστις, the faithful submission of ἔθνη to Rome ensures their status as always around the bottom of Roman society, as defined by its imperial hierarchy.[148]

According to Rome's hierarchy, domination *over*—political, economic, sexual, and social—is a prerequisite for entrance into its upper echelons. Yet, in the mindset of the Romans, all ἔθνη under its control will always be *under*. They are forever peoples who have been and will continue to be dominated by Rome's superior political and military power; they are always penetrated, always feminized. Whether incorporated long ago or just defeated and whether living in their home territory or having migrated to Rome or elsewhere, non-Roman ἔθνη were always under the Roman people; they were always submissive, always conquered, always un-men. The relation of πίστις that Augustus and his successors offer these ἔθνη they conquered requires them to maintain the receptive, feminized, and physically lower positions that Rome forced upon them in defeat: a Briton will always be a version of that female Brittania, held down under Claudius's sword, poised to be penetrated by the emperor as the ultimate representation of dominant Roman masculinity.

Faithful submission is racialized, gendered, and sexualized, as is the good life that πίστις promises. The good life assumes one will be Romanormative, and that means its benefits are best experienced by Rome's mythical norm: freeborn, Roman, citizen, wealthy, male, Romosexual. Citizen or not, a foreigner is repeatedly reminded of the conquered state of their ἔθνος. Even when freed, enslaved wo/men have been forcefully separated

---

148. Looking at imagery in Trajan's rule, Clarke observes how ordinary non-Romans (especially those conquered) were encouraged to read the imagery in Rome's forum. For example, "Trajan's column projected a success story, where the Emperor's virtues and the army's *obedience* to the rules brought about victory *through hard and persistent work*" (Clarke, *Art in the Lives of Ordinary Romans*, 41). From this assessment, Clarke considers how this message encouraged non-Roman viewers to adopt similar mindsets of obedience that results in hard work within the system as a means to victory in the form of social mobility (he also acknowledges it is probable some conquered subjects may resist or find negative interpretations—the vast likelihood being that *both* interpretations existed). See pp. 31–42. Of course, the majority of freeborn, native Romans also inevitably failed to achieve the good life seen among and available only to the wealthy elite; however, the conquered position of the ἔθνη ultimately makes most cruel the πίστις they must show toward Rome and its people.

from their families of origin. Becoming a citizen grants them a Roman *cognomen* at the expense of their original name, a visible invisibility. Even more cruelly, freedwomen were encouraged and expected to prove their successful citizenship through marriage (and children).[149] Evidence attests that they often entered into marriages with their patrons, that is, usually their former enslavers, which ensured the patron would continue to financially benefit from them (since their patron-client relationship would legally dissolve if a freedwoman married).[150] These marriages integrated freedwomen into the sexual morality of Romosexuality: a freedwoman was viewed suspiciously due to her ambiguous moral status as both chaste matron and former sexual object. However, if a woman married her former enslaver, by whom it was presumed she had been used/abused sexually, her *pudicitia* (sexual integrity/honor) was restored.[151]

The benefits of citizenship, freedom, social status, and wealth come with immense emotional costs. "People *are* worn out by the activity of life-building," Berlant stresses, "*especially* the poor and the nonnormative."[152] These affective burdens query the goodness of the good life for those who do not fit the Romosexual mythical norm. The good life may be promised to anyone who is Romanormative enough, but the fantasy will never quite fit since it was never meant for *them*: enslaved, foreign, conquered, non-citizen, poor, female, queer.

Even if subjects never meant to fit into the Roman good life experience some form of Romanormativity hangover, πίστις still urges their Romanormative craving. *Faithfully submit and the good-life fantasy* will *come true.* Unfortunately, this faith in imperial politics implies submission

---

149. "It is unsurprising then that two central issues for jurists were a freedwoman's sexual integrity and her ability to form marriages, which were defining aspects of the iconic Roman woman—the *matrona*" (Perry, *Gender*, 71).

150. Perry, *Gender*, 88–93 (legal aspects), 118–27 (attestations of these marital relations and their dynamics in funerary inscriptions).

151. "Furthermore, associating patron and husband effectively recontextualized the woman's servile sexual duty by associating it with her conjugal relationship" (Perry, *Gender*, 126, see further 22–28, 130–38). In case it was not abundantly clear, this should horrify us with its cruel injustice. *Pudicitia* and its role in Roman sociosexual-political morality will be discussed at greater length in chapter 5.

152. Berlant, *Cruel Optimism*, 44. They emphasize this at the end of their titular chapter (ch.1), right after their discussion of the story "Exchange Value," which draws out ways the good life may not quite fit subjects for whom the life of mythical normativity was never imagined (Berlant, *Cruel Optimism*, 36–43).

from the lower status party in exchange for (the hope of) benefits from the higher. In the case of ἔθνη, their faithful submission entails accepting and maintaining the proper postures of their conquered status as visualized in stylized depictions that were broadcast throughout these territories and in the city of Rome. This underscores the practical impossibility of the good life for these ἔθνη. Proper πίστις for Roman ἔθνη requires submission, and this faithful submission is cruel πίστις. It prevents upward mobility on the Roman hierarchy and sets the terms that make fantastical the ability to flourish as Rome's elite.

Paul's Cruel πίστις

The relation Paul envisions for his audience of ἔθνη involves God and Jesus Christ as opposed to the emperor and the *populus Romano*; however, these Roman conceptions of πίστις as outlined above, particularly in relation to ἔθνη, would have informed how Paul and his audience thought about πίστις-relations with other forms of authority, including divine. Aspects of Paul's theology that express a Roman-without-Rome ideology make possible that πίστις in Romans could become cruel. Paul's vision of the establishment of God's justice on earth retains the structures and hier-archy of the imperial regime while it replaces those who rule with God and Jesus. It is implied that God will restructure the retained hierarchy, making upward mobility possible for these ἔθνη (alongside Jews) upon the coming establishment of God's reign. In order to gain this higher status, ἔθνη should (now) demonstrate their πίστις, their faithful submission, to God's rule and the newly established hierarchy under God and the earthly κύριος Jesus Christ.

Unfortunately, this πίστις, which Paul promises will allow these fol-lowers the hope of a good life, requires submission. The πίστις, exemplified through Jesus, betrays that the relationship envisioned between God and a faithful follower is one where πίστις is unequal and hierarchical. It is like one between emperor and subject, enslaver and enslaved, husband and wife—not one between friends or political allies with equal invest-ment. Though the promised reward is great, the risk incurred is greater for those who faithfully submit than it is for the faithful God (who, unlike the emperor, does not need the faithful submission of loyal subjects to retain control over the empire). To be submissive in this way means that these loyal subjects of God's empire prove their unsuitability for upward mobil-ity according to the logic and ideologies of imperial hierarchies, which requires that those at the top dominate, whether socially, politically, or sexually. Despite the hope engendered by Jesus Christ's πίστις, the submission this πίστις requires ultimately works to inhibit flourishing and the rise of lower class ἔθνη on the imperial hierarchy, whether it is topped by Caesar or God. Jesus's raising is the elite exception that keeps all other ἔθνη in their posture of faithful submission, hoping for a similar rise.

The faithful submission that defines Paul's cruel πίστις becomes especially apparent in the sexual dimensions that undergird Jesus's πίστις in Romans, which subsequently becomes a model for the ἔθνη who are to number among his followers. Reading Rom 3 through the logic of Romosexuality's penetrative axis, Stephen D. Moore argues that Jesus's submissive position vis-à-vis God implies sexual passivity and availability to God.[153] God's authority places God above Jesus on this hierarchy, so that Jesus's sexual position is literally under God, the top (an, or the, "impenetrable penetrator," as Walters would say, or the "Bottomless Top," as Moore prefers).[154] Identifying this as the "sexual substratum of Paul's soteriology," Moore observes, "Stripped naked and spread out on the cross, run though with sundry phallic objects, Jesus in his relationship to God perfectly models the submissiveness that should also characterize the God-fearing female's proper relationship to the male."[155] This substratum connects the overt appearance of Greco-Roman sexual norms in 1:18–32 to the logic of Paul's overall argument in Rom 1–5, in particular the significance of Jesus's death as portrayed in Rom 3 that is central to this argument.[156] Sexual submission according to the pervasive logic of the penetrative hierarchy infuses Pauline theology, particularly as it relates to the significance of Jesus's death.

---

153. Stephen D. Moore, *God's Beauty Parlor: And Other Queer Spaces in and around the Bible*, Contraversions (Stanford: Stanford University Press, 2001), 156.

154. Moore, *God's Beauty Parlor*, 170, see also 169; Walters, "Invading the Roman Body," 30.

155. Moore, *God's Beauty Parlor*, 156.

156. Moore identifies his reading as a logical extension of work on the penetrative hierarchy (particularly deriving from Foucault and Halperin) and Bernadette Brooten's exegesis of Rom 1:18–32 in *Love between Women: Early Christian Responses to Female Homoeroticism* (Chicago: University of Chicago Press, 1996). Moore proceeds to protrude further into Romans and applies this logic to Rom 3 with aid from Stowers's rereading, especially his assertion that self-mastery (ἐγκράτεια) was a central concern in the first century, in particular including Paul's audience (and therefore, Paul). See Stowers, *Rereading of Romans*, 42–82.

This "sexual substratum" underlines the submission that I have shown to be central to the portrayal of πίστις in Romans. In addition to its political and social dimensions, faithful submission, through displays of πίστις toward an impenetrable God, has sexual implications. Jesus's πίστις, according to 3:21–26, permits God to set him out for God's purposes (προέθετο ὁ θεὸς ἱλαστήριον διὰ πίστεως [3:25]); Jesus's body is literally entrusted to God to use as God pleases.[157] Even though God does not use Jesus's body for overtly sexual purposes (at least in Paul's accounting), according to Rome's socio-sexual-political hierarchy, such a trusting relation signals passivity: placement under in one dimension implies that one can be placed under in others. If God is entrusted with the power of placement, then Jesus faithfully submits to being placed into a position that is most beneficial—indeed, pleasing—toward God. Jesus's πίστις provokes God's pleasure.

Since Jesus's πίστις provides a model for his followers—from his πίστις into theirs (1:17)—it follows that πίστις for the ἔθνη addressed by Paul should also be directed toward God's benefit and pleasure. If Jesus willingly places himself under God, so too must those who follow (the model of) Christ. Since πίστις entails faithful submission to God, those who follow Christ Jesus must participate in this sexual availability (penetrable under God) that is implicit in Paul's praise of Jesus's faithful submission unto death.[158] Just as Jesus submits and offers his body as entirely penetrable, not only by his imperial executioners but also by the impenetrable, ever-πιστός God of Romans, in Romans these ἔθνη find πίστις being extended to them by God, who increasingly looks like a more powerful and divine version of Augustus as he extends πίστις to πλεῖστα ἄλλα ἔθνη.[159]

As with Rome's conquered ἔθνη, who were thought of and portrayed as being sexually penetrable (in addition to socially and politically lower), the gentiles—the ἔθνη—of Romans assume a position of submission to

---

157. In the context of his enslaved appearance, connection could be made to the sexual use of enslaved persons and its meaning in terms of a divine master (sometimes called κύριος, though not by Paul). I invoke a similar idea about God's use of Mary of Nazareth in James N. Hoke, "Behold the Lord's Whore? Slavery, Prostitution, and Luke 1:38," *BibInt* 26 (2018): 61, see further 61–63.

158. As Moore's layout of Pauline soteriology suggested.

159. Thus, the character of these ἔθνη in Romans cannot be separated from the political situation of ἔθνη in the Roman Empire: they both refer to persons who come from nations whom the emperor has conquered, as Lopez argues.

God, following the model of Jesus, who is lifted over them as their κύριος. According to Rome's kyriarchal logic, in order to display πίστις, it follows that, like Jesus, the ἔθνη of Romans are under God in the same ways that they are under Caesar, politically, socially, and even sexually. Penetrable and submissive, these ἔθνη assume the posture of Brittania to Claudius, brought into faithful (albeit perhaps more willing) submission to an all-powerful deity.

The πίστις-relation with God described in Romans offers ἔθνη a path toward the good life and upward mobility, especially in the form of δικαιοσύνη ("justice"). The imperial language that occurs throughout Rom 1–5 grounds the argument that Jesus's πίστις is rooted in trusting that God has a plan to make just (or, justly benefit) all ἔθνη ("Jews first then Greeks"). This plan presumes that God will establish God's own reign in Rome, replacing the reigning emperor while retaining the basic structures of empire and its hierarchies. As in imperial πίστις-relations, then, God's πίστις to the ἔθνη produces hope for upward mobility. πίστις in Romans remains Romanormative, as does the good life under God.

This πίστις-relation attaches ἔθνη to God in a relation of optimism, promising them the benefits of justice that have not been realized under Roman rule.[160] The πίστις of these followers trusts not only that God's justice will be established, that God will reign as an all-powerful emperor with all people under God, but also that, once this system is established, those who have displayed proper πίστις to God will be uplifted in the same way as Christ has. Christ's faithful submission unto death results in his rising: not just from death but also from lowest status (as a condemned traitor to empire) to highest status as a κύριος under God's coming reign. He is raised from death to a life that is not only new but that is also *good*. Following Christ, the hope of these ἔθνη is that they, too, will be raised from their low position to that of the elite nearest the top, finally able to achieve the good life.

Unfortunately, just as the πίστις of many ἔθνη and *peregrini* in Rome can be called cruel in light of Rome's imperial hierarchy, the πίστις that Paul portrays in Romans proves cruel. It retains the submissive forces of Romanormative kyriarchy, envisioning a system of power that places all persons under God and then under Christ. The πίστις that properly defines

---

160. Once again, God's promises echo Berlant's theory, offering a fantasy of justice: "just the right way" (Berlant, *Cruel Optimism*, 2).

Christ-followers requires submission. Receiving benefits from God, all the ἔθνη must be led into the obedience of their πίστις (1:5); their πίστις is definitionally submissive, always a πίστις that requires them to be lower than and under the ultimate ruling authority. The literal "placing under" of faithful submission has negative implications for socioeconomic status in a system of imperial kyriarchy, whether Rome's or one that is Roman without Rome.[161] From such a view, the faithful submission of Rom 1–5 must always be a cruel πίστις.

Romans's sexual substrata underscores the cruelness of faithful submission. If Jesus's faithful submission to God's plan for justice demonstrated his penetrability, then the faithful submission of his followers among the ἔθνη proves that they are even more penetrable, being both under God and under Jesus Christ. If, during his first coming, Jesus Christ submissively bent over to be fucked by God, then he (alongside God) will get to top his submissive followers for his second coming.[162] They are faithful bottoms always available to their master-Christ and the impenetrably penetrating emperor-God, who is forever established as a "top without a bottom."[163] Willingly under God and Christ, their faithful submission places them in an endless position of powerlessness and passivity that, according to the Romosexual hierarchy of empire and its πίστις, undermines the hope for upward mobility.

πίστις in Rom 1–5 is cruel because, despite its hope for increased status under God's reign, its portrayal as "faithful submission" under God infinitely inhibits that hope to flourish. Under this imperial and kyriarchal framework, submission and obedience are always connected to those who are less powerful politically, passive and penetrable sexually, and ultimately lower socially. The hope of πίστις attaches these ἔθνη who follow Christ to a fantasy of upward mobility that they hope will be achieved with the establishment of God's justice as emperor. However, it is a fantasy that is impossible so long as God's power is presented in kyriarchally and imperially defined terms, as Paul does.

Throughout Paul's cruel πίστις, where do he and other Christ-followers find themselves? In a *delay* (ἀνοχή)—quite literally an "impasse"

---

161. That God's coming reign is discussed in real, Roman terms means that it cannot be severed from Roman socioeconomic systems, even if God and Jesus are neither Julio-Claudian rulers nor native Romans.

162. Pushing further Moore's language of Paul's sexual substrata in *God's Beauty Parlor*, 146–69.

163. Moore, *God's Beauty Parlor*, 170.

in Berlant's terms—in which God's wrath is held back to permit ἔθνη to enter God's reign. The delay becomes the "temporary housing" of Berlant's impasse, itself an apocalyptic moment wherein "the world is at once intensely present and enigmatic, such that the activity of living demands both a wandering absorptive awareness and a hypervigilance."[164] During this delay (ἐν τῇ ἀνοχῇ τοῦ θεοῦ [3:26]) God promises a "dismissal of previous errors" (τὴν πάρεσιν τῶν προγεγονότων ἁμαρτημάτων [3:25]). God makes time to forgive the impieties, injustices, and unnatural sexual behaviors that proliferated among unfaithful ἔθνη (as 1:18–32 enumerates) by stopping the apocalyptic clock so that ἔθνη can follow Jesus's model, faithfully submit to God, and embody a Romanormative good life.

In this impasse, the ultimate crisis—that is, apocalyptic expectation of God's coming to administer justice and punish the wicked—is delayed, as is the promised good life that is hoped for in the revelation of God's justice. The impending end of the world creates a crisis of apocalyptic urgency to perform faithful submission to bring about the good life under God. But the indefinite delay is an impasse, an infinite crisis state. The delay pauses ἔθνη in the holding pattern of crisis ordinariness to which they faithfully submit in an apocalyptic hope—eager expectation even (see Rom 8:18–25). Apocalypse now settles into a routinized rut of apocalypse (Roma)normal.

πίστις is the posture that is encouraged for ἔθνη following Christ as they wait in this indefinite impasse. It makes possible "'technologies of patience' that enable a concept of the *later* to suspend questions about the cruelty of the now."[165] This patient, faithfully submissive posture ensures ἔθνη remain forever stuck in their penetrably lower status, prolonging the impasse of an imperially structured life. The fantasy of mobility contained in Pauline πίστις (a mobility that can be occasionally realized in insignificant increments, as in the more general situation of Roman ἔθνη) merely sustains the submission that leaves them faithfully frozen in their lower position under imperial terms.

But why continue this cruel πίστις? Does Paul's imperial language betray an intentional alignment with the conquest and domination of Rome? Not necessarily.[166] As they discuss the impasses that often indicate cruel optimism, Berlant observes of their stuck subjects, "Cruel optimism

---

164. Berlant, *Cruel Optimism*, 4–5.
165. Berlant, *Cruel Optimism*, 28.
166. This statement does not forbid the possibility of intentionality on Paul's part,

or not, they feel attached to the *soft hierarchies of inequality* to provide a sense of their place in the world."[167] This insight emerges from Berlant's discussion of film characters who pretend to be living the ideal good life despite their actual inability to achieve such a life. They perform the social, sexual, or political terms of modern capitalist ideology, trusting that it might eventually lead to the flourishing it actually prevents. Likewise, Paul's cruel πίστις in Rom 1–5 provides the holding pattern by which Christ-followers can cling in faithful submission to the hope of flourishing under Roman imperial terms. This cruel πίστις and the imperial ideology it sustains enable an experience of comfortable familiarity during this delay (which one must hope does not turn out to be an infinite impasse). Drawn toward Romanormativity, it ultimately reproduces a soft hierarchy of inequality under the just rule of an imperial God and the obedient lord/master (κύριος) Christ.

Kyriarchy functions as an assemblage: cruel optimism and cruel πίστις permit affective sensations that draw subjects back into holding patterns, promising change, justice, and a good life that will never come so long as one remains attached to normative manifestations of these fantasies. Both cruel optimism and cruel πίστις are sustained by affective attachments to systems and ideologies of imperial domination that have long become normative, a fact of ordinary life that for most subjects is an extended state of crisis. Having created comfort in a state of crisis ordinary, these affective attachments cling to senses of stability, to those structures and patterns that have become and feel normal. Even subjects drawn toward queerness today find themselves craving normativities, showing how assemblages are both promising and threatening: queerness and kyriarchy can and do overlap. Likewise, kyriarchy and ἐκκλησία overlapped. As they are simultaneously drawn toward visions of justice and true change within an ἐκκλησία-l assemblage, Paul and perhaps some of his hearers needed to retain the familiarity of a πίστις-relation that relied on faithful submission to power. Feminist and queer affective critique of Romans can identify the cruelty of its faithful submission under God, but, ultimately, cruel πίστις is often easier to identify than it is to escape. The next chapter turns to the queer wo/men of Rome to proliferate some potential escape routes that swirled alongside these inescapable soft kyriarchies.

---

but the question of intent is irrelevant, as intent is not needed for such alignments to occur.

167. Berlant, *Cruel Optimism*, 194, emphasis added.

4

Faithful Subversion

"No!" she cried triumphantly. "*Like* and *equal* are not the same thing at all."
—Madeleine L'Engle, *A Wrinkle in Time*

Since the imperial context of Paul's πίστις proves it to be cruel, what other theo-christological impulses could have moved in between queer wo/men in Rome's ἐκκλησία? Could hopeful visions for God's justice move beyond a Roman-without-Rome ideology? What other ancient fantasies were possible besides a good life predicated on submission and kyriarchal inequality? What does God's justice (δικαιοσύνη θεοῦ) *feel* like?

This chapter engages the difficulties inherent to achieving egalitarianism. As Meg Murray screams at the imperial-like authority IT in L'Engle's story, making everyone exactly "like" one another does not render them "equal." People can wield equality to perpetuate kyriarchy.

Yet, "people are different," according to Sedgwick's axiom. People sense and experience equality differently. This chapter centers the different impulses around equality and God's justice that moved in between queer wo/men in Rome's ἐκκλησία. Some of these wo/men embraced egalitarianism as well as theo-Christologies that moved toward it.

Egalitarianism denotes impulses that attempt to equalize bodies that are always different. It admits its vision is utopian; egalitarianism exists as an ideal, but its embodiment is always changing as bodies interact and exist in different ways.[1] We can speak of egalitarian impulses that existed in the first century, today, and throughout history.[2] The existence of theo-christological

---

1. On egalitarianism within feminist historiography and the Jesus movement, see especially Mary Ann Beavis, "Christian Origins, Egalitarianism, and Utopia," *JFSR* 23 (2007): 27–49, esp. 31–36, 43–48.

2. Historians often deny the existence of egalitarian impulses, on the grounds that such ambitious ideals (namely, perfect equality) are impossible in societies that are

ideas that were oriented toward egalitarianism offer a basis from which some wo/men in Rome's ἐκκλησία could have embraced a variety of responses to the cruelly optimistic theo-christological vision presumed in Rom 1–5. This chapter decenters the Pauline impulses found in Romans and places them among the impulses of the queer wo/men of Rome.

This chapter proliferates theo-christological *impulses* that plausibly moved in between the queer wo/men around Rome's ἐκκλησία. This ἐκκλησία-l assemblage contained many impulses, some of which differed significantly and, as a result, could produce tensions, conflicts, and debates in between its queer wo/men participants. By suggesting plausible impulses that could have existed around such an assemblage, a more dynamic theo-Christology—really, an assemblage of theo-Christologies—emerges.

I use the term *impulse* to emphasize how ideas and suggestions are inherently affective and embodied. An impulse is a force exerted on the mind ("idea") or body ("feeling") that incites or stimulates action.[3] The theo-christological impulses proliferated below appear as ideas that were plausibly envisioned within Rome's ἐκκλησία. But ideas are never just thoughts or spoken suggestions: a thought is simultaneously a feeling, just as feelings are simultaneously ideas that affect the mind.[4] Ideas move around: they are thought, gestured, expressed, spoken, discussed, hated, liked, chewed upon, spat out, and grasped. They change as they move in between different bodies, objects, and feelings. *Impulse* captures this sensational blur in between ideas and feelings. *Impulses* emphasize how the

---

hierarchical and radically nonegalitarian. Assessing these judgments, Shelly A. Matthews shows their problematic assumption: "Taken together, these positions subject the ancient world to particularly high standards for what constitutes egalitarian strivings and utopian ideals, while assuming that such high standards have been currently met." See Shelly A. Matthews, "A Feminist Analysis of the Veiling Passage (1 Corinthians 11:2–16): Who Really Cares That Paul Was Not a Gender Egalitarian After All?," *LD* 2 (2015), https://tinyurl.com/SBL4531g. See also Beavis, "Christian Origins," 36–42, esp. 40.

3. The language here has been adapted from the definition of *impulse* as found in *OED*.

4. Feminist disability studies employs the concept of bodyminds as a term that insists mind and body are inseparable. My development of impulses has benefited from thinking with Sami Schalk, *Bodyminds Reimagined: (Dis)ability, Race, and Gender in Black Women's Speculative Fiction* (Durham, NC: Duke University Press, 2018), esp. 5–6. Schalk credits the term *bodymind* to Margaret Price, "The Bodymind Problem and the Possibilities of Pain," *Hypatia* 30 (2015): 268–84.

suggestions that follow were plausibly embodied in and in between the bodies and minds of first-century queer wo/men.

We already saw these impulses at work in chapter 2's test case. The brief impulses brought to life there emphasized the different ways queer wo/men embodied, discussed, and thought about sexuality, gender, politics, and theology as they interrupted Paul's Romanormative impulses in 1:18–32. This chapter does not leave those impulses behind. It continues to follow their connections and disjunctions with impulses around God and Jesus.

When brought together through a feminist and queer praxis of ἐκκλησία-l assemblage, different impulses ooze in between these queer wo/men, sometimes in ways that elude our imaginations and confuse our expectations. These impulses and their affective embodiments scramble the sides in between questions of justice and equality, kyriarchy and egalitarianism, and submission and its subversion. They do not end at this chapter's conclusion. These impulses affect the rest of the reading of Romans, and chapter 6 continues to follow these impulses, specifically asking how they became embodied within the ethical practices of Rome's ἐκκλησία.

The impulses I propose are necessarily speculative because there is no evidence to verify their expression in Rome's ἐκκλησία. There is also no evidence to disprove them. I contend that each of my proliferations of different theo-christological impulses holds *speculative plausibility*. Although they contain some elements of imagination that cannot be verified, I am working up from postholes with evidence that makes it plausible that these impulses could have existed.[5]

The evidence from which I draw comes from an eclectic-seeming range of first-century sources, perspectives, and locations. I frequently appeal to Paul's other letters, particularly those containing evidence of impulses originated by other Christ-followers whom Paul cites. I draw from the expressions about God and Christ that are contained in the pre-Pauline liturgical materials that circulated among Christ-followers, which Paul quotes in Gal 3:28 and Phil 2:6–11. While we do not have evidence of the extent of their circulation, it is plausible they reached Rome in some form, and, even if not, they provide evidence upon which different theo-christological expressions can be based.

---

5. On "working up from postholes," see discussion in chapter 2, pp. 132–33. The metaphor comes from Odai Johnson, *Absence and Memory in American Colonial Theatre* (New York: Palgrave Macmillan, 2006), 18.

Evidence from sources beyond the texts of early Christianity also make plausible my alternative proliferations. In this chapter, these sources include Philo and devotion to Isis. These instances show how such impulses could be formulated by numerous parties across the Roman world and, therefore, were not anomalous to a single movement. If these ideas existed and circulated elsewhere in the first century, their existence lends plausibility to their potential effect on the theo-Christologies of Christ-followers in Rome.

In "God's Equals," I work with Jesus being ἴσα θεοῦ ("equal to God" [Phil 2:6]) to consider a plausible egalitarian theo-christological impulse that could arise from such a hymnic form. Then, continuing off the implications of this first impulse and Phil 2:6–8, "Drowning Jesus" considers other christological interpretations of Jesus's death that may avoid some of the crueler fantasies found in Rom 1–5. In "Kyriarchal Christs," we must remember that queer wo/men of Rome were not all perfectly oriented toward egalitarianism. I consider attestations of Jesus as κύριος and query the ways that such an attribution might indicate an ongoing craving for kyriarchy that did not originate with Paul. Finally, in "Assemblaging Theo-Christology," I bring these impulses together, alongside those of Paul in Rom 1–5, through a praxis of ἐκκλησία-l assemblage to display their interactions, alignments, and clashes. This praxis brings these plausible impulses to life and shows how they were embodied, in tandem and in tension, in between the queer wo/men who assembled in Rome's ἐκκλησία.

God's Equals

Feminist historiography has long affirmed the historical existence of egalitarianism among the earliest wo/men Christ-followers.[6] Especially following the work of Elisabeth Schüssler Fiorenza, we sense these egal-

---

6. See especially Elisabeth Schüssler Fiorenza, *In Memory of Her: A Feminist Theological Reconstruction of Christian Origins*, 10th anniversary ed. (New York: Crossroad, 1994); Beavis, "Christian Origins"; Elizabeth A. Castelli, "The *Ekklēsia* of Women and/ as Utopian Space," in *On the Cutting Edge: The Study of Women in Biblical Worlds*, ed. Jane Schaberg, Alice Bach, and Esther Fuchs (New York: Continuum, 2004), 36–52; Melanie Johnson-DeBaufre, "Dreaming the Common Good/s: The Kin-dom of God as a Space of Utopian Politics," in *Common Goods: Economy, Ecology, and Political Theology*, ed. Johnson-DeBaufre, Catherine Keller, and Elias Ortega-Aponte, TTC (New York: Fordham University Press, 2015), 103–23; Matthews, "Feminist Analysis."

itarian impulses in the pre-Pauline baptismal formula of Gal. 3:28: οὐκ ἔνι Ἰουδαῖος οὐδὲ Ἕλλην, οὐκ ἔνι δοῦλος οὐδὲ ἐλεύθερος, οὐκ ἔνι ἄρσεν καὶ θῆλυ· πάντες γὰρ ὑμεῖς εἷς ἐστε ἐν Χριστῷ Ἰησοῦ ("There is no longer Jew nor Greek; there is no longer slave nor free; there is no longer male and female. For all y'all are one in Christ Jesus").[7] This hymn conjures the unrealized potential for a world where differences, here named in terms of status, ethnicity, and gender, are not the basis for divisions. Even though people are different, all can participate in an ἐκκλησία. The individual ἐκκλησίαι where these followers gathered represented spaces where these burgeoning egalitarianisms could proliferate, interact, expand, and clash. Its egalitarian impulses are utopian, both as a historical reality and always anticipating a different future.[8]

Egalitarian impulses impact theo-Christology. They could signal other plausible relations between God and Jesus, who was a model for followers. If oriented in egalitarian directions, some of these relations could differ from and even counteract Jesus's submissive posture found in Paul's pre-

---

7. "I have sought to read the baptismal formula as an articulation of the emancipatory vision of a broad-based egalitarian Jewish movement whose language Paul shares but which he seeks to control.... Methodologically one must read Gal. 3:28 as *the tip of the iceberg that indicates what Paul's text submerges*" See Elisabeth Schüssler Fiorenza, *Rhetoric and Ethic: The Politics of Biblical Studies* (Minneapolis: Fortress, 1999), 169, see further 149–73. See also Schüssler Fiorenza, *In Memory of Her*, 205–41; Sheila Briggs, "Galatians," in *Searching the Scriptures: A Feminist Commentary*, ed. Elisabeth Schüssler Fiorenza with Shelly Matthews (New York: Crossroad, 1994), 2:218–36; Melanie Johnson-DeBaufre and Laura S. Nasrallah, "Beyond the Heroic Paul: Toward a Feminist and Decolonizing Approach to the Letters of Paul," in *The Colonized Apostle: Paul through Postcolonial Eyes*, ed. Christopher D. Stanley, PCC (Minneapolis: Fortress, 2011), 164; Matthews, "Feminist Analysis." For alternative perspectives/histories, which often prioritize Paul and query the hymn's egalitarian potentials (of which both Matthews and Schüssler Fiorenza are especially critical), see Lone Fatum, "The Glory of God and the Image of Man: Women in the Pauline Congregations," in *The Image of God and Gender Models in Judeo-Christian Tradition*, ed. Kari Elisabeth Børresen (Minneapolis: Fortress, 1995), 50–133; Dale Martin, *Sex and the Single Savior: Gender and Sexuality in Biblical Interpretation* (Louisville: Westminster John Knox, 2006), 77–90; Brigitte Kahl, "Der Brief an die Gemeinden in Galatien: Vom Unbehagen der Geschlechter und anderen Problemen des Andersseins," in *Kompendium feministischer Bibelauslegung*, ed. Louise Schottroff and Marie-Therese Wacker (Gütersloh: Chr. Kaiser Gütersloher Verlagshaus, 1998), 603–11.

8. See Elisabeth Schüssler Fiorenza, *Discipleship of Equals: A Critical Feminist Ekklēsia-logy of Liberation* (New York: Crossroad, 1993), 353–72; Castelli, "*Ekklēsia* of Women"; Johnson-DeBaufre, "Dreaming the Common Good/s."

sentation of Jesus's placement, under God's authority, in Romans. One plausible relation that could complement the vision of Gal 3:28 is a relation to God expressed in plausibly egalitarian terms: ἴσα θεοῦ, "equal to God" or even "on egalitarian terms with God." While the Greek adjective ἴσος is frequently used to indicate mathematical equality (often in quite technical terms, such as by Euclid), its meaning extends beyond pure mathematics within sociopolitical contexts to indicate equality based on rights, division of power, or fairness.[9]

While Greek equality terms did not solely convey egalitarian impulses, their usages indicate that the term was not devoid of such a meaning when some wo/men heard or invoked equality. In the first-century, Roman authors were actively debating the meaning of equality. They imbued it with sociopolitical meanings that were both kyriarchal and egalitarian. Debates about equality, as L. L. Welborn maps them, existed along a spectrum wherein equality can be highly "proportional" (κατ᾽ ἀναλογίαν)—one's share of power is determined by one's status, which is a reflection of one's moral worth (ἄξιος)—or more "numerical" (κατ᾽ ἀριθμόν), that is, in ways that share power so that the most people possess the same share, regardless of their status.[10] Oligarchic and imperial equality favors a proportional definition of equality (which can be seen in the writings of Dio Chrysostom, Plutarch, and Philo) while a more democratic rendering of equality (as potentially seen in Ps.-Archytas) tends toward a numerical definition.[11]

Welborn's analysis of equality situates Paul's language of equality (especially ἰσότης in 2 Cor 8:13–15) with this wider Roman context in which (mostly) elite men grappled with how to define equality in light of the shift to an imperial rule under that expanded inequality.[12] Decidedly different from the sociopolitical divisions under democratic rule, imperialism made inequality manifest in ways that were apparent even to those near the top of the kyriarchal pyramid. Welborn is primarily interested in *Paul's* heroic notion of equality as it emerges from this context. In his

---

9. LSJ, s.v. "ἴσος," 839.

10. L. L. Welborn, "Paul's Place in a First-Century Revival of the Discourse of 'Equality,'" *HTR* 110 (2017): 546–553; Welborn, "'That There May Be Equality': The Contexts and Consequences of a Pauline Ideal," *NTS* 59 (2013): 81–82. The terms come from Aristotle's discussion of equality, as detailed in Welborn, "That There May Be Equality," 76.

11. Welborn, "Paul's Place," 546–53.

12. Welborn, "Paul's Place." See also Welborn, "That There May Be Equality."

reading of 2 Cor 8:13–15, the ἐκκλησία—or, at least, its wealthy women participants—becomes the implicitly villainous foil to Paul and his allies, who passively wait for Paul's heroic intervention.[13] For Welborn, Paul does not learn notions of equality *from* his ongoing correspondence with the queer wo/men in the ἐκκλησίαι he has visited; instead, Paul learns about equality from conversations among elite philosophers (in which, implicitly, he alone participates) and adapts them—in original and *unprecedented* ways—to the needs of these ἐκκλησίαι.[14]

It is more plausible that the queer wo/men of these ἐκκλησίαι were *all* participants in this first-century revival. They debated among themselves the different meanings of equality, especially as it pertained to their theo-christological understandings of a just world. Paul's understandings come from some of these wo/men, agreeing with some while responding in disagreement to others. "Recognizing these traditions as at one time independent of Paul," writes Cynthia Briggs Kittredge, "recovers them as possible resources for early Christian visions."[15] Pre-Pauline materials like (but not limited to) Gal 3:28 affirm how Paul integrates egalitarian

---

13. See especially, Welborn, "That There May Be Equality," 88–90; as well as Welborn, "Paul's Place," 560–61. Here the "unprecedented nature" of Paul's ideas is especially emphasized. Welborn does briefly gesture in one final conclusion to the "egalitarian and democratic impulses" already present among early Christ-followers (see "Paul's Place," 561–62), but it is not a central emphasis throughout. Welborn does analyze some of these democratic notions among Corinth's ἐκκλησία in more detail in a later-published article, but he still situates Paul as the heroic defender of the poor and enslaved Christ-followers in this democracy, over and against the elitism that characterizes the slogans found in 1 Corinthians. See Welborn, "How 'Democratic' Was the Pauline *Ekklēsia*? An Assessment with Special Reference to the Christ Groups of Roman Corinth," *NTS* 65 (2019): 289–309, esp. 298–99. Here, despite claiming to have presented a "complex and contradictory portrait of the politics of the Christ groups at Corinth" (299), Welborn oversimplifies the division between elite and impoverished, especially when he characterizes all of the slogans of 1 Corinthians as betraying a uniform elitism with little consideration of their participation in the politics of gender, sexuality, or race/ethnicity. Thus, Paul's critique of these slogans emerges as a heroic democratic counterpoint to their presumed elitism.

14. On the novelty—particularly of Paul's development of an *economic* notion of equality—see Welborn, "That There May Be Equality," 88–90.

15. Cynthia Briggs Kittredge, "Rethinking Authorship in the Letters of Paul: Elisabeth Schüssler Fiorenza's Model of Pauline Theology," in *Walk in the Ways of Wisdom: Essays in Honor of Elisabeth Schüssler Fiorenza*, ed. Shelly Matthews, Kittredge, and Melanie Johnson-DeBaufre (Harrisburg, PA: Trinity Press International, 2003), 331.

ideals—which originated around and among these ἐκκλησίαι of queer wo/men—into his theo-Christology, in both egalitarian and kyriarchal ways. Just as kyriarchy did not originate in Paul's letters, neither did egalitarianism.

Equality (ἴσος) appears directly in Philippians' Christ hymn, which likely circulated among Christ-followers in various ἐκκλησίαι across Rome's territories.[16] The hymn affirms how the ἐκκλησία's impulses about equality, in its many different interpretations, preceded (and influenced) Paul.[17] It proclaims of Christ Jesus: ὅς ἐν μορφῇ θεοῦ ὑπάρχων / οὐχ ἁρπαγμὸν ἡγήσατο / τὸ εἶναι ἴσα θεοῦ ("Who, existing in God's form, / did not consider rape and robbery / in order to be equal to God" [Phil 2:6]). Even if the wo/men who assembled in Rome did not know the exact hymn quoted in Phil 2:6–11, the ideas it espouses—including Jesus's equality with God—were plausibly familiar, just as those held in Gal 3:28 were. What might it mean for first-century theo-Christology in Rome's ἐκκλησία if some followers took seriously the statement that Jesus was ἴσα θεοῦ ("equal to God")?

One plausible interpretation of this impulse moves beyond taking it as solely meaning that Jesus is Godlike in terms of divine powers, knowledge, and abilities. Instead, it takes Jesus and God to be equals in a sociopolitical sense.[18] In such an interpretation, there is no power imbal-

---

16. Such circulation would have meant the hymn had several, slightly differing, oral-based versions.

17. Kittredge discusses the need to take the pre-Pauline designation of the hymn (and other such formulae) seriously, particularly as an alternative source for varying perspectives on authority and leadership (Kittredge, "Rethinking Authorship," 324–26).

18. Contra Stanley K. Stowers, *A Rereading of Romans: Justice, Jews, and Gentiles* (New Haven: Yale University Press, 1994), 219–20. He argues it means "similar to God in some respects" (drawing comparison to a usage of the phrase in Homer), making it similar in effect to μορφή, used soon after: "Paul's wording quite precisely says that Jesus was godlike or Godlike but not equal to God" (220). However, as LSJ attests, the word was used quite frequently, with multiple meanings for this "equality," certainly (as Stowers argues) equal in appearance ("like"), but it can also refer to size, rights, power, authority, strength, and generally "equal relations." I do not deny that Stowers's interpretations is a plausible way this can be (and has been) interpreted, but it is not the only way it may have been heard by first-century audiences, given this wide semantic range and usage, and it seems quite restrictive to limit it to this (very traditionally, theologically charged) meaning based on an example from Homer, who (although influential) used a very different style and version of Greek than that heard on the streets of first-century Rome. See further LSJ, s.v. "ἴσος," 839.

ance between the two (even if one is fully divine and one is of human origin).[19] This denies Jesus's submission *to God*.[20] God's power diverges from the Roman imperial model of power, wherein the godlike emperor must reign over all others.[21] Thinking of Jesus as God's equal opens avenues to conceive God's power and justice differently, as something that is unlimited and sharable. Such an ideal represents one, among many, plausible theo-Christologies that worked to express some of the egalitarian impulses within Rome's ἐκκλησία.

According to Rome's kyriarchal ideology, having an equal (as opposed to being alone on top) makes one vulnerable to exploitation, penetration, and being brought under. Philippians 2:6 proclaims that Jesus did not think that rape and robbery (ἁρπαγμός)—that is, the forced and violent exploitation of others to seize their honor (*pudicitia/pudor*), wealth, and power—was required as proof that he was equal to God.[22] Such an occurrence would have been unexpected based on Roman accounts of human history; he

---

19. Here I will defer from fully speculating on whether Jesus is/was a God, except to note that much of the argument and discourse about this (and particularly ideas of Jesus as "fully God") do not develop in any full sense until well after the first century. To be sure, there is early evidence of Jesus being seen as (always) having divine status/ origin, and it is plausible that some in the ἐκκλησία ascribed to such an idea; but it is equally plausible that others saw Jesus as (solely) "fully human." My reconstructions take most seriously the implications of stressing Jesus's humanity, but I do not think they are incompatible with (at least some) ways of thinking of Jesus as a God who becomes human.

20. As Kittredge likewise argues. See Cynthia Briggs Kittredge, *Community and Authority: The Rhetoric of Obedience in the Pauline Tradition*, HTS 45 (Harrisburg, PA: Trinity Press International, 1998), 78–83.

21. And indeed, the pantheon of the Roman gods has a hierarchy of power and control, which stands above Caesar.

22. My translation of ἁρπαγμός in this verse follows Shaner's analysis of the term's textual *and* material contexts in order to argue the term clearly refers to rape and robbery. See Katherine A. Shaner, "Seeing Rape and Robbery: ἁρπαγμός and the Philippians Christ Hymn (Phil. 2:5–11)," *BibInt* 25 (2017): 342–63. The *hapax legomenon*, ἁρπαγμός, in Phil 2:6—as it has been traditionally defined and interpreted from its limited usage—refers to exploitation as seizing or exploiting (as in robbery or rape in other ancient examples), although the specifics have been long debated (but seem to point to this general meaning, at least). See LSJ, s.v. "ἁρπαγμός," 245. For a history of expositions on this quite difficult word (before Shaner's incisive intervention)— and an overview of scholarly debate and translation—see Michael Wade Martin, "ἁρπαγμός Revisited: A Philological Reexamination of the New Testament's 'Most Difficult Word,'" *JBL* 135 (2016): 175–94. Much of this so-called difficulty has more to do

who is on top is he who has most exceptionally exploited power. Looking to the imagery of Aphrodisias's Sebasteion, Shaner unpacks the Roman theo-ideology wherein the emperor's rape and robbery of conquered ἔθνη (personified as women, as in the depiction of Claudius and Brittania) confirmed his divine status.[23] Caesar is ἴσα θεοῦ (and no other human is ἴσα Καῖσαρ). Many would assume gods and emperors must be able to force all their subjects into submission under them—symbolically and in actuality. If this Romosexual logic applied to Jesus, his equality with God would require the ability to force God (and all others) under him, to fuck the Bottomless Top and rob God of God's wealth and power.[24]

However, according to the Christ hymn, Jesus does *not* ascribe to this way of thinking (οὐχ ἡγήσατο): equality with God is *not* ἁρπαγμός, *not* rape and robbery. Jesus embodies a different, egalitarian-leaning ideal that sharing power does not necessarily entail a reduction of one's own status or control in order to raise another. δικαιοσύνη θεοῦ is not a zero-sum game. If Jesus serves as an example or model for other humans (especially non-Jews) to follow into full participation in δικαιοσύνη θεοῦ ("God's justice"), then it is plausible that some queer wo/men sensed in these impulses a hope that stemmed from this possibility of equality with God in social, political, and economic terms.

What follows from Jesus's equality is Jesus's submission (γενόμενος ὑπήκοος [2:8]) and appearance as enslaved (μορφὴν δούλου λαβών [2:7]). In her essay "Can an Enslaved God Liberate?," Shiela Briggs problematizes the hymn's use of enslavement as a metaphor. The material reality of enslaved wo/men, especially those who heard this hymn in these ἐκκλησίαι, prompts the question of who composed and sang this hymn and how it was heard and interpreted by others.[25] The hymn's emphasis on Jesus's equal

---

with the potential Christian theological offense of associating divinity with rape and robbery (Shaner, "Seeing Rape and Robbery," 345).

23. "Thus in the visual rhetoric of these reliefs, the imperial god's divinity is confirmed in the act of seizure and victory; said another way, robbery and rape equals God" (Shaner, "Seeing Rape and Robbery," 358, see further 350–58). I discussed the image of Claudius conquering the feminized Brittania in chapter 3.

24. On God as a "Bottomless Top" (or the ultimate impenetrable penetrator, à la Jonathan Walters), see Stephen D. Moore, *God's Beauty Parlor: And Other Queer Spaces in and around the Bible*, Contraversions (Stanford: Stanford University Press, 2001), 169–70. See also discussion above in chapter 3.

25. Shiela Briggs, "Can an Enslaved God Liberate? Hermeneutical Reflections on Philippians 2:6–11," *Semeia* 47 (1989): 137–53, esp. 142–43.

status to God makes his enslaved form a contradiction: "Christ as divine was absolutely too worthy to be enslaved."[26] If Jesus should not be enslaved because of his divine equality, the hymn leaves unchallenged the systemic and dehumanizing conditions of real enslaved wo/men.[27] The hymn's use of slavery idealizes the metaphorical experience of enslavement (especially if enslaved folks did not actively participate its composition)—much like the elite characters who find themselves enslaved in Hellenistic novels.[28] Jesus's equality with God emphasizes the cruelty of everyone else's reality, especially enslaved wo/men's.

But what if equality to God was not exclusive to Jesus? Could there be other ways ancient hearers and singers interpreted these verses of the hymn? Another way of hearing, singing, or interpreting the hymn does not deny that wo/men can experience less liberative impulses in these words (such as those to which Briggs draws our attention). Shaner's reconsideration of the Christ hymn acknowledges its "glimmer of liberation."[29] "Thus to Roman imperial eyes, Jesus's form is that of the enslaved barbarian woman. In contrast, Phil 2:6 insists that Christ held a divine form, consonant with imperial depictions of powerful, divinely beautiful bodies, even if Christ did not act out the violence of rape and robbery that usually confirms such power."[30] These different interpretive impulses could have existed alongside one another; they may have been experienced within the same bodies.

Taking their designation as *Christ-followers* a little more literally, if wo/men thought of Jesus as a model to follow (an idea we saw Paul take

---

26. Briggs, "Can an Enslaved God Liberate?," 143. Briggs continues by emphasizing how the fact that Jesus's voluntary enslavement denies the reality that slavery is always an involuntary condition as well as that Jesus is never affected by the moral inferiority that attached to enslaved wo/men; indeed, his enslavement makes him morally superior (146–48).

27. "The dependence of the Philippians text on the mental universe of slaveholding antiquity is attested not only by what it incorporates of the social reality of slavery into its christological metaphor but also by those elements which it excludes. Hence, precisely at the point where Philippians could have challenged the ethical and anthropological assumptions about the slave, it avoids the question of whether slavery is equivalent to moral inferiority" (Briggs, "Can an Enslaved God Liberate?," 148).

28. Briggs, "Can an Enslaved God Liberate?," 146.

29. Shaner, "Seeing Rape and Robbery," 362–63. See also Kittredge, *Community and Authority*, 78–81.

30. Shaner, "Seeing Rape and Robbery," 361.

up in Rom 3:21–31), then it is plausible some assumed that following Christ stemmed from an acknowledgment that *they too* were ἴσα θεοῦ. It is plausible to hear the hymn say that if Jesus is equal to God, then *Jesus's submission is not to God*. His submission only conforms to Roman conceptions of submission as he submits himself *to Roman imperial rule*, being enslaved by them and, therefore, worthy of the most ignoble death for defying the justice of the state.[31] He chooses to live on equal terms with God, despite his submissive, enslaved form (which, according to Roman imperialism, could never be Godlike).[32]

Jesus's status as God's equal does not make Jesus a unique hero who saves the people who are and always will be below him in status and capability. He provides a model by which his followers can envision δικαιοσύνη θεοῦ and work together to continue accomplishing it.[33] This model is one in which all are equal to God and therefore equal to one another: an ἐκκλησία that is a "discipleship of equals" *alongside Jesus and God*, a God whose power is not kinglike or imperial.[34] In this interpretation, God's

31. My suggestion, however, cannot completely avoid the problems Briggs diagnoses. On this point, Jesus's submission and enslavement is still conveyed as voluntary, and—as Briggs emphasizes with slavery and as we have seen above with conquered ἔθνη and their portrayal as women—neither submission nor slavery are voluntary choices people make (Briggs, "Can an Enslaved God Liberate?," 146–48).

32. With this, I am attempting to think about whether the Christ hymn could have been interpreted in such a way so that Jesus's submission and slavery were not voluntary choices, thus taking the hymn's designation of Jesus as enslaved according to reality and not as a metaphor. Instead of Jesus voluntarily choosing slavery, the hymn grants Jesus an agency, as one of God's equals, that Roman ideology would deny him as an enslaved man. Though I have not engaged it closely here, Schalk's emphasis on reading disability as reality—in addition to metaphor—in Black women's speculative fiction has been a valuable resource for thinking through the importance of nonmetaphorical interpretations as well as the interpretive value of holding metaphor and reality together in tension. See Schalk, *Bodyminds Reimagined*, 33–57 (ch. 1, "Metaphor and Materiality").

33. Indeed, one hopes that Johnson-DeBaufre and Nasrallah's move to reveal voices and conversations "beyond the heroic Paul" might reveal—within these conversations—ideas that get beyond the heroic [as an extension of the historical?] Jesus (and perhaps foreground a similar move in biblical studies and Christian theology) (Johnson-DeBaufre and Nasrallah, "Beyond the Heroic Paul").

34. On the term, development, and historicity of the "discipleship of equals," see Schüssler Fiorenza, *In Memory of Her*, esp. 99–104; Schüssler Fiorenza, *Discipleship of Equals*.

power is shared power. δικαιοσύνη θεοῦ summons a world where sharing with God means that power is not exploited to benefit those on top over all others. Instead, *shared* power can realize an actual good life that has more potential to be good for different people.

How does Jesus's relation as ἴσα θεοῦ affect the fact of his submission to Rome (and its imperial authority) that results in his humiliation/lowering in status (ἐταπείνωσεν)? One plausibility is that Jesus's relation with God empowered him to act as God's equal in first-century society, despite the sociopolitical ramifications of his actions within imperial rule. Jesus provides his followers with an example of how being conquered and forced into submission *does not impact* his equality with God. Submission is not the required posture for anyone; it is not a prerequisite for δικαιοσύνη θεοῦ. Submission does not make anyone better in God's—or anyone else's—eyes. Through God's justice, such a conception of "better" becomes impossible because all, including God, are moving toward an egalitarian vision that is yet to be fully embodied. Putting the Christ hymn in conversation with the ἐκκλησία's baptismal formula (Gal 3:28), God's justice, unlike Roman justice, among equals should render submission and slavery impossible: οὐκ ἔνι δοῦλος οὐδὲ ἐλεύθερος, "there is no longer slave nor free." An egalitarian world does not mean everyone will be exactly the same, but it must systemically eliminate and avoid inequity and injustice. An optimistic investment might not hope for the good life—or even a better life—but a just life for all.

Drowning Jesus

Jesus's death held considerable significance among his earliest followers. His crucifixion is central to the proclamations of Phil 2:6–8 (the first half of the Christ hymn) and the miniclimax of Paul's theo-christological explanation in Rom 3:21–31. Jesus's death, alongside his subsequent raising, is one of the few historical details about him mentioned in Paul's letters, and this is the detail Paul emphasizes most consistently.[35] It is highly probable that participants in Rome's ἐκκλησία interpreted the significance of Jesus's death in different ways.[36] This impulse foregrounds how interpretations

---

35. Paul exhibits little interest in the details of Jesus's ministry, teaching, and life such as those accounted for by the gospel tradition, though he does mention in Rom 1:3 that Jesus was born in the lineage of David.

36. It is probable given the evidence of ἐκκλησία-1 debates found in Paul's letters

of Jesus's death could have drawn toward egalitarian impulses like those considered above.

Berlant's image of treading water conveys an aspirational normativity that creates conditions for cruel optimism. But when is a struggle an act of subversion or resistance that is slowly swimming toward change, and when does it become merely a holding pattern that prevents both drowning and swimming? And how would subjects have been able to recognize the cruelty of imperial ideals of social mobility that sustained a rigid, yet flexible-seeming, kyriarchy through ideals like πίστις? If many Roman subjects (in particular, those in the ἐκκλησία) were treading in imperial waters, is there an escape from this pattern that does not move them into another situation of cruel optimism? Perhaps the most popular theo-christological answer, sustained over centuries, is to make Jesus the almighty lifeguard who offers a buoy of salvation to these slowly drowning subjects. Jesus's death and resurrection saves (literally) by overcoming death for all and promising new life (after death) in God's justice.[37]

A different direction for plausible theo-christological impulses in Rome's ἐκκλησία might address the significance of Jesus's crucifixion less optimistically. The suggestions that follow speculate plausible, if unverifiable, interpretations of the evidence found about Jesus's death in early hymns and Paul's letters in ways that might align with the evidence of egalitarian impulses moving in between Rome's queer wo/men. If Jesus submits himself to the bounds of Rome's kyriarchal rule, he is a participant alongside the majority of Jews/conquered ἔθνη who are treading water with little chance of ascending the status scale. Perhaps the significance of Jesus's death is just that: *he dies*. Instead of cruelly hoping for a buoy, he stops treading water. Jesus drowns.

He drowns spectacularly. Instead of slowly sinking further and further underwater, he opts for the more painful dunk of crucifixion, an ultimate public humiliation for crimes against kyriarchy. He is now a known traitor, untrustworthy and undeserving of respect or followers after death. Crucifixion's threat represents one of countless well-known negative consequences for resisting the forces that guided and structured Rome's

---

and the plurality of theo-christological histories and interpretations of Jesus's life and death that proliferated in the first centuries CE.

37. While certainly one possibility that has roots in Rom 3:21–31, the previous chapter showed how such an idea continues cruel πίστις and promises a future justice that still looks rather imperial.

kyriarchal rule. Jesus's death can take on significance by refusing to be contained by that threat—or by finding it more promising than threatening. Maybe he did not know (or even suspect) that God will raise him from this death: he just realized that choosing to be brutally but (more) quickly drowned for swimming against the tide is far less cruel than an otherwise unavoidable slow death.[38]

Why would such an idea have been important to some in Rome's ἐκκλησία, making it worth following this drowner? Regardless of whether these followers had been aware that they were treading water, Jesus's death uncovers a less cruel promise that hides beneath Rome's threat of crucifixion: he is *still* (and always was) equal to the God whom he follows. His actions were not performed primarily as protest or rebellion against (the) empire, even though they may have this effect. His radical, rebellious-seeming choice is to live on egalitarian terms with God (and, therefore, with all others) in a kyriarchal culture that actively resisted such an impulse. For those expected to be submissive under kyriarchy, everyday existence gets perceived as rebellious. Living on such terms risks—but does not require—drowning. Jesus's death is a result of choosing the risk over the rut. Followers of this impulse regarding Jesus's death find permission neither to drown themselves nor to rebel recklessly: they find a model (who need not be singular) to live into and work toward a society based on egalitarian visions of God's justice.[39]

---

38. "What does it mean," asks Berlant, "to consider the ethics of longevity when, in an unequal health and labor system, the poor and less poor are less likely to live long enough to enjoy the good life whose promise is a fantasy bribe that justifies so much exploitation?" See Lauren Berlant, *Cruel Optimism* (Durham, NC: Duke University Press, 2011), 105. For Berlant, "slow death" describes another affective dimension of cruel optimism: "the physical wearing out of a population in a way that points to its deterioration as a defining condition of its experience and historical existence" (95, see further 95–119 [ch. 3, "Slow Death"]). Karen Bray's affective political theology draws upon Berlant's slow death to reclaim Holy Saturday—that is, on the Christian liturgical calendar, the day between crucifixion (Good Friday) and resurrection (Easter Sunday)— as a radical, utopian *queer time*. Her discussions frequently resonate with this plausible theological impulse. See Karen Bray, *Grave Attending: A Political Theology for the Unredeemed* (New York: Fordham University Press, 2020), 30–67 (ch. 2, "Unsaved Time"). Her discussion of Robin James's melancholic reading of "a feminist method of *going into the death*" in Rihanna's song "Diamonds" especially connect to this discussion of drowning (Bray, *Grave Attending*, 53–56). Bray quotes Robin James, *Resilience and Melancholy: Pop Music, Feminism, Neoliberalism* (Alresford, UK: Zero Books, 2015), 126.

39. Bray reads the imagery of drowning in the music video for Rihanna's "Dia-

While this impulse moves away from the cruel optimism of Roman (and Pauline) πίστις and hopes of salvation, there are still potentials for its implications to morph back into cruelty. Though Jesus drowns (in what could be seen as an embrace of the "queer art of failure"), eventually he rises—or, more accurately, God raises him.[40] What looked like failure in the crucifixion is revealed to be success in the resurrection. Or, in the tone of traditional Christian theology, Jesus overcomes death's failure and makes possible something new: the good life after death.

Such a resurrection can become the buoy for drowning subjects to grasp: salvation. How fantastic *is* such a buoy, and is the promise it provides still as cruel as Pauline πίστις? Considering life after death possible is not inherently cruel. But it can become cruel if its promise of the good life after death mitigates the terror of potential crucifixion. If it relieves the risk of death's finality, it may also prevent the risks necessary to attain this resurrected life: cruel optimism. Cruel though it may be, in a society where many were struggling with the burdens of treading in rough imperial waters, some Christ-followers may have needed such an interpretation. Even if this buoy turns out to be a slowly deflating raft, not everyone is ready or able to drown quickly. The risks (and what gets left behind) are heavier for some.

A potentially less cruel option—which it is possible at least a few in the ἐκκλησία entertained in some form—does not rely on this promise of resurrection. Death may still be final. This alternative impulse prioritizes the *risk* of Jesus's model: drowning in an attempt to live as God's equals must be a better life than continuing to tread under kyriarchy. These followers still attach optimistically to a promise for a good life that can only be imagined (is any life possible without having some form of optimism in Berlant's definition?). The good life anticipated here is a sociopolitical life aligned with δικαιοσύνη θεοῦ. It is a good life that requires followers to

---

monds," coming to a similar idea through it: "This is not a request to drown, but rather to block up a flight from that which needs our attending" (Bray, *Grave Attending*, 55).

40. Despite my own hesitation with Halberstam's embrace of failure, aspects of it resonate these implications. See Jack Halberstam, *The Queer Art of Failure*, JHFCB (Durham, NC: Duke University Press, 2011). However, my hesitation toward Halberstam's argument in this book and my critique of resurrection also have similarities: the failure described is often not final and leads to success in a slightly shifted perspective. Further, I suspect such models of failure are most easily embraced and elaborated by those (myself included) with a greater degree of safety net that prevent failure's total ruin (or drowning).

enact it and make it possible. Jesus's death quells the cruelty of what is still a good life fantasy by upholding its possibility without falsely promising its immediate realization. Death is still possible, but it is not (only) a threat. Death in the service of δικαιοσύνη θεοῦ can also be a promise, if not of new and resurrected life, then of *genuine change*—movements and sensations toward egalitarian, just lives on a wider, shared scale. For some, Jesus's death hopefully beckons: *try to swim until you drown; don't tread until it is inevitable.*

Kyriarchal Christs

The impulses that moved in between the queer wo/men in Rome's ἐκκλησία were not equally just. Even the previous two impulses are not devoid of kyriarchal orientations. The ability to drown can be a privilege, and for many, treading water is a necessary survival tactic, one that does not spectacularly detach from submissive postures but also may not necessarily attach to promises that can never be fulfilled by them. If some found in Jesus a model for drowning, others might have found strategies for survival that involved appearances of submission that seem Romanormative. Beyond such strategies, other queer wo/men in Rome's ἐκκλησία clung to kyriarchy and its cruel promises.

The Christ hymn contained many meanings for its first-century hearers and singers (just as it does for contemporary interpreters). Turning to the hymn's conclusion, we see how Christ-followers retained kyriarchal language and ideologies for Christ and God. Here, I proffer plausible ways such language could have functioned within developing theo-Christologies in Rome's ἐκκλησία. This accounts for the affective in-betweenness of these theo-christological impulses with a reminder that Christ-followers could embody kyriarchy even as they critiqued it or sensed and proclaimed egalitarian visions of justice.

If the Christ hymn contains the idea of Jesus's equality with God, it also concludes by touting an image of submission to Jesus as the Christ—indeed, as κύριος.

ἵνα ἐν τῷ ὀνόματι Ἰησοῦ
πᾶν γόνυ κάμψῃ
ἐπουρανίων καὶ ἐπιγείων καὶ καταχθονίων
καὶ πᾶσα γλῶσσα ἐξομολογήσηται ὅτι
κύριος Ἰησοῦς Χριστὸς

εἰς δόξαν θεοῦ πατρός.

So that in Jesus's name
Every knee will bend
Heavenly, earthly, and underworldly
And every tongue will admit that
Jesus Christ is *kyrios*
Toward father-God's glory. (Phil 2:11)

The hymn's conclusion permits the possibility for Jesus's death as God's equal to gain its significance through the lens of his raising: he conquers death's finality. The praise of Jesus as κύριος represents a flavor within the ἐκκλησία's impulsive theo-christological stew. Paul's use of κύριος language in Romans contributed to the spread and development of this impulse. Is Paul's usage the only way early Christ-followers could have thought of κύριος Ἰησοῦς Χριστός? How could some followers have used such language while also encountering alternative impulses about Jesus's death and relation to God?

ἐκκλησία-1 use of kyriarchal language, ideas, and embodiments (including the use of terms such as κύριος and δοῦλος) did not originate with Paul. Just as the queer wo/men in these assemblies developed egalitarian impulses, some of which Paul draws and dissociates from, these same queer wo/men also promulgated different kyriarchal impulses. In a context where being called a κύριος signaled revered status and praiseworthiness, such a designation could be natural. For some, the attribution of κύριος to Jesus may have started as an indication of respectful importance with little or no thought about the kyriarchal submission it implies. Its usage can hold a range of plausible, contradictory meanings, some of which may have implications that are more cruel than others.[41]

The Christ hymn confirms how the ἐκκλησία used and developed kyriarchal ideology, especially when it designates and celebrates Jesus as κύριος. The submissive slave of 2:7–8 becomes the exalted master in 2:11.[42] "The slave-existence of Christ's humanity stands in stark contrast to the

---

41. Thus I argued in the previous chapter that Paul's adoption of kyriarchal language and ideas is among those most cruel.

42. As Briggs puts it: "Christ is the doulos who has been made kurios, or has regained in enhanced form his original status as master" (Briggs, "Can an Enslaved God Liberate?," 143).

acclamation of Christ's lordship at the end of the hymn," writes Briggs.[43] The end of the hymn defies the egalitarian meanings of its beginning: it reorients it back toward kyriarchy. Jesus's freedom allows him to participate in kyriarchal citizenship: once freed, formerly enslaved persons could and did enslave others.[44] The Christ hymn may make some space to imagine an egalitarianism that moves away from cruel optimism, but, taken from start to finish, it retains a fantasy that ends with the Romanormative good life under God and Jesus, as the master-Christ.

The multiple impulses and directions held within the Christ hymn's language and potential interpretations admits the complexity of kyriarchy's hold upon bodies, feelings, and forces. As we saw in chapter 2, queerness, as an assemblage, holds utopian movements alongside its regulatory usages and affects. Likewise, the impulses that move around ἐκκλησία-l assemblage pulsate in between justice and oppression, equality and inequality, submission and subversion. Kyriarchy as its own assemblage intersects and overlaps with this ἐκκλησία-l assemblage and its impulses. These overlaps produce tensions and contradictions that could be held together in between bodies. Some (possibly many) in Rome's ἐκκλησία could call Jesus κύριος while envisioning, advocating, and even enacting egalitarian-oriented ideas and practices within the structure of the ἐκκλησία and beyond.[45] They desired an ἐκκλησία that embodied God's justice, but that justice held multiple, diverging meanings and visions.

---

43. Briggs, "Can an Enslaved God Liberate?," 143.

44. In Briggs's reading, the hymn also effaces any moral inferiority that would have been attributed to Jesus for once having been enslaved: "Philippians is careful to dissociate Christ from the morally defective nature of a slave" (Briggs, "Can an Enslaved God Liberate?," 148). I concur that this is one very likely way ancient (and contemporary) interpreters have interpreted the hymn, especially as we are considering how it moves toward kyriarchal impulses, even as I propose that it is plausible that some ancient interpreters/singers could also have found radical potential in the message of an enslaved Jesus who did take on the moral inferiority of enslavement *according to Rome* (hence his crucifixion as well as the potential shame of the gospel in Rom 1:16) but who takes on *no* moral inferiority or stain *according to God* (since there is "no longer slave nor free").

45. For example, some scholars have recognized and emphasized the subversive nature of using κύριος-type language (largely in Paul's epistolary voice) in and against its Roman imperial context when it portrays Christ as a replacement of Caesar and his elite. Although such a substitution does not undermine the kyriarchal system or eliminate the existence of marginalized and submissive societal bottoms it produces, its (cruel) optimism often derives from serious desires for sociopolitical change and

While some in the ἐκκλησία could have held egalitarian impulses
more easily alongside the proclamation κύριος Ἰησοῦς Χριστός, others
could have recognized—to different degrees—the tensions and contradictions between them and queried the term's usage.[46] These queries
do not have to have been fully articulated, but it is plausible they took
shape within some expression (in words, tone, or gestures) of unease
with a particular term or image; a personal avoidance of the language
when speaking/thinking; a request to reduce or cease some usage (perhaps not being quite able to explain or justify the request beyond a
sensation of discomfort); or simply a sensation or thought of which
one is personally (bodily) aware but not comfortable verbalizing.[47]
Others may have voiced discomfort directly: a complaint about the
fact that they do not like comparing Jesus to their earthly κύριος; pointing to problems of Roman imperial rule and its echoes in a particular
theo-christological expression; or asking whether there is another term
to show reverence for Jesus Christ beyond κύριος. Any of these plausible approaches partially queries the kyriarchal system, its influence
on language, or its tension with equality. These queries could coexist

---

even equality. Unfortunately, and partially due to the retention of such language and
its ideologies, these optimisms cannot detach from the comfortable familiarity of
inequality's soft hierarchies. Elliott, incorporating Schüssler Fiorenza's critique of his
earlier attempts to liberate Paul (alongside that of Horsley), observes that Paul exemplifies such a complex tension between advocating justice yet using the language of
kyriarchy (which, as Johnson-DeBaufre and Nasrallah note, considers such tensions
only in relation to Paul and how they may have been manifested within the entire
ἐκκλησία). See Elisabeth Schüssler Fiorenza, *The Power of the Word: Scripture and the
Rhetoric of Empire* (Minneapolis: Fortress, 2007), 89–95; Neil Elliott, *The Arrogance of
Nations: Reading Romans in the Shadow of Empire*, PCC (Minneapolis: Fortress, 2008),
50–57, 158–59; Johnson-DeBaufre and Nasrallah, "Beyond the Heroic Paul," 165–66.

46. Can someone (i.e., Jesus) be a κύριος in title only? Can God be revered like a
Caesar without actually having attributed to God the dominant status and authority
of a Roman emperor? Questions such as these emphasize important issues that loom
over actual conversations, especially as they consider how language interacts with and
influences reality.

47. Indeed, it is probable that some conversations that tried to consider or begin
to articulate these issues and questions happened in smaller pockets of the ἐκκλησία
community, within and beyond its physical dimensions. Not all ἐκκλησία-l conversation would occur when the full group is present/gathered (if they entirely were!). With
so little known about the formal structure of these gatherings, it is possible that forms
of small-group discussions were a part of gatherings.

alongside contradictory approaches. They provide potential for challenge even while they may also be simultaneously absorbed into the movement of kyriarchy.

Others may have relied more heavily on the language of Jesus as κύριος along with its implicit hierarchal structures and praxes. Thinking alongside the Berlantian notion of attachment to "soft hierarchies of inequality," some need any buoy of safety or security, despite or unaware of its cruel roots. Some of these attachments are necessary tactics that permit survival, even if such survival must occasionally participate in a cruel system while still striving to change it. To even entertain rebellious-seeming impulses could make vulnerable wo/men uncomfortable. The risk is too great compared to the rut.

It is also plausible that some had *no* discomfort with this kyriarchal language and system: they may have wanted to retain it. Some could have responded with an unhesitant desire to overturn, to have the kyriarchal good life for themselves while subjecting their overlords to the struggles of treading waters by making them submit under God and Christ.[48] The evidence of wealthier Christ-followers (indicated in some names from Rom 16 as well as from the later historical accounting in Acts) who helped financially sustain early ἐκκλησίαι indicates that some did have some level of wealth and status that might be upset by an overturning or sharing of power.[49] Some folks may have been among those who were able to gain some status, wealth, manumission, or citizenship via limited avenues of social mobility permitted under Roman rule. If their status felt hard-won, it could be harder to abandon. Although not every wealthier Christ-follower necessarily supported kyriarchal impulses, the benefits they derived from the status quo provides one plausible motivation for sustaining its

---

48. As eventually occurs as Christianity becomes the dominant religion of Rome's empire (and the many that follow it into the present).

49. See Elisabeth Schüssler Fiorenza, "Missionaries, Apostles, Coworkers: Romans 16 and the Reconstruction of Women's Early Christian History," *WW* 6 (1986): 432; Peter Lampe, *From Paul to Valentinus: Christians at Rome in the First Two Centuries*, trans. Michael Steinhauser, ed. Marshall D. Johnson (Minneapolis: Fortress, 2003), 170–83. As Steven J. Friesen notes, this wealth was limited relative to the upper eschelons of Rome's elite and still, by and large, would have been close to subsistence level. See Steven J. Friesen, "Poverty in Pauline Studies: Beyond the So-Called New Consensus," *JSNT* 26 (2004): 323–61.

socioeconomic system.[50] Such persons could have been be insistent on emphasizing language such as κύριος Ἰησοῦς Χριστός.

Assemblaging Theo-Christology

What does God's justice feel like?
This question breezes its way in between these plausible impulses. God promises justice, but will that justice be egalitarian, kyriarchal, drowning, treading, surviving, thriving? The promising question likewise threads its way through Paul's impulses in Rom 1–5. Promises are not just ideas, they are also impulses. They are affective forces that get attached to bodies through optimistic bonds (some of which become cruel). God's justice is one among many questionable feelings winding its way around, through, and among Paul and the queer wo/men of Rome's ἐκκλησία.

How did all these impulses interact? Schüssler Fiorenza's names the ἐκκλησία of wo/men a "radical *democratic* space" that assembled Christ-followers, including the wo/men, queer, and enslaved folks greeted in Rom 16.[51] How does such a radical democracy engage different theo-Christologies, some of which may seem fundamentally at odds? What dynamics could be expected within an ἐκκλησία-l democracy in the first century CE? In *Corinthian Democracy*, Anna C. Miller addresses this question and demonstrates how there was a robust "*ekklēsia* discourse" in first-century Rome, particularly in the Greek East: a democratic impulse that persisted in spite of and in tandem with Roman imperial autocracy.[52] Miller demonstrates that the wo/men in Corinth's ἐκκλησία practiced their own democratic participation in this ἐκκλησία discourse, one that specifically included the free speech of women and enslaved persons.[53] For Miller, the dynamics of (Corinthian) ἐκκλησία-l democracy was one that emphasized

---

50. One could query to what degree such followers would or would not have been interested in bringing their (lower status) cofollowers into their social circles beyond the ἐκκλησία (with any number of possible responses from individual/collective bodies).

51. Schüssler Fiorenza, *Discipleship of Equals*, 369. See further discussion of her claim in chapter 2, n. 134.

52. Anna C. Miller, *Corinthian Democracy: Democratic Discourse in 1 Corinthians*, PTMS (Eugene, OR: Pickwick, 2015), esp. 40–67 (ch. 2, "The First Century *Ekklēsia* in the Writings of Dio and Plutarch").

53. Miller, *Corinthian Democracy*, esp. 115–53 (ch. 5, "The Gendering of Democratic Participation").

and valued free speech (παρρησία) and democratic debate as a decision-making process that involves and includes all people.[54] "Specifically, the baptismal formula of Gal 3:28 undermines the very boundaries separating the truly free and equal male citizen from the *polis*'s noncitizens: slaves and women most visible among them. In turn, this opens the possibility for all to practice citizenship through equal voice and equal discernment in the gathered *ekklēsia*."[55] But was voice/speech the only means for queer wo/men's democratic participation in these ἐκκλησίαι of Christ-followers? Was deliberative debate (followed, presumably, by some form of vote for consensus) the only way these wo/men engaged and interacted with these different impulses?

Theology/theo-Christology often gets imagined taking form as spoken or written ideas that can interact through conversation, debate, spoken (or written) dialogue, and discourse.[56] This is a challenge that my feminist and queer praxis of ἐκκλησία-l assemblages confronts. When bringing to life theo-christological impulses that history has swept away, these impulses must first be reconstructed as speculatively plausible. But then, this speculative plausibility must be stretched further to imaginatively reconstruct their impulsive interactions. When this is done fully, the tautness of these plausible stretchings releases. An ἐκκλησία-l assemblage springs to life.

Schüssler Fiorenza summons a *radicality* that was quintessential to the democracy promised by ἐκκλησίαι that permitted enslaved, women, foreign, and queer participation (as implied in Rom 16, Gal 3:28, and 1 Corinthians, especially 5–7 and 11–14). Such participation refused kyriarchal democracy's restrictions that were reinforced through the ongoing and fairly widespread teaching of ἐκκλησία discourse.[57] What happens

---

54. Miller, *Corinthian Democracy*, esp. 90–114 (ch. 4, "Speech and Wisdom of the Corinthian *Ekklēsia*"). On the general importance of παρρησία in Greco-Roman democratic discourse, see Miller, *Corinthian Democracy*, 48–53.

55. Miller, *Corinthian Democracy*, 161.

56. This imagination is especially due to the influence of white, straight, cisgender men have on the disciplinary discourse. Womanist theologians, in particular, have long emphasized embodiment, alongside Black women's experiences, as central to theology. Queer, feminist, and disability theologies have also regularly insisted on the body's centrality. Among and beyond these theologians, affect theory has offered additional resources for theology that moves beyond thoughts and ideas. See especially Karen Bray and Stephen D. Moore, eds., *Religion, Emotion, Sensation: Affect Theories and Theologies*, TTC (New York: Fordham University Press, 2019).

57. Miller identifies the tension between the radical potential of democracy (as

when the δῆμος (i.e., the "people" of a democracy) expands? How did queer wo/men change the wind when they invoked an ἐκκλησία? When participation expands to include "all y'all" (πάντες ὑμεῖς [Gal 3:28]), participants who were queer, enslaved, and wo/men were not just included in democracy by performing its expected norms. They transformed it through their own radical and egalitarian visions for its promises. These promises accord with their hope for bringing about God's justice. They practiced free speech and voiced their ideas, but *their ἐκκλησία* also thought, moved, gestured, and felt their impulses.

If an expanded ἐκκλησία changed the proper forms for democratic engagement, how did Rome's queer wo/men bring theo-Christology to life around such a space? As Paul's epistle was (presumably) read aloud in Rome's ἐκκλησία, his impulses moved in between the queer wo/men assembled there. The impulses in Rom 1–5 (cruel and otherwise) interacted with other impulses, such as those proffered above. They intermingled in and around the bodies in the room: a phrase gets stuck in one woman's head; some attempt to subtly cover their ears and stop hearing them; others uncomfortably notice they've been turned on by the subtle undertones of sexual submission; a man stifles a groan; someone nods (or nods off). The queer wo/men in Rome's ἐκκλησία were affected by Paul's letter. However, these queer wo/men and their own impulsive theo-Christologies also affected Paul's theo-christological impulses.

Questions may have been spoken aloud to verbally interrupt Paul's epistolary voice, or they could have been thought, whispered, or just hovered in the air—sensed but not quite grasped. Does Jesus display πίστις, and what does a πίστις-relation with God mean? How is πίστις connected to δικαιοσύνη θεοῦ? What hope does (or doesn't) this provide, especially for low-status and enslaved ἔθνη/*peregrini*? These questions could have proliferated alongside ongoing questions that were given a renewed emphasis through Paul's words: what is Jesus's (and our) relation to God? What is

---

seen in Gal 3:28 and summoned by Schüssler Fiorenza) and how it stands in tension to what Schüssler Fiorenza names "kyriarchal democracy"—that is, democracy that is limited to a citizenry that draws rigid boundaries and renders noncitizens as the ultimate Other, especially in terms of race/ethnicity and gender (Miller, *Corinthian Democracy*, 140–41). See further Schüssler Fiorenza, "Introduction," in *Prejudice and Christian Beginnings: Investigating Race, Gender, and Ethnicity in Early Christian Studies*, ed. Laura Nasrallah and Elisabeth Schüssler Fiorenza (Minneapolis: Fortress, 2009), 9–15.

the meaning of his death? How does this relate to Jesus's Jewishness? How do the εἰρήνη ("peace"), πίστις, and δικαιοσύνη that God offers differ from those promised by Roman κύριοι? What should δικαιοσύνη θεοῦ (God's justice) look and feel like?

As these queer wo/men explored the interactions of varying theo-christological impulses, some of Paul's ideas could have been *helpful* in an ἐκκλησία that assembled within the imperial capital. Hearing Paul's framing of πίστις to describe Jesus's faithful submission to God, it is possible something clicked in the bodies of some hearers: suddenly the swirl of shifting ideas on this subject made sense. Paul's voice prompts this shift by adding a vital (but not exclusive or uncontested) piece to their theo-christological puzzle. For some, Paul's πίστις may have been *more* puzzling: they may not have felt any shift (yet or ever) and may have stayed confused and pondering—or even have increased their sense of confusion.[58]

Since some of Paul's compatriots (e.g., Prisca and Aquila) had preceded him to Rome, some versions of his impulses that related πίστις to Jesus could have already been expressed, debated, or even embraced around this ἐκκλησία. These compatriots' impulses also would have diverged and even dissented from Paul's. Some queer wo/men could have been intrigued by these ideas; some may have embraced alternative formulations; others could have rejected them; and more might have been confused or not quite understood how πίστις was significant to following Christ.

One plausible source of tension that fueled some ἐκκλησία-1 impulses prior to Paul's letter could have surrounded the fact of Jesus's crucifixion (by Rome) and its significance. Jesus's death hovers around each of the impulses laid out above. Romans 1:16 hints at this hovering tension. Romans 1:16 begins Οὐ γὰρ ἐπαισχύνομαι τὸ εὐαγγέλιον ("For I am not ashamed of the gospel"), a statement that assumes there *is* something shameful about this message featuring the death of a treasonous criminal.[59] Assuming that some in the gathering were less (or not at all) comfortable with any emphasis on Jesus's crucifixion, Paul's presentation of πίστις in Rom 3:21–31 could have distracted from that emphasis and provided alternate routes to think about Jesus's death. Such routes could have

---

58. This is not meant to be bad. Different bodies think, respond, and comprehend differently. Indeed, there can be benefits to not understanding and confusion, if they lead to greater clarification over time.

59. Robert Jewett, *Romans: A Commentary*, Hermeneia (Minneapolis: Fortress, 2007), 136–39; Elliott, *Arrogance of Nations*, 51. See also 1 Cor 1:18–31.

focused on how his death promises a resurrected good life for Jesus and his followers based on this πίστις relation with God.[60] It is the πίστις that makes the death significant in such an interpretation more than the death itself or its particular manner. In Paul's explanation, the fact that Jesus is *crucified* is less overt: that he entrusts God with his blood is enough mention. While the deeper implications of such a πίστις-based interpretation appear enmeshed in the kyriarchy of Roman cruel optimism, these would have been (quite) difficult to perceive. On the surface, some may have been able to reconcile or hold in tension some of these ideas alongside some degree of an egalitarian vision, plausibly based upon Jesus's equality with God.

Beyond πίστις, Paul's letter could have offered useful ideas that affected those who engaged with them. Perhaps his words offered helpful suggestions to some who were skeptical or confused about impulses they had previously encountered. Some may have found ideas that helped them better advocate for their own feelings and ideas: perhaps some appreciated his ongoing attribution of κύριος to Jesus and used it to support their insistence upon keeping this profession prominent. Others (though perhaps less thrilled about this kyriarchal embrace) could have sensed promises within his ongoing emphasis of δικαιοσύνη θεοῦ, especially if they struggled to articulate its meaning and relevance in practical terms that might distinguish it from their current experiences of justice. Some may have found thrill in this promise even as they felt other parts of the letter were threatening. As queer wo/men listened, pondered, reacted, and engaged, some may have discovered ways to better express their visions of justice. Others may have perked their ears and listened more intently at these mentions. Some may have only appreciated Paul's emphasis on δικαιοσύνη θεοῦ because it provided an entry point for their very different impulses about what God's justice meant.

The impulses in Rom 1–5 open plausible avenues for engaging the role of ethnicity within the ἐκκλησία's burgeoning theo-Christologies. In a socioreligious context where conquered ἔθνη were expected to embrace the Roman pantheon (including its divinized imperial kyriarchy), Jesus, the Christ, as a model for (non-Jewish) ἔθνη offered a theological alternative that did not require complete conformity with Roman rule and its enforce-

---

60. That is, Jesus displays πίστις that God will raise him to a good new life.

ment of ethnic submission.[61] Though certainly not the first or only example, Jesus appears to have been an example to follow in order to be followers of the historical God of Abraham, Israel, and Judea. If these followers in Rome were mostly non-Jewish ἔθνη/*peregrini*, how would their different, non-Jewish backgrounds have influenced their theo-Christologies?

These questions provide background to Paul's presentation of Abraham and his πίστις in Rom 4. Some queer wo/men might have sensed, in seeming agreement with Paul's argument, that Abraham's πίστις plays a different role from that of Jesus. Although all ἔθνη are descendants of Abraham, Abraham's πίστις brings Jews into relationship with God, while Jesus's πίστις is the means by which non-Jewish ἔθνη enter into this relation.[62] It is further plausible, as Israel Kamudzandu and Neil Elliot have suggested was Paul's intent, that hearers would have connected Abraham's story with that of the founding of Rome by Aeneas.[63] Reinforced by Paul's suggestion that all ἔθνη are descended from Abraham (as πατέρα πολλῶν ἐθνῶν ["father of many ἔθνη"] in Rom 4:17, citing Gen 17:5), Christ-followers in Rome could have connected with these stories and figures as sources for understanding the God whom Jesus (and now they) followed. Just as multiple interpretations and theologies based on these texts existed within first-century Judaism, it is quite plausible that numerous interpretations and ideas about these texts and theologies were suggested and debated within Rome's ἐκκλησία, especially if some of these wo/men had already encountered and experienced this theological diversity.

---

61. Yet, as we have seen from Paul's theo-Christology as explained in the preceding chapter, such alternatives are not necessarily any less kyriarchal or cruel, especially to the extent that they reform Roman notions of submission into another sociopolitical religious vision.

62. As Stowers notes in his reading of Romans, according to Paul, the relation (begun with Abraham's πίστις) between God and Jews is unaffected by Jesus, who provides a new and separate path (διὰ πίστεως instead of ἐκ πίστεως) for gentiles/ἔθνη—all of this being consonant within the ideas of Abrahamic descent (See Stowers, *Rereading of Romans*, 227–50, esp. 237–50). For more on Rom 4 and its interpretive history in the late twentieth century, see Gerhard H. Visscher, *Romans 4 and the New Perspective: Faith Embraces the Promise* (New York: Peter Lang, 2009).

63. Israel Kamudzandu, *Abraham as Spiritual Ancestor: A Postcolonial Reading of Romans 4*, BibInt 100 (Leiden: Brill, 2010), esp. 203–36; Kamudzandu, *Abraham Our Father: Paul and the Ancestors in Postcolonial Africa*, PCC (Minneapolis: Fortress, 2013), 83–104; Elliott, *Arrogance of Nations*, 121–41.

Even though these plausible interpretations are inaccessible, such a question was a significant topic for discussion among early Christ-followers, both within the earliest ἐκκλησία-l gatherings and continuing well into the second century and beyond. The fact that Paul retells and quotes the stories and texts of Judaism makes it plausible that, as followers became familiar with the figures and stories about Judaism, they raised questions about the theologies in these texts and how they applied to following Christ. Within Rome's ἐκκλησία, we know that some Jewish Christ-followers, such as Prisca and Aquila, were familiar to this community, based on Paul's greeting of them in Rom 16. Wo/men in Rome's ἐκκλησία could have been familiar with some Jewish texts and theological traditions as a result of having interacted with Jewish wo/men in Rome.

The queer wo/men of Rome's ἐκκλησία may have held a variety of impulsive responses to Paul's presentation of Abraham (among other elements of the Jewish theological tradition) and this story's relation to ethnicity and theo-Christology. With respect to Abraham and Jewish theology, some non-Jews may have been more willing to accept or incorporate Paul's interpretations on this subject given his Jewish background. Others may have been more skeptical. Some might have wanted to hear his ideas affirmed by other Jews whom they had come to know and trust within (or beyond) the ἐκκλησία, with a woman like Prisca being a plausible and prominent example.[64] Some could have ignored his interpretations and developed their own interpretation of these traditions and their theo-christological relevance.

Since it is plausible that this assembly was already discussing Jewish theology, Jewish ideas about theology and ethnicity in multiethnic contexts could have informed participants in Rome's similarly multiethnic (though mostly non-Jewish) ἐκκλησία. If the ancient ἐκκλησία of Christ-followers can be considered an assemblage, then so can first-century Judaisms—as well as the diverse theological stew of impulses that existed in between Judaism and an emerging (but, in the mid-first century, not yet named) Christianity as they engaged and diverged through periods of (re)formations and apparent partitions.[65] As Cynthia Baker has shown, Jews across

---

64. See Rom 16:3–4. On Prisca's prominence in this passage and in the early Christian missionary movement, see Schüssler Fiorenza, *In Memory of Her*, 178–80; Schüssler Fiorenza, "Missionaries, Apostles, Coworkers," 427–32.

65. Daniel Boyarin employs the language of "partitioning" Judaism and Christianity and the process of their becoming two separate "religions," and he establishes

Rome's empire had already expanded their theological views to encompass the ethnic multiplicities of living in diaspora. Philo discusses Jews, alongside their ancestral beliefs and customs, as participants in the societies and cultures that surrounded them.[66] Even Jerusalem, the mother city for Jews, encourages the diversity among its inhabitants and visitors from other ἔθνη (many of whom are also Jews), whose different cultural ideas and practices interacted with those native to the city.[67] Baker observes, "These writers assumed no definitional conflict or categorical contradiction in imagining Jews as *belonging* to a vast multiplicity of *ethne* … through *genos* ('birth,' 'race') and ancestral *syngeneia* ('kinship')."[68]

Returning to Rome's ἐκκλησία, these examples of embracing of Jewish multiethnic existence across the Roman world may have encouraged its participants from other ἔθνη to find ways to embrace their own ethnic identities and interactions as they developed their theo-Christologies.[69]

---

how the borders that separated these two traditions were blurry in the earliest centuries of the common era and (especially after the second century CE) had to be drawn and enforced over a long period of time. See Daniel Boyarin, *Border Lines: The Partitioning of Judaeo-Christianity*, Div (Philadelphia: University of Pennsylvania Press, 2004).

66. Particularly drawing from *Legatio ad Gaium* and *Flaccus*, Baker concludes of Philo: "rather, appropriating the colonial apparatus, he articulates a worldwide Jewish identity in the image of worldwide 'Hellenism' and a Jewish map, the boundaries of which match (and exceed) those of either the 'Hellenic' or Roman *oikoumenē* ('inhabited world')" See Cynthia M. Baker, " 'From Every Nation under Heaven': Jewish Ethnicities in the Greco-Roman World," in *Prejudice and Christian Beginnings: Investigating Race, Gender, and Ethnicity in Early Christian Studies*, ed. Laura Nasrallah and Elisabeth Schüssler Fiorenza (Minneapolis: Fortress, 2009), 91, see further 86–91. Beyond Philo, Baker notes, "In fact, the identification of Jews by diverse ethnic-geographic signifiers occurs in all manner of Greek and Semitic (Hebrew and Aramaic) writings by Jews in the Hellenistic and Roman periods" (83).

67. Baker, "From Every Nation," 88–91. On pp. 91–95, she shows how Acts 2:5–11 offers a similar portrayal.

68. Baker, "From Every Nation," 95.

69. "In the Hellenistic and Roman periods, the worship of many foreign divinities spread from their native lands as commerce and military maneuvers moved multitudes back and forth across the Mediterranean." See Ross Shepard Kraemer, *Her Share of the Blessings: Women's Religions among Pagans, Jews, and Christians in the Greco-Roman World* (New York: Oxford University Press, 1994), 71. Indeed, what Baker says for Luke (writing Acts) could also be applied to Paul and the participants in Rome's ἐκκλησία: "What makes perfect sense to Luke leaves his modern interpreters tied up in exegetical knots" (Baker, "From Every Nation," 95).

Even if ἔθνη fully acknowledge the God of Israel as the only true god—thus turning away from the downward theological spiral as described in Rom 1:18–25—they may have drawn from elements of their former theologies as they figured out what it meant to follow this God through Jesus Christ. Their former beliefs could have helped them develop these new theo-christological impulses.

Connections between the Isis cult and the theo-christological impulses of early Christian texts provide an example of how different ἔθνη in Rome's ἐκκλησία could have drawn from their past theological experiences. Originating in Egyptian religious practices, Isis devotion spread across the Greco-Roman world, was integrated into the religious landscape of the Roman Empire, and had significant popular appeal in the first century.[70] Schüssler Fiorenza has observed that the Christ hymn (among other texts in the Jesus traditions) uses "terms of Wisdom-Isis theology" and shows how "Christians proclaim that, like Isis, Jesus-Sophia is now the ruler of the principalities and powers that have previously enslaved the world."[71]

The hymns of the Isis cult contain phrases that emphasize Isis's justice: "I destroyed reigns of tyranny" (ἐγὼ τυράννων ἀρχὰς κατέλυσα [Kyme Aretalogy, 25]); "I made justice stronger than gold and silver" (ἐγὼ τὸ δίκαιον ἰσχυρότερον χρυσίου καὶ ἀργυρίου ἐποίησα [Kyme Aretalogy, 28]); "I impose retribution on those who practice injustice" (ἐγὼ τοῖς ἄδικα πράσσουσιν τειμωρίαν ἐπιτίθημι [Kyme Aretalogy, 35]).[72] A compendium that invokes the many names and powers of Isis proclaims: "thou art seen by those who invoke thee faithfully" (P.Oxy. 11.1380).[73] Christ-followers' past experiences with these two hymns could have contributed to their emphasis on

---

70. Temples and material evidence of cultic practices related to Isis can be found across Greco-Roman territory, and there have been several significant finds, including a worship complex, in Pompeii. Laura Hackworth Peterson observes that Isis was portrayed as "the people's goddess." See Laura Hackworth Peterson, "The Places of Roman Isis: Between Egyptomania, Politics, and Religion," *Oxford Handbooks Online*, September 2016, https://tinyurl.com/SBL4531h. See also Robert A. Wortham, "Urban Networks, Deregulated Religious Markets, Cultural Continuity and the Diffusion of the Isis Cult," *MTSR* 18 (2006): 103–23.

71. Elisabeth Schüssler Fiorenza, *Jesus: Miriam's Child, Sophia's Prophet* (New York: Continuum, 1994), 147–48.

72. Greek text accessed through "Searchable Greek Inscriptions: A Scholarly Tool in Progress," Packard Humanities Institute, https://tinyurl.com/SBL4531i.

73. Trans. in Kraemer, *Women's Religions in the Greco-Roman World: A Sourcebook* (New York: Oxford University Press, 2004), 455.

God's justice or to the various questions and impulses surrounding πίστις in Rome's ἐκκλησία. The empowerment of a woman as the central deity, alongside the cult's associations with potential gender egalitarianism (discussed further in ch. 6), could have offered insights for queer wo/men to envision a theo-Christology that did not replicate a gendered hierarchy that mostly divinized men.

Theo-christological impulses involving suffering, death, resurrection, and salvation can also trace connections to the Isis cult in the first centuries CE. Apuleius offers a lengthy account of one devotee's initiation, during which he declares of Isis, "Both the gates of hell and the guarantee of salvation lay in control of the goddess. The act of initiation itself was performed as a rite of voluntary death and of salvation attained by prayer" (Apuleius, *Metam.* 11.21).[74] These emphases can offer context for how wo/men might have found appeal in following a savior who suffered and died. They also show that some Christ-followers, including those who may have participated in Isis rituals before turning to God, could have drawn from Isis theologies of death and resurrection in order to help develop these theo-christological impulses.[75] These emphases on salvation and life after death might have produced tension alongside the impulses, such as those proffered in "Drowning Jesus," that attempted to refuse such buoys. Apuleius's description may run counter to the experience of other wo/men in the Isis cult, and it could be that some followers of Isis placed exclusive emphasis on her gender and justice or on the cult's practices of egalitarianism.[76] The resonances between the theological impulses seen in texts expressing devotion to Isis and those among first-century Christ-

---

74. Trans. Kraemer, *Women's Religions*, 448.

75. The connections between suffering and salvation in Isis devotion and early Christianity have been explored with New Testament scholarship. For examples, see David L. Balch, "The Suffering of Isis/Io and Paul's Portrait of Christ Crucified (Gal. 3:1): Frescoes in Pompeian and Roman Houses and in the Temple of Isis in Pompeii," *JR* 83 (2003): 24–55; Lawrence M. Wills, "Wisdom and Word among the Hellenistic Saviors: The Function of Literacy," *JSP* 24 (2014): 118–48.

76. The spread and legitimation of Isis under Roman rule offered the cult significant benefits, but it also came with influence from its encounter with the Roman world and its elite. Peterson observes, "The goddess's ability to regenerate life provided followers with a hope for life after death or eternal life, which was becoming increasingly attractive to Romans, indeed, the Dionysiac mysteries and Platonism, both of which promised such ideals, were already much in vogue" (Peterson, "Places of Roman Isis," 15 [under section "Isis: Ritual and Religiosity"]). It is worth nothing that the bulk of

followers emphasize how wo/men in Rome's ἐκκλησία could and would have engaged impulses from their past religious experiences as ἔθνη as they created and embodied new impulses together.[77]

Prior discussions about sexuality from Rom 1:18–32 would have moved in between and alongside these impulses. Since Paul mentions sexuality early in his epistle, the reactions and thoughts this stimulated affect the conversations around his approach to πίστις and theo-Christology. Just as his ideas about sexuality affected his approach to Jesus's πίστις-relation with God in Rom 3, the approaches to sexuality of those in Rome's ἐκκλησία affect their theo-Christologies and their reactions to Paul's. Though it is unlikely that anyone fully recognized what Moore calls the "sexual substratum of Paul's soteriology," the fact that Paul's opinions on sexuality largely parroted those of Roman imperial society would have made some queer wo/men less receptive to his impulses.[78] They could have been prone to listen for things to critique within his theo-christological arguments that followed Rom 1—if they were still listening at all.

While reactions against Paul's attribution of κύριος to Jesus Christ could have arisen solely from active discomforts and objections to this language, some might have made more specific connections to the sexual dominance of Roman κύριοι, as experienced under the imperial socio-sexual hierarchy. If Jesus is their κύριος, would they be sexually available to him, as was common for those placed into submission under powerful Romans, especially in the case of enslaved wo/men?[79] (Are they Jesus's

---

the emphasis on salvation and Isis comes from accounts from Roman authors (especially Apuleius) as opposed to the evidence from cultic hymns.

77. Theological impulses in Jewish texts from this period also bear traces of Isis devotion, which attests to how all these different traditions influenced one another across multiethnic lines. See Joshua Levinson, "Bodies and Bo(a)rders: Emerging Fictions of Identity in Late Antiquity," *HTR* 93 (2000): 343–72; John S. Kloppenborg, "Isis and Sophia in the Book of Wisdom," *HTR* 75 (1982): 57–84.

78. Moore, *God's Beauty Parlor*, 156. See my elaboration above in chapter 3.

79. In showing how the lived realities of Roman slavery affect New Testament texts/interpretation and the earliest bodies who read and heard these texts, Jennifer Glancy writes, "Sexual access to slave bodies was a pervasive dimension of ancient systems of slavery." See Jennifer A. Glancy, *Slavery in Early Christianity* (Oxford: Oxford University Press, 2002), 21. In addition to the elaboration of this fact in Glancy's monograph, scholarly inquiries since its publication have continued to probe the different dimensions of the sexual use of slaves and its affect on early Christianity. See especially Jennifer A. Glancy and Stephen D. Moore, "How Typical a Roman Prosti-

δοῦλαι?)[80] If some participants were already skeptical of Paul's Christology, such queries could arise more naturally as critique, particularly when considered alongside how Rome's κύριοι would have been visible in their daily lives. If questions along these lines were spoken aloud, grumbled, or gestured toward, other queer wo/men may have found their thoughts and feelings shifting toward less kyriarchal theo-Christologies, perhaps (but not necessarily) due to some disagreement with Rom 1 or to a sensation of confusion about Paul's πίστις. Questions around the sexual implications of Jesus's lordship would not necessarily have been on the minds of all who objected to such language, but it provides an entry point toward these impulses. Theo-Christology, sexuality, and politics would have been inseparable topics in Rome's ἐκκλησία.

Some might have sensed disagreement rooted in an assumption of a more equal relationship between Jesus and God. Some impulsive reactions could quite plausibility be proffered by those whose thoughts and practices around sexuality were less kyriarchally arranged, deviating from Romosexuality. While not always or necessarily the case, a body that was receptive to a more egalitarian approach to sexuality (i.e., nonhierarchal in terms of aligning social and sexual roles) might already be oriented toward considering a similar approach to God, Christ, and the sociopolitical visions of their followers (as well as vice versa).

The dynamic responses that circulated in between Rome's queer wo/men never landed upon firm answers to first-century theo-christological questions. These impulses, responses, ideas, feelings, gestures, and provocations swirled within ἐκκλησία-l assemblage. This praxis demonstrates diverse directions for impulses that moved, shifted, and clashed in between the queer wo/men in Rome's ἐκκλησία. Most (all, even) of the impulses and responses proposed here have not been comprehensive explanations but rather suggestions that contain speculative plausibil-

---

tute Is Revelation's 'Great Whore'?," *JBL* 130 (2011): 551–69; Joseph A. Marchal, "The Usefulness of an Onesimus: The Sexual Use of Slaves and Paul's Letter to Philemon," *JBL* 130 (2011): 749–70; James N. Hoke, "Behold the Lord's Whore? Slavery, Prostitution, and Luke 1:38," *BibInt* 26 (2018): 43–67.

80. On Paul's self-appellation as a "slave of Christ" (part of his epistolary introductions in Rom 1:1 and Phil 1:1), see especially Dale B. Martin, *Slavery as Salvation: The Metaphor of Slavery in Pauline Christianity* (New Haven: Yale University Press, 1990), 50–85.

ity as they were fleshed out with some tantalizing details.[81] Each grasps toward a plausible theo-Christology. Drawn together—as impulses that are simultaneously in tandem and in tension—a fragmentary, partial, and assemblaged theo-Christology shimmers.

Queer wo/men's participation in Rome's ἐκκλησία moved, ebbed and flowed, and changed. Short suggestions could get taken up by others, moved around, remolded, hidden, and rediscovered. A roll of the eyes, a groan, a pleasurable moan, an audible amen, or some nudges could have gestured new impulses into being. Given the transitory nature of this assembly, fleeting ideas and suggestions would have been far more prevalent than watertight, lengthy theo-christological expositions. The disagreement between different, contradictory impulses sparked debates and raised passions, but the in-between nature of ἐκκλησία-l assemblage permits these tensions to exist together, sometimes producing the conflicts we can see in other ἐκκλησίαι. From these tensions, new impulses sprang forth. Regardless, the gathering continued, someone kept reading Paul's letter aloud, bodies moved and changed, and impulses, responses, and tensions proliferated.

As the reading continued, the queer wo/men who gathered alongside Paul's epistolary presence in Rome were still digesting and figuring out their own impulses and Paul's relation to them. They were absorbing new impulses and playing around with them. They remembered some points to consider later in more detail. They forgot small or large pieces that still remained held within and between their bodily assemblages to potentially reemerge in some form (much) later. Nothing about theo-Christology had been firmly decided, even for those (momentarily) occupying a more fixed side.

My feminist and queer praxis of ἐκκλησία-l assemblage works up from the remnants of postholes so that a reconstructed theo-christological framework starts coming to life. My speculative proliferations may seem based on particularly scant evidence, just enough to ground a few plausible theo-christological impulses that would otherwise remain entirely absent. Their concreteness and certainty are hard to track; however, the impulses I proffer remain within the realm of speculative plausibility. Alone, I cannot

---

81. To offer anything firm is impossible and historically inaccurate. Indeed, these questions and their answers have always been in such flux and have been constantly shifting in ἐκκλησία-l assemblages from the first century through the twenty-first and beyond.

represent the entirety of plausible theo-christological impulses in Rome's ἐχχλησία. These proliferations permit us to sense how Paul's impulses were only a few among many. They summon feelings of an enlivened ἐχχλησία of queer wo/men.

As these theo-christological impulses continued moving in between Rome's ἐχχλησία, some may have wondered: *What practical implications do these impulses have? And how do these affect how we—as an ἐχχλησία— live and act in a still very Roman society?* The next two chapters consider how these theo-christological impulses guided and prompted ethics. Those posing questions like these would have found their ethical entry points at the end of Paul's letter. We turn next to Paul's ethics in Rom 12–15, especially his exhortation to ethical submission in Rom 13, and the ways Paul's impulses continued interacting with queer wo/men in a vibrant ἐχχλησία-l assemblage.

5
Ethical Submission

Part of how they make you obey is by making obedience seem peaceful while resistance is violent. But really, either choice is about violence, one way or the other.
—Charlie Jane Anders, *The City in the Middle of the Night*

Romanormativity adheres to a *moral* fantasy: the good life is for good Romans. Yet, as chapter 3 showed, becoming a *good* Roman entailed faithfully submitting to Roman imperial rule. When Caesar graciously extended the "faith of the Roman people" to "many other ἔθνη," he elided the flip side of imperial conquest: *faithfully submit or be crushed.* Faithful submission is enforced on a moral level: submission is good while rebellion is bad. Or, as Anders observes in the voice of her character Mouth, obedience is peaceful while resistance is violent.

Not resisting is only the starting point for peaceful obedience. Peacefulness is proven via proper moral behavior: perform submission by conforming to Roman norms. How can someone be keeping the peace if they are behaving badly? Moral suspicion fuels queries of patriotic fidelity. Immorality itself—whether sexual, political, economic, or social—can be cast as an act of violence. Faithful submission to Roman rule must also be embodied via ethical submission. Obedient or resistant; moral or immoral: every choice involves violence.

These violent fictions are not limited to the *pax Romana*. As we already began to see in the policing of racialized intimacy discussed in chapter 1, Jasbir K. Puar's work scrutinizes the moral violence of what could be called a *pax Americana*. Although there are certainly differences between the first and twenty-first centuries, the echoes cannot be ignored. In this chapter, I argue Paul's ethics in Romans exhibit what Puar terms *homonationalism*.

Homonationalism foregrounds how the good life is a *fantasy of inclusion* into a normativity for which one was never intended. Homonormativity, as laid out in chapter 1, marks how certain queer subjects present themselves as essentially heteronormative in every way except the gender of their partner/ spouse. Homonationalism denotes tactics of homonormative inclusion that specifically rely on *nationalism*, the patriotic production of faithful submission to one's country. By performing a patriotic morality, one that ultimately bolsters the nation's image and power, certain gay subjects can become "subjects worthy of rehabilitation" into a national fantasy of the good life.[1]

As with homonormativity, openly gay (and Christian) US politician Pete Buttigieg's failed 2020 presidential primary campaign offers an excellent, concrete example of homonationalism. At a campaign event in Decorah, Iowa, Buttigieg was asked how he would work with leaders from nations "like Saudi Arabia and Russia, where it's illegal to be gay."[2] He responded, "One great thing about America is that when we're at our best, we have challenged places around the world to acknowledge freedom, and include more people in more ways. And whether it is by policy or just by example, America is at her best when we have done that."[3] The United States' inclusion of LGBTIA2Q+ folks beacons a city on a hill that should provide a moral example (its bestness, in Buttigieg's terms) to challenge countries who seem to provide the public with dictionary definitions of *homophobia*. Ignoring violence against LGBTIA2Q+ folks (especially against Black trans women) and ongoing systemic antiqueerness in the United States, Buttigieg made America morally exceptional by casting its rivals as immoral exceptions (what Puar calls "sexual exceptionalism"). When he continued, "We can't intervene in every country and make them be good to their people," Buttigieg chillingly justified US militaristic interventions to make peace with these hostile exceptions, implying (if it were feasible) these interventions would be the best means of protecting LGB-

---

1. Jasbir K. Puar, *Terrorist Assemblages: Homonationalism in Queer Times*, NW (Durham, NC: Duke University Press, 2007), 38. See also Runions's discussion of "the gay antichrist as political enemy," which considers racialized theo-political and theo-democratic rhetoric that permits some "redeemable humans" by producing "fear of the irredeemable, inhuman, antichristic, beastly, homosexual, and Babylonian." See Erin Runions, *The Babylon Complex: Theopolitical Fantasies of War, Sex, and Sovereignty* (New York: Fordham University Press, 2014), 180, see further 179–212.

2. Chris Johnson, "Buttigieg: Anti-gay Countries Will 'Have to Get Used to' Gay U.S. President," *Washington Blade*, 2 November 2019, https://tinyurl.com/SBL4531j.

3. Johnson, "Buttigieg." He began by quipping, "So, they're going to have to get used to it." This, in particular, was met with enthusiastic praise from the crowd and on social media.

TIA2Q+ folks worldwide.[4] As in the aftermath of 9/11, America remains the militaristic enforcer of democratic morality.[5] Buttigieg is one example of tactics that wed the homonormative with a national morality enforced in a global arena—that is, homonationalism. Good gays are good citizens who pay their taxes, get married, and start a family under US-flag bed-sheets.[6] In America, good gays can live the good life. They can even live in the White House.

In first-century Rome, and specifically in Paul's ethics in Rom 13, Romanormativity weds with Roman imperialism through tactics of homonationalism, as this chapter shows. Paul's ideas in Rom 13 exhibit an ethical submission that complements the faithful dimensions of submission found in Rom 1–5. By performing Roman virtue, certain typically nonnormative subjects might become included in the Roman fantasy of the good life: good citizens who pay their taxes, get married, and submit to the prevailing Roman authorities. Paul exhorts all three of these moral performances of Romanormativity in Rom 13. Paul's direction to submit to political authority in Rom 13 merely makes explicit the submissive and Romanormative affects that weave their way through his theology and ethics throughout Romans. Despite the interpretive acrobatics performed by scholars who situate this submissive posturing within a

---

4. Johnson, "Buttigieg." This one-sided approach ignores the work of LGB-TIA2Q+ activists *within* these countries and assumes that the harm and traumas of military invasion and indefinite wars could not inflict as much (or more) violence and terror on many LGBTIA2Q+ folks. On this point, especially with regard to use of US queer/feminist rhetoric to justify interventions in Afghanistan and Iraq, see Puar, *Terrorist Assemblages*, 3–24, 40–61. In all these cases, the selection of which countries to name speaks volumes: the government *already* viewed them with political suspicion (as enemies/threats or, at least, as hostile to the United States). The illegality of gay-ness, not limited to these places (and still not entirely ended in the United States) is merely an excuse used to justify already desired invasions.

5. As can be seen in the video clip of this moment (found in Johnson, "Butti-gieg"), students from Luther College stand in the background holding red-white-and-blue-striped campaign signs that bear the slogan "Freedom. Security. Democracy." Though Buttigieg was a Democrat, this slogan is reminiscent of Republican US president George W. Bush's post-9/11 and Iraq-War speeches.

6. My use of "US-flag bedsheets" evokes (and riffs on) an image Puar uses as a visual example of homonationalism. In it two young, muscular, shirtless/naked white men wrap themselves together in the US flag. The image is captioned "come together" and was originally displayed as a four-month-long billboard campaign by the website gay.com (Puar, *Terrorist Assemblages*, 42).

liberationist reading of an anti-imperial (and generally heroic) Paul, the obvious interpretation of 13:1–7 is that these words are meant to encourage Christ-followers to submit to the current political regime, namely, Roman rule. This chapter spells out how Paul's ethical submission in Rom 13 employs homonationalism.

Why not call this *Romonationalism* when it occurs in Paul's letters (or other first-century examples)? At some point, the riffing becomes banal. More importantly, changing the analytical terms every time we shift contexts demands difference. It reifies a pure homonationalism that could exist only in the specific contexts out of which Puar develops the term. Every renaming implies that the differences matter more than the similarities, adhering to a rigid historicism that is allergic to any perception of anachronism.[7] It is the similarities that interest me. Using Puar's term admits striking affective resonances across history; it acknowledges the utility of this term for historical analysis; and it draws attention to the ongoing political affects that move in between the past, present, and future. Therefore, I insist on naming ancient examples of homonationalism for what they are: manifestations of the same tactics we see today.

This chapter walks through this comparison between first-century and twenty-first-century homonationalism as I exegete Rom 13. I place imperial, Romosexual *mores* and Rom 13 into conversation with Puar, weaving into this exegesis examples of US sexual exceptionalism and homonationalism. These examples include the politics of the US war on terror, Buttigieg's campaign, and the US Supreme Court's decision in *Obergefell v. Hodges* (2015). The connections forged through these examples draw out the subtler dimensions of ethical submission in Romans and first-century Rome.

In "Praiseworthy Submission in Romans 13," I show how Rom 13:1–10 encourages an ethical submission that is thoroughly Romanormative, especially given the passage's emphasis on the desirability of imperial praise. This Romanormativity forms the foundation for Paul's homonationalism. Next, "Exceptional Sexual Mores" draws out the politics of morality and sexual exceptionalism as used *by* the empire or nation. Elite Romans used moral discourse to establish themselves and their empire as exceptional (in the sense of being excellent). This exceptional status

---

7. *Homonationalism* doubly defies such rigidity, since both *homo* and *nationalism* denote what many historians insist are modern formulations.

depended upon its construction and regulation of sexual *mores* that policed the borders of its ethnically Roman citizenry.[8] "Rome's Sexual Exceptionalism for Jews and other ἔθνη" begins with the flip side of sexual exceptionalism: who is *distinguished from* the empire/nation in order to confirm its excellence? I consider how Rome used sexual exceptionalism to create a morally repugnant, racialized, and queer Other. Then, I turn to these Others and show how some marginalized persons and groups could exploit sexual exceptionalism to curry imperial praise and inclusion. Echoing the homonormative politics of queerness-as-regulatory, ethical self-regulation permitted upwardly mobile first-century Jews (e.g., Philo) to politically position themselves and their ἔθν-ic ethics as Romanormative through tactics of sexual exceptionalism. Finally, in "Homonational- ism in Romans 13," I analyze Rom 13:11–14 and show how Paul's ethical submission hinges around sexualized language that aligns with Rome's elite sexual exceptionalism. Read in tandem with the patriotic loyalty to Roman authority expressed throughout Rom 13, Paul's ethical ideas pres- ent Christ-followers as praiseworthy, sexually respectable subjects worthy of rehabilitation in the eyes of Rome: homonationalism.

Praiseworthy Submission in Romans 13

Contemporary homonationalism conspires with homonormativity. Turning to Paul's letter to the Romans, Pauline homonationalism should stem from Romanormativity. Focusing on Rom 13:1–10, I show how Paul's ethical guidance in Romans is molded to fit into Roman morality. Paul molds goodness into the image of Roman virtue and badness to Roman vice. He exhorts ethical submission for the explicit purpose of receiving praise from Roman authorities. Though the theo-Christology of Rom 3–5 was Roman without Rome, these ethics bask in their Romanormativity and submit fully to a desire to be Roman—under Rome and God.

As we analyze the alignments of Rom 13:1–7 with imperialism and its racist and xenophobic conquest rhetoric, we must remember how the passage

---

8. Marchal has already established that sexual exceptionalism appears in Rome's empire and can shed light on the interpretation of Paul's letters in this context. I am building upon his astute observations to reveal other ways sexual exceptionalism was and is present in Rome and Romans. See Joseph A. Marchal, "The Exceptional Proves Who Rules: Imperial Sexual Exceptionalism in and around Paul's Letters," *JECH* 5 (2015): 87–115.

continues to inflict harm in the name of securing national borders. On June 14, 2018, former US attorney general Jeff Sessions invoked Rom 13 in his galling attempt to defend the terror made visible in images of caged children who had been separated from their parents at the US-Mexico border. "Illegal entry into the United States is a crime—as it should be," Sessions opined. "Persons who violate the law of our nation are subject to prosecution. I would cite to you the Apostle Paul and his clear and wise command in Romans 13, to obey the laws of the government because God has ordained the government for His purposes."[9] This is not the first (nor is it likely to have been the last) time Rom 13 has been used to justify submission—often in the context of horrific injustices—by a nation/empire. Examples of the interpretation of 13:1–7 as encouraging total submission to political authority abound, from its quotation/appearance in early Christian archaeological sites (such as a Byzantine-era mosaic in Caesarea Maritima) to its use in myriad contemporary examples, including but not limited to Sessions.[10]

Though we can call these readings irresponsible, we cannot simply label these horrifically unjust uses of 13:1–7 as incorrect interpretations.[11]

---

9. Jeff Sessions, "Attorney General Sessions Addresses Recent Criticisms of Zero Tolerance by Church Leaders," United States Department of Justice, 14 June 2018, https://tinyurl.com/SBL4531k.

10. Romans 13 has often been quoted against dissent in the modern era, including in the United States (in events such as the Iraq War) but also in South Africa under apartheid. Neil Elliott's description of these verses being cited in 2003, at the beginning of the most recent Iraq War ("It is the duty of all Christians to stand with their president in a time of war [Rom 13:1–7]"), is not, as Elliott notes, an exceptional experience. See Neil Elliott, *The Arrogance of Nations: Reading Romans in the Shadow of Empire*, PCC (Minneapolis: Fortress, 2008), 5–6.

11. Some scholars, who argue that Paul is anti-Rome, emphasize that Rom 13's language and apparent endorsement are out of place in Paul's letter and thought. Elliott exemplifies: "The language of submission and fear that appears here is a startling exception to the rhetoric of the rest of the letter; more typical is the declaration to which it immediately gives way, that obedience to God can be summed up in a single obligation, 'to love one another, for the one who loves the neighbor has fulfilled the law' (13:8–11)" (Elliott, *Arrogance of Nations*, 153). See also Jennifer Wright Knust, *Abandoned to Lust: Sexual Slander and Ancient Christianity*, GTR (New York: Columbia University Press, 2006), 71; T. L. Carter, "The Irony of Romans 13," *NovT* 46 (2004): 209–28. The majority of commentators take a middle stance, to varying degrees: they note that 13:1–7 is not meant to be a theology of the state for all times and places as they emphasize Paul's pragmatic realism and need to keep peace with outsiders to avoid persecution, especially in light of political unrest and instability surrounding

Turning to the text, nowhere is Paul's ethical submission to Rome more explicit than in 13:1.[12]

Πᾶσα ψυχὴ ἐξουσίαις ὑπερεχούσαις ὑποτασσέσθω. οὐ γὰρ ἔστιν ἐξουσία εἰ μὴ ὑπὸ θεοῦ, αἱ δὲ οὖσαι ὑπὸ θεοῦ τεταγμέναι εἰσίν.
Every soul, submit to the prevailing authorities. For there is not authority except by God, and the present ones have been placed by God.[13]

---

either the Edict of Claudius or complaints about taxation in the early years of Nero. Achtemeier's comments are perhaps the best example of the tension such a position attempts to hold together: God's sovereign placement of political authorities who govern by making and enforcing rules is not an endorsement of the major injustices some of these laws enact (so, Jim Crow laws, apartheid, the Holocaust, immoral wars); however, good Christians should, following Romans 13:1–7, "obey traffic lights." See Paul Achtemeier, *Romans* (Louisville, John Knox, 1985), 204. See also Kuo-Wei Peng, *Hate the Evil, Hold Fast to the Good: Structuring Romans 12.1–15.1* (London: T&T Clark, 2006), 211, see further 189–211 for his entire appendix of approaches to this passage; Joseph A. Fitzmyer, *Romans*, AB 33 (New York: Doubleday, 1993), 602–5; James D. G. Dunn, *Romans*, WBC 38, 2 vols. (Dallas: Word, 1988), 2:759, 770–73; Ben Witherington III with Darlene Hyatt, *Paul's Letter to the Romans: A Socio-Rhetorical Commentary* (Grand Rapids: Eerdmans, 2004), 306–7; Philip F. Esler, *Conflict and Identity in Romans* (Minneapolis: Fortress, 2003), 332–33; Richard N. Longenecker, *The Epistle to the Romans: A Commentary on the Greek Text*, NIGTC (Grand Rapids: Eerdmans, 2016), 964–65; Arland J. Hultgren, *Paul's Letter to the Romans: A Commentary* (Grand Rapids: Eerdmans, 2011), 474–75.

12. My emphasis on the obvious meaning of Paul's words in Rom 13 awkwardly situates my progressively queer reading in (partial) agreement with traditional, conservative interpreters, most notably that of Luke Timothy Johnson, *Reading Romans: A Literary and Theological Commentary* (New York: Crossroad, 1997), 186–88. However, we diverge in how much authority and heroic status we grant to Paul and his ideas: Paul encourages submission to empire, as do these commentators; I do not. It is worth noting how Moo and Matera both emphasize *marriage* as an *enduring institution protected by the state that is a part of God's plan* in Rom 13:1–7. The state—whether Roman imperial or US democratic—should have authority to regulate and establish marriages, and this establishment has presumably always followed God's natural definition. See Douglas J. Moo, *The Epistle to the Romans*, NICNT (Grand Rapids: Eerdmans, 1996), 810, see further 790–91; Frank J. Matera, *Romans*, Paideia (Grand Rapids: Baker Academic, 2010), 293–94. Although I query state regulation of hetero- or homonormative marriage, I cannot help experiencing a giddy curiosity at how these commentators consider their positions in light of recent expansions of marriage by the authority of the US government.

13. This third-person imperative is tricky to translate into English because it does not have a grammatical equivalent. Traditionally, this form is translated with "Let,"

As with the empire's conquest and goals, every soul must submit, or be subject, to the authorities who prevail. This description of the authorities as ὑπερεχούσαις, "the ones who prevail [literally meaning 'hold over']" emphasizes their dominion and domination.[14] These "prevailing authorities" refer to the power held by some of the imperial elite, who were seen as authorities.[15] These persons prevailed, overpowered, held over, and benefitted most—politically, economically, and socially—as a result of Roman conquest and rule. These elite imperial authorities also set the ethical rules.

Paul's makes submission explicit using the third-person passive imperative of ὑποτάσσω ("to be placed under," i.e., "to submit"). This verb denotes proper *placement* (as a compound of τάσσω ["to place"]): this

---

that is, "Let every soul submit," but this translation produces both awkward English (a form of speech not used regularly in conversation or prose). Though not perfect, my translation of "Every soul, submit" (almost as if "every soul" were a vocative and "submit" were a second person imperative) better communicates the force of the third person imperative.

14. The term combines ἔχω ("to hold/have") with ὑπέρ ("over, above"). Deriving in part from a mathematical/numerical usage (a certain number "holding over" another), ὑπερέχω often had military meanings, either to denote ability to overpower (and thus prevail) or to denote holding numerical advantage over an opponent. See, for example, its use in Josephus, *B.J.*, 1.45, 124, 412; 2.43, 122; 4.197, 199; 5.9, 156, 287; note sometimes he contrasts this numerical advantage with a strategic advantage not bound to army size. See LSJ, s.v. "ὑπερέχω," 1863.

15. Thus, these authorities are "the Greek equivalents of the Roman *imperia* and *magistratus*" (Fitzmyer, *Romans*, 666). This is evident, despite the fact that 13:1–7 never explicitly mentions Rome or the state as he notes on p. 662. See also Dunn, *Romans*, 2:760; Moo, *Epistle to the Romans*, 795–96; Thomas R. Schreiner, *Romans*, BECNT (Grand Rapids: Baker Books, 1998), 681; Witherington, *Paul's Letter to the Romans*, 310; Hultgren, *Paul's Letter to the Romans*, 471; Longenecker, *Epistle to the Romans*, 955–59; Matera, *Romans*, 294; Leander E. Keck, *Romans*, ANTC (Nashville: Abingdon, 2005), 312–13; Esler, *Conflict and Identity*, 331–32. Mark Nanos has offered an alternative referent for these authorities, asserting that they are the (non-Christian) Jewish leaders of the synagogue where his audience met/worshiped as Christ-followers (gentile and Jewish). In this interpretation, Paul exhorts Christ-followers not to cause trouble, attempt to overthrow/challenge the leaders, or disobey protocol (thus connecting to the questions in chapters 14–15). While Nanos's suggestion has advantages in terms of creating continuity through Romans, especially chapters 12–15 (as he demonstrates), it ultimately seems unlikely, in part due to its dependence on the location of the ἐκκλησία in the synagogue. See Mark D. Nanos, *The Mystery of Romans: The Jewish Context of Paul's Letter* (Minneapolis: Fortress, 1996), 289–336.

theme of placement is central to Rom 13.[16] Proper placement is *passive*, as we saw in 3:25–26a where God's placement of Jesus (as a "display") signaled Jesus's willing, faithful submission to God's authority.[17] It means being placed (by another agent) *under* those who prevail with authority: submission. The posture of submission Paul encourages in 13:1–5 undergirds the ethical ideas encouraged in the rest of the chapter (not just in 13:7): ethical submission to Roman *mores*.

This placement under is not only at the hands of Caesar and the Roman authorities but also (and most directly) by the God whom all Romans and ἔθνη are under: "For there is not authority except by God." "By God" emphasizes God's role as the active agent in the placement and establishment of a hierarchy of authority.[18] In Rom 13, God is the ultimate authority, who places everyone (ὑπὸ θεοῦ τεταγμέναι εἰσίν) in their position in the present Roman kyriarchy (αἱ οὖσαι).[19] With this emphasis on presentness, Paul's Romanormativity comes into bloom: Roman—no longer without Rome.

---

16. The verb comes from τάσσω ("to place") with the prepositional prefix ὑπό ("under"), thus meaning in its passive form to be subjected or placed under, in other words "to submit."

17. See chapter 3, "Faithful Submission."

18. The use of this particular prepositional phrase here is awkward, as ὑπό with a genitive object typically expresses a personal agent in relation to a passive verb (which is not present in this clause). This awkwardness is often smoothed out by translators of this verse, who most often opt to render it as "from God" (implying the preposition ἀπό or perhaps ἐκ). Indeed, some later variants smooth out or clarify this verse by changing it to ἀπό. Fitzmyer notes "by God" is technically correct but prefers "from" (Fitzmyer, *Romans*, 667); also Johnson, *Reading Romans*, 188–89; Keck, *Romans*, 313; Schreiner, *Romans*, 688. Another option, as rendered by Jewett in his commentary, is "under God." See Robert Jewett, *Romans: A Commentary*, Hermeneia (Minneapolis: Fortress, 2007), 789. Rendering this phrase as "under God" would be quite fitting for my argument; however, one would expect θεός to appear in the accusative case, as is typical when ὑπό means "under," and ὑπό with a genitive object (as here) is almost always attested as "by"—indicating a personal agent. Therefore (alas!), despite its *near* possibility, "under God" here is quite improbable on philological grounds, so—despite its awkward sound—"by God" seems both more accurate and preferable. See Herbert Weir Smyth, *Greek Grammar*, rev. Gordon M. Messing (Cambridge: Harvard University Press, 1920, 1984), 387–88 (§1698).

19. Again, τάσσω appears, here as a perfect passive participle (τεταγμέναι) used periphrastically with εἰσίν, to indicate God's placement. αἱ οὖσαι is the present participle of εἰμί having the ἐξουσίαι as its antecedent. God established these authorities' position and rule in the past, and their placement is still in effect in the present.

Ideally, every soul submits to these authorities, but this is not the only possible placement. Romans 13:2 explains:

ὥστε ὁ ἀντιτασσόμενος τῇ ἐξουσίᾳ τῇ τοῦ θεοῦ διαταγῇ ἀνθέστηκεν, οἱ δὲ ἀνθεστηκότες ἑαυτοῖς κρίμα λήμψονται.
As a result, whoever opposes authority stands against God's appointment, and those who stand against themselves, they will receive judgment.[20]

The contrast between submission and opposition (or rebellion/revolt, as other possible translations) again centers on *placement* with respect to authorities, featuring another compound of the root verb τάσσω. Submission, from ὑποτάσσω, is to place/be placed *under*. In Rom 13:2, opposition is expressed with the verb ἀντιτάσσω, to place (oneself) *against*.[21] ὁ ἀντιτασσόμενος, whoever this may be, is the person who does not follow the imperative to submit in 13:1; this person opposes—is placed against—the authorities, τῇ ἐξουσίᾳ. The person is a rebel, one who attempts to overturn or even overthrow the established hierarchy—a potential threat to the prevailing authorities who have previously conquered the person.

Persons who place themselves against such authorities were prone to suspicion from imperial leaders. They represented potential risks to the *pax Romana*. By disturbing the peace, they become morally unworthy of imperial benefits. Their so-called violence lacks the virtue and self-control (i.e., *virtus*) of good Romans. Unable to submit and live as proper subjects (by controlling their rebellious urges), they must *be* controlled, regulated, punished, and made lower on the sociopolitical hierarchy.

---

20. The placement of the reflexive pronoun ἑαυτοῖς here is ambiguous, as it could go with either the main verb (λήμψονται) or with the participle (ἀνθεστηκότες). Given the ambiguity, it seems better to put the dative pronoun with the intransitive participle, as this form often takes a dative to specify against what the subject is set. However, it is possible that τῇ τοῦ θεοῦ διαταγῇ is the implied indirect object of the participle, carrying over from the indirect object of the same verb in the previous clause. See especially Fitzmyer, *Romans*, 687; Moo, *Epistle to the Romans*, 762–63; Keck, *Romans*, 314–15; Dunn, *Romans*, 2:790.

21. Jewett calls ἀντιτάσσω "the opposite" of ὑποτάσσω (Jewett, *Romans*, 790). Often occurring in this middle form, ἀντιτάσσομαι occurs frequently in contexts describing a person or persons who oppose or resist others, especially, in the LXX, referring to groups who are rebelling against an established authority. See Dunn, *Romans*, 2:762.

Philo offers a telling use of ἀντιτάσσω in his description of his delegation to Gaius Caligula, attempting to sway the emperor to a better policy toward Jews in light of anti-Jewish sentiment in Alexandria. He writes:

εἰσελθόντες γὰρ εὐθὺς ἔγνωμεν ἀπὸ τοῦ βλέμματος καὶ τῆς κινήσεως, ὅτι
οὐ πρὸς δικαστὴν ἀλλὰ κατήγορον ἀφίγμεθα, τῶν ἀντιτεταγμένων μᾶλλον
ἐχθρόν.
Immediately upon our arrival, we knew from his glance and his movement that we had come not to a judge but to a prosecutor, much more an enemy of those who had opposed him. (*Legat.* 349)

By stating that Caligula was τῶν ἀντιτεταγμένων μᾶλλον ἐχθρόν ("an enemy of those who had opposed him"), Philo conveys the emperor's prosecuting judgment on the party: their side represented the cause of unrest in Alexandria that opposed the emperor/imperial rule.[22] Caligula's opinion that this party comes from among τῶν ἀντιτεταγμένων, literally the ones who had placed themselves against him, not only shows how this term often denotes rebellion or revolt against (imperial) authority but also conveys an ethical placement against submission to Rome's (moral) *imperium*.

Philo's usage demonstrates why rebellion is antithetical to ethical submission in Romans. Those who oppose the empire and its ruling authority are viewed with suspicion and deserve prosecution and punishment as enemies of the state. For this reason, their needs and concerns are irrelevant to the prevailing authorities, and they themselves should be considered of lower status, unworthy of the attention or care granted to those higher on the social ladder.

Written after Caligula's death, Philo's recounting affirms the ethical submission of Alexandria's Jews. By placing this brash judgment in the persona of a despised emperor, Philo makes clear they were not rebellious.[23] Likewise in Rom 13, by submitting to both God and God's placed kyriarchy, Christ-followers appear less threatening and, hopefully, worthy of upward mobility.

---

22. Indeed, at that moment in the story, according to Caligula, they remain opposed to him, given the perfect tense of ἀντιτάσσω here. Compare this use of the perfect to that found in Rom 13:2.

23. *Legatio ad Gaium* was written to support Caligula's successor, Claudius. Caligula's poor judgment would have been affirmed by most Roman elites under Claudius, and this example appeals to such sentiments. See Maren Niehoff, *Philo on Jewish Identity and Culture* (Tübingen: Mohr Siebeck, 2001), 85–94.

In 13:1–2, Paul presents a binary that is governed by God, the ultimate top of the imperial hierarchy (along with Jesus, the ultimate κύριος), who places all authority.[24] The binary is simple: one either submits to Rome's moral/military authority or one opposes it.[25] The options are to be placed under (ὑποτασσέσθω) or to be placed against (ἀντιτασσόμενος). Paul states that submission is the better, indeed more ethical, option.

It is not just this explicit preference for submission that reveals Paul's ethical alignment with Rome's kyriarchal *mores*. Ethical submission is most effective in the subtle ways its notions of "good" (ἀγαθός) ideas and actions are affectively drawn into Romanormative alignment. Roman imperialism cast morality in binary terms, enforcing an affective gridlock on behavior: *you're either good or you're bad; you're either with us or against us*. Paul's Romanormativity replicates this binary and presents a morality whose "goodness" is consistently "with us." This gridlock affects Paul's theo-Christology and his ethical impulses beyond those found in chapter 13. Paul's ethical submission may be most overt in Rom 13, but his ethical submission is implied in his suggested actions that permit living this Roman good life. Romans 13:1–5's explicit submission continues the ethical ideas of chapter 12, which begins by telling his audience to think according to God's will and discern what is good (τὸ ἀγαθόν), pleasing, and perfect (see 12:2).[26]

Romans 13:3 is central to the ethical submission of Rom 13 and the entire letter.

> οἱ γὰρ ἄρχοντες οὐκ εἰσὶν φόβος τῷ ἀγαθῷ ἔργῳ ἀλλὰ τῷ κακῷ. θέλεις δὲ μὴ φοβεῖσθαι τὴν ἐξουσίαν· τὸ ἀγαθὸν ποίει, καὶ ἕξεις ἔπαινον ἐξ αὐτῆς·

---

24. The opponent stands against (ἀνθέστηκεν) God's appointment or command, τῇ τοῦ θεοῦ διαταγῇ, literally what has been firmly placed by God. As we know from 13:1, what God firmly places or appoints is the authority against which this rebel is placed. Fitzmyer, notes the term's proximity to those used specifically for imperial edicts with the Latin *edictum* having equivalence to the Greek διάταξις or διάταγμα (Fitzmyer, *Romans*, 667).

25. James N. Hoke, "Unbinding Imperial Time: Chrononormativity and Paul's Letter to the Romans," in *Sexual Disorientations: Queer Temporalities, Affects, Theologies*, ed. Kent L. Brintnall, Joseph A. Marchal, and Stephen D. Moore, TTC (New York: Fordham University Press, 2018), 72–73.

26. "Do not be be conformed to [or make your image according to] this age, but be transformed by the mind's renewal so that you discern what God's will is, what is good and pleasing and perfect" (12:2). Here one submits to God by adopting God's (ultimately kyriarchal) mindset and image.

For the rulers are not a terror to good actions but to bad ones. You desire
not to fear authority: do good, and you will have praise from it.

This verse clarifies how Paul's ethical exhortations connect to his submissive theo-political system. The verse's final mandate, "Do good, and you will
have praise from it," neatly summarizes Paul's goal in expounding on what
is good, pleasing, and perfect throughout Rom 12. The person or group who
does what is good receives ἔπαινον—"praise," as in "approval" and "commendation"—from the imperial authority whom God has ultimately placed.
Desire for imperial praise cements Romanormativity into Paul's ethics.

Though Paul defines good actions as God's will, Paul's "good" actions
conform to "goodness" as defined by Rome's ruling authorities. Paul's ethical advice throughout Rom 12–15 would not have been out of the ordinary
to most first-century Roman audiences. This alignment is most apparent in
chapter 13, where Paul specifically exhorts his audience to submit to imperial authority and do good according to its morality. By stating that rulers
are not a "terror" (φόβος) to good acts (τῷ ἀγαθῷ ἔργῳ) but to bad ones (τῷ
κακῷ), Paul turns submission into a position defined by ethics: doing good
and not bad.[27] If one submits to authority, both imperial and divine, then
one also must do good. Alternately, those who do bad (including but not
limited to those who rebel/stand against imperial authority and values) draw
negative attention and provoke "terror" from those in power (οἱ ἄρχοντες).[28]

Vice and rebellion (which often could be found together) needed to
be regulated, policed, and kept under control by Rome. Romans 13:3 is
closely connected to the verse that follows:

θεοῦ γὰρ διάκονός ἐστιν σοὶ εἰς τὸ ἀγαθόν. ἐὰν δὲ τὸ κακὸν ποιῇς, φοβοῦ· οὐ
γὰρ εἰκῇ τὴν μάχαιραν φορεῖ· θεοῦ γὰρ διάκονός ἐστιν ἔκδικος εἰς ὀργὴν τῷ
τὸ κακὸν πράσσοντι.

---

27. In my translation of this phrase, I have chosen to render τῷ ἀγαθῷ ἔργῳ and
τῷ κακῷ as plural in English, as the neuter singular noun seems to refer more to an
ideal than to a single act/deed and therefore is better captured in English using the
plural.

28. Knust's comparison to prevailing kingship theories in relationship to 13:1–7
shows the ways Paul's rhetoric does not deviate from general Roman moral or political thought (Knust, *Abandoned to Lust*, 71–74). On Paul, Romans, and Hellenistic
kingship theories, see Bruno Blumenfeld, *The Political Paul: Justice, Democracy and
Kingship in a Hellenistic Framework* (Sheffield: Sheffield Academic, 2001); for these
theories' application to Rom 13:1–7, see 389–98.

> For God's minister is yours for good. However, if you do bad, fear because
> it does not bear the sword at random. For God's minister is an avenger
> for anger to whoever practices vice.

Together, 13:3–4 emphasize the contrast between good and bad actions
and the consequences that ensue from them: "you will have praise from
it" (13:3, on "good" actions); "it does not bear the sword at random" (13:4,
on "bad" actions). This all-important praise contrasts the fear that comes
from refusal to submit to the *mores* of imperial authorities. This second
statement elaborates the terror: it comes from imperial policing via the
sword, and such policing is not "random."[29] It is for those who act badly.[30]

The ἔπαινος—praise—of 13:3 is the reward of ethical submission: it
is what Christ-followers (like all Romans) want instead of φόβος, terror.
ἔπαινος applies to acknowledgment, rhetorical or otherwise, of noteworthy
action.[31] This praise can be general, but when it comes at the hands of the

---

29. Elliott argues that Paul, by saying that authority does not bear the sword in
vain, makes an ironic reference to Roman propaganda, though his audience would
know that it is actually untrue, as Nero indeed was among Rome's bloodiest emperors (Elliott, *Arrogance of Nations*, 155–56); see further Elliott, "Romans 13:1–7 in the
Context of Roman Imperial Propaganda," in *Paul and Empire: Religion and Power in
Roman Imperial Society*, ed. Richard A. Horsley (Harrisburg, PA: Trinity Press International, 1997), 201–3.

30. Jewett notes τὴν μάχαιραν φορεῖ also draws from the language of policing, as
the technical term μαχαιροφόροι could be used to refer to those who enforced the law
(Jewett, *Romans*, 795). See also Fitzmyer, *Romans*, 669. Commentators generally agree
that this is a broad reference to Rome's authority to punish crimes, especially emphasizing that this reference to "bearing the sword" cannot be limited to the military
enforcement and the death penalties implied by imperial *ius gladii*. See Moo, *Epistle to
the Romans*, 802; Brendan Byrne, *Romans*, SP 6 (Collegeville, MN: Liturgical, 2007),
391; Dunn, *Romans*, 2:764; Schreiner, *Romans*, 684–85; Witherington, *Paul's Letter to
the Romans*, 314.

31. It is often the term used to describe panegyric that praised noteworthy figures in older Greek sources (such as in Isocrates, Aeschines, or Demosthenes). Dunn
calls it the goal of the Greek wisdom tradition (Dunn, *Romans* 2:763). Contrasting it
with Roman sexual slander, Knust notes that ἔπαινος in such Greco-Roman rhetoric
was critical for ideals of Roman virtue. Such praise frequently appealed to the subject's *noble origins* as a primary source for being worthy of praise (and, likewise, lower
status/birth was not worthy) (Knust, *Abandoned to Lust*, 19–20). Bruce Winter argues
that such praise can be related to the act of public inscriptions and benefactions. See
Bruce Winter, "Roman Law and Society in Romans 12–15," in *Rome in the Bible and
the Early Church*, ed. Peter Oakes (Grand Rapids: Baker Academic, 2002), 67–102.

empire, it implies benefits and privileges typically conferred upon more elite subjects who have gained particular notice of the emperor (or those closest to him).[32] By doing good, Paul hopes his audience will gain notice from the empire and its authorities for their moral behavior that conforms to (and perhaps even exceeds) the empire's standards.[33] Paul assumes that this notice will result in praise from those in power, which will hopefully help to confer better social standing and benefits for these Christ-followers.

On the flip side of Paul's binary, αἱ ἀντιτασσόμεναι (whoever place themselves against authority) prove themselves to be no better than those whom Rome deemed "barbarians" in need of conquering and order.[34] They are of low birth and will never rise on the social ladder to praise and power. Returning to Paul's desire for praise (the antithesis to this fear and force), those who submit are also more likely to be praiseworthy, which implies the ability to move upward on the social scale.[35] Doing good requires full ethical submission to the *mores* that make one a good person. It is ethically submissive subjects who are worthy of praise (and potentially of higher status), while those who rebel and do bad/practice vice are clearly only worthy of terror and suspicion.

Paul's encouragement to do good is both a strategy to avoid fear and prosecution *and* a way to receive praise and positive attention from the imperial authorities. Doing good, via ethical submission, represents another potential pathway for Christ-followers to become upwardly mobile under the imperial system: Romanormativity.

How do the ethical mandates of 13:3–4 relate to the exhortation to submission and counterexample of rebellion in 13:1–2? Romans 13:5 connects the dots: Paul's advises submission:

---

32. For example, Josephus describes the praises given to Antipater by Julius Caesar (on account of his military service and prowess), which included Roman citizenship and, later, political positions. See Josephus, *B.J.* 1.193–194.

33. As the expansion on exceptionalism below implies, these stricter emphases in non-elite ethics present *exceptional* self-control in Roman terms, of such a standard that would certainly be unexpected and praiseworthy for those outside the elite. (To be brought into the elite, one may need to be excessive in these ethical embodiments).

34. On the racialized Greco-Roman portrayals of barbarians and their appearance in Romans and other Pauline letters, see Joseph A. Marchal, *Appalling Bodies: Queer Figures before and after Paul's Letters* (Oxford: Oxford University Press, 2019), 162–79.

35. This is, ultimately, a very limited move, as we will see further below and as we already saw in chapter 3 and the fantasies that sustained cruel πίστις (from which these ethical submissions cannot be divorced).

διὸ ἀνάγκη ὑποτάσσεσθαι, οὐ μόνον διὰ τὴν ὀργὴν ἀλλὰ καὶ διὰ τὴν συνείδησιν.

Therefore, it is necessary to submit, not only because of anger but also because of [your] consciousness.

Romans 13:5 reinforces the now explicit connection between ethics and submission. Paul admits that submission prevents wrath (ὀργὴν), but this is not his emphasis; it is not the only (οὐ μόνον), or even the main, benefit. It is simply an obvious outcome.

The major benefit comes from moral awareness (συνείδησις).[36] It comes from knowing what is good and being seen as having adopted the ethical values of the imperial authorities.[37] The ideal embodiment of Romanormativity must affect the mind as well as the body.[38] Paul's audience should submit and do good because of this awareness/knowledge *beyond* the fact that not doing so will result in anger from and fear of authority. The benefit of adopting this mindset is this *praise*. This praise or commendation is a recognition and acknowledgment, from the kyriarchal top, that these Christ-followers go beyond not posing a moral-political threat. They are model loyal subjects who fully embody the virtues and values of the imperial elite citizen: praiseworthy patriotism.

But doesn't God trump elite authority, since God stands at the top of the kyriarchal hierarchy? It is God who placed these authorities at the top of the imperial system, and it is God's ethics—seemingly endorsed in the imperial system—that Christ-followers must ultimately obey. Though this is true, God's ethical standards, as elaborated in Rom 12–15, barely deviate from those already set by the empire. By establishing God as above all

---

36. The term συνείδησις is almost always used to evoke the idea of awareness in a moral sense and is often translated as "conscience," though it can more generally mean "awareness" or "knowledge" in a shared sense (LSJ, s.v. "συνείδησις," 1704). Diodorus Siculus twice uses the phrase διὰ τὴν συνείδησιν, both times in reference to a guilty conscience, which drive its possessor mad (*Bibl. hist.* 4.65.7) or haunts him (*Bibl. hist.* 29.25), due to an immoral act. See further Rom 2:15, 9:1; 1 Cor 8:7, 10, 12; 10:25, 27 (both with διὰ), 28, 29; 2 Cor 4:2, 5:11. Moral awareness submits the transformed mind to God and ultimately, then, to Roman ethics under God. See also Byrne, *Romans*, 388.

37. The benefit comes quite literally from having the same knowledge, συνείδησις, as the authorities. Contrasted with ὀργή, this motivating "conscience" means the awareness of proper moral behavior with relation to the imperial authorities.

38. Though there is not space to draw out fully, we can see this Romanormative mentality in Paul's language of mindsets (φρόνημα) in Rom 8.

and as the one who places all authority, Paul establishes imperial ethics as being equivalent to theo-christological ethics. In so doing, Paul also proves all Christ-followers, as adherents to these theo-christological ethics must be faithful followers of imperial ethics.

Under Roman rule, good people are those who conform to the socio-sexual-political hierarchy. They are good imperial subjects, who *submit* to the rule of the prevailing authorities. The premise of 13:1–5 is that rulers—those prevailing authorities of 13:1—require good behavior and are a terror to those who do bad. Paul's exhortation assumes that ethics are determined by those who have authority to rule: those with the power to praise and punish decide who and what is good and bad. Paul's command for submission is not merely a call to accept imperial authority; his advice submits his audience ethically to imperial standards of behavior. The act of submission is an ethical *placement*, allowing oneself to be placed under others (ὑποτασσέσθω). Paul does not just encourage his audience to submit as a form of nonrebellion, he encourages them to submit fully by adopting and following the moral codes of the empire. He exhorts ethical submission.

Romans 13:1–5 makes explicit the submissive affects that have pulsed through Paul's letter to Rome, starting with *pistis*'s obedience (ὑπακοὴν πίστεως) in Rom 1:5, moving into the spiraling sexual disgust of Rom 1:18–32 and the faithful submission of Jesus and ἔθνη in Rom 3–5, and ending with Paul's ethics. This ethical submission continues through the rest of the chapter, and affects theo-christological ethics in Rom 12–15. Paying one's taxes (13:6–7) is a demonstration of submission, of loyal patriotism to imperial authority.[39] By again referring to these imperial authorities as servants/ministers (διάκονοι) of God, Paul reaffirms both God's position at the top of the imperial hierarchy (placing all others under God) and the alignment of God's idea of "what is good, pleasing, and perfect" with imperial ethics. Romans 13:6–7 transitions from the explicit directive for submission to ethical advice that stems from ethical submission to imperial authority.

---

39. In similar ways, Puar discusses modern gay consumerism, particularly with relationship to the assumptions of access to capital involved in the large gay tourism industry, observing that as white, affluent ("regulatory") queerness aligns more closely with national belonging, the once disruptive aspects of gay tourism are downplayed and replaced by rhetorics of patriotism and loyalty to the American state (Puar, *Terrorist Assemblages*, 61–67).

Romans 13:8 broadens the specific repayment of taxes in 13:7:

μηδενὶ μηδὲν ὀφείλετε, εἰ μὴ τὸ ἀλλήλους ἀγαπᾶν· ὁ γὰρ ἀγαπῶν τὸν ἕτερον νόμον πεπλήρωκεν.
Owe nothing to no one except for loving reciprocally. For whoever loves completes a different law.

The demands to owe nothing continues the submission to imperial ethics, which penalized those who owed money, taxes or otherwise. Owing money conveys lower status and dependence upon those higher on the social ladder. Since wealth is indicative of elite status, the ability to not owe debts proves some level of financial stability. These demonstrations of financial access and stability are a form of what Puar calls "mediated national belonging" and, in the first century, invest in hopes for elite respect and belonging via ethical submission.[40] If Christ-followers are known to owe nothing to anyone (except in their love, which might attract further positive attention), then they are again more likely to be viewed as praiseworthy subjects who submit to imperial demands and live debt-free, as do the wealthier elite.

The one thing that Christ-followers should owe to others is τὸ ἀλλήλους ἀγαπᾶν, "loving reciprocally." This reciprocal owing of love returns to the themes of love already encouraged in chapter 12 (ἡ ἀγάπη ἀνυπόκριτος, "love is unhypocritical" [12:9]). This love is separate from the imperial ethics to which Christ-followers must submit. It is part of—and allows one to fulfill or complete—τὸν ἕτερον νόμον, a *different* law.[41] Based on

---

40. Puar, *Terrorist Assemblages*, 27.

41. This translation deviates from prevailing scholarly opinion, which takes τὸν ἕτερον as the object of the participle ἀγαπῶν, generally because νόμος always refers to the torah for Paul and (since it clearly refers to torah here) there is no need to contrast its otherness to an unmentioned Roman law (in terms of an explicit mention of νόμος previously). See Fitzmyer, *Romans*, 678; Dunn, *Romans*, 2:776; Schreiner, *Romans*, 691–92; Moo, *Epistle to the Romans*, 813, n. 19; Jewett, *Romans*, 807–8. I do not deny the possibility of their translation as being on equal grounds to my selection, but this argument seems weak, as Roman law is *very* implicit in 13:1–7. My translation is not totally unestablished, as these commentators make their arguments against those of Willi Marxsen and James Arthur Walther in particular. See Willi Marxsen, "Der ἕτερος νόμος Röm 13,8," *TZ* 11 (1955): 230–37; James Arthur Walther, "A Translator's Dilemma: An Exegetical Note in Romans 13:8," *Perspective* 13 (1972): 243–46; see also Johnson, *Reading Romans*, 192.

13:9's quotation of the Septuagint form of the Decalogue (Deut 5:17–19, 21; Exod 20:13–15, 17) and of Lev 19:18, it appears that this different law refers to that found in Jewish Scriptures. In 13:8–10, this "different law"— that is, differing from that of the imperial authorities—emphasizes this reciprocal and unhypocritical love in chapters 12–13.[42]

Just because this law is different does not mean that those who complete its commands of love are not also completing the demands of imperial morality. Paul continues in 13:10 by observing: ἡ ἀγάπη τῷ πλησίον κακὸν οὐκ ἐργάζεται ("Love does not work vice toward a neighbor"). Here, Paul combines the scriptural/Jewish law of love with the moral terms of empire, in particular that of vice, τὸ κακόν, which is used alongside the verbal form of the noun ἔργον (used above in 13:3), ἐργάζομαι. Paul aligns Jewish/scriptural values as fulfilling both God's commands and the laws and ethics of the imperial state (whose authority is placed by God). When I introduced Romanormativity in chapter 1, we saw how Philo makes a similar alignment of Jewish laws and customs using the story of Joseph.[43] Through a similar Romanormativity that ethically aligns with imperial authority, Paul positions Christ-followers, alongside Jews, to be seen as being most able to embody and remain under imperial values. They become exemplars of patriotism. They are submissive to authority, live in ways that pose no threat to the state, and support its political project of dominion.[44]

Throughout Rom 13, Paul's stance of ethical submission is Romanormative, aligning Christ-followers with imperial *mores*. As a result of this submission, freedom from punishment (φόβος) is the first of many benefits enjoyed by Rome's exceptional elite. More importantly, as he competes in this imperial arena, Paul molds Christ-followers as superior competitors

---

42. On this passage, Brooten responds to a frequent supersessionist reading that presumes Paul to argue that the love of Lev 19:18 replaces the need to follow the rest of the law. She writes, "The term 'summarize' does not mean 'replace.'" See Bernadette J. Brooten, *Love between Women: Early Christian Responses to Female Homoeroticism* (Chicago: University of Chicago Press, 1997), 287.

43. See chapter 1, pp. 48–50. We will return to Philo's Romanormative construction of Jewish values later in this chapter.

44. Below we will see how Paul's attempts to show the exceptional nature of the Jewish torah that aligns with (and indeed strengthens) Roman *mores* is *un*exceptional among Jews, many of whom (but far from all) also attempted to curry favor and praise from Rome by showing how their ethics (particularly, for Philo, in the torah) are excessively Roman.

(especially compared with other ἔθνη) because they are equipped with an elevated moral code that supplements the Roman moral code. Just as in the case of πίστις, praise from these authorities (for exceptional ethical submission) continues to permit the upward mobility that enables and sustains a good life. In addition to his general ethical submission as seen in 13:1–10 (and preceded by his ethical advice in ch. 12), his language in 13:11–14 continues these Romanormative alignments to imperial ethics, specifically aligning them with the *mores* of Rome's sexually exceptional elite. This paves the way for them to become, via homonationalism, "subjects worthy of rehabilitation."

Exceptional Sexual Mores

To see homonationalism in Paul's letter, we must situate Rom 13 into its broader ethical context under the Roman Empire. Ethical ideals legitimized Rome's *imperium* and affected all of the empire's inhabitants, who were expected to adhere to its values in order to maintain peace. Romosexuality affects and was affected by a wider moral discourse that governed proper behavior for Rome, especially its exceptional elite. A narrative that elite, Roman men were inherently better than all others—and therefore most fit to rule—guided Romosexual morality. In what follows, I describe Romosexual morality and explain how its narrative relied on strategies of what Puar terms *sexual exceptionalism*. This puts Puar into conversation with the broader context of morality under Roman imperialism and prepares us to scrutinize how some of Rome's marginalized subjects drew on homonational tactics by infusing Romanormative ideas with this Roman sexual exceptionalism.

"The stability of the Roman Empire, insofar as ethics contributed to it," Teresa Morgan writes, "depended not only on certain kinds of behavior, but on its members fitting in with one another and taking complementary roles in a kind of vast social jigsaw puzzle."[45] Maintaining Rome's sociosexual-political jigsaw, ethical virtue was as much about politics, that is, perpetuating the structure and stability of empire in order to bolster its prosperity (and, as a consequence, that of its citizens), as it was about living well or properly, as befits *the good life*.

---

45. Teresa J. Morgan, *Popular Morality in the Early Roman Empire* (Cambridge: Cambridge University Press, 2007), 184.

Good or proper living in the empire meant conducting one's affairs in alignment with Rome's kyriarchy, from the emperor and the elite at the top to enslaved wo/men and others of lowest status at the bottom. Though Roman authorities would police ethical standards when necessary, moral stability was effectively maintained by promises of stability and benefit for those who adhered to the ethical dimensions of *pax Romana*. Because the complementary roles on this jigsaw puzzle were stacked since the elite held most of the pieces, this ethical system enforced imperial control and permitted cohesion across the empire in the name of being "good" (ἀγαθός) or having "virtue" (*virtus*, or Gk. ἀρετή). Just as virtue in Rome was thought to be possessed solely by "true men" (*viri*) of noble status, the adjective ἀγαθός is frequently connected with being wellborn when it refers to persons, thus implying that those who do good are intrinsically elite or noble.[46] As we see in his presentation of moral goodness throughout Rom 12–13, Paul's ethical ideas participate in this social jigsaw puzzle of Roman kyriarchy whose *mores* and idealized *virtus* sustained Rome's rule.

Being derived from *vir*, *virtus* was a gendered Roman value. Within imperial discourse, it was a quality possessed by "real"—meaning freeborn and elite—men.[47] Behaviors that were characteristic of a (true) man who possessed *virtus* included eating habits, dress and grooming, household order and control, military bravery and discipline, and "natural" sexual comportment.[48] The ideal of *virtus* (and the *vir*) encompassed prescribed

---

46. LSJ, "ἀγαθός," 4. Indeed, ἀρετή is related to ἀγαθός as the noun form of its superlative, ἀριστός.

47. Catharine Edwards, *The Politics of Immorality in Ancient Rome* (Cambridge: Cambridge University Press, 1993), 57; Jonathan Walters, "Invading the Roman Body: Manliness and Impenetrability in Roman Thought," in *Roman Sexualities*, ed. Judith P. Hallett and Marilyn B. Skinner (Princeton: Princeton University Press, 1997), 32; Craig Williams, *Roman Homosexuality*, 2nd ed. (Oxford: Oxford University Press, 2010), 139; Maud W. Gleason, *Making Men: Sophists and Self-Presentation in Ancient Rome* (Princeton: Princeton University Press, 1995), 159. See further Colleen M. Conway, *Behold the Man: Jesus and Greco-Roman Masculinity* (Oxford: Oxford University Press, 2008), 15–34; Knust, *Abandoned to Lust*, 28.

48. Gleason, throughout *Making Men*, points to the physiognomic and performative (especially via rhetoric) behaviors required of Roman men. In terms of sexual comportment, especially: always being the active/penetrating partner in intercourse and not being perceived as being overeager in one's sexual pursuits (as discussed in the introduction) in addition to and not violating the sexual honor (*pudicitia*) of another person of elite status (as will be discussed later in this chapter). See Williams, *Roman*

norms for proper behavior and excluded persons who did not or could not live accordingly (namely, all wo/men and most men). As a gendered, elite ideal, *virtus* reinforced Romosexuality. It communicated to individuals the ethical *mores* that characterized the ideal, elite man who is able to control and govern his self, household, and the affairs of the state.

Virtus was also racialized. It was a particular possession of Romans that was lacking in the various ἔθνη whom they conquered.[49] "*Virtus* is the *special inheritance of the Roman people*," argues Myles McDonnell, "and it was by this *virtus*, this 'manliness,' that Roman supremacy had been built. The Romans believed they were successful because they were 'better' men."[50] *Virtus* legitimized conquest and maintained Rome's rule. It represented the distinct qualities of the collective *imperium* of the Roman state, governed and embodied by elite men. Imperial morality used *virtus* to distinguish elite Roman men from others, in particular foreigners conquered by Rome, in addition to wo/men, enslaved persons, and those of lower socioeconomic status.[51]

Narratives of Roman *virtus* exemplify *exceptionalism*. "Exceptionalism," Puar explains, "paradoxically signals *distinction from* (to be unlike,

---

Homosexuality, 137–76; Walters, "Invading the Roman Body," 41; Conway, *Behold the Man*, 30–34.

49. "A common theme in ancient texts is that true Roman men, who possess *virtus* by birthright, rightfully exercise dominion not only over women but also over foreigners, themselves implicitly likened to women. An obvious implication is that non-Roman peoples were destined to submit to Roman masculine *imperium*" (Williams, *Roman Homosexuality*, 148). Knust draws attention to how language of virtue (and therefore vice) is a "power-laden process" (Knust, *Abandoned to Lust*, 17).

50. Myles McDonnell, *Roman Manliness*: Virtus *and the Roman Republic* (Cambridge: Cambridge University Press, 2006), 3, emphasis added. Though *virtus* has a Latin derivation and history separate from its typical Greek equivalent (ἀρετή), as McDonnell outlines, the idea of Romans believing that their *virtus* made them better men cannot be completely separated from the fact that the Greek term derives from the superlative of ἀγαθός ("best"). See further McDonnell, *Roman Manliness*, 105–41.

51. Williams, *Roman Homosexuality*, 146. McDonnell observes that the notion of *virtus* in a more ethical context emerges in the rhetoric of the first century BCE, particularly in its turbulent politics and the lack of *virtus* among even elite politicians. It is this ethical notion, then, that becomes much more established in the rhetoric of empire, combining it with the ideals of martial prowess and manliness, as it touts the return of *virtus* to Rome—a *virtus* that, as McDonnell shows, differs from its earlier usages (McDonnell, *Roman Manliness*, 2–9, esp. 5, 385–89; Elliott, *Arrogance of Nations*, 143–45).

dissimilar) as well as *excellence* (imminence, superiority), suggesting a departure from yet mastery of linear teleologies of progress."[52] *Virtus* distinguishes the goodness of elite Roman men as *exceptional*—that is, morally excellent. In the process, it signals their *distinction from* those below them, especially wo/men whom Rome conquered in the process of building a virtuous *imperium*. Rome's social jigsaw was a 3D puzzle that used morality to piece together a pyramid—a kyriarchal pyramid.

This moral exceptionalism infused the presentation of imperial rule by Rome's rulers. Augustus contrasted his restoration of the ancient *mores maiorum* to the immorality that proliferated in the late Republic.[53] This idealized past permitted his regime's novelty.[54] Invoking this idea in his Res gestae, Augustus repeatedly describes the offers he received for political power, which, in his description, he humbly refuses.[55] For example, he narrates, "when the senate and the citizen-body [δῆμος] of the Romans agreed that I should be elected as the sole curator of their laws and ways [τρόπος] with greatest authority, I received no offer of authority [ἀρχή] that was against the ancestral customs [παρὰ τὰ πάτρια ἔθη]" (Res gest. divi Aug. 6).[56] Through his humble presentation of his route to power, Augustus justifies sole imperial rule for himself and his successors by implying that it does not contradict the *mores maiorum*. Roman ethics consistently enact an exceptionalism that created an exceptional elite *imperium*.

---

52. Puar, *Terrorist Assemblages*, 3.

53. Augustus publicly declared (on his Res gestae) this moral restoration and inscribed it across his *imperium*. "Since new laws were produced by me, as their promoter, I brought back many models of the ancestors, which at that time were falling out of use by our generation; and I, myself, handed over to posterity models of many affairs [*rerum*] that should be imitated" (Res gest. divi Aug. 8.4–7). Despite the novelty of his laws, the emperor (an *imperator novis* himself) asserts that he draws from the example of ancient times, before the dissolution of morality as seen in the late republic. See Edwards, *Politics of Immorality*, 34–35.

54. Paul Zanker, *The Power of Images in the Age of Augustus*, trans. Alan Shapiro (Ann Arbor: University of Michigan Press, 1988), 156.

55. The eschewal of empire is equally apparent in American rhetoric, not wanting to admit its imperial resemblances. See Amy Kaplan, "Violent Belongings and the Question of Empire Today: Presidential Address to the American Studies Association, October 17, 2003," *American Quarterly* 56 (2004): 1–18; see also brief discussion in Puar, *Terrorist Assemblages*, 1–3.

56. The Latin for this particular segment is illegible in the extant remnants of the Res gestae.

Exceptionalism can wield sexual morality to enforce its distinction. Puar's *sexual exceptionalism* draws attention to the role sexuality plays in contemporary US exceptionalism: the nation bolsters its excellence by embodying excellent sexual mores; however, this national sexual excellence is produced through its distinction from especially queer and racialized forms of sexual deviance.[57] Sexual exceptionalism regulates race, gender, class, and sexuality in ways that enforce nationalist politics as a means to national prosperity. The United States as nation and the ideal citizens within it embody a heteronormative (and, with growing frequency, homonormative) ideal of the monogamously married family, which is distinguished from the nation's enemies—most notably Middle Eastern "terrorists"— who routinely get cast in racialized deployments of perversely queer sexual expressions.[58] US sexual exceptionalism can be seen in the moral distinction of ideal (white) heteronormative citizens from the threat that promiscuous racialized subjects, frequently implied in discussions of "unwed mothers" and "welfare queens," impose on national prosperity.[59]

This focus on nationalist politics can broaden to comprise imperialism, especially given that contemporary US nationalism is more frequently coming out as imperialism.[60] Whether for a nation or for an empire (or an

---

57. For a detailed overview of political theories of contemporary American exceptionalism and their relations to hetero- and homonormativities in the United States, see Puar, *Terrorist Assemblages*, 3–11.

58. Puar, *Terrorist Assemblages*, 3–11, 37–38.

59. Cathy Cohen, "Punks, Bulldaggers, and Welfare Queens: The Radical Potential of Queer Politics?," *GLQ* 3 (1997): 452–57. Puar refers a similar point when she writes, "Further, moralizing arguments, entrenched within the rubric of culture, obscure economic exploitation." These arguments shift blame onto the exploited, especially focusing on "those marital practices coded as problematic cultural and racial anomalies (polygamy, matriarchy, gender segregation) or coded as failures due to cultural and racial attributes (black welfare queen)" (Puar, *Terrorist Assemblages*, 29).

60. Puar opens with a discussion of how the United States, as a modern nation, both eschews and embraces the term *empire* as a description for its politics. Though they do not exactly correspond, Puar's description of nationalism/nation today could easily be substituted for imperialism/empire in the first-century context. Such a substitution occurs below as I point to how these concepts (already quite malleable in Puar's theorization) do morph and adapt in a different historical and sociopolitical setting (Puar, *Terrorist Assemblages*, 1–30). See also Kaplan, "Violent Belongings"; Marchal, "Exceptional Proves Who Rules," 89–91, 95–99; Hoke, "Be Even Better Subjects, Worthy of Rehabilitation," in *Bodies on the Verge: Queering Pauline Epistles*, ed. Joseph A. Marchal, SemeiaSt 93 (Atlanta: SBL Press, 2019), 85–87.

assemblage that encompasses both), sexual exceptionalism produces narratives wherein norms of sexual morality simultaneously produce certain bodies as excellent, and thus elite and deserving of power and inclusion, and as distinct from, and therefore better than, those presumed unwilling and unable to adhere to these moral standards.

Within Roman moral discourse, an ancient form of sexual exceptionalism operates alongside Romosexuality. The exceptional moral restoration of Rome's empire was emphasized by appealing to the dangers of sexual immorality. The specter of moral degeneration, particularly among the elite, threatened imperial cohesion and control. Horace emphasizes the consequences of unrestrained immorality, which contrasts the return of ethical values and the prosperity their restoration ushered in. "The generations, being fecund with flaws [*culpae*], first pollute marriages, then the race and households; thus, destruction, stemming from this source, flows into the fatherland and its people" (*Carm.* 3.6.17–20).[61] The deterioration of society results from the flaws, or the immoral behaviors, of each generation.[62] Given that marriages (*nuptias*) are corrupted first, Horace has sexual immorality in mind when he refers to the flaws that threaten to overflow and destroy Roman society. Signified by the flooding of the fatherland (*patria*), sexual immorality threatens a social order that represents the fantastic return to an ancestral ideal. Roman anxieties around excessive and unnatural sexuality could diminish the *virtus* of an individual (elite) man, but they also threatened to violate the purity and dominance of Rome's elite *imperium*.

Horace's warning resonates in twenty-first-century fears that same-sex marriage represents a gay pollution of marriage that naturally leads to social degeneration, including incest, bestiality, public sex, and the ruin of civilization. US Supreme Court justice Antonin Scalia's dissent in *Obergefell v. Hodges* (the 2015 decision that legalized same-sex marriage) echoes Horace: "I write separately to call attention to this Court's *threat to American democracy*."[63] He labels the court's opinion "extravagant" and

---

61. For discussions of this passage, see Zanker, *Power of Images*, 156–59; Edwards, *Politics of Immorality*, 45–47; Knust, *Abandoned to Lust*, 40–44.

62. These flaws, *culpa* (often used later for "sin" or "wrongdoing"), refer both to general behaviors that deviated from Roman moral standards, idealized in the *mores maiorum*, and to specifically sexually deviant behaviors, as *culpa* often had sexual implications.

63. Obergefell et al. v. Hodges, Director, OH Dept. of Health, et al., 576 U.S. ____, Scalia, J., dissenting, (2015), slip. op. at 1, emphasis added.

continues, in the footnote read round the world, "The Supreme Court of the United States has *descended* from the disciplined legal reasoning of John Marshall and Joseph Story to the mystical aphorism of the fortune cookie."[64] Scalia's dissent racializes the heteronormative ideal of US sexual exceptionalism, epitomized in its ancestral golden age of Marshall (1801–1835) and Story (1812–1845), through the image of the fortune cookie.[65] As the court descends from the white maleness of Marshall's court, it opens the floodgates of sexual perversions through the lack of reason, a lack that Scalia associates with foreignness. The sexual exceptionalism we see today has ancient roots.

Returning to these roots, the imperial masculinity of Rome's sexually exceptional *virtus* worked in tandem with its emphasis on protecting *pudor*, "modesty" or "a sense of shame." Where *virtus* emphasized male dominance that needed to be established and constantly maintained, *pudor* represented this purity and guarded against the excess that a *vir* must moderate and control.[66] *Pudor* forms the root of the Roman ideal of *pudicitia* ("sexual inviolability" or "chastity").[67] *Pudicitia* idealized "the

---

64. 576 U.S. ____, Scalia, J., dissenting, (2015), at 7–8, emphasis added. This particular quotation was lifted into numerous articles about his dissent, as well as in compendiums of his most pithy statements following his death.

65. The years indicate when each justice sat on the US Supreme Court.

66. Horace lauds Augustus's exceptional return to these *mores*: *iam Fides et Pax et Honor Pudorque / priscus et neglecta redire Virtus / audet, apparetque beata pleno / copia cornu* ("Now Loyalty/Trust, Peace, Honor and ancient Modesty, and neglected Virtue dare to return, and prosperous abundance, with a full horn, appears" [*Saec.* 56–60]). Horace's celebration proclaims that the new imperial regime has ushered in agricultural, economic, political, and social prosperity; however, it further implies that this prosperity is dependent upon the empire's ability to maintain the standards of these values. See also Edwards, *Politics of Immorality*, 58–59.

67. On *pudor*'s relationship to shame and the gendered body in Rome, see Carlin A. Barton, "The Roman Blush: The Delicate Matter of Self-Control," in *Constructions of the Classical Body*, ed. James I. Porter (Ann Arbor: University of Michigan Press, 1999), 212–34. For a detailed overview of *pudor*'s political import and relation to sexuality, see Rebecca Langlands, *Sexual Morality in Ancient Rome* (Cambridge: Cambridge University Press, 2006), 17–29. Williams discusses this at length in relation to the Roman charge of *stuprum*. With compelling evidence, Williams argues that Roman charges of *stuprum* were not exclusively or primarily brought against those who committed homosexual sexual acts (specifically pederastic acts, which were really only a small subset included under the charge) but that *stuprum* was instead a broader charge brought against men who violated another freeborn's *pudicitia* (or

inviolability of the Roman bloodline."[68] *Pudicitia* was easily lost, especially by taking the passive/penetrated role in intercourse (for men) or by being penetrated by anyone who is not one's lawful husband (for women).[69] Those accused of *stuprum*, said to have lost their *pudicitia*, were unfit for political office or social acceptance, according to the arguments of those making the accusations.[70] In line with Roman ethical *mores*, sexuality was primarily concerned with the maintenance of Rome's elite class. Roman morality ensured that those with sociopolitical control or influence were those who were unable to lose their *pudicitia* and, more generally, their modesty or honor (*pudor*).

Sexual pleasures denote a particular site of anxiety for elite Romans who feared social and political decline.[71] Unlike the overt danger posed by Rome's barbarian enemies in battle, sexuality represented a more subtle and dangerous threat that could penetrate the borders of Rome's elite and, by extension, its *imperium*. Preserving *pudor* was crucial to preventing a downward spiral that constantly threatened imperial dominion. As seen in Horace's ode (and echoed in the spirals of Rom 1:18–32), socio-sexual-political deterioration spreads from marriages to the household and the

---

against the person who "allowed" their *pudicitia* to be violated) (Williams, *Roman Homosexuality*, 103–6).

68. Williams, *Roman Homosexuality*, 104. Williams emphasizes that *pudicitia* is "the province of the free" (107) and is the central concern of *stuprum* as a charge. See pp. 104–9.

69. Williams's discussion of *pudicitia* portrays it as a quality that can be lost by both men and women as described above; however, it is possible to infer from his presentation that perhaps *pudicitia* is a quality possessed only by men. Williams argues that when a woman commits adultery, she loses her *pudicitia*, but his evidence implies that the crime of adultery is largely a crime against the husband—implying that his *pudicitia* is potentially lost through his inability to control his unfaithful spouse (Williams, *Roman Homosexuality*, 109–25). Thus, as Edwards summarizes, "It is impossible to disentangle suggestions that a man's wife was unfaithful from attempts to suggest that he was politically or socially weak" (Edwards, *Politics of Immorality*, 57). See further Langlands, *Sexual Morality*, 29–32; Knust, *Abandoned to Lust*, 37–47.

70. Williams, *Roman Homosexuality*, 110–16; Knust, *Abandoned to Lust*, 25–50.

71. Edwards, *Politics of Immorality*, 195. These anxieties and their particular emphasis on sexuality emphasize the ways in which sexuality was (and still is) burdened with an "excess of significance," as Gayle Rubin diagnoses. See Gayle S. Rubin, "Thinking Sex: Notes for a Radical Theory of the Politics of Sexuality," in *Deviations: A Gayle Rubin Reader*, JHFCB (Durham, NC: Duke University Press, 2011), 149.

entire race (*genus*).[72] As one immoral behavior often accompanies another, sexual immorality was an inseparable piece of the Roman moral jigsaw.[73] Rome's sexual exceptionalism exhibits particular anxiety around marriage, a characteristic we also see in US sexual exceptionalism (including in Scalia's dissent). In 18 BCE, Augustus enacted the *lex Iulia*, legislation that regulated various sexual arrangements, most famously marriage but also *stuprum* and adultery.[74] These laws primarily regulated the sexual

---

72. While these anxieties around sexuality heavily influenced the renewed *mores*, the "flaws" that elite Roman authors perceived included more than just sexual immorality. So, in Roman morality, it was assumed that the most moral elite could control their urges for pleasures (sexual especially, but also in other realms, such as food or drink) (Edwards, *Politics of Immorality*, 57). Stephen D. Moore and Janice Capel Anderson note, "Mastery—of others and/or self—is the definitive masculine trait in most Greek and Latin literary texts that survive from antiquity." See Stephen D. Moore and Janice Capel Anderson, "Taking It Like a Man: Masculinity in 4 Maccabees," *JBL* 117 (1998): 250. They discuss the relation of manliness and ἐγκράτεια especially on pp. 258–59. See also Knust, *Abandoned to Lust*, 37–39; Stanley K. Stowers, *A Rereading of Romans: Justice, Jews, and Gentiles* (New Haven: Yale University Press, 1994), 42–82.

73. Recalling Morgan, *Popular Morality*, 184 (quoted above). See also Edwards, *Politics of Immorality*, 4.

74. Though both the laws on marriage and adultery bear the name of Augustus's daughter Julia, the laws were separate texts: the *Lex Julia de maritandis ordinibus* and the *Lex Julia de adulteriis*. The laws were introduced relatively contemporaneously, around 18 BCE. See Susan Treggiari, *Roman Marriage: Iusti Coniuges from the Time of Cicero to the Time of Ulpian* (Oxford: Clarendon, 1991), 60–61, 277–78. The latter set of laws (variously titled in sources, but generally called the *Lex Julia de adulteriis*) stipulated permissible punishments, often harsh, for acts of adultery and *stuprum*. This included punishments for the general acts, included under the label *stuprum*, specific discussions of punishments for adulterers (typically women who cheated on their husbands and the men with whom the affair was conducted), and provisions to punish husbands who caught their wives in an affair and did not prosecute them (this charge was called *lenocinium*, "procuring" or "pandering") (Treggiari, *Roman Marriage*, 277–90). See also discussions in Edwards, *Politics of Immorality*, 34–62; Williams, *Roman Homosexuality*, 130–36 (see further his second appendix, "Marriage between Males," 279–86); Amy Richlin, *Arguments with Silence: Writing the History of Roman Women* (Ann Arbor: University of Michigan Press, 2014), 36–61 (this chapter of Richlin's collection of her own essays updates her original publication, much earlier in her career, under the same title: "Approaches to the Sources on Adultery in Rome," *Women's Studies* 8 [1981]: 225–50); Jane F. Gardner, *Being a Roman Citizen* (London: Routledge, 1993); Brooten, *Love between Women*, 42; Marilyn B. Skinner, *Sexuality in Greek and Roman Culture*, 2nd ed. (Malden, MA: Wiley Blackwell, 2014), 318–20; Knust, *Abandoned to Lust*, 39–41. The most comprehensive ancient source on these

behaviors of free citizens of all genders. They reiterated proper Roman sexual values and established them as essential to Rome's stability.[75] It was assumed that if an elite married woman had an affair (especially with someone of lower status or non-Roman), then her husband also lacked the virtue (as well as virility) and self-control characteristic of men of high status and political influence.[76] Through these laws, Augustus made the regulation of (citizens') sexual behavior a prerogative of the state, just as it regulated more overtly political crimes, such as treason.[77]

The regulation of *stuprum* went hand in hand with Augustan legislation on marriage, seamlessly arranging sexual ethics to maintain kyriarchy.[78] Roman citizens were expected to marry other citizens, and when mixed marriages occur, the status of the parties and their offspring are discussed heavily, to sometimes different conclusions.[79] Status, particularly that of being free, was critical to marriage and to citizenship: "Freedom and citizenship were intertwined" to the point that if one lost one's status as free

---

marriage laws is their quotation by Ulpian (second/third century CE); see also the compilation of ancient sources discussing issues surrounding women and marriage in Judith Evans Grubbs, *Women and the Law in the Roman Empire: A Sourcebook on Marriage, Divorce, and Widowhood* (London: Routledge, 2002), 81–218.

75. Treggiari, *Roman Marriage*, 60–61; see elaboration of its legal details pp. 61–77.

76. Edwards, *Politics of Immorality*, 57. Furthermore and more broadly, she notes, "Female sexuality was a potent danger for Roman moralists because it might disrupt status distinctions" (Edwards, *Politics of Immorality*, 53, 42–47).

77. "The law against adultery bore a disconcerting resemblance to that against treason—and adultery itself took on a much more intimate association with political subversion" (Edwards, *Politics of Immorality*, 61). In the nascent and often fragile political climate of establishing imperial control, these laws enforced a "politics of distraction," addressing growing anxieties around sexual boundaries through stricter regulation and thereby confirming the need for greater imperial control. See Mary Rose D'Angelo, "εὐσέβεια: Roman Imperial Family Values and the Sexual Politics of 4 Maccabees and the Pastorals," *BibInt* 11 (2003): 142.

78. The *Lex Julia de maritandis* (18 B.C.E.) and the *Lex Papia Poppaea* (9 CE) regulated marriages in the Augustan empire. The *Lex Papia* appear to have been introduced in 9 CE following the ineffectiveness of the policies of the *Lex Julia*, loosening some of the more stringent regulations. However, the parts of these laws with the most effect carry through under Augustus and are confirmed by his successors. Unless specified otherwise, I simply refer to the "Augustan marriage laws" to mean the effects and regulations imposed by both sets of laws. For more details on the two specific codes, their stipulations, and effects, see Treggiari, *Roman Marriage*, 60–80.

79. Treggiari, *Roman Marriage*, 44, see further 43–51.

(most commonly a result of being taken captive in war), it meant being stripped of citizenship and its privileges, which included the nullification of marriage.[80]

An important stipulation of Augustus's marriage laws incentivized childbearing and rearing, and these stipulations were reinforced most often in the reigns of successive emperors, including both Tiberius and Claudius.[81] They created incentives, both political and financial, for having a greater number of children, in particular children who reached adulthood.[82] The laws penalized persons who reached old age without having any children, and these penalties were strengthened under successive regimes.[83] These regulations had notable effects in the Roman provinces (where the pool of native citizens was limited): intermarriages between Romans and ethnic others were penalized and discouraged.[84] The main

---

80. Treggiari, *Roman Marriage*, 44. Indeed, the rhetoric of these laws and the anxieties they addressed overshadow the fact that most evidence attests that they affected few changes in practice. See Treggiari, *Roman Marriage*, 77–80; Mary Rose D'Angelo, "Gender and Geopolitics in the Work of Philo of Alexandria: Jewish Piety and Imperial Family Values," in *Mapping Gender in Ancient Religious Discourses*, ed. Todd C. Penner and Caroline Vander Stichele, BibInt 84 (Leiden: Brill, 2007), 66–70.

81. D'Angelo, "Gender and Geopolitics," 77–79. She also notes later refinements under Trajan and Hadrian, attesting to the duration of these laws.

82. For example, the laws stipulated better inheritance provisions for both women and men who had raised a sufficient number of children, ideally to adulthood, and, for the holding of certain political offices (such as senior consul), they made the number of children a candidate had a determining factor for selection, outranking age/seniority as the primary determinant (D'Angelo, "Gender and Geopolitics," 66–75).

83. D'Angelo, "Gender and Geopolitics," 78–79.

84. D'Angelo, "Gender and Geopolitics," 70. On pp. 61–66, she observes that, in terms of the marriage prohibitions, the military was most strictly regulated (soldiers could not marry), and senators and their progeny had specific regulations imposed upon them in terms of not being able to marry from lower classes of free citizens (freedpersons and actors, in particular). Treggiari suggests several plausible reasons for the restriction on soldiers, though none can be confirmed. These include a shortage of eligible women, a preference to keep women in Rome and away from the borders where wars were fought, or a desire to maintain better discipline through military chastity. This final reason, though it cannot be confirmed, does make sense in light of Tacitus's discussion of Roman military discipline in contrast to the revelry of German barbarians (Treggiari, *Roman Marriage*, 63–64). On this, see later discussion in this chapter and in Nancy Shumate, *Nation, Empire, Decline: Studies in Rhetorical Continuity from the Romans to the Modern Era*, Classical Interfaces (London: Duckworth, 2006), 81–127.

emphasis of these childrearing laws was to promote the promulgation of elite citizens by elite citizens since these rewards and penalties had the greatest (if not exclusive) impact upon the most wealthy or those seeking political office and authority.

As it claimed the restoration of the ethical values of *pudor* and *virtus*, Roman propaganda and legislation established a sexually exceptional elite citizenry at the top of its kyriarchy. Roman moral discourse affectively produced a fear of moral degeneration whose cause moves and meshes in between threats of unnatural sex and foreign bloodlines. Sexual exceptionalism relies on blurring anxieties about sexual degeneration and foreign threats, from Horace and Scalia to the *lex Julia* (and their continuations beyond Augustus) and US immigration policies that scrutinize marriages between citizens and not-yet-citizens and have traditionally prioritized family reunification.[85] From the side of those who rule, sexual exceptionalism enforces clear boundaries between the excellent moral citizen and the immorally threatening Other.

Rome's Sexual Exceptionalism for Jews and Other ἔθνη

The boundaries policed under sexual exceptionalism are porous. We just saw how sexual exceptionalism (in Rome and the United States) bolsters the state's power and control by using sexual morality to justify its rule as exceptional. Now, we consider the flip side: how does sexual exceptionalism permit certain marginalized groups to become sexual exceptions to the general rule that declares them morally unfit?

Although for conservatives (like Scalia) gay marriage still represents a threat to US democracy, the nation's legalization and acceptance of gay marriage signals an exception that permits crossing its heteronormative borders. Via homonormativity, same-sex couples conform to the socio-sexual-political norms of marriage in order to be fully included in the rights of US citizenship. Marriage molds homonormative couples into moral citizens, as Anthony Kennedy emphasized in the majority opinion to *Obergefell v. Hodges*. "Far from seeking to devalue marriage, the petitioners seek it for themselves because of *their respect—and need—for*

---

85. On US immigration politics, family reunification, and homonationalism, see Puar, *Terrorist Assemblages*, 29. The Trump administration's limitations that tightened restrictions on legal immigration made immigration based on family reunification more difficult.

its privileges and responsibilities. And *their immutable nature* dictates that same-sex marriage is their only real path to this profound commitment."[86] This sexual exceptionalism renders marriage a marker of respectable, praiseworthy citizenship, especially for same-sex couples whose homonormativity proves their profound respect for the institution—and, by extension, the nation. Kennedy's invocation of "immutable nature" marks a moral distinction between married gays and unwed queers. Thus, the court renders an exception to the sexual rule.

Same-sex couples can exploit this exception and laud it as a route to national justice. Certain LGBTIA2Q+ citizens rely on their homonormativity to emphasize their natural inclination toward marriage, implicitly casting those who do not marry as queers worthy of suspicion. This can be seen in the respectability of the plaintiffs in *Obergefell v. Hodges* (all longtime monogamous couples, many with children, and one a veteran) as well as requests for respectable dress during Pride celebrations (more clothes, less kink—usually with appeals to the presence of families with children). As detailed in chapter 1, the court's decriminalization of sodomy in *Lawrence-Garner* established a "right to privacy" that tasks patriotic citizens with the policing of intimacy.[87] Now via sexual exceptionalism, LGBTIA2Q+ folks prioritize and mandate homonormative intimacy as the primary strategy for rights and inclusion: self-regulation of sexuality. Although national heteronormativity continually deems queerness unfit, homonormative gays present themselves as the sexual exceptions to queerness.

Roman sexual exceptionalism provides a similar route. Despite being deemed worthy of suspicion, via Romanormativity, certain "queer" subjects could mold their *mores* to present themselves as worthy of inclusion under imperial justice. Although the Augustan legislation on both marriage and adultery/*stuprum* primarily regulated the permissible sexual activities of elite citizens with authority, their ethical ideals were disseminated across the empire and were known beyond those most directly addressed.[88] Imperial laws, such as its marriage legislation, were tools

---

86. *Obergefell*, 576 U.S. ____ (2015), slip. op. at 4, emphasis added.

87. See pp. 61–65; Puar, *Terrorist Assemblages*, 114–38.

88. From the eyes of the state, so long as those of lower status (especially non-Roman ἔθνη) did not violate elite *pudicitia*, their sexual practices were irrelevant as they had never possessed much (if any) *pudicitia*. In other words, these regulations primarily concern those who have *pudicitia* to lose—that is, elite citizens—and thus

of political propaganda as much as a means of setting ethical standards. The communication of these values across the empire instills Roman elite *mores* within others across the empire's ἔθνη. If the elite can gain position and prosperity through their ethical actions, then such behavior may prove equally beneficial to others of lower status, proving their ability to live elite-style lives. Fantasies of upward mobility, even though unattainable, can be motivational (what Berlant called "aspirational normativity"). Via proper sexual behavior, one can prove to be the ethnic exception under imperial rule: the flip side of sexual exceptionalism.[89]

The queerness away from which sexual exceptionalism distinguishes is racialized. Homonormative couples seeking marriage are usually imagined as white men: marriage is part of the package of rights inherently presumed to belong to whiteness, just as *Lawrence-Garner's* rendering of a "right to privacy" presumes that one has access to private property

---

preserve a particular elite, ruling class who have neither lost their honor nor mixed it with someone less honorable. Compare, then, the intention of this legislation and its portrayal in propaganda (securing the political stability of Augustus and his regime) to Puar's discussion of media imagery after September 11 and the start of the war on terror to promote American democracy. "From the images of grieving white widows of corporate executives to the concern about white firemen leaving their families to console widows of former coworkers to the consolidation of national families petitioning for bereavement funds to more recent images of broken military homes, the preservation of white heteronormative families has been at stake" (Puar, *Terrorist Assemblages*, 40–41). Likewise, with the Augustan legislation and its propaganda, the preservation of a distinct Roman elite class, who rules alongside the imperial regime, was at stake for the new emperor and his successors.

89. This exceptionalism is already at work in elite narratives where certain lower-class bodies (especially enslaved persons) prove Roman enough (through good, often servile, behavior) to achieve freedom and inclusion among the elite. "Nevertheless," writes Knust, "slaves and freedmen could be 'upwardly mobile,' and an *exceptional* former slave could become a well-known philosopher [i.e., Epictetus]. The fact that such anomalies could occur demonstrates that these categories were not impermeable but were, in fact always dangerously subject to renegotiation" (Knust, *Abandoned to Lust*, 27–28). In my reading, these narratives perpetuate the *possibility of upward mobility* for enslaved persons and others of low status. Indeed, such exceptional examples are usually crafted in the imagination of a more elite author. P. R. C. Weaver discusses in more detail the potentials of upward mobility for slaves and freedpersons and admits the number of enslaved persons who rose upward in status is low compared to the total number of enslaved persons in Rome. See P. R. C. Weaver, "Social Mobility in the Early Roman Empire: The Evidence of Imperial Freedmen and Slaves," *Past and Present* 37 (1967): 3–20.

and that police will not ignore one's right to privacy within it.[90] Sexual deviancy is frequently affixed onto racialized subjects who are rendered queer even as they are presumed straight via homonormativity's regulatory white queerness. In using sexuality to further mark certain gendered, racialized, and classed bodies as threats to US sovereignty, national norms are produced that allow certain of these other bodies to partially or temporarily blend with the norm, thus creating a fiction of social belonging. "Sexual deviancy," explains Puar, "is linked to the process of discerning, othering, and quarantining terrorist bodies, but these racially and sexually perverse figures also labor in the service of disciplining and normalizing *subjects worthy of rehabilitation away from* these bodies, in other words, signaling and enforcing the mandatory terms of patriotism."[91]

A similar deployment of deviancy occurs in Roman discourse. Nancy Shumate has demonstrated how elite Roman literature created the idea of a "composite other," a figure that differed from the elite ideals with respect to race, gender, and sexuality. Analyzing Juvenal's *Satires*, she observes that constructing a "national identity" is achieved negatively, making clear that Roman citizens are distinguished from the deviant and unnatural actions of others. Gender and sexuality play a critical role in this process, taking the form of charges of effeminacy, adultery, or sexual passivity, in order to establish the elite male citizen as the norm over and against these others who practice such unnatural or deviant acts.[92] Shumate observes, "The construction of an enemy of Romanness that he [Juvenal's speaker] so desperately needs to rationalize his own failures hinges on an articulation of the categories of ethnicity, gender, and class that renders all 'outsid-

---

90. On the ways that sodomy and privacy are racialized, see Puar, *Terrorist Assemblages*, 130–51. David L. Eng discusses these dimensions of *Lawrence-Garner* in the context of what he calls "the racialization of intimacy" and, especially in light of the erasure of Tyrone Garner from the narrative and the desexualization of homosexuality, shows how the decision's basis in a right to privacy and intimacy hinges on notions of "whiteness as property" (as theorized by Cheryl I. Harris). See David L. Eng, *The Feeling of Kinship: Queer Liberalism and the Racialization of Intimacy* (Durham, NC: Duke University Press, 2010), 42–47.

91. Puar, *Terrorist Assemblages*, 38, emphasis added (but "away from" is emphasized in the original).

92. Shumate, *Nation, Empire, Decline*, 19, 21, 61–67. It is important to note that Roman imperialism does not necessarily invent the norms, but it uses them in particular ways that reinforce imperial/elite rule. See also Marchal, "Exceptional Proves Who Rules," 95–99.

ers' essentially the same and functionally interchangeable."[93] The general *mores* surrounding Rome's socio-sexual-political hierarchy depended upon elite constructions of barbarian sexualized others, who, preferring uncontrolled deviancy, were unable or unwilling to practice natural (or, as we might say today, normal) sexual behaviors.[94]

This is sexual exceptionalism: morally excellent Roman citizens are produced via distinction from a racialized queerness. What Puar writes of the modern distinction between terrorist/patriot applies also to the Roman distinction between barbarian/citizen: "Without these discourses of sexuality (and their attendant anxieties) ... the twin mechanisms of normalization and banishment that distinguish the terrorist from the patriot would cease to properly behave."[95] The potential fragility of the Roman Empire and its elite is masked by a myth of sexual exceptionalism.

When taken on by ἔθνη, this sexually exceptional imperial context in Rome echoes how more privileged LGBTIA2Q+ citizens explicitly wed their sexual exceptionalism with the objectives of US nationalism. As Puar argues and the earlier discussion of Buttigieg exemplifies, certain queer subjects (most especially white gay cis men of relative affluence) can align their interests with those of the state, presenting themselves as model sexual citizens (i.e., part of a monogamous, married couple) *and* loyal patriots (i.e., serving in the military and supporting US military interventions; condemning terrorist activities, the homophobic actions of enemy nations, or political activism associated particularly with racial minorities). This is homonationalism, arranging sexual exceptionalism in explicit relation to nation (as empire).[96] Through such alignments, these particularly privileged others demonstrate their worthiness of rehabilitation and upward mobility: justice as enjoying every privilege of citizenship—the good life.

Upwardly mobile and homonational ethical positioning, via submission to Roman elite values, can be seen in sources from ἔθνη in the Roman Empire, including several Jewish sources roughly contemporary with Paul's letters.[97] Regulations of sexual activity and their promotion of

---

93. Shumate, *Nation, Empire, Decline*, 20.
94. Marchal, "Exceptional Proves Who Rules," 96–99.
95. Puar, *Terrorist Assemblages*, 37.
96. Puar, *Terrorist Assemblages*, 38–39.
97. Although here I focus on Jewish authors, these strategies were also used by

family values were known in Roman provinces with Jewish inhabitants (Judea and Egypt, in particular).[98] These sources elaborate the connections between Roman values and Jewish Scripture—connections we saw Paul make above in Rom 13:8–10—and detail a sexual exceptionalism within Jewish values that dissociates from racialized queerness in ways that align and appeal to Roman imperialism and its virtues.

One example is the Maccabean literature, especially 4 Maccabees. Although the Maccabean story embodies a revolutionary ethos that seems to contradict submission to Rome, the text's hope for Jewish autonomy is a hope that, like Paul in Rom 1–5, invests in self-rule that is Roman without Rome. Jewish heroes embody a *virtus* that is Roman, and they behave in sexually chaste and self-controlled ways that are emblematic of elite status. The presentation and regulation of gender in 4 Maccabees emphasizes *virtus* and sexual *pudicitia*. As Mary Rose D'Angelo demonstrates, the manly role of the mother in 4 Maccabees is established in her lengthy encomiums and especially her closing speech in 18:7–19, in which she emphasizes her chastity and fidelity to her (absent) husband.[99] This emphasis "echoes the twin Roman concerns expressed in the Julian laws as well as numerous literary texts: control of female sexuality against adultery and *stuprum* (*lex iulia de adulteriis*) and requirement of marriage and remarriage for those of an age

---

Greek authors under Roman rule to align Greek and Roman ethics. See Hoke, "Be Even Better Subjects," 96–97, for my analysis of Dionysus of Halicarnassus's use of περισσεύω through the lens of sexual exceptionalism and homonationalism.

98. See both D'Angelo, "Gender and Geopolitics," and D'Angelo, "εὐσέβεια."

99. D'Angelo draws attention to how 4 Maccabees differs from the earlier (preimperial) 2 Maccabees by giving the mother a prominent role and emphasizing her chastity to this husband who does not receive mention in the earlier versions of the story (D'Angelo, "εὐσέβεια," 155–57, see further 147–57). Moore and Anderson also emphasize the ways in which 4 Maccabees relies upon Greco-Roman virtues, particularly in terms of mastery and definitions of true manliness (Moore and Anderson, "Taking It Like a Man," 256). Elliott, dating 4 Maccabees much earlier than D'Angelo (to 38–41 CE, making it contemporary with the events described in Philo's *Legatio ad Gaium*, to which he compares 4 Maccabees), situates the text—alongside Paul—as anti-imperial and particularly opposing the policies of Caligula (Elliott, *Arrogance of Nations*, 148–49). While the earlier dating of 4 Maccabees is possible (D'Angelo, "εὐσέβεια," 140 n. 3, observes that proposals range from the reign of Tiberius into the third century CE), D'Angelo's argument (along with others') of an early second-century composition seems more likely.

to produce children (*lex iulia de mantandis ordinibus*)."[100] The mother serves as an ideal standard in both Jewish and Roman terms.[101] Never explicitly opposing Rome, 4 Maccabees adapts Roman values into its Jewish narrative.[102] Their revolt stands up against the tyrannical foreign rule of Rome's former rivals. The text's hope for autonomy can be simultaneously invested in presenting virtuous subjects who are worthy of rehabilitation in a world under Roman rule.

Philo offers an especially pertinent example of an author who frames ethnic values alongside Roman elite ideals. His *Legatio ad Gaium* was concerned with making sure that Roman authorities protected Jewish interests, especially for elite Jews in Alexandria.[103] Philo's negative depiction of Caligula in the *Legatio ad Gaium* is not anti-Rome, because it was penned in light of widespread disdain for Caligula in preference for Claudius: one bad emperor (an exception) does not mean Roman imperialism itself is flawed.[104] Philo can argue, as Maren Niehoff summarizes, "The excep-

---

100. D'Angelo, "εὐσέβεια," 156. Moore and Anderson argue that the mother is portrayed as a masculine figure, representing the ideal embodiment of manly virtues, especially self-mastery. Along similar lines as D'Angelo, however, they note that, particularly in the final speech, she is ultimately feminized in the narrative (Moore and Anderson, "Taking It Like a Man," 271–72).

101. Moore and Anderson, taking the position that 4 Maccabees is written to an audience needing an alternative to gentile domination, note the issue of its alignment with Hellenistic/Roman values. "Victory is achieved in 4 Maccabees only by accepting and reaffirming the dominant hierarchical continuum along which ruler and ruled, master and slave, male and female were positioned" (Moore and Anderson, "Taking It Like a Man," 272). Brent D. Shaw shows how 4 Maccabees, along with contemporary Roman and early Christian texts, develops ὑπομονή ("endurance" or "patience") as a value/virtue that embodies ideas of manliness (ἀνδρεία) as active self-control (despite the lack of control martyrs have over their own physical bodies). See Brent D. Shaw, "Body/Power/Identity: Passions of the Martyrs," *JECS* 4 (1996): 269–312, esp. 278–80. See also discussion in Moore, *God's Beauty Parlor: And Other Queer Spaces in and around the Bible*, Contraversions (Stanford: Stanford University Press, 2001), 191–96, where Moore compares 4 Maccabees to Revelation around issues of the construction of masculinity.

102. See also Stowers, *Rereading of Romans*, 60–62, who argues that 4 Maccabees (along with Philo and Paul) presents Jewish law (especially the tenth commandment) as presenting an ethic of self-mastery equivalent to Greco-Roman ἐγκράτεια.

103. Though *Legatio ad Gaium* narrates the presentation of Jewish concerns and values to the Roman authorities, the text was most likely addressed to this Jewish audience (Niehoff, *Philo on Jewish Identity*, 39–42).

104. Niehoff, *Philo on Jewish Identity*, 88. Niehoff then observes, noting that the senate after Caligula was hesitant about continuing imperial rule, "Claudius argued

tional cases of Flaccus and Gaius thus prove the rule: true Romans are beneficent and friendly towards the Jews. They bring peace and civilization to all regions of the empire and are to a high degree congenial to the Jews."[105] The idea of the Romans as bearers of peace and civilization was a crucial part of the propaganda of conquest under Augustus and his successors. Philo's repetition of it demonstrates his own immersion in Roman ideology in addition to his willingness to conform to it in order to better position himself and his community.

Philo's pro-Roman stance, which he is attempting to convince his compatriots to embrace, bears evidence for the ways in which Roman propaganda and its moral exceptionalism could be absorbed by various ethnic others (in this case, elite Jews). "Rome had created a common cultural framework for the whole empire," Niehoff explains. "This unified the different regions and enabled Philo to consider himself, as well as other members of the Eastern elites, as serious partners in a far-reaching and beneficial project of government."[106] Philo's politics show not only that he desired that he (and his Jewish audience) be perceived as model Roman subjects but also that he believed in the imperial promises of peace and prosperity for these subjects. These promises demanded that they adhere to the moral standards of the elite authorities, that is, prove worthy of rehabilitation.

According to Philo, adhering to these moral standards should be no problem for upright Jews, because Jewish morality matches—indeed, exceeds—the standards of Roman ethics. "Philo's construction of Jewish values positioned the Jews within a distinctly contemporary and Roman discourse," observes Niehoff. "Ethnic boundaries were thus shaped and reinforced by a sense that the Jews are congenial and in certain respects superior to the leading nation of the whole *oikoumene*."[107] Philo's descriptions of Jewish law promote the idea that the law requires Jews to live under

---

that only Gaius, and not the imperial system *per se*, must be blamed for the suffering in Rome. The result was a devastating image of his predecessor" (88). In showing how Philo's negative opinion of Caligula conforms with similar Roman rhetoric (particularly that of Seneca), Niehoff notes that Philo's negative statements about Caligula, his hubris and desire to be deified, and his harsh manias often do not entirely match his firsthand accounts of the events of his own embassy (86–93). This confirms that Philo's presentation of Caligula is itself crafted for particular political goals.

105. Niehoff, *Philo on Jewish Identity*, 136.
106. Niehoff, *Philo on Jewish Identity*, 116.
107. Niehoff, *Philo on Jewish Identity*, 76.

the standards of highest virtue (τὴν ἄκραν ἀρετήν).[108] This virtue is fairly Roman. As with his opinions of Roman emperors, Philo's interpretation of Jewish law presents it in conformity with the construction of Roman elite moral standards.

Niehoff's analysis shows how the Roman value of ἐγκράτεια, the self-control critical to maintaining *pudor/pudicitia*, is central to Philo's interpretation of Jewish law, in particular those regarding holidays, food, and—most importantly—sexual relations.[109] Speaking specifically of those who commit adultery, Philo writes, "Such persons must be punished with death as the common enemies of the whole human race, that they may not live to ruin more houses with immunity and be the tutors of others who make it their business to emulate the wickedness of their ways" (*Spec.* 3:11). Philo's condemnation of adultery speaks to the dangers of sexuality that lacks self-control. This passage recalls Horace's description of moral decline and lack of self-control under the late republic. Like with Horace, Philo sees the disease of adultery spreading to infect others, ruining houses, and potentially the whole human race.[110]

While Philo and Roman moralists share disdain for adultery, Philo's ideal of sexual ἐγκράτεια proves much more stringent than that of the Roman elite ideal. Philo ultimately approves of sexual pleasure only if it leads to procreation.[111] Any other sexual act he deems prohibited and unnatural. Even if Philo's ideal for proper sexual behavior is more stringent, this ideal is still framed in the terms that regulated proper Roman sexual behavior. Jewish self-control is equivalent to Roman self-control.[112] To fit into the norm, marginalized subjects must be exceptionally excel-

---

108. In *Spec.* 4, he asserts that these exceptional laws (νόμοι ἐξαίρετοι) of the Jews "are revered out of necessity, seeing that they train the highest virtue" [σεμνοὶ δ' εἰσὶν ἐξ ἀνάγκης, ἅτε πρὸς τὴν ἄκραν ἀρετὴν ἀλείφοντες] (*Spec.* 4.179).

109. Niehoff, *Philo on Jewish Identity*, 94–110. Philo appeals especially to the sixth commandment, which forbids adultery.

110. Niehoff, *Philo on Jewish Identity*, 96.

111. "The Jews, Philo implies, are masters in the art of *aphrodisia*. Striking the right balance, they direct the sexual impulse to a noble purpose" (Niehoff, *Philo on Jewish Identity*, 102, see further 100–102).

112. A comparison can be made here between Philo's presentation of Jewish law and Paul's in terms of the "different law" in Rom 13:8 (discussed above). Note that, to my knowledge, no one has argued that Philo's strengthening of Roman sexual morality represents an implicit imperial critique and positions Philo as anti-Rome (as interpreters do with Paul and Rom 13).

lent; they cannot afford any exceptions. The superiority is not an attempt to subtly critique or overthrow Rome's ruling morality. It is an admission that sexual exceptionalism demands that a rigid Romanormativity appears *even better* than Romosexuality.

The standard of self-control, which also governed Roman conversations of pleasure (sexual, culinary, or otherwise), communicates to elite Jews both proper ethical behavior and the ways in which such behavior helps them present themselves to the Roman elite. Philo's ethics seek to elevate his community's status as they navigate the hierarchies of the Roman Empire and attempt to land on top.[113]

Philo's presentation of Jewish values resonates with the tactics of homonationalism, especially when Philo's distinguishes Jews from other ἔθνη in the empire, especially Egyptians.[114] Philo not only aligned the principles of Jewish law with Roman ethics but also attempted to position Jews as equal to Romans on the social hierarchy by proving them to be more Roman than other ethnic groups.[115] Niehoff argues that, relying on Roman stereotypes and disdain for Egyptians (among whom, of course, the Alexandrian Jews lived), Philo emphasized the otherness of Egyptian politics and values. This sharpens the binary that divided Roman from Egyptian. At the same time that Philo emphasizes Jewish loyalty to the empire and its respect and reverence for its good authorities (i.e., Augustus, Claudius), he mentions the ways in which the Egyptians have less loyalty and that their influence can be seen upon bad emperors, like Caligula. "The acute discrepancy between Egyptian and Roman reactions to Gaius's aspirations provides the first indication that Philo aligned the Jews

---

113. Thus, Niehoff observes, "Philo implied that this definition of Jewish identity was similar to that of the Romans"; and further, "Jewish identity was thus defined in both positive and negative terms, setting the Jews apart as well as playing them among the elite of world civilization" (Niehoff, *Philo on Jewish Identity*, 75). Similarly, Stowers shows how Philo emphasizes this self-mastery in his presentation of Jewish law as a means "to sell the advantages of the Jewish politeia to gentiles on that basis" (Stowers, *Rereading of Romans*, 64). For Philo, again, "the Jewish law is superior because it produces self-mastery" (Stowers, *Rereading of Romans*, 59, see further 58–65).

114. Egypt was famously conquered by Augustus after defeating the forces of Cleopatra and Antony in 30 BCE.

115. See especially Niehoff's third chapter in *Philo on Jewish Identity*, 75–110 ("Jewish Values: Religion and Self-Restraint"); the chapter establishes "the values if the Jews thus emerge as superior to those of other nations and place them at the top of a distinctly masculine Western civilization" (Niehoff, *Philo on Jewish Identity*, 110).

with the Romans. These two nations once more found themselves on the same side of a basic divide."[116]

Philo stresses the *sexual* otherness of Egyptians, as well as other ἔθνη such as Greeks and Persians. While stressing the stringent sexual morals and self-control of the Jews, Philo contrasts this self-control with Roman stereotypes of Egyptian sexual perversity and the prejudices Romans had toward the sexual license found in Greek thought. Philo's alignment relies on the binary between barbarian/citizen discussed above, where one is either morally and sexually self-controlled or one is depraved, deviant, and ultimately penetrable. Like the racialized terrorist of US homonationalism, Philo's Egyptians (and Greeks) become simultaneously the ethnic and sexual other, reifying the terms of the citizen/barbarian binary.[117] This makes space to take advantage of the opening for other ἔθνη (such as the diasporic Jew) to prove worthy of citizenship. Philo's tactics are an apt ancient instance of the transference of stigma typical of sexual exceptionalism and homonationalism.[118]

Philo never mentions Romans as he constructs this hierarchy and presents Jewish values as the most elite in terms of virile self-restraint.

---

116. Niehoff, *Philo on Jewish Identity*, 86. In particular, Philo mentions that Caligula's most heinous acts have clear roots in "foreign" Egyptian practices and, indeed, that Egyptians, unlike the Jews and the Romans, were favorable supporters of Caligula.

117. These ethnic distinctions blur into religious stereotypes and prejudice, particularly surrounding the idea that Egyptian religion worships snakes.

118. While Philo's (elite) Jewish community are *not* homosexuals, as members of an ἔθνος subject to Rome (almost doubly so as Jews living in conquered Egypt), they were similarly othered in ways that make them "queer" to Rome's native elite. Therefore, we can compare Philo's strategies in general to Puar's examples of homonationalisms in the wake of September 11 (Puar, *Terrorist Assemblages*, 40–51). In particular, she observes the binary created between the model homosexuality of American hero Mark Bingham in contrast to the fully deranged terrorist Osama bin Laden (couched and portrayed in stereotypical Orientalist terms). "Indeed, exemplary of the transference of stigma, positive attributes were attached to Mark Bingham's homosexuality: butch, masculine, rugby player, white, American, hero, gay patriot, called his mom (i.e., homonational), while negative connotations of homosexuality were used to racialize and sexualize Osama bin Laden: feminized, stateless, dark, perverse, pedophilic, disowned by his family (i.e., fag). What is at stake here is not only that one is good and the other evil: the homosexuality of Bingham is converted into acceptable patriot values, while the evilness of bin Laden is more fully and efficaciously rendered through associations with sexual excess, failed masculinity (i.e., femininity), and faggotry" (Puar, *Terrorist Assemblages*, 46).

However, he identifies Romans as those elites at the top and works to position his Jewish community alongside them, adopting Roman self-control while insisting that the ideal is historically Jewish. This strategy encourages his audience to think of themselves as elite Romans and to prove themselves as moral exceptions, not belonging to the more degenerate values of the Egyptians.

Philo's emphasis on the Romanness of Jewish values better positions himself and his community at the top of the hierarchy. Thus, writes Niehoff, "he constructs a hierarchy ranging from 'barbarian' to civilized nations. The Jews are placed at the top. They represent the elite of the Western world which promotes the value of virile self-restraint."[119] Philo does this by emphasizing the stark difference between the decency of Jewish sexual ethics and the depravity of other non-Roman ethnic groups, distancing his Jewish community from their identity as ἔθνη. "The factioning, fractioning, and fractalizing of identity is a prime activity of societies of control," Puar argues, "whereby subjects (the ethnic, the homonormative) orient themselves as subjects through their disassociation or disidentification from others disenfranchised in similar ways in favor of consolidation with axes of privilege."[120] Philo's disassociation is similar to this homonational deployment that attempts to align itself with the privilege and power of Rome's normative elite.

Homonationalism in Romans 13

Certainly Paul was not Philo, particularly in terms of social status, location, and writing style. However, Philo's alignment of Jewish and Roman moral standards and his acceptance of the imperial hierarchy illuminate ways in which Paul's rhetoric of ethical submission can be interpreted.[121] Like Philo, Paul is writing to an internal audience, and his advice includes concerns about his audience's relation to imperial authority, exhorting submission to it. Both writers utilize strategies of ethical alignment, partic-

---

119. Niehoff, *Philo on Jewish Identity*, 94.
120. Puar, *Terrorist Assemblages*, 28.
121. Stowers agrees (Stowers, *Rereading of Romans*, 56–70). Johnson also appeals to Philo's embassy as an example that provides context to 13:1–7, in particular that Jews of Paul's era often "turned confidently to the emperor for help" (Johnson, *Reading Romans*, 187–88).

ularly regarding sexual *mores*, that can be compared to homonationalism.[122] While the two ancient Jewish writers remain distinct, since neither author knew of the other and their contexts were quite different, their strategies bear striking, if only partial, similarities. Philo's strategies shed light on the ways in which homonationalism appears in Rom 13.

Paul's ethical exhortations in Romans convey an exceptional impulse, opening the space for sexual exceptionalism and homonationalism to appear.[123] Paul's exhortation to submission in 13:1–10 plays a critical role in aligning his theo-christological ethics (and presumably those of his fellow Christ-followers) with the values of the elite authorities who control the imperial state. By submitting to these prevailing authorities and, ultimately, God, Christ-followers act as model, ethical subjects who present themselves as adhering to the same standards as the authorities. Such a presentation, at least ideally, will prove that they are persons capable of comporting themselves as do the elite, thus making them worthy of rehabilitation, deserving to be included among the elite, ruling authorities.[124]

This rehabilitation is prefaced on the promise that exceptional, Roma-normative *mores* result in a praise that is distinct from the suspicion Rome casts on ἔθνη, against whom Rome was more likely to bear the sword (τὴν μάχαιραν φορεῖ). As we saw above, the praise (ἔπαινος) of 13:3 is contrasted from the fear (φόβος) of 13:4, a fear that comes from the threat of this authoritative sword.[125] In Paul's wording, the threat is a promise: Rome

---

122. Puar observes that homonationalism can appear in such different contexts, and even, I argue, across a wide temporal span: "There is no organic unity or cohesion among homonationalisms; these are partial, fragmentary, uneven formations, implicated in the pendular momentum of inclusion and exclusion, some dissipating as quickly as they appear" (Puar, *Terrorist Assemblages*, 10).

123. Looking at Paul's most famous sex passages (Rom 1:26–27; 1 Cor 6:9–10; 1 Thess 4:3–8), Marchal makes a similar assertion about how Paul's arguments correspond with Roman sexual exceptionalism (Marchal, "Exceptional Proves Who Rules," 99–109, esp. 103).

124. With God at the top, Paul *may* ultimately assume that his audience will prove themselves to be *more* worthy of elite status than the current prevailing authorities and that, eventually, they may replace or supplant the present ones. However, Paul does not discuss the submission in these terms; furthermore, even if he envisions a change in control (i.e., Christ-followers being at the top), he does *not* assume a change in regime. His ideal still operates with the assumption that a basic social and ethical hierarchy will remain.

125. Roman discourse associated fear with corporeal punishment, in particular as it was used by enslavers to enforce obedience and submission. "As Micio comments in

does not police "at random" (εἰκῇ). The logic of these verses echoes the privatized policing of intimacy afforded to certain queer subjects in the undercurrents of homonationalism seen in Puar's discussion of *Lawrence-Garner*. Only those *worthy of suspicion* deserve the threat of the sword; those *worthy of rehabilitation* police themselves and prove praiseworthy. Paul offers this as a promise—those who do good need not fear the sword—yet the "not randomness" also implies a threat. Whomever the state considers threatening and other will always be deemed morally suspicious—regardless of their actual actions. Just as policing in the United States is distinctly *not* random, the "not randomness" of the imperial sword allows Rome to specifically target the ἔθνη it wants to render most exceptionally distinct from Romosexuality.

Paul encourages alignment with imperial *mores* in ways that present Christ-followers as citizens and not barbarians. The praise Paul craves represents one of what Puar describes as "affective modes of belonging to the state" as it acknowledges (positive) interest from the state and a willingness to incorporate these persons into the upper echelons of society and power within it.[126] As we will see in this concluding exegesis of Rom 13:11–14, the ethical submission of Rom 13, propelled by Romanormativity and sexual exceptionalism that patriotically expresses imperial loyalty, is a tactic of homonationalism. As Puar emphasizes and Philo's ethnic othering demonstrates, homonationalism depends on a particular

---

Terence's *Adelphoe*, what distinguishes a father (*pater*) from a master (*dominus*) is that sons are taught to do the right thing 'of their own volition' (*sua sponte*) whereas slaves do so out of fear (*metus*)." See Richard P. Saller, *Patriarchy, Property and Death in the Roman Family* (Cambridge: Cambridge University Press, 1994), 144–45. In Latin, *metus* is roughly synonymous with the Greek φόβος. The distinction between children and enslaved persons within the household is moralized through the rhetoric of *pudor*: sons need not fear punishment because they have been imbued with honor and a sense of shame. Enslaved persons were presumed without honor/*pudor* and therefore required the threat of punishment (Saller, *Patriarchy, Property and Death*, 144).

126. Puar, *Terrorist Assemblages*, 26. Puar continues to note that these are "modes that assuage the angst of unrequited love." Extending Sara Ahmed's work on love ("national love"), Puar observes, "For Ahmed, national love is a form of waiting, a lingering that registers a 'stigma of inferiority' that epitomizes the inner workings of multiculturalism. Unrequited love keeps multicultural (and also homonormative) subjects in the folds of nationalism, while xenophobic and homophobic ideologies and policies fester" (26). See further Sara Ahmed, *The Cultural Politics of Emotion*, 2nd ed. (New York: Routledge, 2014), 122–43; pp. 130–31 are cited by Puar.

use of *sexual* exceptionalism with respect to nation/empire. Paul's advice in 13:11–14 depends upon specifically sexualized language and binaries. It is this sexual element of ethical submission that confirms a first-century version of homonationalism in Romans.

In 13:11–14, Paul encourages his audience to remain sexually upright via the terms of Roman sexual *mores*. This segment begins:

καὶ τοῦτο εἰδότες τὸν καιρόν, ὅτι ὥρα ἤδη ὑμᾶς ἐξ ὕπνου ἐγερθῆναι, νῦν γὰρ ἐγγύτερον ἡμῶν ἡ σωτηρία ἢ ὅτε ἐπιστεύσαμεν. ἡ νὺξ προέκοψεν, ἡ δὲ ἡμέρα ἤγγικεν. ἀποθώμεθα οὖν τὰ ἔργα τοῦ σκότους, ἐνδυσώμεθα δὲ τὰ ὅπλα τοῦ φωτός.

So, knowing this is the time, that it is already the hour for you to be raised from sleep. Our salvation is now nearer than when we believed. The night progressed; the day draws near. Therefore, put away the actions of the dark; wear the armor of light. (13:11–12)

These words communicate important ethical and political messages outside of a (potentially) imminent eschaton.[127] The nearing salvation (σωτηρία) carries the rhetoric of imperial conquest, bringing to mind the figure of the emperor (appointed by God) who established and enforced this ethical system and social hierarchy, thus bringing peace and prosperity—salvation—to barbaric ἔθνη.[128] This coming salvation

---

127. Esler challenges this prevailing assumption (see below) that this section is "eschatological" in tone/force: "The imagery of future salvation serves to tell them who they are or should be in the present, not to warn them that the future is near" (Esler, *Conflict and Identity*, 337, see further 335–38). His point is well-taken in light of my own argument about the present meaning of this passage, but I do not necessarily deny the eschatological urgency: I do de-emphasize it for the purposes of my own interpretation, as much has already been said on this topic. See Elliott, *Arrogance of Nations*, 143–50; Fitzmyer, *Romans*, 681–82; Dunn, *Romans*, 2:785–86; Moo, *Epistle to the Romans*, 818; Witherington, *Paul's Letter to the Romans*, 317; Schreiner, *Romans*, 696–97; Johnson, *Reading Romans*, 193–94; Matera, 299; Kirk, *Romans*, 196; Michael Thompson, *Clothed with Christ: The Example and Teaching of Jesus in Romans 12.1–15.13* (Sheffield: JSOT Press, 1991), 141–49.

128. See Dieter Georgi, *Theocracy in Paul's Praxis and Theology* (Minneapolis: Fortress, 1991), 29–30. Helmut Koester emphasizes the political usage of the apocalyptic term παρουσία, used in 1 Thess 4:13–5:11, which does not appear in Romans, but its meaning is connecting to the idea of salvation here. However, he connects the political ideology of Rom 13:11–14 as similar, even more radical, than that of 1 Thessalonians. Koester emphasizes more a resistant Paul who presents a utopian alternative to Roman ideology through his reframing of its terminology. See Helmut Koester,

offers the peace and prosperity of imperial elite subjects to those who submit themselves both to God and to the emperor—meaning those who live ethically submissive lives that conform to imperial *mores*. If this language of salvation is apocalyptic, then what we find is Apocalypse Romanormal.

Paul's ethical encouragement hinges on a binary metaphor of night (νύξ) and day (ἡμέρα) or, alternately, dark (σκότος) and light (φῶς). He places bad behaviors in the night/dark and good behaviors in the day/light. The ἔργα τοῦ σκότους ("actions of the dark") recalls the earlier contrast in 13:3 between a good action (τῷ ἀγαθῷ ἔργῳ) and a bad one (τῷ κακῷ), marking the night as a time for vice and evil (κακός) of all varieties. From a Roman elite mindset, the dark hours of night also appear to be those most prone to vice, when respectable wo/men remained in their homes. Such an assumption can be seen in the defamations of elite women, like Messalina or Julia of the imperial households, who were accused of extreme sexual license, sneaking out of their marital beds to defile themselves (and, by extension, their husbands) as prostitutes or with any man (of obviously lower status) who will satisfy their "insatiable" lust.[129] Paul encourages an awakening from sleep that coincides with night's end and the day's dawn, an ethical placement away from immoral darkness.[130]

"Imperial Ideology and Paul's Eschatology in 1 Thessalonians," in *Paul and Empire: Religion and Power in Roman Imperial Society*, ed. Richard A. Horsley (Harrisburg, PA: Trinity Press International, 1997), 166.

129. Juvenal's description of [Valeria] Messalina, Claudius's wife, notes that she would crawl out of bed as soon as the emperor, her husband, fell asleep, and would go to a brothel (*Sat.* 6.115–132; see even fuller description, 6.114–135). Messalina is often referred to as *meretrix Augustali*, or the "imperial whore." See further Skinner, *Sexuality in Greek and Roman Culture*, 317; Sandra R. Joshel, "Female Desire and the Discourse of Empire: Tacitus' Messlina," in *Roman Sexualities*, ed. Judith P. Hallett and Marilyn B. Skinner (Princeton: Princeton University Press, 1997), 221–54; Jennifer A. Glancy and Stephen D. Moore, "How Typical a Roman Prostitute Is Revelation's 'Great Whore'?," *JBL* 130 (2011): 562–69. Likewise, Julia's (daughter of Augustus) prostitution, ironic in the aftermath of Augustus's legislation, is portrayed as a vice of the evening, though she appears a respectable member of the imperial family by day (Seneca, *Ben.* 6.32.1). See also Edwards, *Politics of Immorality*, 61–62; Edwards, "Unspeakable Professions: Public Performance and Prostitution in Ancient Rome," in *Roman Sexualities*, ed. Judith P. Hallett and Marilyn B. Skinner (Princeton: Princeton University Press, 1997), 89–90.

130. This placement employs a form of another placing verb τίθημι—ἀποτίθημι, "put away."

Paul urges "wearing the armor of light": acting in morally good ways that befit the day.[131] This respectable living (in the day) contrasts with specific vices, several sexual, which Paul names in the second half of the following clause: μὴ κώμοις καὶ μέθαις, μὴ κοίταις καὶ ἀσελγείαις, μὴ ἔριδι καὶ ζήλῳ· ("not in revelry and drunkenness, nor in sexual pursuits and licentiousness, nor in rivalry and jealousy" [13:13b]).[132] Paul identifies specific examples of the bad deeds he has been naming, ones that belong to the negative side of this binary and that are done by those who practice vice (τῷ τὸ κακὸν πράσσοντι [13:4]).[133] This listing recalls the always compounding number of vices that characterize those on the wrong side of the moral binary.[134]

Elite authors portray Roman discipline/sobriety in contrast to the behavior of barbarians, who cannot control their desire for drink and,

---

131. Paul relies on a similar metaphorical binary in 1 Thess 5:1–11, as part of a passage that also combines eschatological, imperial, militaristic, and ethical language, with 5:4–8 emphasizing a similar night/day binary. In 1 Thess 5:1–11 the eschatological language is more abrupt and urgent than it is in Rom 13:11–14. The day that "draws near" in 13:12 is quite tame compared to the inescapable "sudden destruction" (αἰφνίδιος ὄλεθρος) that springs upon those saying "peace and security" (εἰρήνη καὶ ἀσφάλεια), a Roman political catchphrase according to Koester, in 5:3 (Koester, "Imperial Ideology," 162). Strategies of homonationalism already appear in the eschatological rhetoric of 1 Thessalonians, and apocalyptic language that imagines a new political regime can still replicate the rules and *mores* of the current empire. See Hoke, "Be Even Better Subjects," esp. 101–7.

132. Most commentaries draw attention to the fact that the vices on this list are characteristically perceived as prone to being nighttime activities. See Fitzmyer, *Romans*, 683; Dunn, *Romans*, 2:789–90; Moo, *Epistle to the Romans*, 824–25; Witherington, *Paul's Letter to the Romans*, 318; Johnson, *Reading Romans*, 195; Schreiner, *Romans*, 699–700; Matera, 300; Keck, *Romans*, 197; Thompson, *Clothed with Christ*, 145–49.

133. Knust briefly observes the connection between the ethical submission of 13:1–7 to these specifically sexual vices (Knust, *Abandoned to Lust*, 72). Edwards notes that Seneca connects such pleasures to softness (i.e., effeminacy), which is typically found among slaves and especially within taverns (drinking) and brothels (Edwards, *Politics of Immorality*, 174).

134. As in Roman elite ideology: "Charges of sexual vice tended to appear in lists rather than separately. If a man was condemned for his extravagance, he was also likely to be condemned for adultery, effeminacy, corruption of boys, or some other related charge. If a woman was accused of sexual licentiousness, she was also likely to be accused of excessive adornment and concern for her appearance" (Knust, *Abandoned to Lust*, 32). See further Brooten, *Love between Women*, 260–62.

therefore, drink to excess with disastrous consequence.[135] Connecting the moral language with the militaristic in Roman thought, Tacitus contrasts Romans to the barbarian German other, showing how the typical drunkenness and revelry of the German armies makes them inferior and conquerable to the superior (in terms of might and moral moderation) Roman army.[136] Such a view, which depends on the Roman moral preference to refrain from excess drink, alongside that of the sexual other who must be conquered and controlled, justifies the conquest (and lower social status) of the barbarian ethnic others. They are not only easier to defeat due to their lack of disciplined military strength and planning but also less morally capable of self-control and thus unable to rule themselves or be elite citizens.[137]

Through his day and night contrast, Paul aligns the moral discipline of Christ-followers as similar to that of the superior Roman army. The wearing or donning of "armor of light" (ἐνδυσώμεθα τὰ ὅπλα τοῦ φωτός [Rom 13:12]) denotes the moral uprightness that should be adopted by Christ-followers in the same way that the Roman military comports itself as it brings peace, prosperity, and salvation (σωτηρία) to other ἔθνη. Paul's militaristic language conveys a similar contrast to that made by Tacitus.

---

135. Philo does this as well; see his parody of the Greek symposia in *Contempl.* 40–63, esp. 55, and discussion in Niehoff, *Philo of Alexandria*, 86–88, and Hoke, "Homo Urbanus or Urban Homos? Metronormative Tropes and Subcultural Queernesses around Philo and the Therapeuts," forthcoming. On Philo's juxtaposition of the Greek symposia to the (Stoic) Therapeuts, Niehoff writes, "Devotion to nature, sobriety, and an earnest search for truth are thus the Jewish and Roman alternatives to Greek frivolity." See Maren Niehoff, *Philo of Alexandria: An Intellectual Biography*, ABRL (New Haven: Yale University Press, 2018), 87.

136. Shumate, *Nation, Empire, Decline*, 96–97. Describing an attack on the Germans after scouts reported it was the night of a festival, Tacitus writes, "The clear, starry night was in our favor; the Marsian villages were reached, and a ring of pickets was posted round the enemy, who were still lying, some in bed, others beside their tables, without misgivings and with no sentries advanced. All was disorder and improvidence: there was no apprehension of war, and even their peace was the nerveless lethargy of drunkenness" (*Ann.* 1.50, trans. Moore and Jackson). See further Shumate, *Nation, Empire, Decline*, 97. One could say, based on Tacitus's telling, that the day of the imperial lords came upon these Germans as a thief in the night.

137. In a detailed analysis of Tacitus's corpus, Langlands shows how he connects the Germans to sexual immorality via *impudicitia*—the opposite of Roman *pudicitia*, which was under threat from these barbaric enemies (Langlands, *Sexual Morality*, 320–48).

Once again, Paul associates Christ-followers' values with those of the prevailing authorities.

This emphasis on drunkenness (and the encouragement to avoid it) is associated with imperial *mores* concerning sexual morality. Jennifer Knust observes how both excessive drinking and sexuality come to be portrayed as un-Roman and representative of other ethnic groups, in particular as characteristic of Greeks. "Some Roman authors claimed that wasting money on prostitutes and wild drinking parties was a Greek trait, a characteristic of 'Greek leisure' (*otium*), something that had unfortunately infected Rome."[138] Although the descriptions of sexual vice tended to be most graphic (belying a particular anxiety around sex), Romans depicted persons and entire ethnic groups as engaging in multiple vices. This compounded the reasons and examples of their moral degeneracy and thus their reasons for lower status, at least in the view of elite Roman authors.[139] Drunkenness and revelry, characteristic of Paul's portrayal of nighttime immorality and of anti-Roman barbarians (e.g., Tacitus's Germans), begin the list of vices that are necessarily avoided by those who live in the (respectable) day and who don the armor of light.

Following the discouragement of these vices is the disdain for those that are specifically sexual: κοίτη, meaning "bed" and used as a term for general sexual acts, and ἀσέλγια, which had close connections to desires (ἐπιθυμία).[140] Attributing these behaviors, like drunkenness and revelry, to the night, these illicit sexual deeds (and lack of ability to control the urges to commit them) betray lower status through impulses characterizing both barbarians and Romans condemned and dishonored as sexual deviants. Christ-followers can and should avoid these sexual behaviors, unlike Messalina and Julia, the famed prostitutes of imperial families who committed *stuprum* in their uncontrolled evening sexual frenzies, or the

---

138. Knust, *Abandoned to Lust*, 33.

139. Along similar lines, Marchal observes, "The colonizing (mostly) male authority can claim his superiority, virtue, and civilization by extolling sexual norms (of his own establishment) that the erotically savage or debased colonial people apparently do not embody. Their aberration proves the necessity, even the elevated benefit, of imperial-colonial forces" (Marchal, "Exceptional Proves Who Rules," 96).

140. κοίτη is the act of bedding, as well as the derivation of *coitus* (LSJ, s.v. "κοίτη," 970). In this sense, we can recall Rom 1:18–32, where the sexual excess and lack of control leads to a downward spiral of immorality, with vices compounding as quickly as Paul can list them. ἀσέλγεια generally means "licentiousness" or "wanton violence" (LSJ, s.v. "ἀσέλγεια," 255).

typical foreigners and lower-classed others who committed such acts as an example of their lack of *pudicitia*.[141] Such comportment demonstrates Christ-followers' control of their sexual impulses. Paul implies that, by submitting to the imperial regulation of sexuality and ethics, Christ-followers possess the *pudicitia* typically found among the elite authorities.

Paul's mention of these specifically sexual terms indicates the sexual exceptionalism that underlies his exhortation to ethical submission. As the Roman elite sexually distinguished themselves from lower classes by their pure *pudicitia*, Paul's discouragement of sexual liaisons and wild licentiousness distinguishes the sexual values of Christ-followers as being controlled and pure, as those who live in the respectable daytime. If adopted by Christ-followers as Paul advises, this ethical submission to both Roman authorities and Roman values places them in a position to be seen and considered as praiseworthy—indeed, respectable—for their values. Such consideration could lead to elevated status and authority.

One might wonder to what degree mere tolerance is the goal of ethical submission to Roman *mores*. Just how much elevated status could a Jew or other ἔθνη plausibly hope for in the early years of Nero, still potentially recovering from the fallout from Claudius's edict, which formally expelled all Jews from the city around 49–50 CE?[142] The answer could simultaneously be "not much at all" and "tons" and everywhere in between. As we saw in chapter 3 with Berlant's cruel optimism and Paul's cruel πίστις, fan-

---

141. I am arguing that the sexual distinction made by Paul here is not to prove better than Rome's elite; indeed, it conforms to discourse in order to sexually distinguish Christ-followers from the typical *stuprum* found among lower classes. This is nearly identical to that Roman ideology that requires the tales of these imperial women as warnings that exemplifies the dangers of giving into unrestrained desire (a concession too typical of lower classes). Moral discourse emphasizes these elite falls because they are effectively cautionary in the face of socio-sexual-political anxiety. Thus, Joshel notes of Tacitus's descriptions of Messalina, "Such excess connotes a collapse of social categories as well as epistemic ones: the top of society becomes the bottom, and the object of illicit desire is conflated with its results" (Joshel, "Female Desire," 231). Despite the portrayal of the choice in giving into excess by elite women, few brothel workers (in addition to other lower-classed deviants) had choices when it came to their sexual practices. Commenting on Juvenal's portrayal, Glancy and Moore caution, "Yet this does not imply that Roman sex workers were widely believed to be in the sex trade to satisfy their erotic longings." Glancy and Moore, "How Typical a Roman Prostitute," 567.

142. See discussion of sources/historical context of this edict in chapter 3, n. 94.

tasies of an elevated good life fly in the face of reality and have a stronger affective grasp precisely when circumstances feel direr, such as when the crisis of Claudius's edict became more or less crisis ordinary. The context of Roman sexual exceptionalism fans the flames of ultimately impossible hopes, making it *feel* more possible to attain a good life via potentially praiseworthy ethical submission.[143]

Returning to the sexual exceptionalism of Rom 13:11–14, its homonational tactics become more explicit in Paul's encouragement that precedes this list of specific vices to avoid: ὡς ἐν ἡμέρᾳ εὐσχημόνως περιπατήσωμεν ("Like in daytime, let us live respectably" [13:13a]). Paul stresses that daytime is the time for living εὐσχημόνως, "respectably," deriving from the combination of "good" (εὐ) and "appearance" (σχῆμα). With its emphasis on elegant appearance, the adjective and adverbial forms of εὐσχημόνως typically took meanings to describe decency, and, particularly in its first-century usages, to have implications of honor and nobility.[144] Paul's encouragement to "live respectably"—as one does in the daytime—continues to urge Christ-followers to behave in ways similar to that of the Roman elite. The emphasis that εὐσχημόνως places upon appearance (σχῆμα) demonstrates the opportunities for being noticed and perceived as "good" (εὐ, but also, implicitly, ἀγαθός) that ethical submission to imperial *mores* creates. This respectability and its potential for positive notice continues to stress the potential for ἔπαινος ("praise") from the prevailing, imperial authorities in 13:3. The homonational alignment of Christ-followers' ethical submission and the moral values of the elite imperial authorities continues to foster hope for upward mobility and higher social status.

Paul concludes this segment of ethical advice by exhorting his audience to embody the positive contrast to the uncontrolled immorality, sexual in particular, of lower-status others. He writes:

ἀλλ᾽ ἐνδύσασθε τὸν κύριον Ἰησοῦν Χριστόν καὶ τῆς σαρκὸς πρόνοιαν μὴ ποιεῖσθε εἰς ἐπιθυμίας.
But wear the *kyrios* Jesus Christ, and do not do the intentions of the flesh for desires (13:14).

---

143. See Stowers, *Rereading of Romans*, 74–82; he argues that Paul's use of self-mastery—with echoes of that in Philo and 4 Maccabees—is a strategy of upward mobility for a community that *was* upwardly mobile.

144. LSJ, s.v. "εὐσχημόνως," 734.

Paul employs the language of wearing, like with the donning of armor, to urge the metaphorical donning of a person, presumably indicating they should "wear" his appearance (as an actor dressing for a role).[145] Paul instructs his audience to act like Jesus Christ, their κύριος. These actions include the moral behaviors encouraged previously, as already done by Jesus Christ, presuming his superior ethical behavior making him worthy of the κύριος title.[146]

Paul emphasizes the performative and visible aspects of this ethical submission through this language of wearing. As with the respectable living in 13:13, a notion of proper *appearance* undergirds this advice. Dressing as Jesus implies more than just an imitation of correct moral action. Like clothing or armor, this action is supposed to be *visible*, something that others can notice and potentially praise. This does not mean that such a performance (emphasizing dress and appearance) of proper ethics should not also become a daily habit and lifestyle for Christ-followers.[147] This language of dress and good appearance (εὐσχημόνως) demonstrates an impulse to visibly present Christ-followers as elite-like in their behaviors for the authorities at the top of the hierarchy (both human and divine).

Paul's final exhortation of chapter 13 returns to sexual prohibition, telling the audience not to do the "intentions of the flesh" (τῆς σαρκὸς πρόνοιαν) "for desire" (εἰς ἐπιθυμίας). Paul uses flesh (σάρξ) in a generally negative way, often in binary opposition to the spirit. In Rom 8, Paul con-

---

145. As noted by Jewett, this usage of ἐνδύω with the name of a person is used by Dionysius of Halicarnassus when speaking directly of actors "dressing the role of that Tarquin" (ἀλλὰ τὸν Ταρκύνιον ἐκεῖνον ἐνδυόμενοι [*Ant. rom.* 11.5.2]) (Jewett, *Romans*, 827).

146. While many commentators (Thompson most notably) appeal to the ethical teachings of Jesus (largely meaning those from the gospel tradition) as the ideas behind Paul's ethical exhortations, there are few references to any specific Jesus tradition apart from Paul's appeals to following/imitating Christ (often alongside himself). The parallels to gospels are ultimately echoes at best, and there are not nearly enough specific references to Jesus's lifestyle or teachings to reconstruct these ethical exhortations in alignment with specific content of these teachings that would have been familiar to Paul or Roman Christ-followers. In other words, it is *possible* these followers knew and drew from Jesus's ethical examples in these ways, but it is *equally* probable they did not.

147. Like gender, in other words, ethics are performed, routinized, and ritualized into habitual bodily norms that conform bodies and communities to particular standards, and their influence and effects/affects cannot always be easily discarded. See Judith Butler, *Gender Trouble: Feminism and the Subversion of Identity* (New York: Routledge, 1990; repr. 2006), 190–91.

trasts the mindset (φρόνημα) of the flesh and of the spirit, asserting that it is the flesh that *does not submit* to God's law. In 8:7–8, he writes:

διότι τὸ φρόνημα τῆς σαρκὸς ἔχθρα εἰς θεόν, τῷ γὰρ νόμῳ τοῦ θεοῦ οὐχ ὑποτάσσεται, οὐδὲ γὰρ δύναται· οἱ δὲ ἐν σαρκὶ ὄντες θεῷ ἀρέσαι οὐ δύνανται. Because the mindset of the flesh is hostile toward God, for it does not submit to God's law—indeed it is unable. And those who are in the flesh are unable to please God.

Romans 13:14 recalls this passage: as those with the "mindset of the flesh" in 8:7–8 are unable to "please God" by submitting, those who do the "intentions of the flesh" are unable to please God by submitting their ethical behavior.[148] Both the "mindset" (φρόνημα) of chapter 8 and the "intention" (πρόνοια) of chapter 13 are related in terms of their use of the mind/thought, Paul's use of πρόνοια signals the process of ethical thought and planning that is the emphasis of this section of the letter.[149]

In 8:15, Paul associates this mindset of the flesh with slavery. Enslaved persons were denied the control to make decisions over their own bodies in the way that free persons did, elite citizens especially.[150] Enslaved persons were thought to be in their position because they lacked the ability to adhere to the proper *mores* practiced by the free elite. Though their sexual passivity and loss of *pudicita* was forced upon them, it is such composite others at the bottom of the social hierarchy who embodied the Roman images of lack of self-control, who, to use Paul's terms, would follow the intentions of the flesh in 13:14. The intentions of the flesh, according to Paul, lead toward ἐπιθυμία, "desire," a term that almost always carries implications of sexual longing (see 1 Thess 4:5, as well as Rom 1:24, 6:12, 7:7, 8; Gal 5:16, 24; Phil 1:23).

This idea of a "mindset of the flesh" that leads to "desire" draws upon ethnic distinctions and stereotypes similar to those assumed in elite morality. Having the mindset of these desires is indicative of lower-

---

148. As Paul notes in his introduction to his ethical advice in 12:1–2, the goal of adopting an ethical mindset is to do not only what is "good" (ἀγαθόν) but also what is "pleasing" (εὐάρεστον), particularly in terms of God's will (τὸ θέλημα τοῦ θεοῦ).

149. πρόνοια derives from combining πρό (before) and νοῦς (mind) to give the idea of foresight, planning, or thinking before, thus "intention." See LSJ, s.v. "πρόνοια," 1491.

150. Glancy, *Slavery in Early Christianity* (Oxford: Oxford University Press, 2002) 9–26; Page duBois, *Slaves and Other Objects* (Chicago: University of Chicago Press, 2003), 101–13.

class behavior and broader immorality (as sexual immorality and other vices tended to compound). It is behavior of those who do not or cannot submit to the prevailing authorities and will not be praised for their ethical submission. In order to embody ethical submission and gain status via praise and respectability, Christ-followers must visibly align their behaviors—especially their sexual behaviors—with that of the elite and at the expense of other groups of stereotyped ἔθνη who are lower on the social hierarchy and unable to follow these *mores*: sexual exceptionalism via Romanormativity.

The Romanormative sexual exceptionalism of Rom 13 is explicitly wed to imperial politics via the expression of patriotic loyalty to those who rule, that is, homonationalism. Recalling the donning of the armor of light in 13:12, these exhortations in 13:14 resume the idea that Christ-followers should model themselves (not only in action but also in appearance) after the imperial authorities, the conquerors and the κύριοι, including Jesus as the ultimate κύριος. Just as in the case of submissive πίστις, God, having placed both Jesus and then the imperial authorities, is pleased by ethical behaviors that submit to God's authority. As they adhere to the *mores* that enforce its kyriarchy, these ethical behaviors are *still* Roman (this time, it seems, *with* Rome). In Rom 13 (and 12–15 by extension), as in Rom 3–5, God remains the ultimate impenetrable penetrator who, rather than overturning the imperial system and its social hierarchy, merely creates an avenue by which Christ-followers can rise above others, those who are already low in status.[151]

Just as imperial rule and conquest was not upset by means of faithful submission, Paul's ethical advice for self-control, submission, and respectability—particularly in terms of sexual behavior—reifies the imperial hierarchies that were enforced by rigid ideologies of morality linked to national prosperity. By proving their ability to behave according to elite *mores*, Christ-followers submit to the prevailing authorities (13:1) and do good in order to receive praise (13:3). This good behavior entails conforming to the elite ideals governing sexual morality (13:11–14), as opposed to those who rebel (13:2), do bad (13:4), and are sexual others (13:13). Similar to how contemporary gay subjects patriotically align their exceptional homonormativity with the imperial-like goals of the US nation-state,

---

151. As seen in chapter 3 with Rom 1–5; see again, Moore, *God's Beauty Parlor*, 168–72. See also Marchal, "Exceptional Proves Who Rules," 103–4.

Paul's Romanormative tactics participate in and legitimate the project of empire. Paul's exhortations to ethical submission in chapter 13 (alongside his advice in ch. 12) rely upon the conditions of sexual exceptionalism made possible by imperial morality. Loyalty to Rome is performed through exceptional sexual virtue: homonationalism.

As Puar breaks down strategies of homonationalism, she describes its deployment as follows: "In homonormative narratives of nation, there is a dual movement: US patriotism momentarily sanctions some homosexualities, often through gendered, racial, and class sanitizing, in order to produce 'monster-terrorist-fags'; homosexuals embrace the us-versus-them rhetoric of U.S. patriotism and thus align themselves with this racist and homophobic production."[152] In similar, though also distinctly different, ways, Roman imperialism—and its *mores* and propaganda—produced a notion of an ultimate barbarian, a "composite other," based on racial, gender, class, and sexual stereotypes that are akin to the modern "monster-terrorist-fag." In so doing, the possibility remained open for certain others to be sanctioned as subjects worthy of rehabilitation by submitting to the imperial regime and adopting its us-versus-them ethical binaries. Though the specific strategies and contexts differ from the examples that Puar provides, Roman imperialism and ethics provide avenues for homonationalism. Alongside Philo and others, in Rom 13, Paul attempts to take advantage of these routes.

Paul's homonational tactics assume they can lead to upward mobility and actual integration into Roman imperial culture. To what degree does Rome actually promise rehabilitation? The same can be asked of contemporary homonationalism: does the United States actually promise benefits to patriotic, homonormative gays? The promises, in both the United States and Rome, are unspoken potentials that marginalized groups attempt to exploit. In the contemporary US context, these promises appear to be actual because the tactics seem to have worked for homonormative subjects, especially in light of the nation's praiseworthy acceptance of same-sex marriage in *Obergefell v. Hodges*. Lacking evidence on the ground, we cannot see exactly whether or how Paul's tactics worked—though, it should be noted, we can see how, eventually, Paul's words were central to an ascendant Christianity that became the Roman Empire.

---

152. Puar, *Terrorist Assemblages*, 46.

Their success or failure is not the point. Indeed, it does not matter how realistic Rome's promises were. They are *not* promises. They are *fantasies of inclusion*—into promises for which these subjects were never intended. Despite victories and advances on the front of gay marriage that make these promises *seem* real, Puar emphasizes the fictionality of the inclusive promises homonationalism proffers. "Homonationalism is also a temporal and spatial illusion, a facile construction that is easily revoked, dooming the exceptional queers to insistent replays and restagings of their exceptionalisms."[153] While the homonational other can be rehabilitated into the normal social order, the limited, contingent social mobility is not the largest benefit of this rehabilitation. That ultimate benefit remains in the hands of an already normal elite, who retain their power and control by appearing benevolent and nominally quelling those who might otherwise become rebellious.[154] Rehabilitated subjects, in the eyes of their elite superiors, will *always be lower* on the social hierarchy and, therefore, will always wield less true political power. All the while, these persons truly

---

153. Puar, *Terrorist Assemblages*, 78. The omitted introductory clause to this quotation described Bush-era political circumstances. Though recent gay marriage victories change the specifics, the potential for backlash remains, as is evident in recent discussions of religious-freedom laws (particularly surrounding the RFRA passed in Indiana in March 2015). Joseph A. Marchal's blog ("Statehouse Sodomites, and Other Challenges around 'Religious Freedoms,'" *Feminist Studies in Religion*, 6 April 2015, https://tinyurl.com/SBL4531l) on these laws, the ensuing debates, and issues of race and gender surrounding them especially helps to demonstrate how recent gains (and even potential setbacks) are, as Puar notes they would be, "conservative victories at best, if at all" (Puar, *Terrorist Assemblages*, 78). Such precarity looms in the aftermath of Donald Trump's presidency, which left a significant imbalance on the Supreme Court and made possible a majority that could affirm discrimination of LGBTIA2Q+ persons for the sake of "religious freedom" and even overturn recent victories that prohibit employment discrimination and permit gay marriage. Before this threat, the fact that the major US Supreme Court ruling in favor of gay marriage (*Obergefell v. Hodges*, 2015) came after rulings that major sections of the Voter Rights Act were unconstitutional (*Shelby County v. Holder*, 2013) and that Hobby Lobby had the right to deny contraceptive health care to its female employees (*Burwell v. Hobby Lobby Stores, Inc.*, 2014) is but one (most obvious) example of how certain gay privilege is affirmed while issues of race and gender discrimination (disproportionately affecting poorer persons) continue to abound. All this ultimately continues to affirm Puar's conclusion to this discussion: "The history of Euro-American gay and lesbian studies and queer theory has produced a *cleaving of queerness*, always white, from race, always heterosexual and always homophobic" (Puar, *Terrorist Assemblages*, 78, emphasis added).

154. Puar, *Terrorist Assemblages*, 26.

"on top" of society perpetuate their own (hetero)normative and largely conservative politics. They maintain a rigid social structure that privileges few at the expense of many others. To emphasize the point I have made elsewhere: "Some first-century Christ-followers and some twenty-first century gays may imagine themselves taking over and running the world, but, in their present, they employ [homonational tactics that] rehabilitate the systems they hope to replace."[155]

Though the Roman imperial system was clearly stacked in favor of an essentially predetermined elite, this would not have prevented some excluded others from believing that they could rise through imitation, as modern homonationals do. Similar to the "cruel optimism" of Paul's use of imperial πίστις, the hopes of upward mobility engendered by these exhortations for ethical submission are ultimately a fantasy, one that frequently feels compelling. Certain persons or groups may hope to present themselves as virtuous, able to uphold the same ethical standards as the imperial elite. They may even curry favor and appear to rise above the racial/sexual deviant barbarian. However, this favor merely reinforces the ultimately impossible fantasy, which partially or temporarily includes composite others (with few material consequences for the elite) while quelling the potential of revolt. Rome's ethical system, particularly in its regulation of sexuality, ultimately works to discipline and normalize certain composite others, creating subjects worthy of rehabilitation so that its social hierarchy and political stability remain constant and in control.

Paul's ethical advice at the end of Romans, especially in chapter 13 (but also in the advice given in ch. 12), employs its own brand of homonationalism. Though certainly a strategy for upward mobility for the ἐκκλησία, these homonational ethics are doomed to first-century failure. The fantasy of homonationalism presents the possibility of belonging only to ensure that those already on top remain secure in their positions of power and privilege. Ethical submission may please God, but its material and social benefits are less certain. This is especially the case for queer wo/men in Rome's ἐκκλησία who may have been unable or unwilling to submit to these imperial *mores*. It is among these queer wo/men that the questions of ethical submission and imperial authority must be posed in order to consider what else might have been "good and pleasing and perfect" behavior for first-century queer wo/men.

---

155. Hoke, "Be Even Better Subjects," 107.

6
An Ethical ἐκκλησία

I wanted to tell him that desire was not a distraction. Not something separate from the way we want freedom. I wanted to tell him I had been to a place where anything was possible, and that the only thing more frightening than powerlessness was power.
—Sam J. Miller, "It Was Saturday Night, I Guess That Made It All Right"

What does justice do?

In the last chapter we saw how those in power present ethics as clear and simple rules that can be encapsulated in binary terms: good or bad; submissive or rebellious; peaceful or violent. Powerless people who crave power (like Paul) can perform loyal obedience in hopes of satiating their fantastic cravings. However, these distinctions are fictive: they are all about violence. They make justice, freedom, and desire work for those in power; they keep everyone else powerless under them.

What happens when justice is dislodged from (imperial) power, if some powerless people imbue it with impulsive meanings and actions that move beyond easy binaries? A praxis of ἐκκλησία-l assemblage summons a space "where anything was possible," echoing the realization in Sam Miller's story.[1] Through this reconstructive praxis, the active engagement of queer wo/men in Rome's ἐκκλησία emerges as a place of possibilities. What could these wo/men have *done* with justice?

Ethics embody impulses, since they concern what one does (or doesn't do). But ethical embodiments are also impulses. When these queer

---

1. The realization is voiced by the story's main character, Caul, who has this enlightening experience in the aftermath of a blowjob under a highway overpass. See Sam J. Miller, "It Was Saturday Night, I Guess That Made It All Right," in *A People's Future of the United States: Speculative Fiction from 25 Extraordinary Writers*, ed. Victor LaValle and John Joseph Adams (New York: One World, 2019), 107.

wo/men assembled, they had ideas about ethics; they had feelings about them; they put their different ideas and feelings into motion. In this chapter, I add actions—the more concrete *doing* of ideas and feelings—to the forces that impulses conjure. Queer wo/men reacted and responded to the ideas, feelings, and actions of others in Rome's ἐκκλησία—including but not limited to Paul's ethical impulses.

This chapter reconstructs the ethical impulses that moved in between and were embodied by queer wo/men in Rome's ἐκκλησία. As in chapter 4, I work up from postholes to bring forth four groups of impulses whose existence is speculatively plausible. Beyond the early liturgical materials that Paul quotes in Gal 3:28 and Phil 2:6–11, this chapter's proposals draw evidence from rhetorical reconstructions of other ethical positions to which Paul clearly responds in his other letters. Paul's first letter to Corinth is a particularly helpful resource for these different ideas. In this letter, Paul both identifies and responds to disagreeing positions in ways that have allowed scholars to reconstruct some of the theo-Christologies and ethics of some of the influential Corinthian wo/men whose ideas and practices clearly, at times, diverged from Paul's.[2] While the ἐκκλησίαι in Corinth and Rome certainly differed and were geographically removed, Corinth offers particular relevance (relative to other Pauline epistles) to Rome. It was a port city that featured a great degree of interaction with both Rome and its other territories/ἔθνη.[3] I also appeal to other Pauline

---

2. Most notably, see the reconstructions and development of feminist rhetorical criticism for 1 Corinthians in Antionette Clark Wire, *The Corinthian Women Prophets: A Reconstruction through Paul's Rhetoric* (Minneapolis: Fortress, 1990). Other reconstructive work on 1 Corinthians that follows this tradition includes Joseph A. Marchal, "The Corinthian Women Prophets and Trans Activism: Rethinking Canonical Gender Claims," in *Bible Trouble: Queer Reading at the Boundaries of Biblical Scholarship*, ed. Teresa J. Hornsby and Ken Stone, SemeiaSt 67 (Atlanta: Society of Biblical Literature, 2011), 223–46; Cavan W. Concannon, *"When You Were Gentiles": Specters of Ethnicity in Roman Corinth and Paul's Corinthian Correspondence*, Syn (New Haven: Yale University Press, 2014); Joseph A. Marchal, "How Soon Is (This Apocalypse) Now? Queer Corinthian Velocities after a Corinthian Already and a Pauline Not Yet," in *Sexual Disorientations: Queer Temporalities, Affects, Theologies*, ed. Kent L. Brintnall, Marchal, and Stephen D. Moore, TTC (New York: Fordham University Press, 2018), 45–67.

3. See, for example, the descriptions in Concannon, *When You Were Gentiles*, 47–74; more generally, he assumes that the participants in Corinth's ἐκκλησία were largely ethnic hybrids. Furthermore, it is generally acknowledged as the location from which Paul was writing this letter to Rome.

letters (including 1 Thessalonians, Galatians, and Philippians) when they offer glimpses into differing views and practices.

Other Roman writings and material culture confirm the plausibility of these ethical impulses and show that these impulses were not unique to Christ-followers. Jewish authors, including Philo and Josephus, describe how first-century Jews responded to Roman authority in a variety of ways. These writers offer evidence of the different ethical practices and interpretations held within Second Temple Judaism. Beyond Judaism, examples from other religious cults, particularly that of Isis, provide evidence for the plausible ethical impulses that I proffer. Finally, evidence of Pompeiian material culture—objects, wall paintings, and graffiti—offers insights into the lived experiences and ethical impulses of ordinary Romans, especially regarding their sexual practices.[4]

The impulses I discuss in this chapter *could*, in some form, have guided the thoughts, feelings, and actions of queer wo/men in Rome's ἐκκλησία. "Egalitarian Ethics" explores the ethical implications of egalitarian theo-Christologies (such as the impulses discussed in chapter 4's "God's Equals"), particularly with regard to gender. How could Roman Christ-followers, alongside other first-century movements, have embodied different forms of egalitarianism? "Rethinking Rebels" probes desires for freedom and the different impulses that could embody it. Here, I outline a variety of plausible responses to Roman ethics of submission that included but were not limited to outright opposition. Within these responses, we can discern echoes of theo-christological impulses that arose previously in "Drowning Jesus" and "Kyriarchal Christs." Then, I examine how ethnic backgrounds ("ἔθν-ic Ethics") and questions of sexual practices and orientations ("'Good' Sex?") affected embodiments of theo-Christologies. Some of the impulses assembled here summon connections from the assemblaged theo-Christologies discussed at the end of chapter 4. In both discussions, I acknowledge how race/ethnicity and sexuality cannot be cleaved into discrete impulses. This inseparability leads to "Justice, Queerness, Ethics, and ἐκκλησία-l Assemblage," which brings to life queer wo/men, Paul, and all the impulses moving in between them. I engage a praxis of ἐκκλησία-l assemblage that scrambles the ethical sides to sense what other justices might shimmer in between these wo/men. I

---

4. The remnants in Pompeii represent the most frequently cited material evidence for many reasons, most notably, its preservation in first-century form and its relative proximity to Rome.

claim these divergent, impulsive wo/men in Rome's ἐκκλησία glitter queerness.

Egalitarian Ethics

How could a theo-christological orientation toward egalitarianism have affected the ethics of queer wo/men in Rome's ἐκκλησία? If no longer considered on top or even permanently in the center, it is plausible that God's ethical examples could have been something other than a bullseye on a distant target, which one must hit precisely or else sin.[5] God, following these lines, does not need to assess human adherence to these standards, and God's sensations of anger, patience, or compassion do not require or result in commendation, condemnation, or clemency. If an egalitarian-oriented vision of justice (δικαιοσύνη) arose as a standard for assessing ethics, it is plausible that some in Rome's ἐκκλησία put egalitarian ethical impulses into action.

Wo/men in other ἐκκλησίαι moved toward more egalitarian practices when they assembled. In Corinth, women claimed authority to prophesy and speak in the ἐκκλησία: according to 1 Cor 11:2–16 and chapter 14 (especially 14:34–36), they asserted their bodily presence (with heads uncovered) and made their voices heard in worship and conversation.[6] Paul may acknowledge that wo/men minister (as he admits in Rom 16), but his vision of their participation regulates their freedom to do so within Romanormative boundaries. Assuming these wo/men prophets were familiar with the οὐκ ἔνι ἄρσεν καὶ θῆλυ ("there is no longer male and female") from the baptismal hymn quoted in Gal 3:28, it is plausible this formula justified wo/men's access to leadership.[7] It could also have permit-

---

5. Drawing here from the fact that the Christian term for "sin" comes from the Greek ἁμαρτάνω, which often could be used in the sense of "to err," but in its wider history, it comes from the meaning "to miss the mark," in particular, as a term meant in the context of spear-throwing, that is, not hitting the target/bullseye. See LSJ, s.v. "ἁμαρτάνω," 77.

6. Wire, *Corinthian Women Prophets*, 116–34, 140–49.

7. See Wire, *Corinthian Women Prophets*, 123–28. Note Paul quotes a similar formula (notably without the "male and female" part) in 1 Cor 12:12–13. It is plausible that, even if these wo/men in Rome did not know Gal 3:28 in its exact form, they were familiar with its egalitarian impulses through other hymns or ideas that circulated among early Christ-followers. "I ask here: If the Corinthians did know this formula or something very similar to it, what might such a baptismal formula have meant to

ted wo/men (and some of the Corinthian men) to deviate from gendered expectations for dress and head covering.[8] These egalitarian ethics around gender existed before and continued after the arrival of Paul's letter.

Regarding status, 1 Cor 7:21–24 suggests that some Corinthian Christ-followers were enslaved. Paul advises them, δοῦλος ἐκλήθης, μή σοι μελέτω· ἀλλ' εἰ καὶ δύνασαι ἐλεύθερος γενέσθαι, μᾶλλον χρῆσαι ("If you were called as a slave, do not be concerned about it; rather, even if you are able to become free, make all the more use" [1 Cor 7:21]). It is quite plausible that enslaved folks took their egalitarian experiences in the ἐκκλησία to mean that it should extend to their freedom beyond its walls.[9] Galatians 3:28 (to which Paul alludes in 1 Cor 12:13) demands: οὐκ ἔνι δοῦλος οὐδὲ ἐλεύθερος ("there is no longer slave nor free").[10] The logical (not to men-tion, most just) interpretation of this phrase, especially from an enslaved perspective, is that *there is no longer slave because everyone is free*—that is,

---

a community which also conceived of itself as a democratic *ekklēsia*?" See Anna C. Miller, *Corinthian Democracy: Democratic Discourse in 1 Corinthians*, PTMS (Eugene, OR: Pickwick, 2015), 139–40, see further 130–52.

8. In her queer readings of 1 Cor 11:2–16, Gillian Townsley shows how schol-ars assume only women's dress to be the problem for Paul. Drawing from Monique Wittig, Townsley demands we problematize the men and include them among those disrupting Paul's ideal Corinthian ἐκκλησία. "A rereading of this passage can therefore take into consideration the possibility that the men—by playing with the established sign systems of clothing and coiffure—are as involved in gender-scrambling behaviors as the women." See Gillian Townsley, *The Straight Mind in Corinth: Queer Readings across 1 Corinthians 11:2–16*, SemeiaSt 88 (Atlanta: SBL Press, 2017), 110, see further 110–15.

9. On questions of social status of the wo/men in Corinth, see Wire, *Corinthian Women Prophets*, 62–69. On issues of Paul's rhetoric in this passage as it relates to ancient slave bodies, see Jennifer A. Glancy, *Slavery in Early Christianity* (Oxford: Oxford University Press, 2002), 67–69; Laura Salah Nasrallah, "'You Were Bought with a Price': Freedpersons and Things in 1 Corinthians,'" in *Corinth in Contrast: Studies in Inequality*, ed. Steven J. Friesen, Sarah A. James, and Daniel N. Schowalter (Leiden: Brill, 2014), 54–73.

10. Miller emphasizes how the baptismal formula empowers enslaved Christ-followers as well as the women in Corinth: "Specifically, the baptismal formula of Gal 3:28 undermines the very boundaries separating the truly free and equal male citizen from the *polis'* non-citizens: slaves and women most visible among them. In turn, this opens the possibility for all to practice citizenship through equal voice and equal discernment in the gathered *ekklesia*" (Miller, *Corinthian Democracy*, 161). In a world where gendered oppression intersected with slavery and rendered their invisibility greater than double, it had the potential to doubly empower enslaved women.

slavery is abolished. That Paul must tell enslaved persons not to be concerned about their enslavement and, *twice*, to remain as they are (1 Cor 7:21, 24) indicates that enslaved wo/men *were* so concerned.[11] It implies that enslaved Christ-followers (alongside others, including freedpersons) were demanding, enacting, and embodying their (and others') freedom among the wo/men in Corinth's ἐκκλησία.

While some Christ-followers seemed to take actions that moved toward an egalitarian ἐκκλησία, their movement was never perfect. While many wo/men clearly embodied forms of egalitarianism, they did not go unchallenged. In Corinth, at least according to Paul's rhetoric, there was considerable debate over these more egalitarian practices, to the point of producing what Paul (or a few in Corinth) chose to deem σχίσματα ("divisions" [1 Cor 1:10; 11:18]). Given that Paul responded to reports of these practices, it appears that some wo/men—presumably less comfortable with how egalitarianism was being enacted—complained or appealed to Paul for assistance.

At least according to this report or Paul's perceptions, economic inequality made visible some divisions in Corinth's ἐκκλησία. This points to an ethical arena in which the imperfection of Corinthian egalitarianism may have been made visible. First Corinthians 11:21 suggests that social distinctions were not entirely erased, and this became especially evident when the ἐκκλησία dined together. ἕκαστος γὰρ τὸ ἴδιον δεῖπνον προλαμβάνει ἐν τῷ φαγεῖν, καὶ ὃς μὲν πεινᾷ ὃς δὲ μεθύει ("For, when eating, each receives in advance one's own meal, and one is hungry while the other is drunk.") It appears that communal dining was a regular occurrence during Corinth's ἐκκλησία's gatherings. These meals seem to have made manifest who could afford to eat and drink lavishly and who could not scrape together enough for sustenance.[12]

11. Scholars have long debated whether this passage is oppressive. See discussion in Nasrallah, "You Were Bought with a Price," 63–66. The potential injustice of these lines resonates across history, especially in the context of US slavery, where this passage, among others, was used to condone slavery and tell enslaved persons not to liberate themselves and seek their freedom.

12. L. L. Welborn cites this text as evidence of significant economic inequality that divides the Corinthian ἐκκλησία. See L. L. Welborn, "Paul's Place in a First-Century Revival of the Discourse of 'Equality,'" *HTR* 110 (2017): 555. See also Welborn, "How 'Democratic' Was the Pauline *Ekklēsia*? An Assessment with Special Reference to the Christ Groups of Roman Corinth," *NTS* 65 (2019): 299; Welborn, "Inequality in Roman Corinth: Evidence from Diverse Sources Evaluated by a Neo-Ricardian Model," in *The First Urban Churches 2: Roman Corinth*, ed. James R. Harrison and Welborn (Atlanta: SBL Press, 2016), 189–243.

This potential imperfection is emblematic of the in-betweenness of ἐκκλησία-1 assemblage. Although Paul exhorts unity in 1 Cor 1:10, the divisions in Corinth (if they indeed existed) are not problematic on their own. They arose from attempts to embody egalitarianism, and dissent about whether (or just how) to do it produced tensions in between the wo/men who assembled there. Although these divisions seem to take firm sides (at least according to Paul's rhetorical perception), in reality, there could have been much movement and crossing in between them. As different wo/men felt different impulses, they divided differently depending on the particular issue. Some wo/men prophets may have opposed enslaved persons' demands for freedom; wealthier enslaved wo/men might have been among those who refused to share their food and drink. There were many debates and potential sides to take, and the wo/men of Corinth likely scrambled these divisions as they interacted with each other. Indeed, we see Paul taking up different relations to egalitarianism in his own impulses about Corinthian ethics. While never perfectly realizing the fully egalitarian vision they sensed within theo-christological impulses like Gal 3:28, these egalitarian embodiments—alongside dissent to them—moved the ἐκκλησία in more just directions.

Egalitarian ethics were not unique to Christ-followers and their ἐκκλησίαι. There is evidence of various egalitarian-leaning practices within other groups in the Roman world. The cult surrounding the worship of the Egyptian goddess Isis appears to have encouraged egalitarian impulses among her followers, both in terms of women's participation and with regard to socioeconomic status. "Distinctions of rank and status are not altogether absent, but they often seem based on the achievement of devotees and not on externally determined status criteria. Some degree of egalitarianism exists," writes Ross Shepherd Kraemer. While such egalitarianism may have been ideal, especially since devotees needed some degree of wealth to attain these distinctions, anyone could attain higher status, including wealthier enslaved persons and freedpersons.[13]

Evidence suggests that both men and wo/men practiced devotion to Isis across the Greco-Roman world, and even the most conservative accounting for numbers attests a fairly high percentage of wo/men devo-

---

13. Ross Shepherd Kraemer, *Her Share of the Blessings: Women's Religions among Pagans, Jews, and Christians in the Greco-Roman World* (New York: Oxford University Press, 1992), 78.

tees.[14] An early second-century hymn to Isis praises her because "thou didst make the power of women equal to that of men" (P.Oxy. 11.1380).[15] Such a praise makes clear that some, though not necessarily all, wo/men devotees of Isis found egalitarian inspiration in their practice. However, as Kraemer notes, the impulses contained in the story of Isis also permit a less egalitarian interpretation of wo/men's power and agency. The myth connects Isis's actions to her love for Osiris and attributes some of her veneration to her fidelity to her husband, despite his own infidelity (which she forgives) and the hurdle of his death (which does not prevent her from bearing a son).[16] These elements of Isis's story do not necessarily diminish her power, especially since they could resonate with the women who expressed devotion to her and found empowerment from it.

Another imperfect example of egalitarian religious impulses appears in Philo's *Vita Contemplativa*. This text describes a community of Jews (the Therapeuts) who leave their lives (homes, wealth, families, etc.) to form an ascetic collective centered around full devotion to God by focusing on worship. The system he describes hints at more egalitarian practices, and Philo makes it clear that distinctions are not drawn according to social status. No one is enslaved, and the collective serves one another (see *Contempl.* 70).[17] In terms of gender, he notes that women coexist with the men and practice the same routines, albeit often (but not always) in separated spaces. "And they dine together with women" (*Contempl.* 68).[18]

---

14. See Kraemer, *Her Share of the Blessings*, 75–76. Here she discusses how the number could actually be greater than the percentage of recorded attestations, since women's presence are usually downplayed or unrepresented in official documentation.

15. Ross Shepherd Kraemer, *Women's Religions in the Greco-Roman World: A Sourcebook* (New York: Oxford University Press, 2004), 456.

16. So, as Kraemer observes, emphasis is put far more on Isis's role as wife in the context of marital fidelity and only secondly (with decidedly less emphasis) on her maternal role. This differs from many female goddesses and their cults, notably that of Demeter. See Kraemer, *Her Share of the Blessings*, 74–75.

17. This description is not without Philo's own bias, and it seems that no one serves like a slave because the entire community comes from among those who previously inhabited. Philo praises "equality by erasure." See James N. Hoke, "*Homo Urbanus* or Urban Homos? Metronormative Tropes and Subcultural Queernesses around Philo and the Therapeuts," forthcoming.

18. In the rest of this passage, Philo emphasizes the virginity (and age) of these women participants, which seems to be a prerequisite for such cohabitation and participation in his description.

Philo's description is far from an ideal instance of egalitarianism. His account is idealized (and possibly fictional); he presents the participants as having come from higher socioeconomic background; and the presence of men and wo/men leans toward complementarity as much as egalitarianism.[19] Despite such caveats, the collective seems to come closer to egalitarianism than to those overtly kyriarchal hierarchies. Philo's presentation makes plausible the existence of egalitarian-oriented Jewish communities that would have been roughly contemporary with the forming of Christ-following ἐκκλησίαι.[20]

We can connect all of these attempts to embody egalitarianism to the ethical impulses that would have been enacted among the queer wo/men in Rome's ἐκκλησία. Some could have attempted to embody the theo-christological ideal of ἴσα θεοῦ within this space, even if their embodiments were imperfect and other wo/men dissented. If some queer wo/men imagined God on more egalitarian terms with them, God's example could inspire ethical impulses that anticipate living equally and justly, in ways that slowly redefine the kyriarchal definitions of such terms.[21] It is plausible that similar (if not exactly the same) egalitarian practices as those seen above were formed in response to the emerging theo-Christologies in Rome's ἐκκλησία.

If a few thought in these terms, they might have preferred a different prepositional description of their relation to God: something like παρὰ θεόν ("alongside God") or παρὰ θεῷ ("with/among God"). As an equal, alongside Paul and each wo/man in Rome's ἐκκλησία, God participates more fully in the movements of ἐκκλησία-l assemblage. Such a relation changes ethical positions, rules, and norms—which imply a static desire for perfection—into ethical guide*lines*. Lines are always *moving*: they change, get developed, and become embodied differently as they cross new times and places. The guidance they offer shifts as queer wo/men

---

19. See Kraemer, *Unreliable Witnesses: Religion, Gender, and History in the Greco-Roman Mediterranean* (Oxford: Oxford University Press, 2011), 59–116.

20. See Kraemer, *Unreliable Witnesses*, 116; Hoke, "Homo Urbanus or Urban Homos?" (final section, titled "Queerness Goes Rural: Twisting the Trope with Subcultural Therapeuts").

21. Notably, such ideas should not be assumed to be unique or original to Christ-followers in the ἐκκλησία; they were also present in Jewish ideas in and before [and after] the first century, as they were being debated and developed in tandem and in what could be called συναγωγ-al assemblages.

attempted to embody dynamic egalitarianism that is experienced in small, imperfect sensations. By removing the demands and imposition of divine regulations and rules from above, an embodied ethics—imperfect and incomplete—could emerge as perfection on the move.

Roman wo/men did not just discuss and debate ethics: they embodied and enacted ethical impulses. They postured in ways that changed who took leadership roles and how different wo/men could participate and lead. Different postures reshaped the spaces in which they met: who sits, who stands, and who gets to be in which space? They could reorient the space itself—and how they assembled within it—as they experimented with how to make an assembly—an ἐκκλησία—more egalitarian. As we seem to see in Corinth, these ethical movements would have been imperfect. Freedom is easier to desire than it is to embody; justice is easier to talk about than to do. When one is molded into a system, it is difficult to fully and concretely envision a *different* world beyond it. A praxis of ἐκκλησία-l assemblage reminds us that kyriarchy continues to draw back and produce tensions in Rome's ἐκκλησία at the same time egalitarianism tugs these queer wo/men toward δικαιοσύνη θεοῦ.

Rethinking Rebels

How might some queer wo/men have demanded justice and freedom? How did they respond when imperial virtues collided with some of these emerging ethical impulses? Thinking of Rome's queer wo/men and their ethical impulses as an ἐκκλησία-l assemblage demands we scramble the sides and move beyond a binary of submission or rebellion. Around this assemblage of bodies, feelings, ideas, experiences, and movements, ethical impulses could coalesce into actions of total submission or rebellion, but they also moved toward these postures and shifted away from them. These movements occur by degree. Drawing from more scientific language, substantial action, such as a massive revolt, indicates a "phase shift," a phrase from chemistry that describes when H_2O transforms from liquid water to gas steam: it suddenly boils at a particular point.[22] Here, we look beyond

---

22. Usually at 100°C—however, a number of factors (such as atmospheric pressure) can shift this boiling point so that it is higher or lower. The idea of phase shifts comes from Manuel DeLanda's elaboration of Deleuze and Guattari's theory of assemblage: essentially, as various factors (e.g., temperature, pressure) shift and change within an element that cause it to change state (solid, liquid, gas) at certain points,

this spectacular moment and consider how reaching a boiling point participates in dynamic processes that are considerably longer than the duration of such boiling.[23]

The act of rebellion (ἀντιτάσσω) could be described as representing such a boiling point, and a rebellious response certainly could have emerged among some wo/men in Rome's ἐκκλησία.[24] In terms of ethical impulses, this could result in advocating for rebellion, active resistance, eschewal of imperial virtues and their rewards, and other forms of action against Rome's rule. Beyond Christ-followers, historical evidence affirms that some Romans, largely among conquered ἔθνη, participated in various forms of resistance. Such resistance was only recorded when violence led to visible unrest or upheaval that could not be ignored or construed differently.

Jewish resistance and unrest with regard to Roman rule in the first century CE produced an armed revolt in Jerusalem in 66 CE, aimed at expelling Rome and regaining independent Jewish rule. Though prompted by growing and intensified pressures, this spectacular revolt was an obvious instance of a large group coalescing around and embodying full rebellion against their ἐξουσίαι ὑπερεχούσαι ("prevailing authorities," as in Rom 13:1). Yet decades of differing forms of Jewish dissent and debate

---

even though these different internal factors may shift and change constantly, various parameters move and shift in an assemblage, but the changes are only noticeable at certain critical points—that is, when the phase shifts. See Manuel DeLanda, *Assemblage Theory* (Edinburgh: Edinburgh University Press, 2016), 19–20.

23. In other words, the moment boiling begins is the point of phase shift that occurs after what can be a slow, complex process to reach that critical point. It is the result of an assemblage of gradual or quick temperature rises and falls, movements of place and space, differences of pressure, additions of particles, and myriad other possible factors.

24. In various degrees. Such a reaction is certainly confirmed in historical records and writings, as we know rebellious sentiment existed among Jews (especially leading up and culminating in the rebellion of the Jewish War in 66 CE) and other ἔθνη who did revolt against Rome. The existence of such perspectives in relation to Paul and early Christianity are affirmed by, among others, Neil Elliott, *The Arrogance of Nations: Reading Romans in the Shadow of Empire*, PCC (Minneapolis: Fortress, 2008); Richard A. Horsley, ed., *Paul and Empire: Religion and Power in Roman Imperial Society* (Harrisburg, PA: Trinity Press International, 1997); Horsley, ed., *Paul and Politics: Ekklēsia, Israel, Imperium, Interpretation* (Harrisburg, PA: Trinity Press International, 2000); and Horsley, ed., *Paul and the Roman Imperial Order* (Harrisburg, PA: Trinity Press International, 2004).

regarding Rome's authority preceded it. The impulses that surrounded the revolt resonated far beyond the final conquest and destruction of Jerusalem in 70 CE. This traumatic event continued affecting Jews, Judaism, and others around them.

Josephus makes this build-up apparent in *Bellum judaicum* (*Jewish War*), his lengthy account of the revolt, which begins its narration two hundred years prior with the Maccabean revolts and an account of Hasmonean rule.[25] Given that *Bellum judaicum* begins before Rome's occupying presence in Judea, Josephus presents the ultimate moment of rebellion as the end of a long historical process. He details an *assemblage* of characters, ideas, skirmishes, treaties, debates, consensuses, and unrest that ultimately heated up to the point of phase shift, a boiling over in 66 CE. Susan Sorek writes, "In the final years before the war with Rome, Jews had become divided in their attitude to Roman authority."[26] By accounting for multiple divisions, and varying degrees of them, among first-century Jews in the context of their eventual revolt, Josephus's narrative presents rebellious and submissive impulses as a *continuum* among Jews where few perfectly adhered to either pole.[27] Some Jews were more willing to accommodate to Roman authority (including those who stood to benefit most from it and attain its good life), and others publicly protested it. Many others embodied impulses that moved in between these two poles, as they navigated and negotiated the ideas around various differences within Judaism.[28]

---

25. This account is further supplemented by his *Antiquitates judaicae*, which further highlights Jewish debates and differences—some more and some less related to Roman rule. At various points, these two accounts overlap descriptions (such as those of Jewish sects), though sometimes with divergences and discrepancies. See further Susan Sorek, *The Jews against Rome* (London: Continuum, 2008), esp. 1–13, 27–44; Tessa Rajak, *Josephus*, 2nd ed. (London: Duckworth, 2002), 65–103. On the diversity within Judaism and some ways of thinking of the ideas and practices of ordinary or common Jews as different from those of the few distinct and plausibly small sects, see especially the essays in Wayne O. McCready and Adele Reinhartz, *Common Judaism: Explorations in Second-Temple Judaism* (Minneapolis: Fortress, 2008).

26. Sorek, *Jews against Rome*, 11

27. As Sorek shows, the ruling aristocracy comes closest to being fully submissive (though not always), while the Zealots gain the most attention for their revolutionary stance. But even among the Zealots, there were divisions and differences on how to resist authority (Sorek, *Jews against Rome*, 39–44).

28. On the varying relations of Jews to Roman imperialism, see especially Seth Schwartz, *Imperialism and Jewish Society, 200 B.C.E. to 640 C.E.*, JCMAMW (Princeton: Princeton University Press, 2001), 87–98.

Another continuum of responses to Rome's dominion can be seen in evidence of enslaved persons. There is evidence of active and even violent resistance of enslaved persons against their enslavers. Tacitus discusses an instance of an enslaved man who kills his enslavers, and Roman law addresses the matter as a threat that needed to be prevented.[29] Periodically, enslaved people united and revolted en masse. This included three noteworthy revolts in the late Republican era (135–134 BCE, 104–100 BCE, and 74–73 BCE) and an uprising in 70 CE at a point of political turmoil in the aftermath of Nero's reign. Localized resistance allowed groups of enslaved persons to liberate themselves, flee, and band together in communities that would inhabit less populated areas and sustain themselves, in some cases through banditry. Flight was a common form of active resistance, usually when individual slaves found ways to liberate themselves and either join these communities or flee to densely populated areas where they could pass as freedpersons or those born free.[30]

Not all active resistance is visible. Enslaved resistance could be subtler so as not to attract attention and harsh penalties. Literary records that show enslaved resistance had been shaped almost exclusively by elite Roman interests (i.e., κύριοι/enslavers). These accounts have a vested interest in masking the resistance of enslaved persons in order to confirm their powerful image. Enslavers complained about slaves working slowly, mentioned punishments for forms of disobedience, and crafted tropes of the "lazy, disobedient slave."[31] This indicates that slowness and disobedience formed strategies of resistance, strategies that could be individual or collective.[32]

---

29. Allen Dwight Callahan and Richard A. Horsley, "Slave Resistance in Classical Antiquity," in *Slavery in Text and Interpretation*, ed. Callahan, Horsley, and Abraham Smith, SemeiaSt 83–84 (Atlanta: Scholars Press, 1998), 147–48. These examples, then, do not report that the provocation for slave resistance is particularly poor treatment. Rhetorically, the recounting of such instances (real or embellished) works to support Rome's slave system and provides argument for its brutality (i.e., enslavers reading this could be less likely to promise rewards or freedom, for fear of such retaliation).

30. Callahan and Horsley, "Slave Resistance," 139–43, 145, 147. As a result, enslaved persons might be tattooed or collared for easier identification. Archaeological remains have unearthed collars offering a reward for the return of a enslaved person who self-liberated; some indicate their enslaver was a Christ-follower. See also Glancy, *Slavery in Early Christianity*, 13.

31. See Glancy, *Slavery in Early Christianity*, 102–29. See also the trope of the faithful slave in the gospels (e.g., Matt 25:14–30).

32. Keith R. Bradley, "*Servus Onerosus*: Roman Law and the Troublesome Slave,"

"Considered as a whole," Sandra Joshel and Laura Hackworth Peterson explain, "slaveholders' complaints and attempts to counter slaves' actions suggest a thoroughgoing, constant resistance to slaveholders' strategies."[33] Descriptions of compliant submission to Roman enslavers must be taken with serious suspicion and assumed to be, at most, a very rare exception to the resistant rule.[34]

Roman houses and other buildings similarly masked resistance. Since enslavers wanted attention directed toward themselves and not their enslaved workers, enslaved persons could use the construction to their advantage by avoiding these intended sight lines. Unseen paths, invisible corners, and backdoor routes in between buildings offered spaces to enact resistant tactics (such as not working, leisure, or conspiracies).[35] This demonstrates the variety of forms resistance can take, some of which may *seem* submissive when contrasted to an armed revolt.

Resistant impulses among Jews and enslaved persons in the Roman world took different forms. While some subjects held rebellious ideas that they attempted to enact, others found less overt ways to express and embody concern and discomfort with their forced submission to Rome's rule. From the Jewish evidence, we see how collectives within a subjected ἔθνος debated and disagreed among themselves as to the best approach for responding to Rome's rule. As enslaved persons responded to their forced subjection with similar variety, it is plausible that they felt, imagined, and debated different responses alongside one another, especially when such

---

Slavery and Abolition 11 (1990): 135–57. After elaborating these various situations and resistant responses, he proposes, "The contention I make from the legal evidence surveyed is that Roman slaves constantly and continuously resisted slavery through a broad variety of non-cooperative ways that ranged from sabotage of property (arson, theft, falsification of record books, damage to animals) through vagrancy and time-wasting to feigning illness" (150). See also Callahan and Horsley, "Slave Resistance," 134–39; Keith R. Bradley, *Conquerors and Slaves* (Cambridge: Cambridge University Press, 1978), 121–23; Glancy, *Slavery in Early Christianity*, 133–39; Sandra R. Joshel and Lauren Hackworth Peterson, *The Material Lives of Roman Slaves* (Cambridge: Cambridge University Press, 2014), 13–17.

33. Joshel and Peterson, *Material Lives*, 13.

34. Just as Angela Davis insists must be the guiding assumption about slavery in the United States. "From the numerous accounts of the violent repression overseers inflicted on women, it must be inferred that she who passively accepted her lot as a slave was the exception rather than the rule." See Angela Y. Davis, *Women, Race, and Class* (New York: Vintage Books, 1981), 19–20.

35. Joshel and Peterson, *Material Lives*, 59–84, 97–114.

responses eventually led to organized rebellion. Attention gets drawn to the phase shift, making it easy to miss what else can be found in the longer process that creates, enables, and enacts radical change. The wo/men and impulses in these assemblages could have been debating and embodying forms of rebellion and submission simultaneously.

These instances provide insight into how queer wo/men in Rome's ἐκκλησία interacted with Paul's submissive impulses, such as those in Rom 13:1–7. Among enslaved Christ-followers, some may have insisted on overthrowing the system and demanded the ethical endorsement of liberation through flight.[36] Would they expect the ἐκκλησία to be a space that could or should offer protection? Other wo/men could have preferred Paul's submissive awaiting of Jesus's arrival. Others may have embraced subtler tactics for resistance, solicited funds and aid from free Christ-followers, and found other possibilities. These impulses would provoke feelings, responses, demands, and expectations that would have affected all the wo/men in Rome's ἐκκλησία.

Could Rome's ἐκκλησία have been on the verge of a rebellious phase shift? Could Rom 13 have helped less rebelliously oriented wo/men cool the waters? Paul's words plausibly prompted myriad feelings and responses. Some may have sensed possibilities or voiced questions about rebellion and submission beyond their polar extremes. Others might have felt confused, frustrated, or encouraged by Paul's advice. Though some in the ἐκκλησία experimented with egalitarianism's potentials, its full (or even slight) realization, especially beyond the assembly, may only have been accomplished in minuscule steps moving toward a hopeful phase shift.

Even among those resisting Rome, the most stridently rebellious discourse can still replicate kyriarchal ideology if it desires to invert the identity of the rulers. The oppressed can force the oppressors into submission in a very similar hierarchy under God (the book of Revelation being one stark example). Alluring and intoxicating, power turns out to be the one thing more terrifying than powerlessness.[37] As we saw in the theo-christological impulses of chapter 4, the rebellious potentials of drowning Jesus overlapped and interacted with impulses toward more kyriarchal Christs. Kyriarchal, imperial power works to retain bodies in its hold,

---

36. As we saw in the previous section, it seems some enslaved folks in Corinth may have been doing this. See 1 Cor 7:21–24.

37. As Sam Miller observes in the quotation from this chapter's epigraph. See Miller, "It Was Saturday Night," 107.

especially with its threat of punishments and promise of rewards. Some may have been more willing to risk rebellious postures; others may have needed to be less overt in order to survive; and others may have been content to stay submissive or perhaps even felt they benefitted from Rome's rule.

For some in the ἐκκλησία, this could have manifested with anger and other impatient bodily responses. Kyriarchy frustrates. This less-heartening final plausibility is not to quell the potential promises of sociopolitical ethics in Rome's ἐκκλησία. Rather, it names the difficulties of their movement. These difficulties affected queer wo/men's feelings and actions. Radical visions of justice and freedom have existed, but they have never been fully and permanently achieved.

Any action or impulse could be rebellious and submissive simultaneously. Existing in a dynamic ἐκκλησία-l assemblage, these sociopolitical plausibilities uncover messier realities beyond and in between rebellion or submission. They break down this binary and show why it so readily remains. Rebellion emerges as one among many strategies required to dismantle kyriarchy. Dismantling ethical binaries, this praxis of ἐκκλησία-l assemblage rethinks rebellious impulses as some among many participants in a process. They made it more plausible to move beyond the regulatory norms that, as we have seen with Rom 13, threaten to homonationalize certain queer bodies and impulses in order to place them in closer proximity to power.

ἔθν-ic Ethics

How did the lived experiences of different ἔθνη affect justice in Rome's ἐκκλησία? The ἐκκλησία brought together queer wo/men who came from a plurality of ethnic backgrounds. Just as their ethnic identities affected their theo-christological impulses, these queer wo/men let their multiple ethnic heritages affect the ethical impulses that came to life around Rome's ἐκκλησία. Romans scholars almost always reduce the interactions between different ethnicities to a binary between Jews and gentiles, as a conglomeration of all other ἔθνη: the ethical practices being debated in Rome's ἐκκλησία must either derive from Jewish or gentile backgrounds.[38]

---

38. When addressing ἐκκλησία-l discussions of ethics and (Jewish) ethnicity, focus hones upon and (almost exclusively) prioritizes the binary positions of fairly complete adoption or rejection of Jewish practices. Or, more often, particular sets of

Jewish practices get reduced to "Judaism" as representative of its "core" ethical teach-ings/demands. Romans 14:1–15:13 makes the most overt references to such specific practices, in particular eating meat, drinking wine, and observing holy holidays. Romans assumes a division in approaches to these practices according to being "weak" (ὁ ἀσθενῶν) or "strong" (οἱ δυνατοί, also used to refer to those who are powerful/most able), with the weak corresponding to those who adhere to these practices (all having roots in Judaism) and the strong as those who do not. The more or less standard approach, often assuming derivation from his experiences dealing with similar (spe-cific) questions in Galatia and Corinth, is to assume that Paul's "weak" corresponds to Jewish Christians (i.e., followers who are Jews, which can include some god-fearing gentiles) and "strong" to gentile Christians (i.e., followers who are from non-Jewish ἔθνη and almost always exclusively gentile). See Joseph A. Fitzmyer, *Romans*, AB 33 (New York: Doubleday, 1993), 686–708; Robert Jewett, *Romans: A Commentary*, Her-meneia (Minneapolis: Fortress, 2007), 829–85; James D. G. Dunn, *Romans*, WBC 38, 2 vols. (Dallas: Word, 1988), 2:794–853; Douglas J. Moo, *The Epistle to the Romans*, NICNT (Grand Rapids: Eerdmans, 1996), 826–84; Thomas R. Schreiner, *Romans*, BECNT (Grand Rapids: Baker Books, 1998), 703–60; Ben Witherington III with Dar-lene Hyatt, *Paul's Letter to the Romans: A Socio-Rhetorical Commentary* (Grand Rapids: Eerdmans, 2004), 325–49; Brendan Byrne, *Romans*, SP 6 (Collegeville, MN: Liturgical, 2007), 403–33; John B. Cobb Jr. and David J. Lull, *Romans*, Chalice Commentaries for Today (Saint Louis: Chalice, 2005), 175–79; Richard N. Longenecker, *The Epistle to the Romans: A Commentary on the Greek Text*, NIGTC (Grand Rapids: Eerdmans, 2016), 986–1019; Frank J. Matera, *Romans*, Paideia (Grand Rapids: Baker Academic, 2010), 305–26; Luke Timothy Johnson, *Reading Romans: A Literary and Theological Commentary* (New York: Crossroad, 1997), 196–207; Arland J. Hultgren, *Paul's Letter to the Romans: A Commentary* (Grand Rapids: Eerdmans, 2011), 495–534; Leander E. Keck, *Romans*, ANTC (Nashville: Abingdon, 2005), 334–58. Following Stowers's assumption that Paul's intended audience in Romans is exclusively gentile (though located within a synagogue), Nanos suggests the "weak" refers to the *non-Christ-fol-lowing Jews* in the synagogue. See Mark D. Nanos, *The Mystery of Romans: The Jewish Context of Paul's Letter* (Minneapolis: Fortress, 1996), 85–165. While I agree that Paul's audience is largely gentile, I am less interested in distinguishing firm positions or identities for the strong and the weak (somewhat in line with Stanley K. Stowers, *A Rereading of Romans: Justice, Jews, and Gentiles* [New Haven: Yale University Press, 1994], 321–23), although Paul may have more specific identities in mind. In terms of the realities within the ἐκκλησία (in Rome but likely as much in Corinth of Galatia), there was more likely much ambiguity between positions and many different opinions and practices regarding the adoption (or rejection) of these—and other—specifically Jewish practices (an assumption continued below). Ultimately, I find the following comment of Nanos most instructive: "What we find is that the behavior of those called 'weak' is characterized by their *opinions* of how to practice their faith as differenti-ated from the behavior patterns of the 'strong' (14:1–3, 4ff.), however, it is not their behavior or opinions that are regarded as 'weak,' but their faith" (Nanos, *Mystery of*

A praxis of ἐκκλησία-1 assemblage demands moving beyond this binary reduction and *proliferating* the ethnic identities erased through the imperial term ἔθνη.[39]

Paul's letters to other ἐκκλησίαι attest to a plurality of practice, particularly when it comes to practices related to so-called idols, that is, following the deities of other ἔθνη (such as Isis). In both 1 Cor 12:2 and 1 Thess 1:9, Paul alludes to how participants in these ἐκκλησίαι were "led away" (ἀπαγόμενοι [1 Cor]) by "idols" (εἴδωλατα) from which they have now "turned away" (ἐπεστρέψατε [1 Thess]).[40] In both assemblies, it is unclear to what degree these practices have been fully abandoned. Paul's rhetoric (ὅτε ἔθνη ἦτε, "when [in the past] you were ἔθνη" [1 Cor 12:2]) assumes all forms of devotion to other deities have ceased now that these participants are following Christ and worshiping the God of Israel. This does not mean everyone fully ceased: while his rhetoric may have helped to shape reality, it is does not necessarily describe reality. Perhaps some Thessalonian, Corinthian, and Roman Christ-followers turned simultaneously toward God and other deities/religious practices.

There are hints within Paul's letters, alongside other material evidence, that some Christ-followers adapted or retained elements of their ethnic customs as part of their practices as participants in the ἐκκλησία. Based on Paul's use of magical and cursing imagery in his letter to the Galatians (especially in 3:1), Natalie Webb suggests that Paul crafts his

---

Romans, 103). In other words, it is Paul's rhetorical framing that produces the binary and connects what are ultimately *different opinions about ethical practices* (based in Christo-theological ideas); but they do not necessarily correspond to fixed theological positions (especially since few if any existed).

39. I again draw from Saldhana's use of assemblages to think about race: "Race should not be eliminated, but *proliferated*, its many energies directed at multiplying racial differences so as to render them joyfully cacophonic." See Arun Saldhana, "Reontologising Race: The Machinic Geography of Phenotype," *Environment and Planning D: Society and Space* 24 (2006): 21. Emphasizing the many different languages that wo/men from different nations would have spoken in Corinth's ἐκκλησία, Ekaputra Tupamahu argues that the Corinthian ἐκκλησία (and other ἐκκλησίαι of Christ-followers) would have been multilingual, and Christ-followers would have spoken/worshiped in their (many) own languages. As evidence, Tupamahu reads Paul's attempt to silence those speaking in "tongue(s)" (γλῶσσα) in 1 Cor 14, where, he shows, Paul deploys racialized language of being "barbarian" (βάρβαρος). See Ekaputra Tupamahu, "Language Politics and the Constitution of Racialized Subjects in the Corinthian Church," *JSNT* 41 (2018): 223–45.

40. See Concannon, *When You Were Gentiles*, 31–32, 100–105, 115.

language of the cross to appeal to Christ-followers who were prone to use various physical symbols (e.g., the phallus) to ward off evil (especially the evil eye).[41] If Paul transforms this practice, it is plausible that early Christ-followers from among this ἐκκλησία's ἔθνη used the symbol of the cross, in depiction or as physical objects, for apotropaic effect.[42] Evidence from curse tablets and spells also attests the blending of the language of curses and magic (used to ward off evil spirits or set them upon others) with the traditions of Judaism and appeals to the God of Israel.[43]

We see the blending and incorporation of different ethnic deities in the worship of Isis. One invocation lists the many names of the Egyptian goddess, mapping her spread across the Greco-Roman world: "among the Amazons, warlike, among the Indians, Maia; among the Thessalians, moon; among the Persians, Latina; among the Magi, Kore, Thapseusis; at Susa, Nania; in Syrophoenicia, goddess; in Samothrace, bull-faced; at Pergamum, mistress; in Pontus, immaculate; in Italy, love of the gods" (P.Oxy. 11.1380).[44] This spread of naming shows how, as different people began to worship her, they identified how she embodied their values and incorporated the names of their deities (which, in some Greek locations, include Aphrodite). When it comes to religious practices, both within ἐκκλησίαι and beyond, practitioners frequently incorporated inherited ethnic practices with new ones they encountered and adopted.

Through this diverse ethnic interaction, persons from various ἔθνη, including Jews, could find ways to blend their own ethical customs, beyond religious practices, with these traditions. It is quite plausible that some ἔθνη in Rome did not fully abandon other ethnic practices that may have governed approaches to diet, gender, or behavior toward others, alongside

---

41. Natalie R. Webb, "Powers and Protection in Pompeii and Paul: The Apotropaic Function of the Cross in the Letter to the Galatians," in *Early Christianity in Pompeiian Light: People, Texts, Situations*, ed. Bruce Longenecker (Minneapolis: Fortress, 2016), 93–121.

42. Webb does not weigh in on this plausible implication of her argument and might disagree. Her suggestion leans more into the implication that the (singular) event of the cross replaces the need for physical apotropaic symbols: the event/concept of the cross functions apotropaically (Webb, "Powers and Protection, 114–20).

43. See especially John G. Gager, *Curse Tablets and Binding Spells from the Ancient World* (New York: Oxford University Press, 1992), 184–87. §86 is a curse meant to protect private property, which blends pagan curse language and deities with allusions to the Septuagint, leading Gager to say he is "in some sense a 'Judaizing' Gentile" (185).

44. Trans. in Kraemer, *Women's Religions in the Greco-Roman World*, 455.

these blended approaches to religious practices. While the issue of diet among Christ-followers is frequently considered in terms of Jewish difference from all other ἔθνη, the divisions in Corinth over dining practices (1 Cor 11:20–22) suggest issues surrounding food consumption beyond the Jew-gentile binary. While these divisions are often considered as demonstrations of socioeconomic difference, could it not *also* be plausible that the issue relates to differing approaches to dietary ethics or preferences due to diversity in ethnic heritage? An assembly of wo/men from numerous ethnic backgrounds means that these Christ-followers, including those in Rome, were negotiating questions of ethics with these blending and blended perspectives in mind.

Questions of adopting Jewish practices informs Paul's ethical advice in Rom 14–15. A similar concern arises in his polemical rebuke of Galatian Christ-followers who opted to be circumcised (also addressed more briefly in Phil 3:2–3), and it appears in terms of dietary questions (related to *kashrut*) in 1 Cor 8 and 10:14–30. Along with questions of holiday/Sabbath observance, the ethical questions of circumcision and diet/*kashrut* are those most attested, at least judging from Paul's letters as evidence, to have been concerns of first-century ἐκκλησίαι.[45] These three Jewish practices had, to some degree, become representative of Jews in the Roman world, attracting comment (usually that of ire and confusion) from Roman observers.[46] Jewish ethics extend well beyond these three practices, and wo/men in Rome's ἐκκλησία could have been familiar with Jewish practices and ethical impulses, especially if they interacted with practicing Jews, either in the context of a synagogue, as neighbors, or fellow Christ-followers (e.g., Prisca).

It is plausible that some of these wo/men held biases and stereotypes about Jews and their practices. While some (at least in Galatia, Philippi, and Corinth) clearly adopted commonly known Jewish practices, their decision was a source of ethical tensions and debates in these ἐκκλησίαι. Since Paul has been prompted to provide input, some wo/men in these assemblies were not comfortable with how other wo/men adopted Jewish customs. This discomfort could have had roots in the ire that accompanied

---

45. In addition to the texts described above, see Rom 14–15, where Sabbath/holiday observance is discussed in 14:5–6, alongside questions of diet.

46. See references and discussion in Erich S. Gruen, *The Construction of Identity in Hellenistic Judaism: Essays on Early Jewish Literature and History* (Berlin: de Gruyter, 2016), 318–19.

Roman stereotyping of Jews. They may already have been prone to reject Jewish practices based on sensations that such adoption would signal their ethical or sociopolitical decline. These stereotypes do not have to lead to negative evaluations of Jewish (and other) ethics. If Rome's ethnic hierarchy held some ethical systems with greater esteem than others, it is equally plausible that some felt that appearing more Jewish (according to Rome) would signal a rise in status. By considering an assemblage of ἔθνη, complex ethical impulses emerge. They can account for debates around Jewish theological ethics and make room for a plurality of interactions in between ethnic customs within Rome's ἐκκλησία.

The plurality of these interactions in between wo/men from many different ἔθνη encourages thinking about ethical impulses as temporary. With certain exceptions, these practices could be temporarily adopted and abandoned by different wo/men at different times, and their reasons for doing so could vary.[47] Paul's language of "wearing" (ἐνδύσασθε) Jesus Christ (Rom 13:14) provocatively suggests ethics as a matter of dressing: choose a style, try on another, change out the top, dress in drag. Not everyone wanted or needed a makeover in the form of Paul's Romanormative eye for the queer ἔθνη. As queer wo/men encountered, interacted with, and even tried on different ethical practices in Rome's ἐκκλησία, their impulses could have shifted. Some wo/men might have adopted some practices while choosing not to adopt others. Others may have been ambivalent, seeing little harm in many ethnic customs existing together in the ἐκκλησία.

Since Rome's ἐκκλησία consisted largely of non-Jewish ἔθνη, their experiences of Jewish ethics need to be considered as one piece of a wider conversation. The ἐκκλησία's ethnic diversity would have affected these queer wo/men's disagreements and discoveries.[48] Jewish practices—as the embodied ethics of a particular ἔθνος—existed *alongside other ethnic practices* embodied within Rome's ἐκκλησία. The Jewish practices under

47. Indeed, if debates on these topics were heated, it seems quite probable that some might have attempted to follow the practices (in public or private) to see how the ethical arguments and ideas were experienced and affirmed within their own bodies. Ethics, in other words, seem different in theoretical discussions than when they are actually attempted to be practiced.

48. In other words, if not clear already, ἔθνη-as-gentiles/non-Jews is still an extraordinary broad category as an ethnic distinction, and it represents a vast number of very different ethnicities across a wide geographic expanse. Given such a range, some of these ἔθνη would bear more (even close) similarity and have proximate ethical practice to Jews/Judeans.

scrutiny in Rom 14–15 may have contradicted or made difficult the cultural practices or ethics of some ἔθνη while complementing those of others.[49] Jewish ethics were important impulses in Rome's ἐκκλησία (perhaps especially after these wo/men heard Rom 14–15); however, emphasizing these specific differences to the exclusion of others risks missing the variety of ethics and customs that moved, shifted, and clashed in between these ἔθνη. Within the scope of this ethnic assemblage, Jewish customs were some among many of the ethics embodied by Roman Christ-followers.[50] Ethnicity mattered in the ἐκκλησία: Jewish alongside Greek, Egyptian, Phrygian, Dacian, Ethiopian, and even Roman.

Considering that all of these various ἔθνη had been incorporated under Rome's rule via some form of conquest, their approach to this variety of ἔθν-ic ethics would have been affected by kyriarchy. The empire valued different ἔθνη in hierarchal terms that were based in part on ethical distinctions; this fostered competition and displays of exceptionalism between various ἔθνη desiring upward mobility.[51] We saw in Tacitus and Philo the repetition of Roman stereotypes against particularly dangerous or depraved ἔθνη, like Germans and Egyptians. As these stereotypes circulated, they influenced ordinary Romans. Though Christ-followers from different ἔθνη participated together in Rome's ἐκκλησία, they would, to varying degrees, have been influenced by how moral associations stuck to particular ἔθνη. Sensations from these sticky associations moved in between queer wo/men's impulses and affected what they felt were acceptable ethical practices in their assembly.

---

49. Though Paul's exhortations to abandon ethnic ethics on theological grounds (i.e., move away from other gods) may also imply full abandonment of these ethical systems, it seems improbable that every person from every ἔθνη abandoned these ethics in practices (likely including the worship of other gods).

50. It is worth noting that, if Paul's letters do home in on Jewish ethics most lengthily, this is likely because of his own expertise and experience as a Jew on his specific vector within an assemblage of first-century Jewish theologies and ethics. Of course, the time spent on Judaism and its ethics is also partially due to the fact that Christ-followers adopt a theology that follows the God of Israel and of the Jews/Judeans, and therefore, to a fair degree, Jewish theology (broadly speaking).

51. As seen above (and explained by Niehoff) with Philo's presentation of Jews as an attempt to jockey for better sociopolitical standing under Rome's empire, especially under Claudian rule. Philo's attempts were not exceptional among the various elite of Rome's ἔθνη.

What can this complexity reveal about specific impulses within Rome's ἐκκλησία-l ethics? We can see how ethical impulses are embodied: they involved what people wore, what and how they ate, and what they did. Queer wo/men enacted impulses they heard, saw, thought of, and already knew. They let their hair down, prophesied, sniffed, tasted, and spat things out. They reacted to these enactments, whether they experienced disgust at someone else's action or felt a thrilling shiver when they tried on an impulse for the first time.

ἔθν-ic practices and Roman virtues were embodied in an *assemblage* of ethical impulses that colluded and collided in Rome's ἐκκλησία. Despite many specifics being lost, a variety of ethical impulses and practices would proliferate out of these plausibilities.[52] Christ-followers experimented, created, fixed, or cast aside innumerable ethical customs from many different ἔθνη as they impulsively moved toward different embodiments of justice.

Good Sex?

What makes sex good? The goodness of sex poses a moral question that is not separate from aesthetics. Imperial morality set particular boundaries on the moral goodness of sex, and these boundaries dissociated enjoyable goodness from moral goodness. Romosexuality regulated *desire*, which distracts virtuous men from their control of self, home, and empire. But *desire was not a distraction* for some Roman queer wo/men.[53] Desire extends beyond craving sex, whether it is a craving for food, wealth, or power—or for justice. What others impulses could queer wo/men in Rome's ἐκκλησία have felt about the goodness of sex? Could they connect desires for justice with their sexual desires? What is just sex?

Queer wo/men experienced many different sexual impulses, ones that do not necessarily have to involve intercourse. These experiences folded in between the ethical impulses proliferating among the queer wo/men in Rome's ἐκκλησία, just as their experiences as ἔθνη did. Sexual ethics among Rome's queer wo/men need to be considered beyond more mechanical

---

52. It is always possible that some of these lost specifics were incorporated and changed and could be uncovered in their traces that remain in textual or material evidence, a task unfortunately beyond the scope of this particular reconstructive endeavor.

53. Here I allude again to Miller, "It Was Saturday Night," 107, quoted in the chapter's epigraph.

questions that focus on position and the identities of participants. Unfixed through a praxis of ἐκκλησία-1 assemblage, sexual positions and participants swirl alongside practices, preferences, relationships, consent, and dynamics of power and control, including the negotiation of racialized and gendered differences.

ἔθν-ic ethics included sexual *mores*.[54] Since Roman discourse commonly portrayed depraved sexuality as rampant among ἔθνη (some more than others), perceptions of sexuality in Rome's ἐκκλησία cannot be severed from its participants' experiences as ἔθνη. In other letters, Paul explicitly equates sexual deviance with (all) ἔθνη, who are clearly meant as a negative example.[55] In 1 Thessalonians, he tells wo/men (who came from ἔθνη and had followed idols [1 Thess 1:9]) to approach issues of sexual praxis "not in lust's passion as is in the case of the ἔθνη that do not know God" (μὴ ἐν πάθει ἐπιθυμίας καθάπερ καὶ τὰ ἔθνη τὰ μὴ εἰδότα τὸν θεόν [1 Thess 4:5]).[56] He sticks a similar association of depravity to ἔθνη when he writes to Corinth's ἐκκλησία. He describes certain sexual behaviors there as being so bad they are even unheard of among ἔθνη—that is, the peoples among whom he and his audience could expect to find the worst depravity (1 Cor 5:1). In both cases, Paul constructs another strong, Romanormative border between ἔθν-ic ethics and those of Christ-followers. This border was more porous in practice—especially given that his sexual advice usually reacts to *how* wo/men in these ἐκκλησίαι *were* having sex, most notably in Corinth.

Evidence hints that many ancient queer wo/men enjoyed sex— or, at least, they wanted to.[57] This enjoyment may seem obvious, but

---

54. As can be seen in the ethical codes of Jews, as one of Rome's ἔθνη.

55. A homonational tactic, as we saw above, since Rome also considered its sexual ethics to be superior and contrasted them to the depravity that existed among its various conquered ἔθνη. I discuss Paul's use of ἔθνη as a negative example in 1 Thess 4:5, as another example of Pauline homonationalism, in Hoke, "Be Even Better Subjects, Worthy of Rehabilitation," in *Bodies on the Verge: Queering Pauline Epistles*, ed. Joseph A. Marchal, SemeiaSt 93 (Atlanta: SBL Press, 2019), 88–101.

56. Paul's contrast of how Christ-followers should behave sexually as opposed to ἔθνη in 1 Thessalonians is specifically related to the ambiguous advice "that each of you knows to acquire one's own vessel in holiness and honor" (4:4), a statement that has generally vexed scholars attempting to determine its specific referent. See discussion in Hoke, "Be Even Better Subjects," 88–90. For the purposes here, the fact that the advice clearly pertains to sexual ethics matters more than what Paul means by "acquiring a vessel."

57. We know some Romans enjoyed sex, because they are condemned for doing so;

its emphasis is critical in the context of an ancient culture where the majority of the evidence either renders enjoyment dirty and invisible (by calling it an immoral distraction) or problematic (by only emphasizing the perspectives and pleasures of powerful men who enjoy sex that is abusive and nonconsensual).[58] Queer wo/men trying to *enjoy* sex in (less) problematic ways are left invisible in ancient and scholarly discourses. By warning against the dangers of pursuing pleasure unrestrained, the elite Roman values of ἐγκράτεια (self-control) and σωφροσύνη (moderation) are based upon an unspoken admission that sexual pleasure *is* pleasing: deviant sexuality would not be tempting or alluring if not for its potential for uncontrolled and unmoderated pleasure that overtakes and consumes one's body.[59] Some queer wo/men experienced—or attempted to experience—pleasure through "unnatural" acts, positions, and preferences.

Queer wo/men were *there*. Beyond the philosophies espoused in elite discourse, evidence from Egypt includes love spells that display women's attempts to attract, in sexualized terms, the attentions and desires of other women.[60] One of these spells attempts to bind the desire of one woman (Paitous) to the other (Nike): ʾΩρίων Σαραποῦτος ποίησον καὶ ἀνάγκασον Νίκην Ἀπολλωνοῦτος ἐρασθῆναι Παιτοῦτ[ος,] ἥν ἔτ[εκ] ε Τμεσιῶς ("Orion Sarapous, make and force Apollonous's Nike to pas-

---

furthermore, graffiti in places like Pompeii attest to a more lived discourse of sexuality that includes reference to enjoying "unnatural" "excesses." See Craig Williams, *Roman Homosexuality*, 2nd ed. (Oxford: Oxford University Press, 2010), 151–70, 291–301.

58. Even today, sexual enjoyment is often tinged with guilt and associations with immorality and distraction, thus the "excessive significance" Rubin emphasizes as a burden of sexuality and the need to affirm that desire is not a frivolous distraction. See Gayle S. Rubin, "Thinking Sex: Notes for a Radical Theory of the Politics of Sexuality," in *Deviations: A Gayle Rubin Reader*, JHFCB (Durham, NC: Duke University Press, 2011), 149. Rubin's essay especially rings as relevant for thinking about how queer wo/men, ancient and contemporary, can consensually pursue BDSM and pornographic pleasure in ways that are aware of yet distinct from abusive uses of both.

59. Thus, overshadowing or including the impulses of the rational mind. On such warnings and how they support and comprise ethics of self-control and moderation, see Dale Martin, *Sex and the Single Savior: Gender and Sexuality in Biblical Interpretation* (Louisville: Westminster John Knox, 2006), 65–76.

60. Bernadette J. Brooten, *Love between Women: Early Christian Responses to Female Homoeroticism* (Chicago: University of Chicago Press, 1996), 96–105. As Brooten discusses, these spells are often formulaic and were most likely written by men for the women who commissioned them.

sionately desire Paitous, whom Tmesios bore").⁶¹ The existence of such spells affirms that women desired women for sexual passion/pleasure as much as companionship (if not more so).

While it is plausible, as Brooten argues, that these spells hope to invoke a more long-term, loving attraction between the women involved, the other side of the tablet that bears the first spell specifies in a second spell that it wants only to bind Nike and her desires for a short-term period: ποίησον Νίκην Ἀ[πολ]λωνοῦτος ἐρασθῆναι Παντοῦτος ἥν ἔτεκεν Τμεσιῶς, ἐπὶ ε″ μῆνας ("Make Apollonous's Nike passionately desire Pantous, whom Tmesios bore, for five months").⁶² This limited binding makes more plausible the notion that women pursued sexual pleasures with other women beyond the confines of a permanent relationship.⁶³

Material evidence from Pompeiian graffiti depicts inhabitants frequently pursuing a variety of sexual liaisons, and often enjoying doing so.

> O utinam liceat collo complexa tenere brac[ch]iola et teneris / oscula ferre label[l]is. i nunc, ventis tua gaudia, pupula, crede. (CIL 4.5296)
> O, would that it were permitted to grasp with my neck your little arms as they entwine (it) and to give kisses to your delicate little lips. Come now, my little darling, entrust your pleasures to the winds.⁶⁴

These lines begin a poem written by one woman to another in the entry-way of a small house. This graffito emphasizes the pleasures (gaudia) that pass between these women as they grasp and kiss, and it shows how

---

61. Brooten, Love between Women, 91–92. My translation of the Greek modifies Brooten's slightly: most notably, I translate ἐρασθῆναι as "desire passionately" instead of using "love." While "love" is the typical gloss for this verb, this English term has multiple meanings, extending beyond and often made distinct from sexual desire, and its lexical usage and definition clearly emphasize the desirous and passionate qualities of love that can differ from the meaning Brooten attributes to it within her argument. See LSJ, s.v. "ἔραμαι," 680. While it is plausible that Paitous intended this to attract Nike's love in this way, it is equally plausible that she merely sought a more limited sexual attraction, as the other side of the tablet implies (see further in discussion below).

62. Brooten, Love between Women, 91–92.

63. Contra Brooten, Love between Women, 92–93, who does not fully deny this plausibility but prefers to suggest that Pantous may desire this as a "trial period" for the women before entering a longer relationship or that external factors would prevent their relationship to last any longer.

64. Trans. in Kristina Milnor, Graffiti and the Literary Landscape in Roman Pompeii (Oxford: Oxford University Press, 2014), 197.

Roman queer women expressed and displayed their own pleasurable sexual impulses.

Sexual agency and pleasure could also come from resisting its denial, especially in the case of the abusive conditions faced by enslaved prostitutes. Considering how they interacted with its graffiti, Sarah Levin-Richardson brings to life the wo/men of Pompeii's purpose-built brothel.[65] She argues that these wo/men could have asserted their sexual agency by writing graffiti in first person or reading aloud graffiti inscribed by men.[66] For example, wo/men, as graffiti writers, could proclaim themselves as the subject of the verb "to suck" (*fellare*, e.g., "Fortunata sucks" [*CIL* 4.2259, 2275]).[67] This allowed enslaved prostitutes with little social power to try on, voice, and thereby contest the penetrative agency they usually lacked.[68] Levin-Richardson attends to exploitations of enslaved wo/men that included the denial of their sexual pleasure and permits them to resist via professions of pleasure and agency on their own or among themselves.[69] Both Levin-Richardson and Deborah Kamen and Levin-Richardson show how women could proclaim themselves as *fellatrices* ("suckers") and *fututrices* ("fuckers") in ways that emphasized their agency and their (seeming) desirous enjoyment of the sexual activity.[70] Their readings of Pompeii's graffiti evoke a willful sexual subculture among wo/men, especially enslaved prostitutes, that has its own vocabularies and feelings (of which the brothel's graffiti are merely the tip of the iceberg).

---

65. Sarah Levin-Richardson, "*Futata Sum Hic*: Female Subjectivity and Agency in Pompeian Sexual Graffiti," *CJ* 108 (2013): 319–45; Levin-Richardson, *The Brothel of Pompeii: Sex Class, and Gender at the Margins of Roman Society* (Cambridge: Cambridge University Press, 2019), 111–28 (ch. 7, "Female Prostitutes").

66. Levin-Richardson, "*Futata Sum Hic*," 327–41.

67. Levin-Richardson, "*Futata Sum Hic*," 328–32. On women as subjects of verbs with the root *futu-* (fuck), see pp. 332–34.

68. Levin-Richardson, "*Futata Sum Hic*," 340–42.

69. This is especially the case in her book's chapter on female prostitutes, which draws out enslaved wo/men's agency in the face of exploitation, which extended beyond their sexual labor and included emotional labor with their clients and physical labor in maintaining the brothel. In addition to claiming themselves as subjects, these wo/men also likely framed their clients as objects and formed communities of support/resistance among themselves (Levin-Richardson, *Brothel of Pompeii*, 111–28).

70. Deborah Kamen and Sarah Levin-Richardson, "Lusty Ladies in the Roman Literary Imaginary," in *Ancient Sex: New Essays*, ed. Ruby Blondell and Kirk Ormand (Columbus: Ohio State University Press, 2015), 239–42 (on *fellatrices*), 244–48 (on *fututrices*); Levin-Richardson, "*Futata Sum Hic*," 331–34.

Shorter graffiti, seemingly inscribed by men, that evoke sexual pleasure occur frequently across Pompeiian graffiti. These include *ubi me
iuvat, asido* ("When I want to, I sit on it. [with an image of the phallus]"
[*CIL* 4.950, located in between the entrances to two buildings]) and *hic
ego bis futui* ("I fucked here two times" [*CIL* 4.2217, located on a building facade accessible from a public street]).[71] These proclamations visibly
admit to pursuing sexual pleasures, which can involve being penetrated, as
an embrace of their (deviant) desire for it (especially in the case of "when
I want to").

We have traces that some Christ-followers also enjoyed sex, including
sex that the prevailing authorities called deviant. For example, 1 Cor 5–7
addresses sexuality that deviates from Romosexuality and emphasizes its
power to pollute the ἐκκλησία in Corinth. As Wire's reconstructive method
shows, Paul's rhetoric in this letter is constructed as a response to what is
happening on the ground in this ἐκκλησία. If Paul exhorts φεύγετε τὴν
πορνείαν ("flee sexual immorality/prostitution" [1 Cor 6:18]), this reaction,
among others in these chapters, "may reveal that it is in vogue."[72]

When I say queer wo/men enjoyed sex, I am referring to some of the
unspecified sexual pleasures Paul's lumps into πορνεία—*not* to the specific,
almost always abusive, acts of sexual exchange that occur through Roman
prostitution.[73] While we cannot ignore how term the πορνεία was associated with Greco-Roman prostitution and the sexually abusive conditions
it imposed upon enslaved wo/men, Paul's usage of the term makes prostitution a metonymy for any and all sexual immorality.[74] This is similar

---

71. These graffiti are discussed and compiled in Williams, *Roman Homosexuality*,
294–95, 428 n. 25, 429 n. 29, see further 151–70, 291–301. As evidence, the Pompeiian
graffiti is not without its limitations and biases, most notably our lack of any knowledge
of its authors, particularly in terms of class, gender, or ethnicity. He presumes it to be
overwhelmingly written by men, given the particular perspective espoused (296–97).

72. Wire, *Corinthian Women Prophets*, 1–11, 72; she compares his reactions to a
"No Fishing" sign, which "can signal where there is good fishing" (72).

73. *Paul* characterizes what these wo/men are doing as πορνεία, but we do not
know how these wo/men described their own sexual experiences. If they (or we, as
interpreters) were to reclaim πορνεία, this would be problematic—especially if those
reclaiming the term were not enslaved prostitutes or do not consider the abusive conditions this term can and did describe.

74. For a comprehensive overview of the usage and developing meanings of
πορνεία, from its classical/Hellenistic uses almost exclusively as prostitution, to wid-
ening meanings of sexual immorality in Hellenistic/Roman-era Jewish and Christian

to how society today frequently shames "promiscuous" wo/men as "sluts" and "whores." Paul's concern is Romanormative: he is not concerned about the material conditions of enslaved prostitutes (who, if/when they are addressed by his advice, are not offered viable means for flight). He is concerned that Christ-followers, through their sexual impulses, might be associated with the sexual immorality that the term sticks to these wo/men.

First Corinthians 5:1–6 offers one specific form that Paul's label of πορνεία takes, and it does not seem to involve prostitutes, prostitution, or (necessarily) abuse.[75] The text confirms that participants in Corinth's ἐκκλησία permitted sexual impulses that Paul deems nonnormative. Paul explicitly identifies the instance of a man living with his father's wife:

> ὅλως ἀκούεται ἐν ὑμῖν πορνεία, καὶ τοιαύτη πορνεία ἥτις οὐδὲ ἐν τοῖς ἔθνεσιν, ὥστε γυναῖκά τινα τοῦ πατρὸς ἔχειν.
>
> On the whole, sexual immorality is reported among you: such sexual immorality that is not even among the ἔθνη, to the extent that someone has his father's woman. (1 Cor 5:1)

What is significant here is that, at least from what Paul has heard, enough of the wo/men in Corinth had accepted this situation that they had not

---

texts (usually aligned with prevailing cultural mores and often associated with ethnic/ gentile others), see David Wheeler-Reed, Jennifer W. Knust, and Dale B. Martin, "Can a Man Commit πορνεία with His Wife?," *JBL* 137 (2018): 383–98. See also Wheeler-Reed, *Regulating Sex in the Roman Empire: Ideology, the Bible, and the Early Christians*, CP (New Haven: Yale University Press, 2017), 65–73; Glancy, "The Sexual Use of Slaves: A Response to Kyle Harper on Jewish and Christian *Porneia*," *JBL* 134 (2015): 215–29. For more on the associations between πορνεία and prostitution and how these should inform interpretations of this passage in the context of slavery, see Nasrallah, "You Were Bought with a Price," 59–60; Glancy, *Slavery in Early Christianity*, 65–67; Joseph A. Marchal, "The Usefulness of an Onesimus: The Sexual Use of Slaves and Paul's Letter to Philemon," *JBL* 130 (2011): 768.

75. My reading of πορνεία and 1 Cor 5 resonates with Midori E. Hartman's queer reading the Corinthian ἐκκλησία's so-called πορνεία as alleged and policed by Paul. Hartman argues that the practices Paul characterizes as πορνεία among the Corinthians indicate their embrace of queer pleasures that resist Roman and Pauline sexual norms. She calls attention to the fact that Paul's use of πορνεία is racialized through his use of "not even among the ἔθνη," which makes πορνεία characteristic of Rome's racialized ethnic others. See Midori E. Hartman, "A Little *Porneia* Leavens the Whole: Queer(ing) Limits of Community in 1 Corinthians 5," in *Bodies on the Verge: Queering Pauline Epistles*, ed. Joseph A. Marchal, SemeiaSt 93 (Atlanta: SBL Press, 2019), 143–63.

already expelled or condemned those involved. Despite the fact that this situation is, it appears, more heinous than any depravity seen, imagined, and thrust upon ἔθνη (by Paul and by Rome), the ἐκκλησία has not rejected this sexual situation.[76] It is plausible that they have embraced it under their theo-christological slogan: πάντα μοι ἔξεστιν ("I am allowed to do anything" [1 Cor 6:12]).[77] While Paul may have selected what he considers more extreme examples to discuss in detail, the chapter's opening words make clear that a wide range of sexual impulses (all of which Paul reduces to πορνεία) existed in multiple manifestations among the ἐκκλησία's wo/men.[78] For the wo/men of Corinth, this permissive embrace of multiple sexual impulses, as Midori E. Hartman argues, "is not a bug but a feature" of their ἐκκλησία.[79]

In 1 Cor 7, Paul's tentative embrace of sex within marriage reflects an imposition of or appeal to return to Roman ideals of controlling passions, particularly through moderation. This further supports the plausibility that some wo/men in Corinth were pursuing passion unrestricted. If "it is better to marry than to burn" (κρεῖττον ἐστιν γαμῆσαι ἤ πυροῦσθαι [1 Cor 7:9]), Paul proposes marriage as the only appropriate channel for the Corinthian wo/men's desires, which have been excessive to the point of producing πορνεία.[80] According to Paul, marriage is a suitable (Romosexual and heteronormative) alternative to these desires when completely refraining from sexual pleasure proves impossible.

Even as the Corinthian ἐκκλησία appears to have had some participants who embraced subcultural sexual impulses in various forms, others took the ideal of sexual permissibility as license to refrain from sex entirely,

---

76. Wire discusses this passage and raises issues concerning whether both members of this couple (the man and his father's wife) were participants in the Corinthian ἐκκλησία or whether it may be only the man (since the directives appear to be meant in response to his presence) (Wire, *Corinthian Women Prophets*, 73–76).

77. A more word-for-word translation would be "Everything is allowed for me," but my translation better gets at how such a slogan—at least somewhat idiomatic— would be repeated in less stilted English. On such statements as slogans, see Wire, *Corinthian Women Prophets*, 13–14, 75–76.

78. The adverb ὅλως, from the adjective ὅλος, "whole, entire," is often used in such descriptive contexts as "on the whole" in the sense of "speaking generally" (LSJ, s.v. "ὅλος," 1218).

79. Hartman, "A Little *Porneia* Leavens the Whole," 155.

80. See Wheeler-Reed, *Regulating Sex*, 68–73; Martin, *Sex and the Single Savior*, 65–76.

even among some wo/men who were married (1 Cor 7:1–16).[81] Such an orientation toward nonpraxis could, for some, have been because sexual acts were *not* pleasurable, due to past experience or asexuality.[82] While general scholarly consensus has accepted the option that those refraining from sexuality were expressing a form of asceticism (i.e., refraining from being overcome by any sort of pleasure: sexual, dietary, emotional, etc.), consideration should be given to the plausibility that those who refrained from sex pursued alternative, nonsexual pleasures.[83] While some queer wo/men may have found in Christ an affirmation to embrace their sexual desires through expressions of mutual pleasure, others may have found permission to refuse to engage in the same activities *because* they did not provoke pleasures.

Some wo/men in Rome's ἐκκλησία could have, in somewhat similar ways, explored a plethora of practices and approaches in relation to sexuality (including having none at all). Queer wo/men were *in* Rome's ἐκκλησία, after all, including Tryphaena and Tryphosa (Rom 16:12) as, plausibly, a married missionary pair.[84] This pair gives us a brief glance at the iceberg of potential sexual partners, practices, and embodiments that

---

81. See Wire, *Corinthian Women Prophets*, 72–97. Marchal discusses this passage and Wire's reconstructions of the wo/men prophets, focusing on how their different apocalyptic temporalities and velocities affect their sexual orientations/choices. Marchal, "How Soon Is (This Apocalypse) Now?," 53–55.

82. As in wider queer theory, more exploration could be given to asexuality and queerness in the first century, and asceticism in the ancient world seems to provide a good place for such inquiry, in a way that could see ascetic practice as an embodiment of sexuality related to asexual practice and preference. On wider theoretical issues, see Ela Przybylo and Danielle Cooper, "Asexual Resonances: Tracing a Queerly Asexual Archive," *GLQ* 20 (2014): 297–318. In terms of asexuality and Greco-Roman sexuality, Thomas K. Hubbard and Maria Doerfler have explored asexual orientations in Greek religious cults from the fourth century BCE alongside the early Christian desert fathers of the third and fourth centuries CE. See Thomas K. Hubbard and Maria Doerfler, "From Ascesis to Sexual Renunciation," in *A Companion to Greek and Roman Sexualities*, ed. Hubbard (Chichester, UK: Wiley Blackwell, 2014), 168–87.

83. In other words, the decision to not have sex is determined by an ace orientation not from religious devotion (an assumption that incorrectly presumes that refraining from sex means quelling an innate desire [that for many is not always innate] and, therefore, the only reason to do stems from moral/religious conviction). See Hoke, "*Homo Urbanus* or Urban Homos?"

84. Mary Rose D'Angelo, "Women Partners in the New Testament," *JFSR* 6 (1990): 72–75.

also could have existed among these queer wo/men. When they heard Paul encourage them not to have licentious sexual pursuits so that they could live in respectful submission to Rome in Rom 13, they may have groaned, interrupted, or left (as they plausibly did after hearing 1:18–32). Maybe a few queer wo/men passionately kissed to remind others of their own embodied ethical impulses.

Alongside impulses that envisioned and prioritized egalitarianism, it is plausible that such ideas prompted movements toward more egalitarian expressions of sexuality within some bodies. This might take the form of seeking *mutual pleasure*, as opposed to assertions of dominance and focus on the (more powerful) penetrator.[85] Prioritizing pleasure can be oriented as a rather radical ethical perspective in the context of a culture that cautioned against good sex as lacking moderation and, therefore, debased and lowly.[86] By emphasizing shared pleasures (which might also extend beyond sex), ethical goodness requires fewer mandates that force goodness to be noble or natural. Good sex pleases *all parties involved*, ideally.

Just as egalitarian impulses did not immediately produce a sociopolitical utopia, an ethical orientation toward mutual pleasure did not create some queer utopia where Christ-followers easily and often practiced perfectly pleasing sex with their partners. Good sex takes different forms; it can take time to get just right. Sex is messy; sexual-ethical impulses move

---

85. As Brooten emphasizes can exist beyond and below the radar of the hierarchical paradigms of androcentric, elite Roman sexuality (Brooten, *Love between Women*, esp. (but not limited to) 105–9, 359–60). For more on prioritizing mutual pleasure as an erotohistoriographical approach to Rom 13 specifically, see Hoke, "Unbinding Imperial Time: Chrononormativity and Paul's Letter to the Romans," in *Sexual Disorientations: Queer Temporalities, Affects, Theologies*, ed. Kent L. Brintnall, Joseph A. Marchal, and Stephen D. Moore, TTC (New York: Fordham University Press, 2018), 79–83. See also work on divergent/mutual sexual pleasures in Maia Kotrosits, "Penetration and Its Discontents: Greco-Roman Sexuality, the *Acts of Paul and Thecla*, and Theorizing Eros without the Wound," *JHistSex* 27 (2018); Joseph A. Marchal, "Bottoming Out: Rethinking the Reception of Receptivity," in *Bodies on the Verge: Queering Pauline Epistles*, ed. Marchal, SemeiaSt 93 (Atlanta: SBL Press, 2019), 228–32.

86. Sexual equality could also pertain to sex as gender, in which case the ἐκκλησία offered a space for women's full and equal participation, as discussed in chapter 4 above. There are porous lines between ancient gender and ancient sexuality, and both affected one another—along with issues of race. Thus, penetrative sexual acts and sexual agency are the purview of male, Roman bodies, while female, barbarian bodies are prone to penetration or excessive sexuality that is less manly.

in between bodies that experience feelings and sensations differently—especially when sexual experience (and shame) is intimately entwined with kyriarchal forces. When practiced by real wo/men, mutual-seeming sex acts can still reinforce power imbalance; acts that seem pleasing and mutual in theory may produce problems or awkwardness in actual bodies. Pleasure is perspectival and produced in relation. Some people like to bottom (such as Rome's *cinaedi*); some enjoy topping; others flop and flip. Tastes change. Wo/men scissor, spank, lick, flog, smooch, bind and are bound, cuddle, sniff, and shower. They derive pleasure from desires that are not sexual. Sharing pleasure takes time, effort, patience, and experimentation that may not always be good. "People are different."[87]

It is plausible that some of Rome's queer wo/men connected their pleasurable desires with their theo-Christologies. This could have prompted ethics of sexual equality instead of those that center on God's pleasure as the top. This might have permitted some to pursue their sexual impulses more freely or openly, especially if their praxes defied kyriarchy's nature: women loving—or just loving fucking with—women, for instance.

A variety of risks and factors complicated the ethical embodiments of sexual impulses among queer wo/men in Rome's ἐκκλησία. With sexuality's excessive significance, ethical impulses around whether and how sex could be good would have pulled bodies in strong and different ways. Many would have been attached to Romanormativity, unaware of its kyriarchal and imperial arrangements and affects. This draw might be most apparent in those who stridently adhered to prevailing sexual ethics or those whose sociopolitics leaned toward upholding kyriarchy. Different ethnic upbringings would have engendered different experiences, ideas, and stigmata concerning sexual mores.

Paul's letters imply that some wo/men experienced and expressed their discomfort with queerer pursuits. Paul knows the details of the situation described in 1 Cor 5:1, and it is likely that this is because some participants have raised complaints. The same disagreements and complaints to Paul can be seen in his need to address marriage and more asexual preferences. Some Christ-followers desired some degree of kyriarchy when it came to sexual matters, which also includes their questioning the extent of gender-based egalitarianism (e.g., 1 Cor 11:2–16).

---

87. Once again recalling Sedgwick's antihomophobic axiom. See Eve Kosofsky Sedgwick, *Epistemology of the Closet* (Berkeley: University of California Press, 1990), 22.

While some queer wo/men in Rome's ἐκκλησία may have enjoyed such pleasurable pursuits, the sexual practices of Christ-followers were still affected by kyriarchy and Romosexuality. Even though Rome's legal regulation, enforcement, and propaganda around sexuality targeted and protected elite and citizen bodies (often exclusively), these ideologies grasped bodies across the sociopolitical plane, especially holding those with optimistic attachments to upward mobility.[88] As Puar argues in contemporary contexts, bodies are often regulated by "intimate control" that encompasses not only official scrutiny and policing but also a lack of privacy and access that is assumed in many ideals and arguments for freer pursuits of pleasure.[89] Though different in ancient contexts, a similar point can be made: spaces for sexual praxis for bodies of lower status would often have been more public and less intimate. Depending on one's social location, queerer sexual impulses and practices would have felt freer—and have been more accessible—for some than others. As an assemblage, queerness as regulatory moves in tension alongside queerness's extension toward justice. Impulses that were simultaneously drawing wo/men toward and away from Romanormativity produced pleasures and freedoms as well as disgust, discomfort, and resistance.

In Rome's ἐκκλησία, some queer wo/men would sense their own limitations drawing them back when it came to sexual impulses and embodiments—even among those who embraced egalitarian impulses in general. Sexuality's excesses frequently produce sensations of disgust toward certain sexual thoughts or embodiments, especially when put into embodied practices.[90] Like sex itself, how these ethical impulses

---

88. As seen in the previous chapter with regard to Rom 13.

89. That is, an ethic of "anything is permissible behind closed doors" requires having doors to close. Certainly, Roman authorities were unlikely to sexually police those of lowest status (unless they were defiling elite bodies), especially considering these ἔθνη were already considered sexually immoral and unnatural by definition. However, the social, political, and economic factors that influenced and constrained less elite lives would have had a regulatory effect on sexual practice. Compare to the regulation of intimacy in Jasbir K. Puar, *Terrorist Assemblages: Homonationalism in Queer Times*, NW (Durham, NC: Duke University Press, 2007), 114–65 (discussed in ch. 1 above).

90. See Sara Ahmed, *The Cultural Politics of Emotion*, 2nd ed. (New York: Routledge, 2014), 82–100 (ch. 4, "The Performativity of Disgust") Ahmed largely talks about the performance of disgust in the context of racial prejudice in contemporary society, but it applies equally to disgust around nonnormative sexuality (which, as

would have been felt, embodied, or discussed would have been messy and affected bodies differently. Sex and sexuality affects bodies—whether one is engaging in sexual activities, reacting to it, imagining it, wondering about it, or questioning one's own orientations. Queer wo/men would have sensed these different feelings moving in between them as they struggled with these ethical impulses. As Rome's ἐκκλησία struggled together, their impulses broached—but left ultimately unanswered—the question: *Can sex ever be good?*

Justice, Queerness, Ethics, and ἐκκλησία-l Assemblage

What should God's justice do?
This question whispers behind these ethical impulses as they pulsed in between one another and the queer wo/men in Rome's ἐκκλησία. God's justice (δικαιοσύνη θεοῦ) does not act on its own. It must be done by queer wo/men when they embody ethical impulses. The specific concerns in the ethical impulses elaborated above plausibly prompted more general ethical queries: what could τὸ ἀγαθόν ("goodness") mean when following Christ? Why should this term be upheld or embraced (by Paul or by others)? If, collectively, they embody many different ethical impulses that prompt multiple, contradictory decisions, how and when should the ἐκκλησία take decisive action? When does in-betweenness need to take a side—or, at least, a stand? These questions remind how, as we see them, none of these first-century impulses—including Paul's—represent a finalized ἐκκλησία-l ethics.

To conclude, we continue engaging a praxis of ἐκκλησία-l assemblage to bring these many differing impulses to life. ἐκκλησία-l assemblage moves beyond binary answers to moral questions, including rebellion versus submission; Jew or gentile; ascetic and libertine. In what other ways can this assemblage scramble the ethical sides in Rome's ἐκκλησία? What other affective impulses could have been generated? How were these queer wo/men becoming an ethical ἐκκλησία?

These wo/men would have put theo-christological ethical impulses into practice. They did not just discuss or debate ethics: they chewed,

---

Puar shows, is often combined with racialized—especially Muslim/terrorist—bodies, to emphasize disgust). Such disgust was also produced by Roman elite discourse surrounding both sexuality and its ἔθνη. See also Stephen D. Moore, "Vomitous Loathing and Visceral Disgust in Affect Theory and the Apocalypse of John," *BibInt* 22 (2014): 503–28.

gulped, and fucked with their ethics. Their embodiments of diverging ethical impulses could have been performed in direct (or subtle) opposition to others, making visible the tensions and rifts that are inherent when bodies interact in community.[91] As Paul, potentially alongside other Roman wo/men, expressed criticism and judgment of open sexual depravity, some did precisely these things and admitted to practicing them (or embraced those who did, as in Corinth). Perhaps some declared their unnaturalness to be an embodiment of justice. Other wo/men would have sensed and reacted to tense feelings around them. As they did, some may have ceased following certain ethical impulses—or begged others to stop or join in. These embodiments may have given others permission to temporarily try on an impulse. Wo/men could retain and abandon impulses—and the practices that derive from them—depending on how they felt.

Would having just sex prompt demands for taking decisive action toward freedom, especially for enslaved wo/men? Ideally, it would. However, regulatory queernesses compete alongside sensations of queerness as freedom. Actual ethical practices may have drawn queer wo/men toward a changing experience of justice through one ethical impulse even as they continued grasping at imperial justice through another. Some wo/men's hopes for change would be complicated by their ongoing struggles with risks and rewards tied to their survival in Rome's kyriarchal waters.

Queer wo/men could not limit their ethical political impulses to this ἐκκλησία. Outside influences and experiences—persecution, other rebels or dissenters, friends, or possession of power—affected queer wo/men and the ethical impulses they embodied or rejected. If imperial politics affected their ethical impulses, then experiences of ethics around this assembly also affected their impulses toward Rome beyond it. Some may have advocated more rebellious or radical impulses within the ἐκκλησία's safer space but only mutedly embodied them beyond it.[92] Others could have preferred to wait for change in submissive postures, hoping for praise from God and God's appointed authorities, thereby finding support in the exhortations of Paul (along with others) to submit to Roman authority and align to its ethical hierarchies. Some may have taken rebellious actions or positions in more public spaces (as did other rebels and dissenters in Rome) while

---

91. Appearing in ways like the rifts and disagreements in Corinth or even Galatia, as discussed above.

92. And even the ἐκκλησία was likely a safer space for some bodies more than others.

others may have seemed more submissive while embodying a more subtle ethic of resistance.

As they reacted to and embodied (or did not embody) Jewish teachings, it is plausible that outside factors persuaded and discouraged: Jewish friends, synagogue participation, neighbors who expressed anti-Jewish prejudices, or the presence and influence of Jewish wo/men within Rome's ἐκκλησία (e.g., Prisca). The impulses wo/men sensed may have differed from the practices they embodied: some may have attempted to robustly follow Jewish teachings (including diet, holidays, and circumcision) with the "zeal of a convert" (as seems to have happened in Galatians); others (like many Jews) might have striven to follow some Jewish ethics and found the practice more difficult.[93] It is plausible that many experimented with practices, changed approaches frequently, failed and succeeded, and were largely ambivalent. Attempts, experiments, and experiences of embodiment affected and changed ethical impulses, and Rome's queer wo/men acted upon them. The evidence of difference and debates in these ἐκκλησίαι suggests fluctuation in between bodies and practices.

All of these issues do not neatly separate: an approach to Jewish teachings would affect one's position and perceptions vis-à-vis Rome. Living in a Romosexual world, sexual ethics were always sociopolitical embodiments. One's embodiment of Jewish ethics would also influence, in a variety of interpretive directions, ethical impulses around sexuality.[94] Wo/men embody ethical impulses together and in relation to one another, even when their embodiments contradict. Enslaved persons could resist doing work by slowing down in unseen corners or back alleys: finding a tavern for a drink or taking up time with a willing sexual partner.[95] These different ethical impulses—sensed, experienced, seen, and

---

93. Thus, most first-century Jews acknowledged that they would err. See Stowers, *Rereading of Romans*, 176–93.

94. Though largely more conservative in their sexual ethics, diversity can be seen among some of Second Temple Judaism's major extant texts and authors, including Philo and Josephus. See a compendium of texts that address sexuality in William Loader, *Philo, Josephus, and the Testaments on Sexuality: Attitudes toward Sexuality in the Writings of Philo and Josephus and in the Testaments of the the Twelve Patriarchs* (Grand Rapids: Eerdmans, 2011).

95. See Joshel and Peterson, *Material Lives*, 104–6, where they draw off of John DeFelice's description of taverns as being a "deviant location." See also John DeFelice, *Roman Hospitality: The Professional Women of Pompeii* (Warren Center, PA: Shangri-La, 2001), 149.

embodied—continued interacting, moving forward, and drawing back via in-betweenness. Queer wo/men would continue to ask through their practices, their gestures, and their voices: What is egalitarianism? What do submission and rebellion look like? What is goodness? And who decides? Struggling together as they practiced and experimented with embodied ideas, these wo/men would have been constantly reminded of the unsettled nature of their theo-christological ethics. They were still struggling together toward becoming an ethical ἐκκλησία.

And where is Paul as one among the many wo/men participating in Rome's ἐκκλησία? Paul's ethical suggestions at the end of his letter represent a few firmer impulses that circulated among the many ethical impulses that were engaged around Rome's ἐκκλησία. Paul's impulses are some among many: but Paul is not alone in his impulses either. Some queer wo/men were just as Romanormative as Paul—some could have been more so. Paul would not be the first or the only Christ-follower to engender ethical impulses that veered toward homonationalism (or, for that matter, cruel optimism). Some of them could have already been expressing versions of Paul's ethics: his impulses could reinforce or help them to hone how they engaged them within Rome's ἐκκλησία.

Roman queer wo/men's ethical impulses cannot neatly fit into a binary of agreement or disagreement with Paul. Rome's ἐκκλησία-1 ethics scrambled these sides. Perhaps many agreed with at least some of the pieces within Paul's ethics, even as they dissented to a few, and sensed indecision, indifference, or confusion with others. Some may have found support for their own ethical exhortations while others were groaning, rolling their eyes, or hoping the letter was reaching its end. Even if the differing ethical impulses led the wo/men of Rome's ἐκκλησία to literally arrange themselves on separate sides of a room, their stances would mask the sensations that moved in between them, creating subtle differences, divisions, and alliances across the space.

This ἐκκλησία-1 assemblage, which encompasses the many wo/men, impulses, reactions, and the forces and sensations in between Rome's ἐκκλησία, participates in queerness. If queer, then where's the homo in *homo*nationalism? Already, I have discussed how homonationalism implies sexual arrangements different from those meant by the contemporary homos (i.e., gay, white, affluent men). Roman homonationalism is not the same as US homonationalism, but both can be called homonationalism. Puar's homonationalism exceeds the temporal and spatial container of the twenty-first century United States because queerness, as an assemblage, moves in between time and place, just as it fluctuates from sensations of freedom into a regulatory mode. In its Roman and US manifestations, homonationalism signals similar sexualized and racialized alignments with national/imperial politics and ethics that regulate queernesses across times and spaces via kyriarchal forces.

How does this similarity make wo/men in Rome's ἐκκλησία queer? This question returns us to the tensions between queer and queerness, which simultaneously renders them same and different. For some wo/men (ancient and contemporary), queer is an identity that can be and is chosen. However, under kyriarchy, imperialism, and their gridlocks, ethical systems render some bodies queer despite their being unaware of or resistant to such an identification. Depending on circumstances, sexuality could be a way of asserting bodily control, but it could also signal just how little control one has over one's body and sociopolitical situation.[96] These competing circumstances certainly characterize the contexts of many non-citizen ἔθνη of lower or lowest statuses in first-century Rome. Regardless of whether these wo/men fully fit or embrace a queer designation or lifestyle, they can all still embody *queerness*.

This queerness emerges around the wo/men in Rome's ἐκκλησία. It bubbles and seeps out of the tensions that erupted in between their theo-christological ethical impulses. Their queerness prompted ethical movements characterized by both queer resistance and homonational alignments. Moving, shifting, proliferating, and changing in this ἐκκλησία-l assemblage, the queerness of these first-century wo/men can expose unseen norms that continue to regulate contemporary uses of *queer*.

Through these wo/men and their queerness, these plausible, though not entirely tangible, ethical impulses decenter Paul. His more homonational and cruelly optimistic voice becomes one among many impulses that moved in between and affected the queer wo/men who were pondering, waving, discussing, feeling, and doing their ethics together, not always in the same directions. These queer wo/men (who could include Paul among them) and their many ethical impulses form an ἐκκλησία-l assemblage in Rome. In between them, an assemblage of queerness shimmered as it encompassed their desires for regulation and freedom. As these queer wo/men's ethical impulses proliferated, this ἐκκλησία-l assemblage was querying and *doing* justice.

---

96. And, for many, it was more than likely both.

Conclusion
The Politics of Feminism, Queerness, Affect, and Romans

This book placed stories of first-century Roman politics, which submitted queer wo/men under Rome and under God, alongside reconstructed stories of Rome's queer wo/men who engaged and embodied impulses that moved in between other plausible justices, some of which tried to move out from under God. I told these stories by twirling together feminism, queerness, affect, and Romans. Their interactions enabled engagements with feminist and queer affective critique and a praxis of ἐκκλησία-l assemblage. What should we do with these stories?

Feminist and Queer Affective Critique's Futures

> The futures are much closer to us than any pasts we might want to return to or revisit.
>
> —Jasbir K. Puar, *Terrorist Assemblages*

When reading Romans, it is impossible to deny a desire to revisit and return to first-century pasts. Would it not be fantastic to *ask* Paul his authorial intent? Or to experience the impulsive interactions of Rome's ἐκκλησία, to feel their responses to Paul's letter? Such fantasies optimistically attach biblical scholarship to ancient bodies and pasts, including this subversive endeavor. As with any instance of optimism, these fantastic endeavors always risk cruelty, especially if they hope solely to uncover impossibly lost pasts and forget these much closer futures toward which Puar gazes. My feminist and queer affective critique of Romans has laid bare its cruel optimism and homonationalism. Toward what more just and proximate futures does this critique struggle?

When engaged alongside Romans, feminist and queer affective critique drew out the Romanormative cravings that swim around Paul's letter. Submission to God feels like submission to Caesar; it takes the form of Roman imperialism—both without and with Rome. Romosexuality enforced the submissive politics of kyriarchy, making sure exceptional Romosexual men could wield intersecting norms of gender, sexuality, and ethnicity to rule over anyone who deviated from them. Paul's Romanormativity replicates these submissive norms. These replications start in the first chapter, especially through Paul's description of the "unnatural" (παρὰ φύσιν) sexualities of ἔθνη who spiral out of control due to their lack of submission under God (Rom 1:26–27). His Romanormativity moves beyond Rom 1, as seen through the faithful submission of ἔθνη to God in Rom 1–5, which replicated the gendered submission of Brittania to Claudius. This replication continues into the letter's ending in Rom 12–15 (ch. 13 most notably) where Paul's ethical submission to Roman moral authority demands sexually exceptional ethics to prove Christ-followers to be distinctly moral vis-à-vis the specter of immoral ἔθνη.

Feminist and queer affective critique displays how cruel optimism and homonationalism support the Romanormativity of Paul's submissions, even as Paul's Romanormativity produces cruel optimism and homonationalism. In the case of faithful submission, the conquest-fueled nature of Roman πίστις/fides situated Pauline πίστις within the context of the submission of ἔθνη who were incorporated into Rome's empire under the pretense of mutual trust: submissive obedience to Rome's rule would result in upward mobility. πίστις, when embodied in submissive and conquered ἔθνη in Rome generally and Paul's epistle specifically, proved to be an ancient manifestation of Berlant's cruel optimism. Through "ethical submission," Paul's sexually exceptional Romanormativity exhorted submission to Roman *mores* as a means to gain praise from Rome's ruling authorities. Because they should emphatically exceed Romosexuality in distinction from Rome's sexualized and racialized expectations of depravity, Paul emphasizes how ethically Romanormative Christ-followers *deserve* imperial praise and heightened status under Rome and God. Paul presents them as "subjects worthy of rehabilitation," in Puar's words, and this presentation represents one (less exceptional) instance of homonationalism.

Does Romans need more feminist and queer killjoys? It does.[1] If it is critical that we return and revisit the pasts that Romans summons, we

---

1. Here I recall my discussion of Sara Ahmed's work on the feminist killjoy in chapter 1, as well as the summons of her "Killjoy Manifesto." See Sara Ahmed, *Living a Feminist Life* (Durham, NC: Duke University Press, 2017), 251–68.

must do so critically. If we do not scrutinize the injustices held in between the letter's impulses, then they will continue to drag its sensations of justice back into kyriarchal normativities—Romanormative, heteronormative, and homonormative. Its cruel optimism and homonationalism will be perpetuated. They will continue their historical reproductions in our presents and our futures.

This book drew feminism, queerness, affect, and Romans into a constellation that produced shimmering impressions. Cruel optimism and homonationalism are not just concepts that I am applying to Romans so as to unearth new exegetical meanings. They are not methods for biblical studies. Romans changes how we understand cruel optimism and homonationalism in the past *and in the present*. Despite the urgent proximities of the futures, we cannot abandon these pasts, because they will continue to affect the present. They will affect any futures we hope to inhabit.

In several chapters I drew examples from Pete Buttigieg's (ultimately unsuccessful) 2020 campaign to become the first openly gay Democratic presidential nominee as demonstrations of how terms from feminist and queer affective critique manifest in the present era. These examples emphasize how contemporary homonationalisms and cruel optimisms cannot be distinguished from the cruel optimism and homonationalism that we find in biblical texts and contexts, especially Romans. Buttigieg's campaign not only mobilized his gayness; it also emphasized an image of himself as a devoted Christian who explicitly used biblical texts (especially from the gospels/New Testament) as moral guides for him and for the United States. His homonormativity and homonationalism are inseparable from his biblical interpretation. They feed one another. Buttigieg's monogamous fidelity to his husband was the sexually exceptional background to his criticism of then President Donald Trump's immoral infidelities.[2] Buttigieg was remarkable neither for his gayness nor for his Christianity: he was remarkable for being a *gay Christian*. His notoriety stems from the *in-betweenness* of gayness, biblical interpretation, and Christianity.

There are more interactions in between feminism, queerness, affect, and Romans (as well as other biblical texts) that require critical engagement across the present and pasts. In a culture where biblical (and mostly Christian) values have been woven throughout its texts, politics, and his-

---

2. "I mean, I'm sorry, but one thing about my marriage is that it's never involved me having to send hush money to a porn star after cheating on my spouse, with him or her," Buttigieg said in a CNN town hall on 18 February 2020.

tories, one need not have encountered Romans to have been shaped or affected by its cruel πίστις. Alongside Romans, feminism and queerness have yet to get out of the haze of a Romanormativity hangover.

Biblical scholars may bristle because they sense anachronism in my suggestions of homonationalism and cruel optimism in a first-century text.[3] Similar anachronistic sensations fuel the overall lack of biblical scholarship published within the pages and politics of feminism, queerness, and affect. Whether under Roman imperialism or late capitalism, queer wo/men are treading water under kyriarchies that perpetuate fantasies of the good life while affectively enforcing exceptional conformity to racialized and sexualized norms. Kyriarchy continually manifests as an assemblage: it held first-century bodies under Rome's imperial rule, has held countless other bodies in its shifting but persistent grasps, and continues to captivate contemporary, queer wo/men. Even if the pasts summoned by biblical texts cannot (and even should not) be returned to, ignoring their perpetual affective effects summons them forward into kyriarchal futures. Feminist and queer affective critique beckons resistant killjoys to root out kyriarchal definitions of justice in between the present and the pasts it revisits in order to bring much closer futures that transform what justice means and does.

Subversive Stories and ἐκκλησία-l Assemblages

> Gender, sex, romance, desire, power, nationalism, oppression … they're all just stories we tell ourselves. And we can tell different stories if we choose.
> —Charlie Jane Anders, afterword to Ursula K. Le Guin, *The Left Hand of Darkness*

What justices are plausible when we try to get out from under God? "Stories prime us to search for villains."[4] Stories teach us to crave heroes, to

---

3. On the fear of anachronism in biblical studies and methodology's role in "holding anachronism at bay"—as well as how affect-driven biblical scholarship might challenge methodological rigidity and a strict historicism—see Stephen D. Moore, "The Rage for Method and the Joy of Anachronism: When Biblical Scholars Do Affect Theory," in *Reading with Feeling: Affect Theory and the Bible*, ed. Fiona Black and Jennifer L. Koosed, SemeiaSt 95 (Atlanta: SBL Press, 2019), 187–211.

4. Sam J. Miller, *Blackfish City* (New York: Ecco, 2018), 309. This was part of the epigraph in this book's introduction.

imbibe their characteristics. Such stories oversimplify, whether we are telling stories about Paul and the queer wo/men of Rome's ἐκκλησία; Rome's
rulers and conquered ἔθνη; or contemporary hetero/homonormativities
and queernesses. Feminist and queer affective critique tends to draw out
villainous dimensions that lurk in the in-between spaces around texts and
cultures; it dissects them and carves out a space for subversive struggle.
Critique lays bare the currents to make possible resistance to normativity's
affective riptide. In this carved-up space, a subversive feminist and queer
praxis of assemblage *scrambles the sides* in between normative stories.

"The Heroic Paul" is just a story we have told. To move beyond Pauline
heroism, we have to see how Paul can be a villain, especially how he has
been complicit in kyriarchy and imperialism via Romanormativity. However, "The Villainous Paul" uses the same stale story, just inverting the plot
and the characters. So, as Johnson-DeBaufre and Nasrallah argue, we *move
beyond* the heroic trope and see Paul as one among many Romans, one
among many queer Christ-followers.[5] Through ἐκκλησία-l assemblages, I
have scrambled the sides of Rome's ἐκκλησία. I am choosing to tell different stories—histories—of first-century queer wo/men (among whom Paul
was one of many villainous heroes or heroic villains). *What justices exist
beside God? What moves in between God and justice?*

My praxis of ἐκκλησία-l assemblage brought to life queer wo/men and
the speculatively plausible impulses that moved in between them in Rome's
ἐκκλησία. This praxis involved laying out plausible theo-christological and
ethical impulses—including "God's Equals," "Drowning Jesus," "Good
Sex?" and "Rethinking Rebels"—that could have manifested in Rome's
ἐκκλησία before, after, and alongside hearing Paul's letter. After laying
out their contours and the historical evidence behind them, I brought
these impulses, the queer wo/men around them, and Paul into contact.
In the assemblaged theo-Christologies that shimmered in between these
wo/men, they felt how justice might faithfully subvert submission even
as they clung to kyriarchal impulses under Jesus and God. Through their
querying of what it meant to be an ethical ἐκκλησία, Rome's queer wo/men
brought their theo-Christologies to life as they tried on different embodiments of justice that complemented and collided with their sensations of

---

5. Melanie Johnson-DeBaufre and Laura S. Nasrallah, "Beyond the Heroic Paul:
Toward a Feminist and Decolonizing Approach to the Letters of Paul," in *The Colonized Apostle: Paul through Postcolonial Eyes*, ed. Christopher D. Stanley, PCC (Minneapolis: Fortress, 2011), 161–74.

gender, sexuality, and ethnicity. Across this book, my praxis of ἐκκλησία-l assemblage scrambled binaries and told stories of feminisms and queernesses that encompass kyriarchy and egalitarianism; submission and rebellion; good and bad; regulation and freedom.

ἐκκλησία-l assemblages do not offer simple stories. But the stories they tell feature more than words, written down or spoken: they are stories told through glances, gestures, feelings and thoughts, moans and groans, scents and breezes, entrances and exits. Stories of assemblages are complex because assemblages are never singular: they overlap, contract, and expand. Just as assemblages can proliferate "a thousand tiny sexes," ἐκκλησία-l assemblages give rise to a thousand tiny ἐκκλησίαι.[6] This book's praxis of ἐκκλησία-l assemblage challenges any simple rendering of Rome's ἐκκλησία (and, by extension, early Christianity) as a community. Their impulses moved them into and out of groupings, into and out of an assembly, into and out of feelings and ideas. ἐκκλησία-l assemblages are richly complex, which is not the same as being complicated. ἐκκλησία-l assemblages and the stories they produce are no more complicated than reality: when told well, they summon realities to life.[7]

Kyriarchy, as another assemblage, moved in between and affected these ἐκκλησία-l impulses. As assemblages, kyriarchy and ἐκκλησία are not binary opposites: they ooze together and slide apart; they mesh even when they differ. Despite its oppressive goals, as an assemblage, kyriarchy can occasionally, if unwittingly, subvert itself (in the long run, however, these exceptions have tended to confirm its rule). In between ἐκκλησία-l assemblages, subversive meanings of justice overlapped with impulses toward

---

6. See Elizabeth Grosz, "A Thousand Tiny Sexes: Feminism and Rhizomatics," in *Gilles Deleuze and the Theatre of Philosophy*, ed. Constantin Boundas and Dorothea Olkowski (New York: Routledge, 1994), 187–210; Arun Saldanha, "Reontologising Race: The Machinic Geography of Phenotype," *Environment and Planning D: Society and Space* 24 (2006): 9–24; Jasbir K. Puar, *Terrorist Assemblages: Homonationalism in Queer Times*, NW (Durham, NC: Duke University Press, 2007), 205–11.

7. My goal is to tell the stories that come from my praxis of ἐκκλησία-l assemblages well in ways that spin off the page in richness that is complex but not complicated. But writing well—like egalitarianism—is a work in progress, and I have shaped these stories as well as I will be able to with the anticipation that they will lead me to new stories to work on and new complexities to move toward. I originally used the descriptor "complex but not complicated" to praise Brit Bennett's novel, *The Vanishing Half* (New York: Riverhead Books, 2020), and I highly recommend it, both in general and as a phenomenal example of how one can write complexity well.

Romanormative justice. Paul's impulses can anticipate just worlds; others among the queer wo/men of Rome's ἐκκλησία could summon submission. The stories in between ἐκκλησία-l assemblage and kyriarchy remind us how neither subversion nor justice is simple.

Likewise, queerness and ἐκκλησία-l assemblages entwine messily. Queerness and ἐκκλησία-l assemblages diverge as some, like Paul, rejected and dispelled queerness—especially when many experienced queerness as a label thrust upon them by Romosexuality. Other queer women in Rome's ἐκκλησία embodied their queernesses in ways that renegotiated the boundaries of good sex. Rome's queer wo/men embraced queerness's contradictory proliferations within an ἐκκλησία of impulses, including regulatory queernesses that aligned with kyriarchal norms, subversive queernesses that moved toward freedom, and the unbounded queernesses that cruise in between.

ἐκκλησία-l assemblage was *one among many* assemblages moving in between wo/men, materials, texts, and impulses in the first-century Roman world. In addition to assemblages of queerness and kyriarchy, ἐκκλησία-l assemblages snaked in between συναγωγ-al assemblages, cultic assemblages (e.g., Isis), and ἔθν-ic assemblages—to name a few among the many that accumulate *ad infinitum*.

Are ἐκκλησία-l assemblages restricted to to the first centuries CE? Not at all, because their proliferating impulses will continue to affect our present and futures. ἐκκλησία-l assemblages are no more temporally bound than kyriarchy, queerness, or any other assemblage. Paul's letter to Rome, after all, is one among many impulsive shreds of an ἐκκλησία-l assemblage, so if the epistle is present, then ἐκκλησία-l assemblages are too. Still treading water, many of us urgently seek to subvert kyriarchy's grasps and hope for a justice that strokes toward queer utopias characterized by egalitarianism. If we do not sense more of the impulses that swirled in between Paul's in this ἐκκλησία-l assemblage, we leave Romans to trap us in postures of cruel πίστις, submissively trusting in its story that some source from above can rescue us before we finally drown.

Tales of the heroic Paul are tough to abandon. Making space requires digging holes whose gaps can feel like pits of despair. A heroic Paul beckons diggers to keep refilling the hole because moving Paul away from the center draws out sensations of risk. When we remove the ethical or the faithful foundations that seem essential to Christianity, we abandon centers that have oriented theo-politics for centuries. Their norms have become comfortable cravings that require us to endure and move beyond the hangover they leave in their wake. But, when we just keep swimming, we can build up from the postholes so that a speculatively plausible ἐκκλησία-1 assemblage starts shimmering.

Assemblages matter because we are the stories we tell. The stories we tell determine how we struggle as well as who and what we struggle against. When they represent complexities, stories subvert divisive norms. These struggles involve hard work, movements back and forth and in between. After all, one does not escape a riptide by swimming against it as hard as possible. Successfully moving beyond a riptide involves moving diagonally, swimming sideways, carefully pushing out to avoid exhaustion. Subverting submissions is always engaging a complexly sideways process that moves within and beyond kyriarchy and its hetero-, homo-, and Romanormativities. A praxis of ἐκκλησία-1 assemblage infuses more reality into the stories we can tell about Romans—Paul's letter and the queer wo/men who, alongside it, were listening, feeling, pacing, interrupting, gesturing, snoozing, thinking, tasting, clashing, and changing *impulsively*. My stories of ἐκκλησία-1 assemblages continue the struggle to make the impossible plausible.

Queer Wo/men Everywhere

"Everywhere," Esther whispered to herself. "There are people like us everywhere."
                                    —Sarah Gailey, *Upright Women Wanted*

Queer wo/men were there. This refrain thrums persistently throughout this book. Queer wo/men were there in first-century Rome and in Rome's ἐκκλησία because, as Esther delights in discovering, *there are people like us everywhere.*

Is its incessant repetition necessary? Isn't this statement simple, obvious? It should be obvious, and I wish it were not necessary to affirm queer wo/men's presence ad nauseam. Heteronormativity has spent millennia straightening, dismissing, erasing, and denying it. Kyriarchy has spent so long broadcasting the message "queer wo/men weren't there" that it no longer needs to scroll as a ticker across the screen. It has become a fact that requires no footnote. It demands queer wo/men show their work before undermining us through accusations of anachronistic agendas. Dismissals of this refrain reflect kyriarchy's malicious attempt to murder the thrilling sensations queer wo/men experience when we discover we aren't alone, that we not only have a history: we have histories, herstories, theirstories.

Until queer wo/men's presence thunders on its own throughout the past and present, *QUEER WO/MEN WERE* <u>FUCKING</u> *THERE* can never be said too often.

Feminism, Queerness, Affect, and Romans has always been less about the sum of its constituent parts than it has been about exploring the interactions *in between* these four forces. It generated conversations in between theory and text (as opposed to "applying" theory to biblical text). My book has been about what Romans, affect, queerness, and feminism *do together.* ἐκκλησία-l assemblages and feminist and queer affective critique emerged from this clustering. They interacted with one another. Emphasizing intersectionality, these interactions center first-century queer wo/men who were marginalized by Romosexuality and Romanormativity and remain marginalized within scholarship. Through feminist and queer affective critique, we feel how their oppression operated in overt and subtle ways; with ἐκκλησία-l assemblages, we sense *how* queer wo/men were there. Affect's mingling in between feminism, queerness, and Romans demands that we recognize how queer wo/men's presence affects the historical landscape. Queer wo/men could never *just* be there: they took leadership; they listened and gestured; they interrupted and disrupted. Queer wo/men's historical presence spills out when feminism, queerness, affect and Romans mingle.

The stories of queerness, kyriarchy, and ἐκκλησία-l assemblages that this book proliferated emphasize how queer wo/men's presence was and is far from simple. After all, when it plays in tune with affect and feminism, Puar writes, "Queerness irreverently challenges a linear mode of conduction and transmission: there is no exact recipe for a queer endeavor, no a priori system that taxonomies the linkages, disruptions, and contradictions into a tidy vessel."[8] The same could be said for feminist endeavors and affective ones. Telling the stories of the queer wo/men around Rome's ἐκκλησία showcases how this ἐκκλησία was forming and reforming in a messy *process.* Its speculatively plausible impulses become factual not by their content but by their inclusion and prioritization of queer wo/men whose existence *was* and is verifiable. Accuracy is uncapturable and cannot be found nailing down exact details of theological ideas or creeds, ethical dictums and behaviors. The most accurate historiography must be affec-

---

8. Puar, *Terrorist Assemblages,* xv.

tive and, therefore, always proliferating and never perfect in its professed accuracy.

Queer wo/men were there is more than a simple refrain: it is a political summons. This refrain roused me to write this book—just as it previously summoned many of the feminist and queer scholars cited across these pages. The stories that I have told through feminist and queer affective critique and a praxis of ἐκκλησία-l assemblage were stories that needed to be told, but they were also personal: they were the stories I needed to tell. The personal is political: my academic work is rooted in my feminist and queer commitments to justice and intersectionality; it is fettered to my experiences and activism in between feminism, queerness, affect, and biblical texts.

But the summons of this refrain should resonate across many other folks. My stories are far from perfect; they are limited to the scope of my ever-changing politics. It is my hope that this book amplifies the refrain and summons more stories. There are more stories of queer wo/men—around Rome and Romans and beyond—that are pleading us to tell them. There is more work to be done to place Romans in between feminist and queer affective critique and praxes of ἐκκλησία-l assemblage. This storytelling and the speculative work of reconstruction cannot be limited to those who identify as historians. Every new story—wild and tame, small and great, philological and ideological—proliferates history and can make it work toward justices.

Telling these stories is hard work: it can frustrate and exhaust the teller. I do not deny these challenges. It is important to recognize the labor we do and have done. But, in the end, I want to underscore my pleasure. These ancient stories are *thrilling*. There is glee when we find them, tell them, read and hear them. There is also a giddiness that comes out of critique, when we can finally pinpoint what feels askew. Writing this book may have drained me; working in the crossroads of feminism, queerness, affect, and biblical studies (perhaps *especially* biblical studies) frequently thrusts me on top of my bed as tears hurl out from deep within. *But I have lusted for this work.* I lick my lips during research; I let sentences titillate my body as I wrote them; I've relished many of the moans that pour out when this work spanked me. Affective feminism and queerness coax us to feel these sensations, to luxuriate in the experience, to enjoy our work as much and as often as we can.[9]

---

9. Sami Schalk affirms the importance of affirming pleasure in (and beyond)

Feminism, Queerness, Affect, and Romans: Under God? invites sensations around different and familiar stories. Its theo-politics query submissive relations under God and probe plausibilities that might exist beyond submission, cruel optimism, and homonationalism. Through subversions that refuse to simply overturn oppressive divisions, I have scrambled the sides in between heroes and villains, allowing queer wo/men to overflow. The scrambling of feminism, queerness, affect, and Romans summons political stories that affect the past, present, and future. Queer wo/men were and are there. Queer wo/men will always be there, here, and *everywhere*.

---

the work we do, even when our work changes and complicates our perceptions and relations to texts and other beloved cultural media. Her conclusion emphasizes the pleasure she and we can derive from reading and studying Black women's speculative fiction, even as we confront oppression in and through it. In her book's final sentence, she writes, "So often our work in disability studies and black feminism focuses on oppression, but for this book, I insist on acknowledging and ending with pleasure." See Sami Schalk, *Bodyminds Reimagined: (Dis)ability, Race, and Gender in Black Women's Speculative Fiction* (Durham, NC: Duke University Press, 2018), 145, see further 143–45.

Bibliography

Ancient Works

Apuleius. *Metamorphoses*. Edited and translated by J. Arthur Hanson. LCL. Cambridge: Harvard University Press, 1996.

Augustus. *Compendium of Roman History. Res Gestae Divi Augusti*. Translated by Frederick W. Shipley. LCL. Cambridge: Harvard University Press, 1924.

Diodorus Siculus. *Library of History*. 11 vols. Translated by C. H. Oldfather, Charles L. Sherman, C. Bradford Welles, Russel M. Geer, and Francis R. Walton. LCL. Cambridge: Harvard University Press, 1933–1967.

Horace. *Odes and Epodes*. Edited and translated by Niall Rudd. LCL. Cambridge: Harvard University Press, 2004.

Josephus. *The Jewish War*. Translated by H. St. J. Thackeray. 3 vols. LCL. Cambridge: Harvard University Press, 1927–1928.

Juvenal and Persius. Translated by Susanna Morton Braund. LCL. Cambridge: Harvard University Press, 2004.

Martial. *Epigrams*. Edited and translated by D. R. Shackleton Bailey. 2 vols. LCL. Cambridge: Harvard University Press, 1993.

Ovid. *Metamorphoses*. Translated by Frank Justus Miller. Revised by G. P. Gould. 2 vols. LCL. Cambridge: Harvard University Press, 1916.

Philo of Alexandria. *Philo*. Translated by F. H. Colson. 10 vols. LCL. Cambridge: Harvard University Press, 1929–1962.

Plutarch. *Moralia*. Vol. 10. Translated by Harold North Fowler. LCL. Cambridge: Harvard University Press, 1936.

Seneca. *Moral Essays*. Vol. 3: *De Beneficiis*. Translated by John W. Basore. LCL. Cambridge: Harvard University Press, 1935.

Suetonius. *Lives of the Caesars*. Translated by J. C. Rolfe. Introduction by K. R. Bradley. 2 vols. LCL. Cambridge: Harvard University Press, 1914.

Tacitus. *Annals*. Translated by John Jackson. 2 vols. LCL. Cambridge: Harvard University Press, 1931–1937.

Modern Works

Achtemeier, Paul. *Romans*. Louisville: John Knox, 1985.

Ahmed, Sara. *The Cultural Politics of Emotion*. 2nd ed. New York: Routledge, 2014.

———. *Living a Feminist Life*. Durham, NC: Duke University Press, 2017.

———. *On Being Included: Racism and Diversity in Institutional Life*. Durham, NC: Duke University Press, 2014.

———. *The Promise of Happiness*. Durham, NC: Duke University Press, 2010.

———. *Queer Phenomenology: Orientations, Objects, Others*. Durham, NC: Duke University Press, 2006.

Allen, Amy. *The Power of Feminist Theory: Domination, Resistance, Solidarity*. Boulder, CO: Westview, 1999.

Anders, Charlie Jane. Afterword to *The Left Hand of Darkness*, by Ursula K. LeGuin. New York: Ace, 2019.

———. *The City in the Middle of the Night*. New York: Tor, 2019.

Atwood, Margaret. *The Handmaid's Tale*. New York: Anchor Books, 1986.

Baker, Cynthia M. "'From Every Nation under Heaven': Jewish Ethnicities in the Greco-Roman World." Pages 79–99 in *Prejudice and Christian Beginnings: Investigating Race, Gender, and Ethnicity in Early Christian Studies*. Edited by Laura Nasrallah and Elisabeth Schüssler Fiorenza. Minneapolis: Fortress, 2009.

Balch, David L. "The Suffering of Isis/Io and Paul's Portrait of Christ Crucified (Gal. 3:1): Frescoes in Pompeian and Roman Houses and in the Temple of Isis in Pompeii." *JR* 83 (2003): 24–55.

Barton, Carlin A. "The Roman Blush: The Delicate Matter of Self-Control." Pages 212–34 in *Constructions of the Classical Body*. Edited by James I. Porter. Ann Arbor: University of Michigan Press, 1999.

Beard, Mary. "The Triumph of Flavius Josephus." Pages 543–58 in *Flavian Rome: Culture, Image, Text*. Edited by Anthony Boyle and William J. Dominik. Leiden: Brill, 2002.

Beavis, Mary Ann. "Christian Origins, Egalitarianism, and Utopia." *JFSR* 23 (2007): 27–49.

Benefiel, Rebecca R. "Dialogues of Graffiti in the House of the Four Styles at Pompeii (*Casa Dei Quattro Stili*, 1.8.17, 11)." Pages 20–48 in *Ancient Graffiti in Context*. Edited by Jennifer A. Baird and Claire Taylor. New York: Routledge, 2011.

Bennett, Brit. *The Vanishing Half*. New York: Riverhead Books, 2020.

Berlant, Lauren. *Cruel Optimism*. Durham, NC: Duke University Press, 2011.

Bird, Michael F., and Preston M. Sprinkle, eds. *The Faith of Jesus Christ: Exegetical, Biblical, and Theological Studies*. Peabody, MA: Hendrickson, 2009.

Black, Fiona, and Jennifer L. Koosed, eds. *Reading with Feeling: Affect Theory and the Bible*. Semeiast 95. Atlanta: SBL Press, 2019.

Bloomquist, L. Gregory. *The Function of Suffering in Philippians*. Sheffield: JSOT Press, 1993.

Blount, Brian K., Cain Hope Felder, Clarice J. Martin, and Emerson B. Powery, eds. *True to Our Native Land: An African American New Testament Commentary*. Minneapolis: Fortress, 2007.

Blumenfeld, Bruno. *The Political Paul: Justice, Democracy and Kingship in a Hellenistic Framework*. Sheffield: Sheffield Academic, 2001.

Boehringer, Sandra. *L'Homosexualité féminine dans l'Antiquité Grecque et Romaine*. Paris: Belles Lettres, 2007.

Boyarin, Daniel. *Border Lines: The Partitioning of Judaeo-Christianity*. Div. Philadelphia: University of Pennsylvania Press, 2004.

Bradley, Keith R. *Conquerors and Slaves*. Cambridge: Cambridge University Press, 1978.

———. "*Servus Onerosus*: Roman Law and the Troublesome Slave." *Slavery and Abolition* 11 (1990): 135–57.

Braidotti, Rosi. *Metamorphoses: Towards a Materialist Theory of Becoming*. Boston: Polity, 2002.

Bray, Karen. *Grave Attending: A Political Theology for the Unredeemed*. New York: Fordham University Press, 2020.

Bray, Karen, and Stephen D. Moore, eds. *Religion, Emotion, Sensation: Affect Theories and Theologies*. TTC. New York: Fordham University Press, 2019.

Briggs, Shiela. "Can an Enslaved God Liberate? Hermeneutical Reflections on Philippians 2:6–11." *Semeia* 47 (1989): 137–53.

———. "Galatians." Pages 218–36 in *Searching the Scriptures: A Feminist Commentary*. Vol. 2. Edited by Elisabeth Schüssler Fiorenza. New York: Crossroad, 1994.

Brintnall, Kent L., Joseph A. Marchal, and Stephen D. Moore, eds. *Sexual Disorientations: Queer Temporalities, Affects, Theologies*. TTC. New York: Fordham University Press, 2018.

Brooten, Bernadette J. "Junia … Outstanding among the Apostles." Pages 141–44 in *Women Priests: A Catholic Commentary on the Vatican Dec-*

laration. Edited by Leonard Swidler and Arlene Swidler. New York: Paulist, 1977.

———. *Love between Women: Early Christian Responses to Female Homoeroticism*. Chicago: University of Chicago Press, 1996.

———. "Paul's Views on the Nature of Women and Female Homoeroticism." Pages 61–87 in *Immaculate and Powerful: The Female in Sacred Image and Social Reality*. Edited by Clarissa W. Atkinson, Constance H. Buchanan, and Margaret R. Miles. Boston: Beacon, 1985.

Buell, Denise Kimber. "The Microbe and Pneuma That Therefore I Am." Pages 63–87 in *Divinanimality: Animal Theory, Creaturely Theology*. Edited by Stephen D. Moore. TTC. New York: Fordham University Press, 2014.

Burrus, Virginia. *Saving Shame: Martyrs, Saints, and Other Abject Subjects*. Div. Philadelphia: University of Pennsylvania Press, 2008.

Butler, Judith. "Against Proper Objects." Pages 1–30 in *Feminism Meets Queer Theory*. Edited by Elizabeth Weed and Naomi Schor. Bloomington: Indiana University Press, 1997.

———. *Bodies That Matter: On the Discursive Limits of "Sex."* Routledge: New York, 1993.

———. *Gender Trouble: Feminism and the Subversion of Identity*. New York: Routledge, 1990. Repr. 2006.

Byrne, Brendan. *Romans*. SP 6. Collegeville, MN: Liturgical, 2007.

Callahan, Allen Dwight, and Richard A. Horsley. "Slave Resistance in Classical Antiquity." Pages 133–51 in *Slavery in Text and Interpretation*. Edited by Allen Dwight Callahan, Richard A. Horsley, and Abraham Smith. Semeia 83–84. Atlanta: Scholars Press, 1998.

Carter, T. L. "The Irony of Romans 13." *NovT* 24 (2004): 209–28.

Castelli, Elizabeth A. "The *Ekklēsia* of Women and/as Utopian Space." Pages 36–52 in *On the Cutting Edge: The Study of Women in Biblical Worlds*. Edited by Jane Schaberg, Alice Bach, and Esther Fuchs. New York: Continuum: 2004.

Champlin, Edward. *Nero*. Cambridge: Harvard University Press, 2003.

Chapman, David W. *Ancient Jewish and Christian Perspectives of Crucifixion*. Tübingen: Mohr Siebeck, 2008.

Clarke, John R. *Art in the Lives of Ordinary Romans: Visual Representation and Non-Elite Viewers in Italy, 100 B.C.–A.D. 100*. Berkeley: University of California Press, 2006.

———. *Looking at Lovemaking: Constructions of Sexuality in Roman Art 100 B.C.–A.D. 250*. Berkeley: University of California Press, 1998.

Cobb, Christy. *Slavery, Gender, Truth, and Power: In Luke-Acts and Other Ancient Narratives.* Cham, Switzerland: Palgrave Macmillan, 2019.

———. "A Voice after Death: Gender, Class, and Sexuality on Ancient Funerary Monuments." Paper presented at the Annual Meeting of the Society of Biblical Literature. San Diego, CA, 25 November 2019.

Cobb, John B., Jr., and David J. Lull. *Romans.* Chalice Commentaries for Today. Saint Louis: Chalice, 2005.

Cohen, Cathy J. "Punks, Bulldaggers, and Welfare Queens: The Radical Potential of Queer Politics?" *GLQ* 3 (1997): 437–65.

Collins, Patricia Hill. *Black Feminist Thought: Knowledge, Consciousness, and the Politics of Empowerment.* 2nd ed. New York: Routledge, 2000.

Combahee River Collective. "The Combahee River Collective Statement." https://tinyurl.com/SBL4531a.

Concannon, Cavan W. *"When You Were Gentiles": Specters of Ethnicity in Roman Corinth and Paul's Corinthian Correspondence.* New Haven: Yale University Press, 2014.

Conway, Coleen M. *Behold the Man: Jesus and Greco-Roman Masculinity.* Oxford: Oxford University Press, 2008.

Cook, John Granger. *Crucifixion in the Mediterranean World.* Tübingen: Mohr Siebeck, 2014.

Corrigan, John, ed. *Feeling Religion.* Durham, NC: Duke University Press, 2017.

Crenshaw, Kimberlé. "Demarginalizing the Intersection of Race and Sex: A Black Feminist Critique of Antidiscrimination Doctrine, Feminist Theory, and Antiracist Politics." *UCLF* 139 (1989): 139–67.

Cvetkovitch, Ann. *An Archive of Feelings: Trauma, Sexuality, and Lesbian Public Cultures.* SerQ. Durham, NC: Duke University Press, 2003.

———. *Depression: A Public Feeling.* Durham, NC: Duke University Press, 2012.

D'Angelo, Mary Rose. "εὐσέβεια: Roman Imperial Family Values and the Sexual Politics of 4 Maccabees and the Pastorals." *BibInt* 11 (2003): 139–65.

———. "Gender and Geopolitics in the Work of Philo of Alexandria: Jewish Piety and Imperial Family Values." Pages 63–88 in *Mapping Gender in Ancient Religious Discourses.* Edited by Todd C. Penner and Caroline Vander Stichele. BibInt 84. Leiden: Brill, 2007.

———. "Women Partners in the New Testament." *JFSR* 6 (1990): 65–86.

Das, A. Andrew. "The Gentile-Encoded Audience of Romans: The Church outside the Synagogue." Pages 29–46 in *Reading Paul's Letter to the*

Romans. Edited by Jerry L. Sumney. Atlanta: Society of Biblical Literature, 2012.

———. *Solving the Romans Debate.* Minneapolis: Fortress, 2007.

Davis, Angela Y. *Women, Race, and Class.* New York: Vintage Books, 1981.

DeFelice, John. *Roman Hospitality: The Professional Women of Pompeii.* Warren Center, PA: Shangri-La, 2001.

DeLanda, Manuel. *Assemblage Theory.* Edinburgh: Edinburgh University Press, 2016.

———. *A New Philosophy of Society: Assemblage Theory and Social Complexity.* New York: Continuum, 2006.

De Lauretis, Teresa. "Queer Theory: Lesbian and Gay Sexualities: An Introduction." *dif.* 3 (1991): iii–xviii.

Delany, Samuel R. *Times Square Red, Times Square Blue.* Sexual Cultures. New York: New York University Press, 1999.

Deleuze, Gilles, and Félix Guattari. *A Thousand Plateaus: Capitalism and Schizophrenia.* Translated by Brian Massumi. Minneapolis: University of Minnesota Press, 1987.

Dench, Emma. *Romulus' Asylum: Roman Identities from the Age of Alexander to the Age of Hadrian.* Oxford: Oxford University Press, 2005.

Dodd, Brian J. "Romans 1:17: A *Crux Interpretum* for the πίστις Χριστοῦ Debate?" *JBL* 114 (1995): 470–73.

duBois, Page. *Slaves and Other Objects.* Chicago: University of Chicago Press, 2003.

Duggan, Lisa. *The Twilight of Equality: Neo-Liberalism, Cultural Politics and the Attack on Democracy.* Boston: Beacon, 2000.

Dunn, James D. G. "Once More, *Pistis Christou.*" Pages 730–44 in *Society of Biblical Literature 1991 Seminar Papers.* SBLSP 30. Atlanta: Scholars Press, 1991.

———. *Romans.* 2 vols. WBC 38. Dallas: Word, 1988.

Dzodan, Flavia. "My Feminism Will Be Intersectional or It Will Be Bullshit!" *Tiger Beatdown.* 10 October 2011. https://tinyurl.com/SBLPress4531b1.

Edelman, Lee. *No Future: Queer Theory and the Death Drive.* SerQ. Durham, NC: Duke University Press, 2004.

Edwards, Catharine. *The Politics of Immorality in Ancient Rome.* Cambridge: Cambridge University Press, 1993.

———. "Unspeakable Professions: Public Performance and Prostitution in Ancient Rome." Pages 66–95 in *Roman Sexualities.* Edited by Judith P.

Hallett and Marilyn B. Skinner. Princeton: Princeton University Press, 1997.

Eisenbaum, Pamela. "Jewish Perspectives: A *Jewish* Apostle to the Gentiles." Pages 135–53 in *Studying Paul's Letters: Contemporary Perspectives and Methods*. Edited by Joseph A. Marchal. Minneapolis: Fortress, 2012.

———. *Paul Was Not a Christian: The Original Message of a Misunderstood Apostle*. San Francisco: HarperOne, 2009.

Elliott, Neil. *The Arrogance of Nations: Reading Romans in the Shadow of Empire*. PCC. Minneapolis: Fortress, 2008.

———. *The Rhetoric of Romans: Argumentative Constraint and Strategy and Paul's Dialogue with Judaism*. Minneapolis: Fortress, 1990.

———. "Romans 13:1–7 in the Context of Roman Imperial Propaganda." Pages 184–204 in *Paul and Empire: Religion and Power in Roman Imperial Society*. Edited by Richard A. Horsley. Harrisburg, PA: Trinity Press International, 1997.

Endres, Nikolai. "From *Eros* to Romosexuality: Love and Sex in *Dorian Gray*." Pages 251–66 in *Oscar Wilde and Classical Antiquity*. Edited by Kathleen Riley, Alastair J. L. Blanshard, and Iarla Manny. Oxford: Oxford University Press, 2017.

Eng, David L. *The Feeling of Kinship: Queer Liberalism and the Racialization of Intimacy*. Durham, NC: Duke University Press, 2010.

Eng, David L., with Jack Halberstam and José Esteban Muñoz. "Introduction: What's Queer about Queer Studies Now?" *SocT* 23 (2005): 1–17.

Epp, Eldon Jay. *Junia: The First Woman Apostle*. Minneapolis: Fortress, 2005.

Esler, Philip F. *Conflict and Identity in Romans: The Social Setting of Paul's Letter*. Minneapolis: Fortress, 2003.

Fatum, Lone. "The Glory of God and the Image of Man: Women in the Pauline Congregations." Pages 50–133 in *The Image of God and Gender Models in Judeo-Christian Tradition*. Edited by Kari Elisabeth Børresen. Minneapolis: Fortress, 1995.

Fewster, Gregory P. "The Philippians 'Christ Hymn': Trends in Critical Scholarship." *CurBR* 13 (2015): 191–206.

Fitzmyer, Joseph A. *Romans*. AB 33. New York: Doubleday, 1993.

Foucault, Michel. *The Care of the Self*. Vol. 3 of *The History of Sexuality*. New York: Vintage Books/Random House, 1986. Repr. 1988.

———. *The Uses of Pleasure*. Vol. 2 of *The History of Sexuality*. New York: Vintage Books/Random House, 1985. Repr. 1990.

Fox, Arminta M. "Decentering Paul, Contextualizing Crimes: Reading in Light of the Imprisoned." *JFSR* 33 (2017): 37–54.

———. *Paul Decentered: Reading 2 Corinthians with the Corinthian Women*. PCC. Lanham, MD: Lexington Books, 2020.

Franke, Kathryn M. "The Domesticated Liberty of *Lawrence v. Texas*." *Columbia Law Review* 104 (2004): 1399–1426.

Fredrickson, David E. "Natural and Unnatural Use in Romans 1:24–27: Paul and the Philosophic Critique of Eros." Pages 197–222 in *Homosexuality, Science, and the "Plain Sense" of Scripture*. Edited by David L. Balch. Grand Rapids: Eerdmans, 2000.

Freeman, Elizabeth. *Time Binds: Queer Temporalities, Queer Histories*. PM. Durham, NC: Duke University Press, 2010.

Friesen, Steven J. "Poverty in Pauline Studies: Beyond the So-Called New Consensus." *JSNT* 26 (2004): 323–61.

Gager, John G. *Curse Tablets and Binding Spells from the Ancient World*. New York: Oxford University Press, 1992.

———. *Reinventing Paul*. Oxford: Oxford University Press, 2000.

Gailey, Sarah. *Upright Women Wanted*. New York: Tom Doherty Associates, 2020.

Gardner, Jane F. *Being a Roman Citizen*. London: Routledge, 1993.

Garlington, Don B. *Faith, Obedience, and Perseverance: Aspects of Paul's Letter to the Romans*. Tübingen: Mohr Siebeck, 1994.

Gaston, Lloyd. *Paul and the Torah*. Vancouver: University of British Columbia Press, 1987.

Georgi, Dieter. "God Turned Upside Down." Pages 148–57 in *Paul and Empire: Religion and Power in Roman Imperial Society*. Edited by Richard A. Horsley. Harrisburg, PA: Trinity Press International, 1997.

———. *Theocracy in Paul's Praxis and Theology*. Translated by David E. Green. Minneapolis: Fortress, 1991.

Glancy, Jennifer A. "The Sexual Use of Slaves: A Response to Kyle Harper on Jewish and Christian *Porneia*." *JBL* 134 (2015): 215–29.

———. *Slavery in Early Christianity*. Oxford: Oxford University Press, 2002.

Glancy, Jennifer A., and Stephen D. Moore. "How Typical a Roman Prostitute is Revelation's 'Great Whore'?" *JBL* 130 (2011): 562–69.

Gleason, Maud W. *Making Men: Sophists and Self-Presentation in Ancient Rome*. Princeton: Princeton University Press, 1995.

Goss, Robert E. *Jesus Acted Up: A Gay and Lesbian Manifesto*. San Francisco: HarperSanFrancisco, 1993.

Goss, Robert E., and Mona West, eds. *Take Back the Word: A Queer Reading of the Bible.* Cleveland: Pilgrim, 2000.

Graybill, Rhiannon. "Prophecy and the Problem of Happiness: The Case of Jonah." Pages 95–112 in *Reading with Feeling: Affect Theory and the Bible.* Edited by Fiona Black and Jennifer L. Koosed. SemeiaSt 95. Atlanta: SBL Press, 2019.

Gregg, Melissa, and Gregory J. Seigworth, eds. *The Affect Theory Reader.* Durham, NC: Duke University Press, 2010.

Grieb, A. Katherine. *The Story of Romans: A Narrative Defense of God's Righteousness.* Louisville: Westminster John Knox, 2002.

Grosz, Elizabeth. *Becoming Undone: Darwinian Reflections on Life, Politics, and Art.* Durham, NC: Duke University Press, 2011

———. "A Thousand Tiny Sexes: Feminism and Rhizomatics." Pages 187–210 in *Gilles Deleuze and the Theater of Philosophy.* Edited Constantin Boundas and Dorothea Olkowski. New York: Routledge, 1994.

———. *Volatile Bodies: Toward a Corporeal Feminism.* Bloomington: Indiana University Press, 1994.

Grubbs, Judith Evans. *Women and the Law in the Roman Empire: A Sourcebook on Marriage, Divorce, and Widowhood.* London: Routledge, 2002.

Gruen, Erich S. *The Construction of Identity in Hellenistic Judaism: Essays on Early Jewish Literature and History.* Berlin: de Gruyter, 2016.

Guest, Deryn, Robert E. Goss, Mona West, and Thomas Bohache, eds. *The Queer Bible Commentary.* London: SCM, 2006.

Halberstam, Jack. *Female Masculinity.* Durham, NC: Duke University Press, 1998.

———. *In a Queer Time and Place: Transgender Bodies, Subcultural Lives.* Sexual Cultures. New York: New York University Press, 2005.

———. *The Queer Art of Failure.* JHFCB. Durham, NC: Duke University Press, 2011.

Hall, Donald E., Annamarie Jagose, Andrea Bebell, and Susan Potter, eds. *Queer Theory: An Introduction.* New York: New York University Press, 1996.

Hallett, Judith P. *Fathers and Daughters in Roman Society.* Princeton: Princeton University Press, 1984.

———. "Female Homoeroticism and the Denial of Roman Reality in Latin Literature." Pages 255–73 in *Roman Sexualities.* Edited by Judith P. Hallett and Marilyn B. Skinner. Princeton: Princeton University Press, 1997.

Hallett, Judith P., and Marilyn B. Skinner, eds. *Roman Sexualities*. Princeton: Princeton University Press, 1997.

Halley, Janet. "Reasoning about Sodomy: Act and Identity in and after Bowers v. Hardwick." *Virginia Law Review* 79 (1993): 1721–80.

Halley, Janet, and Andrew Parker, eds. *After Sex? On Writing since Queer Theory*. SerQ. Durham, NC: Duke University Press, 2011.

Harrisville, Roy A., III. "Before ΠΙΣΤΙΣ ΧΡΙΣΤΟΥ: The Objective Genitive as Good Greek." *NovT* 48 (2006): 353–58.

———. "ΠΙΣΤΙΣ ΧΡΙΣΤΟΥ: Witness of the Fathers." *NovT* 36 (1994): 233–41.

Hartman, Midori E. "A Little *Porneia* Leavens the Whole: Queer(ing) Limits of Community in 1 Corinthians 5." Pages 143–63 in *Bodies on the Verge: Queering Pauline Epistles and Interpretations*. Edited by Joseph A. Marchal. SemeiaSt 93. Atlanta: SBL Press, 2019.

Hawthorne, Gerald F. *Philippians*. WBC 43. Waco, TX: Word, 1983.

Hays, Richard B. *The Faith of Jesus Christ*. 2nd ed. Chico, CA: Scholars Press, 2002.

Headley, Maria Dahvana. *The Mere Wife*. New York: Farrar, Straus and Giroux, 2018.

Heliso, Desta. *Pistis and the Righteous One: A Study of Romans 1:17 against the Background of Scripture and Second Temple Jewish Literature*. Tübingen: Mohr Siebeck, 2007.

Hengel, Martin. *Crucifixion: In the Ancient World and the Folly of the Message of the Cross*. Philadelphia: Fortress, 1977.

Hoke, James N. "Be Even Better Subjects, Worthy of Rehabilitation: Homonationalism and 1 Thessalonians 4–5." Pages 83–114 in *Bodies on the Verge: Queering Pauline Epistles and Interpretations*. Edited by Joseph A. Marchal. SemeiaSt 93. Atlanta: SBL Press, 2019.

———. "Behold the Lord's Whore? Slavery, Prostitution, and Luke 1:38." *BibInt* 26 (2018): 43–67.

———. "*Homo Urbanus* or Urban Homos? Metronormative Tropes and Subcultural Queernesses around Philo and the Therapeuts." forthcoming.

———. "Orienting the *Domus*: Queer Materials and ἐκκλησίαι in Rome." Paper presented at the Annual Meeting of the Society of Biblical Literature. San Diego, CA, 25 November 2019.

———. "Unbinding Imperial Time: Chrononormativity and Paul's Letter to the Romans." Pages 68–89 in *Sexual Disorientations: Queer Temporalities, Affects, Theologies*. Edited by Kent L. Brintnall, Joseph A.

Marchal, and Stephen D. Moore. TTC. New York: Fordham University Press, 2018.

Holmes, Juwan J. "Chasten Buttigieg Allegedly Abandons Fundraiser for Pete at 'Inappropriate' Gay Bar." *LGBTQ Nation*. 19 January 2020. https://tinyurl.com/SBL4531e.

Hooker, Morna D. "Πίστις Χριστοῦ." Pages 165–84 in *From Adam to Christ: Essays on Paul*. Edited by Morna D. Hooker. Cambridge: Cambridge University Press, 1990.

hooks, bell. *Ain't I a Woman: Black Women and Feminism*. Boston: South End, 1981.

Hornsby, Teresa J., and Ken Stone, eds. *Bible Trouble: Queer Reading at the Boundaries of Biblical Scholarship*. SemeiaSt 67. Atlanta: Society of Biblical Literature, 2011.

Horsley, Richard A., ed. *Paul and Empire: Religion and Power in Roman Imperial Society*. Harrisburg, PA: Trinity Press International, 1997.

———, ed. *Paul and Politics: Ekklēsia, Israel, Imperium, Interpretation*. Harrisburg, PA: Trinity Press International, 2000.

———, ed. *Paul and the Roman Imperial Order*. Harrisburg, PA: Trinity Press International, 2004.

Hubbard, Thomas K., and Maria Doerfler. "From Ascesis to Sexual Renunciation." Pages 168–87 in *A Companion to Greek and Roman Sexualities*. Edited by Thomas K. Hubbard. Chichester, UK: Wiley Blackwell, 2014.

Hultgren, Arland J. *Paul's Letter to the Romans: A Commentary*. Grand Rapids: Eerdmans, 2011.

Inglehart, Jennifer, ed. *Ancient Rome and the Construction of Modern Homosexual Identities*. Oxford: Oxford University Press, 2015.

———. "Introduction: Romosexuality; Rome, Homosexuality, and Reception." Pages 1–35 in *Ancient Rome and the Construction of Modern Homosexual Identities*. Edited by Jennifer Inglehart. Oxford: Oxford University Press, 2015.

Isaac, Benjamin. *The Invention of Racism in Classical Antiquity*. Princeton: Princeton University Press, 2004.

Jagose, Annamarie. *Queer Theory: An Introduction*. New York: New York University Press, 1996.

Jakobson, Janet. "Can Homosexuals End Western Civilization as We Know It? Family Values in a Global Economy." Pages 49–70 in *Queer Globalizations: Citizenship and the Afterlife of Colonialism*. Edited by Arnoldo Cruz-Malave and Martin Manalansan IV. New York: New York University Press, 2002.

James, Robin. *Resilience and Melancholy: Pop Music, Feminism, Neoliberalism*. Alresford, UK: Zero Books, 2015.

Jennings, Theodore W., Jr. *Outlaw Justice: The Messianic Politics of Paul*. CMP. Stanford: Stanford University Press, 2013.

———. *Reading Derrida/Thinking Paul: On Justice*. CMP. Stanford: Stanford University Press, 2006.

Jewett, Robert. *Romans*. Hermeneia. Minneapolis: Fortress, 2007.

Johnson, Chris. "Buttigieg: Anti-gay Countries Will 'Have to Get Used to' Gay U.S. President." *Washington Blade*. 2 November 2019. https:// tinyurl.com/SBL4531j.

———. "Buttigieg Engages LGBT Crowd by Sharing Personal Struggle of Being Gay." *Washington Blade*. 7 April 2019. https://tinyurl.com/ SBL4531c.

Johnson, Luke Timothy. *Reading Romans: A Literary and Theological Commentary*. New York: Crossroad, 1997.

Johnson, Matthew V., James A. Noel, and Demetrius K. Williams, eds. *Onesimus Our Brother: Reading Religion, Race, and Culture in Philemon*. PCC. Minneapolis: Fortress, 2012.

Johnson, Odai. *Absence and Memory in American Colonial Theatre*. New York: Palgrave Macmillan, 2006.

Johnson-DeBaufre, Melanie. "'Gazing upon the Invisible': Archaeology, Historiography, and the Elusive Wo/men of 1 Thessalonians." Pages 73–108 in *From Roman to Early Christian Thessalonikē*. Edited by Laura Nasrallah, Charalambos Bakirtzis, and Steven J. Friesen. Cambridge: Harvard University Press, 2010.

———. "Dreaming the Common Good/s: The Kin-dom of God as a Space of Utopian Politics." Pages 103–23 in *Common Goods: Economy, Ecology, and Political Theology*. Edited by Melanie Johnson-DeBaufre, Catherine Keller, and Elias Ortega-Aponte. TTC. New York: Fordham University Press, 2015.

———. *Jesus among Her Children: Q, Eschatology, and the Construction of Christian Origins*. HTS 55. Cambridge: Harvard University Press, 2005.

Johnson-DeBaufre, Melanie, and Laura S. Nasrallah. "Beyond the Heroic Paul: Toward a Feminist and Decolonizing Approach to the Letters of Paul." Pages 161–74 in *The Colonized Apostle: Paul through Postcolonial Eyes*. Edited by Christopher D. Stanley. PCC. Minneapolis: Fortress, 2011.

Joshel, Sandra R. "Female Desire and the Discourse of Empire: Tacitus' Messlina." Pages 221–54 in *Roman Sexualities*. Edited by Judith P. Hallett and Marilyn B. Skinner. Princeton: Princeton University Press, 1997.

Joshel, Sandra R., and Lauren Hackworth Peterson. *The Material Lives of Roman Slaves*. Cambridge: Cambridge University Press, 2014.

Kahl, Briggitte. "Der Brief an die Gemeinden in Galatien: Vom Unbehagen der Geschlechter und anderen Problemen des Andersseins." Pages 603–11 in *Kompendium feministischer Bibelauslegung*. Edited by Louise Schottroff and Marie-Therese Wacker. Gütersloh: Chr. Kaiser Gütersloher Verlagshaus, 1998.

Kamen, Deborah, and Sarah Levin-Richardson. "Lusty Ladies in the Roman Literary Imaginary." Pages 231–52 in *Ancient Sex: New Essays*. Edited by Ruby Blondell and Kirk Ormand. Columbus: Ohio State University Press, 2015.

———. "Revisiting Roman Sexuality: Agency and the Conceptualization of Penetrated Males." Pages 449–60 in *Sex in Antiquity: Exploring Gender and Sexuality in the Ancient World*. Edited by Mark Masterson, Nancy Sorkin Rabinowitz, and James Robson. London: Routledge, 2014.

Kampen, Natalie Boymel, ed. *Sexuality in Ancient Art*. Cambridge: Cambridge University Press, 1996.

Kamudzandu, Israel. *Abraham as Spiritual Ancestor: A Postcolonial Reading of Romans 4*. BibInt 100. Leiden: Brill, 2010.

———. *Abraham Our Father: Paul and the Ancestors in Postcolonial Africa*. PCC. Minneapolis: Fortress, 2013.

Kaplan, Amy. "Violent Belongings and the Question of Empire Today: Presidential Address to the American Studies Association, October 17, 2003." *American Quarterly* 56 (2004): 1–18.

Keck, Leander E. " 'Jesus' in Romans." *JBL* 108 (1989): 443–60.

———. *Romans*. ANTC. Nashville: Abingdon, 2005.

Keeling, Kara. *The Witch's Flight: The Cinematic, the Black Femme, and the Image of Common Sense*. PM. Durham, NC: Duke University Press, 2007.

Keuls, Eva C. *The Reign of the Phallus: Sexual Politics in Ancient Athens*. New York: Harper and Row, 1985.

Kittredge, Cynthia Briggs. *Community and Authority: The Rhetoric of Obedience in the Pauline Tradition*. HTS 45. Harrisburg, PA: Trinity Press International, 1998.

———. "Corinthian Women Prophets and Paul's Argumentation in 1 Corinthians." Pages 103–9 in *Paul and Politics: Ekklēsia, Israel, Imperium, Interpretation.* Edited by Richard A. Horsley. Harrisburg, PA: Trinity Press International, 2000.

———. "Rethinking Authorship in the Letters of Paul: Elisabeth Schüssler Fiorenza's Model of Pauline Theology." Pages 318–33 in *Walk in the Ways of Wisdom: Essays in Honor of Elisabeth Schüssler Fiorenza.* Edited by Shelly A. Matthews, Cynthia Briggs Kittredge, and Melanie Johnson-DeBaufre. Harrisburg, PA: Trinity Press International, 2003.

Kloppenborg, John S. "Isis and Sophia in the Book of Wisdom." *HTR* 75 (1982): 57–84.

Knust, Jennifer Wright. *Abandoned to Lust: Sexual Slander and Ancient Christianity.* GTR. New York: Columbia University Press, 2006.

Koester, Helmut. "Imperial Ideology and Paul's Eschatology in 1 Thessalonians." Pages 158–66 in *Paul and Empire: Religion and Power in Roman Imperial Society.* Edited by Richard A. Horsley. Harrisburg, PA: Trinity Press International, 1997.

Koosed, Jennifer L., and Stephen D. Moore, eds. *Affect Theory and the Bible. Biblical Interpretation* 22, nos. 4–5 (2014).

———. "Introduction: From Affect to Exegesis." *BibInt* 22 (2014): 381–87.

Kotrosits, Maia. *How Things Feel: Affect Theory, Biblical Studies, and the (Im)Personal.* BRPBI. Leiden: Brill, 2016.

———. "Penetration and Its Discontents: Greco-Roman Sexuality, the *Acts of Paul and Thecla,* and Theorizing Eros without the Wound." *JHistSex* 27 (2018): 343–66.

———. *Rethinking Early Christian Identity: Affect, Violence, and Belonging.* Minneapolis: Fortress, 2015.

Kraemer, Ross Shepherd. *Her Share of the Blessings: Women's Religions among Pagans, Jews, and Christians in the Greco-Roman World.* New York: Oxford University Press, 1992.

———. *Unreliable Witnesses: Religion, Gender, and History in the Greco-Roman Mediterranean.* Oxford: Oxford University Press, 2011.

———. *Women's Religions in the Greco-Roman World: A Sourcebook.* New York: Oxford University Press, 2004.

Lampe, Peter. *From Paul to Valentinus: Christians at Rome in the First Two Centuries.* Translated by Michael Steinhauser. Edited by Marshall D. Johnson. Minneapolis: Fortress, 2003.

———. *Die Stadtrömischen Christen in den ersten beiden Jahrhunderten: Untersuchungen zur Sozialgeschichte.* Tübingen: Mohr Siebeck, 1987.

Langlands, Rebecca. *Sexual Morality in Ancient Rome*. Cambridge: Cambridge University Press, 2006.

Lavan, Myles. *Slaves to Rome: Paradigms of Empire in Roman Culture*. Cambridge: Cambridge University Press, 2013.

L'Engle, Madeleine. *A Wrinkle in Time*. New York: Square Fish, 1962.

"Lesbian Historiography before the Name?" *GLQ* 4 (1998): 557–630.

Levin-Richardson, Sarah. *The Brothel of Pompeii: Sex, Class, and Gender at the Margins of Roman Society*. Cambridge: Cambridge University Press, 2019.

———. "*Futata Sum Hic*: Female Subjectivity and Agency in Pompeian Sexual Graffiti." *CJ* 108 (2013): 319–45.

Levinson, Joshua. "Bodies and Bo(a)rders: Emerging Fictions of Identity in Late Antiquity." *HTR* 93 (2000): 343–72.

Lightsey, Pamela R. *Our Lives Matter: A Womanist Queer Theology*. Eugene, OR: Pickwick, 2015.

Lin, Yii-Jan. "Junia: An Apostle before Paul." *JBL* 139 (2020): 191–209.

Loader, William. *Philo, Josephus, and the Testaments on Sexuality: Attitudes toward Sexuality in the Writings of Philo and Josephus and in the Testaments of the the Twelve Patriarchs*. Grand Rapids: Eerdmans, 2011.

Longnecker, Richard N. *The Epistle to the Romans: A Commentary on the Greek Text*. NIGTC. Grand Rapids: Eerdmans, 2016.

———. "Πίστις in Romans 3:25: Neglected Evidence for the 'Faithfulness of Christ'?" *NTS* 39 (1993): 478–80.

Lopez, Davina C. *Apostle to the Conquered: Reimagining Paul's Mission*. PCC. Minneapolis: Fortress, 2008.

Lorde, Audre. *Sister Outsider*. Berkeley: Crossing, 1984. Repr. 2007.

Love, Heather. *Feeling Backward: Loss and the Politics of Queer History*. Cambridge: Harvard University Press, 2009.

———. "Wedding Crashers." *GLQ* 13 (2006): 125–39.

MacLean, Rose. *Freed Slaves and Roman Imperial Culture: Social Integration and the Transformation of Values*. Cambridge: Cambridge University Press, 2018.

Marchal, Joseph A. *Appalling Bodies: Queer Figures before and after Paul's Letters*. Oxford: Oxford University Press, 2019.

———. "Bio-Necro-*Biblio*-Politics? Restaging Feminist Intersections and Queer Exceptions." *CultRel* 15 (2014): 166–76.

———, ed. *Bodies on the Verge: Queering Pauline Epistles and Interpretations*. SemeiaSt 93. Atlanta: SBL Press, 2019.

———. "Bottoming Out: Rethinking the Reception of Receptivity." Pages 209–37 in *Bodies on the Verge: Queering Pauline Epistles and Interpretations*. Edited by Joseph A. Marchal. SemeiaSt 93. Atlanta: SBL Press, 2019.

———. "The Corinthian Women Prophets and Trans Activism: Rethinking Canonical Gender Claims." Pages 223–46 in *Bible Trouble: Queer Reading at the Boundaries of Biblical Scholarship*. Edited by Teresa J. Hornsby and Ken Stone. SemeiaSt 67. Atlanta: Society of Biblical Literature, 2011.

———. "The Disgusting Apostle and a Queer Affect between Epistles and Audiences." Pages 113–40 in *Reading with Feeling: Affect Theory and the Bible*. Edited by Fiona Black and Jennifer L. Koosed. SemeiaSt 95. Atlanta: SBL Press, 2019.

———. "The Exceptional Proves Who Rules: Imperial Sexual Exceptionalism in and around Paul's Letters." *JECH* 5 (2015): 87–115.

———. *Hierarchy, Unity, and Imitation: A Feminist Rhetorical Analysis of Power Dynamics in Paul's Letter to the Philippians*. AcBib 24. Atlanta: Society of Biblical Literature, 2006.

———. "How Soon Is (This Apocalypse) Now? Queer Corinthian Velocities after a Corinthian Already and a Pauline Not Yet." Pages 45–67 in *Sexual Disorientations: Queer Temporalities, Affects, Theologies*. Edited by Kent L. Brintnall, Joseph A. Marchal, and Stephen D. Moore. TTC. New York: Fordham University Press, 2018.

———. "'Making History' Queerly: Touches across Time through a Biblical Behind." *BibInt* 19 (2011): 373–95.

———. *The People beside Paul: The Philippian Assembly and History from Below*. ECL 17. Atlanta: SBL Press, 2015.

———. "Queer Approaches: Improper Relations with Pauline Letters." Pages 209–27 in *Studying Paul's Letters: Contemporary Perspectives and Methods*. Edited by Joseph A. Marchal. Minneapolis: Fortress, 2012.

———. *The Politics of Heaven: Women, Gender, and Empire in the Study of Paul*. PCC. Minneapolis: Fortress, 2008.

———. "Statehouse Sodomites, and Other Challenges around 'Religious Freedoms.'" *Feminist Studies in Religion*. 6 April 2015. https://tinyurl.com/SBL45311.

———. "The Usefulness of an Onesimus: The Sexual Use of Slaves and Paul's Letter to Philemon." *JBL* 130 (2011): 751–60.

Marcus, Sharon. "Queer Theory for Everyone: A Review Essay." *Signs* 31 (2005): 191–218.

Martin, Biddy. "Extraordinary Homosexuals and the Fear of Being Ordinary." Pages 109–35 in *Feminism Meets Queer Theory*. Edited by Elizabeth Weed and Naomi Schor. Bloomington: Indiana University Press, 1997.

———. "Sexualities without Genders and Other Queer Utopias." *Diacritics* 24 (1994): 104–21.

Martin, Dale B. *Sex and the Single Savior: Gender and Sexuality in Biblical Interpretation*. Louisville: Westminster John Knox, 2006.

———. *Slavery as Salvation: The Metaphor of Slavery in Pauline Christianity*. New Haven: Yale University Press, 1990.

Martin, Michael Wade. "ἁρπαγμός Revisited: A Philological Reexamination of the New Testament's 'Most Difficult Word.'" *JBL* 135 (2016): 175–94.

Marxsen, Willi. "Der ἕτερος νόμος Röm 13,8." *TZ* 11 (1955): 230–37.

Massumi, Brian. *Parables for the Virtual: Movement, Affect, Sensation*. Durham, NC: Duke University Press, 2002.

Masters, Jeffrey. "We Sat Down with Pete Buttigieg to Talk about Gay Stuff." *Advocate*. 23 April 2019. https://tinyurl.com/SBL4531d.

Matera, Frank J. *Romans*. Paideia Commentaries on the New Testament. Grand Rapids: Baker Academic, 2010.

Matthews, Shelly A. "A Feminist Analysis of the Veiling Passage (1 Corinthians 11:2–16): Who Really Cares That Paul Was Not a Gender Egalitarian After All?" *LD* 2 (2015). https://tinyurl.com/SBL4531g.

———. *First Converts: Rich Pagan Women and the Rhetoric of Mission in Early Judaism and Christianity*. Contraversions. Stanford: Stanford University Press, 2001.

———. "Thinking of Thecla: Issues in Feminist Historiography." *JFSR* 17 (2001): 39–55.

McCready, Wayne O., and Adele Reinhartz, eds. *Common Judaism: Explorations in Second-Temple Judaism*. Minneapolis: Fortress, 2008.

McDonnell, Myles. *Roman Manliness: Virtus and the Roman Republic*. Cambridge: Cambridge University Press, 2006.

Miller, Anna C. *Corinthian Democracy: Democratic Discourse in 1 Corinthians*. PTMS. Eugene, OR: Pickwick, 2015.

Miller, Sam J. *Blackfish City*. New York: Ecco, 2018.

———. "It Was Saturday Night, I Guess That Made It All Right." Pages 93–110 in *A People's Future of the United States: Speculative Fiction from 25 Extraordinary Writers*. Edited by Victor LaValle and John Joseph Adams. New York: One World, 2019.

Milnor, Kristina. *Graffiti and the Literary Landscape in Roman Pompeii.* Oxford: Oxford University Press, 2014.

Moo, Douglas J. *The Epistle to the Romans.* NICNT. Grand Rapids: Eerdmans, 1996.

Moore, Stephen D. *God's Beauty Parlor: And Other Queer Spaces in and around the Bible.* Contraversions. Stanford: Stanford University Press, 2001.

———. *Gospel Jesuses and Other Nonhumans: Biblical Criticism Post-Poststructuralism.* SemeiaSt 89. Atlanta: SBL Press, 2017.

———. "The Rage for Method and the Joy of Anachronism: When Biblical Scholars Do Affect Theory." Pages 187–211 in *Reading with Feeling: Affect Theory and the Bible.* Edited by Fiona Black and Jennifer L. Koosed. SemeiaSt 95. Atlanta: SBL Press, 2019.

———. "Vomitous Loathing and Visceral Disgust in Affect Theory and the Apocalypse of John." *BibInt* 22 (2014): 503–28.

Moore, Stephen D., and Janice Capel Anderson. "Taking It Like a Man: Masculinity in 4 Maccabees." *JBL* 117 (1998): 249–73.

Moraga, Cherríe, and Gloria Anzaldúa. *This Bridge Called My Back: Writings by Radical Women of Color.* 4th ed. Albany: SUNY Press, 2015.

Morgan, Teresa J. *Popular Morality in the Early Roman Empire.* Cambridge: Cambridge University Press, 2007.

———. *Roman Faith and Christian Faith.* Oxford: Oxford University Press, 2015.

Muñoz, Jose Esteban. *Cruising Utopia: The Then and There of Queer Futurity.* Sexual Cultures. New York: New York University Press, 2009.

———. "Feeling Brown: Ethnicity and Affect in Ricardo Bracho's *The Sweetest Hangover (and Other STDs).*" *Theatre Journal* 52 (2000): 67–79.

Nanos, Mark D. *The Mystery of Romans: The Jewish Context of Paul's Letter.* Minneapolis: Fortress, 1996.

———. "To the Churches within the Synagogues of Rome." Pages 11–28 in *Reading Paul's Letter to the Romans.* Edited by Jerry L. Sumney. Atlanta: Society of Biblical Literature, 2012.

Nasrallah, Laura Salah. "'You Were Bought with a Price': Freedpersons and Things in 1 Corinthians." Pages 54–73 in *Corinth in Contrast: Studies in Inequality.* Edited by Steven J. Friesen, Sarah A. James, and Daniel N. Schowalter. Leiden: Brill, 2014.

Niehoff, Maren R. *Philo of Alexandria: An Intellectual Biography.* ABRL. New Haven: Yale University Press, 2018.

———. *Philo on Jewish Identity and Culture*. TSAJ. Tübingen: Mohr Siebeck, 2001.

Novik, Naomi. *Uprooted*. New York: Del Ray Books, 2015.

Noy, David. *Foreigners at Rome: Citizens and Strangers*. London: Duckworth, 2000.

Oakes, Peter. *Philippians: From People to Letter*. Cambridge: Cambridge University Press, 2001.

———. *Reading Romans in Pompeii: Paul's Letter at Ground Level*. Minneapolis: Fortress, 2009.

Oliver, James H. "Text of the Tabula Banasitana, A.D. 177." *AJP* 93 (1972): 336–40.

Oliver, Jen H. "*Oscula iungit nec moderata satis nec sic a virgine danda*: Ovid's Callisto Episode, Female Homoeroticism, and the Study of Ancient Sexuality." *AJP* 136 (2015): 281–312.

O'Rourke, J. J. "*Pistis* in Romans." *CBQ* 36 (1973): 188–94.

Osiek, Carolyn. *Philippians, Philemon*. ANTC. Nashville: Abingdon, 2000.

Packard Humanities Institute. "Searchable Greek Inscriptions: A Scholarly Tool in Progress." https://tinyurl.com/SBL4531i.

Peng, Kuo-Wei. *Hate the Evil, Hold Fast to the Good: Structuring Romans 12.1–15.1*. London: T&T Clark, 2006.

Perry, Matthew J. *Gender, Manumission, and the Roman Freedwoman*. Cambridge: Cambridge University Press, 2014.

Peterson, Laura Hackworth. "The Places of Roman Isis: Between Egyptomania, Politics, and Religion." *Oxford Handbooks Online*. September 2016. https://tinyurl.com/SBL4531h.

Price, Margaret. "The Bodymind Problem and the Possibilities of Pain." *Hypatia* 30 (2015): 268–84.

Przybylo, Ela, and Danielle Cooper. "Asexual Resonances: Tracing a Queerly Asexual Archive." *GLQ* 20 (2014): 297–318.

Puar, Jasbir K. "I Would Rather Be a Cyborg Than a Goddess: Becoming-Intersectional in Assemblage Theory." *philoSOPHIA: A Journal of Feminist Continental Philosophy* 2 (2012): 49–66.

———. *Terrorist Assemblages: Homonationalism in Queer Times*. NW. Durham, NC: Duke University Press, 2007.

Queers Against Pete. "Open Letter." https://tinyurl.com/SBL4531f.

Rabinowitz, Nancy Sorkin, and Lisa Auanger, eds. *Among Women: From the Homosocial to the Homoerotic in the Ancient World*. Austin: University of Texas Press, 2002.

Rajak, Tessa. *Josephus*. 2nd ed. London: Duckworth, 2002.

Rawson, A. Paige. "Reading (with) Rhythm for the Sake of the (I-n-) Islands: A Rastafarian Interpretation of Samson as Ambi(val)ent Affective Assemblage." Pages 126–44 in *Religion, Emotion, Sensation: Affect Theories and Theologies*. Edited by Karen Bray and Stephen D. Moore. TTC. New York: Fordham University Press, 2019.

Reumann, John. *Philippians: A New Translation with Introduction and Commentary*. AB 33B. New Haven: Yale University Press, 2008.

Rich, Adrienne. "Compulsory Heterosexuality and Lesbian Experience." *Signs* 5 (1980): 631–60.

Richlin, Amy. *Arguments with Silence: Writing the History of Roman Women*. Ann Arbor: University of Michigan Press, 2014.

———. *The Garden of Priapus: Sexuality and Aggression in Roman Humor*. Rev. ed. New York: Oxford University Press, 1992.

———. "Not before Homosexuality: The Materiality of the *Cinaedus* and the Roman Law against Love between Men." *JHistSex* 3 (1993): 523–73.

———. "Zeus and Metis: Foucault, Classics, and Feminism." *Helios* 18 (1991): 160–80.

Robinson, Donald W. B. " 'The Faith of Jesus Christ': A New Testament Debate." *RTR* 29 (1970): 71–81.

Roller, Matthew B. *Constructing Autocracy: Aristocrats and Emperors in Julio-Claudian Rome*. Princeton: Princeton University Press, 2001.

Rubin, Gayle S. *Deviations: A Gayle Rubin Reader*. JHFCB. Durham, NC: Duke University Press, 2011.

Runions, Erin. *The Babylon Complex: Theopolitical Fantasies of War, Sex, and Sovereignty*. New York: Fordham University Press, 2014.

———. "From Disgust to Humor: Rahab's Queer Affect." Pages 45–74 in *Bible Trouble: Queer Reading at the Boundaries of Biblical Scholarship*. Edited by Teresa J. Hornsby and Ken Stone. SemeiaSt 67. Atlanta: Society of Biblical Literature, 2011.

Saldanha, Arun. "Reontologising Race: The Machinic Geography of Phenotype." *Environment and Planning D: Society and Space* 24 (2006): 9–24.

Saller, Richard P. *Patriarchy, Property and Death in the Roman Family*. Cambridge: Cambridge University Press, 1994.

Sanders, E. P. *Paul and Palestinian Judaism: A Comparison of Patterns of Religion*. Philadelphia: Fortress, 1977.

Schaefer, Donovan O. *Religious Affects: Animality, Evolution, and Power*. Durham, NC: Duke University Press, 2015.

Schalk, Sami. *Bodyminds Reimagined: (Dis)ability, Race, and Gender in Black Women's Speculative Fiction*. Durham, NC: Duke University Press, 2018.

Schreiner, Thomas R. *Romans*. BECNT. Grand Rapids: Baker Books, 1998.

Schumate, Nancy. *Nation, Empire, Decline: Studies in Rhetorical Continuity from the Romans to the Modern Era*. Classical Interfaces. London: Duckworth, 2006.

Schüssler Fiorenza, Elisabeth. *Discipleship of Equals: A Critical Feminist Ekklēsia-logy of Liberation*. New York: Crossroad, 1993.

———. "The Ethics of Biblical Interpretation: Decentering Biblical Scholarship." *JBL* 107 (1988): 3–17.

———. *In Memory of Her: A Feminist Theological Reconstruction of Christian Origins*. 10th anniversary ed. New York: Crossroad, 1994.

———. "Introduction." Pages 1–23 in *Prejudice and Christian Beginnings: Investigating Race, Gender, and Ethnicity in Early Christian Studies*. Edited by Laura Nasrallah and Elisabeth Schüssler Fiorenza. Minneapolis: Fortress, 2009.

———. *Jesus: Miriam's Child, Sophia's Prophet*. New York: Continuum, 1994.

———. "Missionaries, Apostles, Coworkers: Romans 16 and the Reconstruction of Women's Early Christian History." *WW* 6 (1986): 420–33.

———. "Paul and the Politics of Interpretation." Pages 40–57 in *Paul and Politics: Ekklēsia, Israel, Imperium, Interpretation*. Edited by Richard A. Horsley. Harrisburg, PA: Trinity Press International, 2000.

———. *The Power of the Word: Scripture and the Rhetoric of Empire*. Minneapolis: Fortress, 2007.

———. "The Praxis of Coequal Discipleship." Pages 224–41 in *Paul and Empire: Religion and Power in Roman Imperial Society*. Edited by Richard A. Horsley. Harrisburg, PA: Trinity Press International, 1997.

———. *Rhetoric and Ethic: The Politics of Biblical Interpretation*. Minneapolis: Fortress, 1994.

———. *Transforming Vision: Explorations in Feminist The*logy*. Minneapolis: Fortress, 2011.

———. *Wisdom Ways: Introducing Feminist Biblical Interpretation*. Louisville: Westminster John Knox, 2001.

Schwab, V. E. (Victoria). *Vengeful*. New York: Tom Doherty Associates, 2018.

Schwartz, Seth. *Imperialism and Jewish Society, 200 B.C.E. to 640 C.E.* JCMAMW. Princeton: Princeton University Press, 2001.

Scott, Joan Wallach. *Gender and the Politics of History*. Rev. ed. New York: Columbia University Press, 1999.

Sedgwick, Eve Kosofsky. *Epistemology of the Closet*. Berkeley: University of California Press, 1990.

———. *Touching Feeling: Affect, Pedagogy, Performativity*. SerQ. Durham, NC: Duke University Press, 2003.

Sedgwick, Eve Kosofsky, and Adam Frank. "Shame in the Cybernetic Fold: Reading Silvan Tompkins." Pages 1–28 in *Shame and Its Sisters: A Silvan Tomkins Reader*. Edited by Eve Kosofsky Sedgwick and Adam Frank. Durham, NC: Duke University Press, 1995.

Segovia, Fernando F., and Mary Ann Tolbert, eds. *Social Location and Biblical Interpretation in the United States*. Vol. 1 of *Reading from This Place*. Minneapolis: Fortress, 1995.

———, eds. *Social Location and Biblical Interpretation in Global Perspective*. Vol. 2 of *Reading from This Place*. Minneapolis: Fortress, 1995.

Seigworth, Gregory J., and Melissa Gregg. "An Inventory of Shimmers." Pages 1–25 in *The Affect Theory Reader*. Edited by Melissa Gregg and Gregory J. Seigworth. Durham, NC: Duke University Press, 2010.

Sessions, Jeff. "Attorney General Sessions Addresses Recent Criticisms of Zero Tolerance by Church Leaders." United States Department of Justice. 14 June 2018. https://tinyurl.com/SBL4531k.

Shaner, Katherine A. *Enslaved Leadership in Early Christianity*. Oxford: Oxford University Press, 2018.

———. "Seeing Rape and Robbery: ἁρπαγμός and the Philippians Christ Hymn (Phil. 2:5–11)." *BibInt* 25 (2017): 342–63.

Shaw, Brent D. "Body/Power/Identity: Passions of the Martyrs." *JECS* 4 (1996): 269–312.

Shi, Wenhua. *Paul's Message of the Cross as Body Language*. Tübingen: Mohr Siebeck, 2008.

Skinner, Marilyn B. "Parasites and Strange Bedfellows: A Study in Catullus' Political Imagery." *Ranus* 8 (1979): 137–52.

———. *Sexuality in Greek and Roman Culture*. 2nd ed. Malden, MA: Wiley Blackwell, 2014.

Smit, Peter-Ben. *Paradigms of Being Christ: A Study of the Epistle to the Philippians*. London: Bloomsbury, 2013.

Smyth, Herbert Weir. *Greek Grammar*. Revised by Gordon M. Messing. Cambridge: Harvard University Press, 1984.

Sorek, Susan. *The Jews against Rome*. London: Continuum, 2008.

Stanley, Christopher D. *The Colonized Apostle: Paul through Postcolonial Eyes*. PCC. Minneapolis: Fortress, 2011.

Stendahl, Krister. "The Apostle Paul and the Introspective Conscience of the West." *HTR* 56 (1963): 199–215.

Stone, Ken. *Practicing Safer Texts: Food, Sex and the Bible in Queer Perspective*. QT. London: T&T Clark, 2005.

Stowers, Stanley K. "The Concept of 'Community' and the History of Early Christianity." *MTSR* 23 (2011): 238–56.

———. *A Rereading of Romans: Justice, Jews, and Gentiles*. New Haven: Yale University Press, 1994.

Supp-Montgomerie, Jenna. "Affect and the Study of Religion." *Religion Compass* 9 (2015): 335–45.

Swancutt, Diana M. " 'The Disease of Effemination': The Charge of Effeminacy and the Verdict of God (Romans 1:18–2:16)." Pages 193–233 in *New Testament Masculinities*. Edited by Stephen D. Moore and Janice Capel Anderson. SemeiaSt 45. Atlanta: Society of Biblical Literature, 2003.

———. "Sexy Stoics and the Rereading of Romans 1.18–2.16." Pages 42–73 in *A Feminist Companion to Paul*. Edited by Amy-Jill Levine with Marianne Blickenstaff. London: T&T Clark, 2004.

———. "*Still* before Sexuality: 'Greek' Androgyny, the Roman Imperial Politics of Masculinity and the Roman Invention of the *Tribas*." Pages 11–61 in *Mapping Gender in Ancient Religious Discourses*. Edited by Todd Penner and Caroline Vander Stichele. BibInt 84. Leiden: Brill, 2007.

Tamez, Elsa. "Romans: A Feminist Reading." Pages 698–717 in *Feminist Biblical Interpretation: A Compendium of Critical Commentary on the Books of the Bible and Related Literature*. Edited by Luise Schottroff and Marie-Theres Wacker. Grand Rapids: Eerdmans, 2012.

Taubes, Jacob. *The Political Theology of Paul*. Translated by Dana Hollander. Edited by Aleida Assmann and Jan Assmann, in conjunction with Horst Folkers, Wolf-Daniel Hartwich, and Christoph Schulte. Stanford: Stanford University Press, 2004.

Thompson, Michael. *Clothed with Christ: The Example and Teaching of Jesus in Romans 12.1–15.1*. Sheffield: JSOT Press, 1991.

Thurston, Bonnie B., and Judith M. Ryan. *Philippians and Philemon*. SP 10. Collegeville, MN: Liturgical, 2005.

Tonstad, Sigve. "Pistis Kristou: Reading Paul in a New Paradigm." *AUSS* 40 (2002): 37–59.

Townsley, Gillian. *The Straight Mind in Corinth: Queer Readings across 1 Corinthians 11:2–16*. SemeiaSt 88. Atlanta: SBL Press, 2017.

Treggiari, Susan. *Roman Marriage: Iusti Coniuges from the Time of Cicero to the Time of Ulpian*. Oxford: Clarendon, 1991.

Tupamahu, Ekaputra. "Language Politics and the Constitution of Racialized Subjects in the Corinthian Church." *JSNT* 41 (2018): 223–45.

Varaone, Antonio. *Erotica Pompeiana: Love Inscriptions on the Walls of Pompeii*. Rome: L'Erma di Bretschneider, 2002.

Vines, Matthew. *God and the Gay Christian: The Biblical Case in Support of Same-Sex Relationships*. New York: Convergent Books, 2014.

Visscher, Gerhard H. *Romans 4 and the New Perspective: Faith Embraces the Promise*. New York: Peter Lang, 2009.

Wallis, Ian G. *The Faith of Jesus Christ in Early Christian Traditions*. Cambridge: Cambridge University Press, 1995.

Walters, Jonathan. "Invading the Roman Body: Manliness and Impenetrability in Roman Thought." Pages 29–43 in *Roman Sexualities*. Edited by Judith P. Hallett and Marilyn B. Skinner. Princeton: Princeton University Press, 1997.

Walther, James Arthur. "A Translator's Dilemma: An Exegetical Note in Romans 13:8." *Perspective* 13 (1972): 243–46.

Warner, Michael, ed. *Fear of a Queer Planet*. CP 6. Minneapolis: University of Minnesota Press, 1993.

Weaver, P. R. C. "Social Mobility in the Early Roman Empire: The Evidence of Imperial Freedmen and Slaves." *Past and Present* 37 (1967): 3–20.

Webb, Natalie R. "Powers and Protection in Pompeii and Paul: The Apotropaic Function of the Cross in the Letter to the Galatians." Pages 93–121 in *Early Christianity in Pompeiian Light: People, Texts, Situations*. Edited by Bruce Longenecker. Minneapolis: Fortress, 2016.

Weed, Elizabeth, and Naomi Schor, eds. *Feminism Meets Queer Theory*. Bloomington: Indiana University Press, 1997.

Weheliye, Alexander G. *Habeas Viscus: Racializing Assemblages, Biopolitics, and Black Feminist Theories of the Human*. Durham, NC: Duke University Press, 2014.

Welborn, L. L. "How 'Democratic' Was the Pauline *Ekklēsia*? An Assessment with Special Reference to the Christ Groups of Roman Corinth." *NTS* 65 (2019): 289–309.

———. "Paul's Place in a First-Century Revival of the Discourse of 'Equality.'" *HTR* 110 (2017): 541–62.

———. "'That There May Be Equality': The Contexts and Consequences of a Pauline Ideal." *NTS* 59 (2013): 73–90.

Wheeler-Reed, David. *Regulating Sex in the Roman Empire: Ideology, the Bible, and the Early Christians*. Syn. New Haven: Yale University Press, 2017.

Wheeler-Reed, David, Jennifer W. Knust, and Dale B. Martin. "Can a Man Commit πορνεία with His Wife?" *JBL* 137 (2018): 383–98.

Whittaker, Alexandra. "Pete Buttigieg Wants to Restructure the Supreme Court to Be 'Less Political.'" *Cosmopolitan*. 24 October 2019. https://tinyurl.com/SBL4531b.

Wiegman, Robyn, and Elizabeth Wilson, eds. *Queer Theory without Antinormativity*. Special issue of *dif.* 26, no.1 (2015): 1–187.

Williams, Craig A. *Roman Homosexuality: Ideologies of Masculinity in Classical Antiquity*. Revised and expanded 2nd ed. Oxford: Oxford University Press, 2010.

Williams, Demetrius K. "African American Approaches: Rehumanizing the Reader against Racism and Reading through Experience." Pages 155–73 in *Studying Paul's Letters: Contemporary Perspectives and Methods*. Edited by Joseph A. Marchal. Minneapolis: Fortress, 2012.

Williams, Sam K. "Again *Pistis Christou*." *CBQ* 49 (1987): 431–47.

———. *Jesus' Death as Saving Event: The Background and Origin of a Concept*. Missoula, MT: Scholars Press, 1975.

———. "The 'Righteousness of God' in Romans." *JBL* 99 (1980): 241–90.

Wills, Lawrence M. "Wisdom and Word among the Hellenistic Saviors: The Function of Literacy." *JSP* 24 (2014): 118–48.

Wilson, Nancy. *Our Tribe: Queer Folks, God, Jesus, and the Bible*. San Francisco: HarperSanFrancisco, 1995.

Winkler, John J. *The Constraints of Desire: The Anthropology of Sex and Gender in Ancient Greece*. New York: Routledge, 1990.

Winter, Bruce. "Roman Law and Society in Romans 12–15." Pages 67–102 in *Rome in the Bible and the Early Church*. Edited by Peter Oakes. Grand Rapids: Baker Academic, 2002.

Wire, Antoinette Clark. *The Corinthian Women Prophets: A Reconstruction through Paul's Rhetoric*. Minneapolis: Fortress, 1990.

———. "Response: Paul and Those Outside Power." Pages 224–26 in *Paul and Politics: Ekklēsia, Israel, Imperium, Interpretation*. Edited by Richard A. Horsley. Harrisburg, PA: Trinity Press International, 2000.

———. "Response: The Politics of the Assembly in Corinth." Pages 124–29 in *Paul and Politics: Ekklēsia, Israel, Imperium, Interpretation*. Edited by Richard A. Horsley. Harrisburg, PA: Trinity Press International, 2000.

Witherington, Ben, III, with Darlene Hyatt. *Paul's Letter to the Romans: A Socio-Rhetorical Commentary*. Grand Rapids: Eerdmans, 2004.

Wortham, Robert A. "Urban Networks, Deregulated Religious Markets, Cultural Continuity and the Diffusion of the Isis Cult." *MTSR* 18 (2006): 103–23.

Zanker, Paul. *The Power of Images in the Age of Augustus*. Translated by Alan Shapiro. Detroit: University of Michigan Press, 1990.

Ancient Sources Index

Modern Authors Index

Subject Index

CPSIA information can be obtained
at www.ICGtesting.com
Printed in the USA
FSHW020142110122
87239FS